Unhonored Service:

The Life of Lee's Senior Cavalry Commander, Colonel Thomas Taylor Munford, CSA

Also by Sheridan R. Barringer:

Custer's Gray Rival:
  The Life of Confederate Major General
  Thomas Lafayette Rosser

Fighting for General Lee:
  Confederate General Rufus Barringer
  and the North Carolina Cavalry Brigade

Unhonored Service:

The Life of Lee's Senior Cavalry Commander, Colonel Thomas Taylor Munford, CSA

Sheridan R. Barringer

© 2022 by Sheridan R. Barringer

All rights reserved. No part of this publication may be reproduced, stored in a retrieval system, or transmitted, in any form or by any means, electronic, mechanical, photocopying, recording, or otherwise, without the prior written permission of the publisher.

Publisher's Cataloging-in-Publication Data
provided by Five Rainbows Cataloging Services

Names: Barringer, Sheridan Reid, 1943- author. | Wittenberg, Eric J., 1961- writer of introduction.
Title: Unhonored service : the life of Lee's senior cavalry commander, Colonel Thomas Taylor Munford, CSA / Sheridan R. Barringer ; [introduction by] Eric. J. Wittenberg.
Description: Burlington, NC : Fox Run Publishing, 2022. | Includes bibliographical references and index.
Identifiers: LCCN 2022930746 (print) | ISBN 978-1-945602-22-1 (paperback) | ISBN 978-1-945602-21-4 (hardcover)
Subjects: LCSH: Confederate States of America. Army. Cavalry--History. | United States--History--Civil War, 1861-1865. | United States--History--Civil War, 1861-1865--Biography. | Virginia--History--Civil War, 1861-1865. | BISAC: HISTORY / United States / Civil War Period (1850-1877) | HISTORY / Military / United States. | BIOGRAPHY & AUTOBIOGRAPHY / Military.
Classification: LCC E581.6 .B37 2022 (print) | LCC E581.6 (ebook) | DDC 793.7/42--dc23.

Cover design by Sandra Miller
Cover photographs: Col. Thomas T. Munford (Virginia Military Institute) Oakland Plantation, Uniontown, Alabama (Virginia Historical Society)

Library of Congress Control Number (LCCN): 2022930746

Published by
Fox Run Publishing LLC
2779 South Church Street, #305
Burlington, NC 27215
http://www.foxrunpub.com/

For Shannon and Michael.

Table of Contents

Preface	i
Acknowledgments	ii
Introduction	iii
Abbreviations	v
Chapter 1: The Early Years and Family Life	1
Chapter 2: Life at Virginia Military Institute	9
Chapter 3: Thomas Munford Becomes a Farmer as Virginia Prepares for War	21
Chapter 4: 1861: Outbreak of War–Battle of First Manassas	31
Chapter 5: Aftermath of Battle of First Manassas	49
Chapter 6: 1862 Shenandoah Valley Campaign	59
Chapter 7: The Peninsula Campaign	91
Chapter 8: Battle of Second Manassas, the Maryland Campaign, and the Battle of Fredericksburg	101
Chapter 9: 1863–The New Year Begins; Onward Toward Chancellorsville	129
Chapter 10: Gettysburg Campaign	147
Chapter 11: Remainder of 1863 Campaigns and Cavalry Reorganization	185
Chapter 12: 1864–Kilpatrick-Dahlgren Raid on Richmond and Grant's Overland Campaign	209
Chapter 13: Siege of Petersburg Begins, Battle of Trevilian Station, and Battles for Critical Railroads	229
Chapter 14: 1864 Shenandoah Valley Campaign	245
Chapter 15: 1865: Five Forks–The Waterloo of the Confederacy	279
Chapter 16: High Bridge, Escape to Lynchburg, and Final Surrender	297
Chapter 17: After the War–Farmer, Veterans Supporter, and Church Leader	311
Chapter 18: Thomas Munford's Business Ventures and Legal Challenges	323
Chapter 19: President of the Board of Visitors of VMI and Life in the 1880s	329

Chapter 20: Long Awaited Promotion and Bitter Feud	343
Chapter 21: Plantation Life in Alabama and Remembering a Fallen Soldier	353
Bibliography	367
Index	381
About the Author	409

List of Images

Ashby, Turner (Col.)	79
Beauregard, Pierre G. T. (Gen.)	37
Buena Vista	23
Custer, George Armstrong (Bvt. Brig. Gen.)	261
Early, Jubal A. (Maj. Gen.)	265
Ewell, Richard S. (Maj. Gen.)	85
Jackson, Thomas J. "Stonewall"	17
Lee, Fitzhugh (Maj. Gen.)	301
Munford "Tutor" Home	319
Munford Lynchburg Italian Style Home	320
Munford with son and grandson	358
Munford, Elizabeth Thorogood Ellis	vi
Munford, George Taloe	338
Munford, George Wythe	4, 322
Munford, Thomas Taylor	81, 300, 331, 357, 362
Munford, William (Rev.)	29
Oakland Plantation	355
Oakland Plantation Barbeque	360
Payne, William H. (Brig. Gen.)	270
Robertson, Beverly H. (Brig. Gen.)	111
Rosser, Thomas Lafayette (Brig. Gen.)	267
Smith, Francis H.	334
Stonewall Jackson Memorial at VMI	142
Stuart, James Ewell Brown (J.E.B.)	155

List of Maps

Bull Run, First Battle of	42
Richmond-Petersburg Area	51
Shenandoah Valley 1862-1865 Battles	71
Stonewall Jackson's Valley Campaign 1862	73
Peninsula Campaign	92
Seven Days Battles	97
Area of Operations 1863-1865	135
Chancellorsville, Battle of	141
Brandy Station, Battle of	151
Gettysburg Campaign	171
Gettysburg, Battle of	175
Gettysburg, Retreat from	179
Travelian Station	233
Tom's Brook	258
Dinwiddie Court House, Battle of	286
Five Forks	288
Appomattox Campaign	296

Sheridan R. Barringer

*Unhonored Service: The Life of Lee's Senior Cavalry Commander,
Colonel Thomas Taylor Munford, CSA*

Preface

While writing my biography of Major General Thomas Lafayette Rosser, entitled *Custer's Gray Rival: The Life of Confederate Major General Thomas Lafayette Rosser* a few years ago, I kept encountering animosity, vitriol, and yes, just plain hatred between Rosser and Colonel Thomas Taylor Munford. That relationship certainly makes for fascinating reading. There is a wealth of Munford's written material available in repositories in the form of letters, diaries, reminiscences, and accounts of battles, and as I read more about Munford, I decided I would study this man to see if a full biography of him was warranted.

After doing more research, corresponding, and talking with several historians and authors about Munford, I determined a Munford biography was indeed justified. So, I began the task in earnest, and I must say that I have enjoyed the journey. I hope that you, the reader, enjoys the ride and learns interesting facts you did not already know about this skilled cavalry commander.

Munford was a graduate of Virginia Military Institute, and thus, not a member of the "Virginia West Point elite," a fact he thought worked against him in his military career from day one. He was passed over for promotion to brigadier many times, a point which embittered him. Some reports hold that other officers, particularly "West Pointers," found Munford difficult to get along with, yet he genuinely loved his troopers, and they were quite fond of him.

I believe that this exploration into Colonel Munford's life shows that he was indeed a Virginian whose life accomplishments make his story a worthy narration.

Sheridan R. Barringer

Acknowledgments

I wish to express my sincere thanks to the following individuals and institutions for their contributions in the creation of this book:

To Bryce Suderow, who has become a friend and confidant. Bryce reviewed several war chapters, made suggestions, found additional resources, and kept me from making some embarrassing mistakes. Thanks to my friend, Tonia J. Smith for her review, suggestions, and encouragement. Thanks to descendants of Thomas T. Munford, William Tayloe Munford and Estelle Call for their information and support; To Eric J. Wittenberg for his suggestions and for writing the Introduction to this book. To Edward G. Longacre for his review and suggestions. To Jim Burgess, Robert Trout, Terry Justice, and Michael McCarthy for their individual contributions in reviewing chapters and making suggestions for improvements. To Dr. James R. Jewell for his consultations and information provided regarding Munford; To Hal Jespersen for the maps. To researcher, Steven Wade, for his hard work in sending me materials from Duke's Rubenstein Library. To Elizabeth Dunn at Rubenstein Library of Duke University for her help in finding and sending me letters and other materials from the Munford-Ellis Papers. To editor, Julianne Murphy.

To my wife, Pam, for her encouragement and for putting up with all the time I was away from her while doing research or at the computer updating the manuscript.

Thanks to the staffs at the following institutions: Albert and Shirley Small Special Collections Library, University of Virginia; Library of Virginia; Rubenstein Library at Duke University; Virginia Historical Society; Southern Historical Collection at the University of North Carolina; Reynolds Library at Wake Forest University; Boston University's Howard Gotlieb Archival Center; National Archives; Library of Congress; Penn State University Library; Virginia Military Institute Archives; United States Army History Center at Carlisle, Pennsylvania; United States Cavalry Association at Fort Riley, Kansas; and the National Park Service.

And finally, thanks to my fine publisher, Fox Run, and in particular Keith Jones for managing this project through to release. Thanks to a fine editor, Hailey Bibbee, for her diligent work.

Sheridan R. Barringer

Introduction

Thomas Taylor Munford, of Lynchburg, Virginia, was one of the most important officers to serve in the Army of Northern Virginia's vaunted cavalry arm during the Civil War. Munford, a member of a wealthy and prominent Virginia family and an alumnus of the Virginia Military Institute, was an extremely talented commander of horse. However, the fact that he was not a West Point trained soldier, had a difficult and prickly personality, and had a propensity for arguing with his superiors prevented him from reaching the high rank that his sheer competence and good service warranted. Again and again, Tom Munford watched as officers junior to him were promoted over him, regardless of whether they had any formal military training. Although Munford claimed that Confederate President Jefferson Davis promoted him to brigadier general in the Civil War's waning moments, the Confederate Senate never approved the promotion, and Munford finished the war with precisely the same rank that he began it: colonel.

Along the way, Munford spent almost as much time commanding a brigade, and sometimes a division, as he did in regimental command. His brigade, and later division commander, Gen. Fitzhugh Lee, suffered from health issues, and, in 1864, a major combat wound, meaning that his senior subordinate, Munford, often led Lee's troops in battle. Munford commanded Lee's brigade in some of the Civil War's most important engagements, including the June 9, 1863 Battle of Brandy Station, the largest cavalry battle fought on the North American continent. In command of Fitz Lee's division at the time of the Army of Northern Virginia's surrender at Appomattox in April 1865, Munford's troopers were among the last members of the Army of the Northern Virginia to surrender.

In addition, Munford had a long-standing and fascinating feud with Maj. Gen. Thomas L. Rosser. Rosser, who started out junior to Munford, was a special favorite to Maj. Gen. J.E.B. Stuart, who arranged for Rosser to be promoted to brigadier general. By the fall of 1864, Rosser was a major general and in command of a division, while Munford remained stuck at the rank of colonel. Despite the difference in rank, Munford and Rosser often quarreled and were often at odds. As a consequence of that personality clash, Rosser ignored Munford's warnings on October 9, 1864, leading to the worst defeat suffered by the Confederate cavalry in the Eastern Theatre of the Civil War in the Battle of Tom's Brook. There was no love lost between these two strong-willed men, and it caused significant problems with field operations for the Southern cavalry.

Munford richly deserved promotion, but never received it. He was understandably bitter about it, and that bitterness tainted his post-war observations. Munford documents much of his experiences after the war, and he pulled no punches in doing so. That undoubtedly irked his old Confederate comrades, who had no particular affection for him anyway.

Until Sheridan R. "Butch" Barringer decided to tackle a full-length biography of Tom Munford, he remained the highest-ranking cavalry officer of the Army of Northern Virginia not to be the subject of a full-length biography. Butch Barringer, a relative of Confederate Brig. Gen. Rufus Barringer, has now corrected this oversight with this comprehensive and well-documented biography of Thomas Taylor Munford.

Butch Barringer's masterful biography of this largely overlooked Confederate officer deserves a place on the bookshelf of any serious student of Virginia history, or of Civil War cavalry operations.

Eric J. Wittenberg
Columbus, Ohio

Abbreviations

NCDAH – State Archives, North Carolina Division of Archives and History, Raleigh, North Carolina.

SHC – Southern Historical Collection, Wilson Library, University of North Carolina at Chapel Hill.

DU – Rare Book, Manuscript, and Special Collections, Rubenstein Library, Duke University, Durham, North Carolina.

SHSP – Southern Historical Society Papers, 52 vols., Jones, J. William, et al, editors, Richmond, Virginia, Southern Historical Society, 1876-1959.

LC – Library of Congress

NA – National Archives and Records Administration, Washington, D.C.

OR – The War of Rebellion: A Compilation of the Official Records of the Union and Confederate Armies, 70 vols., 128 parts, Washington, D.C., 1880-1901. All references are to Series I, unless otherwise indicated.

VHS – Virginia Historical Society, Richmond, Virginia.

LVA – Library of Virginia, Richmond, Virginia

UVA – Albert and Shirley Small Special Collections Library, University of Virginia, Charlottesville, Virginia.

Thomas T. Munford's Step-mother, Elizabeth Thorogood Ellis Munford (1818-1910)

Thomas thought of her as his birth mother. His birth mother died in 1900, when Thomas was just four years old.

(Courtesy: Virginia Historical Society)

CHAPTER 1

Thomas T. Munford's Heritage, Early Years, and Family Life

Thomas Taylor Munford, a fourth generation Virginian from a prominent Old Dominion family, was born on March 29, 1831, in Richmond, Virginia. He was the second son of George Wythe Munford, who served as secretary of the Commonwealth before and during the Civil War, and Lucy Singleton Taylor of Richmond, who was related to President Benjamin Harrison. George and Lucy married on November 29, 1828. Lucy died in 1835, when Thomas was only four, and in 1838 George married Elizabeth Thorowgood Ellis. Elizabeth was Mr. and Mrs. Charles Ellis, Sr.'s daughter; they lived at the southwest corner of Franklin and Second Streets.

Thomas embraced his new mother and came to think of her as his birth mother.[1] He had a total of 15 surviving brothers and sisters from his father's two marriages. Among his siblings from George and Lucy were William Munford, George Wythe Munford, Jr. (a twin, George Munford, born with George Wythe Munford, Jr., died at birth), and Lucy Harrison Munford. Siblings from George and Elizabeth were Robert Munford, Charles Ellis Munford, Sallie Radford Munford, Anne Bland Munford, Rosalie Munford, and the following sisters who never married: Margaret Nimmo Munford, Lucy Taylor Munford, Frances Ellis Munford, Jane Beverley Munford, Caroline Homasselle Munford, and Etta Wythe Munford. Two brothers served in the Civil War: Charles Ellis Munford, who was killed at Malvern Hill during the Peninsula campaign, and William Munford, a lieutenant colonel of the 17th Virginia Infantry, who became an Episcopal priest after the war.[2]

By 1840, George Munford had built his home at the corner of Franklin and Fourth Streets in Richmond, designated as "No. 1" West Franklin Street. Richmond neighborhoods initially spread out from

---

1. Anne Trice Thompson Akers, "Colonel Thomas T. Munford and the Last Cavalry Operations of the Civil War in Virginia," 3, Master's Thesis, Virginia Polytechnic Institute and State University (Virginia Tech), Blacksburg, VA; Munford Family Bible pages (copies), Jones Memorial Library, Lynchburg, VA; Robert Beverley Munford, Jr., *Richmond Homes and Memories*, (Richmond, 1936), 5.
2. Robert Beverley Munford, *Richmond Homes and Memories* (Richmond, VA, 1936), 5.

the Capitol building located in the center of the city, with the wealthier citizens moving west of town, opting for the less hilly, more elite sections of Grace, Franklin, and Fifth Streets. For this reason, among others, Munford's residence was for many years considered a Richmond landmark. All of his children from his second marriage were born there, with the exception of his eldest son, Charles Ellis. Charles Ellis Munford was born at the home of his grandparents, Mr. and Mrs. Charles Ellis.[3]

Thomas Munford's ancestor, Thomas Munford (1580-1646), a member of the Second Virginia Company of London, sailed from England with Captain John Smith on at least one of his two resupply and mapping missions of the Chesapeake Bay in 1607-08. Thomas L. Munford's great-grandfather, Robert Munford, served as Halifax County Clerk, justice of the peace in Lunenburg County, a senior magistrate of the newly formed Mecklenburg County, a member of the House of Burgesses, and a member of the House of Delegates. Robert entered the House of Burgesses in 1765, the same year as Patrick Henry, and worked with him on several issues relating to the autonomy of the colony, including the Stamp Act of 1765.[4]

Robert Munford's first military experience came in 1756, when he served as a junior officer under Colonel George Washington in the French and Indian War. In 1765, Robert served as county lieutenant of Mecklenburg County, where his primary task was to defend the area from slave uprisings. Robert owned slaves left to him by his father.[5]

Politically, Robert was a moderate during the pre-revolutionary period, expressing loyalty to the king but protesting taxation; he refused to recognize the absolute authority of Parliament. Because he opposed the war, he was less active in public life for a short period before and after the conflict, but he still served in the House of Delegates in 1779. Robert, despite his opposition to the war, maintained a role with the military throughout this time, and by 1781, he commanded the militias for Mecklenburg, Lunenburg, and Brunswick counties.[6]

In addition to his many military and civic duties, Robert found time to pursue his love of literature. He authored two plays, *The Candidates* (ca. 1770) and *The Patriots* (ca. 1777), considered by many scholars to be the first comedies written in America. These dramatic

---

3. Ibid.
4. M. L. Crawford, "Robert Munford (d. 1783)," *Encyclopedia Virginia*, Virginia Foundation for the Humanities, March 1, 2014, Library of Virginia (LVA), Richmond.
5. Ibid.
6. Ibid.

works are reminiscent of English Restoration comedy. *The Candidates* is also noteworthy as one of the best depictions of elections in Virginia of that era. These plays do not appear to have been publicly performed or published in any form during his lifetime, though it is possible they were performed privately.

Almost none of Robert's literary works can be dated precisely, but based on events described in the plays, they appear to have been written during the 1770s. Also a poet, he published one of his poems in 1779.[7] Among his other literary pursuits is a partial translation of Ovid's *Metamorphoses*. In 1798 Munford's son, William, published a volume of his father's work including the plays, a collection of poems, and Robert's work on *Metamorphoses*.

Thomas's grandfather, William Munford (1775-1825), moved from Mecklenburg County to Richmond around 1800 to seek a living as a lawyer. He studied law under notable scholar George Wythe and established his home at the northwest corner of Fifth and Canal Streets. During his boyhood, William had been a student at the College of William and Mary, where he had the good fortune of residing in the home of the Chancellor, George Wythe. William learned the beauty of classical literature and art from Wythe and a strong friendship ensued. He considered George Wythe to be his mentor and pronounced the oration at his funeral at the state capitol. Furthermore, in admiration, William named his first son after the famous judge. Later, William became Clerk of the House of Delegates, a post he held until his death in 1825.[8]

Thomas's father, George Wythe Munford (1803-1882), was born January 8, 1803, in Richmond, Virginia, to William Munford (1775-1825) and Sally Radford Munford. George's siblings were John Durburrow Munford, Dr. Robert Munford, William Preston Munford, Carlton Munford, Anna Munford, Elizabeth Munford, and Elvira Munford. George studied law at the College of William and Mary under the direction of Wyndam Robertson, who later became governor of Virginia. George W. Munford was employed by his father, who served as clerk of the Virginia House of Delegates. George succeeded his father at this post upon his father's death in 1825 and held that position until 1852, when he became Secretary of the Commonwealth. He remained in that position until the end of the Civil War.

The 1850 Federal Census shows George W. Munford owned nine slaves, including four children. During the time he served as Virginia's

---

7. Ibid.
8. Akers, Thesis, 2–3, Virginia Tech; *Richmond Times Dispatch*, March 17, 1905; Robert Beverley Munford, *Richmond Homes and Memories*, 2.

George Wythe Munford (1803-1882)
Father of Thomas T. Munford

For 12 years, George Wythe Munford was Secretary of the Commonwealth of Virginia. He ran unsuccessfully for Governor of Virginia in 1863. Financially ruined after the war, he struggled to make ends meet.

(Courtesy: Rubenstein Library, Duke University)

Secretary of the Commonwealth, as well as secretary of the Virginia Constitutional Convention of 1829-30. During the Civil War, he reported directly to Governor John Letcher. He became known as "Colonel Munford," and compiled the *Virginia Codes of 1860 and 1873*. He authored a book on early Virginians, entitled *Jewels of Virginia*. George Munford died January 10, 1882, in Richmond and was buried in Hollywood Cemetery.[9]

One of Thomas L. Munford's lifelong friends-to-be, John Esten Cooke (1830-1886), arrived in Richmond in March of 1840. Esten was a son of prominent Virginian John Rogers Cooke and a nephew of future Union Brevet Major General Philip St. George Cooke. This family illustrates how close relations were between the two sides. Gen. Philip St. George Cooke's son, and namesake of his much older brother, was future Confederate Brigadier General John Rogers Cooke. Philip's daughter, Flora was the wife of Major General J.E.B. Stuart.[10]

During this antebellum period, education was primarily the responsibility of each family. Free public schools were scarce, and mandatory education did not exist. Some of Richmond's elite believed their sons could best be educated in private academies in England, although overseas education was in decline. Wealthier citizens sent their children to private boarding or finishing schools in Richmond. Another educational option utilized by Richmond's upper-class was the use of private tutors for both boys and girls. Tutors, often the most expensive form of education, were taken into a family as teacher, friend, and role model for the children. From 1821 until 1852, one of Richmond's best private schools was William Burke's school for boys. Burke served as its first principal and managed the school until about 1845, when Claudius Crozet took over. Crozet would go on to be one of the founders of Virginia Military Institute, and was elected president of its first board of visitors. Burke, who was born in Ireland, gained great respect among the city's citizens. He was an excellent teacher of the classical languages, and later became a physician. His school offered a corps of cadets program for those interested in military training.

In 1835, the Virginia General Assembly incorporated the Richmond Academy, a boys' prep school in the capital city, located at the corner of Tenth and Marshall Streets. The institution prospered quickly. By 1839, there were 69 students over the age of 12, with that number rising to 127 by 1843. The academy curriculum concentrated

---

9. Akers, Thesis, 3, Virginia Tech; *Richmond Times Dispatch*, March 17, 1905; Munford Family Bible, Lynchburg, VA; Robert Beverley Munford, *Richmond Homes and Memories*, 4.
10. "John Esten Cooke," in *Pioneers of Southern Literature*, vol. I (Nashville, TN: Publishing House of the M.E. Church South, 1903), p. 250.

on subjects in English, classics, mathematics, and languages. For those interested in a military career, it also offered the option of enrolling in a corps of cadets in preparation for schools like West Point and Virginia Military Institute.[11] Thomas Munford surely took advantage of this cadet option, one he must have liked, because upon graduation from this academy, he enrolled at VMI.

The academic school year at Richmond Academy was divided into two sessions; one commencing October 1 and ending on February 1; the second beginning on March 1 and ending on July 31. There were two examinations held each year; on February 16 and the other on July 25. Discipline was divided into minor and major infractions. Minor infractions, such as being inattentive or disruptive, drew punishment by either private admonition, admonition before the class of the offender, or dismissal from the school for the day. Only the faculty enforced punishment for major infractions, which were punishable by admonitions before the entire student body, probation, suspension, dismissal, or expulsion.[12]

As a youngster, Thomas Munford grew up in Richmond, first educated at William Burke's private school and then again at the prestigious Richmond Academy. Thomas's father, George Wythe Munford served as a member of the academy's board of trustees. Thomas's good friend, Esten Cooke, had been a classmate at Burke's school and then at Richmond Academy.

Young Esten Cooke's diary recounted adventures in the neighboring woods and swimming trips to the falls of the James River. This picturesque place was soon to be invaded by factories, much to the chagrin of the Richmond schoolboys.[13] Thomas Munford must have participated in many of Cooke's boyhood adventures.

Future famed poet, Edgar Allan Poe, also attended Burke's school. In 1835, Poe applied to Richmond Academy to be the new English teacher, but he was not selected. Poe never held a position outside of literature or literature review, ultimately having no source of income besides his pen. Poe's foster father, John Allan, was the business partner of Charles Ellis, whose daughter, Elizabeth Thorowgood Ellis, was the stepmother of Thomas T. Munford.[14]

---

11. Alfred James Morrison, *The Beginnings of Public Education in Virginia*, 1176–1860, Virginia State Board of Education (Richmond, VA, 1917), 139; Virginius Dabney, *Richmond: The Story of a City* (Charlottesville, 1990), 146.
12. *Journal of the House of Delegates of the Commonwealth of Virginia*, Document No. 31 (January 1, 1836), 69.
13. Beaty, *John Esten Cooke, Virginian*, 15.
14. Edgar Allan Poe Museum, Richmond, Virginia. Elizabeth T. Ellis Munford was given Poe's bed after he outgrew it, and she used it. It is now housed in the Poe Museum in Richmond.

Even though Richmond did not yet have its own university, it maintained a close relationship with the venerable College of William and Mary and with the newer University of Virginia. The number of students at these universities greatly increased with the development of sectional ill-will, and with the subsequent dislike of southern fathers to send their sons to northern universities. Literary societies were of great interest to school boys of this period, as parents viewed oratory as the forte of southern gentlemen. It was natural that young men should emulate the great spokesmen of the day. The Franklin Debating Society, an incorporated literary and debating body, initially met twice a week at Burke's School and later at Richmond Academy. The Society touched the outside world by having men of prominence in the community as honorary members.[15] Cooke carefully recorded the "Records of the Proceedings" of the Society for 1845-46. Once during this period, Cooke was "fined 6 and 1/4 cents for interrupting Mr. Munford."[16]

Thomas Munford matriculated from Richmond Academy in the spring of 1849, preparing him for the next phase of his life as a cadet at Virginia Military Institute. There, he flourished in the military lifestyle, and came to know and serve a new professor at the institute, Thomas Jonathan Jackson. Thomas Munford was Jackson's cadet adjutant during his senior year, preparing him to serve under Jackson in the 1862 Shenandoah Valley campaign.

---

15. Beaty, *John Esten Cooke, Virginian*, 15. Thomas's father and grandfather had been members of the Franklin Debating Society. There does not appear to be a record of Thomas being a member, but it is likely he was.
16. Ibid.

CHAPTER 2

Life at Virginia Military Institute

"I will give my impression of this grand, gloomy and peculiarly good man and great soldier as he then appeared to me, to grow on me, and I flatter myself to have had the extraordinary advantages to learn to honor and to respect and to love him."

–Thomas T. Munford, speaking of Maj. Thomas Jonathan Jackson

After having matriculated from Richmond Academy on July 30, 1849, Thomas Munford entered Virginia Military Institute (VMI) as a third classman of the class of 1852. His father, George Wythe Munford, was then serving on VMI's Board of Visitors. This probably determined Thomas's choice of military academy. He did not try to obtain an appointment to West Point, which his father, as the clerk of the House of Delegates, could have likely arranged for him.

Thomas's class ranking his first year began as 20th in a class of 45. He rose in class standing the next year to number 15 of 31 cadets, and was promoted to sergeant major. When he graduated on July 5, 1852, he stood 14th out of 24 cadets.[1] Included in Munford's class were James A. Walker, the last surviving member of the Stonewall Brigade, and George Smith Patton, grandfather of the legendary World War II general of the same name. Thomas roomed with George S. Patton for two years at the VMI.[2]

By the 1830s, the Commonwealth of Virginia needed some new ideas for its military training. The state militia system in place to defend Virginia had become more of a social club than a military organization. Virginia did not have an institution to teach military skills to militia officers. Alden Partridge, an ex-acting superintendent of West Point, believed a military college in the state would enable the militia to become more professional. The town of Lexington, Virginia,

---

1. Akers, Thesis, 4; *Richmond Times Dispatch*, March 1, 1918.
2. *The Cadet*, Vol. II, October 25, 1913, VMI Archives; Jeffry Wert, "His Dishonored Service." CWTI (June 1985), 29; *Merit Roll*, Virginia Military Institute, Lexington, VA., 1849–1850, 1851–1852; Munford Family Bible. Note: There seems to be some confusion regarding Munford's graduation year. *The Baltimore Sun*, July 8, 1852 reported that Munford received his diploma, but other sources state 1854 as his graduation year, which is incorrect. He had returned to the life of farming by 1853.

provided an ideal location and a good reason to establish a military school. Located at the upper end of the Shenandoah Valley, Lexington in the 1830s was a small village of 1,000 inhabitants. It was also home to one of three arsenals established in 1816 by the state to store large amounts of weapons produced during the War of 1812. The arsenal was then guarded and defended by an independent Virginia company of 28 men, led by one captain.[3]

While the discipline of the guards was strict, many of the soldiers were overly fond of drinking. Members were known to fight amongst themselves, and in 1826 one guard killed another. It became obvious the current guard system needed to be replaced, but the question remained as to what organization would be enlisted instead.[4] The fact that the arsenal provided much needed income to the small town was also of utmost consideration.

During the 1820s, discussions favoring turning the arsenal into an educational institution, with the students serving as the caretakers of the arms, commenced. In December 1834, the Franklin Society, a debating body composed of influential citizens in Lexington, posed the question, "Would it be politic for the State to establish a military school, at the arsenal near Lexington, in connection with Washington College, on the plan of the West Point Academy?"[5] This idea was contemplated, and action voted down once, but a unanimous vote in favor passed by the year's end.

John T. L. Preston, a lawyer in Lexington, realized the issue at stake was whether or not the Lexington arsenal could remain in use as an arsenal while also serving as a literary institution. Preston believed it could and laid out a plan in which young men, 16 to 21 years of age, would replace the present guard system. Instead of receiving pay for guarding the arsenal, they would have the opportunity for a liberal education. The students would be under military discipline to secure the post and, promote "industry, regularity and health."[6]

These students would be appointed from each of the state's senatorial districts. This plan, according to Preston, would greatly benefit the town of Lexington. Instead of a group of guards, "respected by none, considered obnoxious by some and disliked by all," the town

---

3. Michael M. Wallace, LCDR, USN, M.L.A, "The Use of the Virginia Military Institute Corps of Cadets as a Military Unit Before and During the War Between the States," A thesis presented to the Faculty of the U.S. Army Command and General Staff College in partial fulfillment of the requirements for the degree Master of Military Art and Science Military History, Tulane University, New Orleans, LA, 1999, Fort Leavenworth, Kansas, 2006, 4.
4. Ibid.
5. Ibid., 4–5.
6. Ibid., 5.

would instead have a corps of young men, "guided by virtuous principal, ennobled by the ardor of patriotism."[7]

The arsenal's new guards would not have time to create disruption in town, because their time would be spent in academic pursuits. Preston argued that the graduates of this military school would provide Virginia with a growing pool of men from all regions in the state who could instruct and serve as officers in the state militia.

Initially, the idea to turn the arsenal into a military school had substantial opposition. Preston's published articles, combined with strong legislative backing from southwestern Virginia, helped the idea of a military school gain statewide support. On March 22, 1836, the Virginia Legislature passed an act to reorganize the arsenal into a military school; however, problems with the legislation kept the school from a timely opening.[8]

Finally, in March 1839, the legislature approved a new law which solved the problems with the previous regulation. The arsenal and its appropriation would be transferred to the new military school. Additionally, the professors and military students were to be held responsible for the safekeeping, protection, and preservation of the grounds, buildings, arms and other property the state had located at Lexington. When asked to name the new school, Preston recommended Virginia Military Institute, a state organization, neither sectional nor affiliated with any one branch of the military. Being called an institute indicated something different and more regulated than either a college or university.[9]

A board of visitors was established in 1837 to organize the school under the original legislative act. VMI began with a very meager endowment, and its graduates would not enter a single profession but rather the varied work of civil life. To many young men, this was not as attractive or as secure as a military career. Discipline could not be enforced with the same rigor as at West Point. The military portion of the school, still essential for discipline, would not be the primary focus in the education. It was expedient to take West Point as a model, but also to provide for necessary variations.[10]

Besides establishing the military division of the school, the board of visitors had another task: to find a principal professor who would run day-to-day operations. The board eventually chose Francis H. Smith, a professor of mathematics at Hampden-Sydney College. Smith, born in Norfolk, Virginia, on October 18, 1812, was an 1833 graduate

---

7. Ibid.
8. Ibid., 6.
9. Ibid.
10. Ibid., 8.

of West Point. He had served in the artillery branch and as a mathematics instructor at West Point before leaving the Army in 1836 to accept the professorship at Hampden-Sydney.[11]

The board elected Smith principal professor on May 30, 1839, with the rank of major in the state militia. His title was later changed to superintendent with the rank of colonel by the legislature in July 1842.

The law establishing VMI provided for two types of cadets to attend the school: state (or regular paying) cadets and pay (irregular) cadets. The state cadet program was intended for indigent youths to receive a higher education. Each of the 32 district state senators would be able to appoint one cadet. State cadets would have most of their fees paid by the state, and they would then serve the Commonwealth for a period of two years after graduation, often by teaching in Virginia schools. Pay cadets would be accepted on a space-available basis and would be charged full fees of $225 per year.[12]

Professor Smith believed that more pay cadets should be accepted at the institute and recommended changes to the infrastructure. His ideas were accepted by the board and in two years, pay cadets overtook the number of state cadets admitted. Smith conferred with Col. Sylvanus Thayer, the former superintendent of West Point for suggestions on academics, uniforms, arms, and equipment. As a result, the course of education mirrored that of West Point and included mathematics, mechanics, chemistry, engineering, tactics, French and German languages, as well as English and German literature.[13]

On November 11, 1839, 17 regular cadets and six irregular cadets were admitted to the new school. VMI was the second public college in Virginia, and among the first colleges in the south to offer engineering and math courses.[14] Even though VMI was initially created to provide a replacement for the state military arsenal guard, it became the primary college in Virginia for graduating engineers, teachers, and officers for the state militia. The popularity of VMI and the military school concept soon spread throughout the south and offered as a model for all subsequent institutions. The institute offered cadets a spartan, physically demanding environment, combined with strict military discipline and has been called by some the "West Point of the South."[15]

---

11. Ibid., 9.
12. Ibid., 9–10.
13. Ibid., 11.
14. Ibid., 11–12.
15. Several other schools were known as the "West Point of the South," including Georgia Military Institute, the University of Alabama, and The Citadel.

VMI regulations decreed there would be an encampment, with the instruction being exclusively military after graduation exercises on July 4 until September 1 of every year. Summer encampment consisted of tents on the parade ground located next to barracks, where new cadets received instruction in military drills as well as in academic subjects, preparing them for placement examinations in late August.

The military system began for the matriculating VMI cadets during summer encampments before the start of the regular school year because the arsenal had to be continuously guarded. This was the first and most important military training that new cadets received—and VMI regulations made no provision for a summer furlough for rising sophomores.

New cadets often wrote to their parents about the summer encampment. One cadet wrote:

> We have to get up every morning at 5 o'clock, go to squad drill at 5 1/2, drill for an hour, come back, go to breakfast at seven, and then we go to squad drill again at nine, drill until ten, come back and study until twelve, and then go to recitation, go to dinner at 1 o'clock, study until four, go to recitation, and then go to squad drill again at five, drill until six, come back and go to dress parade half past six, go to supper at 7 o'clock and then we go to bed at ten. You can see we have not got much time to spare—tell you it keeps me busy as a bee."[16]

First-year cadets also had to face the established practice of hazing, beginning with the summer encampments. Hazing was very tough on the "Rats," and sometimes resulted in injury, first year cadets resigning, or the perpetrators being dismissed from the Institute. One typical hazing incident happened after supper, when the corporal of the guard would order a Rat to go on guard at an outer post and let no one pass without the countersign. The Rat would be given his gun, but unloaded. After the corporal left, about 25 cadets surrounded the poor plebe and attempted to take his gun away from him. Frightening the first-year cadet, the upper classmen succeeded most of the time, but occasionally a Rat would fight back and injuries would occur. Cadet Thomas Munford hated this cruel activity when he was a Rat. When he later served as president of the board of visitors from 1884 to 1888, he took a firm stance and fought for the elimination of all hazing. He described it as a "vulgar, cowardly, bullying practice."[17]

---

16. Richard M. McMurry, *Virginia Military Institute Alumni in the Civil War*, (Lynchburg, VA, 1999), 23.
17. Thomas T. Munford to James T. Murfee, March 4, 1911, Private Collection of David Center, Highland Home, Alabama. Thomas's brother, George

As a cadet, Munford remembered that he experienced "the strangeness of new surroundings, the stir of cadets arriving, and perhaps a tinge of homesickness." He first roomed with Stapleton Crutchfield, who became Stonewall Jackson's chief of artillery. Twenty-one graduates of VMI served under Munford in the Civil War. He recalled fondly his friendships with fellow VMI cadets Raleigh E. Colston, Robert E. Rodes, among others.[18]

Thomas Munford entered VMI after the summer encampment of 1849. He went into the superintendent's office to register as a cadet at Virginia Military Institute. He made his deposit at the Treasurer's office and lined up to sign his name to the Roll of the Corps. He recalled, "a cadet in front of me stepped aside and courteously handed me the pen which he had just used. It was Cadet James T. Murfee. He stood until I had signed my name, asked about some mutual friend, and we went together to the Officer of the Day's tent, who assigned us to the same tent. We were later assigned to the same company and the same table in the mess hall." Munford and Murfee remained lifelong friends, both serving in the Civil War. During their senior year, Murfee became the orderly sergeant for Company A at a time when Munford was adjutant of the corps.[19]

While a senior at VMI, Munford came to be closely associated with Major Thomas Jonathan Jackson, the new professor of natural and experimental philosophy (physics) and artillery. Munford recalled that in mid-August 1851, Superintendent Smith ordered him, as adjutant of the cadet corps, to read an order to all cadets at dress parade, informing them of Jackson's appointment. Smith, in his order proclaimed, "it is hereby directed that he will assume command of the Corps of Cadets tomorrow morning as acting Commandant in the absence of Colonel William Gilham, granted a leave of absence of 30 days. Major Jackson will be obeyed and respected accordingly."[20]

Munford later quizzed Commandant William Gilham as to what kind of man Jackson was and how much latitude he would allow or tolerate. Gilham, his eyes twinkling, laughed, and answered, "Wait and see! He was very distinguished in the late war with Mexico. How he will do here will depend entirely upon himself. We have a gay set to handle, but they are easily managed if understood."[21] As Gilham bid

---

Wythe Munford, Jr., Class of 1856, resigned from the Institute after a experiencing a hazing incident in August 1852. Reference: VMI Archives.
18. Ibid.
19. Thomas T. Munford, "Address to the Graduates and Corps of Cadets of Marion Institute, May 23, 1916," Munford–Ellis Papers, DU.
20. Thomas T. Munford, "How I Came to Know Major Thomas Jonathan Jackson," Munford–Ellis Papers, DU, Box 18, 1.
21. Ibid.

Munford goodbye, he told him to "help Major Jackson out all you can."[22]

William Gilham, who had served in the Mexican-American War, began his teaching career at the Institute in 1846. In November 1859, at the request of the Virginia Governor Henry A. Wise, Major Gilham led a contingent of the VMI cadet corps to Charles Town, Virginia (now West Virginia), to provide additional military security for the hanging of militant abolitionist John Brown on December 2, 1859, following Brown's raid on the federal arsenal at Harpers Ferry.

Munford remembered the morning of Jackson's arrival: "While engaged in marching in the new Guard, the usual crowd had assembled to hear the music of the band in front of the camp on the parade ground."[23] Jackson had just arrived in Lexington one day before the August 14 review of cadets and was not yet known by them. Jackson slipped in among the spectators unnoticed. Munford was in charge of the encampment that day. A ruckus occurred during the daily morning parade review when a cadet yelled at the unbeknownst substitute commandant, "Come out of them boots, they are not allowed in this camp."[24] Munford heard this and to his horror realized that the remark was aimed at Jackson, who was standing among the spectators. Almost panic-stricken, Munford turned over command to the Officer of the Day, Capt. Thomas R. Thornton, and rushed over to salute Jackson, apologizing for the insolent cadet. Munford couldn't help but notice the enormous size of Jackson's feet in those worn and well-blackened artillery boots. Later he recalled of the contrast between Jackson and Gilham, "one stride of (Jackson's) would equal two of Gilham's; his foot occupied double the space."[25]

To Munford's great relief, he saw that Jackson had paid no attention to the cadet's yelling. The new professor had not intended to formally review the cadets during the exercise, but preferred just to watch to see how things were done. He stated he was glad matters worked out the way they did, but Munford was left shaken by the experience. Munford had been charged by Gilham to be Jackson's aide and assist him in getting established with the cadet corps, and as far as he was concerned, things were not off to a very good start.[26]

Munford took his new assignment very seriously. He later explained to Jackson at the corps office that Jackson was expected to

---

22. Ibid.
23. Ibid.
24. Thomas T. Munford, "How I Came to Know Major Thomas Jonathan Jackson," Munford–Ellis Papers, DU, Box 18, 2.
25. Frank E. Vandiver, *Mighty Stonewall* (College Station: TX, 1995), 74.
26. Munford, "How I came to Know Major Thomas Jonathan Jackson," 1–2.

give daily orders to the corps, plan its activities, and establish the drill and instruction routine. Jackson carefully looked over the order book and asked for a copy of the cadet regulations. He soon had a thorough knowledge of them.[27]

Jackson told Munford, "Adjutant, I am here amid new men, strange faces, other minds, companionless. I shall have to rely upon you for much assistance until I can familiarize myself with the routine duties, and the facilities for executing them; there is a great similarity I see to West Point, where I was educated. I trust ere long to master all difficulties."[28]

The young adjutant learned quickly that discipline was Jackson's byword. He was "painfully exacting in details," Munford recalled. "Yet there was an earnestness in his manner and precision in his commands that indicated unmistakably what he meant." Munford exhibited the same characteristic of being a man of few, but well-chosen, words when he became Jackson's cavalry chief in the 1862 Shenandoah Valley campaign.[29]

Munford also described Jackson as "a wonder of contradiction and full of eccentricities or idiosyncrasies, but of exalted character as to right and justice, but he was intolerant if he ever became prejudiced."[30] Jackson was "slow in making up his mind, but when he had arrived at a conclusion, he was generally immovable in his opinions about men."[31]

Munford was instantly sympathetic with Jackson's plight, and within a few weeks became a devoted and loyal fan, remembering, "I will give my impression of this grand, gloomy and peculiarly good man and great soldier as he then appeared to me, to grow on me, and I flatter myself to have had the extraordinary advantages to learn to honor and to respect and to love him."[32]

Munford enjoyed his intimate association with Jackson until the corps went into barracks in September 1851. Jackson took meals with the staff, and Munford remembered, "I was privileged to sit at the table with him. I, a thoughtless cadet drinking in his every word, little dreamed that a few years later I would follow that gallant leader through deadly rain of shot and shell and would glory in his abandon

---

27. Ibid., 2.
28. Ibid.
29. Thomas T. Munford, "How I Came to Know Major Thomas J. Jackson," 2; James I. Robertson, Jr., *Stonewall Jackson: The Man, The Soldier, The Legend* (New York, 1997), 115–16.
30. Munford, "How I Came to Know Major Thomas J. Jackson," 3.
31. Ibid.
32. Munford, "How I Came to Know Major Thomas J. Jackson," 2; Vandiver, *Mighty Stonewall*, 75.

and daring in facing every danger until his tragic end at Chancellorsville, where my regiment led his advance."³³ Munford later recalled, "during that time I was the Executive Officer and saw more of him than any man there, and as Adjutant had the best opportunity to study his disposition, and his knowledge of men—for he was taxed by a gay set who in those days were generally the sons of Gentlemen able to supply more money than young men have had since the war."³⁴

Munford thought Jackson, although a notoriously poor professor, was at his best when he instructed cadets in artillery tactics. He recalled, "when he would give the command to the cannoneers to 'Fire,' the ring of his voice was clear enough to be heard and to burn amid the rumbling of the wheels, giving life and nerve to the holder of the lanyard."³⁵ Munford also thought Jackson "was alone; always, the same grand and peculiar, Christian soldier and gentleman."³⁶ He also remembered much later, "I doubt very much if there is a man at the Institute at any time who had been thrown more directly with him [Jackson] or who knew him personally better than I did."³⁷

Major General Thomas Jonathan "Stonewall" Jackson circa 1863

Cadet Thomas T. Munford was Jackson's Adjutant while a senior at Virginia Military Institute. He got to know Jackson intimately and Jackson liked him. Munford was at the front with Jackson on Jackson's flanking maneuver at Chancellorsville.

(Courtesy: Library of Congress)

---

33. Thomas T. Munford, "Address to the Graduates and Corps of Cadets of Marion Institute, May 23, 1916," Munford–Ellis Papers, DU.
34. Ibid.
35. Vandiver, *Mighty Stonewall*, 75.
36. Thomas T. Munford to John C. Ropes, December 7, 1897, in John C. Ropes Papers, Howard Gotlieb Archival Center, Boston University, Boston, MA.
37. Thomas T. Munford to E. W. Nichols, July 23, 1911, Munford Papers, VMI, Lexington, VA.

Professor Gilham, unlike Jackson, was popular with the cadets. Cadet Munford wrote that Gilham "was the brightest professor we had in his day—scientifically—and was a superb drill master, the best I ever saw."[38]

During the academic year, military duty continued as "cadets daily practiced in military exercises, at such hours as not interfere with their regular studies." Military drill was held daily at 4 p.m. Monday through Thursday, with Friday reserved for a full-dress parade and inspection on Saturday.[39]

In addition to academics and military duties, cadets were also expected to perform guard duty, a tiring and tedious detail that was far from being a favorite among cadets. Cadets constantly complained about guard duty, but VMI's administration was unmoved.

Third classmen (rising sophomores) were employed as instructors to teach the new cadets military basics such as the manual of arms and small unit drill. This system had benefits for both the new and seasoned cadets, as it allowed new cadets to get their first taste of military life while providing senior cadets valuable experience in training men. In addition to the summer encampments, the Corps also undertook long marches throughout the upper Shenandoah Valley.[40]

At the beginning of 1852, during Munford's senior year, there was a revolt of the first classmen. The grievance sprang from the action of the overly aggressive First Captain of the Cadet Corps, William M. Gordon, who was unhappy with the cadets' in-formation performance. He ordered a cadet private to "keep his eyes to the front." Still steaming from a quelled mutiny of the cadet corps the previous year, most of the senior class rallied behind the private. Cadet Adjutant Munford supported his fellow officer, Captain Gordon. Gordon was relieved of his command. After several months of investigation by a review board, the captain's actions were deemed proper, and to the utter disappointment of his classmates, he was reinstated. Feelings ran so high that the captain's life was threatened, and he had to carry a weapon to defend himself.[41]

Matters were not settled as far as most of the senior class were concerned. Several fights ensued, and when time came to purchase class

---

38. Francis H. Smith, *History of the Virginia Military Institute* (New York, 1912), 111.
39. Michael M. Wallace, "The Use of The Virginia Military Institute Corps of Cadets as a Military Unit Before and During the War Between the States," 18.
40. Ibid.
41. Byron Rarwell, *Stonewall: A Biography of General Thomas J. Jackson* (New York, 1992), 95; *The Cadet*, February 3, 1895.

rings, many seniors of the 28-member graduation class refused to buy the normally inscribed class ring. Instead, most decided to have their rings inscribed "One of 26," not "28," thereby disowning Gordon and Munford. Munford and several others determined to have their own rings marked "One of 28."[42]

Upon graduating from VMI in 1852, Thomas Munford had to choose a career path. He could have, like his father and grandfather, studied law. He could venture into business. Since he was a civil engineer, he could have made that his profession. The part of his life spent in Lexington at VMI probably helped him realize he preferred the mountains and country living to urban city life. Even so, he tried clerking in Richmond for Judge John Y. Mason of the I. R. & K. Railroad for a brief period in 1853. He abandoned that effort soon after, moving back to the country to join his younger brother, Wythe, in the farming business.[43]

The next chapter in Thomas Munford's life saw him find success as a farmer. He married and began his life as a family man. As the threat of a civil war loomed, he faced making some life-changing decisions.

---

42. *The Cadet*, February 3, 1895, February 7, 1914.
43. Vandiver, *Mighty Stonewall*, 74; Douglas Southall Freeman, *A Study in Command*, I, 707; R. A. Brock, *Virginia and Virginians: Eminent Virginians*, 579; Biographical Sketch, Munford Papers, VMI; Akers, Thesis, 6.

CHAPTER THREE

Thomas Munford Becomes a Farmer as Virginia Prepares for War

"I do hope that there is yet patriotism enough in the North to save us from the horrors of a Civil War . . . The people up here are not united, nor are they in Roanoke or Botetourt. I fear Virginia is in a bad way."

— Thomas Munford to his stepmother.

Return to the Farming Life

By October 1853, Tom Munford and his brother, Wythe, were busily engaged in the farming life. Tom wrote his father, who had provided financial backing for the brothers' farming enterprise, that his corn crop was in first-class condition. He was concerned about the price of wheat and how his crop would fare against the "joint worm and fly" pests. He boasted of having 27 shoats he guaranteed to weigh in at 180 pounds the next year and 25 more that would weigh an average of 140 pounds. He confidently wrote his father, "You may rest assured that the last pack of corn has been bought for the place that will come out of your pocket—Everything was improving when I left home."[1]

The 1,000-acre farm, called "Rock Spring," was located on Old Buckingham Road, two miles north of the Powhatan County Court House in the village of Powhatan, Virginia. Tom and his brother may have been renting the land at this point, perhaps seeing if they could make a go of it as farmers. At any rate, Tom soon wrote his father of news other than farming; he wrote on October 14, "I think the 25th will be the day for my marriage [to Elizabeth Henrietta Tayloe]."[2]

---

1. Thomas Munford to George Wythe Munford, October 14, 1853, Munford–Ellis Papers, DU.
2. Thomas Munford to George Wythe Munford, October 14, 1853, Munford–Ellis Papers, DU; Article of Agreement between George Wythe Munford and Thomas Munford, January 1, 1854, Munford–Ellis Papers, DU; Lizzie Munford to Powhatan Ellis, Jr., September 14, 1853, Munford–Ellis Papers, DU; Akers, Thesis, 6–7, Virginia Tech; Weekly *Richmond Enquirer*, November 12, 1858.

After a September visit to Thomas's farm, his stepmother, Elizabeth T. Ellis Munford, wrote to her brother, Powhatan Ellis, Jr., about her soon-to-be daughter in law: "It seems right strange to think of Tom's getting married, but he is really a true farmer and intends to remain so, I think his present life too lonely, and I am delighted at the change in his prospects. She is said to be quite pretty and a remarkably intelligent accomplished girl."[3]

For whatever reason, Thomas and Elizabeth Tayloe did not marry until November 7, 1853. Thomas's bride, Elizabeth Henrietta "Etta" Tayloe, was the daughter of Colonel George Plater Tayloe of Roanoke County and Mary Elizabeth Langhorne Tayloe of Roanoke, Virginia. Tom was 22 and Etta was 18 when they married at the Tayloe family home, "Buena Vista," in Botetourt County, Virginia. Buena Vista, located on Ivy Creek on the road leading from Boonsboro to Forest, Virginia, was built in 1833 on one of the oldest estates in the vicinity of Roanoke. Originally spanning 1,500 acres, the land had been in the Tayloe family for five generations. Etta's mother, Mary Elizabeth L. Tayloe, died in childbirth at age 37 in 1848; Elizabeth's father, George, however, was a founding board member of Roanoke Valley Union Seminary, today's Hollins University. He served in that capacity from its inception in 1842 until his death in 1897. He was also a charter board member of Roanoke College and an avid promoter of the development and establishment of the City of Roanoke, particularly through the Buena Vista Land Company.[4]

Thomas received a gift of $10,000 from his father-in-law for the purpose of buying a home. Thomas and his bride purchased the Rock Spring farm, where their marriage flourished. In September 1854, Etta bore their first child, George Tayloe Munford. Thomas assured his parents, "Etta is very well, but is very busy."[5] The couple also had four additional children: Carlton Beverly Munford, Emma Tayloe Munford, George Wythe Munford, and William Munford.

Although Thomas and Wythe were successful farmers in Botetourt County, Thomas began to yearn for the gently rolling hills and mountainous views of Bedford County. He had an uncle who lived there whom he visited often. Before making a final decision to move, however, the brothers decided to try their hand at cotton planting, which they did on a farm in Cassell County, Mississippi. The Yazoo River farm had been given to Tom and Etta by Etta Munford's father.

---

3. Lizzie Munford to Powhatan Ellis, Jr., September 14, 1853, Munford–Ellis Papers, DU; Akers, Thesis, 7. Note: Elizabeth T. Munford was known by her family and others as "Lizzie."
4. Copy of Munford Family Bible records, Jones Memorial Library, Lynchburg, VA.
5. Thomas Munford to George Wythe Munford, September 6, 1854, Munford–Ellis Papers, DU.

Buena Vista
Built circa 1820

Home of George Plater Tayloe and wife, Mary Elizabeth (Langhorne) Tayloe, parents of Thomas T. Munford's first wife, Elizabeth Henrietta Tayloe.

In 1858, Thomas and Etta Munford moved from Rock Spring and acquired land closer to his uncle in Bedford County. They sold the Rock Spring farm and on February 6, 1859, purchased the large and valuable "Glen Alpine" plantation estate from Albert McDaniel and wife, Catherine S. McDaniel, for about $60,000. The Munfords had to borrow substantial additional money to make the purchase, and Etta's father made them a generous loan of $30,000.[6]

Glen Alpine was situated near the town of Coffey between Boonsboro and Perrowville, Virginia. At the foot of the Blue Ridge Mountains, the home was surrounded on three sides by beautiful, aspiring hills with a gap in between two of them immediately in front of the front porch, providing a view of one of the peaks of Otter, and a mountain to the left.

The Munford farm was almost as hilly and rolling as Rock Spring, but the land was fine, producing wheat and tobacco without the need for guano, though Munford still used some for poorer spots. Their house was an elegant brick mansion, with three Corinthian columned-porches, ornamental iron balustrades around the windowsills and caps,

---

6. Copy of Bill in Real Estate Suit, 1918, p. 2; Akers, Thesis, 6, fn9, Virginia Tech; Munford Family Bible; VMI Thomas Munford biography; Thomas T. Munford to E. W. Nichols, July 5, 1857, Munford Papers, VMI.

and front steps of the best granite, cut out of a quarry on the property. There was a handsome, spacious hall running through the center of the first floor, with a massive mahogany stairway to the hall above. Two of the principal bedrooms were cut off from the private stairway, having no doors through the partition wall, thus allowing no communication with the other half of the house. The house had a large, commodious, brick kitchen. There were also three large houses for raising fowl, with doors that one could walk into like other houses, very unlike the typical hole-like doors of other coops. These were all framed and underpinned around with brick about 12 feet wide, 20 feet in length, and well-proportioned in height.[7]

A large dairy had two rooms; under one was the icehouse, though they were both consistent in style and architecture. There was a spacious smoke house, a large pigeon house, and a brick house for holding ashes, prepared for making lye and soap. There was a sizeable stable, two stories high and underpinned with stone. There were 18 stalls for horses and an upper story for hay and oats. The stable was a double house, nine stalls on each side, and every stall separated by a door. Oddly, the stable was placed almost in front of the house. The slave cabins were to the left of the house, there being six to eight of them, bolstered by brick underpinnings. These cabins were well-framed, attractive, with well-constructed brick chimneys and windows and doors with glass in them. All were painted lead color, with planks running upright in modern style. There was a corn house and carriage house. The carriage house was the dwelling in which the proprietor had lived before the present mansion was erected. A barn had yet to be built. There was an uncommonly large orchard, producing excellent fruits, including apples, peaches, pears, cherries, and quinces.

Tom Munford incurred a heavy debt to purchase Glen Alpine, but he worked "like a Trojan and seems disposed to economize as far as possible to pay and work himself out of debt." He had a fine stock of hogs, upwards of 100. His cattle were equally first rate, about 40 of all sizes, as well as a large flock of sheep, and a considerable number of mules and oxen.[8]

In a letter to his stepson Charles Ellis, George Wythe Munford wrote, "His [Thomas's] house is an elegant brick mansion about sixty by fifty feet."[9] Thomas Munford busied himself on the farm, writing his father, "I have a heavy crop of everything that we raise, & as my

---

7. George W. Munford to his wife "Liz," August 19, 1859, Munford–Ellis Papers, DU.
8. Ibid.
9. George Wythe Munford to Ellis Munford, August 20, 1859, Munford–Ellis Papers, DU.

hands are yet green, have but little time to devote to anything. Am in my hay harvest & have a splendid crop. My tobacco is almost too forward—am topping regularly in my first planting. Have about 150,000 planted. Will begin my oat harvest on Friday . . . as you see I have plenty to do"[10]

The 1860 Federal Census lists Thomas (age 29), Elizabeth (age 25) and their children, George Tayloe Munford (age six), C. Beverly Munford (age four), Emma Munford (age two), and Wythe Munford (age six months) residing in the Northern District of Bedford County. Their farm was valued at $83,000, "Par Value" $63,500.[11] In the fall of 1858, Thomas purchased 35 slaves, costing $24,500, from Colonel Thomas N. Burwell of Botetourt County. By 1860, Thomas T. Munford owned 43 slaves who worked his farm.[12]

Virginia's Attitude Towards Slavery

By 1860, the looming crisis of slavery and secession came to the forefront of everyone's life. After Abraham Lincoln's election to the presidency of the United States, most citizens and officials in the Virginia took a "wait and see" attitude, wondering what Lincoln would do. Secession was not on their minds; they hoped for a peaceful resolution to the mounting secessionist movement.

The United States Census for 1860 cited the white population of Virginia at 1,047,299 and the number of slave holders at 52,128.[13] F. E. Chadwick, in his work, *Causes of the Civil War*, wrote, "Of the 52,128 slave holders in Virginia, one-third held but one or two slaves; half held one to four; there were but one hundred and fourteen persons in the whole state who owned as many as a hundred each, and this out of a population of over a million whites."[14]

By this same census, the area of Virginia was fixed at 64,770 square miles, divided into 148 counties. An analysis of the census returns showed that in the "portion of the state lying west of the Blue Ridge

---

10. Thomas T. Munford to George Wythe Munford, July 5, 1857, Munford–Ellis Papers, DU.
11. 1860 Federal Census for northern Bedford County, Virginia.
12. Federal Slave Schedule for 1860 for Bedford County, Virginia. Munford's name was incorrectly spelled "Mumford" in the Schedule; *Richmond Whig*, October 26, 1858.
13. 8th Federal Census for Virginia, 1860.
14. F. E. Chadwick, *Causes of the Civil War, American Nation Series* (New York, 1906), vol. 19:33; Beverley Bland Munford, *Virginia's Attitude Toward Slavery and Secession* (New York, 1909), 125.

Mountains, embracing eighty counties and 37,992 square miles, there were 596,293 whites and only 66,766 slaves; while in the remaining 68 counties containing 26,778 square miles, there were only 451,006 whites and 424,099 slaves, of which 173,109 were in 22 counties situated between the James River and the North Carolina border, known as the 'Black Belt,' where the white population of which was only 128,303."[15] A small percentage of the people of Virginia were owners of slaves, and a still less proportion of slave holders were counted among the soldiers that the Commonwealth contributed to the armies of the Southern Confederacy. In 1860, out of 12,500,000 persons represented in slave-holding communities, only about 384,000 persons—or one in 33—was a slaveholder."[16]

The census returns for Virginia showed that of the 52,128 slaveholders in the state, one-third held but one or two slaves, half one to four, and 114 people held as many as 100 each. A great majority of the slaves in Virginia descended to their owners by the laws of inheritance, just as the plantations of which they were a vital part.[17] Slavery made its home among the great plantations spreading their broad acres far from the centers of population, their owners living distant one from the other.[18]

President Lincoln calls for Southern troops to help quell the Rebellion

After President Lincoln's election, seven states seceded from the Union. Following President Lincoln's call for 75,000 troops to put an end to the rebellion, four more states seceded, including Virginia. Upon the President's requisition for Virginia to provide its quota of troops to put down the rebellion, Virginia Governor John Letcher replied to the Secretary of War:

> I have only to say that the militia of Virginia will not be furnished to the powers at Washington for any such use or purpose as they have in view. Your object is to subjugate the Southern States and the requisition made upon me for such an object—an object in my judgment not within the purview of the constitution or the act of

---

15. Munford, *Virginia's Attitude Toward Slavery and Secession*, 126.
16. Albert B. Hart, ed., *The American Nation: Slavery and Abolition, 1831–1841* (New York, 1906), 67; Munford, *Virginia's Attitude Toward Slavery and Secession*, vol. 16:154.
17. Munford, *Virginia's Attitude Toward Slavery and Secession*, vol. 16:160.
18. Ibid., 177.

1795, will not be complied with. You have chosen to inaugurate civil war; and having done so we will meet you in a spirit as determined as the Administration has exhibited toward the South.[19]

As events unfolded and the possibility of war loomed ever more probable, George Wythe Munford wrote his stepson, Charles Ellis, at the University of Virginia:

> All these things demonstrate the necessity that our young men should furbish up their armour. Not literally their swords and spears, but that mental armour which will enable them to take the lead and direct the unthinking masses. . . . You are fast hastening to the time when you must take your position. Leave no stone unturned to gain all the knowledge you may now. . . . Examine every question thoroughly—never go off half-cocked—a gun that does is the most dangerous weapon.[20]

Thomas voiced his concern to his stepmother, "I do hope that there is yet patriotism enough in the North to save us from the horrors of a Civil War. . . . The people up here are not united, nor are they in Roanoke or Botetourt. I fear Virginia is in a bad way."[21]

In 1859 Bedford, like so much of Virginia, was divided over the question of secession, but by April of 1861 all that had changed. Thomas wrote his step-brother, Charles Ellis Munford:

> I'm happy to inform you that Old Bedford was disenthralled and with her arms on, ready for conflict, before the Gauntlet was thrown down by our would-be-masters. I feel better contented now than I have been for several months, all of my friends are with us at heart and soul and we shall all stand together as a band of brothers. . . . With each son in the field, old Virginia will soon retake her position as the first state and first people of the world.[22]

The escalating tensions between north and south moved the Commonwealth of Virginia to call a special convention to deal with

---

19. Munford, *Virginia's Attitude Toward Slavery and Secession*, 282; Horace Greeley, *American Conflict*, (New York, 2005), vol. I:459; *OR*, Series 3, vol. 1:67–78.
20. George Wythe Munford to Charles Ellis Munford, December 9, 1860, Ellis–Munford–Young Papers, Manuscript, Albert and Shirley Small Special Collection Library, Charlottesville, VA.
21. Thomas Munford to Elizabeth T. Munford, January 10, 1859, Munford–Ellis Papers, DU; Akers, Thesis, 9, Virginia Tech.
22. Thomas Munford to Charles Ellis Munford, April 18, 1861, Munford–Ellis Papers, DU.

the secession crisis. The convention opened on February 13, 1861, after seven seceding states had formed the Confederacy on February 4. Unionist delegates dominated the convention and defeated a motion to secede on April 4. The convention had deliberated for several months, but on April 15, President Lincoln called for troops from all states still in the Union in response to the Confederate capture of Fort Sumter. On April 17, the Virginia convention voted to secede, pending ratification of the decision by the voters. With the entry of Virginia into the Confederacy, the leaders decided in May to move the Confederate capital from Montgomery, Alabama, to Richmond, in part because the defense of Virginia's capital was deemed strategically vital to the Confederacy's survival regardless of its political status. Virginians ratified the Articles of Secession on May 23.

Even though his position on the coming conflict had hardened, Thomas had the responsibilities of family and his farm to consider. His heart was pulled in different directions from the pressures at hand. His finances in the spring of 1861 were certainly a primary consideration. His wife Etta was attuned to his worries and wrote anxiously to her mother-in-law:

> These are indeed sad . . . times that have befallen us. One yet can foretell what the end will be . . . but I do not trust that Civil War may be averted and that matters yet may be settled satisfactorily and peacefully. Mr. Munford feels gloomy at the prospects and is trying to find what course will be best for him to pursue—with his heavy debts but I trust a merciful provider may watch over to provide for us all.[23]

In the end, Thomas Munford laid aside his farmer's work and "exchanged his plow for a sword." On May 8, Thomas enlisted in the army of the South, leaving his wife and their five children, including an infant son, on the farm in Bedford County. They were protected by his older sister and her husband, Mr. and Mrs. W. M. Gwalthmey. Munford traveled to Lynchburg to become the first lieutenant of Company G, the Radford Rangers, a cavalry company from Bedford County.[24]

Thomas's older brother, William, also enlisted and was promoted after the First Battle of Manassas, being named lieutenant colonel of the 17th Virginia Infantry, commanded by Col. Montgomery D. Corse. William also served as lieutenant colonel of the 24th Virginia

---

23. Etta Munford to Elizabeth T. Munford, Spring 1861, Munford–Ellis Papers, DU. Thomas and Etta Munford must have had financial backing from George Plater Tayloe and/or George Wythe Munford.
24. Compiled Service Record for Thomas T. Munford, NA.

Infantry Regiment for a while. He was dropped from the rolls of the 24th Virginia Infantry during a reorganization in April 1862; he was not re-elected to his former rank. He was instead listed as a private of the Richmond Otey Battery from 1862-65. Three months before the end of the war, then-adjutant William Munford was sent through the lines to Canada on special service for the Confederate government, which he performed satisfactorily. In returning, William ran the blockade via Nassau, reaching the South just as Robert E. Lee surrendered.[25] William became an Episcopal minister and practiced in Dallas, Memphis, and New Orleans after the war. He died in Annapolis, Maryland, on March 8, 1904. Thomas's younger brother, Charles Ellis Munford, a member of the Letcher Light Artillery, was killed by artillery shrapnel at the Battle of Malvern Hill on July 1, 1862 during the Peninsula campaign.[26]

Rev. William Munford (1829-1904)
Episcopal priest

Older Brother of Thomas T. Munford

(Courtesy: Rubenstein Library, Duke University)

The year 1861 saw Thomas Munford's military fortunes rise as he was appointed lieutenant colonel of his regiment, leading several companies at the First Battle of Manassas. He gained valuable experience as a cavalry commander, leading to his promotion as colonel of the 2nd Virginia Cavalry.

---

25. *Richmond Times Dispatch*, April 21, 1907.
26. Ibid.

Chapter Four

1861: Outbreak of War
Battle of First Manassas

Munford recalled he "had the honor of delivering to his Excellency the President of the Confederate States ten rifled guns, their caissons, and forty-six horses."

–Lieutenant Colonel Thomas T. Munford
at the battle of First Manassas.

During 1861, Thomas Munford's military fortunes rose as he achieved the rank of lieutenant colonel of his regiment and led several companies at the battle of First Battle of Manassas. He gained valuable experience as a cavalry commander, resulting in his promotion as colonel of the 2nd Virginia Cavalry.

On April 15, 1861, President Abraham Lincoln's call for 75,000 troops from all loyal states to put down the rebellion in the lower South resulted in Virginia switching allegiances from being pro-Union to pro-Confederate almost overnight. Two days later, Governor John Letcher refused Lincoln's request, called out the militia, and volunteer regiments formed. Virginia quickly became an armed camp and formally seceded from the Union on May 22.[1]

Lynchburg, a railroad hub in central Virginia, became a strategic training ground for Virginia soldiers. On May 16, Col. Jubal A. Early was placed in command of arriving troops. On May 9, Gen. Robert E. Lee, in command of all military forces in the state, signaled to Early that West Point graduate and Mexican War veteran, Col. Richard C. W. Radford, would report to him, assume command of a regiment of volunteers, and move them to Culpeper Court House. The volunteers being mustered into service at that time by Lt. Col. Daniel A. Langhorne were organized by Early into three armed regiments: the 24th Virginia Infantry Regiment led by Early; the 28th Virginia Infantry Regiment under Col. R. T. Preston; and the 30th Virginia Cavalry Regiment commanded by Col. Richard C. W. Radford.

---

1. Carol Berkin, Christopher Miller, Robert Cherny, and James Gormly, *Making America: A History of the United States* (Boston, 2005), vol. 1:347.

Radford's regiment were subsequently designated the 2nd Virginia Cavalry.

Originally, the 30th Virginia Volunteer Regiment was to have been an infantry outfit. Radford's prewar service, however, had been as a dragoon—a soldier armed, equipped, and trained to fight mounted and afoot with equal effectiveness. Through Colonel Early in Lynchburg, Radford appealed successfully to Gen. Robert E. Lee to allow the 30th to instead be recruited as cavalry. Early turned over the troops at Lynchburg to Radford and directed him to join his own regiment in the field at Manassas.[2]

The 30th Regiment Virginia Volunteers first mustered into state service between May 9 and June 9, 1861, at Lynchburg. Its companies volunteered from the counties of Bedford, Campbell, Botetourt, Amherst, Franklin, Appomattox, and Albemarle.[3]

The companies making up the regiment had, with one exception, prior service as cavalry in the Virginia Militia. Company A, the "Clay Dragoons" under Capt. William R. Terry, a VMI graduate, led this Troop. Capt. John S. Langhorne commanded Company B, the "Wise Troop." Capt. Andrew L. Pitzer, who had attended VMI, led Company C, the "Botetourt Dragoons." Capt. Giles W. B. Hale, a student at Randolph-Macon College, commanded Company D, "The "Franklin Rangers." Capt. Edgar Whitehead led Company E, the "Amherst Mounted Rangers." Capt. James Wilson commanded Company F, the "Bedford Southside Dragoons." The "Radford Rangers," named in honor of their captain, Edmund W. Radford (brother of Col. Richard C. W. Radford), who had attended VMI and Washington College entered state service as Company G. First Lt. Thomas T. Munford served in this company. Capt. Joel L. Flood, who had attended Emory & Henry College and the University of Virginia, commanded Company H, the "Appomattox Rangers." The "Campbell Rangers," became Company I, under Capt. John D. Alexander. Capt. Eugene Davis, a University of Virginia graduate, led Company K, the "Albemarle Light Horse."[4]

Richard H. Burks, who had attended VMI and served in the Mexican War, served as adjutant of the 30th Volunteer Regiment. The regimental surgeon was Samuel H. Meredith, a graduate of the University of Virginia and the University of Pennsylvania Medical

---

2. Edward G. Longacre, *Lee's Cavalrymen* (Mechanicsville, PA, 2002), 5; *OR* 2/1:806, 822, 852-53, 858; Lieutenant General Jubal Anderson Early, *Autobiographical Sketch and Narrative of the War Between the States* (Philadelphia, PA, 1912), 2.
3. Robert J. Driver, *2nd Virginia Cavalry* (Lynchburg, VA, 1995), 2–3.
4. Irving P. Whitehead, "The Campaigns of Munford's 2nd Virginia Cavalry," 2, UVA; Robert J. Driver, *2nd Virginia Cavalry*, 2–3.

School. William H. Trent of Appomattox County was appointed captain and quartermaster. Albert McDaniel of Bedford County was named captain and commissary officer. William Steptoe of the "Radford Rangers" served as sergeant-major. Lomax Tayloe, who had attended the University of Virginia, was named color sergeant. The quartermaster sergeant, Francis Merriweather, was a graduate of the University of Virginia. John S. Kasey of Company G served as bugler. Reverend William W. Berry was later appointed chaplain. The field officers elected were Col. Richard C. W. Radford and Lt. Col. Thomas T. Munford.[5]

Munford recalled Radford as the best camp officer he had ever seen: "a good disciplinarian, a fine horseman, an excellent swordsman, and a thorough drill master. Personally, he was a brave officer . . . but he had an exalted opinion of the regular service, and underestimated the value of volunteers, which made him very unpopular with his command." Long after the war, Munford recalled, "I was commanded by eight or ten [West Point] men, who regarded 'us' as militia—and there was envy, hatred and malice whenever occasions arose for display of what Institute men could do. . . . Fitz Lee, Rosser and Lomax never seemed to comprehend that anything [not] out of West Point was equal to themselves as soldiers."[6]

Unlike Radford, Munford believed the volunteers who comprised the 30th Virginia were "the best material in the land, mountain men, expert marksmen, accomplished horsemen. Many of them could cut the head off a squirrel on the top of the highest tree, or kill a running deer with a rifle, and all had been accustomed to horses from early infancy, and could ride as well without saddles as with them."[7]

The 30th Virginia Volunteer Regiment, with 23 VMI graduates, officially transferred into Confederate service on July 1, 1861. On or about October 31, 1861, the regiment was re-designated as the 2nd Virginia Cavalry.[8]

During the war, the 2nd Virginia was brigaded, at different times, under Generals Beverly H. Robertson, William E. Jones, Fitzhugh Lee, Williams C. Wickham, and Colonels Thomas T. Munford, and Cary Breckenridge. The 2nd Virginia saw action at First Manassas, Jackson's

---

5. Whitehead, The Campaigns of Munford's 2nd Virginia Cavalry," 2-3; Driver, *2nd Virginia Cavalry*, 2.
6. Thomas T. Munford, "Reminiscences," *Cavalry Journal*, vol. 4 (September, 1891), 279; Thomas T. Munford to "My Dear [E. W. Nichols], February 14, 1914," VMI Archives, Lexington, VA.
7. Thomas T. Munford, "Reminiscences," *Cavalry Journal*, September, 1891, vol. 4:280.
8. Driver, *2nd Virginia Cavalry*, 29.

Valley campaign, the Peninsula campaign, Second Bull Run, Antietam, Fredericksburg, Kelly's Ford, Chancellorsville, Brandy Station, Aldie, Upperville, Gettysburg, and Shepherdstown. After participating in the Bristoe Station and Mine Run campaigns, it fought at Todd's Tavern, Spotsylvania, Yellow Tavern and other actions of Sheridan's Richmond Raid, Haw's Shop, Cold Harbor, and Trevilian Station. The 2nd fought in the Shenandoah Valley with General Jubal Early in the latter half of 1864, and later, in the closing days of the siege of Petersburg and the Appomattox campaign.[9]

On June 8, 1861, Colonel Early summed up the regiment's readiness in a communication to Robert E. Lee:

> There is no company of cavalry here fully armed. Two companies have double-barreled shot-guns, bought by their counties, but no sabers, and are but beginning to drill. There are two companies tolerably well drilled, with forty or fifty sabers each. One has no guns and the other a few. There are two other companies, one of which has about forty sabers and a few guns, just commencing to drill. There are about a hundred flint-lock pistols, which have been gathered from old companies. A number of sabers, of old patterns, have also been collected. All the companies want cartridge-boxes and cap-boxes. . . . All the companies here are well mounted, and would make fine companies if there were arms for them.[10]

In Lynchburg, companies of the 30th Volunteer Regiment guarded the munitions magazines and drilled until ordered to Manassas by Gen. Robert E. Lee. Companies A and B left Lynchburg on June 10; Companies C and D on June 17; and Companies E and F departed about the end of June. Some companies bypassed Lynchburg after forming and headed directly for Manassas Junction.[11]

By mid-June, Radford's companies had arrived at their respective camps in northern Virginia. Companies E, F, G, H, and I camped at Milford Mills, near Camp Pickens. Company D deployed at Leesburg, guarding the Potomac River crossings. Company C served with the headquarters of the advanced Confederate forces near Fairfax Court House. Company A positioned itself at "Camp Radford" at Frying Pan Church. Company B camped near Centreville.[12]

On June 19, Jubal Early reported to Gen. Pierre G. T. Beauregard at Manassas and deployed his regiment, the 24th Virginia Infantry, four

---

9. Civil War Soldiers and Sailors System (CWSS–NPS–CW-S7SS).
10. *OR* 2:912.
11. Driver, *2nd Virginia Cavalry*, 6.
12. Ibid., 10.

miles east of Manassas Junction. Here, the regiment guarded the fords of Bull Run immediately above its junction with the Occoquan. At this time, brigades had not yet been formed, but in a few days, the regiments under Beauregard's command organized into six brigades: one made up of South Carolina troops under Brig. Gen. Milledge L. Bonham; another comprised of Alabama and Louisiana troops under Brig. Gen. Richard S. Ewell; a brigade of South Carolina and Mississippi troops under Brig. Gen. D. R. Jones; a brigade of Virginia troops under Col. George H. Terrett (subsequently replaced by Brig. Gen. James Longstreet); a brigade of Virginia troops under Col. Philip St. George Cocke; and a brigade composed of the 7th and 24th Virginia, and the 4th South Carolina Regiments under Early's command. The 4th South Carolina had been sent to Leesburg in Loudoun County and did not join Early's brigade; it was subsequently replaced by the 7th Louisiana Regiment.[13]

After this organization, the troops deployed as follows: the 4th South Carolina Regiment and Maj. Chatham R. Wheat's Louisiana battalion at Leesburg under Col. Nathan Evans; Bonham's brigade at Fairfax Court House, Cocke's at Centreville, and Ewell's brigade at and near Fairfax Station, all in front of Bull Run. Meanwhile, Brig. Gen. David R. Jones's brigade encamped on the south side of the Run near the railroad, at a place called Camp Walker, Longstreet's at the Junction, and the 7th and 24th Virginia Regiments of Early's brigade, camped separately, northeast and east of the Junction, three to four miles apart. The cavalry, consisting of Colonel Radford's regiment of nine companies and several unattached companies, mainly scouted and picketed with Evans, Bonham, and Ewell. One company on Early's right watched the lower fords of the Occoquan, and the landings on the Potomac below the mouth of the Occoquan. There, another company subsequently joined it.[14]

Just prior to the great battle at Manassas on July 21, General Beauregard, commander of the Army of the Potomac, promised Colonel Radford, the most senior cavalry officer, the command of all of the cavalry; but on July 16, Lt. Col. James Ewell Brown Stuart of Gen. Joseph E. Johnson's army at Winchester was appointed to the post, receiving his colonel's commission and promotion with the support of Johnston. This rejection so soured Radford that he eventually decided to leave the army upon its reorganization in April 1862.[15]

---

13. OR 2/1:806, 822; Early, *Autobiographical Sketch and Narrative of the War Between the States*, 3–4.
14. OR 2/1:806, 822; Early, *Autobiographical Sketch and Narrative of the War Between the States*, 4.
15. Munford, "Reminiscences," *Cavalry Journal*, 280.

On the eve of the first major battle of the war, Colonel Radford commanded a mixture of cavalry companies, primarily from the 30th Virginia, but also including the "Chesterfield Troop" and the "Black Horse Troop;" in September these would become companies B and H, respectively, of the 4th Virginia Cavalry, and some independent cavalry squadrons. Radford's combination of cavalry companies was assigned to Gen. Bonham's 1st Brigade of the Confederate Army of the Potomac under Beauregard. Bonham assigned Lt. Col. Munford a squadron of the "Black Horse Troop," under Capt. William H. Payne and the "Chesterfield Troop," under Capt. William B. Ball. Munford's squadron was joined the day of the 21st by the Wise Troop (Company B of the 30th Virginia), led by Capt. John S. Langhorne and the Franklin Rangers (Company D of the 30th Virginia), under Capt. Giles W. Hale. Langhorne's company, had been detailed to the Loudoun Artillery in the morning, but joined Munford about 5:00 p.m.[16]

Meanwhile, by early July 1861, Union Brig. Gen. Irvin McDowell had amassed five divisions numbering nearly 36,000 troops in Alexandria, Virginia. McDowell's plan was to march westward in three columns and make a diversionary attack on the Confederate line at Bull Run with two columns. The third column would move around the Confederate right flank to the south, cutting the railroad to Gordonsville, and threatening the rear of the Rebel army. Successful execution of this plan would result in isolating the Confederate force at Manassas from potential support from Gen. Joseph E. Johnston's army in the Shenandoah Valley, as well as troops from the south. McDowell reasoned that the Confederates would be forced to abandon Manassas Junction and fall back 40 miles to the Rappahannock River, the next defensible line in Virginia, relieving pressure on Washington. From Alexandria, the Federal commander planned to proceed with 31,000 troops through Fairfax Court House and Centreville, before sending Col. Samuel P. Heintzelman's 3rd Division across the Occoquan at Wolf Run Shoals to unleash a surprise attack on Beauregard's right flank at Manassas. McDowell's forward movement began on July 16, and on the morning of July 17, his forces reached the outskirts of Fairfax Court House.[17]

Confederate General Beauregard assembled some 21,000 Confederates—Virginia regulars and militia troops—along Bull Run to oppose McDowell. The majority of Beauregard's troops deployed behind Bull Run, guarding the various fords between the Warrenton Turnpike and the railroad bridge, 25 miles southwest of Washington.

---

16. *OR* 2/1:534–35, 552.
17. John Hennessy, *The First Battle of Manassas* (Lynchburg, VA, 1989), 9; Longacre, *Lee's Cavalrymen*, 8.

Beauregard posted two outposts to monitor McDowell's march south. At the first outpost was Bonham's 1st Brigade, positioned at Fairfax Court House, 14 miles west of Washington and 10 miles north of Manassas. The second outpost was manned by Brig. Gen. Richard S. Ewell's 2nd Brigade, located near Sangster's Station and along Braddock Road up to its intersection with Little River Turnpike, five miles south of Bonham's position.[18]

Aware that he was heavily outnumbered, on July 14 General Beauregard sent his aide-de-camp, James Chesnut, to meet with President Jefferson Davis, Robert E. Lee, Adjutant and Inspector General Samuel Cooper, and Col. John S. Preston (of Beauregard's staff) to discuss Beauregard's plan for the impending battle. Beauregard proposed that Davis reinforce him with Gen. Joseph E. Johnston's 11,000-man (8,334 effectives would be on the battlefield at Manassas) Army of the Shenandoah Valley. Under the plan, Beauregard and Johnston would first defeat McDowell's army at Manassas. Then, Johnston was to return to the Valley, aided by part of Beauregard's forces, to destroy Maj. Gen. Robert Patterson's Union army. Next, Johnston and Beauregard would unite with Brig. Gen. Richard S. Garnett in northern Virginia for an invasion of Maryland. Finally, the combined forces would launch an assault on Washington. But Davis rejected Beauregard's entire plan, including Johnston's reinforcement at Manassas, after Gen. Robert E. Lee and Adjutant and Inspector

General Pierre G. T. Beauregard Post War Photo

Beauregard blamed Jefferson Davis for failing to follow up on the victory at First Manassas. His battle report was leaked to the press, inflaming passion in Davis, who felt blindsided.

(Courtesy: Library of Congress)

---

18. Ibid., 18.

General Samuel Cooper advised against it. Instead, Davis reinforced Beauregard with Col. Eppa Hutton's 8th Virginia Infantry, Brig. Gen. Theophilus Holmes's two regiments at Fredericksburg, Col. Wade Hampton's Legion, and the 6th North Carolina under Col. C. F. Fisher in Richmond.[19]

In his official report of the July 21 battle, Beauregard claimed he had proposed to Davis that they follow up the victory at Manassas by invading Maryland and capturing Washington. Although Beauregard filed the report on August 26, 1861, Davis did not read it until after Adjutant General Cooper received Beauregard's report through official channels in October. Prior to that, however, Davis saw a newspaper synopsis of the account in the *Richmond Dispatch* and perhaps other papers in October, that depicted him in an unfavorable light. He began an urgent call for Beauregard's report. Finally, upon reading Beauregard's account, Davis was surprised that it sustained the newspaper accounts. President Davis scrambled to preserve his reputation, claiming he had not actually rejected the plan because it was never presented to him in writing. After the appearance of the report, Davis's feelings toward Beauregard soured, bringing on a long-lasting feud.[20]

After the July 14 meeting with Davis, Beauregard revised his plans. His advance force at Fairfax Court House was to make the appearance of a confrontation, but not to engage the enemy. From there, Beauregard's forward soldiers would gradually pull back along a predetermined path in order to lure the Union army to Bull Run at Mitchell's Ford, where Confederate forces occupied the higher ground.[21]

At dawn on the 17th, Colonel Radford was informed by Bonham of the approach of McDowell's forces at Fairfax Court House. Bonham followed Beauregard's orders to fall back along the preplanned line of retreat to Centreville and then Manassas.[22]

To strengthen his rear guard, Bonham split the cavalry into three parts. He assigned one squadron, composed of the companies of Captains Williams C. Wickham and Joel W. Flood, to report to Col. Joseph B. Kershaw, commander of the 2nd South Carolina Infantry Regiment. He ordered Lieutenant Colonel Munford and his squadron

---

19. *OR* 2:485, 487, 505–08; Hennessy, *The First Battle of Manassas*, 10.
20. *OR* 2:485, 504–14; *Richmond Dispatch*, October 23, 1861; *Richmond Whig*, October 23, 1861; *Shreveport Daily News*, November 5, 1861; *New York Times*, November 13, 1861; Varina Davis, *Jefferson Davis, Ex-President of the Confederate States of America: A Memoir* (New York, 1890), 120–37.
21. Hennessy, *The First Battle of Manassas*, 9.
22. *OR* 2/1:457.
23. Ibid., 457–58.

to join Col. Thomas G. Bacon's 7th South Carolina Infantry Regiment, and three of Radford's companies to cooperate with Col. E. B. Cash's 8th South Carolina Infantry Regiment. Radford reported that Colonel Munford helped lead the retreat in "perfect order and to my entire satisfaction, bringing off everything."[23]

McDowell's Union force, unopposed, gained control of Fairfax Court House sometime after 9:00 a.m. on the morning of July 17, 1861. Realizing his troops were already tired from the summer heat and the long march from Alexandria, McDowell ordered them to march slowly westward towards Centreville. They unhurriedly followed the Confederate retreat.[24]

On the night of the 17th, McDowell came up with a plan for a reconnaissance the next day to determine if a turning movement around the Confederate right would succeed. McDowell ordered Brig. Gen. Daniel Tyler to march to Centrerville and give the impression that he intended to cross Bull Run at Blackburn's Ford and then move to Manassas. The reconnaissance was to be conducted by General Heintzelman's division. McDowell wanted to turn the Confederate right by crossing the Occoquan at Wolf Run Shoals and then cut the Orange and Alexandria Railroad.[25]

Although McDowell expressly told Tyler to take Centreville and remain there while watching the roads to Bull Run and Warrenton, Tyler exceeded his orders. McDowell cautioned him about not bringing on a general engagement. On July 18, taking a squadron of cavalry and two light companies of Col. Israel B. Richardson's brigade, with Colonel Richardson, Tyler proceeded on a reconnaissance down the road toward Manassas Junction all the way to Blackburn's Ford on Bull Run. He detected only a battery of artillery and some pickets on the opposite side. But the opposite side of the ford was in fact defended by Longstreet's brigade, consisting of the 1st, 11th, and 17th regiments of Virginia Volunteers, with reinforcements readily available. Tyler ordered up artillery support and the remainder of Richardson's brigade to feel out the enemy, setting off the general engagement he was ordered not to start. The Union attack commenced with 30 minutes of cannon fire, followed by an assault with 3,000 infantry, which Longstreet's troops repelled with difficulty. After a few minutes, the Federal forces launched a second attack, which again was repulsed by Longstreet's skirmishers. After Longstreet beat back a third attack, he took the offensive with artillery fire from the Washington Artillery, driving the invaders back towards Centreville.[26]

---

24. Hennessey, *The First Battle of Manassas*, 9.
25. Ibid., 9, 12–13.
26. *OR* 2:310–12, 461–62.
27. Ibid., 478; Hennessy, *The First Battle of Manassas*, 9.

After learning of McDowell's advance on Fairfax Court House, President Davis changed his mind, and at 1:00 a.m. on July 18th, he requested Adjutant and Inspector General Samuel Cooper, the senior officer, to telegraph Johnston to immediately move his army from the Shenandoah Valley to Manassas and support Beauregard. Johnston, without presidential approval and in direct contact with Beauregard, had been preparing to leave the Valley since the 15th, and so he easily slipped away from the overly cautious Maj. Gen. Robert Patterson and headed for Manassas Junction. Meanwhile, the delay caused by the slow march of McDowell's army from Fairfax Court House proved crucial in allowing reinforcements from Johnston's Army of the Valley to rendezvous with Beauregard and his men.[27]

Before daybreak on the 18th, as General Bonham neared Bull Run Creek and under pressure from McDowell during the retreat, he fell back across Bull Run at Mitchell's Ford. Radford occupied the position between Col. Philip St. George Cooke and General Bonham. In late morning, Capt. R. B. Ayers's Union artillery battery pummeled the Confederate forces at Mitchell's Ford crossing for two hours. Private Rufus Peck of the 2nd Virginia Cavalry recalled the Union cannonade on the morning of July 18:

> During the night we marched across Bull Run at Mitchell's Ford and laid down for the remainder of the night in front of the guns at Manassas Junction. We were awakened next morning by the firing of one of the enemy's guns called "Long Tom." As this was the first big gun I had seen fired, I remember well the appearance of that shell to me. It looked more like a gate-post flying through the air than anything else I could compare it to. After hissing through the air about a mile it exploded, and I told the boys I knew it had blown Manassas Junction to "kingdom come" and she would need no more protection.[28]

While the fighting raged at Mitchell's Ford, Heintzelman's reconnaissance showed the roads to be too narrow and winding to facilitate movement of troop columns and artillery. McDowell abandoned his plan for a surprise attack on the Confederate right flank and decided instead to make a diversionary attack with Gen. Daniel

---

28. Rufus H. Peck, *Reminiscences of a Confederate Soldier of Co. C of the 2nd Virginia Cavalry* (Fincastle, VA, 1913), 4. Note: the 30-pounder Parrott known as "Long Tom" was not engaged on July 18 but two 20-pounder Parrotts under Lt. S.N. Benjamin were engaged at Blackburn's Ford. Peck may have been mistaken about the date, and was actually recalling events of the morning of July 21.

29. *OR* 2:307, 489; Hennessy, *The First Battle of Manassas*, 27.

Tyler's 1st Division at Stone Bridge on the Warrenton Turnpike. McDowell planned to turn the Confederate left with the divisions of brigadier generals David Hunter at Sudley Springs and Samuel P. Heintzelman at Poplar Ford. From here, these two divisions could march into the Confederate rear. The brigade of Col. Israel B. Richardson continued to harass the Confederates at Blackburn's Ford, preventing them from thwarting the main attack. Major General Robert Patterson had expected to tie down Johnston in the Shenandoah Valley so that reinforcements could not reach Beauregard. McDowell's plan required close coordination but ultimately failed due to poor execution by his inexperienced officers and men. Despite this failure, the Confederates, who had been planning to attack the Union left flank, found themselves at an initial disadvantage.[29]

Soon after President Davis decided to support Beauregard with Johnston's troops, Confederate reinforcements began arriving from the Shenandoah Valley by railroad, including Brig. Gen. Thomas J. Jackson's brigade of 2,500 on July 19. At sunrise on the 20th, more of Joseph E. Johnston's reinforcements pulled in—the 7th and 8th Georgia regiments of Col. Francis S. Bartow's brigade, numbering 1,400 men. At about noon, the Commander of the Army of the Shenandoah, Johnston himself arrived, accompanied by Brig. Gen. Barnard Elliot Bee's 3rd Brigade, as well as the 4th Alabama, 2nd Mississippi, and two companies of the 11th Mississippi.[30]

Early on July 21, McDowell began his attack, preempting Beauregard's planned attack of that same morning. At about 5:15 a.m., Israel Richardson on the Confederate right fired a few harassing artillery rounds across Mitchell's Ford in his planned diversionary strike. It was hoped this would prevent the Confederates there and at nearby Blackburn's Ford from reinforcing the Confederates at Stone Bridge. Bonham and Radford, under fire, remained at Mitchell's Ford, holding the position against a possible Federal attack while Longstreet, not knowing of the pending action above Stone Bridge, crossed Blackburn's Ford after receiving his attack orders at 7:00 a.m.[31]

Meanwhile, McDowell's planned flanking maneuver of the Confederate left began late, as a result of the entanglement of troops on the Warrenton Turnpike. By taking a wider detour than originally planned, Heintzelman missed the road to Poplar Ford, where he had been assigned to cross, and ended up following Hunter all the way to Sudley. Colonel William B. Franklin's brigade, leading Heintzelman's column, did not begin crossing at Sudley Ford until late morning.

30. OR 2:486; Hennessy, *The First Battle of Manassas*, 28, 32–33.
31. Hennessey, *The First Battle of Manassas*, 35, 43.
32. Ibid., 40, 44.

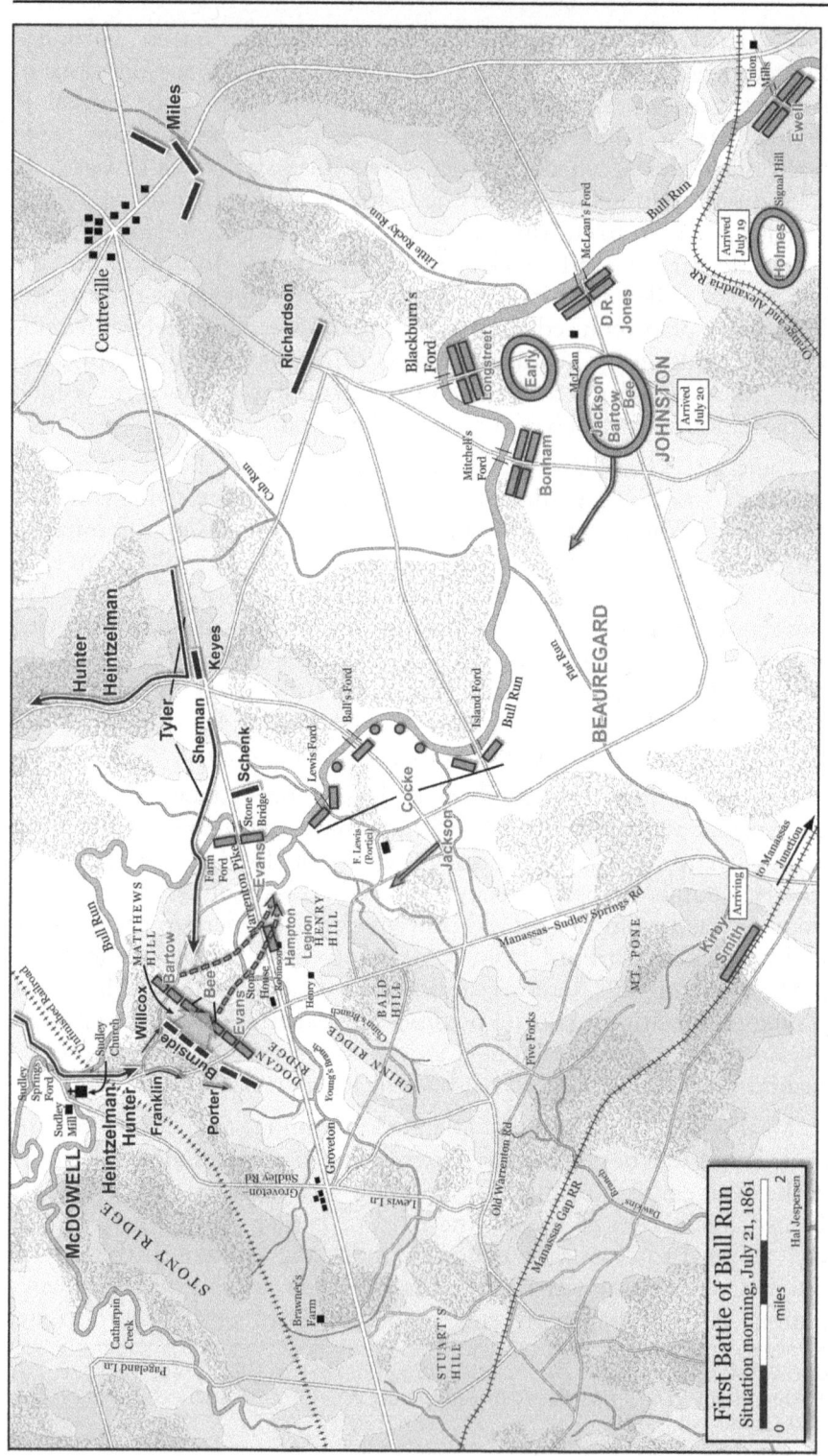

Heintzelman and Hunter did not begin crossing Sudley Ford until 9:30 a.m. Tyler reached Stone Bridge about 6:00 a.m. and began demonstrating, but failed to draw an expected response from the Confederates.[32]

From a hill on the Confederate right flank, signal officer Capt. Edward Porter Alexander observed the main Union column marching toward Sudley Springs. Using signal flags, he alerted Col. Nathan Evans at Stone Bridge. McDowell's element of surprise was lost. All that stood in the way of the advancing 18,000 Union troops (only half that number got across Bull Run before the afternoon) was Evans's brigade. Evans headed for Matthews Hill and Henry Hill to intercept the Union column with 900 of his 1,100 men, with several companies of the 4th South Carolina having been left at Stone Bridge. Evans was eventually reinforced about 11:00 a.m. by Bee's brigade and Bartow's two Georgia regiments. The resulting clash on Matthews Hill was a bloody fight in which neither side could initially prevail. The battle went back and forth until finally, about noon, the Federals drove the Confederates off the hill, forcing them to retreat to Henry Hill. Meanwhile, Beauregard had been transferring troops from his center and right to block the Federals crossing at Sudley Ford as he and Johnston headed for the main battleground.[33]

Fortunately for the Confederates, McDowell did not press his advantage and attempt to seize the strategic ground immediately, choosing instead to bombard Henry Hill from Dogan's Ridge with the batteries of Captains James B. Ricketts's Battery I, 1st U.S. Artillery, and Charles Griffin's Battery D, 5th U.S. Artillery. The Confederates on Henry Hill held on against the Federal fire, preventing the Union army from reaching the Confederates' rear. Finally, more of Beauregard's reinforcements arrived around noon. They were met by Generals Johnston and Beauregard, who had just arrived on the field themselves. Jackson headed for Henry Hill on his own volition, having heard the troops there were in trouble.[34]

Noon also brought Brig. Gen. Thomas J. Jackson's Virginia brigade in support of the disorganized Confederates, who had earlier been joined by Col. Wade Hampton and six companies of Hampton's Legion and several companies of Col. J.E.B. Stuart's cavalry. Some of Stuart's command had been left in the Shenandoah Valley to watch Patterson. Jackson posted his five regiments on the reverse slope of Henry Hill, where they were shielded from direct fire, and managed to assemble 13 guns for the defensive line, which he posted on the crest of

---

33. Ibid., 45–47, 62–64.
34. Ibid., 45–47, 64, 68.
35. Ibid., 68–71.

the hill. Meanwhile, McDowell ordered the batteries of Ricketts and Griffin to move from Dogan's Ridge to Henry Hill for close infantry support. Their 11 guns engaged in a fierce artillery duel against Jackson's 13, set a mere 300 yards away. The Union pieces were now within range of the Confederate smoothbores, and the predominantly rifled pieces on the Union side were not as effective weapons at such close ranges. Many shots fired well over the heads of their targets. The battle raged on. Following Radford's orders, at about 3:00 p.m., Munford supported Colonel Radford on Gen. Thomas J. Jackson's counterattacking right flank.[35]

By 3:00 p.m., the tide of the battle shifted with Jackson's troops capturing Rickett's and Griffin's batteries on Henry Hill. McDowell had two fresh brigades, one was William T. Sherman's, the other, Col. Orlando Willcox's. McDowell was determined to reclaim his lost batteries, and so fighting intensified on Henry Hill. Finally, around 4:00 p.m., Col. Oliver O. Howard's brigade arrived on the field after a fatiguing march. McDowell placed Maj. George Sykes's battalion of regulars on the west slope of Henry Hill to cover the potential withdrawal of the Federals located there. Realizing the futility of sending Howard against the Confederates on Henry Hill, McDowell directed him up Chinn Ridge to gain the Confederate left.[36]

Simultaneously, two of Bonham's regiments—the 2nd South Carolina under Col. Joseph Kershaw, and the 8th South Carolina, led by Col. E. C. B. Cash—arrived and took position along the Sudley Road on the west side of Henry Hill. Other reinforcements arriving were Philip St. George's Cocke's brigade and Capt. Del. Kemper's battery.[37]

Also, at this critical time Col. Arnold Elzey and Col. Jubal Early's brigades joined Cash and Kershaw. Johnston ordered them to attack the Union right. To the west of Sudley Road, Chinn Ridge had been occupied only briefly by Colonel Howard's brigade from Heintzelman's division. At 4:00 p.m., the two Confederate brigades that had just arrived—Early's and Kirby Smith's (now commanded by Col. Elzey after Smith was wounded)—drove Howard's brigade from Chinn Ridge. Beauregard then ordered his entire line on Henry Hill forward. This left Sykes's regulars, the only organized Federal troops on the field. Driven from Chinn Ridge, Howard left the Regulars to cover the retreat. As the Union troops began withdrawing under fire, many panicked and the retreat turned into a rout.[38]

---

36. Ibid., 74, 77, 102.
37. Ibid., 107–10.
38. Ibid., 110–11, 116.
39. *OR* 2:534; Longacre, *Lee's Cavalrymen*, 23.

Radford soon crossed Bull Run just south of Stone Bridge and headed for the turnpike until he was redirected by Johnston to head more eastward for the Cub Run bridge. Munford crossed at Ball's Ford and, upon converging with Radford's forces, he found the enemy in "wild confusion" and charged, capturing 20-some prisoners and several horses.[39]

After capturing the prisoners, Radford and Munford's columns were met by a heavy volley of musketry, disabling four horses and slightly wounding four men. Two cannons on a hill beyond Bull Run then opened fire on the horsemen, killing Radford's brother, Capt. Edmund Winston Radford of Company G of the 2nd Virginia; another officer; and five enlisted men. Dismounted troopers were sent after the guns. The Federals abandoned the guns and fled.[40]

Next, Munford mistook Col. Joseph B. Kershaw's command and Capt. Del. Kemper's battery, located at his rear, for the enemy. Withdrawing his command, Munford watched the mistaken enemy's movements until Kemper opened fire upon the real enemy. Discovering his mistake, Munford recalled his squadron and joined Colonel Kershaw. Upon Kemper's ceasing fire, Munford advanced, finding Maj. John Scott, in command of Capt. Eugene Davis's Company D, which had advanced along the turnpike to the bridge on Cub Run. Munford assumed command of the cavalry there and ordered them to dismount, while sending Capt. William H. Payne's Black Horse Troop to Colonel Kershaw for assistance. As soon as the captured cannons on Munford's side of the creek were hitched up, Major Scott, without consulting Munford, marched off with his Company D troops and the captured guns. Munford continued with the Black Horse and Chesterfield Troops until five more pieces of cannon, caissons, and forges were all hitched up. Munford later boasted as a result of his performance, that he "had the honor of delivering to his Excellency the President of the Confederate States ten rifled guns, their caissons, and forty-six horses."[41]

Munford's command, being exhausted in numbers and condition, withdrew from Cub Run. Afterwards, Munford conducted the train back to Manassas. In his report of the battle, Munford singled out Lt. John Langhorne, praising him for charging an enemy soldier who was behind a cedar tree and, killing him before he could fire. He also commended Pvt. John Taliaferro, of the Black Horse, whose horse was

---

40. Longacre, *Lee's Cavalrymen*, 24; *OR* 2:497, 533. Note: The Federal artillery fire probably came from guns of Capt. J. H. Carlisle's battery near Mrs. Spindle's house.
41. *OR* 2/1:525, 534–35.
42. Ibid., 534–35.

killed under him, and in falling, broke his collar bone. But, "he sprang to his feet, pursued and killed his man with his pistol, running at full speed."[42]

Colonel Radford reported:

> I have no hesitation in saying that the charge made by my own command, in connection with that made by the command under Lieutenant-Colonel Munford, composed of Captains Payne, Ball, Langhorne, and Hale, caused the jam at Cub Creek Bridge, which resulted in the capture of fourteen pieces of cannon, their ammunition and wagons, five forges, thirty wagons and ambulances, and some forty or fifty horses. I base this opinion on the fact that we were in advance of all our forces, and by our charge the enemy were thrown into wild confusion before us, their vehicles of all sorts going off at full speed and in the greatest disorder.[43]

An ensuing attempt by Gen. Joseph Johnston to intercept the retreating Union troops from his right flank, using the brigades of Generals Bonham and James Longstreet, was a failure. The two commanders squabbled with each other and when Bonham's men received some artillery fire from the Union rear guard, and found that Gen. Israel B. Richardson's brigade blocked the road to Centreville, Bonham called off the pursuit.[44]

Officers of the 17th Virginia Infantry won the praises of their superiors for their performance at Blackburn's Ford. Longstreet noted that several officers in his brigade, including Col. Montgomery D. Corse, Lt. Col. William Munford (Thomas T. Munford's brother), and Maj. George W. Brent from the 17th Virginia, "displayed more coolness and energy than is usual amongst veterans of the old service." He was "particularly indebted to Lieutenant-Colonel Munford and Major Brent, who having a spare moment and seeing my great need of staff officers at a particular juncture, offered their assistance." Corse also singled out Munford and Brent, among other officers, for their "gallant conduct" where "the fire was hottest."[45]

The Confederate victory of July 21 was followed by a day-long hard rain as Union troops passed through Fairfax Court House during the night, strewing the roads with clothing, food, arms and camp equipage. McDowell's men, along with panic-stricken northern civilians who had come down to watch the battle, continued their frantic retreat in the direction of Arlington and Washington. Both

---

43. Ibid, 532–33.
44. Ibid., 476, 498.
45. Ibid., 463; *OR* 51/1:34.

armies were sobered by the fierce fighting and high casualties, and they realized the war was going to be much longer and bloodier than anyone had anticipated.[46]

On July 22 Davis, Johnston, Beauregard, and Col. T. J. Jordan (adjutant for Beauregard) held a conference at Beauregard's headquarters in Manassas to discuss the battle and what should be done subsequently. One option—that of crossing the Potomac and taking the fight to Washington City—was discussed, but Beauregard advised against it, warning that the crossing would be perilous due to the strong Federal fortifications along the river. The truth was these fortifications did not even exist and were not even begun until Gen. George B. McClellan was named commander of Washington and troops within the city on July 26. The Confederates pursued instead a more cautious approach in northern Virginia.[47]

---

46. Hennessy, *The First Battle of Manassas*, 121-22; William Marvel, *Mr. Lincoln Goes to War* (Boston, 2006), 149.
47. Davis, *Jefferson Davis, Ex-President of the Confederate States of America: A Memoir*, 112–13.

CHAPTER FIVE

Aftermath of the Battle of First Manassas

On one occasion, Lt. Col. Munford, while reporting to Gen. Joseph Johnston, was invited to dine on turkey and brandy with the commanding general. Munford recalled the usually formal and stern [General Joseph] Johnston as "simply charming; full of life and graces . . . an elegant host."

From the victory at First Manassas through the remainder of 1861, the Confederate Army of Northern Virginia continued to defeat the Federal armies. General Robert E. Lee named J.E.B. Stuart as commander of cavalry of his army. Thomas Munford continued to prove himself a reliable officer, gaining the trust of his men and superiors.

Even though Radford's 30th Virginia had been the first regiment mustered into service in September 1861, Stuart's regiment was designated the 1st Virginia Cavalry. In October, Radford's regiment was re-designated the 2nd Virginia Cavalry. It was the custom of the military to have the commanding officer assigned to the 1st Battalion, 1st Regiment, 1st Brigade, etc. As Stuart was promoted over Radford, it would be humiliating to have a commanding officer assigned to the 2nd Cavalry, whereas a subservient officer of lesser rank be in charge of the 1st Cavalry. A few days later, Col. William E. Jones took over command of the 1st Virginia. Radford was infuriated, and he never forgave Stuart for preempting the naming of his regiment as the 1st Virginia. More likely, the beef was not the Cavalry designation, but rather Radford being passed over as a senior colonel and a junior colonel being promoted instead.[1]

On September 24, 1861, Stuart received a promotion to brigadier general in charge of all mounted forces; his appointment was confirmed in early December. Stuart now commanded all cavalry protecting the Alexandria Line. By October, Stuart commanded about 2,400 troopers, and as additional companies and regiments were added over the next few months, the number of horsemen increased rapidly, especially after including the newly created horse artillery.[2]

1. Munford, "Reminiscences," *Cavalry Journal*, vol. 4 (Sept. 1891), 279.
2. McClellan, *Stuart's Cavalry*, 42; Longacre, *Lee's Cavalrymen*, 54–55.

The battle of First Manassas was followed by eight months without a major battle in Virginia. In Brig. Gen. Irvin McDowell's Union army, discipline broke down and morale sank so low that it became impossible to undertake another offensive. President Lincoln called for 500,000 new volunteers for the army, and thousands of new recruits immediately poured into Washington at a rate of about 10,000 per week. Major General George B. McClellan, who had won a series of victories in western Virginia, replaced McDowell on July 26, 1861.[3]

On November 1, commanding Gen. Winfield Scott retired, and McClellan ascended to command all Union armies, except the Department of Virginia, which comprised the area within 60 miles of Fort Monroe. McClellan spent this relatively quiet period restoring discipline, organizing, and training what became known on August 20 as the Army of the Potomac. He made it a priority to take better care of his troops, endearing himself to them. McClellan found only four forts on the Virginia side of the Potomac and only one on the northern side; no organized defensive line had yet been established anywhere. He began immediately building fortifications around Washington—a series of 48 forts and redoubts to guard the city's 37-mile perimeter. He also established a defensive line, positioning these infantry divisions: Maj. Gen. Nathaniel Banks on the far right on the Maryland side of the Potomac near Sandy Hook opposite Harpers Ferry; Brig. Gen. Charles P. Stone on the river between the Capital and Sandy Hook; and Brig. Gen. George A. McCall to the left of Stone near Langley, Virginia.[4]

After the Confederate victory at Manassas, Jefferson Davis adopted a defensive policy. Like their Federal counterparts, the Confederates took advantage of the long absence of major battles and recruited, reinforced, and trained what would become in 1862 the Army of Northern Virginia. On October 21, the Confederate government organized the Department of Northern Virginia, commanded by Maj. Gen. Joseph E. Johnston. This department was in turn divided into three districts: Valley, Potomac, and Aquia, commanded respectively by Major Generals Jackson, Beauregard, and Holmes. On October 22, Jackson was ordered to proceed to Winchester, where he assumed command of 10,000 troops, including the "Stonewall Brigade," Brig. Gen. William W. Loring's 6,000 troops, and Col. Turner Ashby's cavalry.[5]

Following the battle of Manassas, Johnston edged closer to Washington, occupying Centreville, Fairfax Court House, Vienna,

---

3. *Battles and Leaders*, vol. 2:160; James A. Rawley, *Turning Points of the Civil War* (Lincoln: University of Nebraska Press, 1966), 58.
4. *Battles and Leaders*, (New York, 1956), 2:162.
5. *Battles and Leaders*, 2:282; *OR* 5:913–14, 936, 938.

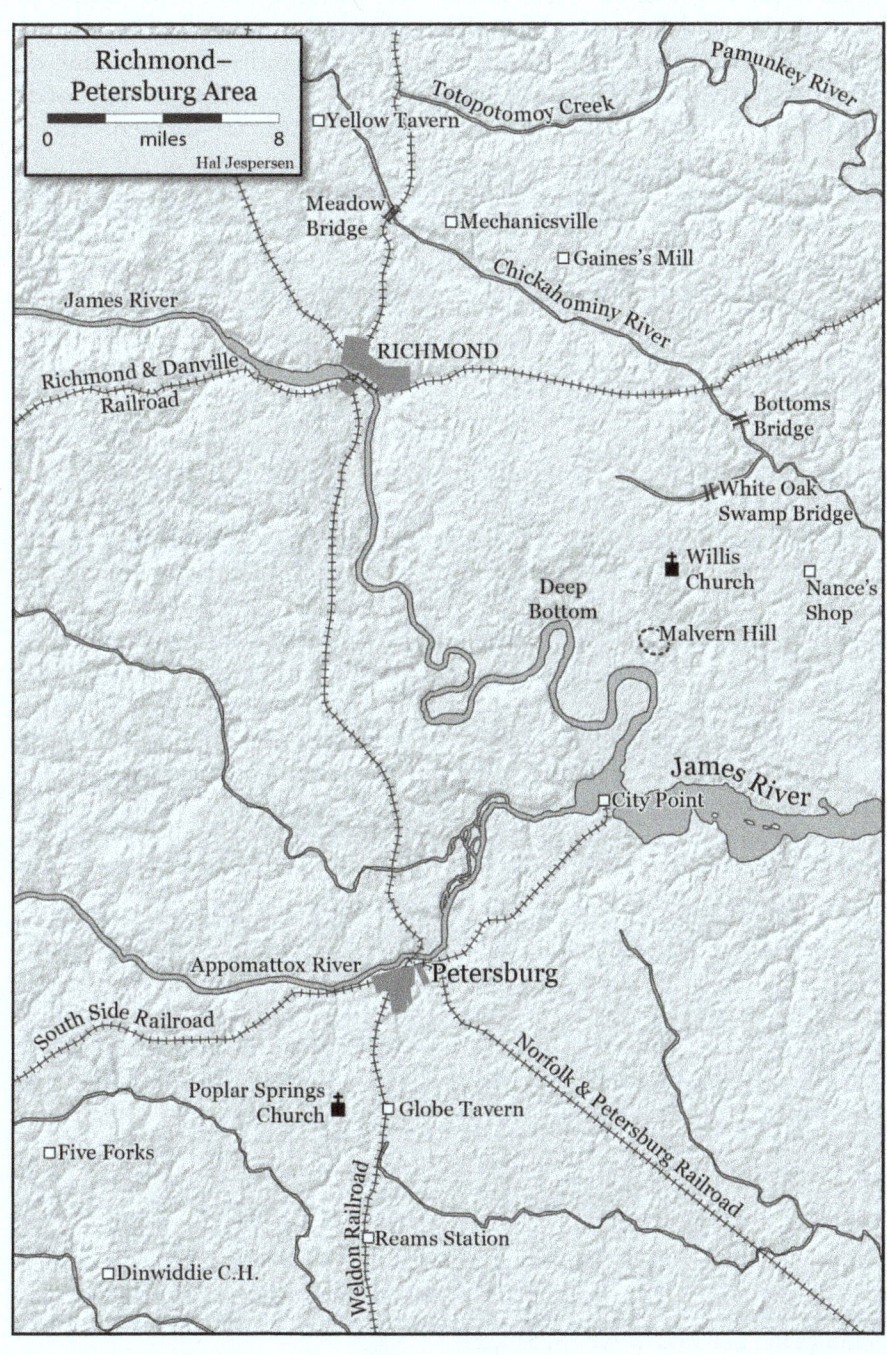

Germantown, Leesburg, and Waterford. Probing further, he established a presence even closer to Washington, with outposts between Annandale on the Little River Turnpike and Falls Church. At this point what came to be known as the Alexandria Line—a line of outposts and picket stations stretching almost 30 miles to the north and west, ending at Leesburg on the upper Potomac—formed. Stuart and Radford's horsemen played a key role in defending the Alexandria Line, often alone. There was no infantry or artillery support; if under a surprise attack, these defenders would clear out quickly. Stuart established his headquarters along the road between Centreville and Fairfax Court House. Stuart's command at this juncture was his nine companies of the 1st Virginia Cavalry and some of the independent companies that had served under Radford before and during the Manassas battle.[6]

Beauregard's forces, including General Bonham, occupied a front about six miles from Flint Hill, through Fairfax Court House and Fairfax Station, to Sangster's Cross Roads. An advance guard of 11 regiments of infantry and Stuart's cavalry was stationed at Falls Church, Munson's and Mason's Hills, at Padgett's (where the Columbia Turnpike enters from Alexandria to Fairfax), and at Springfield Station on the Orange and Alexandria Railroad. This was a good defensive position, and Beauregard recommended that offensive operations not be undertaken. Back in May 1861, the Confederates had erected batteries on the lower Potomac in order to close the river to Federal vessels proceeding to and from Washington. In September, additional batteries were constructed near Evansport. The blockade was effective for unarmed boats but not for armed vessels. It remained in place until March 1862, when the Confederates withdrew to the line of the Rappahannock River.[7]

McClellan fretted constantly, fearing an attack on Washington itself. He continually overestimated the Confederates' strength, believing it to be three to four times his number. In actuality, Johnston, with fewer than 40,000 soldiers, had no plans to attack Washington without substantial reinforcements, while McClellan had about 60,000 troops during August. By October, McClellan had 140,000 men and pressure began mounting for him to take the offensive, pressure which he largely ignored. He would decide when it was time to move on the Confederates.[8]

On September 27, the Confederates' growing concern for the size of McClellan's army convinced them to abandon their outpost at

---

6. Longacre, *Lee's Cavalrymen*, 51–52.
7. *OR* 5:881–82; *Battles and Leaders*, 2:143.
8. David. G. Martin, *The Peninsula Campaign, March-July 1862* (Conshohocken, PA, 1992), 13, 22, 27.

Munson's Hill, within sight of the Capital, and withdraw to Fairfax Court House. On October 17, Johnston again withdrew, consolidating his 40,000 soldiers in a triangular area with Centreville at the apex and a base running from Manassas Junction to the Manassas battlefield. McClellan noticed one position the Confederates had not abandoned was an outpost at Leesburg, the extreme left flank of their line. He thought he could simply demonstrate in front of it and take it without a fight, but he was badly mistaken. On October 19, McClellan ordered Brig. Gen. Charles P. Stone to make the demonstration at Ball's Bluff, but Stone exceeded his authority and before long, a full engagement was underway, one in which the Federals lost half their force of 1,700. The Confederates, however, under Col. Nathan G. Evans, lost only 155 troops. The engagement, though not large, surprised McClellan not to mention President Lincoln. It was another embarrassing setback for the Union Army.[9]

After Manassas, Munford's command consisted of four companies: D and E from the 30th Virginia under Captains Giles W. B. Hale and Edgar Whitehead, respectively; the Black Horse Troop (Company H of the 4th Virginia after September 4) under Capt. William H. Payne; and the Chesterfield Light Dragoons (known as Company B of the 4th Virginia after September 4) under Capt. William B. Ball. They were attached to Gen. James Longstreet's 4th Brigade, stationed from mid-August to mid-October at Fairfax Court House. Munford's troopers moved to Centreville from mid-October to late November.[10]

On November 13, a grand review of all of the cavalry of the Army of the Potomac was held at Centreville, under inspection by Generals P. G. T. Beauregard and Joseph Johnston. One 2nd Virginia trooper recalled, "About 1,200 on review. The grandest sight I ever saw; the men were well mounted and well dressed, and appeared to be in good fighting condition. . . . No more than one-third of the Cavalry turned out; balance on picket & sick."[11]

Another 2nd Virginia trooper worried about the strong possibility of moving from the Centreville camp:

> I have ordered a small stove which I intend to put in my tent as soon as we are settled for the winter, which will make it much more comfortable. . . . they have been talking for the last few days of sending us up to

---

9. *Battles and Leaders*, 2:124; *OR*, vol. 5, 347; Alfred Roman, *The Military Operations of General Beauregard in the War Between the States, 1861-1865* (New York, 1883), 2:155.
10. *OR* 2:534–35, 552; Catherine M. Wright, ed., *Lee's Last Casualty: The Life and Letters of Sgt. Robert W. Parker, Second Virginia Cavalry* (Knoxville, TN, 2008), 22–39.
11. Diary of 1st Corporal James H. Hopkins, Munford–Ellis Papers, DU.

Waterford to take the place of the Loudoun Cavalry, which has been stationed there for some time, and which has been ordered to Centerville, but I hope we will not have to go. . . . I have been talking with Col. Munford about it and he wishes to keep us here.[12]

Lieutenant Edwin R. Page had reason to worry; the very next week Munford's troopers relocated to Waterford in Loudoun County, where they picketed and supported outposts.

On November 17, Lt. Col. Munford had been ordered on detached service to newly minted Brig. Gen. Nathan G. Evans at Leesburg, where he would serve from late November through January 1862. Evans had been ordered to Leesburg on August 8 to take command of Confederate forces in Loudoun County and protect them against Federal army incursions. In early December, Brig. Gen. D. H. Hill relieved Evans at Leesburg.[13]

General Beauregard maintained his headquarters at Fairfax Court House from August into October, when the army fell back to Centreville. On February 2, 1862, Beauregard was transferred to the Army in West Tennessee under Maj. Gen. Albert Sidney Johnston. On October 7, 1861, Longstreet was promoted to major general and assumed command of a division in the Confederate Army of Northern Virginia—four infantry brigades and Hampton's Legion. Radford's six companies, including Companies A, C, G, and I of the 30th Virginia, the Hanover Light Dragoons under Capt. Williams C. Wickham, and the Fairfax Cavalry under Capt. E. B. Powell, were assigned to the 1st Brigade under Gen. M. L. Bonham.[14]

Things remained mostly quiet for Munford's command throughout the fall of 1861. His troopers spent much of their time drilling and entertaining one another. They also took their turn on picket duty and fought in small skirmishes. Life in camp was good for the men of the 2nd Virginia. Trooper Rufus Peck recalled that Munford had a cook, hostler, and man-servant, "a boy of about sixteen, by the name of Billy. They all called him the 'Colonel's cup-bearer.' Well, if ever there was a black boy, he was the one; so black until he was blue, and charcoal was ashamed of itself by the side [sic] of him."

---

12. Edwin R. Page to his wife Olivia, November 24, 1861, Albert and Shirley Small Collections Library, MSS 8937, UVA; Wright, *Lee's Last Casualty*, 41–44.
13. Munford's CSR File, Special Order 498, NA; Wright, *Lee's Last Casualty*, 49–68; Roman, *The Military Operations of General Beauregard in the War Between the States, 1861–1865*, vol. 1:131, 172.
14. Roman, *The Military Operations of General Beauregard in the War Between the States, 1861–1865*, vol. 1:131; Driver, *2nd Virginia Cavalry*, 25; *OR* 2/1:532–33, 552–53, 562, 564, 573.

Peck, a notorious prankster who often consumed alcohol, sometimes stole liquor from the regimental supply (primarily intended to be used for wounded soldiers), blaming the theft on poor Billy.

Another soldier wrote to his wife of the "easy times we have now besieging us with so many blessings not deserved by us such good and kind officers especially our captain and Colonel Munford is one of the finest men I know. . . . haven't been under Colonel Radford since the Battle of Manassas and I hope we will not be under him again soon. Have plenty to eat and that is good . . . it is very quiet with us now." Shortly afterwards he wrote from Fairfax Court House, "We have splendid living for soldiers. Flour, pickle, pork, and beef, coffee, sugar, roasting ears, and Irish Potatoes by the barrel."[15]

Throughout the winter, Munford's command picketed the roads from Stone Bridge to Dranesville. On one occasion, Munford, while reporting to General Johnston, was invited to dine on turkey and brandy with the commanding general. Munford recalled the usually formal and stern Johnston as "simply charming; full of life and graces . . . an elegant host."[16]

There was time during this quiet period for social activities. Munford, like many officers, apparently enjoyed flirting with the ladies. Captain Charles M. Blackford, of Munford's command, wrote that he and Munford took great amusement in being introduced to young women while failing to mention their own marital status. They would proceed to impress the ladies by saying "gallant things." Then, when they had the women particularly interested, they would allude to their wives and children, catching the unsuspecting ladies completely off guard. There was lots of socializing, dances, and parties that included music. Munford had under his command a talented musician, banjo player Sam Sweeney, who with a band provided grand entertainment for the social events.[17]

All the cavalry units assembled near Manassas had been without brigade organization until December 1861. Brigadier General J.E.B. Stuart formed the 1st Cavalry Brigade, composed of the 1st Virginia commanded by Col. William E. Jones; the 2nd Virginia (including Munford) commanded by Col. Richard C. W. Radford; the 4th

---

15. *OR* 2/1:532, 1000; Peck, *Reminiscences of a Confederate Soldier of Co. C 2nd VA Cavalry*, 11; Robert W. Parker to his wife, August 7, 18, 1861, Southern Historical Collection, UNC, Chapel Hill, NC; Wright, *Lee's Last Casualty*, 21.
16. Munford, "Reminiscences," *Cavalry Journal*, 280–81; Akers, Thesis, 16, Virginia Tech.
17. Charles Minor Blackford, III, ed., *Letters from Lee's Army* (New York, NY., 1947), 62–63; Akers, Thesis, 16, Virginia Tech; Irving P. Whitehead, "Campaigns of Munford's 2nd Virginia Cavalry," 3.

Virginia led by Col. Beverly H. Robertson; the 6th Virginia led by Col. C. W. Field; the 1st North Carolina Cavalry Regiment led by Col. Robert Ransom; and the Jeff Davis Legion commanded by Col. William T. Martin. Robertson's promotion to lead the 4th Virginia caused some morale problems with other officers, including Capt. Williams C. Wickham, who considered resigning their commissions. Stuart, however, was able to cajole the protesters into staying and supporting the new colonel. Robertson was something of a prima donna, and within a few weeks, Stuart was complaining he was "by far the most troublesome man I have to deal with."[18]

During this period of picketing near Leesburg, one 2nd Virginia trooper wrote his wife of escorting Col. Munford across the Potomac to visit Gen. Charles P. Stone, who had commanded the Union forces during the Ball's Bluff battle. Stone was then commanding the right of Gen. McClellan's army across the Potomac where Munford's troopers, then under D. H. Hill's command, were picketing. Trooper Edwin R. Page wrote from camp near Leesburg:

> Yesterday about noon Col. Munford came out from Leesburg, where he had been at Head Quarters, and told me that he had orders to deliver some letters and dispatches to Genl. Stone under a flag of truce, that it might be necessary for him to cross the River, and that he wanted me to go with him. I very readily consented, when we got to the River at Edward's Ferry, with our white flag, they sent a boat over, and hearing that Genl Stone was on the opposite side, the Col. concluded to go over. Several of us went with him, and when we got over we were surrounded by some hundreds of Yankees. We had a long and quite a pleasant conversation with them, and returned safe and sound. Genl Stone seems to be a very nice and courteous gentleman, and think the Yankees seemed to look upon us as something very superior to them.[19]

---

18. *OR* 5:1029; H. B. McClellan, *The Campaigns of Stuart's Cavalry* (Edison, NJ, 1993), 43; Longacre, *Lee's Cavalrymen*, 54; Williams C. Wickham to his father, September 8, 1861, Wickham Papers, Library of Virginia (LVA), Richmond, Va.; J.E.B. Stuart to Flora Cooke Stuart, October 21, 1861, Stuart Papers, Robert W. Woodruff Library, Emory University, Atlanta, GA.
19. Edwin R. Page to his wife, December 7–8, 1861, MSS 8937, UVA Special Collections Library, Charlottesville, VA.; *Journal of the Military Service Institution of the United States*, Volume XLIX, July–August (Governor's Island, New York, 1911), 419. Note: General Stone was shortly thereafter arrested and imprisoned for almost six months, mostly for political reasons. He never received a trial, and after his release he would not hold a significant command during the war again.

On December 14 at Centreville, General Stuart presented the 2nd Virginia and five other regiments with their flags during a grand ceremony. On a cloudy and mild December 18, a brigade drill was held at Mechan's field near Centreville. About 700 troopers paraded for General Beauregard and other officers.[20]

On a clear and pleasant December 20, one 2nd Virginia trooper wrote:

> a Confederate foraging party led by Stuart headed for Dranesville with 250 wagons and several hundred cavalry, and 1,500 infantry, 4 pieces of artillery. Met with a foraging party of the Yankees at Dranesville. Had a heavy engagement; fought two and a half hours. The Yankees had about 4,000 infantry, 500 cavalry, and 7 pieces of artillery. Our loss was 35 killed & some 75 wounded. The Yankees lost from what could be found out was 50 killed and 75 or a hundred wounded. Our side had 12 horses killed, the Yankees lost none. The Yankees had advantage of position and ground.[21]

During 1861, Munford continued to hone his skills as a junior commander; skills that he needed to assume command of the 2nd Virginia Cavalry in 1862.

---

20. Diary of 1st Corporal James H. Hopkins, 2nd Virginia Cavalry, Munford–Ellis Papers, DU.
21. Ibid.

Chapter Six

1862 Shenandoah Valley Campaign

"I became colonel of what I believed to be the best cavalry regiment in the army, and was more in love with it than ever."
—Colonel Thomas Munford
on being elected Colonel of the
2nd Virginia Cavalry, April 1862

As 1861 ended, commanders and troops alike must have wondered what the New Year would bring. Colonel Thomas Munford saw action in Stonewall Jackson's 1862 Valley campaign, the Peninsula campaign, Second Manassas, Antietam, and Fredericksburg. Munford's competence as a commander continued to be demonstrated, but he faced more disappointment as his promotion to brigadier general failed to materialize. Other officers, some with less seniority and less competence, bypassed Munford to receive the coveted brigadier rank.

The New Year found big events shaping up as both armies sought to formulate their strategies and strengthen their commands to carry out successful campaigns after winter quarters. Throughout the early winter months of 1862, Munford's troopers saw little fighting in northern Virginia. From their camp at Waterford, seven miles northwest of Leesburg, Munford's horsemen took their turn picketing around Dranesville on the Loudoun and Leesburg Turnpike. Brigadier General D.H. Hill, commanding Confederate forces in the Leesburg area of Loudoun County, requested additional cavalry support. Hill had only dispatched Munford's four companies, Capt. Elijah V. White's partisan cavalry (which became 35th Virginia Battalion), and the Madison Virginia Cavalry. The Union 28th Pennsylvania Infantry Regiment, commanded by Col. John W. Geary, with headquarters at Point of Rocks, Maryland, made frequent raids across the Potomac River into Loudoun County.[1]

---

1. Irving P. Whitehead, "The Campaigns of Munford and the 2nd Virginia Cavalry," 4; Driver, *2nd Virginia Cavalry*, 35; Peck, *Reminiscences of a Confederate Soldier of Co. C 2nd Virginia Cavalry*, 12; Briscoe Goodhart, *History of the Independent Loudoun Virginia Rangers: U. S. Vol. Cav.*

Stuart's cavalry brigade was then encamped near Stone Bridge, with two of the regiments under command of Colonels Charles W. Field and Richard Radford. Stuart wanted to send all of Radford's companies to Hill's aid, but Johnston objected, and so on January 9 General Stuart sent Colonel Radford and two of Radford's companies to join Munford's four companies already at Waterford. A cavalryman of the 2nd Virginia wrote his wife from Waterford, "Two more companies of our regiment have come up and Col Radford with them, so colonel Munford has to leave us—I am very sorry indeed to part with him he is an excellent man." Private George H. Caperton echoed, "Munford left us today; much regret at his departure." On January 11, Munford left Waterford to take charge of Radford's cavalry companies still positioned near Stone Bridge. In parting with Munford, D. H. Hill expressed "sincere regret at losing the services of so able, zealous and efficient officer, ever ready to discharge his duty and in a pleasant way." In March, Munford headed for the Shenandoah Valley with these companies to be joined later by the remainder of the companies then at Waterford.[2]

As the army went into winter quarters, General Beauregard caused considerable friction with the Confederate high command. He had initially strongly advocated an invasion of Maryland to threaten the flank and rear of Washington. With his plan rebuffed as impractical, he requested reassignment to New Orleans, which he assumed would be under Union attack in the near future, but his request was denied. He had enraged President Davis when his report about the Manassas battle was printed in the newspapers, which suggested that Davis's interference with Beauregard's plans prevented the pursuit and full destruction of McDowell's army and the capture of Washington. He quarreled with Commissary Gen. Lucius B. Northrop, a personal friend of President Davis, about the inadequate supplies available to his army. He issued public statements challenging the ability of the Confederate Secretary of War to give commands to a full general. Having become a political liability in Virginia, on January 30, 1861, Davis had Beauregard transferred, effective March 14, 1862, to Tennessee to become second-in-command to Gen. Albert Sidney Johnston.[3]

(Scouts) 1862–65 (Washington, D. C., 1896), 26; Frank M. Myers, *The Comanches: A History of White's Battalion, Virginia Cavalry, Laurel Brig., Hampton Div., A.N.V., C.S.A.* (Marietta, GA, 1956), 33.

2. Robert W. Parker to his wife, January 10, 1862, SHC, UNC; Driver, *2nd Virginia Cavalry*, 35–36; Wright, *Lee's Last Casualty*, 59; *OR*, vol. 5:1025; D. H. Hill orders, January 11, 1862, LVA, Richmond, VA; Peck, *Reminiscences of a Confederate Soldier*, 12.
3. *OR* 5:1053. When the Confederate States Army was first established, its highest rank was brigadier general. It quickly became apparent that the large

On February 24, Col. John W. Geary led his 28th Pennsylvania Infantry Regiment across the Potomac at Harpers Ferry and occupied Lovettsville. Aiding Geary's columns was Samuel C. Means, an antisecessionist Waterford miller who had been forced to flee from his home the year before and was acting as a Union guide on these raids. This so incensed the Confederates that a reward was offered for the capture of the "renegade Sam Means." The occupation of northern Loudoun County increased the pressure on the Waterford Confederate garrison; the outposts could no longer be held. General D. H. Hill moved his brigade from Leesburg to follow the withdrawing Southern army, but he left the cavalry companies at Waterford to watch and delay Geary's advance.[4]

Notwithstanding the urgent warning of President Davis's letters of early February to not retreat from Manassas and Centreville, on March 8 General Beauregard began his retreat from Manassas unbeknownst to the President. Davis had advised Beauregard he need not abandon his posts until the weather had cleared and the roads were in better condition, because McClellan was unlikely to follow due to the same obstacles Beauregard's moving troops were facing. Beauregard's troops suffered from excessively cold weather on their march south. The retreat continued to the south bank of the Rappahannock, where a halt was called, and the troops encamped. In the undue haste to retire from the front of McClellan, who neither followed nor interfered with General Beauregard's rear guard, the Confederates abandoned and burned stores, arms, and clothing. Davis, General Early, and others lamented the unnecessary loss of the huge stores. Radford's and Munford's commands served as part of the rear guard during the Confederate retreat to their new defensive position on the south bank of the Rappahannock River. After the massive burning of the stores upon evacuating Manassas, Munford's companies who had been encamped earlier at Stone Bridge were ordered to keep up the vidette line from Manassas Junction to Strasburg.[5]

Before destroying the meat packing plant during the Confederate retreat from Manassas, Maj. B. P. Nolan, Commissary of Subsistence,

---

size of the armies being created would need larger units and higher ranks to command them. On May 30, 1861 Albert Sidney Johnson was authorized to the rank of full General.

4. Goodhart, *History of the Independent Loudoun Virginia Rangers*, 26; Myers, *The Comanches*, 33. By order of the Secretary of War, Edwin M. Stanton, Means would later be given a Union captain's rank and command of an independent cavalry company, the Independent Loudoun Virginia Rangers.

5. *OR* 5:526–28; Varina Davis, *Jefferson Davis, Ex–President of the Confederate States of America: A Memoir*, 188–90; Driver, *2nd Virginia Cavalry*, 38–39; Bradley T. Johnson, ed., *A Memoir of the Life and Public Service of Joseph E. Johnston* (Baltimore, MD, 1891), 75–76.

6. *OR*, Series 4, 1:1038.

received authorization from General Johnston to use his discretion and try to save as much meat as possible from destruction by hauling it to Warrenton and giving it away. He placed combustibles under every pile of meat for immediate destruction if Federals neared the area. Meat was offered to every person who would send a wagon. On March 10, nearly 30 wagons full were hauled off. The next day, Lieutenant Colonel Munford arrived with orders from Stuart to destroy all the property along the line of railroad. Seeing that Nolan was scurrying off as much meat as he could to civilians, Munford and his men pitched in, impressing all the wagons that could be found. Another 50 wagons full were saved that day, but Munford had to follow his orders later on, setting fire to the plant. Perhaps 200,000 pounds of beef and bacon were saved, while 170,000 pounds were destroyed.[6]

Trooper Rufus Peck recalled the burning of the meat packing facility at Thoroughfare Gap:

The citizens told us that 600,000 lbs. of bacon was stored in the building. We were ordered to burn this also, which we did and when the lard ran out into the creek it chilled and formed a damn across Broad Run. . . . I was bitterly opposed to all this destruction but we had to carry out orders. . . . We also had orders to blow up the big stone bridge. . . . It took 40 kegs of powder to destroy the bridge.[7]

When General Ewell retreated from Warrenton Junction to Orange Court House, Munford and his companies joined him to get their orders. Henceforth, Munford and his cavalry were assigned to Ewell. The cavalrymen crossed the Blue Ridge at Snicker's Gap in a soaking downpour, encamping at Elks Run Church. Munford remained there a few days on scout duty before crossing the mountain and riding as far as Linden Station.[8]

McClellan's Grand Strategy

With a mere 100 miles separating the two capitals and their armies, Virginia was fated to become a major theater of the war. The ground between Washington and Richmond, particularly from the Rappahannock River to the James River, was low, swampy, and covered with woods and underbrush. The roads were deep in mud throughout the winter and much of the spring; many were impassable.

---

7. Peck, *Reminiscences of a Confederate Soldier of Co. C 2nd Virginia Cavalry*, 12; OR 12/1:412.
8. Driver, *2nd Virginia Cavalry*, 39.
9. Richard W. Stewart, ed., *American Military History, Volume 1: The United*

Following a relatively quiet winter, the spring of 1862 brought a renewed determination to take the rebel capital, but a Union offensive against Richmond presented formidable difficulties. There were two primary approaches to Richmond: a direct approach by land through Manassas and Fredericksburg and down the Richmond, Fredericksburg and Potomac Railroad; or an approach by sea to the tip of the peninsula formed by the James and York Rivers and then up the peninsula to Richmond.[9]

The overland approach to take Richmond had failed at the Battle of First Manassas, when Confederate forces under Generals Beauregard and Johnston routed those of General McDowell. On July 27, 1861, Lincoln had replaced McDowell, due to his defeat at Manassas, with 34-year-old Maj. Gen. George Brinton McClellan. Already popular with his men, McClellan's past victories in western Virginia placed him in high regard with the Northern people, but more importantly, with the President, Cabinet, and Northern press.[10]

McClellan's first order of business after taking over from McDowell had been to restore the army's faith in itself. McClellan's organizational ability was unmatched. Within weeks he had the ragtag army that had raced to the safety of Washington from the plains of Manassas looking as an army should. Next, he turned his sights on restoring discipline to Washington. On November 1, McClellan succeeded Gen. Winfield Scott as commander of the entire army.[11]

The Union Army, twice the strength of General Johnston's, looked better than it ever had, but still McClellan was reluctant to take the offensive. While everyone clamored for action, he stayed near Washington. Desperate to get his commander moving, Lincoln issued President's General Orders No. 1 and 2, specifically ordering McClellan to move on Manassas Junction by February 22.[12]

Instead of preparing to move his army as ordered, McClellan wrote a multi-page letter to Secretary of War, Edwin M. Stanton, recommending against another move on Manassas. He offered instead his "Urbanna Plan," designed to shift his army down the Chesapeake Bay to Urbanna, Virginia, on the south bank of the Rappahannock, just 50 miles from Richmond. From there he planned to cut off the Rebels

---

States Army and the Forging of a Nation, 1775–1917 (Washington, D. C., 2004), 221–23.
10. Donald Stoker, *The Grand Design: Strategy and the U.S. Civil War* (New York, 2010), 52–53.
11. Steven W. Sears, *George B. McClellan: The Young Napoleon* (New York, 1988), 97, 100, 125.
12. Ethan S. Rafuse, *McClellan's War: The Failure of Moderation in the Struggle for the Union*, (Bloomington and Indianapolis, IN, 2005) 177.
13. George McClellan to Edwin Stanton, January 31, 1862; Stephen Sears, ed.,

holding the lower Virginia peninsula between the York and James Rivers. Next McClellan planned a short march to attack Richmond.[13]

In March, after eight months of preparations, McClellan still was not ready to attack the Confederate Army. Frustrated, and with political pressure building, President Lincoln summoned General McClellan to the White House for a March 6 conference so that he could "talk plainly" to his commander. After a contentious meeting about his grand plan, McClellan declared that he would appoint the group of his brigadier general commanders, meeting that very morning with Chief of Staff Randolph B. Marcy as a council of war with authority to decide all questions of his grand strategy. He wanted his plan judged on its merits, and the decisions sent to the President for review.[14]

McClellan was forced to abandon his Urbanna Plan when General Johnston, on March 11, preempted him by crossing to the south side of the Rappahannock River first. His plan now useless, McClellan was forced to fall back on the less desirable alternative of approaching Richmond from the peninsula formed by the James and York rivers. On March 17, McClellan began moving his men to Fortress Monroe. He concentrated his troops, numbering about 122,000 men, at the Union fort and nearby Hampton and Newport News, in preparation for his June Peninsula campaign. McClellan's plan also called for Brig. Gen. Irvin McDowell, with 30,000 men near Fredericksburg, to advance on Richmond from the north. Also, Brig. Gen. Ambrose Burnside planned on capturing New Berne, North Carolina, on March 14, 1862, cutting the Atlantic and North Carolina Railroad that connected the coast with the interior. A short distance north, at Goldsboro, the line crossed the Weldon Railroad, noted for keeping the Confederate Army of Northern Virginia supplied throughout the war. Thus, if New Berne were to fall into Federal hands, an important link in the supply chain of that army would be broken. In addition, Maj. Gen. Robert Patterson would tie up Jackson in the Shenandoah Valley so that Confederate reinforcements could not be sent to the south of Richmond.[15]

With the coming of the spring campaign, the days of leisure ended. Munford recalled:

> On the 12th of March, 1862, "saddle up" and "boots and saddles" sounded with a spirit that will be long remembered. Our "wild campaign" had now begun. I

The Civil War Papers of George B. McClellan: Selected Correspondence 1860–1865, (New York, 1992), 169.
14. Stephen W. Sears, *To the Gates of Richmond* (New York, 1992), 4–5.
15. Ibid., 6, 18.
16. Munford, "Reminiscences," *Cavalry Journal*, 282.

left Centerville [20 miles west of Washington] with Colonel Fitz Lee. At Gainesville we parted, he going to Warrenton, to the immediate rear of Longstreet, while my orders were to follow the Manassas Gap Railroad and destroy the [Confederate] meat packing establishment at Thoroughfare Gap [just outside of Gainesville] and to remain there as long as I could. Then to fall back on the left flank of our army, via White Plains and Orleans, but to watch the left flank and, if possible, to keep up communication with General Jackson then retiring from Winchester.[16]

Jackson's Shenandoah Valley Campaign

The Shenandoah Valley was important to the Confederacy as a source of provisions and a potential launching point for any invasion north. The Federals intended to deny use of the valley to the Confederate Army. After Jackson's lackluster winter campaign in the snow-covered mountains of "West" Virginia, he returned to Winchester, having failed to capture the isolated Union garrisons at Bath and Romney. He did, however, collect a substantial quantity of supplies and damaged the canal and railroad near Bath. He left Brig. Gen. William W. Loring and a detachment to block communications between Maj. Gen. Nathaniel Banks and Maj. Gen. William S. Rosecrans.[17]

In early March, General Banks moved up the valley and occupied Winchester, which Jackson had evacuated. On March 11, Brig. Gen. James Shields's division of 9,000 troops advanced to Strasburg, while Brig. Gen. Alpheus S. Williams's division of 7,000 soldiers remained at Winchester. Brigadier General John Sedgwick's division of 7,000 was at Harpers Ferry. Banks intended to leave the Valley for the Peninsula. Williams started for Manassas on March 20, while Shields dropped back from Strasburg and prepared to follow. Jackson's mission was to hold Banks's troops in the Valley. Finding out the Federals intended to leave, Jackson made a forced march, attacking Shields at Kernstown on March 23.[18]

---

17. Mark M. Boatner, III, "Shenandoah Valley Campaign of General Stonewall Jackson, May–June '62," *The Civil War Dictionary* (New York, 1991), 739.
18. *OR* 5:1098.

Kernstown

The first battle of Kernstown was fought on March 23, 1862, in Frederick County and near Winchester, Virginia. It was the opening battle of Confederate Maj. Gen. Thomas J. "Stonewall" Jackson's campaign throughout the Shenandoah Valley. Jackson dispatched Col. Turner Ashby's cavalry on a feint on the Confederate right. Ashby, however, sent his commander incorrect intelligence that a small detachment under Union Col. Nathan Kimball was vulnerable, but it was in fact a full infantry division more than twice the size of Jackson's force. Jackson ordered Col. Samuel V. Fulkerson's small brigade and Brig. Gen. Richard B. Garnett's "Stonewall Brigade" to attack the Union artillery position on Pritchard Hill. The lead brigade under Fulkerson was repulsed, so Jackson decided to move around the Union right flank, about two miles west on Sandy Ridge, which appeared to be unoccupied. If this was successful, his men could move down the spine of the ridge and get into the Union rear, blocking their escape route to Winchester. Union Col. Erastus B. Tyler's brigade, however, countered this movement, and when Col. Nathan Kimball's brigade moved to Tyler's assistance, the Confederates were driven from the field. The Federals hotly pursued Jackson's force, doing more damage as they went. Confederate losses were about double that of Union forces.[19]

Federal spirits soared at this initial defeat of Jackson. This was Jackson's sole loss of the war. Although the battle was a Confederate tactical setback, it represented a strategic victory for the South by preventing the Union from transferring forces from the Shenandoah Valley to reinforce the Peninsula campaign against the Confederate capital, Richmond. Little did the Union leadership know that "Stonewall" would soon become seemingly invincible.

As a result of the battle, Federal authorities in Washington decided to withhold McDowell's 40,000 troops from McClellan, and Brig. Gen. Louis Blenker's division was withdrawn from McClellan and sent to the valley to oppose Jackson. A hodgepodge of separate Federal commands was established, which contributed to Jackson's subsequent successes. These separate and independent commands were McDowell's Department of the Rappahannock; Banks's Department of the Shenandoah; and the Mountain Department under Fremont, who succeeded Rosecrans on March 29. These commands reported directly

---

19. *OR* 12/1:335–39.

to Washington; there was no overall commander on the scene to coordinate operations.[20]

On March 27, Munford wrote Stuart from Middleburg that Union forces were apparently headed for Aldie in Loudoun County, Virginia. Munford learned from an apparent deserter that "[t]hey are about 7,000 strong and have in immense train. I understand twenty of their wagons are loaded with ammunition. The scamp [Col. John W.] Geary commands the advance. General [John J.] Abercrombie's brigade at Mountville, and it is reported that Banks is there with him." Stuart reported: "He [Munford] is doing admirable service there."[21]

Stuart praised Munford and the 2nd Virginia, reporting that "the detachment of Second Virginia, under Lieutenant Colonel Munford, has performed distinguished service along the Piedmont region and I commend to the notice of the general that officer's activity, good judgment, and unceasing vigilance, conspicuously displayed in the signal service he has rendered."[22]

Munford's regiment, assigned to Ewell's division, was stationed at Lamont Point, five miles west of Gordonsville. Ewell, tasked with watching Brig. Gen. John J. Abercrombie and General McDowell at Fredericksburg, "was held in readiness to go to Fredericksburg, or join General Jackson, as the exigencies of service might require." Also assigned to Ewell's 8,000-man division was the 6th Virginia Cavalry under Col. Thomas S. Flournoy, a well-known Virginia resident who had served a term in Congress and had made an unsuccessful bid for governor in 1855.[23]

On April 1, Sgt. Robert Parker wrote from Oak Shade, 13 miles east of Culpeper Court House, that the regiment was on a scout when they received orders to fall back to Fauquier Springs in the face of advancing Federal columns, probably of the 28th Pennsylvania Infantry. They accomplished this during nightfall. The next morning, they received orders to support General Stuart at Rappahannock Station as Union troops advanced on him. As the regiment approached and re-crossed the Rappahannock, the Yankee columns appeared and began shelling Munford's troopers just as they reached the riverbank.

---

20. *OR* 12/1:335–39; Robert G. Tanner, *Stonewall in the Valley: Thomas J. 'Stonewall' Jackson's Shenandoah Valley Campaign, Spring 1862* (Mechanicsburg, PA, 1996), 303–04; Byron Farwell, *Stonewall: A Biography of General Thomas J. Jackson* (New York, 1992), 242–43.
21. *OR* 11/3:407.
22. *OR* 5:511-14, vol. 11, part 3:407, vol. 12, part 1:417; Munford, "Reminiscences," *Cavalry Journal*, 282; Akers, Thesis, 16, Virginia Tech.
23. Munford, "Reminiscences," *Cavalry Journal*, 282; Michael P. Musick, *The 6th Virginia Cavalry* (Lynchburg, VA, 1990), 11.

The shelling continued until nightfall; no casualties occurred. Munford's horsemen expected a clash the next morning, but the Federals had moved back; there was no fight. Munford's troopers remained in the area for a day or two before returning to Oak Shade.[24]

Subsequent to Kernstown, on April 14, Geary's 28th Pennsylvania Infantry reported, "Munford's regiment of cavalry was scouting daily in the vicinity of the [Manassas Gap Rail]road at various points, threatening to obstruct and destroy it." Captain Frank M. Myers of Elijah V. White's 35th Virginia Cavalry Battalion, "The Comanches," added, "Col. Munford kept Geary's forces in constant fear and trembling, so that his cavalry never ventured out of hearing of the infantry." Myers reported his company captured all the baggage of the 28th Pennsylvania at Salem and carried it off. He added:

Col. Munford soon after, came down on his commissary stores at Piedmont, making a heavy capture in flour and many other articles, as well as some negroes whom the Pennsylvania hero [Geary] had stolen away from their homes. . . . In the latter part of April, Munford was ordered end his detached service with his squadron of the regiment at Middleburg and report to the 2nd Virginia, then lying on the Rappahannock, near the O. and A.R.R. [Orange & Alexandria Railroad].[25]

Meanwhile, the 2nd Virginia finally left their Oak Shade camp on April 20, marching near Gordonsville during a two-day rain, followed by a day of mixed rain and snow. They remained there for a couple of days before proceeding to Liberty Mills, six miles north of Gordonsville, where they struck camp.[26]

During April 1862, the Confederate Congress ordered an election of regimental and company officers throughout the army. Very few troopers had enlisted for more than one year, and the army was in dire straits. A reorganization was thought to be required, and though it was carried out with great difficulty, it was deemed a success. One trooper wrote, "Col. Radford, I understand, is not a candidate for re-election." Munford was elected colonel of the 2nd Virginia Cavalry, without opposition. Munford recalled, "I became colonel of what I believed to be the best cavalry regiment in the army, and was more in love with it than ever." An embittered Radford resigned from the service, retiring to his farm in Bedford County until his death in 1886. Munford served as colonel of the regiment during the last three years of the war; two-

---

24. Wright, *Lee's Last Casualty*, 72–73.
25. *OR* 5/1:516; Driver, *2nd Virginia Cavalry*, 40; Myers, *The Comanches*, 27–28.
26. Jesse T. Rusher to his father, April 22, 1862, as quoted in Driver, *2nd Virginia Cavalry*, 40–41; Wright, *Lee's Last Casualty*, 73.

thirds of the time commanding a brigade. He was wounded by saber-cuts at Second Manassas, and at Turkey Ridge, June 2, 1864, by a spent grape shot.[27]

Munford also bemoaned the election. "Some of the best and most conscientious officers," he wrote, "were retired or had to return to the ranks; untried men, sometimes politicians and demagogues were placed in command of regiments, which completely disorganized the old order of the workings."[28]

During this period, Munford reported his headquarters was then at "Swift Run Gap [a natural wind gap in the Blue Ridge entering the Shenandoah Valley], and his pickets extended from Culpeper Court House to the mountains on the east side of the Blue Ridge, and from Harrisonburg to Wolftown on the west [side]."[29]

On May 7, Pvt. William H. Burnley wrote from near New Market, in the vicinity of Madison Court House, "We are being shelled all the time. . . . We have a great deal of Cav–26 Companies of Ashby's 6th and 2nd Regt too." Also on May 7, Ewell ordered Munford, then near Madison Court House, to Conrad's Store, close to Swift Run Gap. On May 15, Munford reported from Washington in Rappahannock County that a small squadron of his pickets attacked a Federal foraging party near Gaines's Cross Roads but were ultimately driven back. Munford reinforced them; they struck down seven arriving Union horsemen. He then led a charge down the road until stopped by Colonel Geary's regiment of Maj. Gen. James Shields's division. The Federal soldiers, with a large train of wagons, were between Flint Hill and Gaines's Cross Roads. The Union soldiers pressed Munford too closely for him to capture any valuable and needed loose Union horses; he used almost all of his ammunition and retreated with only two slightly wounded. The next day Munford captured 15 prisoners, two wagons, and nine horses on the Manassas Gap Railroad. Munford then crossed the mountain between Chester Gap and Thornton's Gap, occupying Chester Gap with a picket.[30]

Munford later recalled an amusing incident involving Generals Ewell and Jackson. Jackson was notorious for keeping his plans and troop movement destinations to himself. This frustrated many, especially Richard Ewell. Once, during this period, Jackson had

---

27. Susan Lee Blackford and Charles Minor Blackford, *Letters from Lee's Army* (Lincoln, NE, 1998), 81; Munford, "Reminiscences," *Cavalry Journal*, 283.
28. Munford, "Reminiscences," *Cavalry Journal*, 282–83.
29. *OR* 12/1:729; Driver, *2nd Virginia Cavalry*, 41.
30. William Henry Burnley to his mother, May 7, 1862, Special Collections, MSS7871, UVA, Charlottesville, VA; *OR* 12/1:498–500, 502; Driver, *2nd Virginia Cavalry*, 41–42.

ordered Ewell to remain east of the Blue Ridge, near the railroad junction at Gordonsville, about 45 miles due east of Staunton. Ewell knew that Maj. Gen. Nathaniel Banks's army of 19,000 soldiers was approaching his position. He wanted to move his men away from the approaching Banks but knew he had better follow Jackson's strict order to remain there until he returned. Frustrated, Ewell, speaking to Col. James A. Walker, struck out at Jackson, "Banks' whole army is advancing on me, and I do not have the most remote idea how to communicate with General Jackson. I tell you, sir, he is crazy, and I will march my division away from here. I do not mean to have it cut to pieces at the behest of a crazy man." But Ewell, despite his outburst, remained mindful of Jackson's order and stayed exactly where he was.[31]

Ewell became even more frustrated with his enforced inaction when he learned from a Union deserter that Maj. Gen. James Shields's division of Banks's army was going to leave the valley and proceed to Fredericksburg. Realizing the importance of his information, he sent a report to Jackson and dispatched Munford to harass Shields. As Munford was about to leave, he stopped by Ewell's headquarters for any final instructions. Ewell was already in bed for the night. Suddenly, Ewell "leaped from the sheets in his nightshirt, spread out a map in the lamplight on the bare floor, and got down on his knees." According to Munford, "his bones fairly rattled; his bald head and long beard made him look more like a witch than a Major General. He became much excited, pointed out Jackson's position, General Shields's and General McDowell's." Ewell continued, "Why I could crush Shields before night if I could move from here. This man Jackson is a crazy fool, an idiot. . ."[32]

On May 16, Munford reported from Gaines's Cross Roads, "General Shields is advancing on Warrenton with 6,000 men, thirty-six pieces of artillery, and a very small cavalry force. He crossed at Chester Gap from Front Royal, and it is generally believed that his destination is Fredericksburg or Culpeper Court House."[33]

On May 17, Munford's regiment left Swift Run Gap on a scout, rode 15 miles down the south side of the Shenandoah, crossing at Columbia bridge, continuing down the north side of the river to Sperryville bridge and down the Sperryville Turnpike to Luray. Here, the troopers fed their horses and rested. Their advance guard spotted Union forces, firing into their rear guard, sending them towards Newmarket. Munford's horsemen pressed on towards Sperryville,

---

31. Alf J. Mapp, Jr., *Frock Coats and Epaulets: The Men Who Led the Confederacy* (Lanham, Md.: Rowman & Littlefield, 2015), 292.
32. Ibid., 294.
33. *OR* 12/3:894.

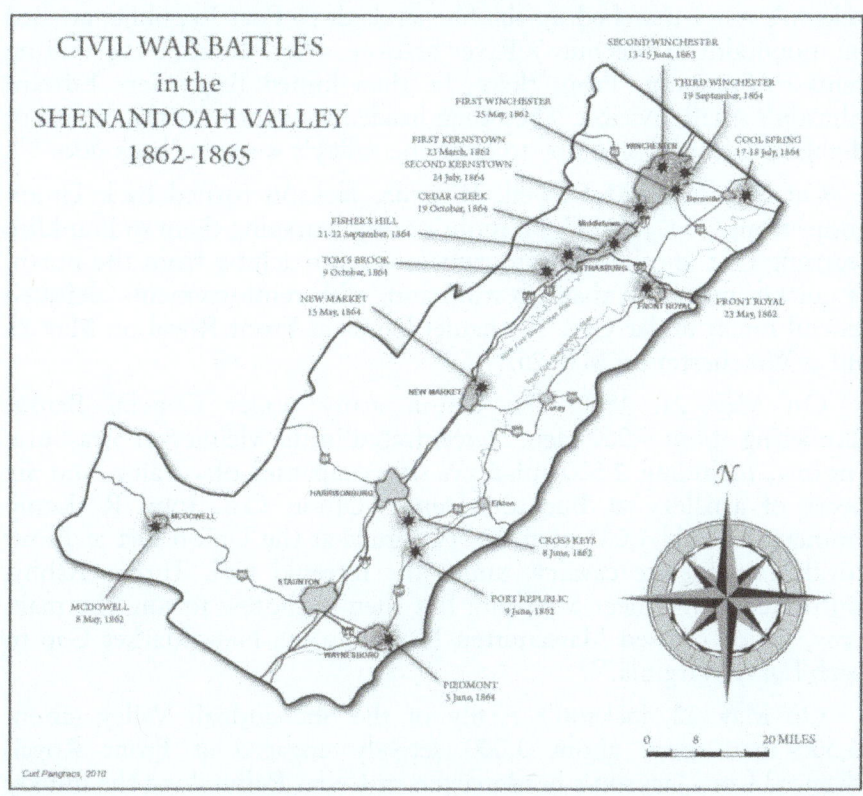

staying in the Blue Ridge mountains that night. The next morning, the troopers crossed the mountain, proceeded to Washington, rested, and then marched to Flint Hill, where they spent the night. The following morning, they travelled along the Manassas Gap Railroad. Nearing the station, Munford sent out troopers to find out if any Federals were there. There were. Spotting some, Munford ordered a charge, taking 14 prisoners, a wagon, and eight horses. Having to leave a considerable amount of plunder due to the expected arrival of Yankees by train, the scouting party returned with the prisoners by way of Washington to Madison Court House.[34]

Front Royal

Despite the initial tactical setback on March 23 at Kernstown, Jackson quickly recovered, choosing to move south, pausing only at Conrad's Store (present-day Elkton) to develop a plan for what would be known as his 1862 Valley campaign. To deceive Federal forces,

---

34. Driver, *2nd Virginia Cavalry*, 42–43; Wright, *Lee's Last Casualty*, 75.

Jackson's army marched up the Shenandoah to Port Republic, crossed the mountains at Mechum's River Station, where he rode the waiting trains to Staunton. From there, he then joined Brig. Gen. Edward Johnson's small division. They then headed west into the mountains of Highland County, planning to close the valley's western "back door."[35]

On May 8, at McDowell, Virginia, Jackson turned back Union troops from Gen. John C. Fremont's army, pursuing them to Franklin. Learning that another Union army was approaching from the north, he quickly moved in that direction and, with reinforcements, defeated Federal forces under Gen. Nathaniel Banks at Front Royal on May 23 and at Winchester on May 25.[36]

On May 21, 1862, the Union army under General Banks, numbering about 9,000 men, concentrated in the vicinity of Strasburg, Virginia, including 2,500 infantry, six companies of cavalry, and six pieces of artillery at Buckton Depot. Union Col. John R. Kenly commanded only 1,063 men and two guns at the Union fort at Front Royal. Confederate cavalry, under the intrepid Col. Turner Ashby, confronted Banks near Strasburg but then withdrew to join the main army, which crossed Massanutten Mountain via New Market Gap to reach Luray, Virginia.[37]

On May 22, Jackson's Army of the Shenandoah Valley (about 16,500 men--only about 3,000 actively engaged at Front Royal) advanced from Jackson's headquarters at Cedar Point along the muddy Luray Road to within 10 miles of Front Royal. Jackson's intention was either to destroy the garrison at Front Royal and get in Banks's rear, or to force Banks to give up Strasburg, about nine miles to the west. The Confederates marched north and bivouacked 10 miles south of Front Royal.[38]

The Confederate cavalry, under Colonel Ashby and Col. Thomas S. Flournoy of the 6th Virginia Cavalry, crossed the South Fork of the Shenandoah River at McCoy's Ford, north of the enemy's position, for the purpose of destroying the railroad and telegraphic communications between Front Royal and Strasburg. They also wanted to check the advance of any reinforcements from Strasburg or the retreat of any portion of the enemy in that direction from Front Royal.[39]

Brigadier General George H. Steuart, who temporarily commanded the 2nd and 6th Virginia Cavalries, had been previously dispatched to Newtown, a point nine miles north of Winchester, with

---

35. Rafuse, *Stonewall Jackson: A Biography*, 84.
36. Ibid., 89, 91.
37. *OR* 12/1:523; *New York Times*, May 27, 1862.
38. Rafuse, *Stonewall Jackson: A Biography*, 90–91.
39. *OR* 12/1:702.

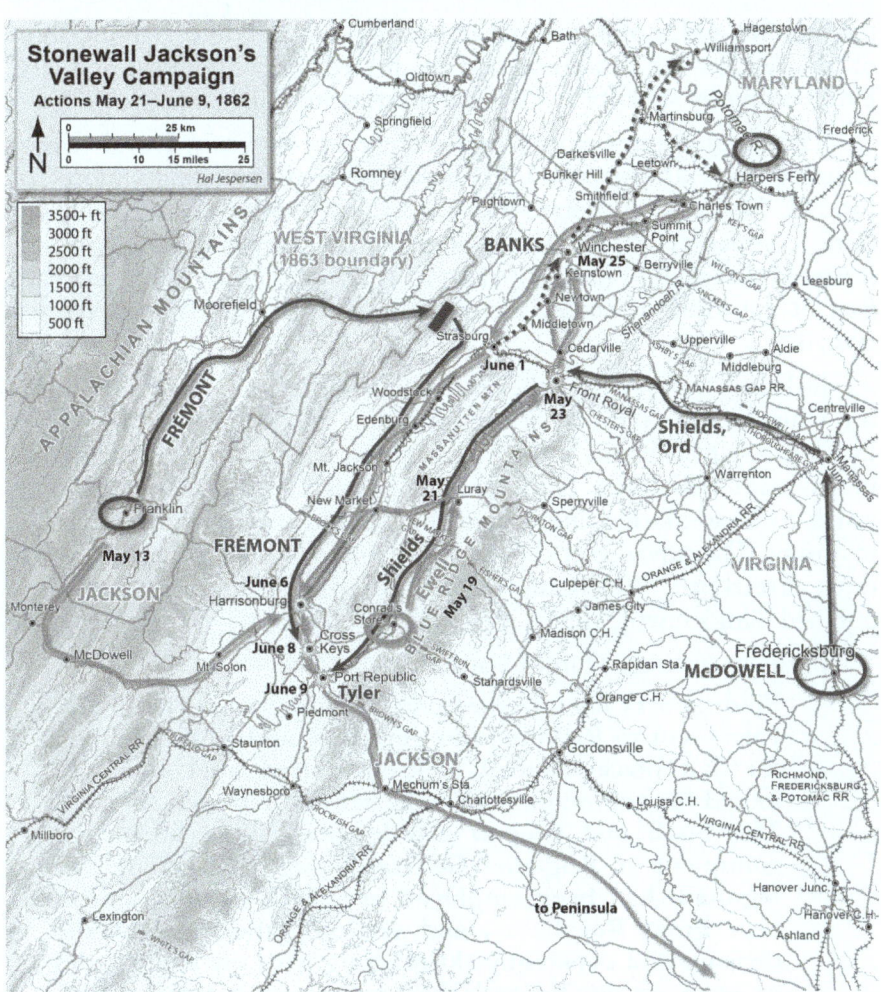

instructions to observe the movements of the enemy. At Newtown, Steuart succeeded in capturing some 225 prisoners, several wagons, ambulances, arms, and medical stores. He also advised Jackson of movements which indicated that Banks was preparing to leave Strasburg. A newspaper reported that Munford's that cavalry regiment was sent east to close off Manassas Gap and cut communication between Front Royal and Washington. Specifically, Munford's 2nd Virginia "wrecked track and bridges as far east as Thoroughfare Gap."[40]

The Battle of Front Royal was fought May 23, 1862, in Warren County, Virginia. Front Royal demonstrated Jackson's use of valley

---

40. *OR* 12/1:702–03; Angus James Johnston II, *Virginia Railroads in the Civil War* (Chapel Hill, NC. for the VHS, 1961), 53; *New York Times*, May 27, 1862; Michael P. Musick, *6th Virginia Cavalry* (Lynchburg, VA, 1990), 15.

topography and mobility to unite his own forces while dividing those of his enemies. At a minimal cost, he forced the withdrawal of a large Union army by striking at its flank and threatening its rear.[41]

The Confederates won a lopsided victory at Front Royal. Union casualties were 773, of which 691 were captured, including Union Col. John R. Kenly. Confederate losses numbered 36 killed and wounded. Nine companies of the 1st United States Maryland Infantry were scattered pell-mell. Two companies of the 29th Pennsylvania Infantry, part of the Pioneer Corps, and some of the 5th New York were also routed.[42]

Jackson's victory over the small Union force at Front Royal forced the main Union Army at Strasburg under Banks into abrupt retreat. Jackson deceived Banks into believing that the Confederate army was in the main valley near Harrisonburg; instead he had marched swiftly north to New Market and crossed Massanutten via New Market Gap to Luray. The advance to Front Royal placed Jackson in position to move directly on Winchester in the rear of the Union army. Jackson pursued Banks north, almost to Harpers Ferry.[43]

In the meantime, Munford reported:
> Finding over 100 unarmed recruits added to my regiment, I was sent to Richmond to get arms, and while en route for that place General Jackson started after Banks. I joined his command at Winchester and reported for duty. The Sixth and Second Cavalry were then under the command of Brigadier General George H. Steuart. My regiment had been employed in tearing up the railroad near Front Royal . . . and guarding the flank of the division and constantly skirmishing with the enemy, and as soon as the Federals had commenced their retreat, they were pursued by the Sixth and Second on the turnpike to within 5 miles of Winchester.[44]

On May 24, Banks retreated down the Valley Pike to Winchester, harassed by Confederate cavalry and artillery at Middletown and Newtown (Stephens City), setting the stage for the First Battle of Winchester the following day.

The confusion produced by Jackson's appearance at Front Royal and the hasty Union retreat from Strasburg to Winchester contributed materially to the defeat of Banks's army at First Winchester on May 25. Jackson's infantry scored another notable triumph, driving Banks's

---

41. Rafuse, *Stonewall Jackson: A Biography*, 90–91.
42. Musick, *6th Virginia Cavalry*, 14.
43. Rafuse, *Stonewall Jackson: A Biography*, 92–93.
44. *OR* 12/1:701–08, 730.

frightened troops out of the town. When the Southern commander looked about for cavalry to reap the harvest of the day, however, none was found. He sent his aide, Lt. A. S. "Sandie" Pendleton, in search of Steuart and his two regiments. He found them; the men were dismounted, and the horses were grazing. Steuart declared that he was under Ewell's command; orders to pursue would have to come through Ewell. Ewell was finally located and put his stamp of approval on the order to advance, but by then Banks's main force was too far away for a successful chase. General Jackson was not pleased. Meanwhile, Banks retreated to Martinsburg, crossing the Potomac at Williamsport on May 26.[45]

Upon returning from picket duty at Stone Church, two miles west of Harpers Ferry, the 2nd Virginia passed through Winchester, which had been abandoned by General Banks during his retreat. The troopers were excited to come upon all of the sutlers' supplies. One trooper recalled:

> You can well imagine how the Confederates immediately took possession of everything. The dress goods were sent back home as gifts to the widows, mothers and sisters of the boys. I think it was the next day that we were encamped in an old orchard, and were asleep, when our lovable and gallant Col. Munford, came in person and awakened the command. We started for Strasburg on the double quick.[46]

On May 29, Munford's regiment marched to Charlestown while supporting the batteries on Bolivar Heights, which were engaged in shelling the Federals under General Fremont. Munford reported:

That evening I was driven from the heights [by elements of the First New York Artillery]. My regiment was performing heavy picket duty on all the roads on the Key Ferry road and the Harper's Ferry road. . . . We were shelled nearly all night, and had nothing for men or horses to eat for twenty-four hours. . . . We marched from Charlestown to Kernstown on the 30th; had no feed for our horses; and on the morning of June 1st we started at early dawn to cover our retreat to Strasburg, at which place we were kept in line of battle nearly the whole day, watching for the approach of both Shields and Fremont. Then we got about a third of a ration of corn for our horses. That very night the pickets of the 6th Virginia were approached by

---

45. *OR* 12/1:701-708; Whitehead, "Campaigns of Munford's 2nd Virginia Cavalry," 18; Musick, *6th Virginia Cavalry*, 15.
46. W. A. Rucker, "A Sketch of My War Experiences," From the *Rucker Family Society Newsletter*, Volume 12 Number 3, September, 2001.

Union troopers who identified the challenge question as "Ashby's cavalry." The Sixth Virginia Cavalry . . . was thrown into confusion and suffered some loss.[47]

The weary horsemen of the 2nd Virginia were asleep when the firing began, and the 6th stampeded through their camp. To make matters worse, some of the 7th Louisiana Infantry, camped just beyond them, fired into the 2nd Virginia. Munford recalled, "Many of our men were nearly exhausted from hunger and loss of sleep. We had been in the saddle and had had no regular rations for three days. My command was soon formed, and we drove them back, capturing three or four, who in the dark mistook us for their friends."[48]

On June 2, during a retreat from Kernstown to Strasburg, near Woodstock, Munford's 2nd Virginia mistakenly came under fire from the Confederate forces of the 42nd Virginia Infantry during an ordered retreat. The withdrawal turned into a stampede of Colonel Ashby's and General Steuart's cavalry and an artillery battery. Munford was infuriated, speaking of Steuart, "Such management I never saw before. . . . Mortified and annoyed at such management, Colonel Flournoy, of the Sixth, accompanied me to see General Ewell, who was kind enough to intercede with General Jackson and have us at once transferred to General Ashby's command." On June 3, Trooper Burnley wrote from near New Market, in the vicinity of Madison Court House, "We are retreating to Newmarket, rear guard fighting all the time, our Regt. was charged upon by Yankee Cavalry very unexpectedly could not form. We were shunning their artillery at the time. We will make a stand at New Market, retreating in haste."[49]

Port Republic

In early June, two separate Union armies of 20,000 each moved to unite near Strasburg and hoped to crush Jackson in a trap. Jackson raced south, eluding the trap. The two northern armies pursued him on either side of Massanutten Mountain, which runs down the spine of the Shenandoah Valley. At Massanutten's southern tip, Jackson's army fought masterful back-to-back battles with Maj. Gen. John C. Frémont's army at Cross Keys on June 8 and Port Republic on June 9, preventing the Federals from combining their armies. After these defeats, Union forces withdrew from the valley. Jackson, having

---

47. *OR* 12/1:640, 730–31; Driver, *2nd Virginia Cavalry*, 45.
48. Ibid.
49. *OR* 12/1:731; William Henry Burnley to his mother, June 3, 1862, Special Collections, MSS7871, UVA, Charlottesville, VA.

accomplished his mission, then moved east and joined Gen. Robert E. Lee in front of Richmond for the Peninsula campaign.[50]

The hamlet of Port Republic lies on a neck of land between the North and South Rivers, which connect to form the South Fork Shenandoah River. On June 6 and 7, 1862, Jackson's army, numbering about 16,000 strong, bivouacked north of Port Republic. General Ewell's division situated along the banks of Mill Creek near Goods Mill, and Brig. Gen. Charles S. Winder's division kept on the north bank of North River near the bridge. The 15th Alabama Infantry regiment was left to block the roads at Union Church. Jackson's headquarters was in Madison Hall at Port Republic. The army trains parked nearby.[51]

On June 6, as Stonewall Jackson's army withdrew from the pressure of General Frémont's superior forces, moving from Harrisonburg toward Port Republic, Colonel Turner Ashby commanded the rear guard. There was, as a result, a short skirmish at Good's Farm, just east of Harrisburg, in which the intrepid leader of Jackson's cavalry, Col. Turner Ashby, was killed. Nearer to Harrisonburg, the 1st New Jersey Cavalry, under the Englishman, Col. Sir Percy Wyndham, attacked Ashby's position at Good's Farm. Wyndham had previously boasted that he would capture Ashby. Although Ashby and the 2nd and 6th Virginia regiments fended off the cavalry attack, capturing Colonel Wyndham, a subsequent infantry engagement resulted in Ashby's horse being shot and Ashby charging ahead on foot, shouting for his men, "Charge men; for God's sake, charge!" Within a few steps, he was shot through the chest and side, killing him.[52]

On June 8, William Burnley wrote from near Port Republic:

> We are fighting nearly every day, we met with heavy loss day before yesterday. General Ashby was killed and will be buried in Charlottesville. None in our Co. was hurt. We took 41 cavs prisoners, 1 Col, major and 3 or 4 capts. Our Cav. [Company A] did not lose a man. Good many Yankee Cav were killed, after we charged the infantry. The infantry on each side were rushed in & it was a very hot fight. Our loss was 40 killed, I think.[53]

---

50. James I. Robertson, Jr., *Stonewall Jackson, The Man, The Soldier, The Legend* (New York, 1997), 454–55.
51. *OR* 12/1:721–23.
52. John H. Eicher and David J. Eicher, *Civil War High Commands* (Stanford, CA, 2001), 588; Whitehead, "Campaigns of Munford's 2nd Virginia Cavalry," 20.
53. William Henry Burnley to his mother, June 8, 1862, Special Collections, MSS7871, UVA, Charlottesville, VA.

Munford reported on the June 6 fight:

> Leaving me in command of the brigade, he [Ashby] marched with the First Maryland and Fifty-eighth Virginia Infantry under cover of the woods to my right, intending to flank the Yankees, instructing me that as soon as he had dislodged them from the hill to charge them with my whole force. In that enterprise he was baffled and ambushed himself. As soon as our forces became engaged, the Yankee cavalry advanced to the support of the [Pennsylvania] Bucktails. I advanced with my command to meet them, and getting within easy range, I opened with two pieces of [Roger Preston] Chew's battery, which had been masked in rear of the cavalry, and drove them from their position. Finding that a severe engagement had taken place, and that the brave Ashby had fallen, General Ewell ordered me to retire, making a heavy detail from my regiment to bear off our wounded on horseback.[54]

Munford recalled Ashby, "I believe Ashby was more than a partisan leader, and was a peer of the best of the officers in his sphere of service."[55]

Munford added:

> the cavalry furnished at first their own horses, and were required subsequently to furnish their own horses at their own expense. . . . I do not think that even General Jackson fully appreciated Ashby's troubles, because he complained of his disorgaNIZED COMMAND AND NO ORER for the organization of his command was ever given until after Ashby was killed. He was as brave and as modest about it as Hampton, with all the dash and fire of Fitz Lee or Stuart. Neither of them had a better eye for defense. They could not swoop down quicker when a flank was exposed or an opportunity given than he. They had better advantages in camp and by education, but he WAS A NATURAL SOLDIER AND HAD HIS LIFE BEEN SPARED WOULD have equaled Forrest in his boldest moves.[56]

Munford remembered that "crusty old Dick Ewell was deeply moved when Ashby fell, and remained on the field with me until all the prisoners and wounded men were taken back; [he] assisted many of the wounded to mount behind the cavalry, who carried them from the

---

54. Munford, *Reminiscences of Jackson's Valley Campaign*, SHSP (Richmond, VA, 1879), Vol. VII:523–524, 528–29; *OR* 12/1:712, 732.
55. Munford, *Reminiscences of Jackson's Valley Campaign*, 523–24.
56. Ibid.

*Colonel Turner Ashby
General Jubal Early's Cavalry Chief
in the 1862 Shenandoah Campaign*

Ashby, a fearless and beloved warrior, was killed on June 6, 1862 in a skirmish at Good's farm just east of Harrisburg, Virginia. Thomas T. Munford took over command of Ashby's independent minded cavalry.

(Courtesy: Library of Congress)

---

field, and I saw him give what money he had to some of the Maryland troops who were too badly wounded to be carried from the field on horseback."[57]

Robert E. Lee, in writing the Secretary of War Randolph, lamented the loss of Ashby:

> I grieve at the death of General Ashby. I hope he will find a successor. I doubt whether Radford would be. Ransom cannot be spared from his brigade nor would he, I presume, exchange his command for the cavalry of Jackson. We must endeavor to find someone. General Stuart mentions Col. Fitz. Lee, of the First Virginia

---

57. Ibid., 528.

Cavalry. . . . P.S.–How would Col. Thomas T. Munford, of Second Virginia Cavalry, answer? He seems to be a good officer, judging at this distance, and was elected in place of Radford.[58]

Following the death of Ashby on June 6, 1862, the command of the "Ashby Cavalry" was placed temporarily in the hands of Colonel Munford. Ashby's death left only one officer in the "brigade—" Maj. Oliver Ridgeway Funsten. Funsten had no previous military training, although he had been in service since the beginning of the war.[59]

With the death of Ashby, General Jackson was now able to implement his plans to reorganize and discipline the companies of Ashby's command, which up to that point in time operated more or less as an independent partisan outfit. He had attempted it once before, during late April 1862, and both Ashby and Funsten had submitted their resignations. After a rapprochement between Ashby and Jackson, however, Jackson agreed to let well enough alone, and their resignations were withdrawn. On June 12, Jackson wrote to Colonel Munford and informed him that he had "directed Inspector General [of the Valley District] to organize the cavalry now under Major Funsten."[60]

This organization took place at Swift Run Gap, 15 miles on the Luray side of Port Republic on June 16 and 17, 1862. The 7th and 12th Virginia Regiments and the 17th Battalion were created from Ashby's old command, in addition to a battery of artillery. The 17th Battalion was also known as the 1st Battalion of Virginia Cavalry and consisted of the companies of Capt. George W. Myers, Company A; Capt. William H. Harness, Company B; Capt. T. L. M. Chipley, Company C; Capt. Edward H. McDonald, Company D; and Cap. Joseph T. Hess, Company E.[61]

Command of the 17th Battalion was given temporarily to Capt. William H. Harness, who performed the duties of that office until he was relieved by Maj. William Patrick after July 11, 1862. Major Funsten at this time was attached to the 7th Virginia Cavalry.[62]

The brigade then consisted of the 2nd, 6th, 7th and 12th Regiments of Cavalry, the 17th Battalion of Cavalry, and Chew's Battery of Artillery, all under the command of Brig. Gen. Beverly H. Robertson as of June 18. When Jackson pulled out for eastern Virginia

---

58. *OR* 12/3:907. Ashby's promotion to brigadier general was not confirmed before his death.
59. Richard L. Armstrong, *11th Virginia Cavalry* (Lynchburg, VA, 1989), 8.
60. Ibid.
61. Ibid.
62. Ibid.

Colonel Thomas T. Munford,
dressed in a brigadier general's uniform.

VMI Class of 1852
circa 1875

(Courtesy: Virginia Military Institute Archives)

after the June 9 battle at Cross Keys, the cavalry was left behind to guard the roads near Harrisonburg. Robertson, a strict disciplinarian, drilled the companies every chance he got. This was a bitter pill for the men of Ashby's Cavalry, who were accustomed to a free and easy lifestyle. As a result, Robertson was not well liked by Ashby's men.[63]

Cross Keys

The Battle of Cross Keys was fought on June 8, 1862, in Rockingham County. Moving up the Shenandoah Valley on June 8 in pursuit of Jackson's army, General Frémont's army encountered General Ewell's division at Cross Keys. Munford, in temporary command of the cavalry brigade as of June 8, protected Ewell's right flank. Union Brig. Gen. Julius Stahel's brigade, attacking on the Union left, was stunned by a surprise volley from Brig. Gen. Isaac R. Trimble's command and driven back in confusion. After testing other parts of the Confederate line, Frémont withdrew to Keezletown Road under protection of his batteries. The next day, Trimble's and Col. George S. Patton's brigades held Frémont at bay while the rest of Ewell's force crossed the river to assist in the defeat of Gen. Erastus B. Tyler's command at Port Republic. Although the triumphs of the day belonged to the Infantry, the 6th Virginia Cavalry contributed to the success by protecting the baggage train; following the routed enemy; and scooping up numerous prisoners, arms, and wagons. Union casualties totaled 557 killed and wounded and 100 captured, while the Confederates lost fewer than 300 men.[64]

The Confederate cavalry, led tirelessly in these last battles by Colonel Munford of the 2nd Virginia Cavalry, finally camped on the summit of a nearby peak at midnight of June 9. Over the next few days Munford garnered prisoners and plunder in the vicinity of Harrisonburg, New Market, and Mount Jackson, until he was relieved of command by the freshly promoted Brig. Gen. Beverly H. Robertson on June 18th.[65]

Munford recalled the night after Cross Keys:

> The night after the battle of Cross Keys, I was at General Jackson's headquarters with Ewell, and heard the orders given for the next morning's work. My orders were to send and ascertain whether the road to Brown's gap was open, and to see if a bridge could be thrown across the

---

63. Ibid.
64. Musick, *6th Virginia Cavalry*, 16; *OR* 12/1:653–54, 658, 658, 783, 785–86.
65. Musick, *6th Virginia Cavalry*, 16.

South of the river. The Quartermaster ran a half-dozen wagons in the water, upon which some very long and thick planks were placed, so that, with their cadence step, the men were in a swing. This really impeded the march, AND CAUSED OUR TROOPS TO GO INTO THE FIGHT IN DETAIL instead of in compact body.⁶⁶

On June 9, 1862, Jackson concentrated his forces east of the south fork of the Shenandoah River against the isolated brigades of General Tyler and Col. Samuel Carroll of General Shields's division, with Tyler commanding. Confederate assaults across the bottomland were repulsed with heavy casualties, but a flanking column turned the Union left flank at the Coaling. Union counterattacks failed to reestablish the line, and Tyler was forced to retreat. Confederate forces at Cross Keys marched to join Jackson at Port Republic, burning the North River bridge behind them. Frémont's army arrived too late to assist Tyler and Carroll, instead watching helplessly from across the rain-swollen river. On the morning of the 12th, Munford entered Harrisonburg, where, in addition to wagons, medical stores, and camp equipage, he captured some 200 small-arms. Additionally, his troopers took about 200 of Frémont's men prisoner; many of them had been severely wounded on the 8th, and most of the others had been left behind as sick. The sick and the Federal surgeons attending them were released as paroled.⁶⁷

After these dual defeats at Cross Keys and Port Republic, the Union armies retreated, leaving Jackson in control of the upper and middle Shenandoah Valley, freeing his army to reinforce Lee in the Seven Days' battles outside of Richmond. Union losses were put at 1,002 killed and wounded, while the Confederates lost 816.⁶⁸

Munford recalled what happened subsequently:

> The next day was a rough one for our army. Shields had secured a splendid position. . . . There was no field for the cavalry to operate in. When the enemy retired, it WAS THROUGH A PINEY COUNTRY WITH A SINGLE WAGON ROAd. 7 E COULD ONLY FOLOW IN A COLUMN OF TWOS 7 E FOLLOWED THEM TO NEAR #ONRADS' STORE SECURING MANY STRAGGLERS wagons and several pieces of artillery. That night I returned to Ewell's quarters and took supper with him.⁶⁹

Munford also remembered, "This was the first time his [Jackson's] infantry had had a day's rest since the campaign opened, but there was

---

66. Munford, *Reminiscences of Jackson's Valley Campaign*, 529–30.
67. *OR* 12/1:716.
68. National Park Service, "Battle of Port Republic."
69. Munford, *Reminiscences of Jackson's Valley Campaign*, 530.

no rest for the cavalry. We pushed on to Harrisonburg, and followed the enemy towards New Market, capturing many stragglers, wagons, horses, and plunder abandoned by the enemy." Munford also wrote of what it meant to serve in the cavalry and artillery under Jackson:

> Jackson, the "wagon hunter," never gave up one after it came into his possession. If a tire came off a wagon, he would stop the whole train and wait for it to be fixed on, and let the "rear guard" hold its position. A man who never served in the cavalry under Jackson knows little of what was required of them. We skirmished all day and half the night, retiring en echelon. There was one eternal picking at each other. The artillery would seize a position and hold it as long as they could, then fall back to another, covered by the cavalry. I do not believe the world has ever produced a grander, braver, nobler band of patriotic soldiers than the artillery in the Army of Northern Virginia.[70]

The night of June 12, Munford wrote Jackson and received a reply:

> Colonel, I congratulate you upon your early reoccupation of Harrisonburg. I have directed the Inspector-General to organize the cavalry now under Major Oliver R. Funsten, and hope it will soon be of service to you. You had better order forward Chew's battery and your train in time to pass Mount Crawford before 12 o'clock M. tomorrow. In the morning I trust that I will make a timely move for the Valley pike, and expect to encamp this side of Mount Crawford.[71]

During Stonewall Jackson's memorable 1862 Valley campaign, his battles with Pope, and the fight at Leesburg, Company B of Munford's regiment was detailed with General Longstreet's Corps as his bodyguard. Company A of the 1st Maryland Cavalry, under Capt. Ridgley Brown, served with Munford's regiment in their absence. Munford remembered, "A more chivalrous and gallant band of soldiers never flashed a blade or answered a bugle's call. It is with especial pride that I enroll them with my old regiment, since they add a luster to its fame."[72]

---

70. Ibid., 528, 531.
71. Ibid., 530.
72. Postwar letter from Thomas T. Munford to H. B. McClellan, printed in W. W. Guggenheimer, *The Maryland Line in the in the Confederate Army,*

Maj. Gen. Richard S. Ewell

Colonel Thomas T. Munford had a good relationship with the sometimes difficult Ewell.

Munford recalled Ewell: "I have a most kind remembrance and affection for General Ewell, Jackson's senior lieutenant, commanding his right wing, and wish to recall some of his oddities. He possessed more eccentricities than he thought Jackson displayed. He was a hard old customer, and could swear, when he chose to exercise that faculty, in a style that defies description. He spared no one when he was cross, but was nobly generous at all other times. My relations with him were always of the kindest character..."

(Courtesy: Library of Congress)

So, during Jackson's Valley campaign, Munford's regiment had served under Maj. Gen. Richard S. Ewell, of Jackson's Corps. Munford recalled Ewell:

> I have a most kind remembrance and affection for 'E NERAL% WEIL* *A CKSON'S SENIOR LIEUTENANT COMMANDING his right wing, and wish to recall some of his ODDITIES ™(E POSSESSED MORE ECCENTRICITIES THAN HE thought Jackson displayed. He was a hard, old customer, and could swear, when he chose to exercise that faculty, IN A STYLE THAT DEFIES DESCRIPTION (M E SPARED NO ONE WHEN he was cross, but was nobly generous at all other times. My relations with him were always of the kindest character.[73]

Jackson's successful valley campaign had convinced even Richard Ewell of Jackson's brilliance. Ewell confided in Munford one night after dinner, "Look here Munford, do you remember a conversation

---

1861–1865 (Baltimore, MD, 1900), 228; McClellan, *The Campaigns of Stuart's Cavalry*, 445.

73. Munford, *Reminiscences of Jackson's Valley Campaign*, 523.

we had one day at Conrad's Store?" "To what do you allude?" asked Munford, as if he could forget sight of Ewell on his knees in his white nightshirt. "Why to General Jackson," replied Ewell. "Very well," said Munford. "I take it all back," said Ewell, "and I will never prejudice another man. Old Jackson is no fool; he knows how to keep his own counsel, and does curious things; but he has a method in his madness."[74]

On June 13, Colonel Munford received instructions from Jackson, then near Mount Meridian:

> It is important to cut off all communications between us and the enemy. Please require the ambulances to go beyond our lines at once, and press our lines forward as far as practicable. It is desirable that we should have New Market, and that no information should pass to the enemy. I expect soon to let you have two more companies of cavalry for the Army of the Northwest. I will not be able to leave here today, and possibly not for some time, so you must look out for the safety of your train. Please impress the bearers of the flag of truce as much as possible with an idea of a heavy advance on our part, and let them return under such impression. Whilst it is desirable for us to have New Market, yet you must judge of the practicability. The only true rule for cavalry, is to follow as long as the enemy retreats.[75]

On June 16, Jackson sent a note to Colonel Munford, instructing him "to meet him at ten that night at the north end of the street at Mount Sidney, and not to ask for him or anybody." The story goes that Colonel Munford received the note, set out alone, and, at the appointed hour, entered Mount Sidney, which, at that late hour of the night, looked dark and deserted. The moon shone, however; and at the head of the street, in the middle of the highway, a solitary figure on horseback awaited him, motionless, and in silence. The hand of the figure went to his cap, and in the curt and familiar tones of Jackson came the words, "Ah, Colonel, here you are. What news from the front?" "All quiet, General," replied Colonel Munford. "Good! [Now] I wish you to produce upon the enemy the impression that I am going to advance." And Jackson then gave his orders in detail, after which the figures parted and went different ways—Jackson back to Port Republic, Colonel Munford went to Harrisonburg. But, according to Maj. Jedediah Hotchkiss's diary, it was Hotchkiss himself who met

---

74. Mapp, Jr., *Frock Coats and Epaulets: The Men Who Led the Confederacy*, 300; "Reminiscences of Jackson's Valley Campaign," *Southern Historical Society Papers*, vol. VII:530.
75. Ibid.

Jackson at Mount Sidney that night. Munford did not attend, due to a severe bout of neuralgia.[76]

In a letter from Jackson to Munford, dated June 18, Jackson stated he regretted to hear that Munford was suffering from the effects of neuralgia. He noted Munford acted prudently in not venturing out "last night," which was rendered unnecessary because Brig. Gen. Robertson had just reported for duty. Jackson assigned Robertson the instructions he had written for Munford.[77]

As Jackson slipped away from the valley, he relied on Munford to accomplish a bit of the subterfuge they had discussed to entice the Federals into believing that they were initiating a "heavy advance" further up the valley. Under a flag of truce, General Frémont sent 28 ambulances under an escort with surgeons, asking to take their wounded back to their lines. Munford, communicating with Jackson using only couriers, held the Federals overnight, telling them that he must obtain General Jackson's permission. He also made sure that they overheard a feigned verbal report from local citizen, William Gilmer, of a heavily reinforced Jackson moving up the valley. He had also, per Jackson's orders, let it be widely known to folks in the area to keep the road to Winchester open for a few days for use by Jackson's army. Munford's and others' ruses worked, because the Federals bolted for Strasburg and immediately began fortifying the town. All the while, Jackson was heading towards Richmond.[78]

In preparation for leaving the valley to join Lee in the Peninsula campaign, Jackson ordered Munford to have his cavalry "picket from the Blue Ridge to the Shenandoah Mountain or the mountain west of Harrisonburg." Soon, Jackson ordered him to march his regiment to Port Republic. There, he received orders to report to the quartermaster at Charlottesville Junction. Jackson "did not want the cavalry to know their final destination."[79]

---

76. *OR* 12/3:914; John Esten Cooke, *Stonewall Jackson: A Military Biography* (New York, NY, 1866), 202-03. Note: This story appears inaccurate. Jackson gave his instructions to Jedediah Hotchkiss who delivered them to Munford; *OR* 12/3:912, 914; George Francis Robert Henderson, *Stonewall Jackson and the American Civil War* (New York, 1919), Vol. I, Chapter XI, 518; Thomas T. Munford to R. L. Dabney, December 31, 1865, SHC, Richmond, VA; Douglas Southall Freeman, *Lee's Lieutenants*, (New York, 1970), vol. 1:469fn; Jedediah Hotchkiss to Thomas T. Munford, August 19, 1896, August 3, 1897, Munford–Ellis Papers, DU.
77. T. J. Jackson to Colonel Munford, June 18, 1862, Thomas H. Ellis Papers, Accession 41008, Letters of Thomas T. Munford, LVA, Richmond, VA.
78. *OR* 12/1:732; part 3:912, 914–15. SHSP, Vol. IX, 366-67; Munford, "Reminiscences," *Cavalry Journal*, vol. V:74-75; Thomas J. Jackson to Thomas T. Munford, December 31, 1865, SHC; Whitehead, "Campaigns of Munford's 2nd Virginia Cavalry," 28.
79. Driver, *2nd Virginia Cavalry*, 51; Munford, *Reminiscences of Jackson's Valley Campaign*, 523.

Munford reflected upon the recent Valley campaign:

> The weather had been extremely hot. . . . The roads macadamized and the cavalry unprovided with horseshoes and being compelled to subsist them mostly on young grass without salt, I found my command in a most deplorable condition, our work had been eternal day and night. We were under fire twenty-six out of thirty [days] having gone in with more than 100 [men] unarmed, we returned generally well-equipped.[80]

Munford remembered the cavalry battles and Stonewall Jacksons's slogan for the cavalry, "A bold front and a dash at their weakest point." He also recalled:

> I have seen scores of men tumble from their horses in a charge in Jackson's Valley campaign of 1862, who were more afraid of their horses then of our men; they would stand after they got on the ground; they were put into the Union Army to fill up companies. The time came when the Union cavalry officers would have none such in their commands, and the Confederates were then deprived of a source of supply of good accoutrements and equipment so much needed in our Army.[81]

By virtue of Jackson's vigorous offensive in the Shenandoah Valley, McDowell was forced to remain in Fredericksburg. Jackson successfully wrested the initiative away from the Federal campaign. Jackson made use of rapid, unpredictable movements on interior lines and flanking maneuvers, culminating in his 17,000 "foot cavalry" marching 646 miles in 48 days. They won key battles as they successfully engaged three Union armies, preventing them from reinforcing the Federal offensive against Richmond. Jackson inflicted twice as many casualties as he suffered, seized countless supplies, and tied up elements of three separate Federal armies totaling more than 60,000 men, who would otherwise have been used against Richmond.[82]

---

80. *OR* 12/1:732; Akers, Thesis, 18, Virginia Tech.
81. *Journal of the Military Service Institution of the United States,* Vol. X (March 1889) No. XXXVII, 528.
82. Robert Stevens, *The Bracken Rangers: Company K, 28th Regiment, 1st Indiana Cavalry, and Essays on the American Civil War* (Los Angeles, 2010), 216–17.

Although Munford had led the brigade admirably after Ashby's death, permanent command had gone to West Pointer, Brig. Gen. Beverly H. Robertson. Jackson probably would have accepted the promotion of Munford to fill the vacancy, but President Davis selected Robertson. This was just the first of a long string of disappointments for Munford concerning a promotion to brigadier general. Robertson remained in charge at Harrisonburg, while Munford followed Jackson to Richmond. After an exhausting march for both man and beast, on June 25 Munford's 2nd Virginia joined Jackson at Ashland.[83]

---

83. *OR* 12/2:552, part 1:733.

Chapter Seven

The Peninsula Campaign

"Yes, sir; but I ordered you to be here at sunrise, and I have been waiting for you for a quarter of an hour."
— Stonewall Jackson to Thomas Munford, on why he [Munford] was late in meeting him at White Oak Swamp.

In the coming months, Col. Thomas Munford led his regiment during the Peninsula campaign, revealing himself as a maturing cavalry leader with distinction. He continued to learn his trade, lessons he brought to bear during the upcoming campaigns.

When on the Virginia lower peninsula, the only thing that stood between General George McClellan and a clear road to Richmond were the 11,000 Confederates posted at Yorktown under the command of Maj. Gen. John B. Magruder. Despite the overwhelming Union numbers heading his way, Magruder stood his ground and bought precious time by implementing a bold ruse. "Prince John" created the illusion that his force was a formidable one by splitting his command, sending half of it racing through the woods with orders to show themselves often enough that the enemy would take note. As soon as one half made the route, he sent in the other. Round and round they went for hours, long enough to bring McClellan's advance to a standstill. By the time the commander of the Army of the Potomac realized he had been fooled by a clever subterfuge, substantial reinforcements had arrived from Richmond.[1]

Finally, on May 4, McClellan began his slow movement up the Virginia lower peninsula, and by the end of the month, he had worked his way up to within about nine miles of Richmond. When he became entangled in the swamplands of the Chickahominy River, Gen. Joseph E. Johnston's forces moved out to meet him. The Battle of Seven Pines, or Fair Oaks, which occurred May 31-June 1, was badly fought

---

1. Paul D. Casdorph, *Prince John Magruder: His Life and Campaigns* (New York, 1996), 143–45; Sears, *To the Gates of Richmond*, 36–39.

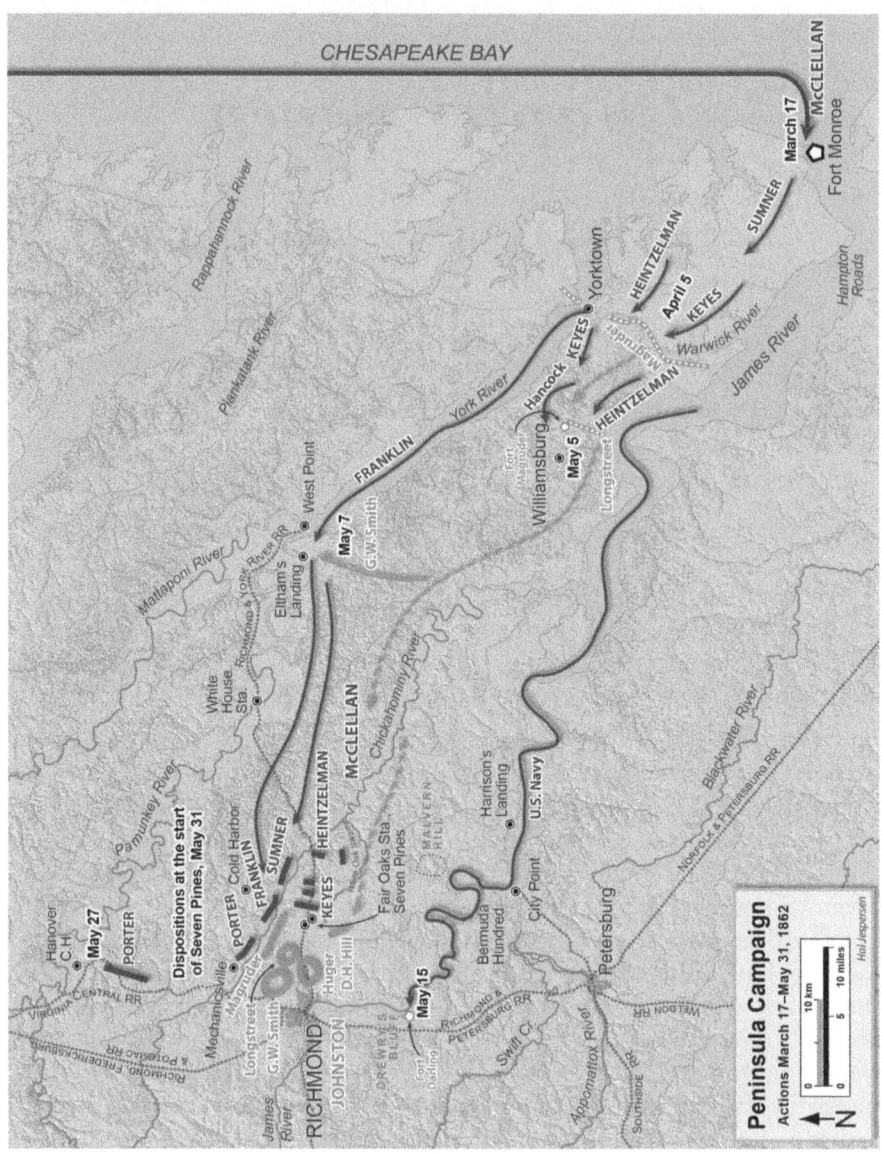

on both sides and indecisive. Johnston was severely wounded at Seven Pines on May 31, and on June 1, Confederate President Jefferson Davis assigned Robert E. Lee to replace Johnston in command.[2]

On June 25, McClellan launched an attack at Oak Grove in a failed attempt to get his siege guns within striking distance of Richmond. This attack opened what became known as the "'Seven Days' Battles."[3]

---

2. Sears, *To the Gates of Richmond*, 118, 138, 140, 145.
3. Clifford Dowdey, *Seven Days: The Emergence of Robert E. Lee and the Dawn of a Legend* (DE, 2012), 2–3.

General Lee sought to mitigate the disparity in numbers by building a series of fortifications requiring fewer defenders. His goal was to drive McClellan off the peninsula, thus relieving the pressure on Richmond. He was aided in his quest by information provided by Stuart's famous reconnaissance ride of June 12-15 around McClellan's army, which showed that McClellan's right flank was "in the air" and thus vulnerable to attack. In addition to reinforcements from Georgia and the Carolinas, Lee called on General Jackson from the Shenandoah Valley. Despite Jackson's late arrival, Lee launched his first attack of the Seven Days' Battles on June 26 at Mechanicsville, Virginia. Darkness and Jackson's failure to arrive contributed greatly to Lee's loss in that battle. Following the attack at Mechanicsville, Lee struck the Federals at Gaines's Mill. Although McClellan's forces greatly outnumbered Lee's, the new commander maneuvered and dispatched 57,000 troops against about half as many Federals under Brig. Gen. Fitz John Porter. Porter's V Corps had become isolated on the north side of the Chickahominy River, and while those forces fought valiantly, the Federals had no choice but to retreat across the Chickahominy by sundown of June 27.[4]

By mid-June, McClellan had shifted his supply base from White House Landing on the Pamunkey River to Harrison's Landing on the James, 12 miles southeast of Richmond. Lee learned that McClellan was moving his troops to the James and tried unsuccessfully to turn the Federal retreat into a rout. He attacked the Federals at Savage's Station and Frayser's Farm on June 29 and 30, but the attacks were uncoordinated and failed in their purpose. During the night of the June 29, McClellan retreated across White Oak Swamp, a shallow tributary of the Chickahominy.[5]

White Oak Swamp on June 30, 1862

As the Union Army of the Potomac retreated southeast toward the James River, its rear guard, under Maj. Gen. William B. Franklin, stopped Stonewall Jackson's divisions at the White Oak bridge crossing. An artillery duel ensued while the main battle of Glendale raged two miles farther south around Frayser's Farm. Resistance from General Franklin's VI Corps prevented Jackson from joining a consolidated assault on the Union Army at Glendale that Gen. Robert E. Lee had ordered, producing an inconclusive result. The Union

---

4. Sears, *To the Gates of Richmond*, 174, 208, 252.
5. Ibid, 307–10, 336.

Army avoided destruction and assumed a strong defensive position at Malvern Hill.[6]

A story relating what happened during the fight at White Oak Swamp reveals a characteristic of Jackson: He was almost never late. One of General Jackson's soldiers recalled, "Jackson did everything promptly himself, and he expected his men to do the same." Jackson was immovable by reasons given for delays. As an example, Colonel Munford recalled the following story: Munford parted with General Jackson on the evening of June 29, 1862, during the Peninsula Campaign. Jackson told Colonel Munford to "report the next morning at sunrise, ready to precede the troops." Munford remembered that a violent thunderstorm came up the during the night, and his troopers were scattered by the blasts of the night, and in the thickly pine-wooded country, "it was so dark that one could hardly see his horse's ears." When the first gray streak appeared, Colonel Munford sent his adjutant and officers to gather up his broken regiment; but, at sunrise, only 50 had reported. They were a half-mile from the crossroad.

To Colonel Munford's horror, he found General Jackson sitting there waiting for him. In Colonel Munford's own words: Jackson "was in a bad humor," and said to him, "Colonel, my orders to you were to be here at sunrise." Colonel Munford replied, "the command had no provisions, and the storm and the dark night had delayed him." Jackson's reply was, "Yes, sir; but Colonel, I ordered you to be here by sunrise. Move on with your regiment. If you meet the enemy drive in his pickets, and, if you want artillery, Colonel [Stapleton] Crutchfield will furnish you." Colonel Munford started with his 50 troopers. As other cavalrymen came straggling on to join in the marching body, Jackson observed it and sent two couriers to tell their commander his men were straggling badly. Colonel Munford rode back and repeated his former story. Jackson listened, but answered, "Yes, sir; but I ordered you to be here at sunrise, and I have been waiting for you for a quarter of an hour." Colonel Munford then made the best of the situation, re-formed his men, drove in Federal pickets, captured a number of wounded and secured a large quantity of stores. This was accomplished so rapidly that the Federal battery, located on the other side of the White Oak Swamp, could not fire on the Confederate cavalrymen without endangering their own. Jackson rode up smiling. In about an hour he ordered Colonel Munford to move his regiment over the creek to capture some Federal cannon. He rode with Colonel Munford to the swamp, where they saw the bridge torn up, its timbers lying in a tangled mass. Colonel Munford said he did not think they could pass, but Jackson looked at him, waved his hand, and said, "Yes,

---

6. *OR* 11/1:491–92.

Colonel, try it." Jackson went in and struggled and floundered partway over, even before Colonel Munford could form his men. Jackson called on him to move on the Federal guns. Colonel Cary Breckinridge went forward with what men had already crossed, and Colonel Munford followed with another squadron. They encountered a Union infantry regiment supporting the battery, and a hitherto unseen battery on the right flank of the Confederates opened on them. The small band of horsemen had to retreat along the bank of the swamp for a quarter of a mile, and then, with great difficulty, re-cross by a cowpath.[7]

Colonel Munford, in a post war letter to Gen. Wade Hampton, wrote:

> At the battle of White Oak Swamp, after Col. Crutchfield's artillery had disabled one gun, and driven the cannoneers from the battery which commanded the crossing at the old bridge at White Oak Swamp, Gen. Jackson directed me to cross the creek, with my regiment, at the ford, and to secure the guns in front of us. The enemy's sharpshooters were stationed in rear of the building overlooking the ford; and as soon as we neared the abandoned battery of the enemy, these sharpshooters, and another battery stationed in the road at the edge of the woods, and commanding the road and the ford over which we had passed, opened a furious fire upon us, and I was forced to move a quarter of a mile lower down the creek, where I found a cow path which led me over the swamp. . . . Thirty-nine years is too long a time to attempt to say what I wrote him, but I know that I thought, all the time, that he could have crossed his infantry where we recrossed. I had seen his infantry cross far worse places, and I expected that he would attempt it. . . . We remained near where we recrossed all day, with a vidette on the other side of the swamp. He put his sharpshooters in on the right of the ford, and made no attempt to cross where we recrossed. Why, I never understood.[8]

---

7. C. A. Fonerden, *A brief history of the military career of Carpenter's Battery: From its organization as a Rifle company under the name of the Alleghany Roughs to the ending of the war between the States* (Baltimore, MD, 1983), 20–22; Thomas T. Munford to H. B. McClellan, August 4, 1884, printed in McClellan, *Stuart's Cavalry*, 80–82; Thomas T. Munford to John C. Ropes, December 7, 1897, Howard Gotlieb Archival Research Center, Boston University.
8. Colonel Thomas T. Munford to General Wade Hampton, March 23, 1901, Munford–Ellis Papers, DU.; E. P. Alexander, *Military Memoirs of a Confederate, A Critical Narrative* (New York, 1907), 148-49.

Much later after the war, Munford speculated that because Jackson had been in whirlwind of fighting for six weeks, "his endurance simply gave out, and that he was not at his best." Countering Munford's opinion that Jackson could have crossed the swamp was Dr. Hunter McGuire, who stated, "Jackson himself, accompanied by three or four members of his staff, of whom I was one, followed the cavalry across the Swamp. The ford was miry and deep, and impracticable for either artillery or infantry."[9]

Just before Munford forwarded his report of the battle at White Oak Swamp, Army Headquarters issued an order requiring "all Cavalry reports be sent through Gen'l J.E.B. Stuart." Up until this point, Munford's cavalry was part of Jackson's corps. Munford complied with the order; Jackson was much annoyed, informing Munford, "he belonged to his corps and not to Gen'l Stuart." Munford's report did not appear in the Official Records; it was either lost or suppressed. Jackson did not release his cavalry forces to General Stuart until August 10, 1862. At that time, despite his dislike for General Beverly Robertson, Stuart allowed him to retain the command of his brigade and gave only general instructions.[10]

The final attack of the Seven Days' battles occurred on July 1 at Malvern Hill. Lee was determined to destroy the retreating Federals before they reached the James and safety, but the ensuing battle proved to be a disaster from start to finish for General Lee. A lack of coordination and communication among the Confederate commanders allowed the Union artillery to take advantage of its superiority in numbers and its position to pound the Confederate gunners, effectively destroying the Rebel batteries, one by one, as they came on the field. The Confederate infantry, too, was cut to pieces as they charged up the long slope toward the entrenched Federals.[11]

William Pegram's Battery at Malvern Hill July 1, 1862:

A gallant and fearless Capt. William R. J. Pegram fought a hopeless artillery duel with Federal artillery, often alone with his single gun on Malvern Hill. Joined by the Virginia Letcher Light Artillery, the Confederate gunners peppered the Federal line against overwhelming

---

9. Thomas T. Munford to John C. Ropes, December 7, 1897, Howard Gotlieb Archival Research Center, Boston University, Boston, MA; Henderson, *Jackson*, 51; *OR* 11/1:556–57.
10. Thomas T. Munford to John C. Ropes, December 7, 1897, Howard Gotlieb Archival Research Center, Boston University, Boston, MA.
11. Sears, *To the Gates of Richmond*, 333–37.

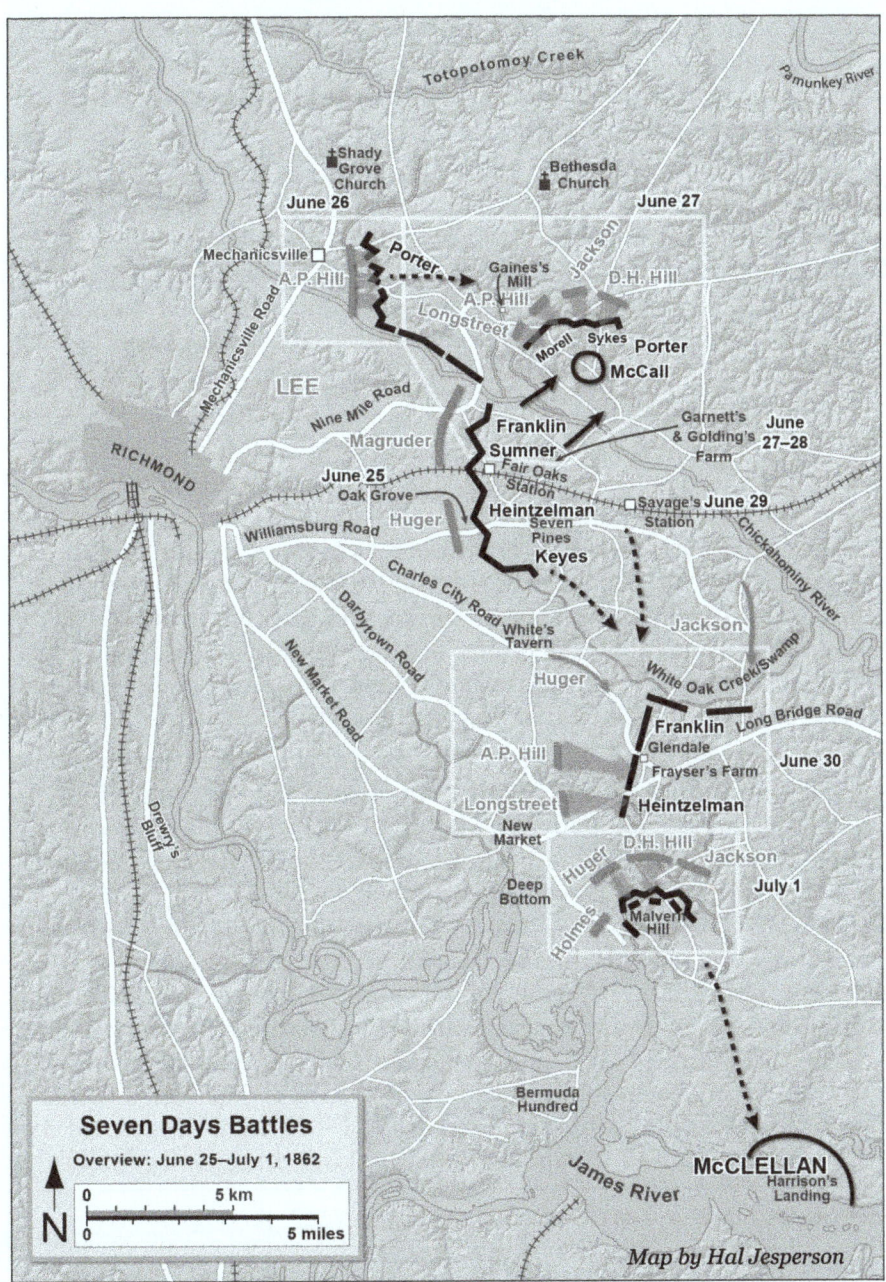

forces. "Willie" Pegram's friend, Lt. Charles Ellis Munford, was Thomas T. Munford's youngest brother and had been assigned to Letcher's artillery. Ellis Munford had been Willie's classmate at the University of Virginia and was engaged to Willie's sister, Jennie. The two friends stood within sight of each other, firing away at the Union forces, but were vastly outgunned by Federal artillery. During the fight, a spherical shell exploded directly over Ellis Munford, spraying shrapnel balls. Munford was hit. One ball passed through his eye, another through his head, and the last struck his thigh. Ellis Munford crumbled to the ground, dead.[12]

Elizabeth Thorogood Ellis Munford, Thomas Munford's stepmother, was at home in Richmond on July 1, 1862, and heard cannon fire from the battle at Malvern Hill. Her 23-year-old son, Lt. Charles Ellis Munford, was fighting with the Letcher Light Artillery. She expected to "hear from Ellis tonight," she wrote her daughters. Later that evening, his comrades brought her son's body to her doorstep, directly from the battlefield.[13]

Confederate casualties during the Seven Days' Battles were nearly two to one compared to those of the Federals. However, McClellan ceded the field to the Confederates, due to his earlier decision to set up a new base on the James at Harrison's Landing. This relieved the pressure on Richmond; it was another two years before Richmond again came under Federal attack. McClellan continued his retreat even before receiving his subordinates' reports of the successful battle at Malvern Hill, and in spite of his officers' protests. Major Generals Philip Kearney and Fitz John Porter believed that they could hold the ground and then attack Lee, forcing him back to Richmond.[14]

After the battle of Malvern Hill, an amusing incident involving Jackson and Munford was recalled by Esten Cooke. According to Cooke, on the morning after the battle of Malvern Hill, Jackson was riding on the left of his line when he met Colonel Munford, and after some words upon military matters, asked him if he had managed to secure some breakfast. Munford informed him that he had, and Jackson asked, "I should like to have some myself. I wonder if I could get some buttermilk?" "Yes, General, come with me," was Colonel Munford's answer, and they rode to the plain mansion in which an old lady of the humbler class had furnished Colonel Munford with his breakfast. "Can I get some breakfast for General Jackson, madam?" asked Munford. "He has had none to-day." "For whom?" exclaimed the good woman, pausing in her work and looking earnestly at Munford.

---

12. William J. Miller, *The Peninsula Campaign of 1862, Yorktown to Seven Days* (Cambridge, MA, 1995), vol. 2:37; John H. Munford to Sally Munford, July 6, 1862, Munford–Ellis Papers, DU; *Battles & Leaders of the Civil War*, Vol. II:448. Note: Willie Pegram was killed in action at Five Forks on April 1, 1865, and Willie's older brother, General John Pegram, was killed in action during the battle of Hatcher's Run late in the war.

13. Clint Schemmer, *Richmond Times Dispatch*, February 3, 2011; *Battles & Leaders of the Civil War*, Vol. II:448.

14. Joseph P. Cullen, *The Peninsula Campaign, 1862* (Harrisburg, PA, 1973), 20–21, 168–69; David G. Martin, *The Peninsula Campaign* (Conshohocken, PA, 1992), 229–30.

"For General Jackson," was Munford's reply. "General Jackson! That is not General Jackson!" she exclaimed, pointing to the man in the dingy uniform. "Yes, it is, madam." The old lady gazed at the General for a moment in silence; her face flushed red, and raising both hands, she suddenly burst into tears. Everything in her house was produced without delay, including the longed-for buttermilk; but nothing, evidently, in the old lady's estimation was good enough for her hero. These things touched Jackson more than the plaudits of victory.[15]

After Malvern Hill, on General Lee's orders, Stuart's cavalry relentlessly pursued the retreating Federals, while providing a steady flow of information of the enemy's movements to the Confederate chieftain. On July 3, Stuart discovered that Evelington Heights, an area towering some 60 feet above Herring Creek and separating Harrison's Landing from the mainland, was only lightly defended. Possession of the heights would afford Lee an excellent position from which to launch an attack that could conceivably trap McClellan. Stuart lost no time in relaying this valuable piece of intelligence to Lee, who immediately ordered Longstreet and Jackson to ready their troops for a march to meet Stuart. Perhaps out of pique due to Jackson's poor performance during the bulk of the Seven Days' Battles, Lee decided to put Longstreet's troops ahead of Jackson's for the march, necessitating a needless delay as the two bodies of troops traded positions. In the meantime, Stuart prematurely ordered his favorite artillerist, Capt. John Pelham, to open fire with a single howitzer on the slight Union force holding Evelington Heights. Stuart obtained the desired effect of driving those troops off the heights, but at the same time it alerted McClellan to his vulnerability from that direction. McClellan immediately dispatched nearly half his army to Evelington Heights and the surrounding area. Poor command decisions, on both Stuart's and Lee's part, effectively put a stop to the Confederate commander's last chance to destroy McClellan's army on the banks of the James.[16]

With the successful containment of McClellan's army at Harrison's Landing, the Confederates withdrew to a more favorable defensive position closer to Richmond. General Lee ordered Stuart's cavalry the task of observing McClellan's army and spending July and August on picket and scouting duty.[17]

McClellan's failure in the Peninsula campaign led to changes in the Union army. On June 27, Major General John Pope, who had achieved

---

15. John Esten Cooke, *The Life of Stonewall Jackson* (New York, 1866), 248-49. Cooke states that he was told this story by Munford.
16. *OR* 11/2:519-20; Douglas Southall Freeman, *R. E. Lee*, (New York, 1934), Vol. II:225; Brian K. Burton, *Extraordinary Circumstances: The Seven Days Battles*, (Bloomington, IN, 2001), 380–84.
17. Sears, *To the Gates of Richmond*, 356.

a measure of success in the West, assumed command of the three Valley armies now designated the Army of Virginia. Pope was a physically imposing man with a talent for telling clever stories, but boastful to the point of being arrogant and obnoxious. Pope desired to step up the assault and announced his intention to make short work of the Confederates.[18]

Barely two weeks into his command, Pope issued a series of general orders which provoked bitter resentment in the South and shock among his more conservative fellow officers. The orders, however, met with little opposition among the enlisted men and lower grade officers, for the orders encouraged his troops to seize food and supplies from Virginia farmers and threatened to hang, without trial, anyone suspected of aiding the Confederates. Lee later called the blusterous Pope "a miscreant" who needed to be "suppressed."[19]

---

18. John J. Hennessy, *Return to Bull Run: The Campaign and Battle of Second Manassas* (Norman, OK, 1993), 3–6; Peter Cozzens and Robert I. Girardi, ed., John Pope, *The Military Memoirs of General John Pope* (Chapel Hill, NC, 1998), 129.
19. Peter Cozzens, *General John Pope: A Life for the Nation* (Chicago, IL, 2000), 86–87, 89.

Chapter Eight

Battle of Second Manassas, the Maryland Campaign, and the Battle of Fredericksburg

"They absorbed us . . . the shooting, running, cursing and cutting that followed cannot be understood except by an eye witness."

–Colonel Thomas T. Munford
at the battle of Lewis Ford (Farm),
August 30, 1862.

During 1862, Colonel Thomas Munford was called upon often to provide valuable leadership, often leading cavalry charges or supplying critical support. These valuable experiences enabled him to raise his skills to levels affording capabilities to command his regiment and brigades.

Battle of Second Manassas

After defeating McClellan in the Seven Days Battles, General Lee turned his forces on General Pope. This campaign became known as "Second Bull Run" or "Second Manassas," and was fought August 28-30, 1862.

The Union Army of Virginia consisted of three corps of 51,000 men: the I Corps under Maj. Gen. Franz Sigel; the II Corps led by Maj. Gen. Nathaniel P. Banks; and the III Corps commanded by Maj. Gen. Irvin McDowell, who had led the losing Union army at First Manassas. Parts of three corps (III, V, and VI) of McClellan's Army of the Potomac, along with Maj. Gen. Ambrose Burnside's IX Corps (commanded by Maj. Gen. Jesse L. Reno), eventually joined Pope for combat operations, raising his strength to 77,000 soldiers.[1]

---

1. Scott C. Patchan, *Second Manassas: Longstreet's Attack and the Struggle for Chinn Ridge* (Washington, D. C., 2011), 3.

On the Confederate side, Gen. Robert E. Lee's Army of Northern Virginia organized into two "wings" or "commands," totaling about 55,000 men. Maj. Gen. James Longstreet commanded the "right wing," while Maj. Gen. Stonewall Jackson led the left. The Cavalry division, under Maj. Gen. J.E.B. Stuart, was attached to Jackson's wing.[2]

Pope's objective was two-fold: protect Washington and the Shenandoah Valley, and draw Confederate forces away from McClellan by moving in the direction of Gordonsville. Based on his experience fighting McClellan in the Seven Days' Battles, Robert E. Lee realized McClellan was no further threat to him on the lower Virginia peninsula, and so he felt no compulsion to keep all of his forces in direct defense of Richmond. This allowed him to relocate Jackson to Gordonsville to block Pope and protect the Virginia Central Railroad.[3]

Lee had even larger plans in mind. Since the Union Army was split between McClellan and Pope and they were widely separated, Lee saw an opportunity to destroy Pope before returning his attention to McClellan. He committed Maj. Gen. Ambrose P. Hill to join Jackson with 12,000 men. On August 3, Union General-in-Chief, Henry W. Halleck, directed McClellan to begin his final withdrawal from the Peninsula and to return to northern Virginia to support Pope. McClellan protested and so did not begin his redeployment until August 14.[4]

Meanwhile, on August 9, Maj. Gen. Nathaniel Banks's corps attacked Jackson at Cedar Mountain, gaining an early advantage, but a Confederate counterattack led by General A. P. Hill drove Banks back across Cedar Creek. Jackson's advance was stopped, however, by the Union division of Brig. Gen. James B. Ricketts. By now, Jackson had learned that Pope's corps were all together, foiling his plan of defeating each in separate actions. Jackson remained in position until August 12, then withdrew to Gordonsville. On August 13, Robert E. Lee sent General Longstreet to reinforce Jackson.[5]

On August 21, Robert E. Lee instructed Jackson to have Munford's regiment report directly to Gen. J.E.B. Stuart. The 2nd Virginia had been on Jackson's left flank after the Confederate's

---

2. Ibid., 2.
3. Ibid., 4
4. Ibid., 4–5.
5. Ibid., 5.

capture of Culpeper Court House. Munford proposed that he and his regiments be permitted to go after General Pope's wagon train, but his request was denied.[6]

From August 22-25, the two armies fought a series of minor actions along the Rappahannock River. Swollen by heavy rains, Lee was unable to forge a river crossing. By this time, reinforcements from the Army of the Potomac began arriving from the Peninsula. Lee's new plan in the face of all these additional forces outnumbering him was to send Jackson and Stuart with half of the army on a flanking march to cut Pope's line of communication, the Orange & Alexander Railroad. Pope would be forced to retreat and could be defeated while moving and vulnerable. Jackson departed before dawn on August 25, with Colonel Munford leading his 2nd Virginia at the head of Jackson's miles-long column. Munford's troopers picketed the roads until Jackson's infantry, artillery, and wagons passed. Jackson's army marched from Jeffersonton to Amissville, crossing the Rappahannock at Hinson's Mill, through Orleans toward Salem (present-day Marshall), arriving that night.[7]

The march resumed at daylight on August 26, through the Bull Run Mountains at Thoroughfare Gap and down its eastern slope. Arriving at Gainesville in late afternoon, they were overtaken by Stuart with Fitz Lee and Robertson. When they had arrived at Salem, Stuart had overtaken the wagon train, clogging the road for Jackson to continue to Thoroughfare Gap. Stuart, seeking to unclog the road, and with the help of a guide, moved by way of backroads, passing through the mountains, probably at Glascock's Gap, a mile and a half south of Thoroughfare Gap.[8]

Meanwhile, at about 4:00 a.m. on August 20, under a full moon, Brigadier Generals Fitzhugh Lee's and a portion of Robertson's brigades moved across the Rapidan River at two adjacent fords and pushed rapidly forward. Robertson crossed at Tobacco Stick Ford with

---

6. T. J. Jackson to Colonel Munford, August 21, 1862, Thomas H. Ellis Papers, Accession 41008, Letters of Thomas T. Munford, LVA, Richmond, VA.
7. Patchan, *Second Manassas: Longstreet's Attack and the Struggle for Chinn Ridge*, 5; OR 12/2:643, 747; Wert, *General James Longstreet*, 162-63; Jeffry D. Wert, *Cavalryman of the Lost Cause* (New York: Simon & Shuster, 2008), 130.
8. *OR* 12/2:643, 733-34; *Supplemental OR* 2:597; Wert, *Cavalryman of the Lost Cause*, 130-31.

the 6th, 7th, and 12th Virginia Cavalry Regiments. Fitzhugh Lee's brigade, with Pelham's artillery, crossed at Raccoon Ford, in the direction of Kelly's and Ellis's Fords on the Rappahannock River. Robertson's brigade, which Stuart accompanied, marched via Stevensburg, a village four miles east of Culpeper Court House, then moved toward the railroad depot at Brandy Station. One of Robertson's regiments, Munford's 2nd Virginia, with Roger Chew's battery of his brigade, remained on the upper Rapidan to guard its crossings, keep open a return route for Stuart, and provide support for Jackson's infantry.[9]

Soon, Fitz Lee's brigade encountered the rear guard of Pope's army, Brig. Gen. John Buford's brigade. Lee made a "vigorous attack" and "secured several prisoners and a cavalry color." Meanwhile, Robertson's brigade encountered Federal pickets of Brig. Gen. George D. Bayard, Chief of Cavalry of the III Corps, between Stevensburg and Brandy Station. The immense dust raised by Robertson's troopers prevented his movement from being conducted in secrecy. Colonel William E. Jones's 7th Virginia Cavalry, being in advance, made a spirited attack, driving in Bayard's outpost on their reserve. Heavy skirmishing on both sides then ensued and lasted several hours. The Federals finally retired and were followed beyond Brandy Station, where a brigade of Union cavalry commanded by John Buford appeared, drawn up in line of battle on a commanding hill. Buford intended to dispute Robertson's progress, and fired upon his advance column with long-range guns. Robertson soon led the 12th Virginia Cavalry, under Col. A. W. Harman, in a charge directly against the center of the Federal line, while the 6th and 7th Virginia regiments were directed against Buford's flank. The Confederate horsemen charged gallantly and after a brief hand-to-hand contest, the Federal cavalry was routed with several killed, a number wounded, and 64 prisoners captured, including several commissioned officers. Robertson's loss was three killed and 13 wounded. Stuart, who did not like Robertson, nevertheless forced a compliment for him, lauding the "superior discipline, organization, and drill" Robertson had imparted on his brigade.[10]

---

9. *OR* 12/2:725, 745; Longacre, *Lee's Cavalrymen*, 113–14.
10. *OR* 12/2:726–27; Longacre, *Lee's Cavalrymen*, 114–15.

On the evening of August 26, after passing around Pope's right flank via Thoroughfare Gap, Jackson's wing of the army struck the Orange & Alexandria Railroad at Bristoe Station. Before daybreak on August 27, they marched to capture and destroy the massive Union supply depot at Manassas Junction. This surprise movement forced Pope into an abrupt retreat from his defensive line along the Rappahannock River. During the night of August 27, Jackson marched his divisions north to the Manassas battlefield, where he took position behind an unfinished railroad grade below Stony Ridge. The defensive position was a good one. The heavy woods allowed the Confederates to conceal themselves while maintaining good observation points of the Warrenton Turnpike, the likely avenue of Union movement, only a few hundred yards to the south. There were good approach roads for Longstreet to join Jackson, or for Jackson to retreat to the Bull Run Mountains if he could not be reinforced in time. Lastly, the unfinished railroad grade offered cuts and fills that could be used as ready-made entrenchments.[11]

In the August 26 fight, the 2nd Virginia Cavalry reached the United States Military Railroad at Bristoe Station. Colonel Munford, 31 years of age with premature gray hair and a drooping mustache led the advance. Munford was a highly capable officer who had earned Jackson's respect and trust. He ordered his forces forward against the Union soldiers holding the station just as a supply train pulled by the Taunton Locomotive Works engine "Secretary" arrived on the scene. Coming in behind Munford was a brigade from Major General Richard Ewell's division. The Confederates tried to stop the train with a hasty barricade of railroad ties, but with bullets whistling around him, the engineer opened the throttle wide and threw himself down on the cab floor. That train escaped, but the Confederate raiders captured three other trains, 43 prisoners, killing seven, and wounding seven.[12]

In the battle of Thoroughfare Gap on August 28, Longstreet's wing broke through light Union resistance and marched through the gap to join Jackson. This seemingly inconsequential action virtually

---

11. Patchan, *Second Manassas: Longstreet's Attack and the Struggle for Chinn Ridge*, 6; McClellan, *The Campaigns of Stuart's Cavalry*, 95–96, 102–03.
12. *OR* 12/2:741, 747; McClellan, *The Campaigns of Stuart's Cavalry*, 95–96; Wert, *Cavalryman of the Lost Cause*, 131.

ensured Pope's defeat during the coming battles, because it allowed the two wings of Lee's army to unite on the Manassas battlefield.[13]

Pope was convinced he had Jackson trapped and assembled the bulk of his army against him. He wanted to attach Jackson and perhaps capture him before Longstreet could reinforce him. On August 29, Pope ordered a series of attacks against Jackson's troops along an unfinished railroad grade. These assaults were repulsed with heavy casualties on both sides. By noon, Longstreet had broken through light Union resistance and arrived on the field from Thoroughfare Gap, taking up a position on Jackson's right flank. On August 30, Pope renewed his attacks, seemingly unaware that Longstreet had arrived on the field. Massive Confederate artillery devastated a Union assault by Gen. Fitz John Porter's V Corps, resulting in Longstreet's wing of 25,000 men in five divisions counterattacking in the largest simultaneous mass assault of the war. The Union left flank was crushed with the army being driven back to Bull Run. Only an orderly withdrawal of Pope's army prevented a repeated debacle similar to First Manassas. Pope's army retreated to Centreville, defeated.[14]

In the August 30 fight, Robertson's brigade reached the Lewis farmhouse on the ridge overlooking Bull Run. The 2nd Virginia, under Colonel Munford, led the advance over Lewis Ford. They spotted a small body of Federal cavalry, General Buford's advance guard. Lieutenant Colonel James W. Watts of the 2nd Virginia took one squadron, charged and routed it, but before he had gone far discovered Buford's brigade of four regiments of cavalry, including the 1st Michigan, 4th New York, and the 1st West Virginia. The rest of the 2nd Virginia came up and soon the whole regiment was engaged with the blue-clad horsemen, meeting their charge with a countercharge. As the 4th New York joined the fray, Munford ordered a retreat back to the remainder of his brigade. Just then, General Robertson arrived with the rest of the brigade. A terrible hand-to-hand fight ensued, and the Federals, with greatly superior numbers, began to force the Confederates back. The 7th Virginia, under Capt. S.B. Myers, the 12th

---

13. McClellan, *Campaigns of Stuart's Cavalry*, 108; Hennessy, *Return to Bull Run*, 424–38.
14. Ibid.

Virginia, under Col. Asher W. Harman, and the 6th Virginia, under Col. Thomas S. Flournoy, came to the rescue. The Federals were soon forced from the field, and the 7th and 12th Virginia continued the pursuit until the enemy was driven beyond the turnpike at Stone Bridge. Colonel Munford, whose horse was killed in this fight, was wounded by several saber cuts on his head. He later recalled, "They absorbed us . . . the shooting, running, cursing and cutting that followed cannot be understood except by an eye witness." Buford was wounded by a gunshot to the knee. Private Thornton R. Baxter of the 2nd Virginia wrote, "Our regiment charged four regiments of yankee cavalry and they charging at the same time. We had a regular hand to hand sabre fight." Baxter's horse was killed in the melee, and his leg injured when his mount fell atop him. Also wounded with saber cuts were Lt. Col. James Watts and Maj. Cary Breckinridge.[15]

The Confederates captured 300 prisoners with many horses, arms, and equipment at Lewis Ford. The loss in Robertson's brigade was five killed and 40 wounded. Pope was now in full retreat. Early the following morning, Jackson left Longstreet to bury the dead and followed in pursuit. Stuart, with Fitz Lee and Robertson's brigades, preceded Jackson, harassing the enemy's rear. Pope fell back behind the defenses at Washington.[16]

Munford commended his troopers after the August 30 fight at the Lewis farm, "My regiment went up in splendid order, and made as gallant a charge as ever was seen." Stuart reported, "Munford . . . (and others) were wounded in the action, conspicuously displaying great gallantry and heroism." Robertson called Munford's charge "brilliant and dashing," while Fitz Lee noted that Munford had led the charge "with great gallantry."[17]

---

15. *OR* 12/2:748; *Richmond Times Dispatch*, April 6, 1913; McClellan, *The Campaigns of Stuart's Cavalry*, 105–06; Charles L. Convis, *The Honor of Arms: A Biography of Myles W. Keogh* (Tucson, AZ, 2010), 19; Heros von Borcke, *Memoirs of the Confederate War for Independence* (Philadelphia, PA, 1867), 109; Whitehead, "Campaigns of Munford's 2nd Virginia Cavalry," 36.
16. *OR* 12/2:559, 747–49; Dennis E. Frye, *12th Virginia Cavalry* (Lynchburg, VA, 1988), 12.
17. *OR* 12/2:558–59, 737, 746–48.

The Maryland Campaign

After a stunning victory at the battle of Second Manassas at the end of August 1862, Confederate Gen. Robert E. Lee planned to take the war onto northern soil. Lee invaded Maryland for two specific reasons: to relieve Virginia of the burden of feeding his Army of Northern Virginia, and to possibly earn diplomatic recognition from Great Britain and France, thereby establishing Southern independence. He also wanted to exert pressure on Washington and Baltimore to recall any remnants of Pope's army from Virginia. As an added option, and assuming the Maryland campaign went well, Lee was considering threatening Pennsylvania, which he hoped would cause Union troops to abandon in the Shenandoah Valley.[18]

On the day following the August 30 fight, Robertson's brigade scouted toward Fairfax Court House. The 2nd Virginia remained nearby until called to Leesburg four days later.[19]

Leesburg

On September 1, Robert E. Lee summoned Munford to his headquarters and showed him a letter he had just received from an old friend, John Janney, of Leesburg. Janney asked Lee for protection for Leesburg citizens from the marauding Loudoun Rangers, commanded by Capt. Samuel Means. Means was threatening to "arrest and carry away prominent Confederates the next day." "We must crush these people," Lee told Munford, ordering him to leave his wagons behind so he might travel quickly. "I shall expect to have a good report from you tomorrow." Lee, indicating his concern for feeding his army, added that upon Munford's return he should help the Commissary department "to collect beef cattle for his army."[20]

---

18. Joseph L. Harsh, *Taken at the Flood: Robert E. Lee and the Confederate Strategy in the Maryland Campaign of 1962* (Kent, OH, 2000), 83–84.
19. Frye, *12th Virginia Cavalry*, 12.
20. Thomas Tayloe Munford, "Lee's Invasion of Maryland," in address Delivered Before the Confederate Veterans Association in Savannah, Georgia, (Savannah, GA, 1893-1902), 5 Volumes, 3:36–37; Joseph L. Harsh, *Taken at the Flood: Robert E. Lee and the Confederate Strategy in the Maryland Campaign of 1962*, 14.

On September 2, 1862, Robert E. Lee's advance troops, Munford's 2nd Virginia Cavalry, found Leesburg occupied by Union Capt. Samuel C. Means's independent cavalry company and supported by 200 men of Maj. Henry A. Cole's Maryland cavalry battalion.[21]

Corporal William A. McIlhenny of Company C, part of Henry A. Cole's Maryland Union Cavalry recalled, "We formed into line and charged the force that attacked us in the rear, but when we had done that we looked around and found that a rebel force had gotten around us and was coming at us from the other side. We suddenly found that we were surrounded by a largely superior force, so Major Cole gave the command 'every man for himself.'"[22]

Munford's troopers drove the Union cavalry a mile north of town to "Mile Hill," where the blue-coats suffered casualties, and eventually retreated to Waterford, less than 10 miles south of Point of Rocks on the Potomac. Of Munford's 163 troops on the field, two were killed and five wounded. Means, meanwhile, lost 30 or so men, with one man killed, six wounded, and four captured. Cole's Cavalry, estimated at 150 strong, reported six killed, 27 wounded, and 11 captured. A significant number of those casualties were officers. Stuart reported, "The enemy's papers acknowledged that their entire force of 150 men of the First Maryland and Means' company were, all but 40, killed or captured, stating that our force was 2,000. Colonel Munford's entire force was 163 men, of whom but 123 were in the charge." Two days later, Lee arrived with the rest of his army prior to crossing the Potomac on September 6.[23]

Robert E. Lee reorganized the Army of Northern Virginia for the Maryland Campaign. The Cavalry was led by Gen. J.E.B. Stuart. Stuart's command consisted of three brigades of cavalry under Brigadier Generals Wade Hampton, Fitzhugh Lee, and Beverly Robertson. Robertson's brigade was temporarily commanded by Colonel Munford until November 8, when Brig. Gen. William E. "Grumble" Jones assumed command. Capt. John Pelham led the Horse Artillery, including Roger P. Chew's, James F. Hart's, and Pelham's own battery.[24]

---

21. McClellan, *Stuart's Cavalry*, 109.
22. 2nd Lieutenant William A. McIlhenny, "Diary of a Soldier," Emmitsville (Maryland) Historical Society. Article by Mark Dudrow, nd.
23. McClellan, *Stuart's Cavalry*, 109; *OR* 19/1:814; *OR* 12/2:745, 749.
24. *OR* 12/2:546–51; part 3:933.

Finally, Stuart had had enough of Robertson, and he convinced Lee that Robertson was not effective. On September 5, Robertson was relieved of his command and ordered to report to the Department of North Carolina. Unpopular with his troopers and with General Stuart, Robertson was a strict disciplinarian who could drill men better than he could lead them in battle. His troopers were some of the best trained and drilled troopers in Stuart's command. He was, however, unreliable in battle. Stuart concurred in Jackson's assessment of Robertson; he was incompetent. Stuart and Robertson had disliked each other from the beginning. In earlier years, Robertson had courted Stuart's future wife Flora and, even after her marriage to Stuart, he remained cordial to her. This was perhaps a motivating factor for Stuart's as he sought to get rid of Robertson. Little did Stuart know that General Robertson would return in nine months for the epic cavalry battle at Brandy Station on June 9, 1863. There, Robertson would disappoint Stuart again.[25]

Munford took command of the brigade and reported, "On the 4th [of September] I was ordered to take command of the brigade [Robertson's], then en route for Maryland. I joined General Stuart at Urbana, and on the morning of September 8, I was ordered to Poolesville, with instructions to drive the enemy from that place." Munford's advance guard of the 7th and 12th Virginia had just entered the crossroads village of Poolesville when Union Col. Elon J. Farnsworth's command appeared in force with three regiments of cavalry and four pieces of artillery. Colonel Munford selected an elevated position to the left of the town, and, as soon as the Federals came within range, a section of Capt. Roger Chew's artillery opened on them. Munford added:

> In a few moments they replied with two heavy pieces, and at the same time advanced and drove in my pickets to the left and rear of my advance gun. Not knowing the country, and having had but a few moments' notice, I had some difficulty in extricating my guns, one a howitzer, the other a Blakely. The enemy charged up near the howitzer, but two rounds of canister sent them hurriedly back. Captain [Frank] Myers, commanding the Seventh,

---

25. Musick, *6th Virginia Cavalry*, 17; W. W. Blackford, *War Years with JEB Stuart* (Baton Rouge, LA, 1993), 229; Longacre, *Lee's Cavalrymen*, 110.

Brigadier General Beverly H. Robertson
circa 1863
Robertson was a strict disciplinarian and not liked by his men. Stuart did not like Robertson and finally had him transferred at the start of the 1862 Maryland Campaign.
(Library of Congress)

charged them handsomely. They also charged the rifle piece supported by the Twelfth, when Colonel [Asher W.] Harman repulsed them with some loss.[26]

During the fight, Farnsworth dispatched his 8th Illinois, which threatened the rear of the 12th Virginia. The troopers of the 12th Virginia began to precipitously retreat, but some rallied momentarily, providing enough time for Chew's artillery to withdraw. The collapse of the 12th Virginia left Munford in disgust, reporting, "they behaved very badly" and forced Munford's command to retreat toward Monocacy Church, leaving eight killed, 16 wounded, and six prisoners.[27]

Harman's Confederate loss was eight men killed, wounded, and missing. His regiment had been reduced by detail and other causes to about 75 men. For three days Munford's troopers held the Poolesville cross-roads, skirmishing every day, guarding Sugar Loaf Mountain.[28]

Artillerist Maj. Henry H. Matthews of Stuart's Horse Artillery recalled his thoughts of Munford, "It goes without saying that General Munford was second to none as a cavalry leader----strategic and cautious--always prepared to strike the enemy at his weakest point, when he was least prepared to be attacked." Matthews knew "Munford was loved not only by every member of his regiment, but by every officer and man of the brigade that he loved so well." Matthews, thinking of Munford's performance throughout the war, spoke of Munford as a general officer, even though Munford never received his commission.[29]

On September 11, Munford, under pressure from Union Maj. Gen. Henry W. Slocum's infantry, fell back to a point three miles from Frederick City on the Buckeystown Road. The 6th Virginia Cavalry, having been left at Centreville to collect arms, was not in Maryland with the brigade. The 17th Battalion was on detached service, and on September 10, the 7th Regiment had been ordered to report to General Jackson. They did not join the brigade again until the brigade re-crossed into Virginia.[30]

---

26. *OR* 19/1:825.
27. David S. Hartwig, *To Antietam Creek: The Maryland Campaign of September 1862* (Baltimore, 2012), 174.
28. Ibid.
29. Robert J. Trout, ed., *Memoirs of the Stuart Horse Artillery Battalion, Vol. 2: Breathed's and McGregor's Batteries* (Knoxville, TN, 1910), 21, 30.
30. *OR* 19/1:825; McClellan, *Stuart's Cavalry*, 111.

On September 12, Munford's greatly reduced command moved to a gap in the Catoctin Mountain range at Jefferson. Here they remained until the next day, continually skirmishing with Brig. Gen. Alfred Pleasonton's cavalry. Franklin's infantry pressed them on three roads as they fell back to Burkittsville. The Union forces advanced on Jefferson by the Point of Rocks Road, on the main road from Poolesville, and by a road over a gap which intersects the road leading to Middletown about one and one-half miles from Jefferson. Munford's troopers were pursued nearly the whole way to Burkittsville by elements of Pleasonton's cavalry. Munford reported:

We had the brigade train to protect. I kept them back with the sharpshooters of the Second Regiment, under Captain [T. B.] Holland, and hurried Colonel Harman's command on to Burkittsville to protect the road leading directly from Jefferson to that point. Captain Holland, finding himself heavily pressed and with a mere handful of men, made a dash at a regiment of the enemy's cavalry, driving them back with loss.[31]

Munford sent his wagon train safely over a mountain at Crampton's Gap. After the Federals were repulsed by Capt. T. B. Holland, General Hampton, coming in on their rear, drove them off. Munford remained on the mountain that night, and the next morning received orders from General Stuart to hold the gap at all hazards. Munford wrote many years later that Stuart's order was "easier said than done with such odds."[32]

Battle of Crampton's Gap

Forces under Confederate Brig. Gen. Howell Cobb and Union Maj. Gen. William B. Franklin fought the battle of Crampton's Gap in central Maryland as part of the battle of South Mountain on September 14, 1862.[33]

As part of the siege of Harpers Ferry, units under Maj. Gen. Lafayette McLaws marched to take Maryland Heights and then

---

31. *OR* 19/1:416–17, 825.
32. Ibid., 818, 826; Thomas T. Munford to E. A. Carmen, December 10, 1894, Carman Papers, New York Public Library; Jeffrey D. Wert, *Cavalryman of the Lost Cause* (New York, 2008), 149.
33. Wert, *Cavalryman of the Lost Cause*, 150; Harsh, *Taken at the Flood*, 275–81.

bombard the Union garrison in the town. To protect his rear flank, McLaws stationed a small guard at Brownsville Gap (a smaller gap a few miles south of Crampton's Gap) and at Crampton's Gap, both of which allowed access to Pleasant Valley and the eastern slope of Maryland Heights. The Confederate force at Crampton's Gap consisted of one battery of Pelham's artillery, two fragments of regiments of Brig. Gen. William Mahone's infantry under Col. William A. Parham, one brigade under Brig. Gen. Howell Cobb, and a small cavalry detachment under Col. Thomas T. Munford.[34] Stuart told Munford, "Well Munford, you have had a rough time. You can take your choice--either remain here and hold the Gap or go with me to Harper's Ferry as you please. You or Hampton must go with me."[35]

Years later, Munford recalled the situation quite differently. According to Munford, Stuart was supposed to be with Confederate forces at South Mountain and Crampton's Gap, but "had completely bottled himself up" with McLaws and was "out of place and in a bad fix and was to blame for not remaining with the army at South Mountain and me at Crampton's Gap." Munford complained, "there never was any excuse for Genl. Stuart being off at Maryland Heights with McLaws." He thought Stuart "a light-hearted, dashing, rollicking young fellow devoted to administration, fond of dancing and pretty young girls--fond of music and full of fun, ambitious as Caesar and took care of his own interest under all circumstances."[36]

Regardless of who was supposed to stay at Crampton's Gap, Munford did remain. The small Confederate force used the terrain to its maximum advantage, with Munford's cavalrymen initially stationed behind a stone fence at the eastern base of the mountain, and Capt. Roger P. Chew's battery and a portion of the Portsmouth artillery halfway up its slope. The Confederate infantry entrenched at the summit. From their vantage point on the mountain, they watched throughout the morning as Union Maj. Gen. William B. Franklin's VI

---

34. *OR* 19/1:826-27.
35. Ibid.; Stuart to Munford on who should stay and hold Crampton's Gap, September 14, 1862; Thomas Munford, "History of the 2nd Virginia Cavalry," Munford–Ellis Papers, DU.
36. Thomas T. Munford to John C. Ropes, December 10, 1894; May 21, 1898; January 15, 1899, Howard Gotlieb Archival Center, Boston University, Boston, MA.

Corps marched, with clouds of dust rising above the trees on the roads across the Middletown Valley, toward them.[37]

When the Federals reached Burkittsville around noon, the Confederate artillery opened up on them. Franklin assembled his troops into three columns. At 3:00 p.m., after a delay of nearly three hours, the VI Corps finally began its assault. Four brigades of Maj. Gen. Henry W. Slocum's division, Brigadier Generals Joseph J. Bartlett, John Newton, Alfred Torbert, and William T. H. Brooks were sent forward, with Col. H. L. Cake's 96th Pennsylvania of Bartlett's brigade leading the charge. Their superior numbers quickly overwhelmed the Confederate cavalry and artillery on the slopes of the mountain. The retreating Confederates briefly rallied at the summit, but the weight of the Federal advance was too much. Once the VI Corps reached the peak, they drove the Confederates from their positions, inflicting heavy casualties, in just 15 minutes of fighting. Munford's command retired towards Boonsboro, and on the following day took a position covering the approaches to Keedysville.[38]

Tactically, the Federals were successful in driving the Confederates from the gap––the first time any portion of Lee's army had been driven from the field up until this point in the war—inflicting heavy casualties as they did so. Strategically, the Confederate force was able to stall the Federal advance for three hours, even though they were outnumbered nearly six to one. The delay was long enough to ensure the safety of McLaws on Maryland Heights and the capture of Harpers Ferry the following morning. During the night preceding the surrender of Harpers Ferry, Union Col. Benjamin F. "Grimes" Davis led the garrison's 1,300-man cavalry force in an escape using an unguarded road below Maryland Heights. Munford later blamed Stuart for the escape, noting that by scattering his cavalry units he could not seal off the roads from Harpers Ferry. Despite Jackson being three days late on Robert E. Lee's timeline, Harpers Ferry had finally been captured.[39]

---

37. *OR* 19/1:826, *McClellan, The Campaigns of Stuart's Cavalry*, 120-23; Philip F. Brown, *Reminiscences of the War of 1861–1865* (Richmond, VA, 1917), 32.
38. *OR* 19/1:826; McClellan, *The Campaigns of Stuart's Cavalry*, 122; E. P. Alexander, *Military Memoirs of a Confederate: A Critical Narrative*, 234.
39. Thomas T. Munford to John C. Ropes, January 21, 1898, Howard Gotlieb Archival Research Center, Boston University; Jeffrey D. Wert, *Cavalryman of the Lost Cause*, 151.

Thomas Munford believed that General McLaws never received the credit he deserved for his pivotal performance in the Maryland campaign. Colonel Munford wrote, "I am constrained to say that if Pleasant Valley been under a less determined officer–had General McLaws flickered, one moment in his trying position, the ruin of the whole army of northern Virginia was inevitable." Perhaps, Munford exaggerated, but if Col. Dixon S. Miles at Harpers Ferry had known on September 15 that Franklin was nearby and would be able to support him before Jackson could force him to surrender, there may have been no surrender of Harpers Ferry. The Confederate Maryland campaign would have ended in a humiliating failure and quite possibly McLaws command could have faced dire consequences.[40]

In total, the VI Corps suffered 115 killed, 416 wounded, and two missing, for a total of 533 casualties. The Confederate forces suffered 130 killed and 759 wounded, for a total of 887 casualties.[41]

Long after the war, Munford recalled the Crampton's Gap Fight. "I had orders to hold, with ten times our numbers [of enemy] visible. Today, those scenes are forgotten, except by the handful who witnessed them—that campaign was written in blood—as precious as soldiers could furnish, and General Lee's audacity as a great soldier was never crowned more brilliantly."[42]

Munford's troopers, with an inferior force that day, had performed remarkable service, preventing the Federals from getting in Stuart's rear along the National Road, thus keeping the Federals from discerning the how weakly held were the passes at Burkittsville. They had also delayed the Union forces from reaching the base of South Mountain.[43]

---

40. Thomas Munford, "The Maryland Campaign,"Address to the Confederate Veterans Association of Savannah, Georgia, typescript, McLaws Papers, SHC; David S. Hartwig, *To Antietam Creek: The Maryland Campaign of 1862* (Baltimore, MD, 2012), 476.
41. Campton's Gap National Battlefield, Frederick County, Maryland.
42. Phillip F. Brown, *Reminiscences of the War of 1861-1865* (Richmond, Va.: Whittet & Shepperson, Printers, 1917), 32.
43. Hartwig, *To Antietam Creek: The Maryland Campaign of September 1862* (Baltimore, 2012), 280.

Antietam

Munford's troopers engaged in active skirmishing during the battle of Antietam on September 17-18. The 2nd and 12th Virginia Cavalry regiments reached the field on September 16, taking a position on the extreme right of the Army of Northern Virginia to cover the lower crossings of Antietam Creek. On the evening of the 16th, the 7th Virginia deployed on the Hagerstown Pike, northwest of Sharpsburg. It joined the brigade on the right on the 17th. Robertson's former brigade (it would come to be known as the Laurel Brigade), still temporarily commanded by Munford, remained on the right of Lee's army, guarding the fords that crossed Antietam Creek, until the close of the battle.[44]

During the Confederate retreat from Antietam on the night of September 18, the cavalry acted as rear guard for Lee's army. Munford made a narrow escape from skirmishing along the canal on the right because a courier sent to notify him of the order to withdraw could not locate him.[45]

As Lee's army crossed the Potomac near Shepherdstown back into Virginia, they realized their campaign into the north had failed. They had entered Maryland with high hopes of support from the populace, and indeed many greeted them with cheers, but no one mourned their leaving. This was hard for some soldiers to take, and thus created some bitter feelings. One of Munford's troopers summed up the feelings of many, writing his sister, "I never want to go back again. I would like to go through into Pennsylvania but I don't want to stop in Maryland five minutes longer than I can help."[46]

Munford's brigade next took a position of the Confederate right near Boteler's Ford, a shallow crossing of the Potomac River less than a mile downstream from Shepherdstown, Virginia (now West Virginia). Near this ford, Lee's reserve artillery, under the command of Brig. Gen. William Pendleton, Lee's chief of artillery, covered the retreat with 44 guns. Pendleton set up his guns atop the high bluffs

---

44. McClellan, *Campaigns of Stuart's Cavalry*, 122.
45. Ibid., 133-34.
46. Thomas M. Garber to his sister, September 17, 1862, Garber Manuscript, LVA, Richmond, Va.; Longacre, *Lee's Cavalrymen*, 137.

overlooking the ford on the Virginia side. The artillery was supported by the infantry brigades of Brigadier Generals Lewis A. Armistead and Alexander Lawton. On the evening of September 19, four regiments of Federals from Gen. Fitz John Porter's V Corps crossed Boteler's Ford, vigorously attacking the Confederates, capturing four guns. Munford covered the forced retreat of the Confederate infantry and artillery, preventing certain disaster. Munford's command was last to ford to the south bank of the Potomac under the protection of the artillery, which had previously crossed.[47]

A lack of Union aggressiveness during the greater part of October ushered in a period of unusual leisure. Lee's army, however, was not altogether idle. As soon as stragglers had been brought in, the ranks of the divisions swelled, allowing several missions to be undertaken. The II Army Corps was entrusted with the destruction of the Baltimore and Ohio Railway, a duty entrusted to Jackson, which he carried out successfully. Jackson also tore up the rail line from Harpers Ferry to Winchester, as well as that from Manassas Junction to Strasburg. These preparations for defensive warfare were not, however, of such concern to the Federal army as the action of the Confederate cavalry. Stuart's three brigades, after the skirmish at Boteler's Ford, picketed the line of the Potomac River from the North Mountain to the Shenandoah, a distance of 40 miles: Hampton's brigade was at Hedgesville, Fitzhugh Lee's at Shepherdstown, Munford's at Charlestown, and headquarters near Leestown.[48]

On October 8, General Lee, suspecting that McClellan was considering some movement, ordered the cavalry to cross the Potomac and reconnoiter. Stuart's headquarters was then at his friend Stephen Dandridge's estate "The Bower." The next day, General Stuart selected 600 men from each of three of his brigades, along with four horse-artillery guns, for a raid into Pennsylvania. Brigadier General Wade Hampton and Col. W. H. F. "Rooney" Lee participated. Stuart took a detachment of Munford's brigade, but Munford did not go along; Colonel William E. Jones commanded Munford's detached troopers.

---

47. William N McDonald, *A History of the Laurel Brigade* (Baltimore, MD, 2002), 96; McClellan, *The Campaigns of Stuart's Cavalry*, 133–34.
48. George Francis Robert Henderson, *Stonewall Jackson and the American Civil War* (New York, 1908), vol. 2:290–91.

Stuart's forces rendezvoused on the night of the 9th at Darkesville. As the day dawned, he crossed the Potomac at McCoy's Ford, drove in the Federal pickets, and broke up a signal station near Fairview.[49]

On October 10, marching due north, Stuart's troopers reached Mercersburg at noon, and Chambersburg, 46 miles from Darkesville, at 7:00 p.m. Chambersburg, although a Federal supply depot of some importance, was without a garrison. Here, Stuart's raiders paroled 275 sick and wounded, requisitioned 500 horses, cut telegraph wires, obstructed the railroad, and destroyed machine shops, several trains of loaded cars, and a large quantity of small arms, ammunition, and clothing.[50]

This brilliantly conducted expedition was as fruitful of results as the ride round McClellan's army in the previous June. The information obtained was most important. Lee, besides being furnished with a sufficiently full report of the Federal dispositions, learned that no part of McClellan's army had been detached to Washington. In fact, it was being reinforced from that quarter, effectively barring any over-sea expedition against Richmond. Several hundred fine horses from the farms of Pennsylvania furnished excellent remounts for the Confederate troopers.[51]

Stuart returned to Virginia on October 12, resuming camp at The "Bower." Here, he enjoyed socializing, music, dancing, and a leisurely lifestyle with his good friends. He had his favorite musician, banjo player Sam Sweeney and his band, to provide music for the social functions that would last through the month. Sweeney was officially attached to Munford's 2nd Virginia. Munford stated that the music provided by Sweeney and their band "afforded my regiment much pleasure in dissipating the ennui of camp life." Stuart enjoyed them so much that, on December 1, he had the gifted Sweeney and his musicians detailed to his headquarters. They led Stuart's musical entertainment henceforth. Munford bristled at the abduction, especially when his good friend, Stuart's staff officer John Esten Cooke, goaded him with an invitation to come over and listen to Sweeney's music. Munford recalled, "When Capt. Cooke was on

---

49. *OR* 19/2:31, 52; McClellan, *Stuart's Cavalry*, 137.
50. *OR* 19/2:31, 52.
51. Ibid., 54.

Stuart's staff, he used to laugh at me for 'not coming over to enjoy our music,' until it came to be a sore subject to me." Munford added, "Stuart's feet would shuffle whenever he was in Sweeney's presence, or even at the calling of his name."[52]

While Stuart had been on his Pennsylvania raid, Munford reported, "My brigade [the remainder that did not participate in Stuart's raid into Pennsylvania] was stationed near Cabletown, on the pike between Charleston and Berryville, and picketing from Walper's Cross-Roads, on the Baltimore and Ohio Railroad, to Berry's Ferry."[53]

On October 16, two columns of the Federal army advanced on a reconnaissance mission: Brig. Gen. Andrew A. Humphreys led one column from Shepherdstown to Smithfield; Brig. Gen. Winfield S. Hancock commanded the other column from Harpers Ferry to Charlestown. Stuart ordered Fitz Lee's brigade, reinforced by Brig. Gen. Charles S. Winder's infantry brigade against the advance of Humphreys's column. The next day, Hampton's brigade joined Stuart. Meantime, Colonel Munford with the 6th, 7th, 12th, and a portion of the 2nd Virginia cavalry opposed the advance of Hancock's column. A single gun from Chew's battery and three guns of the Richmond Howitzer Battalion supported Munford's troopers. Munford stubbornly resisted Hancock's advance, forcing him to deploy three brigades of infantry to drive Munford back to Charlestown.[54]

Protesting William E. Jones's September 19 promotion to brigadier, on October 24, 1862, J.E.B. Stuart reiterated his support for Munford's promotion to brigadier general and assignment to command the brigade then commanded by him as colonel. Stuart stated:

> My reasons for this recommendation are that no colonel in the brigade has been as deserving. He is a gallant soldier, a daring and skillful officer, and is thoroughly identified with the brigade as its leader. As a partisan he has no superior. While others not in the brigade might command a higher tribute for ability and military genius,

---

52. Thomas T. Munford to Anne Bachman Hyde, August 29, 1915, SHC, University of North Carolina, Chapel Hill, NC; Burke Davis, *JEB Stuart-The Last Cavalier* (New York, 1957), 70; Thomas T. Munford to John O. Beaty, January 14, 1917, Munford–Ellis Papers, DU, as quoted in John O. Beaty, *John Esten Cooke, Virginian*, 81.
53. Driver, *2nd Virginia Cavalry*, 62; *OR* 19/2:96–97.
54. *OR* 19/2:94; McClellan, *The Campaigns of Stuart's Cavalry*, 167–68.

> yet when I consider the claims of the Colonel for this promotion, and the gallant service he has rendered, I am constrained to ask that he receive this merited reward. The assignment of a junior to this position would be prejudicial to the best interests of the service.[55]

Virginia Governor John Letcher recommended Munford's promotion on December 9, 1862, perhaps in deference to Thomas Munford's father, George Wythe Munford, Secretary of the Commonwealth of Virginia. Munford, however, did not receive the promotion; it had been given to William E. Jones. Stuart despised Jones, making his decision to recommend Munford easy.[56]

The respite which Stuart had gained for his troopers at The Bower was not, however, of long duration. On October 26, McClellan, having ascertained by means of a strong reconnaissance in force that the Confederate army was still in the vicinity of Winchester, commenced the passage of the Potomac. The principal point of crossing was near Berlin, so as soon as it became evident that the Federal line of operations lay east of the Blue Ridge Mountains, Lee ordered Longstreet to Culpeper Court House. Jackson, taking post on the road between Berryville and Charlestown, was to remain in the valley.[57]

Meanwhile, a Federal cavalry force spotted Munford on October 25 near Purcellville, with patrols out toward Waterford, Leesburg, and Middleburg. The next day, Munford was at Snickersville. On October 28, Gen. Alfred Pleasonton reported Munford, with 1,500 men and two guns, had passed through Middleburg toward Upperville.[58]

On November 7, the Army of the Potomac, which was assembled between the Bull Run Mountains and the Blue Ridge, numbered 125,000 officers and men present for duty, together with 320 guns. The Confederates were not only heavily outnumbered by the force immediately before them, but along the Potomac, from Washington westward, was a second hostile army, not as large as that commanded

---

55. SHSP, Vol. III:191. Richmond, Virginia, April, 1877. No. 4, Field Letters From Stuart's Headquarters; McClellan, Stuart, 186-87; Compiled Service Record for Thomas T. Munford. Jones had been promoted on September 19, 1862, without Stuart's backing.
56. SHSP, Vol. III:191. Richmond, Virginia, April, 1877. No. 4, Field Letters from Stuart's Headquarters; McClellan, Stuart, 186–87; Compiled Service Record for Thomas T. Munford.
57. *OR* 19/2:103.
58. *OR* 19/2:514; Driver, *2nd Virginia Cavalry*, 63.

by McClellan, but larger by several thousand than those commanded by Lee. The Northern capital held a garrison of 80,000; at Harpers Ferry were 10,000; in the neighborhood of Sharpsburg more than 4,000; and along the Baltimore and Ohio Railroad 8,000. Thus, the total strength of the Federals exceeded 225,000 men. Yet in face of this enormous force, and with Richmond only weakly garrisoned behind him, Lee had actually separated his two wings by an interval of 60 miles.[59]

On November 7, Lee decided to unite his army. As soon as the enemy advanced from Warrenton, Jackson began to ascend the valley, cross the Blue Ridge at Fisher's Gap, and join with Longstreet, who retired from Madison Court House to the vicinity of Gordonsville. The Confederates would then be concentrated on McClellan's right flank should he march on Richmond, ready to take advantage of any opportunity for attack; or, if attack were considered too hazardous, to threaten his communications, and compel him to fall back to the Potomac.[60]

On the night of November 7, however, at the very moment when McClellan's army was concentrating for an advance against Longstreet, McClellan was ordered to hand over his command to a reluctant Maj. Gen. Ambrose Burnside. Lincoln had yielded to the insistence of McClellan's political opponents, to Secretary of War Edwin Stanton, and to General-in-Chief Henry Halleck.[61]

On November 8, 1862, Robert E. Lee placed newly promoted Brig. Gen. William E. Jones in command of Munford's brigade. Stuart had wanted Munford to keep the position as commander and be promoted, but Confederate authorities had passed over Munford again. Two days later, the 2nd Virginia Cavalry, with Munford in charge, was transferred from Jackson's command to Fitz Lee's brigade. Munford would gain the respect of his and others' troopers. Captain John Lamb of the 2nd Virginia recalled, "A private of my own company, who was detailed as a courier to Colonel Munford, when he returned to his command, never tired of telling his messmates how kind and considerate the General was to the private soldiers of his command."[62]

---

59. G. F. R Henderson, *Stonewall Jackson and the American Civil War*, 294–95.
60. Ibid., 297.
61. William Marvel, *Burnside* (Chapel Hill, 1991), 159–161.
62. R. A. Brock, ed., *Captain John Lamb, SHSP, Vol. XXXII, Address of Honorable John Lamb*, 6; *OR* 19/2:705; Driver, *2nd Virginia Cavalry*, 63.

As of November 10, 1862, Munford's 2nd Virginia was brigaded under Fitzhugh Lee, whose brigade consisted of the 1st, 2nd, 3rd, 4th, and 5th Virginia Cavalry Regiments. On November 12, Fitz Lee's Cavalry brigade, along with Capt. John Lane's artillery battery, were ordered to accompany McLaw's and Gen. Robert Ransom's infantry divisions to Fredericksburg.[63]

On November 18, Union Maj. Gen. Franz Sigel reported, "Munford's cavalry and a part of Stuart's cavalry are with them [McLaws, Jackson, and Early], and came yesterday as far as New Baltimore, Rectortown, and Middleburg."[64]

On November 21, the 2nd Virginia left Brandy Station in the direction of Fredericksburg, sometimes picketing along the Rappahannock. By November 29, they camped near Spotsylvania Court House. After a snowstorm on December 5, they moved their camp five miles south of the courthouse.[65]

Battle of Fredericksburg, December 11-15, 1862

On December 13, Robert E. Lee's Army of Northern Virginia and Ambrose Burnside's Army of the Potomac fought the battle of Fredericksburg, in and around Fredericksburg. The Union army's futile frontal attacks against entrenched Confederate defenders on Mayre's Heights behind the city became one of the most one-sided battles of the war, with Federal casualties more than twice as heavy as those suffered by the Confederates.[66]

Burnside had planned to cross the Rappahannock River at Fredericksburg in mid-November and race to the Confederate capital of Richmond before Lee's army could stop him. Bureaucratic delays prevented Burnside from receiving the necessary pontoon bridges in time, and so Lee moved his army to block the crossings. When the Union army was finally able to build its bridges and cross under fire, urban combat resulted in the city on December 11-12. Union troops

---

63. *OR* 21/1:544, 550.
64. Ibid., 771.
65. Driver, *2nd Virginia Cavalry*, 64–65.
66. David J Eicher, *The Longest Night: A Military History of the Civil War* (New York, 2001), 405.

prepared to assault Confederate defensive positions south of the city and on a strongly fortified ridge just west of the city known as Marye's Heights.[67]

Burnside organized his Army of the Potomac into three so-called "Grand Divisions," organizations including infantry corps, cavalry, and artillery, comprising 120,000 men, of which 114,000 would be engaged in the Fredericksburg battle. Robert E. Lee's Army of Northern Virginia had nearly 85,000 men, with 72,500 engaged.[68]

A trooper of the 2nd Virginia, whose family lived in Fredericksburg, recalled the lead up to the battle:

> After leaving [Fitz] Lee's headquarters I rode into Fredericksburg, and a sad site it is. The people, as far as possible, are all leaving and are carrying away everything they can possibly get off. A large detail of wagons and ambulances is sent into town every day to help them move, and it is amusing to see the soldiers helping them. As far as I have heard any expression of opinion the citizens prefer the place to be burnt to the ground rather than it should be surrendered to the yankees.[69]

On December 13, the "Grand Division" of Maj. Gen. William B. Franklin pierced the first defensive line of Confederate Stonewall Jackson to the south but was finally repulsed by Jackson's second line. Burnside ordered the grand divisions of Major Generals Edwin V. Sumner and Joseph Hooker to make multiple frontal assaults against Lt. Gen. James Longstreet's position on Marye's Heights, all of which were repulsed with heavy losses. One 2nd Virginia trooper recalled, "Awful cannonading at this moment. Shells falling as thick as hail." On December 15, Burnside withdrew his army, ending another failed Union campaign in the Eastern Theater.[70]

The Union army suffered 12,653 casualties (1,284 killed, 9,600 wounded, 1,769 captured or missing). Two Union generals were mortally wounded: Brigadier Generals George D. Bayard and Conrad F. Jackson. The Confederate army lost 5,377 (608 killed, 4,116 wounded, 653 captured or missing), most of them in the early fighting

---

67. Ibid., 396-98.
68. Ibid., 405.
69. Charles Minor Blackford, *Letters from Lee's Army*, 137 (November 30, 1862).
70. Peter L. Huddleston Diary.

on Jackson's front. Confederate Brigadier Generals Maxcy Gregg and T. R. R. Cobb were both mortally wounded.[71]

In the battle of Fredericksburg, Robert E. Lee's cavalry effectually guarded his army's right, annoying the enemy by hanging on his flank, and attacking when opportunity occurred. The nature of the ground and the relative positions of the armies prevented them from doing more. The fords of the Rappahannock north of Fredericksburg were closely guarded by the confederate cavalry; the brigade of Gen. W. H. F. "Rooney" Lee was stationed near Port Royal to watch the river above and below.[72]

Munford wrote his sister, Sarah, "We were not in the fight at Fredericksburg. My Regt was on the right & under fire all day." Colonel Munford desired the Secretary of War to place his regiment under detached service, telling his sister, "I like Genl [Fitz] Lee very well, he is certainly a gentleman and a good officer, but I would greatly prefer being on detached service than cramped and starved to death." He spelled out the hard conditions for man and beast and bragged about his regiment, "Since I joined this command, we have very little to do, but are constantly moving about, starving out both men and horses as rapidly as possible. . . . My regiment is the largest in the division and is nearly equal to the brigade before I joined it and need I tell you best in the service, less you think me vain."[73]

In the same letter, Munford told of Stuart issuing "a circular asking that a subscription be taken up in his division for the benefit of the suffering poor of Fredericksburg, and in an hour, I had in my tent $2037--we will see what regiment will do more in the whole army. Many of my men are poor, but they are generous & brave."[74]

After the battle at Fredericksburg, both armies licked their wounds and shortly began to settle into winter quarters. The cavalry, however, remained active on picket duty. Notwithstanding winter quarters, and after the success of the battle of Fredericksburg, Gen. J.E.B. Stuart planned a Christmas raid to disrupt Federal supply lines, cut telegraph communication at three points between Aquia Creek and Occoquan,

---

71. Eicher, *The Longest Night: A Military History of the Civil War*, 405.
72. *OR* 21/1:551.
73. Thomas Munford to his sister-in-law, December 22, 1862, Private Collection, RR Auctions, Catalog 426, Item 402, April 2014, Boston, MA.
74. Ibid.

deny General Burnside provisions, and force him to weaken his position on the Rappahannock by sending countering forces. Other benefits of Stuart's foray would be keeping his men sharp, active, and well-supplied with captured stores.[75]

Before the raid, in fact on Christmas Eve, it was time for celebrating, and Stuart had a party going on at his big tent located 12 miles away from the main house on the Corbin plantation at Moss Neck. His band of musicians and entertainers were ready: the guitarist, the bird mimic, the bones player, the "Virginia breakdown" dancer, and a couple of fiddlers. On such occasions, the star attraction was banjo player Sam Sweeney. While the party was in full swing, Stuart's tent was filled with cavalry officers. Stuart's wife, Flora, was also there, along with other officers' wives. The band played on and on. The feast was bountiful, with grateful neighbors providing chickens, turkeys, hams, sweet potatoes and dozens of eggs. Liquid spirits were hidden from Stuart, who was a lifelong teetotaler and allowed no drinking, swearing, or dissolute behavior. As Stuart celebrated, he alone knew his men would be in the saddle by dawn on the day after Christmas.[76]

At dawn on December 26, Stuart crossed Kelly's Ford with 1,800 cavalrymen, including a detachment of the 2nd Virginia under Lt. Col. James W. Watts, and four artillery pieces. They camped Christmas night at Mooresville. From there, Fitz Lee's brigade moved toward the Telegraph Road between Dumfries and Aquia on December 27. The troops skirmished until dark with Federal cavalry. The Confederate horsemen then camped near Cole's Store.

On the 28th, the brigade encountered a band of troopers of the 2nd Pennsylvania Cavalry and the 17th Pennsylvania Cavalry, in all about 300 horsemen at Greenwood Church, before it crossed the Occoquan at Davis Ford. After fording the stream and destroying a Union campsite, killing eight to 10 Federals and taking 100 prisoners, Company A of the 4th Virginia burned the bridge over the Accotink. They captured four Federals, including a lieutenant. After reaching Fairfax Court House, Fitz Lee was forced to withdraw because of a heavy Federal defensive fire from two companies of the 15th Vermont, under Brig. Gen. Edwin H. Stoughton, who were concealed in a piece

---

75. McClellan, *Campaigns of Stuart's Cavalry*, 197–202.
76. Burke Davis, *JEB Stuart: The Last Cavalier*, 161.

of woods. The Confederate horse soldiers rode through Frying Pan and Middleburg on their way to Culpeper Court House. Stuart's troopers returned to Fredericksburg on the first day of 1863 with a dozen wagons, many prisoners, and a large quantity of arms and equipment. They had failed, however, in their mission: to attack and capture the Union supply base at Dumfries; and they were repulsed at Fairfax Court House.[77]

After Fredericksburg, things settled down as the armies began to go into winter quarters. Robert E. Lee reported:

> After the battle of Fredericksburg, the army remained encamped on the south side of the Rappahannock until the latter part of April. The Federal army occupied the north side of the river, opposite Fredericksburg, extending to the Potomac. Two brigades of Major General Richard H. Anderson's division, those of Brigadier Generals William Mahone and Carnot Posey, were stationed near the United States Mine or Bark Millford; and a third, under command of General Cadmus Wilcox, guarded Banks's ford. The cavalry was distributed on both flanks--Fitzhugh Lee's brigade picketing the Rappahannock above the mouth of the Rapidan, and W. H. F. Lee's near Port Royal. Hampton's brigade had been sent into the interior to recruit. General Longstreet, with two divisions of his corps, was detached for service south of James River in February, and did not rejoin the army until after the battle of Chancellorsville.[78]

As 1862 drew to a close, Munford reflected upon the past year in a letter to his sister, "I should like so well to be with the family circle to enjoy the quiet of a home feeling again, but this miserable war interferes with all our plans and wishes and we have given up everything deeply for our cause." Indeed, the coming year required more sacrifices for the Munfords and other families as the war dragged on ceaselessly.[79]

---

77. Kenneth L. Styles, *4th Virginia Cavalry* (Lynchburg, VA, 1985), 22; McClellan, *The Campaigns of Stuart's Cavalry*, 200; *New York Times*, December 30, 1862.
78. *OR* 25/1:795.
79. Thomas Taylor Munford to Sallie Munford, December 23, 1862, Munford–Ellis Papers, DU.

Chapter Nine

1863: Onward To Chancellorsville

General Jackson ordered Colonel Munford "to guard his left flank and, if possible, seize and hold Ely's Ford Road, which we did, and when I left, Jackson said to me,
'The Institute will be heard from today.'"
– Stonewall Jackson to Munford during
Jackson's flanking maneuver at
Chancellorsville, May2, 1863.

1863 revealed Colonel Thomas Munford facing increasing responsibilities, often while acting as a brigade commander. He rejoined General Jackson at Chancellorsville in May, riding at the head of Jackson's flanking column in support of Robert E. Lee's greatest victory of the war. Unfortunately for Munford, his disappointment continued being with not receiving a coveted promotion to the brigadier rank.

General Ambrose Burnside initiated a new offensive in January 1863, hoping to redeem himself from his disastrous defeat at Fredericksburg. He set out along the Rappahannock, trying to flank Lee's strong positions north of Fredericksburg. His new campaign, however, quickly bogged down in the winter mud with hundreds of horses dying trying to slog through the knee-deep mire. The abortive "Mud March" and other failures led to General Burnside's replacement by Maj. Gen. Joseph Hooker on January 26. Hooker, age 48 and a West Point graduate of the class of 1837, was a distinguished veteran of the Mexican War, where he had demonstrated strong leadership and administrative skills. Hooker immediately began reorganizing and training his army in winter quarters outside of Fredericksburg. The new army commander adopted nearly all of the recommendations of Gen. Alfred Pleasonton concerning the cavalry service. On February 6, 1863, Hooker issued his General Order Number 6, consolidating all of the cavalry of the Army of the Potomac into a single corps under the command of the army's senior cavalry officer, Maj. Gen. George Stoneman, who was universally liked by officers and enlisted troopers alike.[1]

Meanwhile, on January 10, 1863, General Stuart held a cavalry review, attended by Robert E. Lee and James Longstreet. It was raining as the troopers of the 2nd Virginia rode 15 miles to the site of the review ground. After the review, the troopers slogged back to camp over muddy roads. One trooper recalled, "The weather was so bad that it destroyed all interest in the sight. . . . It rained so hard we could see only fifty yards ahead of us down the line." Commenting on the usefulness of such a review, the same soldier wrote, "The men and horses had been roused before daylight, marched 15 miles through the mud, and then thoroughly wet and worn had to march back. Could anything be more foolish, and all for the sake of a 'grand review,' by which a parade might be made before a few women? I have little patience for such vanity, and I think Fitz Lee and his command agree with me."[2]

The next day Fitz Lee communicated to Munford, "I desire to express to you officially my warmest thanks for the excellent marching and military bearing of your regiment upon review yesterday. The commander-in-chief, General R.E. Lee, was particularly complimentary on your large numbers, the discipline exhibited, and fine appearance of your regiment."[3]

Finally, the 2nd Virginia went into winter quarters at Hanover Court House, broken by occasional tours of picket duty along the Rappahannock. On January 14, the brigade moved five miles in order to find an area where they could better forage for their horses. The brigade could muster only 618 troopers out of 1,900 on the rolls. Munford wrote his mother that "his transportation for the brigade had been reduced to 14 wagons, all of which were captured from the Yankees. There were 175 horses unfit for duty." In the same letter, Munford penned that his troopers were being kept "in a constant state of expectancy" by the Yankees.[4]

By the beginning of the third year of the war, the toll of the war began to wear on Munford's psyche. His soldiers and their horses were in a deplorable state. He counted three of every four horses dying daily (an exaggeration), including his own beloved horse "Ewell," who

---

1. *OR* 25/2:51; Eric J. Wittenberg, *The Union Cavalry Comes of Age* (Washington, D.C., 2003), 9–13.
2. Charles Minor Blackford to his wife, January 10, 1863, *Letters from Lee's Army*, 157–58.
3. *SHSP*, vol. 16:354-55; Driver, *2nd Virginia Cavalry*, 68.
4. Thomas T. Munford to Mrs. Elizabeth Tayloe Munford, January 27, 1863, Munford–Ellis Papers, DU; Driver, *2nd Virginia Cavalry*, 69.

perished from lung fever. Rations for his men were so reduced that Munford "was mortified to see the poor fellows suffer." Even though the entire Confederate cavalry was experiencing extreme suffering, he complained as if his was the only regiment going through these ordeals. "I am becoming like a camel's back which was broken by a continued piling on of the agony," he reported. He wanted to relocate his regiment to an area where he and his men could get subsistence off the land or from the enemy, instead of his men having to buy food for themselves and their mounts. If refused, Munford aimed to demand it "as a right," and if that was not respected, he planned "to go to Richmond en route for home." He then proclaimed, "I have a splendid regiment, and one that I love; the men too are fond of me."[5]

Munford also wrote of his disdain for the management skills of "West Pointers," complaining, "I have made several formal complaints [on behalf of his troopers] but can get no redress. . . . I cannot and will not submit to such management. Stuart is a good general, but like many of these West Pointers with little experience, has but little sense—two weeks ago, I applied for permission to allow the dismounted men of my regiment to go home for twenty days to get fresh horses." Munford's request was denied by R. E. Lee—"no furloughs." As the morale of these dismounted men and others whose horses needed replacing declined, they became complaining and indifferent.[6]

On February 4, Adjutant Lomax Tayloe echoed Munford's concern about feeding the starving troopers and their mounts, writing from a new camp near the Pamunkey River, not far from Hanover Court House, "We have nothing to do here but cuss the Yankees and quarrel with the Qu. Masters and Commissaries for starving man and beast. Our horses are dying every day for want of food."[7]

On February 9, Fitzhugh Lee moved his brigade to near Culpeper Court House to relieve Hampton's brigade on picket duty along the Rappahannock from Griffinsburg to Richard's Ford. The next day, the troopers of the 2nd Virginia picketed along the river. Private Peter L. Huddleston remembered, "Snowing in the morning, hailing and raining," weather that would continue for most of the month.[8]

---

5. Thomas Taylor Munford to Mrs. George Wythe Munford, January 27, 1863; Elizabeth Tayloe Munford to Mrs. George Wythe Munford, March 4, 1863, Munford Family Papers, DU; Akers, Thesis, 21, Virginia Tech.
6. Ibid.
7. Driver, *2nd Virginia Cavalry*, 69. The problem's resolution for the entire army did not rest solely on the shoulders of Stuart or even the officers of the Commissary and Quartermaster's departments, but on the Confederate government and its inability to furnish supplies or the means of transporting them to the army.

On February 24, Fitzhugh Lee led troopers from his brigade from Culpeper across the Rappahannock at Kelly's Ford on a scout, seeking to determine what movements, if any, the Union Army of the Potomac was undertaking around Fredericksburg. The mission's directive had come from Robert E. Lee himself. Four hundred cavalrymen, detachments from the 1st, 2nd and 3rd Virginia Cavalry, splashed across the icy waters of the Rappahannock River in central Virginia, moving through deep snow northward into Union territory. Col. J. H. Drake led the 1st Virginia, Colonel Munford commanded the 2nd Virginia, and Lt. Col. William R. Carter led the 3rd Virginia. The Confederate cavaliers dealt with the bitter cold and heavy snowfall as they marched. Lieutenant Colonel Carter recorded, "On account of the 18 inches of snow roads were miserable and almost impassable."[9]

Despite the snow and treacherous roads, Fitzhugh Lee and his men made good time. Reaching Morrisville on the Warrenton Post Road (today's Route 17), they spent the night, poised to strike east the next day and challenge any Federal cavalry they encountered. Early the next morning, Lee and his troopers set out for the Union lines. In the vicinity of Hartwood Church, four miles north of the Rappahannock and eight miles west of Falmouth, at the junction of the Telegraph Road and Ridge Road, Fitz Lee's horsemen struck the inexperienced picket line of the 16th Pennsylvania Cavalry. These Pennsylvanians were anchoring the far-right flank of the Army of the Potomac. Fitz Lee's horsemen captured a group of them, sending the rest stampeding for the rear. The 1st and 3rd Virginia regiments led the advance.[10]

As fate would have it, the 16th Pennsylvania Cavalry Regiment belonged to the division of Fitz Lee's former West Point classmate and friend, Brig. Gen. William W. Averell. Taking control of the area around the church, Lee then split his force. The 1st and 2nd Virginia continued the advance along Ridge Road, which ran parallel and just north of the Warrenton Post Road. Another detachment of the 2nd, along with the 3rd Virginia, moved along the Post Road itself. Next, Lee's troopers ran into the Union picket reserve, which consisted of the 3rd and 4th Pennsylvania, another contingent of the 16th Pennsylvania, the 1st Massachusetts, the 4th New York, and the 1st Rhode Island. Fighting immediately broke out. Charge met countercharge as troopers in blue and butternut shot and slashed at each other through the woods and thickets between and along the

---

8. Peter L. Huddleston Diary, typescript on file at Fredericksburg and Spotsylvania NMP, 10; Driver, *2nd Virginia Cavalry*, 69.
9. *OR* 25/1:25; William R. Carter, *Sabres, Saddles and Spurs*, Walbrook D. Swank, ed. (Shippensburg, PA, 1998), 46.
10. *OR* 25/1:25.

Ridge and Warrenton Post roads. It was not long before the sounds of battle reached the lines of Federal infantry. Moving out from their position at Berea Church, four companies of the 124th New York Infantry under Lt. Col. F. M. Cummins, part of Maj. Gen. Daniel Sickles's III Corps, came to the support of the Union cavalry. The appearance of foot soldiers on the scene was enough to convince Fitzhugh Lee it was time to withdraw from the fight.[11]

Hooker's Chief of Staff, Maj. Gen. Daniel Butterfield, telegraphed Maj. Gen. Alpheus S. Williams, commander of the 1st Division of the XII Corps, to relay the message to all cavalry commanders in the area (Pleasonton and Averell) to vigorously pursue the retreating Confederate horsemen and capture Fitz Lee's whole command. He thought it should not be difficult, stating that the invaders had "marched from 12 miles the other side of the Rappahannock last night, made a long circuit today, and horses very tired. We ought to capture every one of them." The prickly Butterfield added, "Say to Pleasonton, a major-general's commission is staring some cavalry officer in the face in this business."[12]

Surmising the Federals would pursue rather than return by the route which he had come, Lee moved off to the north and encamped that night near the old battlefield of Second Manassas. Lee crossed the Rappahannock at Kelly's Ford—without being captured—and reported to his uncle Robert E. Lee that the Army of the Potomac remained across the Rappahannock, and no major operation was underway.[13]

General Fitzhugh Lee reported:

> On the 25th, I drove in the enemy's [16th Pennsylvania Cavalry] pickets near Hartwood Church, and attacked his reserve and main body. Routed them, and pursued them within 5 miles of Falmouth, to their infantry lines. Killed and wounded many of them. Captured 150 prisoners, including 5 commissioned officers, with all their horses, arms, and equipments. I then withdrew my command slowly, retiring by detachments. Encamped at Morrisville that night, and on the 26th recrossed the river, and returned to camp with my prisoners. The successive charges were splendidly executed. My loss in killed, wounded, and missing was 14.[14]

---

11. *OR* 25/1:21, 25, part 2:103–04.
12. *OR* 25/2:101, 103–04.
13. Ibid.; McClellan, *Campaigns of Stuart's Cavalry*, 204.
14. McClellan, *Campaigns of Stuart's Cavalry*, 204; *OR* 25/1:25–26.

Averell reported losses in the skirmish of 36 killed, wounded, and missing.[15]

Munford's adjutant, Lomax Tayloe, reported Munford's action:

> Col. Munford saw another regiment coming up on our flank as if trying to cut us off, so he cut off all of the Reg't except the 1st Squadron, and went at them, who no sooner saw him coming than they put to flight. I was with the squadron that was charging the first Reg't that we saw; we pitched ahead thinking the whole Reg't was coming, but lo and behold, this squadron of about 60 men was chasing a Yankee Reg't of about 400 men.[16]

The reconnaissance determined the Federal infantry was still concentrated opposite Fredericksburg.[17]

Meanwhile, there were troubles at the Munford home front. Typhoid fever raged at Glen Alpine. Etta Munford and four of the servants fell sick to the disease. The children were also ill with terrible colds and croup. Etta cried out in desperation in a letter to her mother-in-law, "If this terrible war would only end! I miss Mr. Munford each day of my life and more." Etta Munford, also thinking of the situation regarding her husband's deserved promotion, further lamented, "I am beginning to despair of Mr. M's promotion—though my heart is quite set upon it, and I can but think it strange that his claim should be overlooked."[18]

Echoing his wife's concern, Thomas Munford had cause to wonder when and if he would receive his promotion to brigadier general. Up to this point, he had commanded a brigade much of the time and had previously been recommended for promotion by General Stuart and Governor Letcher. Munford felt that because he was not a "West Point" officer, Stuart and others were biased against him. He believed he was being passed over by others, some less qualified than him.[19]

Before the end of March, Munford was hit by overwhelming sadness due to the loss of his second son, seven-year-old Beverly Carlton. He wrote, "My precious little boy was so gentle and affectionate, and clung to me that I feel his loss sadly indeed. What a mighty gap it leaves in my dear little circle—and how hard it will be to forget his gentle ways. . . . Surrounded as I am by men, hardened by

---

15. Ibid.
16. Ibid.
17. Ibid.
18. Elizabeth Taylor Munford to Mrs. George Wythe Munford, March 4, 1863, Munford–Ellis Papers, DU.
19. Stuart had previously recommended Munford for promotion in the Fall of 1862.

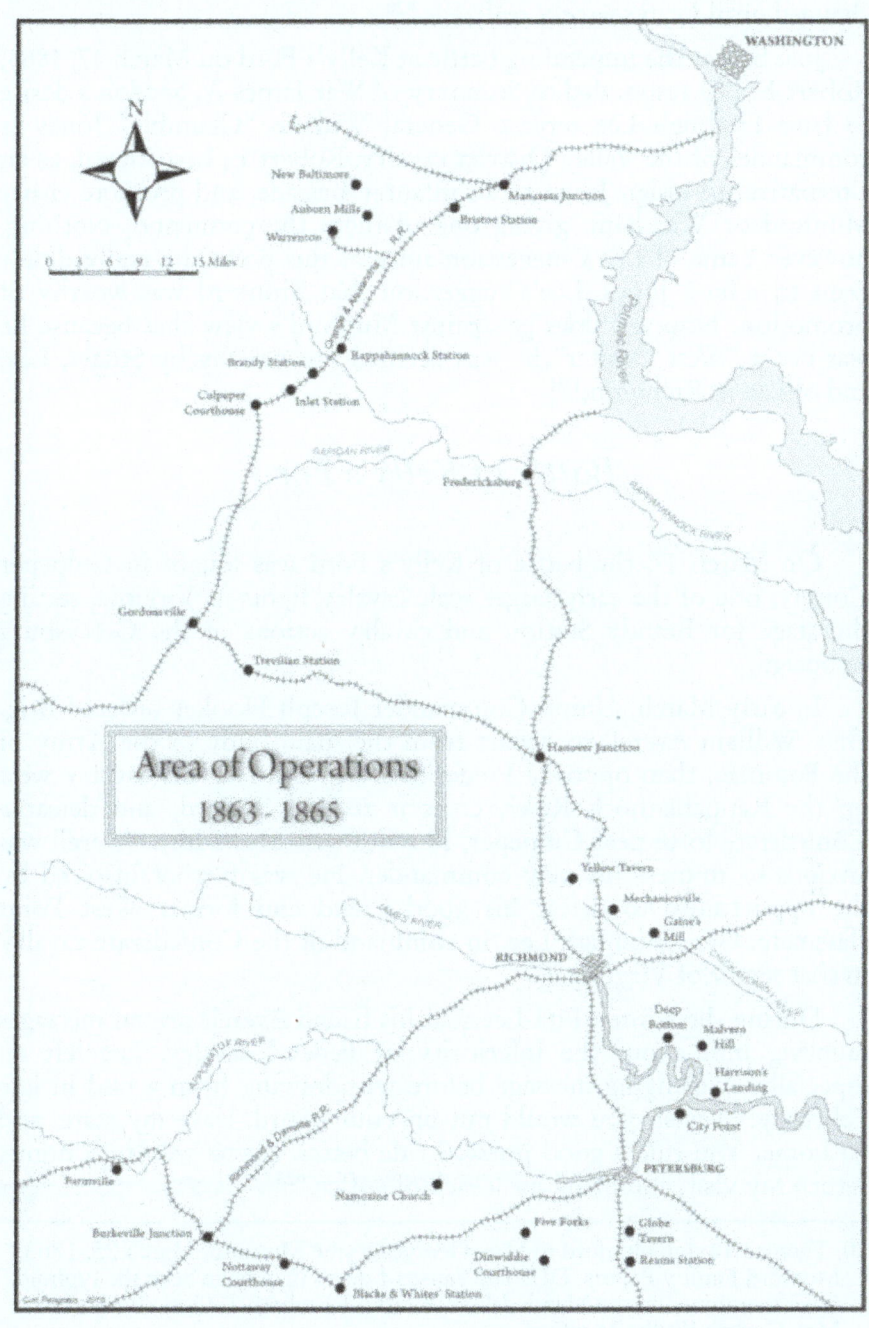

the circumstances of war--my own heart and feelings, blinded and changed until I can scarcely realize it."[20]

Just before the impending battle at Kelly's Ford on March 17, 1863, Robert E. Lee responded to Secretary of War James A. Seddon's desire to have Fitzhugh Lee replace General William "Grumble" Jones as commander of the Valley District cavalry. Robert E. Lee offered, as an alternative, to assign Jones to an infantry brigade, and promote either Munford or Wickham, giving one of them the command. Nothing, however, came of Lee's suggestion since at this point, he really didn't want to relieve Jones. Lee's suggestion that Munford was worthy of promotion, however, does go against Munford's view that because he was not a "West Pointer" he was deemed not worthy by Stuart, Lee, and others in Richmond.[21]

Battle of Kelly's Ford

On March 17, the battle of Kelly's Ford was fought in Culpeper County, one of the early larger scale cavalry fights in Virginia, setting the stage for Brandy Station and cavalry actions of the Gettysburg campaign.

In early March, Union Commander Joseph Hooker ordered Brig. Gen. William Averell to depart from the main body of the Army of the Potomac, then opposite Fredericksburg, and lead his cavalry west up the Rappahannock River, cross it at Kelly's Ford, and defeat a Confederate force near Culpeper, 10 miles west of the ford. Averell was anxious to impress his new commander. He was further inspired by the opportunity to defeat his good friend and former West Point classmate, Gen. Fitzhugh Lee, in command of the Confederate cavalry in that sector of Virginia.[22]

During the winter, Fitz Lee sent his friend Averell several messages taunting him about the inferiority of Federal cavalry. Lee left an especially challenging message before withdrawing from a raid in late February: "I wish you would put up your sword, leave my state, and go home. You ride a good horse, I ride better. If you won't go home, return my visit, and bring me a sack of coffee."[23]

---

20. Thomas Taylor Munford to Mrs. George Wythe Munford, March 25, 1863, Munford Family Papers, DU. The cause of death may have been the typhoid fever mentioned in the March 4th letter from Elizabeth Tayloe Munford to Mrs. George Wythe Munford.
21. *OR* 25/2:654; Driver, *2nd Virginia Cavalry*, 71.
22. NPS, "Battle of Kelly's Ford."
23. George Gordon Meade, ed., *Life and Letters of George Gordon Meade* (New York, 1913), vol. 1:361.

With his 3,000 horsemen and a battery of six cannons, Averell set out on March 16 to accept Lee's challenge. Fearing that a significant enemy force to the northwest might threaten his right flank, Averell expeditiously detached 900 of his troopers to Catlett Station, 15 miles north of Kelly's Ford.[24]

Fitz Lee quickly learned of Averell's movement, but was unsure whether he would attempt to cross the river at Kelly's Ford or at Rappahannock Ford, four miles farther upstream and north of Kelly's. Lee reinforced the 20 Confederate pickets guarding Kelly's Ford. Lee's available sharpshooters were poised to move to either ford. Lee posted the bulk of his command, 800 horsemen and Capt. James Breathed's four-cannon battery, in Culpeper. The Kelly's Ford defenders, about 85 members of the 2nd and 4th Virginia cavalry regiments, found shelter in a dry millrace and blocked the approaches to the ford along both river banks with abatis[25]

At dawn on March 17, General Averell led 2,100 troopers, along with several artillery batteries, and splashed across the swollen Rappahannock River at Kelly's Ford to attack the Confederate cavalry. It had rained overnight, followed by snow with a depth of five inches. Fitzhugh Lee counterattacked with his brigade of about 800 men. Confederate Maj. John Pelham, known as the "Gallant" Pelham and perhaps the best artillerist of the war up to that point, was mortally wounded after returning from some time off duty. The loss of Pelham was a crushing blow to the Confederacy, as the young cannoneer everyone loved had not even had enough time to rejoin his "battalion" before mortally wounded. After achieving success, Union forces withdrew in mid-afternoon. The inconclusive battle, which proved the Federal cavalry would be a force to be reckoned with in the future, resulted in an estimated 200 total casualties. Munford was presiding at the seemingly never-ending court martial of Col. Henry C. Pate, commander of the 5th Virginia Cavalry, at Culpepper Court House. He did not know of the action in time to join his command until the fight was nearly over.[26]

After Kelly's Ford, the Confederate cavalry was stretched thin; their pickets extended from the Blue Ridge Mountains east to the Chesapeake Bay. The majority of this picket duty along the Rappahannock fell on the shoulders of Rooney Lee and Fitz Lee. The work was hazardous for troopers on both sides of the river. Munford recalled that when his pickets manned their posts, they often excelled in a deadly game. In a postwar letter, the 2nd Virginia commander

---

24. NPS, "Battle of Kelly's Ford."
25. Ibid.
26. *OR* 25/1:60, 62; Driver, *2nd Virginia Cavalry*, 71, 76. The horse artillery had not yet been officially formed into a battalion.

remembered, "I had a great many Mountaineers that could kill a running deer with their rifles or cut off a wild turkey's head, and if well posted, it was not safe for any man to come within range of their rifles. It was a cruel kind of fun, but it was war, and they could enjoy the practice."[27]

As the hard times of supplying the Confederate army continued, on March 31, Secretary of War James A. Seddon wrote Robert E. Lee urging that Colonel Munford's cavalry, "whose horses are now suffering greatly from want of adequate supplies of forage, should be allowed to go into or on toward Loudoun to protect them [the citizens] . . . he and his men are especially familiar and influential in that county, and could in every way render them most essential aid, while recruiting and refreshing themselves and their animals." The lack of adequate cavalry to replace the 2nd Virginia prevented Lee from acting on this suggestion and therefore the men of the 2nd continued to suffer, along with many others.[28]

Echoing the problems with supplies, Capt. Thomas B. Holland of Company D reported:

> The company would be more efficient and report a larger number of men for duty if the horses could be properly fed, but they have suffered a great deal with hunger and are thus some rendered unfit for service. The men whose horses are thus disabled for the want of forage are detailed to go home and furnish themselves with fresh one which diminishes our numbers and imposes a very heavy expense on the men.[29]

In mid-April, the men returned from horse detail, and with paroled prisoners and new recruits, raised the strength of the brigade to 1,500 troopers. The 2nd Virginia numbered about 400 present for duty.[30]

On April 11, Munford and his 2nd Virginia went on a scout, arriving at Amissville the next day, camping near Cobbler's Mountain. They returned on the 14th, encountering Federal cavalry, but drove them from the hamlet. Captain Edgar Whitehead of Company E recalled, "weather bad, raining torrents, and no forage." He reported the regiment rode to Sperryville on April 17, returning to Culpeper Court House on April 20.[31]

---

27. Thomas T. Munford to E. A. Carmen, December 10, 1894, Carmen Papers, New York Public Library; Jeffrey D. Wert, *Cavalryman of the Lost Cause*, 213.
28. *OR* 25/2:693–94.
29. Driver, *2nd Virginia Cavalry*, 77; *OR* 25/2:693–94.
30. Ibid.
31. Driver, *2nd Virginia Cavalry*, 77.

Battle of Chancellorsville

The battle of Chancellorsville was fought from April 30 to May 6, 1863, in Spotsylvania County near the village of Chancellorsville. Two related battles occurred nearby on May 3 at Fredericksburg and Salem Church. The main fight at Chancellorsville pitted Joseph Hooker's Army of the Potomac against an army less than half its size: Robert E. Lee's Confederate Army of Northern Virginia. Chancellorsville became known as Lee's greatest victory because of his risky decision to divide his army in the presence of a much larger enemy, a judgment which resulted in a momentous Confederate victory. This triumph, a product of Lee's audacity and Hooker's tentativeness, was tempered by heavy casualties and the mortal wounding of Lt. Gen. Thomas J. "Stonewall" Jackson as a result of friendly fire, a loss that Lee reportedly likened to "losing my right arm."[32]

The Chancellorsville campaign began with the crossing of the Rappahannock River by the Union army under Maj. Gen. Henry W. Slocum on the morning of April 27. Simultaneously, Union cavalry under Maj. Gen. George Stoneman began a long-distance raid against Lee's supply lines. This combined offensive was ineffectual. Three days later, Federal infantry crossed the Rapidan River via Germanna and Ely's Fords, concentrating near Chancellorsville. Combined with the Union force facing Fredericksburg, Hooker planned a double envelopment, attacking Lee from both his front and rear.[33]

On April 28, Maj. Gen. Joseph Hooker began crossing the Rappahannock at Kelly's Ford. Stuart notified Robert E. Lee and then concentrated his cavalry near Brandy Station. The next day, Fitz Lee's brigade skirmished with William Averell's Federal cavalry at Stevensburg. Stuart detached Fitz Lee's brigade, ordering them to Raccoon Ford, where they camped for the night.[34]

General Hooker's army was in possession of Chancellorsville. Stuart marched his command toward Todd's Tavern, where he planned to camp for the night. As Stuart's troopers rode along at night, they encountered the 6th New York Cavalry, which was returning from a scout to Spotsylvania Court House. Stuart ordered his 2nd, 3rd, and 5th Virginia regiments to charge the New Yorkers, but the Federal horsemen escaped to Chancellorsville, leaving pickets at a fork in the road. Stuart ordered the 2nd Virginia to charge the pickets, resulting in

---

32. NPS, "Battle of Chancellorsville."
33. Stephen W. Sears, *Chancellorsville* (Boston, 1996), 120–24, 137–38.
34. Ibid.

capture of the pickets and freeing some of their own troopers who had been taken prisoner earlier by the New Yorkers.³⁵

Lieutenant Colonel James W. Watts remembered the charge as follows: "Very soon we encountered the picket or advance guard, when the charge was ordered, and gallantly made, scattering the command in our front which we learned was the 6th New York, commanded by Lt. Col. [Duncan] McVicar who acted very gallantly. . . . After the fight we were ordered to Spotsylvania Court House with the [captured] prisoners." The highly respected McVicar was mortally wounded in the fight. Stuart's Adjutant, Maj. Heros Von Borcke, had his horse shot and killed under him at the head of Stuart's column.³⁶

On May 1, General Hooker advanced from Chancellorsville toward Robert E. Lee, but Lee split his army in the face of superior numbers, leaving a small force at Fredericksburg to discourage Maj. Gen. John Sedgwick from advancing, while he attacked Hooker's advance with three-quarters of his army. Despite strong objections from subordinates, Hooker, wanting reinforcements, withdrew his army to defensive lines around Chancellorsville, allowing Lee to determine the next step. Hooker wanted to entice Lee to attack while he was in a strong defensive position.³⁷

On May 2, Lee divided his army again, retaining 15,000 soldiers; he sent Stonewall Jackson's entire 30,000-man corps on a flanking march around the right flank of the Union XI Corps under Maj. Gen. Oliver O. Howard. On the morning of May 2, Jackson began to move his corps to accomplish the flanking mission. Munford, just detailed to Jackson that morning, rode at the head of the advance infantry column with Jackson and his chief of artillery, Col. Stapleton Crutchfield, while Maj. Cary Breckinridge led the 2nd Virginia. Munford wrote, "My regiment was all the cavalry that Jackson required."³⁸

About 1:00 p.m., Munford's troopers reached the Orange Plank Road, where it angled northwest towards the Turnpike and the

---

35. Ibid.
36. Driver, *2nd Virginia Cavalry*, 78; Eric J. Wittenberg, *The Union Cavalry Comes of Age*, 156. McVicar was so respected by all that the historian of the 6th New York recorded that the Confederates "paid every respect to his remains." His body was conveyed to the nearby Alsop farm and "tenderly cared for." General Fitzhugh Lee sent Rev. Dabney Ball, Chaplain of the 1st Virginia Cavalry, who prayed over the remains of the gallant McVicar. It has been told that "even General J.E.B Stuart patted the forehead of the Colonel and said, 'Brave man, brave man.'" Reference: William B. Besley and Gilbert Guion Wood, *History of the Sixth New York Cavalry: Second Brigade – First Division – Cavalry Corps* (Boston, Ma, 2010), 107.
37. NPS, "Battle of Chancellorsville."
38. Driver, *2nd Virginia Cavalry*, 79; Whitehead, "Campaigns of Munford's 2nd Virginia Cavalry," 59.

1863–The New Year Begins; Onward Toward Chancellorsville

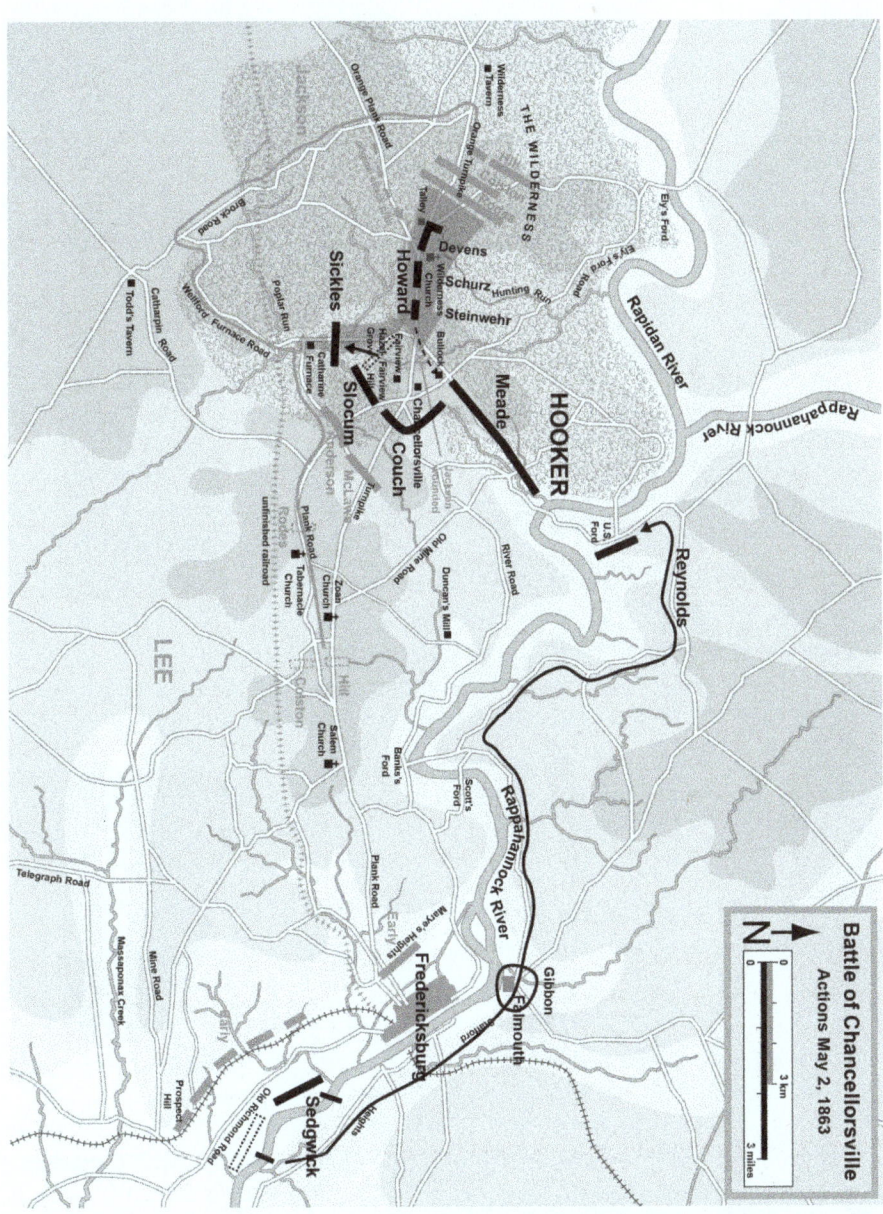

Map by Hal Jespersen

Stonewall Jackson Memorial at V.M.I., Lexington, Virginia
Inscribed with the famous words Jackson said to Munford and other VMI graduates on his flanking maneuver of the Union Army at Chancellorsville:
"The Institute will be heard from today."

(Courtesy: Virginia Military Institute Archives)

position of Maj. Gen. Oliver O. Howard's line on the extreme end on the right flank of the Union army. This was the path Jackson expected to use. Munford led his regiment up that road, stopping at Hickman's farm just a mile and a quarter from the Turnpike. Munford sent a squadron further up the road, striking a picket of the 8th Pennsylvania Cavalry, driving it in. Munford's troopers got a good look at Howard's line, noticing it was unanchored. They reported back to Munford just as Fitz Lee rode up. Fitz Lee quickly rode to tell Jackson, marching up the Brock Road. Lee accompanied Jackson to see the situation for himself.[39]

Earlier that morning, Munford had been at Jackson's headquarters with Brigadier Generals Robert E. Rodes, Raleigh E. Colston, and Major Stapleton Crutchfield to get his orders just before Jackson's attack of Hooker's army. Jackson knew these VMI grads and former professors and trusted their abilities. Munford had been Jackson's cadet adjutant, while Raleigh Colston had been a senior at the Institute when Munford was there. Stapleton Crutchfield had roomed with Munford. Colston, Rodes, and Crutchfield, like Jackson, also had been VMI professors. There were 20 or more officers in the 2nd Virginia who had attended VMI. Jackson knew all these soldiers personally, and these men had served him in the 1862 Valley Campaign, the Seven Days' campaign, and at Second Manassas. Jackson ordered Munford "to guard his left flank and, if possible, seize and hold Ely's Ford Road, which we did, and when I left, Jackson said to me, 'The Va. Military Institute will be heard from today.'"[40]

Lieutenant Colonel James Watts quoted Munford on the flanking march, "After the 2d Va. Cavalry had cleared the Brock Road the enemy [17th Pennsylvania Cavalry] in a sharp skirmish, Gen. Fitz Lee came up to Jackson, who told him, 'This road must be held until my troops pass.'" Jackson left the Stonewall Brigade to support the cavalry. "The column moved forward," continued Watts, "the 2d Va. Cavalry leading, across the pike, two miles north. Here the column turned east and the 2d Va. Cavalry again encountered and drove in the [17th Pennsylvania] cavalry picket, supported by artillery."[41]

Munford added, "When we struck the Plank Road, we found a picket of the 17th Penn. Cavalry, and Breckridge's and Whitehead's squadron of my regiment charged and drove them back on their

---

39. Ernest B. Fergurson, *Chancellorsville 1863: The Souls of the Brave* (New York, Vintage Books, 1993), 164.
40. Whitehead, "The Campaigns of Munford's 2nd Virginia Cavalry," 59–60; *OR* 25/1:885–87; Driver, *2nd Virginia Cavalry*, 80. Many historians and the VMI Archives report Jackson's quote as, "The Institute will be heard from today."
41. Driver, *2nd Virginia Cavalry*, 79.

infantry support." At this point, Jackson's line of battle was formed, with General Rodes first, supported by General Colston, and then by Maj. Gen. A. P. Hill's division in column, ready to go where most needed.[42]

Munford recalled:

> We moved with [Brigadier General Alfred] Iverson's brigade and on its left, but my regiment was ordered to bear to the left and to guard the left flank. We, of course, could not make headway until we got to the road, but we captured the Commissary Department of [Major General Oliver O.] Howard's Corps with some six or eight slaughtered beeves and as many stragglers as we could well guard, and held Ely's Ford road before night, driving the enemy's cavalry picket to the ford.[43]

Jackson's flanking maneuver surprised the Federal XI Corps under the ineffectual General Howard; Jackson rolled them up, routing them. Union III Corps commander Maj. Gen. Daniel E. Sickles reported, "The fugitives of the Eleventh Corps swarmed from the woods and swept frantically over the cleared fields, in which my artillery was parked. The exulting enemy at their heels mingled yells with their volleys, and in the confusion which followed it seemed as if cannon and caissons, dragoons, cannoneers, and infantry . . . Ascertaining the enterprise of cutting us off from the army to be hopeless, the enemy sullenly withdrew to the line of rifle pits and breastworks formerly held by the Eleventh Corps." As Jackson sought continuing to roll up the right flank, he ran up against a stubborn I Corps under Maj. Gen. John F. Reynolds. The guns of the XII Corps brought Rodes's division to a standstill. Jackson's attack stalled. The positioning of Daniel E. Sickles's III Corps and Pleasonton's cavalry on the right flank of Jackson's cavalry cut off direct communication with General Lee's right.[44]

Jackson wanted to continue the fight after darkness closed in. While performing a personal reconnaissance in advance of his line, Jackson was mortally wounded by fire from his own men. Major General J.E.B. Stuart temporarily replaced him as corps commander. The battle continued the next day, under the temporary command of Stuart, who turned in an excellent performance as an infantry commander.[45]

---

42. Ibid.
43. Ibid., 80.
44. *OR* 25/1:200-201; 384–85.
45. Major General Robert Rodes actually replaced Jackson at first, but three hours later Stuart claimed the mantle of Jackson. Munford thought it was "a great piece of injustice." Ref: Darrell Collins, *Major General Robert E.*

On May 3, Lee launched multiple attacks against the Union position at Chancellorsville, resulting in heavy losses on both sides. The same day, General Sedgwick forded the Rappahannock River, defeated the small Confederate force at Marye's Heights in the Second Battle of Fredericksburg, and then moved to the west towards Salem Church. There, Confederates fought a successful delaying action, and by May 4 had driven Sedgwick's men back to Banks's Ford, surrounding them on three sides. Early on May 5, Sedgwick withdrew across the ford. Hooker subsequently withdrew the remainder of his army across U.S. Ford the night of May 5-6. The campaign ended on May 7 when George Stoneman's cavalry reached Union lines east of Richmond.[46]

J.E.B. Stuart reported, lauding Fitz Lee, "The cavalry was well managed by Brigadier General Fitz Lee, who seized Ely's ford, and held the road to within two miles of Chancellorsville, driving the enemy's cavalry from the former place. His men, without rations or forage, displayed a heroism rarely met with under any circumstances, and guarding the two flanks, accomplished an indispensable part of the great success." Munford claimed his and Wickham's reports were delivered to Rosser in the presence of Jedediah Hotchkiss but were never received by the war department. Neither Fitz Lee nor Rosser wrote a report.[47]

By this point, some troopers were growing extremely tired of the war. Robert W. Parker wrote his wife about the unlikelihood of being able to purchase a substitute to take his place in the 2nd Virginia Cavalry, even though he was willing to spend "twenty-five hundred and even more if I could get out of this war, even if it didn't last six months longer."[48]

Rodes of the Army of Northern Virginia: A Biography (New York, 2008), 220.
46. NPS, "Battle of Fredericksburg."
47. *OR* 25/1:889; Thomas T. Munford to Charles Blackford, May 23, 1901, Munford–Ellis Papers, DU.
48. Robert W. Parker to his wife, May 17, 1863, Robert W. Parker Papers, 1858-1889, SHC, UNC, Chapel Hill, NC; Wright, ed., *Lee's Last Casualty*, 102.

Chapter Ten

Gettysburg Campaign

"Colonel Munford's delay in coming to the field has not been satisfactorily accounted for, as the distance was not very great."

— General Stuart, speaking of Munford's late arrival to Fleetwood Hill during the battle of Brandy Station.

After Chancellorsville, the Army of Northern Virginia invaded the north once again, this time in Pennsylvania. Stuart blamed Munford for being late to Fleetwood Hill at the battle of Brandy Station. Munford led his regiment at Aldie as the army headed north. He accompanied Stuart on the cavalry commander's raids in Pennsylvania in the lead-up to the epic battle at Gettysburg. Afterwards, Munford became even more critical of Stuart.

Following Chancellorsville, Robert E. Lee and Jefferson Davis decided to carry the war into Northern territory again. The first northern invasion had resulted in the terrible battle at Antietam and subsequent retreat back to Virginia. An invasion northward would relieve Virginia of the enemy's presence by drawing the Federals north of the Potomac. Union troops might be moved away from the coasts of Virginia and North Carolina. In addition, they might have to alter their Mississippi and Tennessee campaigns (Vicksburg, Mississippi, was then under siege by Ulysses S. Grant) to meet the new Confederate offensive. Equally important, ravaged by war for two years, Virginia was unable to feed General Lee's troops much longer.

After the battle of Chancellorsville, both armies reorganized. The Army of Northern Virginia, with additional men obtained by conscription, divided into three corps commanded by Lieutenant Generals James Longstreet, Richard S. Ewell, and Ambrose P. Hill. By the end of May, Lee had 76,000 men and 272 artillery pieces. Each corps had three divisions, with each division consisting of four brigades—except Longstreet's corps, which had three. The corps of the Army of the Potomac were about half the size of their Southern counterparts. On May 22, Maj. Gen. Joseph Hooker replaced his cavalry chief Stoneman with Brig. Gen. Alfred Pleasonton. Stoneman had been discredited at Chancellorsville, and Pleasonton had enhanced the effectiveness of the Union cavalry by virtue of his skills as a gifted administrator and organizer.[1]

On May 11, Gen. Robert E. Lee ordered Stuart to move his cavalry north from Orange County to Culpeper County in preparation for his planned invasion of the Keystone State. After his success at Chancellorsville, Lee planned to lead his army through the Shenandoah Valley for his second invasion of the North, where he was determined to capture horses, equipment, and food for his men. He was also hoping to threaten as far north as Harrisburg, Pennsylvania, or even Philadelphia, thereby influencing Northern politicians to give up their prosecution of the war. By May 22, Stuart had moved nearly 7,000 troopers from Wade Hampton's, Rooney Lee's, and Fitzhugh Lee's brigades to Culpeper, and by June 5, another 3,000 from Robertson's and Jones's brigades joined them. Robertson's brigade camped southwest of Brandy Station near the John Minor Botts farm, while Jones came from the Shenandoah Valley. Lee's invasion plan called for Stuart to position his Confederate cavalry on the right flank of his army to screen the infantry and protect its rear.[2]

Lee's army was then at Fredericksburg, across the Rappahannock from Falmouth. He intended to march north to Pennsylvania. Hooker wanted to uncover Lee's plans. He knew Lee was at Culpeper, but would he head north, or would he suddenly turn east and move toward Washington? Hooker assigned his entire cavalry corps—two brigades of infantry, and four artillery batteries—to determine Lee's intentions by conducting a raid.[3]

Munford's 2nd Virginia continued to picket the area along the Rappahannock until General Hooker had withdrawn across the Rappahannock on May 6. By May 20, the 2nd Virginia went back into camp near Culpepper Court House. The next day, a review of Fitzhugh Lee's brigade was held, followed on May 22 on John Botts's farm by a 4,000-man cavalry review by Stuart of the brigades of Fitz Lee, W. H. F. Lee, Wade Hampton, and the horse artillery of Maj. Robert F. Beckham. Shortly after the review, Robertson's brigade from North Carolina and William E. Jones's brigade from the Valley arrived, effectively doubling the size of cavalry under Stuart's

---

1. Wert, *Cavalryman of the Lost Cause*, 240-41; Wittenberg, *The Union Cavalry Comes of Age*, 237–38.
2. Heros Von Borcke, *Memoirs of the Confederate War for Independence*, vol. 2:264-65; *OR* 25/2:792.
3. Wert, *Cavalryman of the Lost Cause*, 240.

command. Stuart scheduled another review for June 5, when it was expected Robert E. Lee would attend.[4]

Responding to an order from Robert E. Lee on the condition of the horsemen, Stuart reported that as of May 25, the 2nd Virginia had 28 officers and 443 men effectively mounted, three officers and 194 men non-effectively mounted, and eight officers and 191 men absent, most on horse detail.[5]

On June 5, General Stuart held another review of his corps on an open field near the little hamlet of Inlet Station, four miles northeast of Culpeper. The review was not only a military parade, but also one of those magnificent pageants and splendid social events which the flashy Stuart loved to stage. The entire division passed in review with three bands playing and a flag waving at the head of each regiment. Then, the column divided into brigades and regiments that performed drills. In a climactic finale, the troopers, yelling, sabers drawn, charged at the artillery, which was posted at intervals around the perimeter of the field. The artillery fired blank cartridges at the charging horsemen in a noisy closing. The day ended with another ball "on a piece of turf near headquarters, and by the light of enormous wood fires, the ruddy glare of which upon the animated groups . . . gave the whole scene a wild and romantic effect."[6]

Not all were happy with these reviews. Some, such as Wade Hampton and the irascible "Grumble" Jones, considered them a waste of resources. Jones and his brigade had just arrived on June 3 and 4, and the men and horses were tired and needed rest. The review of June 5 did not allow for a respite.[7]

Robert E. Lee had been invited to review the troops, but he was unable to attend. General Lee ordered another review, and it was held on June 8. Lee surveyed all of his cavalry, some 9,500 troopers, at Inlet Station. According to Munford, Stuart was "as untiring on horseback as a Centaur—setting his steed as if part of his existence. No more dashing soldier ever drew a sabre." Munford, however, complained, "In a fight, he was clearheaded, and inspired by word and example implicit

---

4. Driver, *2nd Virginia Cavalry*, 80; McClellan, *The Campaigns of Stuart's Cavalry*, 261.
5. Driver, *2nd Virginia Cavalry*, 60. Meanwhile, on May 28 the election of governor, lieutenant governor and attorney general, of the State of Virginia was held. Thomas Munford's father, George Wythe Munford was on the Conservative Democratic ticket for Governor. Thomas Stanhope Flournoy was again a candidate for Governor. Munford and Flournoy were defeated by William "Extra Billy" Smith, who had commanded the 49th Virginia Infantry.
6. Von Borcke, *Memoirs of the Confederate War for Independence*, vol. 2:264-65.
7. Longacre, *Lee's Cavalrymen*, 188.

confidence in his men, but his 'Leprechonian' tendencies would allow him to forget his men and horses. He kept [them] on picket all night—without rations—while he with jingling spurs and twinkling eyes reveled in the dance."[8]

The Confederate plan for the next morning, June 9, called for two full corps of infantry, under Lieutenant Generals James Longstreet and Richard S. Ewell, to march west into the Shenandoah Valley and then north towards Pennsylvania. Lieutenant General A. P. Hill's corps would temporarily remain on the banks of the Rappahannock to cover the movement. The cavalry command, under orders to screen Lee's invading forces, included the brigades of Brigadier Generals Wade Hampton, "Rooney" Lee, Beverly Robertson, "Grumble" Jones, Fitzhugh Lee (under Col. Thomas Munford due to Lee's bout with inflammatory rheumatism); and Capt. James F. Hart's battery of Maj. Robert F. Beckham's horse artillery. Lee wanted Stuart's cavalry to cross the Rappahannock at Beverly Ford, four miles northeast of Brandy Station, on the morning of June 9.[9]

Meanwhile, Gen. Joseph Hooker had ordered most of his cavalry and two brigades of infantry, totaling about 11,000 men and led by newly appointed Federal cavalry commander Brig. Gen. Alfred Pleasonton, to attack the Confederates. Pleasonton devised a plan that assumed the gray horsemen were still near the village of Culpeper Court House, having heard of the Confederate cavalry's recent assembling there. His scheme consisted of attacks by two cavalry columns under Brigadier Generals John Buford and David M. Gregg. Buford, supported by infantry—all crossing at Beverly Ford, while Gregg would cross at Kelly's Ford. The two Federal cavalry commands would then link up at Brandy Station. From there they intended to push to Culpeper. The plan was doomed from the start because Stuart was, in fact, bivouacked on Fleetwood Hill near Brandy Station, and Grumble Jones's brigade and Robert Beckham's artillery were camped just southwest of Beverly Ford itself. The Federals would find themselves trying to concentrate their forces while in the midst of Confederate cavalry.[10]

On the evening of June 8, 1863, a large Union cavalry column under Gen. John Buford positioned itself for a surprise move across Beverly Ford the next morning, where, unbeknownst to the Federals, the Confederate cavalry was also planning to cross. Some six miles

---

8. Thomas T. Munford to Anne Bachman Hyde, August 29, 1915, SHC, University of North Carolina, Chapel Hill.
9. *OR* 27/2:692.
10. Longacre, *Lee's Cavalrymen*, 190; Stephen W. Sears, *Gettysburg* (New York, Houghton Mifflin, 2004), 64-66.

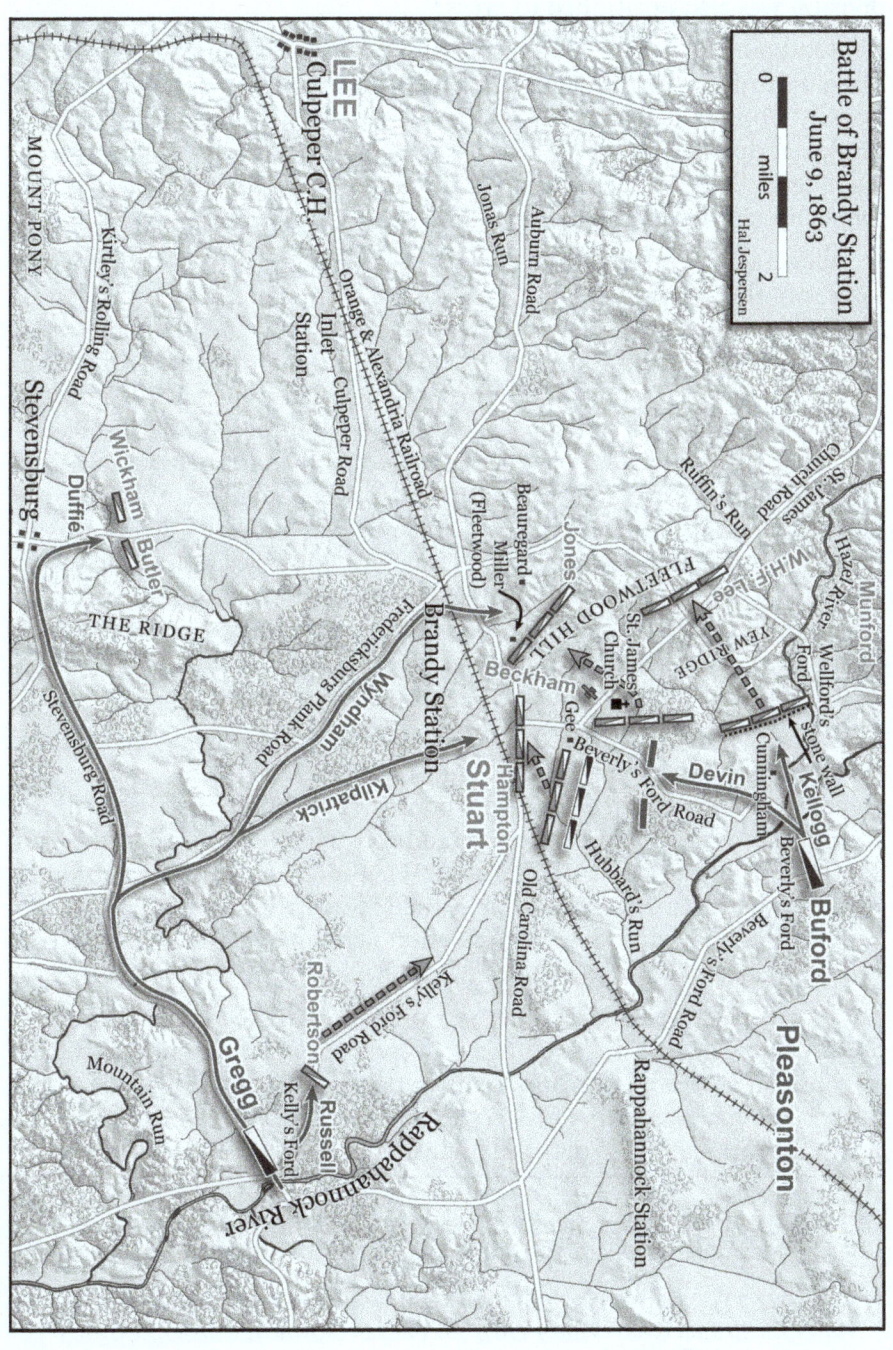

south at Kelly's Ford, General Gregg's 2,400-man Union cavalry division was also positioned to cross.[11]

On command, at 4:30 a.m. on June 9, Col. Benjamin F. "Grimes" Davis's 8th New York Cavalry led the Union column splashing across Beverly Ford in a thick fog. The battle of Brandy Station, the largest single cavalry battle of the Civil War, including about 2,000 infantry, had begun. The immense plains at Brandy Station were perfectly suited for such a cavalry engagement.[12]

General Buford was not expecting the presence of a Confederate force on the other side, but his attack surprised the Confederates. Many were still sleeping or cooking breakfast when the first shots were fired. Buford's attack was stalled by two guns from Hart's Battery, while Beckham's battalion, in imminent danger of being captured, made good an escape to higher ground at St. James Church, just as the surprised Confederates of the 6th and 7th Virginia Cavalry of Grumble Jones's brigade arrived on the scene. During the opening moments of the fight, Col. Grimes Davis was mortally wounded on Beverly Ford Road. Davis's 8th New York, now leaderless, began to retreat. Soon, the Federals regrouped and again attacked the Confederate brigades of Grumble Jones and Rooney Lee. Lee, at the first sound of gunfire, moved his troopers from Welford's Ford just west of Beverly Ford nearer to St. James Church.[13]

General Stuart ordered Hampton, whose troopers at Brandy Station were awakened by the gunfire at Beverly Ford, to support Generals Jones and Lee, under attack at Beverly Ford Road. In accordance with Stuart's orders, Hampton left one regiment, the 2nd South Carolina under Col. Matthew C. Butler, in reserve at Brandy Station. His three remaining units, the 1st North Carolina, the Cobb Legion, and the Jeff Davis Legion, soon arrived at Beverly Ford Road and took position on the right of Major Beckham's horse artillery.[14]

In the renewed Federal attack on Rooney Lee and Jones, the Confederates at first suffered heavy losses before rallying quickly and established a strong position against the Union forces. Beckham's horse artillery was two miles southwest of Beverly Ford on a slight ridge near St. James Church. Hampton's brigade positioned itself just

---

11. *OR* 27/1:949–52.
12. Major H. B. McClellan gives the Federal force as 10,981 and Stuart's as 9,536. McClellan, *The Life and Campaigns of Major-General J.E.B. Stuart*, 293.
13. *OR* 27/2:721–22; Clark B. Hall, "The Battle of Brandy Station," *Civil War Times Illustrated* (May/June 1990), 35; Fairfax Downey, *Clash of Cavalry* (New York, 1959), 94.
14. *OR* 27/2:721–22; U. R. Brooks, *Stories of the Confederacy* (Columbia, S.C., 1912), 145–46.

east of the cannon on the ridge. Jones's brigade was to the west of the church, and Rooney Lee's brigade faced east along a north-south ridge named Yew Ridge. Rooney Lee positioned additional artillery one mile north of St. James Church at Dr. Daniel Green's residence. He also ordered dismounted troopers to a position behind a low stone wall 300 yards below and east of Green's house.[15]

Gregg, who had come up from Kelly's Ford, had easily slid past Beverly Robertson's force with little opposition. Robertson believed his orders were to simply hold Kelly's Ford Road. Stuart assumed Robertson would have stopped the Yankee advance at Kelly's Ford, and thus, he ignored several calls for help from the rear. Stuart was totally surprised when he learned the facts. Gregg's troopers began attacking Fleetwood Hill, Stuart's headquarters, the highest ground. Whoever controlled it would dominate the battlefield. Hampton, pressed by Buford from the north and Gregg from the south, knew he would be entirely surrounded if the enemy gained control of Fleetwood Hill. Stuart ordered Hampton to withdraw his regiments, one at a time, from their positions and proceed to Fleetwood Hill.[16]

Faced with this situation, Rooney Lee had to abandon his defensive line along the Yew Hills northwest of St. James Church, since his right was now dangerously unsupported. He pulled back through the Yew Hills toward higher ground at the northern end of Fleetwood Hill. Buford's blue-coated warriors followed, fighting Lee's rear guard all the way.[17]

Stuart, knowing that whoever held Fleetwood Hill would win the day, ordered Jones to send two regiments to hold the heights. The Federal force advancing on Fleetwood Hill was larger than expected. Stuart ordered Hampton and Robertson to move up their brigades, with Jones to follow, and Rooney Lee to move on the left. Also involved in the mounted attack were Pierce Young's Cobb Legion and Colonel John L. Black's 1st South Carolina. Colonel A. W. Harman's 12th Virginia Cavalry and Lt. Col. Elijah V. White's 35th Virginia Cavalry Battalion, both of Jones's brigade, led the assault. The contest for the hill was spirited and prolonged. Hampton moved the 1st North Carolina and the Jeff Davis Legion into position to turn Buford's right.[18]

The charging Confederate troopers swept the 2nd and 10th New York Regiments off the hill and recovered the ground south and east of

15. *OR* 27/2:721–22; Brooks, *Stories of the Confederacy*, 146–48; Hall, "The Battle of Brandy Station," 37.
16. *OR* 27/2:721–22, part 1, 949–52; Brooks, *Stories of the Confederacy*, 145–48.
17. *OR* 27/2:721–22.
18. Ibid., 681, 721–722.

the railroad at Brandy Station. Then, as the Federals were attempting to escape down the side of the hill, Hampton attacked with Capt. William H. H. Cowles leading Company F and the rest of the 1st North Carolina, supported by the Jeff Davis Legion. The fight intensified on the southern flanks of the two-and-a-half-mile-long Fleetwood Hill. After ferocious hand-to-hand combat between two brigades of blue and gray horsemen, the Confederates drove the Federal cavalry off the hill.[19]

Finally, Munford, hearing all the noise at Fleetwood Hill, raced to the scene of the fierce afternoon battle. Stuart reported the late arrival of Munford to the battle:

> This [close quarters hand-to-hand fighting] continued 'till Munford's brigade, which, having been anxiously expected, arrived opposite this portion of the field and was ordered in at once to the attack in flank. The enemy fell back, and Munford's sharpshooters pressed him all the way to Beverly Ford, on the left. Our whole line, followed the enemy to the river, skirmishing with his rear, and our line of pickets was reestablished that night. Our infantry skirmishers, advancing through the woods, did not engage the enemy.[20]

Because the Federal cavalry was not retreating from the field, but were instead assembling about a mile south of Fleetwood Hill, Stuart was determined to drive them off. He ordered Rooney Lee to counterattack Gregg's forces. In the resulting charge at Buford's lines, Rooney Lee was severely wounded in the leg. The Confederates, now including Fitz Lee's brigade under Colonel Munford, pressed Buford's horsemen back as Buford was ordered to pull back across Beverly Ford and did so, unmolested.[21]

The day-long epic battle of Brandy Station was over. The Confederates lost 515 killed or wounded, and the Federals lost 868. The 1st North Carolina lost five killed, 12 wounded, and 14 missing. Among Hampton's brigade, the losses were put at 15 killed, 55 wounded, and 50 missing. Stuart's division also lost an unusually high number of officers. Colonel Solomon Williams of the 2nd North Carolina and Gen. Wade Hampton's brother, Lt. Col. Frank Hampton, of the 2nd South Carolina, were killed. Brigadier General Rooney Lee, Col. M. C. Butler, and Col. A. W. Harman were severely wounded.[22]

---

19. Blackford, *War Years with J.E.B. Stuart*, 215.
20. *OR* 27/2:682–83.
21. Blackford, *War Years with J.E.B. Stuart*, 216; *OR* 27/2:683.
22. Clark, *NCR*, 1:424; *OR* 27/1:726, part 2:723.

Brigadier General James Ewell Brown Stuart

Stuart blamed Munford for being late at Brandy Station on June 9, 1863, and forever held it against him.

(Courtesy Library of Congress)

Stuart reported, "Colonel Munford's delay in coming to the field has not been satisfactorily accounted for, as the distance was not very great." Stuart had expected Munford much earlier, and his tardiness was held against him by Stuart, which could have affected Munford's future opportunity for promotion to the brigadier rank. Stuart, however, would again recommend Munford for promotion in September. Munford felt Stuart made him "the scapegoat for his misfortunes."[23]

---

23. *OR*, vol. 27, part 2, 683; J.E.B. Stuart to Robert E. Lee, September 10, 1863, Adele Mitchell, ed., *Letters of Major General James E.B. Stuart* (Stuart–Mosby Historical Association, 1990), 340–41; Thomas T. Munford to unidentified Major (probably Henry B. McClellan), circa 1885, Munford–Ellis Papers, DU.

It does appear that Stuart's orders were too vague for Munford to be able to understand exactly where Stuart expected him to bring his brigade. Stuart should have been more specific. Instead, the cavalry commander blamed Munford entirely for being tardy on the scene of the battle for Fleetwood Hill. At 7:00 a.m., Stuart had sent an order through Fitz Lee's headquarters aide, Henry C. Lee, for Munford, who was at that time stationed at Oak Shade on the upper ford of the Rappahannock River, some eight miles from Fleetwood Hill. "The enemy have crossed at Beverly Ford, and are now fighting around the church," Lee's order read. "He desires you to pack up your train, and keep everything ready to move; to bring your command a little farther in this direction, and keep up communication with him, and to look out well for your picket line."

At 10:15 a.m., Lt. R. H. Goldsborough was sent forward with a second order for Munford: "General Stuart wishes all of Colonel Munford's regiments but one brought this way, leaving a guard for the baggage, which can be sent toward Culpeper." Thirty years after the war, Munford wrote that Goldsborough was captured, and the order never reached him. Stuart wrote in his report of the battle that Goldsborough was captured delivering an important message to Williams Wickham.[24] Munford reported that while no specific location was given in the orders, he presumed Stuart meant Welford's Ford. Munford led his brigade immediately to the ford and arrived there just as a brigade of the enemy's cavalry, supported by a battery, were pressing Col. Lucius Davis's 10th Virginia Cavalry, near Dr. Green's house.[25]

In his report of the action, Munford stated:

> Captain Breathed's battery was now put in position, and a few well-directed shots checked the enemy's advance, the head of his column turning toward Barbour's house. At this time, I received a verbal message from General W. H. F. Lee, to move around toward Barbour's house, and at the same time informed him of the advance of the enemy on his extreme left. I now learned for the first time that General Lee's pickets on the Rappahannock had been withdrawn, which caused me to instruct Colonel

---

24. Thomas T. Munford to an unknown "Major" (probably H. B. McClellan), circa 1885, Munford–Ellis Papers, DU.
25. McClellan, *The Campaigns of Stuart's Cavalry*, 283; William R. Carter, *Sabres, Saddles, and Spurs*, 66; Longacre, *Lee's Cavalrymen*, 192; George William Beale, *A Lieutenant of Cavalry in Lee's Army* (Boston, MA, 1918), 96; Driver, *2nd Virginia Cavalry*, 81; Thomas T. Munford to an unknown "Major" (probably H. B. McClellan), circa 1885, Munford–Ellis Papers, DU; OR 27/2:737; Whitehead, "Campaigns of Munford's 2nd Virginia Cavalry," 64–65.

Rosser, who was picketing above Warrenton Springs, to withdraw his command to Rixey's Ford, and picket the Hazel River. Moving in the direction ordered, I came up just as the Ninth Virginia Cavalry made a charge. Not knowing our position, and the indefinite orders I had received as to location, made me apprehend a collision with our own troops, which did occur to a limited extent. As soon as General Lee's left was ascertained, a squadron of the Second Virginia Cavalry was advanced, and became engaged with the enemy's sharpshooters, who were strongly posted in a heavily timbered piece of woods and a pine thicket. The sharpshooters of the brigade, under Captains [C. T.] Litchfield, James Breckinridge, and [G. D.] White, of the First, Second, and Third Regiments, were now ordered to the front, to dislodge the enemy [who had wounded several of Colonel Watts's men], which object they effected, after a stubborn resistance on the part of the enemy. They encountered both infantry and dismounted cavalry skirmishers. A good opportunity now presenting itself, three of Captain Breathed's guns were run up by hand, and opened simultaneously on a brigade of cavalry supporting a battery, which caused them to stampede. Seeing this, I pressed on the sharpshooters, and hurried the brigade down the road to Welford's house, at the same time sending Captain Ferguson, the efficient assistant adjutant-general of this brigade, with the Whitworth gun and two squadrons of the Second Virginia Cavalry, to cut off the enemy's retreat by Welford's Ford. Our sharpshooters, though contending against double their numbers, drove the enemy steadily back, and, on arriving on the hill below Welford's house, I saw between that place and Green's house a division of cavalry, a brigade of infantry, and two or three detachments of dismounted cavalry. Here again Captain Breathed used his artillery with effect. The enemy's right flank being protected by infantry, artillery, and twice our number of sharpshooters, made it impracticable at any time to engage them in a hand-to-hand fight; but they were driven until they crossed the river, the infantry and dismounted men moving down the railroad and crossing at the bridge.[26]

---

26. *OR* 27/2:737–38. Munford noted that only the sharpshooters of his brigade were actually engaged; Whitehead, "The Campaigns of Munford's 2nd Virginia Cavalry," 65.

The battle of Brandy Station has been called a tactical draw by many historians. The Confederates had been surprised but were still able to drive off the Federals while suffering fewer losses. Before Kelly's Ford on March 17 and Brandy Station, the Federal cavalry was seen as clearly inferior to the Confederate cavalry. At Brandy Station, the Union troopers proved they could ride and fight with the South's best. They gained confidence in themselves and their commanders. This proved invaluable in upcoming battles.

The predawn attack by the Federals had surprised Stuart at Brandy Station, but after a day-long fight, the Confederates held the field after suffering substantial losses. The Union cavalry was also surprised. Stuart's reputation was tarnished in the eyes of the press; his aura of invincibility was destroyed. Some claimed this turn of events might have played on Stuart's mind, leading to what some claimed as his "puzzling performance" during the days up to and including the battle of Gettysburg. The Union cavalry fought on even terms at Brandy Station that day, and they would be a force to be reckoned with for the rest of the war.[27]

Robert E. Lee always believed that the Confederacy could not win the war by remaining on the defensive, and instead but must achieve a decisive victory on Northern soil. The morale of Lee's soldiers was high after the victories at Fredericksburg and Chancellorsville. Southern soldiers and their commanders, thought they were more or less invincible. Meanwhile on June 27, after the battle of Brandy Station, Lincoln replaced General Hooker with Maj. Gen. George Gordon Meade as commander of the Army of the Potomac.[28]

At the outset of Lee's northern invasion, Ewell's II Corps led the Confederate advance to Pennsylvania, while Longstreet's I Corps marched to Culpeper. A. P. Hill's III Corps remained at Fredericksburg until Hooker's intentions could be ascertained. Hooker, ordered to protect Washington, soon left the Fredericksburg area. J.E.B. Stuart's role was to operate on Lee's right flank and screen the Army of Northern Virginia's movements from the Union army. Pleasonton was ordered to determine Lee's movements by fighting through Stuart's screen.[29]

Wade Hampton's and Grumble Jones's cavalry brigades remained on the Rappahannock in order to maintain contact with A. P. Hill. Meantime, Stuart took Robertson's, Fitz Lee's (still under Munford),

---

27. Sears, *Gettysburg*, 73–74; Wert, *Cavalryman of the Lost Cause*, 251; Eric J. Wittenberg, *The Union Cavalry Comes of Age* (Washington, D. C., 2003), 311.
28. Sears, *Gettysburg*, 90, 123.
29. Ibid., 83–84, 94, 97, 105.

and Rooney Lee's troopers to guard Longstreet's right and front. Rooney Lee (replaced by Col. John R. Chambliss) suffered a severe wound at Brandy Station and was taken to Col. Williams Wickham's residence in Hanover County to recuperate, but a Federal raiding party learned of his location and captured him. He was later exchanged. Fitz Lee was suffering a bout of inflammatory rheumatism of the knee, and Colonel Munford, now a reliable, experienced cavalry officer, took over temporary command of Lee's brigade.[30]

Munford dispatched a picket with instructions to hold a reserve at the intersection of Leesburg and Little River pike, with vedettes out on each road. He recalled, "Three miles below Middleburg, I moved the command to the Snicker's Gap pike, remaining on the pike myself, and sent the command to Mr. Franklin Carter's to feed their horses and to bring corn enough for [the] night and morning before we went into camp."[31]

Battle of Aldie

The battle of Aldie occurred on June 17, 1863, in Loudoun County as part of the Gettysburg campaign. Stuart's cavalry screened Gen. Robert E. Lee's infantry as it marched north in the Shenandoah Valley behind the sheltering Blue Ridge Mountains.[32]

Late in the spring of 1863, tensions grew between Union commander General Hooker and his cavalry commander Pleasonton because of the latter's inability to penetrate Stuart's cavalry screen. Pleasonton failed to gain access to the Shenandoah Valley to locate the Army of Northern Virginia, which had been on the move since the battle of Chancellorsville. On June 17, Pleasonton decided to push through Stuart's screen. To accomplish his goal, he ordered Brig. Gen. David McMurtie Gregg's division from Manassas Junction westward down the Little River Turnpike to Aldie. Aldie was tactically important because the Little River Turnpike intersected both Ashby's Gap Turnpike and Snicker's Gap Turnpike, which respectively led through Ashby's Gap and Snicker's Gap of the Blue Ridge Mountains into the valley.[33]

Stuart ordered Colonel Munford, temporarily commanding Fitz Lee's brigade, toward Aldie, via Middleburg, with the view, if possible,

---

30. Longacre, *Lee's Cavalrymen*, 197; McClellan, *Campaigns of Stuart's Cavalry*, 296.
31. *OR* 27/2:739; Driver, *2nd Virginia Cavalry*, 83, 85.
32. Sears, *Gettysburg*, 83–84, 94, 97, 105.
33. Mark Nesbitt, *Saber and Scapegoat: J.E.B. Stuart and the Gettysburg Controversy* (Mechanicsburg, PA, 1994), 46.

to hold the gap in Bull Run Mountain as a screen to Longstreet's movements. Lee, having yet another bout of inflammatory rheumatism, rode in an ambulance until June 22, whereupon he resumed command of his brigade. W. H. F. "Rooney" Lee's brigade was kept near the plains, reconnoitering to Thoroughfare Gap, while Robertson's brigade was halted near Rectortown, to move to the support of either. Stuart accompanied Munford as far as Middleburg, where he remained to close up the command and keep in easier communication with the rear.[34]

Early on June 17, Munford led the 2nd and 3rd Virginia eastward on a reconnaissance and forage mission, across Loudoun Valley from Upperville, through Middleburg, to Aldie in the Bull Run Mountains. He established a line of pickets east of Aldie to watch for enemy activity and then withdrew his two regiments northwest of town on the Snicker's Gap Turnpike to camp on the farm of Franklin Carter.[35]

About 4:00 p.m., Brig. Gen. H. Judson Kilpatrick's brigade of the 2nd and 4th New York, 6th Ohio, 1st Maine, 1st Rhode Island, and 1st Massachusetts arrived in Aldie. Just west of the village, the 1st Massachusetts encountered Munford's pickets and drove them back. Around the same time, the rest of Munford's brigade—the 1st, 4th, and 5th Virginia Cavalry, under the command of Col. Williams C. Wickham—arrived at Dover Mills, a small hamlet on the Little River west of Aldie. Wickham ordered Col. Thomas L. Rosser to take the 5th Virginia, which had arrived at Dover Mills, to pass beyond and select a campsite closer to Aldie. As they moved east, Rosser's 5th Virginia ran into the Massachusetts horsemen and easily drove them back through Aldie to the main Union body, relieving pressure on Munford's pickets. Rosser positioned his sharpshooters (50 men of Company I under Capt. Reuben F. Boston) east of William Adam's farmhouse on the right of the Snickersville Road. He then deployed west along a ridge that covered the two roads leading out of Aldie and awaited the arrival of the Federals, as well as for Munford and Wickham. As Munford arrived, he stationed Lt. William Walton of the 2nd Virginia, with one reserve picket of 15 men, behind a stone wall on the left of Snickersville Road. Munford ordered Walton to hold the position "until death," against all odds until the remainder of the 2nd

---

34. *OR* 27/2:688; George N. Bliss, "A Review of Aldie," Maine Bugle (1894), vol. 1:131; Thomas T. Munford to Robert E. Lee, March 18, 1866, Robert E. Lee Collection, Leyburn Library, Washington and Lee University. Munford recalled many years later that Fitz Lee had been earlier kicked by a mule or horse, incapacitating him). Munford commanded the brigade until June 22.
35. *OR* 27/2:688, 739–40; Thomas Munford to George Bliss, April 26, 1884, *The Maine Bugle*, Campaign I, Call 1 (published by the Maine Association, 1894), 131–32; McClellan, *The Campaigns of Stuart's Cavalry*, 296–97.

and 3rd Virginia regiments arrived to assist. Artillerist Maj. Henry H. Matthews recalled Munford at Aldie:

> Those of us knew the material that Tom Munford was made out of can fully realize what he meant when he gave Lt. Walton those orders. He did not play with words. On the contrary, he was a man of few words. Like the great Stonewall Jackson, he spoke only when he intended his orders should be carried out to the letter. Such was the noble soldier and gentleman that led the 2nd Virginia Cavalry on many a bloody field of battle.[36]

In the meantime, Colonel Wickham was positioning the 1st and 4th Virginia and Capt. James Breathed's battery to dispute any Federal advance up the Middleburg Road. As Rosser withdrew west, the 1st Massachusetts, with aid from the 4th New York, charged against what they believed to be a retreat. Rosser's line held, and he mounted a countercharge in concert with a sharp volley from the sharpshooters he had placed on his left. He easily drove the Federals back, securing his hold on the Ashby's Gap Turnpike. Munford then repositioned Rosser's 5th Virginia, 4th Virginia, and one gun from Breathed's battery so as to command Snickersville Road.[37]

Judson Kilpatrick turned his attention towards the Snicker's Gap Turnpike. An artillery duel ensued as more cavalry on both sides arrived. A furious fight erupted, which at first went in favor of Munford as Federal charges were met, stopped, and then forced back by the withering volley of sharpshooters entrenched along the stone wall. The 1st Massachusetts Cavalry was trapped in a blind curve on the Snicker's Gap Turnpike and practically destroyed, losing 198 of 294 men in the eight companies that were engaged. One detachment of the 1st Massachusetts, under Maj. Henry Lee Higginson, was virtually wiped out in hand-to-hand fighting. Captain Charles Adams of the 1st Massachusetts described the horrific destruction of his squadron's men and their mounts:

> My poor men were just slaughtered and all we could do was to stand still and be shot down, while the other squadrons rallied behind us. The men fell right and left and the horses were shot through and through, and no man turned his back. . . . I fell slowly back to some woods. Here I was ordered to dismount my men. . . . I gave the order and the men were just off their horses . . .

---

36. *OR* 27/2:688, 739–41; McClellan, *The Campaigns of Stuarts Cavalry*, 297-98; Trout, ed., *Memoirs of the Stuart Horse Artillery Battalion, Vol. 2: Breathed's and McGregor's Batteries*, 83.
37. *OR* 27/2:688, 739–41; McClellan, *The Campaigns of Stuarts Cavalry*, 297–98.

and in a second the rebs were riding yelling and slashing among us. . . . In twenty minutes . . . I lost thirty- two as good men and horses as can be found in the cavalry corps.[38]

The tide of battle finally turned as Union reinforcements of David M. Gregg's cavalry charged into the fray in the fading light. Colonel William Stedman's 6th Ohio overran Boston's detachment on the Ashby's Gap Turnpike, capturing or killing most of his men. The fighting died down around 8:00 p.m. Stuart, who was not involved in the Aldie fight, ordered Munford to disengage, because his troopers were needed at another engagement at nearby Middleburg. The "engagement" turned out to be Stuart's near capture by the 5th Michigan, while Stuart was dining with Brig. Gen. Asa Rogers at his residence.[39]

Munford wrote of capturing 168 prisoners and 137 horses, moving his dead and wounded back as he retired, while 30 to 40 Union dead were left on the field. Mumford's total losses were 119, of which 58 came from Rosser's 5th Virginia. Munford also reported, "I do not hesitate to say that I have never seen as many Yankees killed in the same space of ground in any fight I have ever seen, or any battlefield in Virginia that I have been over." General Stuart added, "at Aldie ensued one of the most sanguinary cavalry battles of the war, and at the same time most credible to our arms and glorious to the veteran brigade of Brig. Gen. Fitz Lee." It was Munford who gallantly led Fitz Lee's brigade at Aldie, fully responsible for solid leadership on the field of battle and without the aid of Stuart.[40]

Munford did not consider Aldie a defeat, because his withdrawal coincided with an order from Stuart to retire as more Federal cavalry had been sighted at Middleburg. Union casualties were 305 dead and wounded, with one colonel, three captains, five lieutenants, and 129 non-commissioned officers and privates captured, with their horses and arms, representing seven regiments. The Confederates losses were 119, including Lt. Col. James W. Watts, who was seriously wounded in the right arm and henceforth disabled. Watts had been riding at the head of the regiment with Munford when he ran at a fence, cleared it,

---

38. Robert F. O'Neill, "Aldie, Middleburg, and Upperville," *Gettysburg: Historical Articles of Lasting Interest,* Issue Number 43:20; Worthington C. Ford, ed., *A Cycle of Adams Letters, 1861–1865,* 2 Volumes (Boston, MA, 1920), vol. 2:25, 30, 36–37; Longacre, *Lee's Cavalrymen,* 197–98.
39. OR 27/2:741; McClellan, *The Campaigns of Stuart's Cavalry,* 302–03; Thomas T. Munford to Robert E. Lee, March 18, 1866, Robert E. Lee Collection, Washington and Lee University; Thomas T. Munford to an unidentified Major, circa 1885, Munford–Ellis Papers, DU.
40. OR 27/2:739–41; Thomas T. Munford to Robert E. Lee, March 18, 1866, Robert E. Lee Collection, Washington and Lee University.

and landed among the enemy. One trooper "saw him, standing in his stirrups knock a Yankee off his horse with his sabre," before he was shot by one of the blue horsemen. Aldie was the first in a series of cavalry fights along the Ashby's Gap Turnpike in which Stuart's forces successfully delayed Pleasonton's thrust across the Loudoun Valley, thereby depriving him of the opportunity to locate Lee's army.[41]

Munford's brigade continued to defend the approaches to Snicker's Gap. On June 21, Munford's troopers were challenged by Col. William Gamble's cavalry brigade, composed of the 8th New York, 8th Illinois, three squadrons of the 3rd Indiana, two squadrons of the 12th Illinois, and one section of the 1st United States Artillery, in all some 1,600 strong. Gamble's brigade, detached from Buford's 1st Division and assigned to David M. Gregg's division, was on a reconnaissance mission headed for Snicker's Gap. Gamble's cavalry skirmishers met Munford's cavalry near the bridge over Goose Creek, west of Middleburg, and succeeded in driving Munford's troopers to Philomont. The blue troopers pushed Munford's riders on through the streets and beyond the town a short distance. Here, Munford's troopers stiffened at the base of a mountain west of Upperville. As Gamble's regiments charged, hand-to-hand fighting ensued. Finally, Munford's horsemen overpowered the Union cavalry, attempting to turn both flanks. Squadrons of the 8th Illinois and 3rd Indiana were deployed to cover the flanks. After a sharp exchange, Munford pulled his regiments back and headed for Ashby's Gap, two miles to the rear. Gamble had won the fight, but failed in the object of the expedition—locating Gen. Robert E. Lee's latest position. Munford, though pushed by Gamble, succeeded in holding him back from the approaches to Snicker's Gap. To the east lay Robert E. Lee's headquarters, situated in the Shenandoah Valley. Thwarted, Gamble's command returned to their camp at Aldie the next day. That evening Jones camped near Bloomfield while Munford bivouacked near Union.[42]

Munford remained at his post guarding the approaches to Snicker's Gap during the June 12 battle at Upperville. Fitz Lee returned to health and assumed command of his brigade on June 22.[43]

Stuart sought guidance from Robert E. Lee for the raid into Pennsylvania and received vague suggestions from Longstreet and orders from Lee, stating, "If you find that he [Hooker] is moving northward, and that two brigades can guard the Blue Ridge and take

---

41. "Autobiography of St. George Tucker Brooke," 2, VHS; *OR* 27/2:741; Whitehead, "Campaigns of Munford's 2nd Virginia Cavalry," 70–71.
42. *OR* 27/1:932–33.
43. Driver, *2nd Virginia Cavalry*, 89.

care of your rear, you can move with the other three into Maryland, and take position on General [Richard] Ewell's right, place yourself in communication with him, guard his flank, keep him informed of the enemy's movements, and collect all the supplies you can for the use of the army."[44]

Stuart had ordered the brigades of Beverly H. Robertson and Grumble Jones to guard the passes in the Blue Ridge Mountains, certain that they could join Lee before any general battle ensued. Robertson's brigade was a small one, consisting of two under-strength North Carolina regiments. Stuart despised Jones, and Robertson outranked Jones by date of promotion; thus, Robertson led the two brigades of 2,700 troopers on their mission. These brigades would not be able to do the necessary scouting and screening for Robert E. Lee that he needed. Stuart had been given wide latitude by Lee; a general engagement was not planned for Gettysburg. Lee's army, now in Pennsylvania, became blind to the disposition and movement of the Northern army. Stuart, under orders to report to Ewell, had taken a long, circuitous raid around the Union Army and was not able to hook up with Ewell. The movements of the Federals had forced Stuart so far east that he had to cross the Potomac only 20 miles from Washington.[45]

Three cavalry brigades were assigned to march with Stuart; Fitz Lee's, Rooney Lee's, and Hampton's. The three brigades rendezvoused near Salem Depot on June 24, marched through Glascock's Gap, and proceeded to Haymarket the next morning. Encountering Federal infantry of Gen. Winfield Scott Hancock's II Corps, Stuart withdrew, went south and around them, and camped at Gum Springs for the night. Stuart ordered Fitz Lee's brigade to Gainesville on the Manassas Gap Railroad, where it bivouacked for the night.[46]

Stuart's southeasterly detour around Hancock's army continued the next day, crossing the Orange & Alexandria Railroad at Bristoe Station before continuing to Brentsville. Turning north, Stuart's troopers headed for Wolf Run Shoals on the Occoquan River, where they spent the night. The next day, Stuart re-crossed the Orange & Alexandria Railroad west of Alexandria and he, Hampton, and Chambliss headed for the depot at Fairfax Station. Stuart ordered Fitz Lee's brigade to Burke's Station to cut telegraph lines and demolish tracks. Having completed his assigned task, Fitz Lee's brigade headed

---

44. Robert E. Lee to J.E.B. Stuart, June 22, 1863; *OR* 27/3:913.
45. Edward G. Longacre, *The Cavalry at Gettysburg: A Tactical Study of Mounted Operations during the Civil War's Pivotal Campaign, 9 June–14 July, 1863* (Lincoln, NE, 1986), 154.
46. Driver, *2nd Virginia Cavalry*, 89; *OR* 27/2:688, part 3:913–915, 923.

for Annandale, northwest of Stuart's position. Both raiding parties seized and plundered food goods and sutlers' stores. Stuart and Fitz Lee let their hungry troopers eat for a while before resuming the march. Rejoining at Dranesville, Stuart and Fitz Lee's cavalrymen headed for the Potomac, crossing in darkness at Rowzer's Mill Ford, north of Dumfries. Completing their crossing at 3:00 a.m., they were then in Pennsylvania. Esten Cooke recalled watching the rear guard's crossing from the Maryland side of the Potomac, "The picture was picturesque. The broad river glittering in the moon, and on the bright surface was seen the long, wavering line of dark figures, moving in 'single file;' the water washing to and fro across the backs of the horses, which kept their feet with difficulty."[47]

Stuart immediately put his horsemen to work destroying the boats and docks on the Chesapeake and Ohio Canal, a major supply route to Hooker's army. Here, they captured 300 prisoners, and with the group taken at Fairfax Station, were sent under escort to Rockville, Maryland. While there, Stuart's hungry soldiers gathered rations for their empty haversacks and ate plenty. Corporal Charles E. Watts of the 2nd Virginia remembered, "During this time it was necessary to stop and graze the horses several times because there was no food in the country." Rufus Peck of the 2nd Virginia recalled:

> Eight packet boats had been sent up with provisions for Hooker's army, and when they came into the docks not knowing we were there, we turned the wickets and let the water out and burned the boats. We had been marching four days without any provisions at all, so we took what we could in our haversacks, before burning the boats. We took the mules, 24 in number, on with us[48]

The next morning, Stuart's raiders headed for Rockville, only eight miles northwest of Washington. In Rockville, Hampton's brigade spied a supply column of more than 150 wagons, laden with goods for Hooker's army. Hampton's riders corralled the train. William Blackford, riding at the head of the column, wrote, "you could see nothing but the long ears and kicking legs of the mules sticking above bags of oats emptied from the wagons." Stuart was very pleased; he could now take 125 (25 had been overturned) of the wagons in tow and deliver some quality goods to Lee's army. The wagon train slowed

---

47. Longacre, *The Cavalry at Gettysburg*, 154; Longacre, *Lee's Cavalrymen*, 205, 207; *OR* 27/2:693–94; John Esten Cooke, *Wearing of the Gray* (Bedford, MA, 1867), 235.

48. *OR* 27/2:694; Longacre, *Lee's Cavalrymen*, 207; Driver, *2nd Virginia Cavalry*, 89; Peck, *Reminiscences of a Confederate Soldier, of Co. C of the 2nd Virginia Cavalry* (Fincastle, VA, 1913), 32.

Stuart's speed as they continued north, but the grain and other materials were badly needed by soldiers and mounts alike.[49]

On the morning of June 29, Stuart's slowing pace brought his command to the Baltimore & Ohio Railroad at Hood's Mill and Sykesville. Here, the Confederate raiders destroyed tracks, the railroad bridge at Sykesville, depot buildings, and trains. They also had to chase off a Union patrol farther south near Cookesville. Stuart's column, dragging the captured wagons, headed north and by 4:00 p.m. approached Westminster, Maryland. Stuart realized by this time he could have been in Pennsylvania aiding Ewell. Entering town, Stuart encountered 95 determined troopers of Companies C and D of the 1st Delaware Cavalry of the VIII Corps. They were led by Maj. Napoleon B. Knight, with Capt. Charles Corbit and Lt. Caleb Churchman as company commanders. In Major Knight's absence, Captain Corbit led a charge of his men through the streets of Westminster to Washington Road. Expecting to overcome a small unit of Confederates, they found themselves facing a large body of General Stuart's veteran cavalry. The unwavering Federal troopers charged Stuart's advance guard, igniting a fierce skirmish. The Delaware unit, however, was quickly overpowered. Many were captured, including Captain Corbit and Lieutenant Churchman. Sixty-seven Union troopers were killed, wounded, or taken prisoner. Two Confederate officers of the 4th Virginia were killed and four others badly wounded. Instead of proceeding into Pennsylvania to inform Gen. Robert E. Lee about the major Union troop movements, Stuart's cavalry was delayed long enough, as the result of the skirmish, to make it preferable to spend the night just north of Westminster. Fitz Lee's brigade, leading the advance guard, stopped at Union Mills, midway between Westminster and Littlestown on the Gettysburg Road. Stuart's scouts determined that Federal cavalry had encamped for the evening at Lillestown, seven miles north of Union Mills.[50]

The next morning, June 30, Stuart headed for Hanover, Pennsylvania, with Rooney Lee's brigade in the advance, Hampton in the rear of the wagon train, and Fitz Lee moving on the left flank. At 10:00 a.m., the head of the column approached Hanover and ran into the rear of Brig. Gen. Elon J. Farnsworth's cavalry brigade. The Union horsemen were heading straight for the gap in the mountains that Stuart intended to use. Upon seeing Stuart's column, the Union troopers demonstrated, as if preparing to attack. Chambliss's brigade, led by Lt. Col. Jefferson C. Phillips's 13th Virginia, promptly attacked

---

49. William W. Blackford, *War Years with JEB Stuart*, 224; *OR* 27/2:694; Longacre, *Lee's Cavalrymen*, 208; Longacre, *The Cavalry at Gettysburg*, 155.
50. *OR* 27/2:694–95, part 3:396, 403–04; Longacre, *Lee's Cavalrymen*, 208–09.

and repulsed Farnworth's horsemen. The Virginians drove the 18th Pennsylvania Cavalry pell-mell through Hanover, capturing a large number of prisoners and their ambulances. Behind the Union cavalry advance was a larger body of Meade's cavalry, which Stuart would have charged if his elongated column had closed up, but they were spread out. Besides, Stuart was now very anxious to proceed and get to the Susquehanna River as quickly as possible.[51]

Stuart faced a dilemma as his path intersected with the Federal horsemen of Kilpatrick's 3rd Division, who had an hour earlier entered Hanover, heading west for the 12-mile distance to Gettysburg. Stuart faced Kilpatrick's troopers protecting the center of Meade's army, while David M. Gregg covered the right and John Buford the left. Stuart was determined to keep his captured wagon train. Lacking the possibility of turning around, he had to face straight ahead and fight the blue horsemen to get through town. Chambliss was counterattacked by Farnsworth's New Yorkers. To prevent Chambliss from being swept back, Stuart brought forward two cannons from McGregor's battery, placing them to the left on Plum Creek. The guns kept the Yankee cavalry at bay, while Lt. Col. William H. Payne's 2nd North Carolina flanked them, attacking the remaining portion of the 18th Pennsylvania and scattering it.[52]

Payne pursued them, but soon was stopped by reformed 18th Pennsylvanians and Farnsworth's New Yorkers. Unable to support Payne with either Hampton's or Fitz Lee's troopers due to their positions covering the wagon train and about 400 prisoners, Payne and his North Carolinians had to withdraw. Soon the retreating Tarheels, without Payne, who had been captured, were fleeing town and Chambliss's line appeared ready to collapse. Finally, at about 2:00 p.m., the 1st Virginia regiment arrived, along with Stuart's other four guns from Breathed's battery. Soon, Hampton had the guns set up at Mount Olivet Cemetery and began firing at a large detachment of horse soldiers, who seemed ready to attack. The shelling, along with the ready-to-charge Col. Pierce Young's horsemen of Cobb's Legion, discouraged the blue troopers from attempting to flank Hampton.[53]

Soon, Hampton had dislodged the Federal horsemen from their position. Meanwhile, Fitz Lee was facing part of George Armstrong's Custer's brigade on his left. Part of Custer's Michigan cavalry brigade broke through Stuart's line twice on the Union right, but countercharges drove them off. The Wolverines soon moved over to

---

51. *OR* 27/2:695.
52. McClellan, *Campaigns of Stuart's Cavalry*, 327–28; Longacre, *Lee's Cavalry*, 210.
53. *OR* 27/2:696; McClellan, *Campaigns of Stuart's Cavalry*, 328–29; Longacre, *Lee's Cavalry*, 211; Longacre, *The Cavalry at Gettysburg*, 177.

the right side. As a precaution, Stuart formed his wagons in close quarters, prepared to burn them if he had to abandon them. Stuart's right, having been relieved by Hampton, permitted the cavalry commander to send Fitz Lee to move forward with the train, through Jefferson toward York, Pennsylvania. Pressured to join Ewell and Lee, Stuart held on until dark, then quietly slipped away. Kilpatrick, having had enough, did not hinder Stuart's movement north.[54]

As soon as the sun set, Stuart transferred custody of the wagon train to Fitz Lee and sent him on towards Jefferson. During the night march through Jefferson, the nearly 400 prisoners, many loaded in the wagons, and the wagon train itself were a further hindrance. The mules pulling the wagons were starving and often unmanageable. Everyone was fatigued. Whenever the column stopped for any reason except fighting during the entire Pennsylvania march, the troopers and horses were fast asleep. When Fitz Lee reached the road leading from York to Gettysburg, he discovered that Ewell had retraced his steps and headed west. It appeared at that time that the Confederate army was concentrating its forces near Shippensburg. Meanwhile, after a short hiatus at Dover on the morning of July 1, Stuart pressed on towards Carlisle, hoping he could get provisions for his starving troopers. One trooper remembered, "All the provisions we had on this march, except what some of us got at the boats [at Annandale], was what we could beg from citizens. Some of us nearly starved."[55]

Stuart pushed on and, upon arriving at Carlisle, fired some artillery shells into the Union-held town, burning the United States Government barracks. His troopers also destroyed a Federal supply depot. On the evening of July 1, Stuart learned that Lee's army was concentrated at Gettysburg. He immediately set out with his command for the scene of the main battle. When he arrived on July 2, he and his men and horses were exhausted from hard riding and frequent fighting, and were in no condition to effectively battle the Federal Army. Rufus Peck recalled, "As we had been marching so much and had so little rest since June 20, we all laid down in a stubble field and were soon fast asleep." Peck was so exhausted that the cannon fire during the night did not awaken him, nor the fact that he had been dragged 30 yards by his horse seeking grass. Rosser recalled, "Stuart had been marching constantly, almost day and night, on scant forage and little rest for man or horse, for eight days, within the enemy's

---

54. *OR* 27/2:696; Edward G. Longacre, *The Cavalry at Gettysburg*, 174–178; McClellan, *Campaigns of Stuart's Cavalry*, 329; Longacre, *Lee's Cavalry*, 211.

55. Peck, *Reminiscences of a Confederate Soldier*, 32; *OR* 27/2:696; McClellan, *Campaigns of Stuart's Cavalry*, 330; Longacre, *Lee's Cavalry*, 213; Longacre, *The Cavalry at Gettysburg*, 178.

lines, and while his conduct displayed a daring almost to recklessness, he accomplished little, save the wear and fatigue of long marches. He had undoubtedly impaired the strength and vigor of his command."[56]

What happened when Stuart and Robert E. Lee met on July 2 has long been the subject of controversy. As there were no known witnesses at Lee's headquarters besides Lee and Stuart; only Lee and Stuart knew what was said between them. If Henry B. McClellan had accompanied Stuart to Lee's headquarters, Lee certainly would have dismissed him from the meeting with Stuart. Lee would also have dismissed his aides, Charles Marshall and Charles Venable. Neither Lee nor Stuart (nor Marshall or Venable) ever talked or wrote about the meeting. According to Thomas Munford, however, Maj. H.B. McClellan did witness the exchange and told him of it, because many years later Munford told details of the event. Perhaps McClellan overheard a heated conversation between Lee and Stuart. According to the unsubstantiated account by Munford, McClellan thought the meeting "was painful beyond description." The story goes that "Lee reddened at sight of Stuart and raised his arm as if he would strike him. 'General Stuart, where have you been?'" "Stuart seemed to 'wilt,' and explained his movements to Lee. 'I have not heard a word from you for days,' Lee said, 'and you the eyes and ears of my army.' 'I have brought you 125 wagons and their teams, General,' Stuart said. 'Yes, General, but they are an impediment to me now.'" His manner abruptly became one "of great tenderness," and he said to Stuart, "Let me ask your help now. We will not discuss this matter longer. Help me fight these people." According to Munford, McClellan is the only person who witnessed the exchange between Lee and Stuart. Munford recalled that McClellan later told him about the meeting.[57]

---

56. Peck, *Reminiscences of a Confederate Soldier*, 32–33; Driver, *2nd Virginia Cavalry*, 90; Thomas L. Rosser, *Addresses of Gen'l T. L. Rosser, at the Seventh Annual Reunion of the Association of the Maryland Line, Academy of Music, Baltimore, Md., February 22, 1889, and on Memorial Day, Staunton, Va., June 8, 1889* (New York, 1889), 41. Rosser also despised Stuart, but only behind his back to his wife. Stuart probably never knew of Rosser's loathing of him.

57. Burke Davis, *JEB Stuart: The Last Cavalier*, 334, says, "Major McClellan and Colonel Munford, among others, witnessed their meeting." Munford, however, was at least 20 miles away from Gettysburg with the main column of Stuart's cavalry when Stuart arrived in Gettysburg. Davis's footnote, on page 435, says, "This striking, and perhaps astonishing, scene is created almost verbatim from an account in the Anne Bachman Hyde Papers, University of North Carolina's Wilson Library." Actually, it was in a letter from Munford to Anne Bachman Hyde, dated July 24, 1915. Stuart never mentioned such a dressing-down by Lee, even to his wife, Flora. John Esten Cooke recalled that Stuart rode on to Gettysburg alone after camping out with his staff the night before (*Wearing of the Gray*, p. 246), on the way to report to Lee–if so, McClellan would not have been with Stuart to hear such a

Munford thought McClellan "a gentleman, and a scholar, a chivalrous soldier who acted well his part in all the relations of his career. He and I were always friends." Munford recalled McClellan's "sweet tenor voice."[58]

Munford believed Stuart "was a splendid fighter and in a raid and with a small command in action handled his troops with dash—but he did not foster his horses. Worked them for glory and newspaper notoriety—always had a Bohemian to blow a trumpet. His vanity was intense."[59]

In preparation for the resumption of battle on July 3, Robert E. Lee ordered Stuart to protect the Confederate left flank and to attempt to move around the Union right flank. This flanking maneuver would hopefully draw Union strength away from the center, where Pickett was to attack. Lee ordered Stuart to attack the Federal rear if a breakthrough was achieved. If Stuart's horsemen could proceed south from the York Pike along the Low Dutch Road, they would soon reach the Baltimore Pike, the main avenue of communications for the Union army. They could then observe the Union rear and launch

---

conversation. Allen C. Guelzo (*Gettysburg: The Last Invasion*, p. 571) states, "In 1913 Walter Kempster (who had been a lieutenant in the 10th New York Cavalry at Gettysburg) put exactly the same words in Lee's mouth, based upon seeing "a letter" when Kempster had been "in Gettysburg recently." Kempster claimed the letter was written by one of Stuart's brigadiers, who was present with Stuart when he reported his arrival to Gen. Lee." It may be significant that the 50th anniversary reunion of Gettysburg had just taken place that summer, and Munford had attended. Adding to the mystery, Thomas Nelson Page recorded the same words and the same meeting in his 1911 biography, Robert E. Lee, Man and Soldier, and adds some additional dialogue, "When Stuart explained and mentioned his capturing over two hundred wagons . . . Lee exclaimed, "Two hundred wagons! General Stuart, what are two hundred wagons to this army!" It's hard to believe Lee would dress down Stuart in this manner, as from his perspective, Lee had a "father-son" relationship with Stuart. Then again, it's difficult to believe, but possible, Munford would just make up the story. It's true Munford despised Stuart after Gettysburg, but to hold such a grudge for fifty years is also hard to imagine. Also, it is difficult to believe McClellan would invent such a tale. Perhaps, the story got started from speculation as to what was said in Lee's tent, and then the story took on a life of its own. The mystery will most likely never be solved. A letter from Theodore S. Garnett to Munford, dated July 1913, proves Munford, even though 82 years old at the time of the Gettysburg Reunion in 1913, attended the event; Thomas T. Munford to Anne Bachman Hyde, July 24, 1915, Anne Bachman Hyde Papers, University of North Carolina, Chapel Hill. This is the most detailed known account of the famed confrontation of Lee and Stuart, and the one the 1993 movie, "Gettysburg," is based upon.

58. Thomas T. Munford to Anne Bachman Hyde, August 29, 1915, Anne Bachman Hyde Papers, University of North Carolina, Chapel Hill.
59. Thomas T. Munford to John C. Ropes, May 21, 1898, Howard Gotlieb Archival Center, Boston University, Boston, Massachusetts.

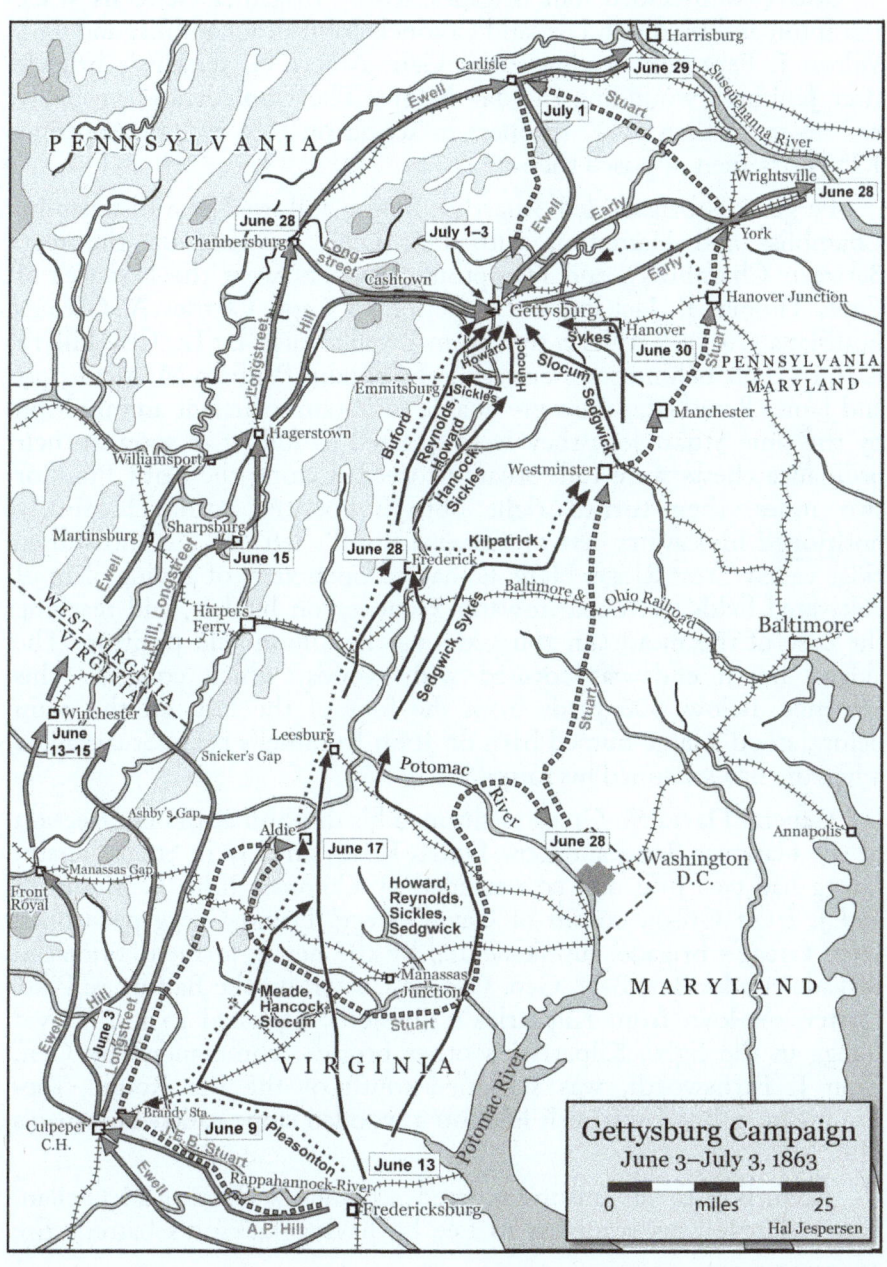

devastating attacks against the rear of Meade's army, perhaps even a breakthrough, if Lee's attack on the Union center was successful.[60]

Stuart commanded four brigades, led by Brigadier Generals Wade Hampton and Fitzhugh Lee, and Colonels John R. Chambliss and Col. Milton J. Ferguson, leading Brig. Gen. Albert G. Jenkins's brigade after Jenkins's wounding the day before. The Confederates probably had no more than 3,400 troopers in action on July 3rd. Pleasonton's 3,250 horsemen opposed them.[61]

Ferguson's brigade led Stuart's column, followed at a distance by Chambliss and Hampton, with Fitz Lee's bringing up the rear. Between Chambliss's and Hampton's troopers were the batteries of Capt. Thomas E. Jackson and a section of Capt. Charles A. Green's Louisiana Guard Artillery, sent from Ewell's corps by Lt. Col. Hilary P. Jones. Left behind were batteries of Captains William M. McGregor and James Breathed, who were unable to obtain sufficient ammunition by the time Stuart left; they were ordered to follow as soon as their ordinance chests were full. Stuart proceeded along the York Pike for two miles, then turned right onto a country road. He finally positioned his cavalry left of General Ewell's left, on a commanding ridge called Cress Ridge. Here, he had an open view of a wide plain of cultivated fields stretching towards Hanover on his left, and reaching the base of the mountain spurs among the Union-held position. The ridge's north end was covered with woods, which concealed his presence. Below, 300 yards from the foot of the hill, on the plain below, stood a large-framed barn on John Rummel's farm. Stuart liked where he had stationed his forces.[62]

General David M. Gregg positioned his division at the intersection of the Hanover Road and Low Dutch Road, directly in Stuart's path. Gregg had two brigades, commanded by Colonels John B. McIntosh and J. Irvin Gregg, cousin of David Gregg. David Gregg positioned Irvin Gregg's brigade, supplemented by the newly formed "Michigan Brigade" under Bvt. Brig. Gen. George Custer, on the Baltimore Pike. Custer, on loan from Kilpatrick's division, requested to join David Gregg in the fight. Kilpatrick's other brigade, commanded by Gen. Elon J. Farnsworth, was stationed south of the Big Round Top-Emmitsburg Road skirmish line, on a wooded slope called Bushman's Hill.[63]

According to an unsubstantiated account by Henry McClellan, Stuart signaled his readiness to Lee by having Jackson's battery fire

---

60. *OR* 27/2:697–98.
61. Ibid., 698.
62. Longacre, *Lee's Cavalrymen*, 217; McClellan, *The Campaigns of Stuart's Cavalry*, 337–38.; Trout, *Galloping Thunder*, 290–91.
63. Longacre, *Lincoln's Cavalrymen*, 196–97.

four cannon shots from the East Cavalry Field at about 11:00 a.m. This would have also alerted David Gregg to his presence had not Gregg already known it. Gregg, commanding about 3,000 cavalrymen, ordered McIntosh and Custer into a blocking formation, opposing Stuart's 3,500 horsemen. The two sides engaged in an artillery duel, with the Union gunners of Lt. Alexander C. M. Pennington's Battery M of the 2nd U. S. Artillery having a decided advantage because of their longer-range guns and superior ordnance. Stuart wanted to pin down the Union troopers and swing around their left flank. The Michigan horsemen, however, armed with Spencer repeating rifles with increased firepower, prevented Stuart's flanking move. At about 1:00 p.m., Fitzhugh Lee's brigade made a direct charge, pushing back the Union skirmish line. Fitz's charge forced Stuart to commit Hampton to support him. Gregg ordered Custer to counterattack. Custer led the charge, shouting, "Come on, you Wolverines!" The fighting became furious with about 700 cavalrymen clashing at point-blank range. Custer's horse was shot out from under him; he quickly commandeered a bugler's mount. Stuart then sent in three regiments: Chambliss's 9th and 13th Virginia, Laurence Baker's 1st North Carolina, along with Hampton's Jeff Davis Legion, and squadrons from Fitz Lee's 2nd Virginia. This forced the Michigan troopers to retreat. The 2nd Virginia held the extreme left of the Confederate line northeast of John Rummel's farm.[64]

According to Pvt. Edward Colston of Company K of the 2nd Virginia, the mounted portion of the regiment moved to several locations but was not engaged that day. The dismounted troopers of the 2nd Virginia, however, were positioned on the extreme left of Lee's army. Here, two companies of the regiment fought with Federal sharpshooters, driving them back into the woods at the end of a large open field. Fitz Lee rode up to alert them that a squadron of between 15 to 20 mounted Union troopers was nearby. Lee ordered the Confederates to drive the Federal horsemen out of the woods, assuring them the enemy was only a small force. Fitz was wrong, and soon two regiments of Federal cavalrymen charged, nearly capturing Lee. Luckily, mounted Confederate horsemen came to the rescue, saving Lee and the dismounted troopers.[65]

When Stuart ordered the bulk of Hampton's brigade forward, Custer and Col. Charles Town led the 1st Michigan Cavalry into the

---

64. McClellan, *The Campaigns of Stuart's Cavalry*, 339, 344; Jeffrey D. Wert, *Cavalryman of the Lost Cause*, 287. McClellan is in error here. Guns from Jackson's battery of horse artillery were there, but Charles Griffin's battery was not anywhere near this area.
65. Edward Colston to Thomas T. Munford, April 15, 1886, Munford–Ellis Papers, DU; Edward Brugh to Thomas T. Munford, April 27, 1886, Munford–Ellis Papers, DU.

fray. McIntosh led his regiment against the Confederate right flank. Hampton was seriously wounded with a saber cut to his head and a gunshot to his thigh. His brigade withdrew when they were assaulted on three sides.[66]

The losses in 40 minutes of intense close-quarter fighting on the East Cavalry Field were as follows: 254 Union casualties, 219 of them from Custer's brigade; 181 Confederate. The fight was a strategic loss for Stuart and Robert E. Lee, whose hopes to successfully attack the Union rear were foiled. Lee sent word to Stuart he was going to withdraw the Army of Northern Virginia and head for Virginia. Stuart, failing to attack the Union army rear, maintained his position until nightfall, when he withdrew to the York Pike, leaving the 1st Virginia on picket duty. Stuart sent Fitz Lee's brigade to Cashtown to protect the wagon trains congregated there. He sent word to Robertson, who was on the right near Fairfield, to hold the Jack Mountain passes open.[67]

Meanwhile, southwest of Big Round Top Mountain, Brigadier Generals Wesley Merritt and Elon Farnsworth, under orders from Alfred Pleasonton, led two brigades on the left flank of the Union army. Merritt commanded the Reserve Brigade of Buford's division,

---

66. Longacre, *The Cavalry at Gettysburg*, 238. Wade Hampton, commenting on Stuart's Gettysburg Report, wrote Munford after the war, "I never read a more erroneous–to call it no harsher name–one that it was." Reference: Wade Hampton to Thomas T. Munford, December 18, 1897. Hampton was thought by many to be jealous of Stuart. At any rate, the two did not like each other. Ref: H. B. McClellan to Thomas T. Munford, February 20, 1904, Munford–Ellis Papers, DU.
67. *OR*, vol. 27, part 2, 699; McClellan, *The Campaigns of Stuart's Cavalry*, 341, 346. While the East Field cavalry fighting was raging, Thomas Munford's half-first cousin, Lieutenant John Henry Munford, of the Letcher Artillery, received a mortal head wound in Lee's July 3 attempt to storm Cemetery Ridge. He was brought back to Richmond where he died on August 8. Ref: Douglas Southall Freeman, *The South to Prosperity: An Introduction to the Writing of Confederate History* (Baton Rouge, LA, 1998), XX; Richmond Whig, August 18, 1863. Note: John Munford's half-cousin, Sallie Radford Munford (younger half-sister of Thomas T. Munford) had written John H. Munford a few days earlier, but her letter was not delivered. In it, Sallie told of the times in Richmond, "raids, and intended attacks by the Yankees upon our town, caused a good deal of excitement last week, which culminated when we learned the Yankees, reported 20,000 strong, were advancing in our direction. The Militia, were all called out, and yesterday, Sunday, the entire male population from 16 to 55, were occupied in drilling and manning the fortifications. There has been no alarm at all for no one dreamed that the city could be taken, but as Gen. Lee has telegraphed for more troops, before we could send them, it was necessary to find out what militia force we could count upon, and the display has been a most satisfactory one." Ref: Sallie Munford to John Munford, June 29, 1863, Munford–Ellis Papers, DU.

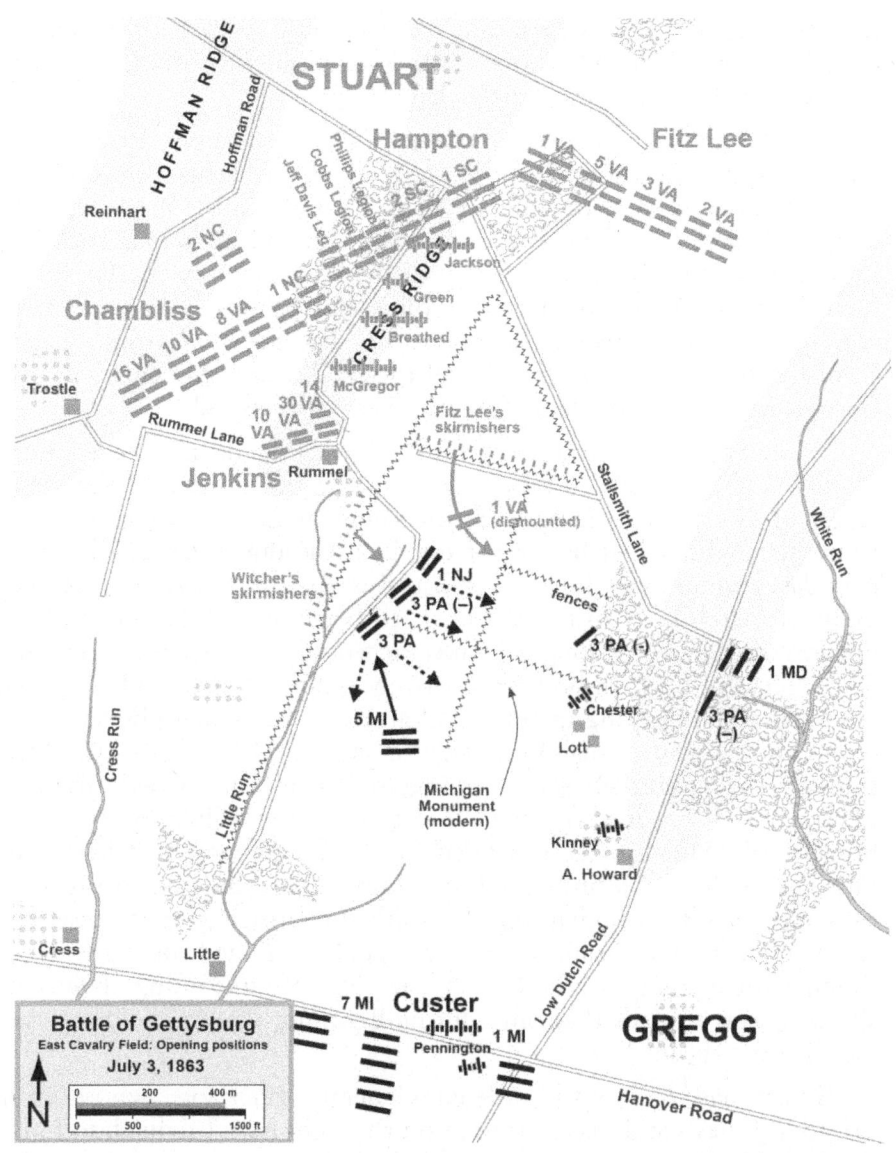

Map by Hal Jesperson

while Farnsworth led a brigade of Kilpatrick's division. About 1:00 p.m., Farnsworth's 1,925 troopers arrived at their assigned position in a line south of George Bushman's farm just as the Confederate bombardment of Cemetery Ridge commenced. Farnsworth's regiments were, west to east: 18th Pennsylvania Cavalry, 1st West Virginia, and the 1st Vermont. Battery E of the 4th U. S. Artillery occupied a small, rocky knoll in the rear, while the 5th New York Cavalry positioned itself in a nearby ravine to guard the artillery.

Kilpatrick joined Farnsworth and together they waited for Merritt's brigade, which arrived about 3:00 p.m., quickly straddling the Emmitsburg Road to Farnsworth's left.[68]

The Confederate forces to the east of Emmitsburg Road were infantry only. The four brigades of Brig. Gen. John Bell Hood's division, under the command of Brig. Gen. Evander W. Law, had escaped Round Top, through Devil's Den, and had regrouped back on Emmitsburg Road the day before. Initially, Law had only the 1st Texas Infantry facing Farnsworth to the south, but he was soon reinforced with the 47th Alabama Infantry, the 1st South Carolina, and Confederate artillery. To the west of the road, facing Merritt, was the Georgia brigade of Brig. Gen. George "Tige" Anderson.[69]

While Stuart was encamping on the York Pike during the evening of July 3, General Lee was withdrawing the main army to the west ridges of Gettysburg. Stuart did not know of Lee's movement until later that night, when he sought out Lee's headquarters. During the next day, a quite rainy July 4, Lee issued written instructions as to the order of march back to the Potomac, to begin at nightfall. The main portion of the 17-mile-long wagon train would be under the charge of Brig. Gen. John D. Imboden's relatively fresh troopers and mounts, who had accompanying infantry and artillery. Lee sent Imboden on a cross-country route, marching west along the Chambersburg Pike through the Cashtown Pass, turning south at Greenwood towards Marion, and passing through Greencastle to Williamsport. The brigades of Hampton (commanded by Gen. Laurence S. Baker) and Fitz Lee, including Munford's 2nd Virginia, were ordered to proceed by way of Cashtown, guarding the flank and bringing up the rear on the road from Greenville to Williamsport. It rained all night, one thunderstorm after another, with the rain often coming down in sheets. It was so dark that only during lightning flashes could anyone see what lay ahead.[70]

Stuart had previously ordered General Robertson, whose two brigades (Jones's and his own) were on the right near Fairfield, to hold the Jack Mountain passes open. This included two roads: one north, the other south of Jack Mountain (a peak in the Blue Ridge chain).[71]

---

68. Jeffery D. Wert, *Gettysburg, Day Three* (New York, 2002), 272.
69. Ibid., 273–75.
70. *OR* 27/2:699; McClellan, *The Campaigns of Stuart's Cavalry*, 349; Eric Wittenberg, J. David Petruzzi, and Michael F. Nugent, *One Continuous Fight: The Retreat from Gettysburg and the Pursuit of Lee's Army of Northern Virginia, July 4-14, 1863* (New York, 2008), 3,5; Diary of I. Norval Baker, 18th Virginia Cavalry, VMI Archives.
71. *OR* 27/2:699.

In the order of the retreating army march, Gen. A. P. Hill's Corps preceded everyone else across South Mountain through Monterey Pass; the baggage and prisoners of war were escorted by another corps. Longstreet occupied the center, and Ewell brought up the rear. The cavalry was dispatched as follows: two brigades (Hampton's and Fitz Lee's) on the Cashtown Road under Fitz Lee, with Munford commanding Fitz Lee's brigade. The remaining brigades, Jenkins's and Chambliss's, under Stuart's direct supervision, were to proceed by way of Emmitsburg, Maryland, guarding the retreating army. Stuart halted his command at dark, when it became extremely hard to see in the heavy rain and dense woods. He halted for several hours and procured the services of a good local guide. Resuming the march at daylight, Stuart's troopers reached Emmitsburg a little after dawn. They stopped for a short time and procured rations. Resuming the march on the road to Frederick, they reached the small village of Cooperstown, and paused to feed and rest the much-fatigued and hungry horses. After an hour, Stuart's horsemen continued, marching through Harbaugh's Valley, by Zion Church, and past the Catoctin Mountain.[72]

The road then forked before debauching from the mountain, one fork leading to the left by Smithtown, the other to the right bearing towards Leitersburg. Here, Stuart purposely divided his command in order to more likely assure at least half of the retreating cavalry would reach safety in Virginia. He sent Colonel Ferguson, commanding Jenkins's brigade, to the road on the right, while Chambliss's brigade, accompanied by Stuart, took the left road. Stuart's column met resistance from some of Kilpatrick's cavalry at the pass in the mountain, but with the aid of his artillery, he drove them away. Ferguson also met resistance, broke through, but was directed by Stuart to retreat and followed his path.[73]

Just before nightfall, Stuart sent dependable Pvt. Robert W. Goode of the 1st Virginia to inform Robert E. Lee of his position and what Lee needed to look out for en route. Stuart, after waiting for Colonel Ferguson to come up, proceeded towards Leitersburg in darkness.[74]

Fitz Lee's brigade, under Munford, was the last to leave Gettysburg on July 5. His mission was to act as rear guard for Lee's army as they retired along the Cashtown Road, heading for a crossing of the Potomac at Williamsport. The next day Munford's troopers skirmished with Union cavalry at Greenwood.[75]

---

72. *OR* 27/2:700; Driver, *2nd Virginia Cavalry*, 92; McClellan, *The Campaigns of Stuart's Cavalry*, 349–51.
73. *OR* 27/2:700; McClellan, *The Campaigns of Stuart's Cavalry*, 351.
74. *OR* 27/2:700; McClellan, *The Campaigns of Stuart's Cavalry*, 351–52.
75. Driver, *2nd Virginia Cavalry*, 92.

Meanwhile, on July 5, Kilpatrick's cavalry, including Custer's brigade, reached the road between Emmitsburg and Fairfield where Ewell's train was moving towards Williamsport. The Union troopers captured and destroyed a large number of wagons and took 1,360 prisoners. On July 6, Col. John Irvin Gregg chased Imboden's trains, albeit at a pace leading some to believe he really did not want to fight. At Greenwood, the Confederate caravan turned south, and Gregg's advance came up against Imboden's rear guard, including the 2nd Virginia. A small skirmish ensued, with the Federals claiming they took 100 prisoners and "a large quantity of wagons."[76]

On the morning of July 6, Stuart, being notified by Fitz Lee at Leitersburg that Kilpatrick's cavalry had headed towards Boonsboro, immediately set out for the town. Jones was nearly captured the previous night while getting separated from his brigade when it was attacked by Kilpatrick's troopers. Jones arrived from Williamsport, where he had taken the portion of his train that had escaped capture (60 wagons were lost—some reports put the figure much higher). Jones informed Stuart of Imboden's arrival at Williamsport. Having then reached Cashtown, Stuart ordered Jones to proceed on the Boonsboro Road a few miles and then head for Funkstown. Jones was then to hold Funkstown, covering the eastern front of Hagerstown.

Munford was relieved by Fitz Lee on July 7, taking command of his brigade and concentrating them at Funkstown. In an all-night fight, Stuart's troopers attempted to drive Federal cavalry from Boonsboro, neither side gaining the upper hand. Stuart's exhausted troopers camped near Funkstown. Chambliss's and Robertson's commands proceeded directly from Leitersburg to Hagerstown. Kilpatrick headed to Hagerstown to confront Stuart, while Buford started for the wagon trains at Williamsport. Meanwhile, Stuart diverged from Jones's line of march at Cashtown and proceeded with Jenkins's brigade by way of Chewsville towards Hagerstown.[77]

The next day, July 8, Stuart proceeded to Downsville on the road to Sharpsburg, joined there by Brig. Gen. William T. Wofford's infantry brigade of Longstreet's corps. Stuart positioned Jenkins's cavalry in front of the retreating Confederate infantry. The Confederate vanguard then approached Hagerstown, only a few hours' march to Williamsport. Stuart covered the front of Lee's army in its march back to the Potomac at Williamsport. There, Lee's army constructed a formidable line of earthworks from Williamsport,

---

76. McClellan, *The Campaigns of Stuart's Cavalry*, 352–53; *OR* 27/1:917, 1019; Longacre, *The Cavalry at Gettysburg*, 250–51; Driver, *2nd Virginia Cavalry*, 92.
77. *OR* 27/2:701, 703; McClellan, *The Campaigns of Stuart's Cavalry*, 356-57; Driver, *2nd Virginia Cavalry*, 93.

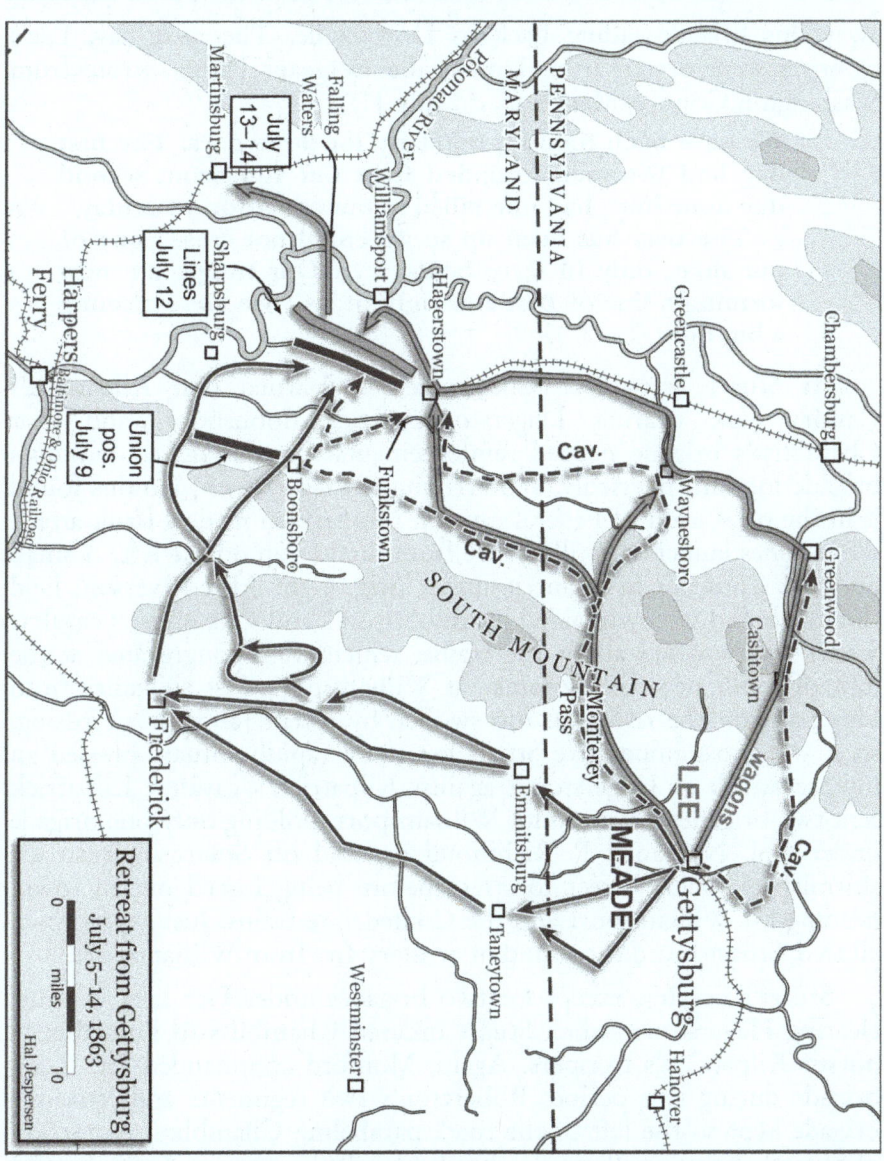

downriver four miles to Falling Waters, and waited for the swollen waters of the Potomac to recede. The Federals had earlier destroyed a pontoon bridge at Falling Waters; another would have to be built. Trooper Charles Blackford wrote, "The rise in the river prevents the wagon train from crossing."[78]

Fitz Lee led his brigade against Union cavalry the next day at Boonsboro, but finding them too strong, he retreated back to Funkstown. On July 10, a large Federal cavalry force drove Fitz Lee

---

78. *OR* 27/2:702-03; Blackford, *Letters from Lee's Army*, 189.

away, his brigade falling back to Downsville. The next day, Lee's troopers were driven from Downsville. Sergeant Parker wrote from Washington County, Maryland, on July 11:

> We have been fighting regularly for three days. The first day had five men wounded from our squadron; second day none hurt; had one killed in our squadron yesterday. . . . The river has been up so we could not cross none of our men, only in ferry boats. . . . Our troops are now forming a line of battle in sight of us. We are expecting a big fight.[79]

As Stuart arrived at Chewsville, he learned that Kilpatrick's Cavalry was nearing Hagerstown from Boonsboro, and that Chambliss's brigade needed reinforcements. He dispatched Jenkins's brigade forward hurriedly, and arriving at Hagerstown, Jenkins found it in the possession of Federal cavalry. His brigade made a flank attack while Jones launched artillery fire from further up on the left. A small body of Confederate infantry, under Brig. Gen. Alfred Iverson, held the north end of town, aided by Robertson's and Chambliss's cavalry. Stuart was worried about the trains, which were congregated at the foot of a hill near the Potomac at Williamsport, just six miles from Hagerstown. The river was too swollen by recent rains for a crossing, so it was most imperative Stuart get there rapidly. Stuart pressed an intense attack at Hagerstown against Kilpatrick's cavalry. Kilpatrick sent two brigades on ahead for Williamsport, holding only one brigade under Col. Nathaniel P. Richmond to hold off Stuart. Kilpatrick's skirmishers fought street to street before being forced out of town, heading for Williamsport and the Confederate trains. Just as the town cleared, Stuart heard the sound of artillery fire from Williamsport.[80]

Stuart's cavalry, except for two brigades under Fitz Lee, was just clearing Hagerstown when Stuart ordered Chambliss to immediately pursue Kilpatrick's troopers. Again, Munford commanded Fitz Lee's brigade during this period. Robertson's two regiments and Jenkins's brigade kept to the left of the road, paralleling Chambliss. A portion of Stuart's horse artillery also headed for Williamsport. Soon, part of Chambliss's leading brigade, the 9th and 13th Virginia, charged the Union horsemen of Kilpatrick, followed by a flank attack begun by Jenkins's brigade; they were stalled by the many post-and-rail fences. They were delayed long enough for the Federal riders to rally along a crest of rocks and fences, from which they opened up with artillery, raking the road. Jenkins's horsemen dismounted and deployed over

---

79. Wright, *Lee's Last Casualty*, 110; Driver, *2nd Virginia Cavalry*, 93.
80. *OR* 27/1:1006–07, part 2:701–02; McClellan, *Campaigns of Stuart's Cavalry*, 357–58.

difficult ground, finally dislodging the blue-clad troopers while Confederate mounted troopers pressed them. The Union cavalry made one countercharge but was ultimately repulsed by Col. James B. Gordon, who was commanding a portion of the 5th North Carolina Cavalry. Colonel Lomax's 11th Virginia of Jones's brigade joined in, sending the Union cavalry stampeding for the rear. Lomax's troopers charged down the turnpike with sabers drawn, under supporting Confederate artillery fire.[81]

Kilpatrick's horsemen headed for Williamsport, followed by Stuart's command, reaching the edge of the river crossing town just as darkness began to set in. Kilpatrick, with Buford's help, planned on capturing and destroying the Confederate wagon trains there, before relief could reach them. Buford was already in a fierce fight less than a mile from Williamsport when Kilpatrick arrived and positioned his troopers on Buford's right. Fitz Lee's horsemen arrived in the vicinity of Williamsport by the Greencastle Road. The Federals were being attacked in the rear by Jones's troopers, artillery, and some infantry. At the same time, Confederate infantry began to move on Kilpatrick's right flank. Buford sent word to Kilpatrick that he was about to retire, fearing the Confederates would move down the Sharpsburg Pike, cutting off their retreat. Slowly the Union soldiers retreated, fighting off Confederate attacks until dark, when Kilpatrick and Buford merged, proceeding to encamp near Jones's Crossing. Stuart had saved the main wagon trains. The Federals lost an aggregate of nearly 400 men, while Stuart reported losses of 254, exclusive of Jones's brigade, from which no report was received.[82]

One trooper of the 2nd Virginia was in good spirits despite the loss at Gettysburg. "Well here I am [in Williamsport] in sight of dear old Virginia," he wrote. "The wagon trains have pretty much all arrived and the troops are but a little way behind, all marching in perfect order and without molestation by the enemy. There are only two regiments of infantry here at this time, but all the wagons, and they [wounded troops] are crossing the river quite rapidly."[83]

From July 8-12, severe fighting took place between Stuart's cavalry and the divisions of Buford and Kilpatrick, at Boonsboro, Beaver Creek, Funkstown, and on the Sharpsburg Road. The cavalry fought mostly dismounted, aided on both sides by small bodies of infantry. Stuart reported an aggregate loss of 216 troops in these hotly contested engagements, while Buford, Kilpatrick, and Col. Pennock Huey

---

81. OR 27/2:702; McClellan, *Campaigns of Stuart's Cavalry*, 358.
82. OR 27/1:708, 928, 935, 995, part 2:702; McClellan, *The Campaigns of Stuart's Cavalry*, 359-61.
83. Blackford, *Letters from Lee's Army*, 188.

reported a total loss of 158. Stuart successfully delayed the advance of the pursuing Federal army until General Lee had established a strong position. On July 12, Stuart uncovered Lee's front, but the pursuing Union forces found it too strong to attack.[84]

General Imboden pressed two local ferries into service, and as soon as the wounded were treated and fed, those who believed they could walk towards Winchester were ferried across the river to Virginia. Eventually, three additional ferries were built and began carrying wounded across. A new pontoon was constructed at Falling Waters for crossings; the majority of Lee's army would cross there. The bulk of the infantry, artillery, and wagons, however, were not able to complete the crossing to Maidstone, Virginia, until July 14.[85]

Captain Charles Blackford of the 2nd Virginia wrote from Williamsport on July 12, "There is now a pontoon bridge at Williamsport, and by tomorrow there will be one at Falling Waters, below this point. It happened there was a large amount of timber at Williamsport and out of it we built twenty boats and on them built a pontoon bridge in four days." Blackford crossed the next day at Falling Waters during a violent rainstorm. He wrote that most of the soldiers and wagons crossed that day. Fitz Lee's brigade was the last to cross in a persistent rain before the rear guard of the 2nd Virginia. Buford's cavalry kept "a very sharp cannonade upon us. After we crossed, our rear guard, under the command of [Brig.] Gen. [James J.] Pettigrew, of South Carolina, was sharply attacked and the General was killed."[86]

On July 13, Fitz Lee's troopers posted on the west bank reconnoitered Union positions. During the evening, Fitz Lee's regiments manned Longstreet's entrenchments while the infantrymen slogged through pouring rain to cross the Potomac at Falling Waters. Adjutant Tayloe described the crossing, "It was quite a picturesque sight when we crossed to see men wading the River up to their necks, and then a train of ambulances, and then two or three regiments of Cavalry one below the other."[87]

On July 14, both Buford's and Kilpatrick's divisions pursued the Confederates to Falling Waters, capturing many of the prisoners and abandoned property that was left behind. When Lee's army had

---

84. McClellan, *Campaigns of Stuart's Cavalry*, 363-64; Wert, *Cavalryman of the Lost Cause*, 296-297; *OR* 27/1:118, 925, 936, part 2:716.
85. Wittenberg, Petruzzi, and Nugent, *One Continuous Fight*, 25.
86. Blackford, *Letters from Lee's Army*, 190, 193; "Autobiography of St. George Tucker Brooke," 32. General Pettigrew was actually mortally wounded, dying three days later. It should be noted that North Carolina also claimed Pettigrew, because he was born in North Carolina and attended the University of North Carolina.
87. Driver, *2nd Virginia Cavalry*, 93–94.

crossed the Potomac by 8:00 a.m., Stuart's cavalry acted as rear guard, making an obstinate resistance near Falling Waters where the main crossing took place. The next day, Buford's and Kilpatrick's divisions, having arrived at Falling Waters too late, moved to Berlin to obtain supplies. The pursuit of Lee's soldiers through Loudoun Valley to the Rappahannock River would be made by Union cavalry in detachments.[88]

Trooper John W. Lakes wrote his wife after crossing back into Virginia, "I never had my saddle off of my horse one hour at a time for three weeks and the most sleep that I got was on my horse's back. We travelled more at night than in the day . . . we lost every wagon we had while we was in Md and Pa. What the yankees did not get we lost in the river. . . . cows, sheep and bread is all we live on."[89]

Trooper I. Norval Baker of the 18th Virginia recalled the terrible condition of the horses before they crossed into Virginia, "the green flies were around us all the time and orders were not to unsaddle or unbridle our horses and be ready for duty at all times. Our blankets were under our saddles and soaked with water and the green flies were working under the rawhide covering of our saddles and ulcerated backs of our horses." After crossing into Virginia, the troopers were ordered to unsaddle their horses. "Our horses' backs were raw with ulcers one and two inches deep and full of maggots." After a thorough cleaning and drying out of blankets, saddles and horses' backs, "it took months before the horses backs were cured."[90]

The Army of Northern Virginia's trek into Pennsylvania had been extremely hard on the troops and horses. They had escaped back into Virginia, but the cost had been horrific. Never again, with the exception of Jubal's Early's raid near Washington in 1864, would the South be able to mount an attack in the North. Soon, they were fighting the fall campaigns of Bristoe Station, Mine Run, and North Anna.

---

88. *OR* 27/1:917.
89. Driver, *2nd Virginia Cavalry*, 94; John W. Lakes letter, July 15, 1863, Collection of James I. Robertson, Virginia Tech, Blacksburg, Virginia.
90. Diary of I. Norval Baker, 18th Virginia Cavalry, VMI Archives.

Chapter Eleven

Remainder of 1863 Campaigns and Cavalry Reorganization

"Stuart will not hear of anything but his foolish and absurd orders. If he had agents or officers who knew their business and would attend to it, we might get along tolerably well—but with his set of men who are wholly unfit for their places. I throw out these hints—hoping to see them connect some of these days—if I can only get out from under him."

—Thomas Munford on General Stuart after Gettysburg.

Thomas Munford temporarily commanded Fitzhugh Lee's brigade during the march to Gettysburg, performing well during the entire campaign, including the exhausting and dangerous return to Virginia. The experience helped prepare him for even more responsibilities in the campaign's aftermath. Obtaining the coveted brigadier's rank, however, would continue to elude him—frustrating him more and more.

After crossing the Potomac in the aftermath of the Gettysburg campaign, General Stuart assigned Hampton's (under Laurence Baker) and Fitz Lee's cavalry the duty of picketing the Potomac from Falling Waters to Hedgesville. Stuart's other brigades moved towards Leestown, while Beverly Robertson was sent to the fords of the Shenandoah River. Harpers Ferry was again in Union possession, though Col. Asher W. Harmen and the 12th Virginia engaged the Federals there, resulting in Harmen's capture. Meanwhile, on July 15, Stuart headed for the Stephen Dandridge estate, the "Bower." Upon arriving there, he learned a large force of Union cavalry was between Shepherdstown and Leestown. He rushed off to position with his cavalry to attack them in order to thwart any intentions they might have towards Martinsburg. Stuart ordered Fitz Lee to proceed through Charlestown to Leestown. Stuart directed Chambliss's, Jones's, and Jenkins's brigades to support the attack on the Federal cavalry. Robert E. Lee called urgently for Stuart to report to Lee's headquarters at Bunker Hill; Fitz Lee led the Confederate cavalry operations. Fitz Lee, leading his and Chambliss's brigades, attacked the Union horsemen on the Leestown Road within a mile of Shepherdstown and drove them back. Jenkins's brigade arrived, moving up to support Fitz Lee. Once the Federal command realized the small number of riders in Lee's brigade, they ordered a counterattack. Company C of the 2nd Virginia could supply only 13 men as part of a skirmish line. Chambliss's brigade arrived, driving the Union cavalry from the field. The Union horsemen retreated to Harpers Ferry and re-crossed the Potomac. The 1st Virginia's leader, Col. James H. Drake, was killed in the action. Munford reported the 2nd Virginia's loss of one officer, nine enlisted men wounded, and two troopers captured. Adjutant Tayloe added, "we [Fitz Lee's brigade] lost 75 to 100 men killed and wounded."[1]

Between July 16 and 22, Federals demonstrated at Hedgesville, forcing back Laurence Baker's North Carolina Cavalry Brigade. Cavalry skirmishing there kept up for several days, while the Confederate infantry engaged in tearing up track of the Baltimore and Ohio Railroad near Martinsburg.[2]

Stuart then realized that the Union army was moving upon his right flank, taking advantage of the rain-swollen Shenandoah River to interpose between Robert E. Lee's army and Richmond, by marching along the east side of the Blue Ridge Mountains. Lee had already sent Longstreet's corps to counteract the Federal movement. Sufficient cavalry was also dispatched, under Brig. Gen. Beverly Robertson, as his advance guard through Front Royal and Chester Gap, while Baker's brigade brought up the rear of Ewell's corps. Jones's brigade picketed the lower Shenandoah to protect that flank of the army and then followed the movement of the army. Fitz Lee's, Rooney Lee's, and Jenkins's brigades proceeded by forced march from near Leestown, through Millwood, and on to Manassas Gap. The Confederate cavalry, however, found Manassas Gap already in possession of the Federal army. The Shenandoah River, still high, had to be crossed south of Front Royal.[3]

Confederate cavalry reached Chester Gap on July 23, and with difficulty and a forced march, reached south of Gaines's Cross Roads, holding the Rockford road and the Warrenton Turnpike up to near Amissville. There, Federal cavalry concentrated in large force. The

1. McClellan, *The Campaigns of Stuart's Cavalry*, 368-70; *OR*, vol. 27, part 2, 706-07. Lt. Lomax Tayloe was Thomas Munford's wife's brother. He was killed at Raccoon Ford, Culpeper, Virginia on October 11, 1863. After General Wickham's resignation on October 5, 1864, Munford commanded Wickham's brigade, and another of Etta Munford's brothers, John William Tayloe, became Munford's Assistant Adjutant General.
2. McClellan, *The Campaigns of Stuart's Cavalry*, 369.
3. McClellan, *The Campaigns of Stuart's Cavalry*, 369–70; *OR* 27/2:706–07.

gray horsemen bivouacked for the night. The Confederate cavalry moved to Fredericksburg and established a picket line on the Rappahannock until the middle of September, while Lee's army withdrew behind the Rapidan. During this period, the cavalry rested with interruptions only for picket duty. The 2nd Virginia also rested, since the troopers and their mounts were completely worn out. The respite permitted additional recruits to be added to the roster, as well as the return of men from horse details and hospitals.[4]

On July 29, 1863, Stuart issued General Order No. 25, abolishing the "Company Q" system. "Company Q" for J.E.B. Stuart's cavalry placed some of the less seriously wounded soldiers, sick men, and disabled horses under separate units, most of which were generally located at a safe, albeit sometimes far distance from their regiments. This system also fostered opportunities for shirkers to hide and avoid battle. Frustrated with this situation, Stuart implemented a new scheme requiring far more hierarchal oversight. It utilized a command structure requiring approvals to insure that badly needed serviceable horses were cared for and available for duty in a timely manner. The disabled horses were to be located in a centralized division camp, away from their regiments and under the control of a division quartermaster, often unfamiliar with the proper care of the animals. The less severely wounded and sick troopers were separated from control of their mounts (often privately owned horses) and sent to different locals, often separated by great distances from their commands. Their equipment was placed with the regimental and brigade trains under the control of provost guards. Frequently, when a soldier returned to duty, his horse was not to be found.[5]

Munford was a proponent of a "rear pasture" system, which kept the sick troopers, their equipment, and the disabled horses all together at a reasonable distance in the rear of their commands. He became incensed over the new system and was very vocal about it. He truly cared for the men of his command and obviously had a deep appreciation for and love of the cavalry horse. He was a good administrator. His anger with Stuart might have further jeopardized his chances for a promotion to brigadier, if Stuart knew about it. Munford was argumentative with his superiors; so, it is likely that Stuart at least knew about it, but perhaps not the full extent of Munford's loathing for him. It likely added to Stuart's peeve that Munford was unacceptably late at Brandy Station. Stuart, however, was

---

4. McClellan, *The Campaigns of Stuart's Cavalry*, 370-71; *OR* 27/2:707; Driver, *2nd Virginia Cavalry*, 95.
5. General Order No. 25, July 29, 1863, Munford–Ellis Papers, DU; *OR* 27/3:1049–50.

able to separate personal disputes from leadership, for the good of the service.⁶

On July 30, the day after Stuart's General Order abolishing "Company Q," Munford wrote to his father, from Culpeper Court House, of rumors of a cavalry reorganization and complained about his being passed over for promotion earlier:

> Genl Hampton and Fitz Lee will be promoted to Major General and several other officers will be made Brigadier. My name is in connection with this command of this Brig. I have been more in command of a Brig during the past yr than in command of my Regt and as I am the senior Col from brig. I will always be in the absence of Brig Genl comdy [commanding] my Brigade. Twice I have been overadvanced by West Point men. Should it happen again, nothing would induce me to retain command of my Regt. The officers all agree with me and have volunteered to advise me not to submit again. I believe I have been highly recommended for the place. I understand Cols Lomax, Rosser and myself are each recommended, one to command this Brig—the other to command Jones' Brig, he having offered his Resignation and the other will have a Brig which is yet to be formed. Please get some friend to see that my claims are represented. Mr. Tucker I'm sure will do it for me.⁷

In the same letter, Munford related the appalling condition of the cavalry:

> I'm sorry to tell you that the cavalry is in a very crippled condition and has suffered very much. My own Regt, the strongest in the Brig, can't mount more than 350 men and the question of recruiting is getting more serious daily. Poor men cannot buy horses at $1,000 and no man who attends to his duty can do with less than two horses a year. The great difficulty is the management and providing for the command, horse shoes, & corn is what we require and all unnecessary trips and raids to be dispensed with altogether.⁸

---

6. Ibid.
7. Thomas Munford to George W. Munford, July 30, 1863, Munford–Ellis Papers, DU. Munford was "venting" here; he had no real intention of leaving his beloved 2nd Virginia. He was getting his hopes up again regarding a promotion. Tucker is probably family friend, Nathaniel Beverly Tucker, a diplomat, and influential politician.
8. Ibid.

Munford next called attention to the care of the wounded men's horses:

> [What is needed is] A horse pasture in the rear, and manned with a few careful men under a good officer to see that they get rest, quiet and attention. Let the horses of the sick men be sent there and their saddles and equipment be kept there until they can return. I have always had such a system, and have it now, "against orders," but it is the only way I have kept up my command. The orders now are for all horses to be kept at their wagon train where anything starves or is ruined or stolen. The idea of leaving a sick man's horse with a quartermaster is perfectly absurd. His horse will inevitably be ruined as always has been the case he returns from his home or a hospital, weak and never in condition for a march or poorly follows our trail for days and gets to his wagon to find his fine animal a mere skeleton unfit for duty & all of his equipment gone.[9]

In early August, Munford wrote from Fredericksburg to an unidentified individual who Munford thought might prevail on President Davis to make some badly needed changes. He spoke of his concern for the care of the wounded and sick soldiers, and temporarily unserviceable horses:

> I enclose you a "Bull[etin]" abolishing Company "Q"—emanating from him [Stuart] who "is determined to spare no effort to secure his command in which he feels so much pride from the impending fate." Alas! He now sees the danger, but does not know the remedy." Munford thought Stuart had created a horrible new system for handling the temporarily unserviceable horses. Munford outlined the new scheme, "An institution entirely of his own making. A mighty congregation of lame, broken down sore back, crippled and who knows of the sick and absent men, ever hanging nearest to his wagon train & farthest from his enemy—a command exceeding the effective strength of each Brig from 3 to 5 to one. Let him deny it, if he will and in the meantime let us inquire, how many men this country is losing from the field?[10]

Munford cited what was needed was "a good officer—one who would husband closely with his men and horses and much more than

---

9. Ibid. Sometimes, adequate forage was not available nearby, requiring horses to be taken some distance away.
10. Thomas Munford to an unidentified individual, August 9, 1863, Munford—Ellis Papers, DU.

their men's wives and daughters—one who has more care and less selfishness, more brains and less vanity, ready to sacrifice himself, but to preserve his command for his country's good."[11]

Munford then turned his attention back to his difficulties with Stuart:

> These are the difficulties we have to contend with—and Stuart will not hear of anything but his foolish and absurd orders. If he had agents or officers who knew their business and would attend to it, we might get along tolerably well—but not with these set of men who are wholly unfit for their places. I throw out these hints–hoping to see them connect some of these days—if I can only get out from under him.[12]

Thomas Munford's ill feelings towards J.E.B. Stuart had been brewing since Stuart had blamed him for being tardy at Brandy Station. Stuart's performance during the Gettysburg campaign amplified Munford's feelings of resentment. Munford felt Stuart was not helping Robert E. Lee with his extended raids on the way to join Lee in Pennsylvania. He felt Stuart was a glory seeker who mistreated his men and their horses. Munford's letter of July 30 to his father revealed in striking detail his gripes, showed his animosity towards Stuart, and his disdain of "West Pointers."[13]

James Longstreet agreed with Munford's assessment of Stuart, writing, "I often spoke of him to General [Robert E.] Lee, as of the best material for cavalry service, but needing an older head to instruct and regulate him. The General was fond of him, and gave way to him to the disadvantage of both." Longstreet thought Fitz Lee "a poor substitute."[14]

Munford continued, striking out at the "know-it-all West Pointers":

> All this amiss from a want of confidence, a desire of power, and the envy, hatred and malice most of those men feel towards each man in the regular service and a proper appreciation of his wants of the service. These

---

11. Ibid.
12. Ibid.
13. Thomas Munford to George W. Munford, July 30, 1863, Munford–Ellis Papers, DU.
14. James L. Longstreet to Thomas T. Munford, November 8, 1891, Munford–Ellis Papers, DU.

men know everything because they were at West Point, but not many of them were at or in a war before this guerilla commenced and very few ever knew the wants of a horse or can supply them.[15]

Munford spoke again of the men and their mounts:

> Most of the Cavalry keep two horses—one at home and one here,—one horse will not stand and perform the service required of him more than six months--many not so long under the present management. Every Regt has a good many first-rate men who are poor and unable to remount themselves at the present high prices of horses and never have gotten pay for their horses which they have been compelled to abandon on some pointless raid. Ever since I have had a regiment, I have always had the strongest regiment in the field when I was not cramped and by such stupid orders. This order has broken us all up. Genl Jackson recently approved this plan [rear pasture system] and allowed it in his army. Genl Beauregard allowed it. But the great horse killer disapproves it in toto.[16]

Munford continued, urging the addressee of the letter to help. "I do not wish, he wrote, "this used as mine but, if you can do anything with this—put them in any shape and call the resident's attention to our condition which he cannot and does not know, you will do your country much good."[17]

Munford felt like an outsider, perhaps even envious of "West Pointers," concluding, "I confess I have very high admiration for West Point—but the present voluntary service is different from the old Regular Service and the wants of this service should be studied, as it was not taught at West Point. The Gallant Hampton is the only Brig. who is not a West Pointer and is 2nd to none of them and is superior to all I have seen."[18]

---

15. Ibid.
16. Ibid.
17. Ibid.
18. Ibid. In speculating to whom this letter was addressed, I am inclined to think it could have been sent to John Letcher. Thomas Munford's father, George Wythe Munford, was Secretary of the Commonwealth under Governor (1860-1864) John Letcher. Letcher and George Wythe Munford were close associates, and Letcher was a family friend. The letter could have been forwarded from George Munford to Letcher. I do not believe this letter was sent to Robert E. Lee, at least not directly.

Reorganization and Aftermath

During early September, Stuart's Cavalry Corps reorganized. Wade Hampton and Fitzhugh Lee were promoted to major general rank, heading up divisions. Colonels Laurence S. Baker, Matthew C. Butler, Lunsford L. Lomax, and Williams C. Wickham were promoted to the brigadier rank, leading brigades. Colonel Thomas Munford was bypassed for promotion to brigadier a third time, which greatly embittered him. Stuart had recommended back in February that a new brigade be formed as part of a reorganization, with Munford heading it. Robert E. Lee had nixed the formation of an extra brigade.[19]

Prior to the September reorganization, many thought Munford of the 2nd Virginia was to get the brigade. A Munford family member wrote, "Everyone says it is most unjust" that Munford was passed over for Wickham. Wickham was tiring of the service and had been elected to the Confederate Congress while commanding his regiment at the front. He was talking of resigning the service to take his elected seat. Lee and Stuart did not want to lose his services. This may be part of the reason he was promoted to brigadier over Munford. Wickham finally took his seat in October of 1864, resigning from the service.[20]

By Special Order 226, from the headquarters of the Army of Northern Virginia, dated September 9, 1863, the cavalry divisions were reorganized as follows:

Hampton's Division:

William E. Jones's brigade: 6th Virginia, 7th Virginia, 12th Virginia, and 35th Battalion Virginia Cavalry.

Laurence S. Baker's brigade: 1st North Carolina, 2nd North Carolina, 4th North Carolina, and 5th North Carolina. Baker did not lead the brigade due to a disabling arm wound inflicted on August 1. Colonel James B. Gordon was promoted to brigadier general to command the brigade.

M. C. Butler's brigade: Cobb Georgia Legion, Philips Georgia Legion, Jeff Davis Legion, 2nd South Carolina. Butler was in South Carolina, recovering from a leg amputation after Brandy Station. Pierce M. B. Young assumed temporary command of the brigade.

---

19. J.E.B. Stuart to Robert E. Lee, September 10, 1863, Adele Mitchell, ed., *Letters of James E. B. Stuart* (Stuart-Mosby Historical Association, 1990), 340–41.
20. Kenneth L. Styles, *4th Virginia Cavalry*, 36.

Fitzhugh Lee's division:

W. H. F. "Rooney" Lee's brigade: 1st South Carolina, 9th Virginia, 10th Virginia, and 13th Virginia.

Lunsford Lomax's Brigade: 5th Virginia, 1st Battalion Maryland Cavalry, 11th Virginia, and 15th Virginia.

Williams Wickham's brigade: 1st Virginia, 2nd Virginia (under Munford), 3rd Virginia, and 4th Virginia.[21]

Stuart disliked Jones and had been trying to get rid of him since February. Stuart's complaint with Jones was in part due to Jones's failure to adequately protect the passes of South Mountain during the retreat from Gettysburg. As a result, Union General Kilpatrick was able to capture 45 wagons and 1,000 Confederate prisoners from Ewell's corps. Jones offered to resign, but he was needed by Robert E. Lee, and the commander was able to defer his departure from the army. Relations between the two strong-headed cavalrymen continued to be strained until it culminated in a verbal clash in September. Stuart had Jones arrested and court-martialed. Jones let it be known that even if he were acquitted, he would never serve under Stuart again. The military court found him guilty of disrespect to a superior officer, and he was stripped of his command and ordered to take charge of the cavalry in southwest Virginia.[22]

Given the vacancy that accompanied Jones's transfer, Stuart recommended to Lee that Rosser be promoted. In a September 30 letter to Rosser from Stuart, the cavalry chief stated:

> Should another vacancy occur in my command, it is my earnest desire to have you fill it, and I have written to Col. Munford, who felt himself slighted at Wickham's promotion, that I should recommend you in preference to him. There is no difference of opinion with General officers under whom you have served that on the field of battle, in coolness or capacity to "control happening events," and wield troops, you have no superior. . . . You deserve promotion more than any Col of a Va Regt in my command, and if Brig Gen Jones should be sent elsewhere, you are my choice for the post this made vacant.[23]

---

21. OR 29/2:707–08; McClellan, *The Campaigns of Stuart's Cavalry*, 371–72.
22. McDonald, *Laurel Brigade*, 168.
23. J.E.B. Stuart to Thomas L. Rosser, September 30, 1863, Thomas L. Rosser Papers, UVA; Mitchell, ed., *The Letters of James E. B. Stuart*, 349.

Within a month, Stuart managed to push through Rosser's promotion. On Rosser's birthday, October 15, 1863, he was promoted to brigadier general, to rank from September 28. Munford had been bypassed for promotion to brigadier time and time again; it must have felt like a terribly stinging wound to him, one that would not heal during his lifetime. This was the start of bitter feelings between Munford and Rosser that carried on after the war, indeed for the remainder of their lives.

Munford's father, Secretary of the Commonwealth, wrote Robert E. Lee concerning his disappointed son. Friends of the family also wrote the commanding general. Lee, answering one of Munford's supporters, assured him he would recommend promotion of Colonel Munford "whenever I can do so consistently with those principles by which I am guided in these matters. . . . I necessarily consult the opinions of those whose opportunities of knowing what will best promote the interests of the service are better than my own. Many things in addition to services and capacity have to be considered in the appointment of a brigade commander, those of course are chief." In response to Munford's father, Lee wrote, after repeating much of the same sentiments:

> **All personal feelings and aspirations should be subordinate to the great end of rendering all the service in every man's power to the common cause. The man who is actuated by this principle will I think find in the end, ample compensation for any disappointment of his personal wishes and aspirations, in the consciousness of duty faithfully performed, and it will generally happen that it is the most certain to honorable advancement. That such will be the action of your son, his previous conduct leads me to expect, and the result will meet his expectations and those of his friends, I have no doubt.**[24]

Regardless of Robert E. Lee's assurances, Munford felt that he was surrounded by West Point men who treated him, or any other VMI soldiers, as militia who were not up to their West Point standards. He observed "envy, hatred and malice whenever occasions arose for display of what 'militia men' could do." Munford complained, "Fitz Lee, Rosser and Lomax never seemed to comprehend that anything not out of West Point was equal to themselves as soldiers."[25]

---

24. Robert E. Lee to Beverly Tucker, October 28, 1863, Private Collection of Thomas T. Munford's great-grand-daughter, Estelle Call.; quoted in Freeman, *Lee's Lieutenants*, vol. 3:214–15.
25. Thomas T. Munford to Superintendent General E. W. Nichols, February 14, 1916, VMI Archives.

Rosser was everything Munford was not; tall and solidly built, colorful, even flamboyant, jovial, seemingly gregarious, bold to the point of being brash and, in the opinion of some, reckless. These traits had endeared him to J.E.B. Stuart, who probably saw something of himself in Rosser, save for Rosser's drinking. Stuart apparently did not see the jealous side of Rosser, evident in Rosser's letters to his wife. Stuart took Rosser under his wing and advanced his career. Stuart never warmed to Munford, nor Munford to Stuart.[26]

Subsequent to the cavalry reorganization, in early September, Robert E. Lee dispatched two divisions of Lt. Gen. James Longstreet's corps to reinforce the Confederate Army of Tennessee in the battle for Chickamauga. Major General George Meade, knowing Lee had been weakened by Longstreet's departure, planned to take advantage and advance his army to the Rappahannock River. On September 13, Meade sent strong columns forward to confront Lee along the Rapidan. Meade then occupied Culpeper, Virginia, following a battle at Culpeper Court House, planning to use numerical superiority in a turning movement of Lee's army. On September 24, however, the Union also had to deplete its forces, sending the XI and XII Corps to the Chattanooga campaign in Tennessee.[27]

On September 22, John Buford's cavalry marched from Madison Court House toward Liberty Mills. Stuart, with a portion of his cavalry, attacked him on the road to Jack's Shop with several charges, both mounted and dismounted, but failed to break his lines. While engaged with Buford, Stuart discovered that a large body of Kilpatrick's cavalry under Brig. Gen. Henry E. Davies, Jr., had turned his left flank and gained possession of the road to his rear. Stuart was cut off from an escape route using the ford at Liberty Mills. He was pressed from front and rear, seemingly trapped. The fighting soon focused in an open field, where Stuart positioned artillery on a small nearby hill. Henry B. McClellan wrote, "Stuart's artillery was firing in both directions from the hill, and within sight of each other his regiments were charging in opposite directions." Two of Stuart's regiments, the 1st and 5th North Carolina, charged but were repulsed. Another charge by the 5th North Carolina and the 9th Virginia was also stopped. Finally, a third charge, this time by the 7th, 11th, and 12th Virginia regiments pushed Davies back, forcing him to give up the road and retire in the direction he had advanced. Stuart quickly disengaged from Buford and retreated on the just-opened escape route

---

26. James R. Jewell, "In Rivulets of Gray Ink: The Bloody Battles About the War (The Munford-Rosser Feud)," n.p., 2, in the author's possession; Rosser letters to his wife, Thomas L. Rosser Papers, UVA.
27. John H. Atkins, ed., *1863 Civil War Diary of Corporal John Irving* (Salem, OR, 2014), 165.

and across the Rapidan at Liberty Mills, where he was reinforced by Cadmus Wilcox's infantry. Wickham's brigade rode to Stuart's assistance, reaching Barboursville by nightfall.[28]

The next day, Wickham's troopers engaged Federal cavalry at Robinson River, suffering slight losses. His troopers drove the Union horsemen back across the stream, capturing 30 to 40 prisoners. Notwithstanding the diminished size of the regiment, the remaining men of the 2nd Virginia wanted to make a mounted cavalry charge, but could not due to timber and underbrush. Trooper Rufus Peck wrote, "We charged them on foot and drove them across the river, capturing a few of them and having a few wounded and killed." Wickham's brigade camped near Orange Court House that night.[29]

Wickham led his brigade to near Verdiersville on September 24. Dress parades and drilling resumed, and soon more plentiful rations returned. On October 1, the brigade marched to the vicinity of Orange Springs. They moved again on October 9 to the area of Somerville Ford on the Rapidan, where they rested for a couple of days.[30]

The Bristoe Campaign

On October 9, 1863, Gen. Robert E. Lee positioned his army 12 miles south of Culpeper, Virginia, south of the Rapidan River near Rapidan Station. Here, Lee began an offensive sweep around Cedar Mountain with his remaining two corps, attempting to turn General Meade's right flank. Lee hoped to get between Meade and Washington, severing Union lines of communication with the capital. By observing Lee's troop movements, Meade discerned Lee's trap and moved his army of 90,000 troops northward along the Orange & Alexandria Railroad toward Manassas. All the way from Rappahannock Station to Warrenton, Meade cautiously looked for an opportunity to attack Lee's 60,000-man army. Lee, likewise, looked to strike a fatal blow to Meade's army.[31]

The Bristoe Campaign was a series of minor battles fought in Virginia during October and early November 1863, involving the infantry and cavalries of Robert E. Lee and George G. Meade. First, Gen. A. P. Hill struck at Bristoe Station on October 14, but without

---

28. McClellan, *Campaigns of Stuart's Cavalry*, 375; Driver, *2nd Virginia Cavalry*, 97; Wert, *Cavalryman of the Lost Cause*, 311–12.
29. Peck, *Reminiscences of a Cavalryman*, 41; Driver, *2nd Virginia Cavalry*, 97.
30. Driver, *2nd Virginia Cavalry*, 97.
31. William D. Henderson, *The Road to Bristoe Station: Campaigning with Lee and Meade, August 1–October 20, 1863* (Lynchburg, 1987), 82, 85–86, 104.

proper reconnaissance, he suffered losses in two brigades and withdrew. As Meade moved south, his army struck a Confederate defensive bridgehead at Rappahannock Station on November 7, driving Lee back across the Rapidan River. Neither Lee nor Meade had achieved their primary objective of bringing on a decisive battle under favorable circumstances. Lee had a chance to inflict a serious blow to the Union army, but the Confederates failed to effectively coordinate their movements and attacks.[32]

The mission assigned to a large portion of the Confederate cavalry during this campaign was to lead the Confederate Army. They also harassed Alfred Pleasonton's cavalry during its withdrawal across the Rappahannock. In addition, they protected the right and rear of Lee's army as the commander of the Army of Northern Virginia flanked Meade. Several cavalry fights occurred during this Bristoe campaign, including Auburn, Buckland Mills, James City, Morton's Ford, Raccoon Ford, Stevensburg, Culpeper Court House, Brandy Station, and others. Two of the more major fights involving the cavalry occurred on October 14 at Auburn Mills, five miles east of Warrenton, and the second on October 19 at Buckland, five miles north of Auburn Mills.[33]

During the engagements at Bristoe, Brandy Station, and Buckland Mills, General Wickham and his brigade were on guard on the Rapidan and Rappahannock rivers. On October 11, Wickham's brigade, under temporary command of Col. Thomas H. Owen in Wickham's absence, crossed the Rapidan at Raccoon Ford. Trooper Rufus Peck wrote, "When we crossed the river the enemy opened fire on us with three or four pieces of artillery and the first ball that was fired cut Sergeant [James P.] McCabe's leg off and the ball went on through his horse and killed it instantly." Colonel Owen reported, "finding the enemy [Buford's cavalry] in line of battle near Stringfellow's House, I was ordered to charge the enemy battery and take it." Owen ordered the 1st Virginia, supported by the 3rd to charge up the road, and the 2nd and 4th regiments to position themselves on the left-hand side of the road in support of Breathed's battery. Fitz Lee, seeing the strength of the Union lines, countermanded Owen's orders to the 1st and 3rd regiments. Owen then dismounted the sharpshooters of those two regiments, sending them forward while positioning the mounted portions of those two regiments behind Breathed's guns. When enemy sharpshooters advanced, Owens ordered the 4th Virginia to break the lines. Captain William B. Newton, commanding the 4th Virginia, was

---

32. Ibid., 150, 163–193; McClellan, *Campaigns of Stuart's Cavalry*, 397.
33. McClellan, *Campaigns of Stuart's Cavalry*, 388–95.

killed and his regiment was forced back. Owen sent his sharpshooters forward, driving Buford's cavalry back to Stevensburg, where they made a stand.[34]

Sergeant Robert W. Parker wrote, "a running gunfight ensued to Brandy Station, [the Federals] leaving their dead and wounded on the field a distance of eight or ten miles. At Brandy they made a stand, being largely re-enforced [by] another command coming down [from] Culpeper CH and here one of the hardest cavalry fights of cavalry and artillery I have ever witnessed." Trooper Peck recalled, "They continued to retreat until they joined the main army. We camped near Brandy Station that night."[35]

The next day, Parker wrote:

> We were sent to the front between Brandy Station and the Rappahannock and kept up a line of skirmishers till an hour or two by sun in view of their skirmishers, when they commenced advancing and made us fall back to within 2 miles of Culpeper CH, where we made a stand, and as they advanced our artillery soon let them know and then our sharpshooters that we were ready for them. A brisk fight ensued which soon sent them back.[36]

That evening Colonel Owen led Wickham's brigade through Jeffersonton, clearing Federal cavalry from Fox's Ford on the Hedgeman River, camping near Warrenton Springs. Continuing their advance the next day, Wickham's brigade moved through Warrenton and along the Orange & Alexandria Railroad to Catlett's Station. The brigade ran into a large Union force guarding their trains near Auburn. Colonel Owen was forced to use his sharpshooters to engage the Federals; he quickly withdrew and camped about four miles from Catlett's Station.[37]

Meanwhile, on October 11, Stuart attempted to get in the Federals' rear at Brandy Station in order to gain the high ground at Fleetwood Hill. Stuart sent the 12th Virginia to attack Federal cavalry near Fleetwood, but a squadron of Union cavalry attacked the flank of his 4th and 5th North Carolina regiments and routed them, forcing them to flee. The Federals established a strong position on Fleetwood Hill, and with artillery, were able to thwart all Confederate attacks. At nightfall, the Federal cavalry under Pleasanton retreated across the

---

34. Peck, *Reminiscences of a Confederate Soldier*, 421; *OR* 29/1:112-113, 471; Driver, *2nd Virginia Cavalry*, 97, 99; Driver, *2nd Virginia Cavalry*, 97, 99.
35. Wright, *Lee's Last Casualty*, 118–19; Peck, *Reminiscences of a Confederate Soldier*, 42.
36. Wright, *Lee's Last Casualty*, 119.
37. Driver, *2nd Virginia Cavalry*, 100–01.

Rappahannock. During the cavalry fight at Brandy Station, Fitzhugh Lee's cavalry division and two brigades of infantry forced Union Gen. John Buford back across the Rapidan at Morton's Ford.[38]

Stuart had succeeded in screening Robert E. Lee's army from the prying eyes of the Union cavalry. Meade thought Lee was at Culpeper Court House, and on the afternoon of the 12th, he sent out the 2nd, 5th and 6th Corps, with Buford's cavalry, for Culpeper intending to fight Lee there.[39]

In late afternoon of October 13, General Stuart, 1,500 troopers, and Captains William M. McGregor, Wiley H. Griffin, and Roger Preston Chew's batteries (all under the command of Maj. Robert F. Beckham), on a reconnaissance mission, found themselves trapped between two of General Meade's corps near Auburn Mills. Escape seemed impossible, but since his troops had not yet been seen, Stuart decided that he and his men would move off the road to concealing woods nearby and remain silent in-place through a very cold night.[40]

Concealment in daylight was impossible, so before sunrise on October 14, Stuart sent Major Beckham's horse artillery up to an elevated hill. It was quite foggy at dawn when Stuart heard infantry musketry fire from the west. He hoped it was Robert E. Lee advancing. It was not. He then ordered his artillerymen on the hill to open fire on the nearby Federal encampment, expecting that the resulting confusion would offer him an avenue of escape. The Federals, though surprised, recovered quickly, sending infantry skirmishers toward Stuart's guns and threatening to capture his whole command. Stuart then ordered Brig. Gen. James B. Gordon's North Carolina Brigade to charge the oncoming 125th New York and break through. The 1st North Carolina made two gallant charges, providing Stuart and most of his troopers an escape route. Stuart then joined Fitz Lee southwest of Auburn.[41]

Meanwhile, Gen. A. P. Hill's corps encountered two corps of the retreating Union army at Bristoe Station. He attacked without sufficient reconnaissance and too far ahead of support. On October 14, Union soldiers of the Warren's II Corps, posted behind the Orange & Alexandria Railroad embankment, mauled two brigades of Maj. Gen. Henry Heth's division, capturing a battery of artillery. Hill finally reinforced his line but could make little headway against Warren's soldiers. After this victory, Meade continued his withdrawal to Centreville virtually unmolested. Meade positioned himself behind

---

38. *OR* 29/1:442-44, 448; McClellan, *Campaigns of Stuart's Cavalry*, 382.
39. McClellan, *Campaigns of Stuart's Cavalry*, 383.
40. Ibid., 388–89.
41. Clark, *NCR*, 1: 426–27.

well-developed entrenchments. Robert E. Lee had outrun his supplies. After minor skirmishing near Manassas and Centreville, the Confederates retired slowly to the Rappahannock River, destroying the Orange & Alexandria Railroad as they proceeded. Meade was soon under pressure from general-in-chief Henry W. Halleck to pursue Lee, but it took almost a month to re-lay the railroad track behind Lee's army.[42]

Also on October 14, Owen led Wickham's brigade through New Baltimore and Gainesville, camping at Langyher's Mill on Broad Run. The next day, the brigade drove Union forces from Manassas. With the aid of his own and Lomax's sharpshooters, Owen forced the Federals to retreat across Bull Run. After establishing a picket line, Owen camped his troopers near Manassas.[43]

Things remained quiet until the evening of October 16, when the same Federals crossed Bull Run but were driven back by Owen's brigade. The brigade camped near Manassas Junction that night. Sergeant Parker wrote, "here we came in contact with their infantry. We held our position till we were ordered back to camp . . . our horses are very much fagged." The Federals advanced again the next day from Groveton, forcing Owen's troopers to retreat back to Gainesville. Owen reported: "I threw out my skirmishers and soon drove them back." Leaving the pickets to face the enemy, Owen removed his brigade back to Ellis's place near Langyher's Mill and bivouacked.[44]

On October 18, Owen moved Wickham's brigade to Langyher's Mill and encamped for the rest of the day and night, leaving the 4th Virginia still on picket at Gainesville. Late that evening, Federal cavalry advanced in considerable force, driving in Owen's pickets. Captain Robert Randolph positioned all of his sharpshooters and skirmished with the Union foes until late that night before withdrawing with the brigade along the pike toward Buckland, leaving a strong picket at Gainesville.[45]

Robert E. Lee's army was unable to sustain itself in barren northern Virginia any longer; he retired his infantry toward Warrenton. The pursuing Federals, emboldened by the Confederate withdrawal, pressed Lee. Meanwhile, Stuart's and Fitz Lee's commands had withdrawn from Bristoe by separate routes and planned to meet in the vicinity of Warrenton. Stuart had ordered Hampton's division toward Warrenton and Fitz Lee's to Auburn. Fitz Lee came up with a

---

42. Atkins, *1863 War Dairy of Corporal John Irving*, 166; NPS "Bristoe Station."
43. *OR* 29/1:472; Driver, *2nd Virginia Cavalry*, 101.
44. Wright, *Lee's Last Casualty*, 119; *OR* 29/1:472; Driver, *2nd Virginia Cavalry*, 101.
45. *OR* 29/1:472–73.

plan to trap the Union cavalry, and Stuart approved. On October 18, Judson Kilpatrick attacked Stuart's outposts, and the Confederate cavalry commander withdrew his troopers to the south bank of Broad Run at Buckland on the Warrenton Pike. Here, Stuart planned to make a stand until Fitz Lee could join him.[46]

On October 19, Stuart and Kilpatrick's 3rd Division of cavalry fought the second major cavalry battle of the Bristoe Campaign at Broad Run, on the Warrenton Pike, near the village of Buckland. The Federal cavalry of Brig. Gen. Henry E. Davies, Jr.'s First Brigade, led by Kilpatrick, pursued Stuart's cavalry, which was shielding the withdrawal of Lee's army. In accordance with the plan devised by Fitz Lee, Stuart feigned a retreat toward Warrenton while trying to draw Kilpatrick's troopers after him. He had arranged with Fitzhugh Lee, stationed three miles south at Auburn, to attack the Federals on their flank and rear when they least expected it. The plan for a trap being set, Stuart then pulled back, with slight skirmishing, to within three miles of Warrenton. Here, at Chestnut Hill, he paused for the expected signal from Lee as General Kilpatrick's troopers rapidly pursued Stuart. Kilpatrick instructed Custer to follow Davies, but Custer refused to move immediately. His men had been fighting all morning and had not eaten breakfast, even though it was past noon. Custer also seemed to sense a possible ambush, based on the ease of the Federal advance on Stuart. Custer remained at Buckland.[47]

Meanwhile, Fitz Lee had ordered Owen forward, with the 2nd Virginia in front, capturing the Federal pickets at Greenwich. Wickham's brigade, under Owen, led Fitz Lee's cavalry as they advanced to attack Kilpatrick's horsemen on their flank. Owen dismounted his sharpshooters, deploying them on the right and left sides of the road. He ordered up Breathed's artillery battery, positioning it to support the attack. While Fitz Lee led the division, Munford commanded Lee's brigade.[48]

At the sound of Breathed's guns, Stuart's entire command remounted, and with sabers drawn, they charged the oncoming Yankee ranks. James B. Gordon's North Carolina brigade was in front and center, with Thomas Rosser's and Pierce Young's brigades on either flank and a little to the rear, in support.[49]

Stuart turned to Gordon and ordered him to advance rapidly along the pike. General Gordon rode to the head of his brigade, ordering

---

46. Adrian Tighe, *The Bristoe Campaign: General Lee's Last Strategic Offensive with the Army of Northern Virginia October 1863* (Bloomington, IN, 2011), 343.
47. Henderson, *Bristoe Campaign*, 202; NPS "Buckland Mills."
48. *OR* 29/1:473.
49. *OR* 29/1:382, 387; Clark, *NCR*, 1: 427–28.

Major Rufus Barringer's 1st North Carolina to charge the Yankee line. The Federals were about 300 yards down the pike, "drawn in a beautiful line, with Stars and Stripes flaunting gaily in the breeze." In a few moments, Stuart's whole command closed, with drawn sabers, on the brigade of General Davies, uncovered by Custer's withdrawal. Davies's troops bravely stood their ground until the column led by the 1st North Carolina, followed closely by the remainder of Hampton's division, came within about 50 yards. Then the whole Yankee line emptied their pistols and carbines on Barringer's troopers before turning and retreating. The volley slowed the speed of the 1st North Carolina Cavalry's advancing lines.[50]

Meanwhile, Fitz Lee's flank attack from the south struck Custer's brigade at Broad Run. Custer was ready and able to check Lee's horsemen. It was Stuart's attack, not Fitz Lee's, that forced a general Federal retreat, as Custer became uncovered by Davies's withdrawal. The 1st North Carolina was momentarily stopped by Federal fire. Barringer, however, rapidly reformed his lines and resumed the pursuit. The Yankees preserved good order, wheeling and firing at occasional intervals for more than a mile. At last Barringer ordered Captain Cowles of Company A to break the Federal ranks. This was speedily accomplished, and the orderly Union retreat became a rout. The pursuit extended several miles and lasted until late into the night.[51]

As Fitz Lee attacked Kilpatrick's flank, Colonel Owen pressed forward with his sharpshooters and took possession of the bridge and ford at Buckland. This forced the Federals, who were now cut off, to leave the road to their right and flee across the run above the bridge and ford. The stampeding blue horsemen raced to save themselves any way they could. Many, however, were captured, killed, or drowned, and a number of their wagons and ambulances were captured.[52]

Fitz Lee, seeing that the rout was on, ordered Owen to pursue the retreating Union cavalry. Owen's brigade took a good position on a hill beyond the run, firing several shells into the fleeing blue horsemen. Advancing at a trot until within about 100 yards of them, he ordered a charge by the 3rd Virginia, followed by the 2nd, and then the 1st. The Federal blue-coats were driven back upon their infantry reserve; many were captured or killed. After driving them about three miles and nearing darkness, upon Fitz Lee's orders, Owen withdrew his troopers with a good many prisoners, horses, equipment and arms—leaving a picket behind—while he and the remainder of the brigade encamped for the night near Buckland. Owen reported, "Thus

---

50. Brooks, *Stories of the Confederacy*, 206; Clark, *NCR*, 1: 427–28.
51. Clark, *NCR*, 1: 428; *OR* 29/1:461.
52. *OR* 29/1:473.

ended a fight which crowned our arms with the most signal cavalry victory of the war, as the enemy's cavalry, supported by infantry, was worse routed and demoralized than I have ever known them before."⁵³

The Buckland rout was completed with the capture of General Custer's headquarters train, many prisoners, about 350 horses, and a large stack of arms and equipment. This segment of the Bristoe Campaign became known as the "Buckland Races."⁵⁴

On the next day, October 20, Owen moved Wickham's brigade to Auburn and then to the Rappahannock, where they crossed at Beverly Ford at 9:00 p.m., encamping at Dr. Green's Farm. Munford reported losses for the 2nd Virginia of eight killed and 33 wounded since October 11.⁵⁵

Following the Bristoe campaign, the Army of Northern Virginia returned to Culpeper County and camped on both sides of the Orange & Alexandria Railroad. The 2nd Virginia resumed picket duty along the river at the Rappahannock Bridge. On November 3, Pvt. James W. Magruder of Company K wrote from Welford's farm that they were busy making camp, building chimneys for their tents, and "making themselves generally comfortable." On November 4, there was a review of Gordon's brigade. Another review near Brandy Station was held the next day; this time of Fitz Lee's and Hampton's Cavalry divisions by Stuart, General Lee, and Virginia Governor John Letcher⁵⁶

Long after the war, Capt. John Lamb recalled that during this mission of picket duty along the Rappahannock:

> Colonel Munford, Colonel W. R. Carter (who fell at Trevilian's Station), Captain [Edward] Fox, of Gloucester and Captain [George N.] Hammond of the 2nd regiment and myself, served on a court-martial occupying the same hotel with Colonel Munford, and often consulting him upon trying and distressing cases that came before us, I learned to know and love the man, and there began a friendship that lasted throughout the war, and has continued to this day. Many of us were anxious to see Colonel Munford promoted. When I guardedly referred to this no word of complaint fell from his lips. Only the good of the service and an ardent desire to contribute all in his power to this end seemed to move him.⁵⁷

---

53. Ibid.
54. Henderson, *The Bristoe Campaign*, 202.
55. Ibid., 413; Driver, *2nd Virginia Cavalry*, 102.
56. Driver, *2nd Virginia Cavalry*, 102.
57. R. A. Brock, ed, *SHSP*, "Address of Captain John Lamb", Vol. Vol. XXXII, 8.

Meanwhile, after repairing needed railroads, on November 7, the Army of the Potomac crossed the Rappahannock at Kelly's Ford and Rappahannock Bridge. They inflicted heavy losses on the Confederate infantry when they captured the fortifications north of the river. Robert E. Lee withdrew his army beyond the Rapidan and prepared for winter quarters. Stuart's cavalry acted as rear guard for Lee's army during the retreat.[58]

On November 10, Wickham's brigade moved to Orange Court House. By November 17, they camped between Robinson River and the Rapidan, with their pickets guarding the fords of the Rapidan. That very night, the brigade was ordered to the Shenandoah Valley. They marched to Miliam's Gap in the Blue Ridge before being surprisingly ordered to return to the Rapidan. The 2nd Virginia camped near Twyman's Mill in the mountains, where their orders were countermanded again. They proceeded on to Mount Zion Church, where they picketed. On November 23, trooper John W. Lakes wrote from camp near Robinson's River that four members of his company were across the Rapidan, attempting to capture horses from Federal cavalry. He also reported the regiment had petitioned Robert E. Lee, requesting that they be sent home during the winter to obtain new horses. Another trooper complained of the lack of long forage for the horses, with corn being their only feed. Captain Whitehead reported the weather during the march was "intensely cold."[59]

Mine Run Campaign

On November 26, General Meade, prodded by superiors and led by David Gregg's cavalry, crossed the Rapidan at Germanna and Ely's Fords and proceeded on Robert E. Lee's right flank toward Orange Court House. Meade's plan was to sweep west of The Wilderness toward open ground beyond to get in the rear of Lee. Meade hoped to surprise Lee by quickly gaining the high ground behind a north-south running tributary of the Rapidan known as Mine Run.

Due to the vigilance of Lee's cavalry, however, the element of surprise was lost. Hampton's cavalry division, supported by A. P Hill's corps, stalled the Federal advance, while Jubal Early's forces advanced on the left as far as Locust Grove. There, Federals were found in strength, and on November 27, General Lee decided to retire to a more defensive position on the west side of Mine Run. Believing that Meade

---

58. McClellan, *Campaigns of Stuart's Cavalry*, 397.
59. Driver, *2nd Virginia Cavalry*, 102–03.

would attack, Lee ordered his soldiers to entrench. On the morning of the 28th, Meade did advance on the Confederate position, but he also ordered entrenchments. For four days the armies faced each other, with neither side attacking in force. Meade then withdrew his forces and recrossed the Rapidan.[60]

Also on the 26th, Fitz Lee was ordered to relieve Ewell's infantry at Raccoon and Ely's Fords. Munford's 2nd Virginia marched all night as part of Wickham's brigade, and relieved Ewell's pickets at Raccoon Ford the next day. Federal cavalry crossed the Rapidan soon after Wickham's horsemen arrived, but the brigade drove them off. The sharpshooters of both sides continued to skirmish across the Rapidan until December 1, when the Union army retreated. After remaining four days, Wickham led his cavalry back to near Barrett's Ford, where they bivouacked. Munford's 2nd Virginia camped on Twyman's farm. Private Magruder wrote that 15 or 20 men had been wounded during the skirmishing at Raccoon Ford.[61]

On December 11, the 2nd Virginia marched to Long's Depot in Albermarle County, expecting to get a much-needed rest. Union Bvt. Lt. Col. William Woods Averell's raid into western Virginia quickly ended the short respite. Averell's mission was to attack the Tennessee and Virginia Railroad. Robert E. Lee ordered Stuart to dispatch some cavalry to the defense of the Valley. Stuart ordered Fitz Lee's division to make the journey.[62]

Private Henry St. George Tucker Brooke wrote, "The weather was bitter cold . . . we camped near Ivy Station, on the Va. Central RR. . . . Notwithstanding the cold, the rain came down in torrents. It was impossible to build a fire and I shivered with cold all night, wet to the skin. When day at length broke, I found my hat had been washed down the hill some distance."[63]

On December 15, the 2nd Virginia continued their march across the Blue Ridge to Miller's Furnace. The long journey took the 2nd Virginia through Staunton and Greenville "in sleet, and cold. Marched night and day to Lexington."[64]

Reaching Lexington on December 18, Margaret Junkin Preston recalled:

> At 3 p.m. General Fitzhugh Lee's cavalry (2,700) passed through. Their horses were in better condition [than

---

60. McClellan, *Campaigns of Stuart's Cavalry*, 397-98; Longacre, *Lee's Cavalry*, 262–63.
61. Driver, *2nd Virginia Cavalry*, 103.
62. Ibid.
63. Driver, *2nd Virginia Cavalry*, 103; Brooke, "Autography of St. George Tucker Brooke," VHS.

Imoden's Brigade]. All the men in both divisions looked in fine spirits, and cheered vociferously as the ladies waved their scarves and handkerchiefs on their passing. People brought out waiters of edibles for the poor tired men.[65]

Lee's march continued that day through Collierstown toward Clifton Forge. He then received word that Averell's horsemen were approaching Buchanan. Lee reversed his direction and led his half-frozen troopers in a forced march over ice-covered roads to Buchanan. Private Brooke recalled, "The cold was intense. My wet clothes had frozen. I could catch hold of my coat or trousers and they would break."[66]

Fizhugh Lee's troopers quickly fed their horses in Buchanan before proceeding through the night to Fincastle. There, Lee learned of Averell's location and hustled the next day to Covington, arriving on December 22. Brooke remembered, "We crossed Craig's Creek a number of times. It was so high that my stirrups got wet and my boots froze to them. I would have to break my feet loose in order to get off my horse. I would have to get off and walk frequently in order to keep from freezing."[67]

Unable to catch Averell, Fitz Lee marched his exhausted troopers back to the valley. Before leaving Covington, Munford received authority to disband his regiment until the beginning of the New Year. They were to meet two months later in Lynchburg. Lee proceeded with the rest of his division to pass through Brownsville on Christmas Eve, where the townspeople fed them. The division reached Staunton on Christmas Day. Just 1,200 horsemen rode with Fitz Lee the next day to New Market.[68]

The year 1863 had been one which started out with promise of continued Confederate successes, but Gettysburg became the turning point in the war. Although the Confederate Army of Northern Virginia would achieve victories in many more battles, their only remaining invasion of northern soil would be Jubal Early's daring raid to the outskirts of Washington in 1864. They suffered from declining resources of manpower, horses, food, and supplies against the backdrop

---

64. Driver, *2nd Virginia Cavalry*, 103–04.
65. Elizabeth Preston Allan, *The Life and Letters of Margaret Junkin Preston* (New York, 1903), 173; Driver, *2nd Virginia Cavalry*, 104.
66. Driver, *2nd Virginia Cavalry*, 104; Brooke, "Autography of St. George Tucker Brooke," VHS.
67. Driver, *2nd Virginia Cavalry*, 104; Brooke, "Autography of St. George Tucker Brooke," VHS, 34.
68. Brooke, "Autobiography of St. George Tucker Brooke," VHS, 35.

of seemingly inexhaustible Union resources. The Federal cavalry had come of age and was no longer easily defeated by Stuart; they would more and more often defeat him.

Chapter Twelve

1864: Kilpatrick-Dahlgren Raid on Richmond and Grant's Overland Campaign

"He feels so heartbroken at home, where everything reminds him of his heavy loss . . . how desolate it is for him here, and it makes me tearful to look at his sad and almost hopeless expression as he sits by the fire in his room"

—Sally Munford on Thomas Munford after his wife Etta Munford's death in January, 1864.

Colonel Thomas Munford, although a competent and reliable senior colonel, had been passed over for promotion by Robertson, Jones, Wickham, and his soon-to-be life-long nemesis, Thomas Rosser. In the coming year, the Confederate cavalry was hard-pressed to keep the Union horsemen at bay, and lost several key commanders, including J.E.B. Stuart.

While the 2nd Virginia Cavalry was disbanded over the winter, Thomas Munford's wife, Etta, died on January 30, 1864, at the age of 30, after a long illness (possibly typhoid fever). Munford's leave was extended on February 1, 1864. He remained on furlough at the family estate, Glen Alpine, in Hamner Parish in Bedford County, to attend to the burial of his wife and other family matters. The children were stricken with "torpid liver" (liver inflammation). Tom, suffering from the effects of his bout with boils since the previous fall, went to Lynchburg and obtained an extension of his furlough. In mid-February, he and his sister Sallie, along with Thomas's children, went to the Tayloe estate at Buena Vista. Etta was buried in the Tayloe Cemetery on the Tayloe estate in southeast Roanoke. Munford remained on furlough or leave of absence from February 1-24, 1864. Major Cary Breckinridge assumed temporary command of the 2nd Virginia.[1]

---

1. Copy of Bill of Real Estate Suit and Bible record, Munford Papers, Jones Memorial Library, Roanoke, Virginia; Sallie Radford Munford to sister

Tom Munford was deeply distressed over his wife's death. His sister, Sallie wrote, "He feels so heartbroken at home, where everything reminds him of his heavy loss . . . how desolate it is for him here, and it makes me tearful to look at his sad and almost hopeless expression as he sits by the fire in his room . . . he told me it was harrowing to him to look around on all the familiar objects and in the room, and to miss her in them all."[2]

The 2nd Virginia remained disbanded until February 1864. Fitz Lee's entire brigade, however, had not been on leave and instead had made raids into Hardy and Hampshire Counties during January. On February 2, most of the returning 2nd regiment troopers regrouped in Charlottesville. The regiment, one squadron at a time, picketed along Robinson River from Graham's Shop to the junction with the Rapidan River. Trooper Rufus Peck wrote, "We camped in a heavy piece of timber and built a wind brake back of the encampment. . . . We kept up picket duty, of course, and had fairly good rations, principally bread and pork with some beef. The country had been so over-run that we couldn't expect to fare as well as we had previously."[3]

Private Henry Brooke wrote from camp at Montpelier, the former home of James Madison:

> We were very insufficiently supplied with tents. I occupied one with five or six others. . . . Some of the men had no tents and built little hovels to protect themselves from the snow. . . . One day when snow was on the ground our regiment marched out of camp and found a South Carolina regiment drawn up in a line of battle on the banks of a little stream. . . . But the South Carolinians, gallant fine fellows they were, had not fought snow ball battles since childhood and this was probably the first time they had ever made a snow ball. Both sides fought until they became tired of the sport and then each side withdrew claiming victory. Perfect humor was preserved throughout.[4]

On February 15, Munford's 2nd Virginia relieved troopers of Lunsford Lomax's brigade on Robertson River. Private Beverly K. Whittle wrote, "Our men are re-enlisting rapidly. . . . Our whole

---

Margaret "Mag" Munford, February 15, 1864, Munford–Ellis Papers, DU; Thomas T. Munford, CSR. Graves from this cemetery were moved to Fairview Cemetery in Roanoke during the 1930s.
2. Sallie Radford Munford to "Mag," February 15, 1864.
3. Peck, *Reminiscences*, 42; Driver, *2nd Virginia Cavalry*, 107. Munford was listed as present on April 1, 1864.
4. Brooke, "Autobiography," VHS, 35; Driver, *2nd Virginia Cavalry*, 107–08.

regiment is armed with guns and is as large as the brigade was before. We are getting 1/4 pound of meat and 3/4 of flour per day."[5]

Kilpatrick—Dahlgren Raid on Richmond

On February 28, Brig. Gen. Judson Kilpatrick, with the assistance of Col. Ulric Dahlgren, led a division size force of Union cavalrymen out of their winter camps at Stevensburg toward Richmond. The invaders crossed over the Rapidan at Ely's Ford, capturing Brig. Gen. Pierce M. B. Young's pickets. South of the river, Kilpatrick and Dahlgren parted, with the flamboyant Kilpatrick commanding 3,600 troopers against Richmond from the north and Dahlgren leading 500 horsemen across the James River west of the capital. The plan was to link up on March 1 for an attack on the city, freeing Union prisoners and assassinating Jefferson Davis and members of his cabinet, according to papers found on Dahlgren's body after he was killed on March 2. Kilpatrick became unnerved upon reaching the outskirts of Richmond, and unable to hook up with the stalled Dahlgren, retreated across the Chickahominy to the safety of Mechanicsville.[6]

Meanwhile, Generals Meade and George A. Custer created diversions to keep Stuart's cavalry busy. Meade and Custer made simultaneous demonstrations in Albemarle County, well northwest of Richmond. Meade advanced with the VI Corps and a portion of the III Corps from Culpeper to Madison Court House. Custer led 1,500 troopers across Robinson River headed for Charlottesville. He pushed Fitz Lee's pickets aside and marched into Madison County. Advancing on Charlottesville on the 29th, Custer's troopers were being watched by Lt. J. N. Cunningham of the 1st Virginia Cavalry, ever since they left Madison Court House. About three miles from Charlottesville, near the Rivanna River, four batteries of Stuart's horse artillery were still in winter quarters. Captain M. N. Moorman was in command of Captains Roger Chew's, James Breathed's, William McGregor's, and his own batteries.[7]

Captain Moorman dispatched pickets to Rio Bridge, but they were driven back to camp. There were no soldiers, infantry or cavalry, in

---

5. Beverly K. Whittle Papers, UVA; Driver, *2nd Virginia Cavalry*, 108.
6. McClellan, *Campaigns of Stuart's Cavalry*, 402; Longacre, *Lee's Cavalrymen*, 270–71; *OR* 33/1:51, 167–68, part 2, 823. Kilpatrick and Meade denied knowing of any such Dahlgren order, as did Dahlgren's troopers. Secretary of War Edwin Stanton, after examining the papers and questioning Kilpatrick and Meade about the alleged assassination plot, denied the plot had existed and had the papers destroyed.
7. McClellan, *Campaigns of Stuart's Cavalry*, 398–99; Longacre, *Lee's Cavalrymen*, 270–71; *OR* 33/1:167–68, vol. 51, part 2, 823.

Charlottesville. Moorman positioned a portion of guns from each of his four batteries and opened up on the Federals' advance, checking them until the remainder of the guns could escape to the rear. These guns were positioned on the road to Charlottesville. The Union troopers approached in two columns: one crossed Cook's Ford and set fire to Moorman's camp while the other charged across Rio Bridge. One of Capt. Roger Chew's caissons exploded, which the Federal horsemen mistook as the reopening of Confederate artillery fire. The two Federal columns mistakenly began firing at each other and broke for the rear, pursued by Chew and Breathed.[8]

Stuart received tardy information about the Federal march towards Charlottesville. The cavalry chief took Wickham's brigade and headed for Charlottesville, but Custer and company had already retired before Stuart could get there. Stuart headed northward, hoping to intercept the Union raiders near Stannardsville. Stuart's chasing troopers ran into cold rain and sleet on their way to the road taken by Custer's retreating horsemen. When Custer became aware of Confederate troopers in his front, he ordered a charge, easily brushing aside Stuart's cavalrymen. Custer then proceeded unmolested towards Madison Court House.[9]

On March 5, the 2nd Virginia, still under the temporary command of Maj. Cary Breckinridge, resumed picket duty along Robinson River. By March 13, many of the disbanded troopers were not yet back in camp. Private Peter Huddleston recalled that on March 22 it snowed 12 inches deep. On April 1, Pvt. John W. Lakes reported from camp that men of his company were still crossing into Union-held territory and attempting to steal horses for themselves.[10]

On March 30, Rooney Lee was exchanged from imprisonment and rejoined Stuart's cavalry. He was promoted to major general and given his own division, consisting of his old brigade (then under Brig. Gen. John R. Chambliss), the 9th, 10th, and 13th Virginia from Fitzhugh Lee's division, and James B. Gordon's brigade of the 1st, 2nd, and 5th North Carolina from Hampton's division. Hampton retained Pierce Young's brigade of the Jeff Davis Legion, Cobb Legion, and two new units, the 7th Georgia and the 20th Georgia Battalion. Also in Hampton's division was Rosser's Laurel Brigade of the 7th, 11th, and 12th Virginia Regiments and the 35th Virginia Battalion. Rosser's brigade, however, had been sent to the Shenandoah Valley and was not at Hampton's calling.[11]

---

8. McClellan, *Campaigns of Stuart's Cavalry*, 399–401; *OR* 33/1:167–68.
9. McClellan, *Campaigns of Stuart's Cavalry*, 401.
10. Driver, *2nd Virginia Cavalry*, 110; Peter L. Huddleston Diary.
11. Longacre, *Lee's Cavalrymen*, 273–74.

Fitz Lee's division, stationed in the Shenandoah Valley, then consisted of Wickham's brigade of the 1st, 2nd, 3rd, and 4th Virginia regiments. Lunsford Lomax's brigade changed slightly, giving up the 1st Maryland Battalion to Bradley Johnson's new brigade. Months earlier Lomax had exchanged the 11th Virginia to Rosser for the 6th Virginia.[12]

On April 14, trooper Beverly K. Whittle wrote, "every disabled horse and worn out horse must be condemned today, and the men sent home after fresh ones. . . . I had been on picket some days. We had awful weather, and were wet day and night; but the river was so high that the Yankees did not bother us any." Whittle mentioned Colonel Munford, who had returned to duty by April 1.[13]

Large numbers of horses of the regiment were condemned or continued to die, as Private Lakes noted on April 23. "The army is quiet yet," he wrote. "They are condemning horses every day. Some of the horses are dieing[sic] too. There are three or four in this company died lately. I shall have mine condemned by the next board before she dies, and bring her home, and then I think I will get a transfer to artillery."[14]

Troopers of Munford's regiment, and indeed, the whole of Fitz Lee's brigade, continued to hunt for horses, and those on foot walked many miles in their search for mounts. Private Huddleston wrote on April 26 that he started on a scout into Federal lines on foot on such a search. He walked 21 miles and stayed the night in Criglersville. The next day he walked 12 miles, spending the night in Pealy Mills. He continued walking many more miles, ending up in Sperryville on May 4 without a horse. While Huddleston and other troopers continued their search for mounts, on April 28 Fitz Lee's brigade moved to near Hamilton's Crossing.[15]

Meanwhile, Colonel Munford's father, still anxious about his son's failure to be promoted, wrote a letter to J.E.B. Stuart expressing his concern. Stuart responded, "I assure you that your anxiety is unnecessary. As far as my action is concerned, it has been my intention in case of Genl Wickham's resignation to recommend Col Thos T Munford for promotion. I agree with you entirely in attributing the high qualities you mention to your gallant son."[16]

---

12. Ibid., 274.
13. Beverly K. Whittle Papers, UVA; Driver, *2nd Virginia Cavalry*, 110.
14. Driver, *2nd Virginia Cavalry*, 111.
15. Huddleston Diary; Driver, *2nd Virginia Cavalry*, 111. Finally, on June 25, Private Huddleston was able to buy a horse, after having had to walk behind the brigade for a couple of months; he paid $1,800 for the horse. Reference: Peter Huddleston Diary, entry 70, June 25, 1864.
16. J.E.B. Stuart to George W. Munford, April 24, 1864, Private Collection of Estelle Call.

The Wilderness Campaign

The Overland campaign was Ulysses S. Grant's 1864 spring offensive against Robert E. Lee's Army of Northern Virginia. The two sides fought an inconclusive battle at the Wilderness and engaged in heavy fighting at the battle of Spotsylvania Court House.

With the 1864 spring campaign approaching, President Abraham Lincoln decided to transfer Maj. Gen. Ulysses S. Grant from the Western Theater to take command of the entire Union Army. Grant was promoted to the rank of lieutenant general, the first United States military man since George Washington to hold that rank. Grant's strategy was to attack the Army of Northern Virginia and Joseph Johnston's Army of Tennessee, not attempting to capture and occupy cities. Not satisfied with the performance of the Federal cavalry in the East, Grant transferred Maj. Gen. Philip H. Sheridan from Tennessee to take command of the Cavalry Corps of the Army of the Potomac. Sheridan's cavalry corps had three divisions: Alfred Torbert's 1st Division, consisting of three brigades; David M. Gregg's 2nd Division; and James H. Wilson's 3rd Division. Brigadier General Henry J. Hunt commanded the artillery reserve.[17]

Grant attached himself to the Army of the Potomac, leaving the task of defeating Johnston to Maj. Gen. William T. Sherman. Grant reduced the Army of the Potomac from five to three Corps—the II, V, and VI—commanded by Major Generals Winfield S. Hancock, Gouverneur K. Warren, and John Sedgwick, respectively. The IX Corps, commanded by Maj. Gen. Ambrose E. Burnside, was not incorporated into the Army of the Potomac until May 24, 1864, although it served with that army in the Wilderness and Spotsylvania campaigns. Grant's army in Virginia consisted of about 116,000 men, including the IX Corps.[18]

In the meantime, Robert E. Lee did not reorganize his army in preparation for the spring campaign. The Army of Northern Virginia still consisted of three infantry corps, commanded by Lieutenant Generals James Longstreet, Richard Ewell, and Ambrose P. Hill, respectively. A single cavalry corps was commanded by Maj. Gen. J.E.B. Stuart. Brigadier General William M. Pendleton commanded the artillery. The Confederacy was unable to add many recruits as the war

---

17. John. A. McClernand, *Journal of The Military Service Institution of The United States (JMSIUS)*, vol. 30 (May, 1902):321–22.
18. *OR*, vol. 36, part 1, 198, 915; McClernand, *Journal of The Military Service Institution of The United States (JMSIUS)*, vol. 30:321–22.

of attrition was taking its toll on manpower. Lee's army could only muster about 64,000 soldiers in its ranks.[19]

In late March 1864, Grant established his headquarters at Culpeper Court House, while Lee set up his at Orange Court House. Lee positioned his army in a defensive arrangement south of the Rapidan River behind fortified entrenchments. Grant, encamped on the north side of the Rapidan, observed that he could not make a frontal assault, so he decided to turn one of Lee's flanks, hoping to force Lee out of his entrenchments to fight or face a Union attack from his rear. Grant decided to try to turn Lee's right flank. He hoped to get through the Wilderness undiscovered and quickly cross the Rapidan to the south side. That way, his superiority in numbers could be more advantageous than in the Wilderness.[20]

The Wilderness, 50 miles north of Richmond, was a wooded rectangular shaped tract of land, south of the Rapidan River, approximately 14 miles long by 10 miles wide. Most of the original timber had been cut, and the vegetation consisted of secondary growth cedar, pine, black oak, and undergrowth that made it almost impenetrable. Troop movements and dispositions in this region were extremely difficult. Grant preferred his army to clear the Wilderness before fighting the Confederates. Robert E. Lee wanted to strike before Grant's subordinate, Meade, cleared the trees.[21]

The long lull in fighting for the cavalry lasted until May 4, when Ulysses S. Grant sent his army, under the immediate direction of General George Meade, across the Rapidan at Ely's and Germanna Fords. The Federal V Corps, under Maj. Gen. G. K. Warren, and the VI Corps under Maj. Gen. John Sedgwick, all with Brig. Gen. James H. Wilson's cavalry leading the advance, crossed at Germanna Ford; Sedgwick's VI Corps followed Warren. The II Corps, under Maj. Gen. Winfield Scott Hancock, screened by David Gregg's cavalry, crossing six miles below Germanna at Ely's Ford. Marching in advance with the 4,000-wagon train was Maj. Gen. Philip Sheridan's cavalry, who positioned Maj. Gen. Alfred Torbert's division at the head of the marching Federal columns. General Ambrose Burnside brought up the rear with his IX Corps, crossing at Germanna early the morning.[22]

Stuart received intelligence from his pickets along the Rapidan that the Federals were crossing and immediately rushed to the scene, meanwhile ordering his cavalry to break camp at their winter quarters

---

19. Freeman, *Lee's Lieutenants*, 3, 345.
20. Bushong, *Fightin' Tom Rosser*, 82–83.
21. Ibid., 83.
22. McClernand, *Journal of The Military Service Institution of The United States (JMSIUS)*, vol. 30:324; Longacre, *Lee's Cavalrymen*, 275–76; OR 36/1:18.

near Orange Court House and head for the front. Fitz Lee's brigade, including Munford's 2nd Virginia, broke camp at Hamilton's Crossing and marched via Massaponax Church to Spotsylvania Court House, where they camped for the night. The next morning, the 2nd Virginia marched to Todd's Tavern and dismounted in support of Lomax's brigade. Here, during the evening, they felled trees and built breastworks and fortifications across the road from Spotsylvania Court House. Munford recalled after the war that Confederate cavalry "never had tools with which to make entrenchments, but relied upon fence rails, stones, dead logs and other obstacles. . . . We sometimes had a few axes, but in four years of war I never saw a cavalryman with a spade or anything better than a shingle pulled from a roof of some house nearby with which to throw up breastworks."[23]

Stuart, with half of Rooney Lee's division, spent most of the day scouting rather than fighting. Hampton's, Gordon's, and Young's troopers had a few small skirmishes on the way to Shady Grove Church, reaching there on May 7.[24]

On May 5, Ewell's corps made first contact with the Federals when it encountered Warren's V Corps in their front moving along the Germanna Plank Road. Also on May 5, Grant ordered Sheridan to take David M. Gregg's and Alfred T. Torbert's divisions of cavalry and march toward Hamilton's Crossing to engage Stuart. Grant sent James H. Wilson's cavalry division to Craig's Meeting House on the Catharpin Road four miles southwest of Parker's Store, and ordered Wilson to reconnoiter the Orange Turnpike and Plank Road, as well as other roads converging on the Federal army's line of march. Meade ordered Hancock's corps to march by Todd's Tavern to Shady Grove Church, Warren's corps to Parker's Store, and Sedgwick's corps to Old Wilderness Tavern. Sedgwick left a division of infantry to protect Germanna Ford until Burnside arrived with the IX Corps. The Union troops moved out as ordered and were extended in long columns along the narrow roads. The Union forces advanced as follows: Sedgwick's corps extended from Germanna Ford southeast to the Wilderness Tavern; Warren's corps was at Belmont Farm; Hancock's corps at the Chancellorsville battleground. The Union army formed in a line running northwest and southeast, with Hancock on the left, Sedgwick on the right, and Warren in the center. General Lee planned to attack Grant's forces while they were strung out on the roads in the

---

23. Driver, *2nd Virginia Cavalry*, 111; McClellan, *Campaigns of Stuart's Cavalry*, 406; Munford, *Journal of the United States Cavalry Association* (Leavenworth, KN, 1889), vol. IV:198.
24. Longacre, *Lee's Cavalrymen*, 277–78.

Wilderness, ill-suited to cavalry fighting. He did not want a full engagement until Longstreet's corps arrived on scene.[25]

Lee moved to strike first, sending Ewell to advance against Warren, who was pressing on southward toward the Plank Road. Warren requested a delay in attacking to permit Sedgwick's VI Corps to arrive. Meade, frustrated at the wait, finally ordered Warren forward to attack Ewell, who had entrenched. Warren dispatched Brig. Gen. Charles Griffin's 1st Division to engage Ewell. Attacks and counterattacks occurred, with no clear winner; both sides by 4:00 p.m. disengaged to construct earthworks. General A. P. Hill also pressed forward on the Plank Road, but he too was preempted by an attacking II Corps under Sedgwick, as well as by Hancock's infantry. A bloody battle ensued and lasted from late afternoon until after dark, with neither side winning a conclusive advantage.[26]

Munford's 2nd Virginia fought from behind their fortifications at Todd's Tavern, beating back charge after charge of Sedgwick's soldiers. Trooper Rufus Peck wrote that the 2nd's losses were slight, but "the ground over which they [Union soldiers] charged was left blue with their slain. . . . The first day I receipted for 100 rounds of ammunition and shot it all and the next day for 115 and used all that the 2nd day. . . . They had removed the dead during the night and charged over the same ground all the second day." The fighting continued for about half of the third day when the breastworks caught fire, and Munford's troopers were ordered to fall back to Lomax's breastworks. The Federals pursued them, but only their sharpshooters came within sight of Munford's men. Munford, in turn, ordered the 2nd's sharpshooters to advance and charge the Yankee soldiers who were occasionally firing from hidden positions in the trees. Munford's dismounted horsemen continued to advance until they ran into Union skirmish lines, at which point they quickly retreated back to the breastworks. Trooper Peck garnered a nice silver watch from what he thought was a dead Union colonel (it turned out he wasn't dead). When Munford later examined the watch, he realized he knew the Union soldier—E. L. Sindler of the 1st Virginia United States Cavalry; Munford had graduated from West Point [VMI] with him.[27]

At nightfall, the fighting ceased. The next morning, Confederate infantry arrived from Richmond to relieve Munford's and Lomax's

---

25. Rev. S. L. Gracey, *Annals of the Sixth Pennsylvania Cavalry* (Philadelphia, PA, 1868), 232–233; Bushong, *Fightin' Tom Rosser*, 83, 85; *OR* 36/2:427–28.
26. Longacre, *Lee's Cavalrymen*, 377; Gracey, *Annals of the Sixth Pennsylvania Cavalry*, 233.
27. Peck, *Reminiscences*, 44–45. Peck is mistaken here; Munford graduated from VMI.
28. Peck, *Reminiscences*, 46.

dismounted troopers. Stuart sent a dispatch to Munford, informing him that General Sheridan was advancing on Richmond with 15,000 men and 90 pieces of artillery. Stuart ordered Munford to head for Richmond, which he and his troopers did at once. They had galloped for about 12 miles when they approached Sheridan's rear. This part of Virginia was filled with a lot of broomsage, which Sheridan had set afire for miles, slowing down their pursuit. Munford's troopers rushed through the fiery grass, singeing some of the horses' manes and tails. The hard-riding horsemen got through the fires in time to close in on Sheridan's rear as well as to allow some of their troopers to get in front of him at Beaver Dam.[28]

Rosser's brigade fought his old West Point rival, James H. Wilson, at Craig's Meeting House, situated across the Po River from Todd's Tavern. Wilson was dangerously far from any support. Rosser drove Wilson's advance guard but was repulsed by his main body. Rosser was able to rally his troopers for a second attack, and Wilson unwisely held his position, expecting support from Hancock's infantry. Hancock, however, had his own battle with A. P. Hill, which kept him from assisting Wilson. Rosser pressed Wilson back, routing about half of his command in a well-coordinated attack, causing many of the Union horsemen to flee 20 miles north to Parker's Store. Finally, a pair of Union horse artillery batteries stalled Rosser's attack for over an hour. Rosser regrouped in perhaps his finest hour on the battlefield during the war, and he struck between Wilson's right flank and the rest of the Union army. Rightfully concerned for his safety, and after learning that Fitz Lee was approaching from the south, Wilson disengaged and headed northeast toward Todd's Tavern. Rosser pressed Wilson, but he made good his escape, crossing the Po River at Corbin Bridge. When he reached Todd's Tavern, he learned that Meade had sent Gregg's cavalry to his aid.[29]

When Fitz Lee's troopers arrived at Todd's Tavern, his and Rosser's forces attacked Wilson and Gregg. Fitz Lee's horsemen made headway on the right, but Gregg's line held, forcing Rosser and Lee back, and then they were counterattacked by Gregg. The retreating Confederate troopers dashed across the Po River, and Gregg gave up the chase. Wilson suffered nearly 100 men killed and more than 400 wounded, while Rosser lost a total of 114 men.[30]

The fighting in the battle of the Wilderness on May 5 had been fierce, but neither side won an advantage. Early on May 6, Stuart led

---

29. *OR* 36/2:428; Wilson, Under the Old Flag, I:382–83; Longacre, *Lee's Cavalrymen*, 278.
30. Longacre, *Lee's Cavalrymen*, 279.

Rosser's Laurel Brigade westward, up the Brock Road leading to Todd's Tavern. Nearby on the Orange Road, A. P. Hill's infantry, supported by Longstreet, was fighting Hancock's corps. Stuart hoped to threaten Hancock's southern flank, thereby aiding Hill and Longstreet. South of Todd's Tavern, Stuart halted his column of horsemen, and after scouting and finding Union cavalry at the intersection of the Brock and Catherine Furnace Roads, he ordered Rosser to attack. Rosser sent Lige White's small 35th Battalion to go up against Custer's Michigan Brigade. White's Comanches made a brilliant charge, driving Custer's troopers back into thick underbrush. White's horse, however, was shot and went down, stalling the charge. Custer's troopers regrouped and sent the Confederates reeling. White escaped, but he lost many of his men killed, wounded, or captured.[31]

The remainder of Rosser's command, with Funsten's 11th Virginia in front, covered the retreat of White's battalion. Funsten held off the charging Union horsemen, until Custer was reinforced by Col. Thomas Devin's brigade of Torbert's division. Funsten was then relieved by the 7th and 12th Virginia, whose troopers stalled the Union advance. Stuart unlimbered Captains James W. Thomson and John J. Shoemaker's guns, whereby Custer's horsemen retreated.[32]

Day two of the battle of the Wilderness ended much as day one had done—with no clear winner. In the first two days of savage fighting, Grant had about 18,000 casualties while Lee had only half that number. Grant was no closer to interposing between Lee and Richmond than he had been at the start of this campaign. In past similar situations, Grant's predecessors had retreated north of the Rapidan. Grant, however, was not about to follow suit, instead opting on May 7 to move his army southeast towards Spotsylvania Court House. Stuart reported Grant's movement to Robert E. Lee, who raced to get ahead of Grant.[33]

On May 6, Meade, in response to erroneous reports that Confederate infantry had gotten in between Hancock's infantry and Sheridan's cavalry, ordered Sheridan's cavalry to withdraw from Todd's Tavern. The next morning, Grant ordered Sheridan to retake the position at Todd's Tavern, so that his march to Spotsylvania Court House could commence from there. Sheridan discovered that Rosser's troopers had evacuated their position, but Fitz Lee's dismounted horsemen had occupied the works the Federals had abandoned and had

---

31. Longacre, *Lee's Cavalrymen*, 279–80; S. Roger Keller, *Riding with Rosser* (Shippensburg, PA, 1907), 22; Frank Myers, *A History of White's Battalion, Virginia Cavalry*, 200; OR 36/1:788–89.
32. Longacre, *Lee's Cavalrymen*, 279–280; Keller, *Riding with Rosser*, 22; Armstrong, *11th Virginia Cavalry*, 70.
33. Longacre, *Lee's Cavalrymen*, 280; OR 36/1:4.

reinforced the fortifications. Sheridan immediately attacked with Torbert's and Gregg's divisions. With supporting artillery, the advancing Union dismounted soldiers drove and pursued Lee's defenders from one line of works to another. Lomax and Wickham's troopers abandoned the works, remounted, and retreated two miles back to a previously occupied position. In this fight, Col. Charles R. Collins of the 15th Virginia was killed, and Colonel Owen of the 3rd Virginia was seriously wounded.[34]

South of Todd's Tavern, retreating Confederates hid amongst the roadside trees, hoping to slow Sheridan's advance. Sheridan's horsemen marched steadily south, chasing the Confederate troopers of Fitz Lee from their hiding places. Fitz Lee's division of cavalrymen faced certain disaster but were saved by the afternoon arrival of Wade Hampton's Virginia and North Carolina regiments. Sheridan's troopers succeeded in occupying the crucial Todd's Tavern intersection for Meade's infantrymen. Hampton wanted to press his advantage, but Sheridan was not about to face the reinforced Confederates in the darkness. He had control of the intersection and disengaged his dismounted troopers.[35]

Beaten on May 7, Fitz Lee reoccupied the breastworks south of Todd's Tavern once Sheridan withdrew. Lee's presence on the Brock Road, however, did impede Sheridan's troopers and Warren's infantrymen the following day on their march to Spotsylvania Court House. Lee's valiant horsemen, fighting dismounted, held up Brig. Gen. Wesley Merritt's cavalry division, leading Warren's V Corps for more than three hours. Seeing the enemy was difficult in the dense undergrowth. Sometimes the battle lines were only 40 feet apart. Most of Lee's horsemen were armed with sabers, revolvers, and musketoons, while the Union cavalry carried seven-shot, breech loading Spencer rifles. Some of the muzzle-loading musketoons became so foul by so much firing that they couldn't be reloaded. One of Munford's troopers tried to hammer the rod against a tree in order to get the cartridge fully loaded in the barrel, but the ram rod bent and the weapon had to be thrown away. The trooper reached down and picked up a musketoon of a dead comrade and continued fighting.[36]

When the Federal V Corps approached the Union cavalry's rear at 3 a.m. on May 8, the horsemen had hardly progressed past Todd's Tavern. Confederates clogged the Brock Road with dismounted

---

34. *OR* 51/1:248–49; Longacre, *Lee's Cavalrymen*, 280–81.
35. *OR* 51/1:248–49, part 2:897–98; Longacre, *Lee's Cavalrymen*, 281.
36. *OR* 36/1:540-41; Longacre, *Lee's Cavalrymen*, 281–82; Driver, *5th Virginia Cavalry*, 73–74; Stiles, *4th Virginia Cavalry*, 45–46; Brooke, "Autobiography," VHS, 38–39, 41.

troopers and horse artillery. Sheridan and Warren furiously demanded that their own cavalry clear the road, which was done at a steep price.[37]

Spotsylvania

The battle of Spotsylvania, the second major battle in General Grant's Overland campaign, followed the bloody battle of the Wilderness. With Lee winning a tactical victory, Grant's army disengaged from Robert E. Lee's army and marched to the southeast, attempting to lure Lee into battle in the open and away from entrenchments. Grant wanted to steal a night march on Lee and get to Spotsylvania Court House first, threatening Richmond.

By May 8, Grant and Meade had lost an opportunity to steal a march on Robert E. Lee and beat him to Spotsylvania. Lee had ordered Maj. Gen. Richard Anderson, commanding Longstreet's I Corps due to its commander's wounding on May 6, to march 10 miles to Spotsylvania. Anderson did not get underway until the morning of May 8, too late to beat the Federals to Spotsylvania had not large parts of the Wilderness been set ablaze by sparks from both Confederate and Union shooting. These fires did not permit Anderson to stop and bivouac for the night and, so his soldiers marched all night. Stuart, knowing that Fitz Lee could not hold back the Federal troops very long, rushed the next morning to urge Anderson and his soldiers on to Spotsylvania. Anderson's infantry, prodded by Stuart, arrived at Spotsylvania prior to the Union army. Fitz Lee led his battle-weary troopers south and took up a defensive position behind Spotsylvania Court House. Just an hour later, Warren's soldiers arrived and challenged Fitz Lee and Anderson. Fighting side by side, the Confederates repulsed Warren's attack.[38]

General Warren's slow progress towards Spotsylvania frustrated Sheridan so much that he feuded with General Meade, complaining that Stuart had too easily outwitted and outfought the Federals for the past three days. Sheridan complained that if he were just permitted to cut loose from Meade, he would draw Stuart into an open fight and whip him. Grant, learning of Sheridan's challenge, gave the cavalry commander authority to proceed. Phil Sheridan set out the morning, May 9, to make good on his boast.[39]

---

37. *OR* 36/1:540-41; Longacre, *Lee's Cavalrymen*, 281–82; Driver, *5th Virginia Cavalry*, 73–74; Stiles, *4th Virginia Cavalry*, 45–46; Brooke, "Autobiography," VHS, 38.
38. Longacre, *Lee's Cavalrymen*, 282; McClellan, *Campaigns of Stuart's Cavalry*, 408–09.
39. McClernand, *Journal of The Military Service Institution of The United*

On May 10, the 2nd Virginia fought the 5th United States Cavalry on Beaver Dam Road. Trooper William H. Stratton, who had just drawn a supply of bacon for his company, recalled:

> Just as we reached the regiment with these rations, we heard Col. Munford's voice ring out: "Attention regiment! From fours! Draw Sabre! . . . Forward, Trot! March!" . . . I soon heard the charge of cavalry coming down the road [Beaver Dam Road]. All of the boys had their sabres drawn, ready to rush into the fighting. . . . Col. Munford rode down the line and said, "Capt. [Edgar] Whitehead, lead your squadron into that charge." Just then the leader of the Yankees came charging down the road a little ahead of his command. I drew my pistol and fired at him and he went tumbling across the fence into the woods. Our boys had sabres and went at the Yankees, who used carbines. Capt. Whitehead's horse was struck in the face and knocked down, so he led the charge on foot. About that time my horse was shot and I had to jump off. With balls flying in front and fences afire on both sides of the road, we drove the Yankees back.[40]

According to trooper St. George T. Brooke, Munford was always at the head of the regiment when they charged the enemy.[41]

Stuart led Fitz Lee's weary division onward to Hanover Junction. There, they rested and slept until 1:00 a.m. on May 11, and then they resumed their march. The 2nd Virginia reached Ashland at 3:00 a.m., spotting Federal cavalry in and around the village. Wickham ordered Munford to drive the Union cavalry from the town. Munford sent troopers down the main street from the north, with the Federal horsemen defending the south end. Munford ordered Whitehead's squadron to lead the attack dismounted, concealing themselves as much as possible, using the honeysuckle bushes on both sides of the street. Lieutenant E. P. Hopkins of the 1st Massachusetts Cavalry led a mounted attack on the advancing Confederates. Captain Joseph W. Carson of the 2nd Virginia wrote his wife, "We were charging them on foot in Ashland . . . when I was struck (which was stopped by an inkwell and comb in his pocket) . . . then the Yankees charged us mounted. I must say I did forget I was wounded until the fight was over. I tell you I gave the best I had, carbine and pistol."[42]

States (JMSIUS), vol. 30:330–31; Longacre, *Lee's Cavalrymen*, 283; *OR* 36/1:788–89, part 2:553; Philip H. Sheridan, *Personal Memoirs of P. H. Sheridan* (New York, 1888), 1:366–67.

40. Driver, *2nd Virginia Cavalry*, 115; Whitehead, "Campaigns of Munford's 2nd Virginia Cavalry," 92; Brooke, "Autobiography," 42, VHS.
41. Ibid.
42. Driver, *2nd Virginia Cavalry*, 116.

Fitz Lee reported, "the 2nd Va . . . was quickly dismounted and under its efficient Colonel, gallantly charged this force, and drove them from the village, killing eight, wounding many, and capturing some prisoners."[43]

Munford's regiment marched on with Lee and Stuart. The Confederate troopers crossed a bridge over the Chickahominy and at 10:00 p.m., arrived at Yellow Tavern, located at the intersection of the Telegraph and Mountain roads, six miles northeast of Richmond.[44]

Battle of Yellow Tavern: May 11, 1864

Before daylight on May 9, the Union's powerful cavalry force—more than 10,000 Union troopers in three divisions, with six batteries of horse artillery—rode to the southeast to move behind Lee's army. Sheridan's goals were to disrupt Lee's supply lines by destroying railroad tracks and supplies, threaten Richmond itself, and most importantly, defeat Stuart. The defending Confederate forces were severely outmanned and outgunned.[45]

The Union cavalry column, stretching more than 10 miles, reached the Confederate forward supply base at Beaver Dam Station on the evening of May 9. The Confederate troops had been able to destroy many of the critical military supplies before the Union troopers arrived. Sheridan's horsemen destroyed railroad cars, six locomotives of the Virginia Central Railroad, telegraph wires, and rescued almost 400 Union soldiers who had been captured.[46]

Stuart moved his 4,500 troopers to get between Sheridan and Richmond. The two combatants met at noon on May 11 at Yellow Tavern, an abandoned stagecoach inn, located six miles north of Richmond and near the intersection of Telegraph and Mountain Roads. Union forces outnumbered the Confederates by three divisions to two brigades. Additionally, they had superior firepower—all were armed with rapid-firing Spencer carbines. Lomax's brigade dismounted and manned the bed of Telegraph Road, facing west. Wickham's dismounted troopers, the 1st, 2nd, 3rd, and 4th Virginia regiments, deployed left to right, with the left flank linking with Lomax's horsemen. Breathed's artillery was in support.[47]

---

43. Ibid.
44. Ibid.
45. Wert, *Cavalryman of the Lost Cause*, 346–47.
46. Ibid., 347; Longacre, *Lee's Cavalrymen*, 284–85.

The Confederate troopers tenaciously resisted from the low ridgeline bordering the road to Richmond, fighting for over three hours. A countercharge by the 1st Virginia Cavalry pushed the advancing Union troopers under Wesley Merritt back from the hilltop as Stuart, mounted on horseback, shouted encouragement. A fleeing dismounted Union trooper turned and shot Stuart as he passed by the Confederate cavalry chief. Stuart, mortally wounded, died in Richmond the following day.[48]

The fighting kept up for an hour after Stuart was wounded, with Fitzhugh Lee taking temporary command. Union cavalrymen suffered 625 casualties, but they captured 300 Confederate prisoners and recovered almost 400 Union prisoners. Sheridan disengaged his men and headed south toward Richmond. He resisted any temptation to attack the modest defenses of the Confederate capital, continued south across the Chickahominy River to link up safely with Maj. Gen. Benjamin Butler's force on the James River. In the meantime, Brig. Gen. James B. Gordon's North Carolina Cavalry Brigade had been dogging the heels of David Gregg's Second Division, preventing him from joining Sheridan at Yellow Tavern. Stuart, however, had badly needed Gordon at Yellow Tavern, but it was not to be. Gordon was mortally wounded at Meadow Bridge the day after Stuart was shot. After resupplying with [Benjamin] Butler on May 24, Sheridan's men returned to join Grant at Chesterfield Station. Sheridan's raid achieved a victory against a numerically inferior opponent at Yellow Tavern, and had killed Confederate cavalry chief J.E.B. Stuart, which deprived Robert E. Lee of his most experienced cavalry commander.[49]

Early on a dismal, cold, and rainy May 12, Fitz Lee assumed command as Stuart lay dying nearby. Lee, probably a bit overwhelmed, did not immediately pursue Sheridan as a dense fog fell before daylight. Instead, he gathered the Confederate troopers that had been scattered by the Union cavalry. Fitz Lee also had to provide for protecting Richmond from Butler's forces, posted six miles south of the city near Drewry's Bluff and, of course, Sheridan, heading south for Butler's supply depot at Haxall's Landing after the fight with Gordon at Meadow Bridge. At Meadow Bridge, Fitz Lee brought a few hundred troopers and held the far shore of the span, which Sheridan had to cross. The span was partially dismantled, so Sheridan's horsemen shored up the bridge with timber stripped from nearby houses. Under pressure from Gregg and Sheridan, Fitz Lee was forced to withdraw, allowing Sheridan's army to cross the Chickahominy,

---

47. Wert, *Cavalryman of the Lost Cause*, 350–51.
48. Ibid., 357-58; Rhea, *The Battles for Spotsylvania Court House and the Road to Yellow Tavern May 7–12, 1864*, 209.
49. Eicher, *The Longest Night: A Military History of the Civil War*, 674;

heading for the James River. On May 13, Fitz Lee marched his remaining 2,400 troopers toward Mechanicsville, where he joined forces with Gordon's brigade, now under the command of Col. Clinton Andrews. For the next several days, Fitz Lee continued to garner the remaining troopers of the cavalry corps and recover from the effects of nine days of marching and fighting with insufficient rations and ammunition.[50]

On May 20, Grant ordered Hancock's II Corps to march to the railroad line between Fredericksburg and Richmond and then to turn south. If Robert E. Lee pursued Hancock directly, Grant would unleash the remainder of his army to chase Lee and strike him before the Confederates could entrench again.[51]

Before Hancock began to move, however, Robert E. Lee ordered Ewell to conduct a reconnaissance in force to locate the northern flank of the Union army. Ewell took the majority of his II Corps divisions under Major Generals Robert Rodes and John B. Gordon up the Brock Road and swung widely to the north and east to Harris farm. There they encamped, awaiting the arrival of Hancock. When Hancock's II Corps appeared, Ewell's men charged them, encountering relatively green Federal troops, who had recently been converted from artillery soldiers to infantry. Soon, the Federal force was reinforced by the Union 1st Maryland Regiment, followed by Brig. Gen. David B. Birney's infantry division. The fighting lasted until about 9:00 p.m. and Robert E. Lee, concerned that Ewell was risking a general engagement while separated from the main army, recalled his men.[52]

Grant's intended advance of Hancock's corps was delayed by the Harris farm engagement, so the troops did not begin their movement south until the night of May 20-21. Lee did not fall into Grant's trap of attacking Hancock but traveled instead on a path parallel to the North Anna River. The Overland campaign continued as Grant attempted several more times to engage Lee, found himself stymied by strong defensive positions, and moved again around Lee's flank in the direction of Richmond. Major engagements occurred at the battle of North Anna and the battle of Cold Harbor, after which Grant crossed the James River to attack Petersburg. The armies then faced each other for nine months in the Siege of Petersburg.[53]

Longacre, *Lee's Cavalrymen*, 289.
50. Longacre, *Lee's Cavalrymen*, 289–90; OR 51/1:250; *Richmond Times Dispatch*, May 19, 1905; Driver, *1st Virginia Cavalry*, 85–86.
51. Gary W. Gallagher, ed., *The Spotsylvania Campaign* (Chapel Hill, 1998), 55.
52. Ibid., 55–56. Birney was promoted to major general on May 20, 1864.
53. Gordon C. Rhea, *To the North Anna River: Grant and Lee, May 13–25, 1864*

Battle of North Anna

After disengaging from the stalemate with Robert E. Lee at Spotsylvania Court House, Grant moved his army southeastward, hoping to lure Lee out of his defensive position to fight out in the open. Grant lost the race to Lee's next defensive position south of the North Anna River. Lee, unsure of Grant's direct intention, opted not to prepare significant defensive works. On May 23, the Union V Corps, under Maj. Gen. Gouverneur K. Warren, crossed the river at Jericho Mills. A Confederate division under Lt. Gen. A. P. Hill's corps was unable to push them back. Meanwhile, Maj. Gen. Winfield S. Hancock's II Corps stormed a small Confederate force at "Henagan's Redoubt" to seize Chesterfield Bridge, crossing on the Telegraph Road, but did not ford the North Anna River.[54]

That night, Robert E. Lee devised a scheme for defensive earthworks in the shape of an inverted "V" that could split the Union army when it advanced, allowing the Confederates to use interior lines to attack and defeat one wing while preventing the other wing from reinforcing it in time. As Hancock's men failed to carry the Confederate works on the eastern leg of the "V" on May 24, a brigade under Brig. Gen. James H. Ledlie was repulsed from an ill-executed assault against a strong position at Ox Ford. Unfortunately for the Confederates, Lee was disabled with an intestinal illness, leaving his subordinates to execute his planned attack. After two days of skirmishing, the inconclusive battle ended when Grant ordered another wide movement to the southeast, this time in the direction of the crossroads at Cold Harbor.[55]

Meanwhile, on May 23, Fitz Lee marched his division to Atlee's Station. The next day, Lee's brigade of dismounted troopers, under Wickham, aimed to attack a Federal garrison (Fort Powhatan) at Kennon Landing on the James River. They attacked the fort, without artillery support, from the side opposite the river, but were pummeled by the "enormous elongated shells" that seemed like lamp posts fired from the gunboats lying in the river. The Confederates were beaten back; they then tried an assault on another side of the fort but were repelled again. After these unsuccessful dismounted attacks, Lee withdrew and led his troopers to Charles City Court House and camped. Hampton's and Rooney Lee's divisions joined them the following day.[56]

(Baton Rouge, 2000), 251–52.
54. Ibid., 260–61, 266, 291, 296.
55. Ibid., 324–25, 337–41, 353–54, 361–62.

Haw's Shop

The battle of Haw's Shop (or Enon Church) was fought on May 28 in Hanover County. Grant abandoned his standoff with Robert E. Lee following the May 23-26 battle of North Anna. Disengaging from Lee and swinging widely around Lee's right flank, Grant used the Pamunkey River to screen his movements to the southwest. Lee's army moved directly south, taking positions on the southern bank of Totopotomoy Creek. The Confederate commander ordered a cavalry force under Wade Hampton to gather intelligence about Grant's next moves. On May 28, Hampton's troopers encountered Union cavalry under Brig. Gen. David McM Gregg. Fighting predominately dismounted and utilizing earthworks for protection, neither side achieved a decided advantage. Gregg was reinforced by two brigades of Brig. Gen. Alfred T. A. Torbert's division. The brigade under Brig. Gen. George A. Custer launched a spirited attack, just as Hampton was ordering his men to withdraw.[57]

Also on May 28, having just arrived from South Carolina a few days earlier, part of Brig. Gen. Matthew C. Butler's brigade, including the 5th South Carolina Cavalry, joined Wickham's and Rosser's brigades for the fight at Haw's Shop. The untested and stubborn South Carolinians, fighting with Rosser, performed admirably in the seesaw fight between Fitz Lee's and David Gregg's horsemen, which lasted until mid-afternoon. Almost cut-off, Hampton rode to the front to reel the South Carolinians in, ordering them to the rear. Lee ordered a retreat when he encountered dismounted Union cavalry, mistaking them for infantry.[58]

Trooper Brooke recalled he had just finished his "scanty breakfast of three crackers or hard tack . . . and a small slice of bacon which had been stuck on a stick and held in the fire while the bacon grease dripped on the crackers which put on the ground to catch it." Brooke then sat on his horse in a line of battle as the squadron was ordered by Lt. Robert C. Wilson to drive the Union pickets. Munford was astride his horse, facing the road as they passed. The squadron forced the lonely cavalry picket into a hasty retreat. They were then fired upon by sharpshooters on both sides of the road, making a hasty retreat. Brooke was wounded in the leg, fell off his horse, and was captured.[59]

The seven-hour cavalry battle at Haw's Shop was inconclusive, but still was one of the bloodiest of the war. Both sides claimed victory.

---

56. Driver, *2nd Virginia Cavalry*, 120, 122; Brooke, "Autobiography," 43, VHS.
57. Longacre, *Lee's Cavalrymen*, 294–95.
58. Ibid.

Union Cavalry Corps commander Maj. Gen. Philip Sheridan asserted that his men had driven Hampton from the field, demonstrating the superiority of the Union cavalry. Hampton, however, had held up the Union cavalry for seven hours, preventing it from achieving its reconnaissance objectives. In turn, Hampton had provided Lee with important intelligence about the disposition of Grant's army. Meade, meanwhile, was crossing the river at Hanovertown.[60]

---

59. Brooke, "Autobiography," 45, 50–52, VHS.
60. Longacre, *Lee's Cavalrymen*, 295.

Chapter Thirteen

Battles for Critical Railroads, The Battle of Trevilian Station, and The Siege of Petersburg Begins.

"Sheridan was fairly and completely beaten, and all of his apologies for his retreat, 'ammunition exhausted and presence of infantry,' are unworthy of a great soldier. Why was he there without ammunition? Didn't he expect to have some fighting? . . . These excuses are really too ridiculous to be discussed."

–Colonel Thomas Munford
after the battle of Trevilian Station.

In June 1864, the siege of Petersburg began. Another epic cavalry battle was fought at Trevilian Station, where Munford led his regiment in capturing four out of the five Union caissons that day, as well as George Armstrong Custer's wagons and personal effects. Munford later returned the private things to Custer's wife, Libbie, after Custer's death at the battle of Little Big Horn.

In May, before General Hampton's promotion to cavalry corps commander, General Grant attempted to flank General Lee's army and force from its entrenchments at Spotsylvania and then again along the North Anna, but failed both times. In June, the Federal commander continued to try to flank Lee, forcing the Army of Northern Virginia back towards Richmond, thus denying Lee room to maneuver. Grant then initiated a series of marches southward, trying to flank Lee's army, but each time the Confederate commander moved successfully to block his attempts. On June 2, during the skirmishing at Turkey Ridge that led up to the climactic battle of Cold Harbor on June 3, Thomas Munford was wounded by spent grape shot.[1]

At Cold Harbor on June 1-3, Grant thought he had discovered a weak spot in Lee's well-entrenched army, but blundered by attacking it. Unable to take Richmond from the north or east, the hard-driving Union commander decided to try from the south. If he could not

---

1. H. B. McClellan, *Life and Campaigns of J.E.B. Stuart*, 424.

destroy Lee's defending army in battle, he might wear it down by siege. Lee realized this too, remarking to Gen. Jubal Early, "If Grant moves his army south of the James, it will become a siege, and then it will be a matter of time."[2]

By June 7, Grant's movements had been fairly well-developed in moving south and east of Richmond. Robert E. Lee ordered the Confederate cavalry to harass him. Brig. Gen. Rufus Barringer's North Carolina Cavalry Brigade was detached and hastened to the lower fords of the Chickahominy. Under the protection of Federal gunboats prowling the river, on June 13 Grant forced in Barringer's pickets at Long Bridge on the Chickahominy and began moving his army south of the James. The entire Tar Heel brigade hurried to support the pickets, but Grant was advancing with cavalry and infantry and pushed Barringer back to White Oak Swamp. Near Riddle's Shop, Rooney Lee sent in the remainder of his division to reinforce Barringer and was able to hold the Federals in check until Southern infantry came up and relieved the cavalry. Barringer's brigade then followed the main Federal column to Wilcox's Landing, skirmishing daily until June 18 at places like Crenshaw's; Nance's Shop (also known as Samaria Church, 13 miles southeast of Richmond); and near Harrison's Landing at Herring Creek. On June 18, Rufus Barringer's brigade crossed the James and took up position two miles south of Petersburg.[3]

Grant realized that if he could take Petersburg with its rail networks to the south and west, Richmond would be isolated and Lee's supplies from the south would be cut off. The Army of Northern Virginia could then be defeated. Meanwhile, Sherman was driving toward Atlanta, pushing Joe Johnston's army before him.

Once south of Petersburg, Grant's basic strategy was to continue to push his lines ever farther to the west, cutting the railroads that fed Lee's Army and forcing Lee to extend his lines. This seemed possible, especially since Grant's forces carried a numerical superiority over Lee's of about two to one. Eventually, Lee's 35-mile-long defensive works extended from northeast of Petersburg, around the city, to Hatcher's Run, 10 miles southwest of the city.[4]

The siege of Petersburg lasted nine months, the longest siege of the war. It was punctuated by a series of battles for the railroads leading to

---

2. Robert Stiles, *Four Years Under Marse Robert* (New York, 1904), 308; Rev. J. William Jones, D. D., *Personal Reminiscences, Anecdotes, and Letters of Gen. Robert E. Lee* (New York, 1875), 40.
3. *OR* 36/1:902, 1035; Clark, *NCR*, 2:430–31; 3:609; *The Daily Confederate* (Raleigh), February 22, 1865.
4. Richard Sommers, *Richmond Redeemed: The Siege at Petersburg, The Battles of Chaffin's Bluff and Poplar Spring Church, September 29–October 2, 1864* (El Dorado Hills, CA, 2014), 2.

the south and west, the lifeblood of Confederate resistance. These crucial railroads were the Norfolk and Petersburg; the Petersburg and Weldon, which ran south to North Carolina; the South Side, which ran southwest to Lynchburg (then to Bristol via the Virginia & Tennessee Railroad); and the Richmond and Danville, which ran from the capital city intersecting the South Side Railroad at Burkeville Junction (50 miles west of Petersburg) and continuing south to Danville. None of these battles for control of these vital arteries were major in scope, but together they wore down Lee's army by attrition. At the same time, sickness and desertion reduced the besieged Confederates.[5]

Trevilian Station

On June 7, General Grant's strategy sent General Sheridan to the Shenandoah Valley with the cavalry divisions of David M. Gregg and Alfred Torbert, totaling about 9,300 troopers and 24 artillery pieces. Their first objective was to raid and destroy the railroads at Gordonsville and Charlottesville. Grant hoped that Maj. Gen. David Hunter, who replaced Maj. Gen. Franz Siegel after his defeat at New Market, would advance on Lynchburg and Lexington, and join Sheridan in Charlottesville. Sheridan traversed the eight-mile-long Federal column, making sure the horses were not overworked, as hot billowing clouds of dust plagued the march. Even so, the horses began breaking down just hours into the walking-paced march. Following the practice previously established, broken-down horses were shot and left along the road, their riders walking off to search the countryside for a new mount or joining the ranks of the dismounted.[6]

Wade Hampton, with information from scouts, correctly concluded that the Federals' immediate objectives were the important railroad towns of Gordonsville and Charlottesville. Robert E. Lee ordered Hampton to follow with an additional cavalry division. Hampton ordered Fitzhugh Lee to join him as soon as possible, and on June 8 proceeded to get between Gordonsville and Sheridan. Hampton, with about 6,400 horsemen and 15 guns under his command, managed to outmarch Sheridan and camped the night of June 10 at Green Spring Valley, three miles from Trevilian Station on the Virginia Central Railroad. Fitz Lee camped the same night at Louisa Court House. General Rosser bivouacked for the night two miles west of Trevilian.[7]

---

5. Ibid., 3-4; Edward G. Longacre, "The Wilson-Kautz Raid," *Civil War Times Illustrated* (May 1970), 32.
6. Wittenberg, *Glory Enough for All*, 37–38, 44, 59.
7. *OR* 36/1:1095–97; *Philadelphia Weekly Times*, April 19, 1884; Eric Wittenberg, *Glory Enough for All*, 43–44, 51.

Hampton learned during the night that Sheridan had crossed the North Anna River at Carpenter's Ford; he decided to attack at dawn. Hampton ordered Fitz Lee's division to march up the Marquiz Road (Virginia Route 22) from Louisa Court House to Clayton's Store, while Hampton, with his division, planned to assault Sheridan on the road leading from Trevilian Station to Clayton's Store. With this disposition, Hampton hoped to "cover Lee's left flank and my right flank, and drive the enemy back if he attempted to reach Gordonsville, by passing to my left, and to conceal my real design, which was to strike him at Clayton's Store after uniting the two divisions."[8]

At the coolness of dawn on June 11, Hampton had his troopers in the saddle. He moved out with Calbraith Butler's and Pierce Young's brigades, while Rosser's command was sent to cover the Gordonsville Road on Hampton's left. Hampton attacked and pressed the Union troopers of Alfred Torbert's division until 9:00 a.m.; pushing them back up the Trevilian Station Road towards Clayton's Store, where they positioned themselves behind breastworks.[9]

Meanwhile, Fitz Lee's division, which had bivouacked four miles from Hampton at Louisa Court House, encountered George A. Custer's brigade on the Louisa Court House Road, a few miles east of Trevilian Station. After establishing contact with Custer, Lee fell back, opening a dangerous gap between himself and Hampton. Lee, therefore, failed to immediately fight through Custer and join Hampton as planned. Hampton's staff officers, and perhaps even Hampton, later regarded Lee's tardiness as proof of his unwillingness to support any superior other than J.E.B. Stuart.[10]

Meanwhile, at mid-morning of what would be a clear, hot day, George A. Custer's brigade exploited the gap between Hampton and Lee. Custer interposed his forces between the rail depot and Louisa Court House by way of a diagonal track through the forest, positioning them in the rear of Butler's and Col. Gilbert J. Wright's Georgia brigades. Custer had left one of his four regiments to deal with the tardy Fitz Lee while proceeding on until he was in a position to strike Hampton from the rear. Hampton was being pressed by the rest of Torbert's troopers in his front. Custer's 5th Michigan came upon lightly guarded ambulances, caissons, wagons, and the 1,500

---

8. *OR* 36/1:1096.
9. Ibid., William McDonald, *A history of the Laurel brigade: originally the Ashby cavalry of the Army of Northern Virginia and Chew's Battery* (Baltimore, 2002), 251.
10. Longacre, *Lee's Cavalrymen*, 300; Wade Hampton to Edward L. Wells, January 18, 1900, Wells Manuscript, Charleston Library Society, Charleston, SC.; Edward L. Wells, *Hampton and His Cavalry in 1864* (Richmond, VA., 1899), 198–99; Keller, *Riding with Rosser*, 38.

Trevilian Station Map

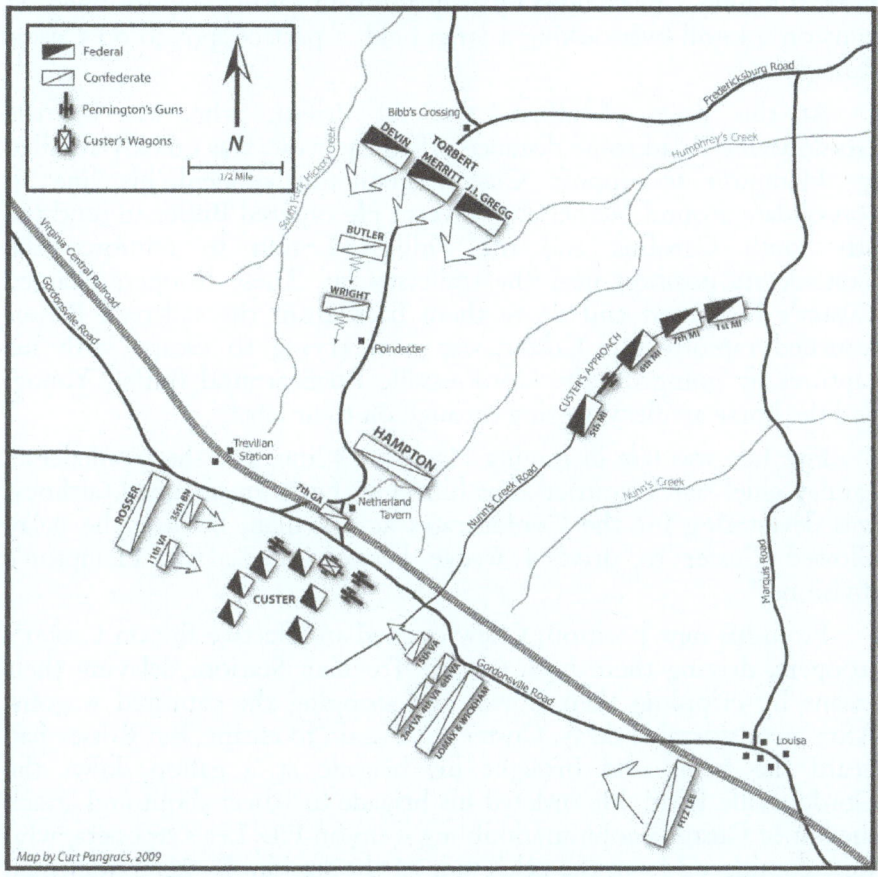

horses of Hampton's division. The 5th Michigan captured several hundred prisoners, the 1,500 horses, six caissons, 40 ambulances, and 50 army wagons.[11]

Custer spotted Maj. James W. Thomson's artillery battery of Butler's brigade behind him on his right, near Netherland Tavern, and decided to take the unattended battery. Lieutenant Colonel Roger P. Chew, of the Horse Artillery, recalled, "Butler was at this time hotly engaged in front. I went back rapidly and found Custer's men advancing from the rear to capture the guns."[12]

Fortunately for the Confederates, Custer overlooked Thomson's two guns, which Thomson immediately repositioned on the Gordonsville Road. Meanwhile, Butler facing more firepower than he

---

11. Longacre, *Lee's Cavalrymen*, 300–02; *OR* 36/1:784–85, 800-01, 806-08, 823-24, 849–51; Wittenberg, *Glory Enough For All*, 101.
12. McDonald, *Laurel Brigade*, 251–52; Wittenberg, *Glory Enough for All*, 104.

could handle, retreated toward Trevilian Station and withdrew James F. Hart's guns. Chew, aided by a squadron of cavalry, repositioned six guns on a knoll overlooking a large field, a perfect spot to do Custer damage.[13]

At this stage of affairs, General Rosser, who was on the Gordonsville Road some distance off to the west, was quickly recalled by Hampton to oppose Custer. Hampton ordered his line to consolidate around Netherland Tavern. He ordered Butler to send the 6th South Carolina and the Phillips Legion to reinforce the Confederate position near the train station. These troopers charged Custer's horsemen and drove them back from the railroad. Rosser returned rapidly, but Custer was now trying to escape with his captures by going off the Gordonsville Road around Butler, Young, and the horse artillery, getting through on their left.[14]

Fitz Lee was late in joining Hampton's line, and the Confederate cavalry chief sent a courier after him. Fitz Lee's unexplained tardiness was devastating for the Confederates at Trevilian, because the delay allowed Custer to drive a wedge between Lee's and Hampton's divisions.[15]

From his new position, Chew opened an effective fire on Custer's troopers, driving them back toward Trevilian Station, delaying their escape by crippling their horses and stopping the captured wagons. After a considerable delay, Custer tried again to escape, but Rosser had heard the firing and brought his brigade at a gallop down the Gordonsville Road. He ordered his brigade to wheel about and attack the left of Custer's column, doubling it up on Fitz Lee's troopers, who were coming up from the other side of the station. Rosser's horsemen attacked vigorously, pushing Custer back and recapturing five caissons and several wagons. Rosser's well-timed assault was made in double columns, the 11th Virginia on the front right of the Gordonsville Road, and Lige White's battalion in front on the left.

Fitz Lee, finally on the scene with Lomax's brigade, captured Custer's headquarters wagon, supply wagons, horses, and prisoners. Upon his arrival, Lee ordered Munford to support Breathed's gunners. Munford, however, spotted a large portion of Custer's brigade nearby and ordered Breathed's batteries to open fire. Munford, without waiting for further orders, pitched into the fray. He led his 2nd Virginia Cavalry column in breaking through Custer's line, "scattering them like sheep," and bore down on Union Capt. Alexander

---

13. Trout, *Galloping Thunder*, 497; Wittenberg, *Glory Enough for All*, 106.
14. *OR* 36/1:1095.
15. McDonald, *Laurel Brigade*, 253; Keller, *Riding With Rosser*, 38; Wittenberg, *Glory Enough for All*, 105.

Pennington's guns. Lieutenant Charles H. Almond recalled that the 2nd Virginia struck the right and rear of Custer's troopers, capturing countless led horses and mules. Munford's troopers captured four out of the five caissons lost by Sheridan that day. They also captured Custer's headquarters wagons, his sash, private wagon, and papers. The wagon was retained and used by Munford until a few days before the surrender at Appomattox.[16]

Munford also attacked Union Battery M, considered by many as their best. Munford's 2nd Virginia captured four caissons, with their drivers and cannoneers, horses, baggage, and 50 men. The Virginians also re-captured two of Chew's caissons and three of his wagons, which had been taken from Hampton in the morning fighting. Munford lost two killed and nine wounded.[17]

Butler's 6th South Carolina, along with the Phillips Legion of Col. Gilbert J. Wright's brigade, attacked Custer from the north. Custer, driven from the field, suffered 11 killed, 51 wounded, and 299 captured before being supported by Generals Merritt and Devin. He was fortunate to have escaped at all. Custer wrote his wife, Libbie, "My Brigade was completely surrounded, and attacked on all sides. I had captured over 1500 horses with saddles, complete; 6 caissons of artillery filled with ammunition, 250 wagons & several hundred prisoners, but against overwhelming odds and lack of support, could not retain our captures. . . . Never has the Brigade fought so long or so desperately."[18]

Confederate artilleryman George M. Neese later recalled, "The enemy had already pierced General Hampton's line . . . when General Rosser, who had been hurriedly dispatched for, dashed on the field with gleaming saber at the head of his brigade of gallant trusty veterans, all rushing to the rescue with naked sabers or drawn pistols, with teeth set and knit brow, determined to do or die." After a tough fight, the blue line retreated, and Neese concluded, "The timely arrival of General Rosser at the head of his brigade was all that saved our side from sustaining a disastrous defeat."[19]

16. R. A. Brock, ed., *SHSP*, Vol. 30 (Richmond, VA, 1902), 286; Wittenberg, *Glory Enough for All*, 116; Driver, *2nd Virginia Cavalry*, 124–25.
17. *Richmond Examiner*, July 1, 1864.
18. *OR* 36/1:1095; *Philadelphia Weekly Times*, April 19, 1884; Trout, *Galloping Thunder*, 495–96; Rod Andrew, *Wade Hampton: Confederate Warrior to Southern Redeemer* (Chapel Hill, NC, 2008), 210; J. H. Kidd, *Personal Recollections of a Cavalryman Riding with Custer's Michigan Cavalry Brigade* (Ionia, MI, 1908), 222; Marguerite Merington, ed., *The Custer Story: The Life and Letters of General George A. Custer and His Wife Elizabeth* (New York, 1950), 104; Wittenberg, *Glory Enough for All*, 116.
19. George M. Neese, *Three Years in the Confederate Horse Artillery*, 285.

Confederate horsemen hotly pursued Custer toward Trevilian Station, 25 miles northeast of Charlottesville. There, Custer formed his men, controlled the approaches, and positioned artillery effectively. Rosser formed his regiments and prepared to attack. Lieutenant Colonel Chew observed that Custer had only about 1,200 troopers with him and so informed Rosser. Rosser, who eagerly envisioned capturing Custer, ordered Elijah "Lige" White's troopers to charge, but just then Hampton rode up and countermanded the order. Custer remained at Trevilian Station, while Sheridan's entire command advanced against Hampton's right flank.[20]

If Fitz Lee, with Munford leading the 2nd Virginia, had been on time, it is likely that Custer's Wolverines would have been nearly destroyed with many captured. Generals Butler and Rosser asked Hampton to seek a court-martial of Fitz Lee, but Hampton declined.[21]

That evening, Sheridan attempted unsuccessfully to dislodge Hampton from his new position. After one of the Federals' failed assaults, Rosser, still believing he could drive Custer from his position, ordered a charge, but at once suffered a bad leg wound at the hands of a Federal sharpshooter. The bullet broke the leg bones below the knee. Rosser, reeling in the saddle, finally sought safety, but his injury put a stop to any thoughts of assaulting Custer. The Confederate horsemen spent the remainder of the day of June 11 repelling Sheridan's limited assaults. Colonel R. H. Dulany of the 7th Virginia took over for the wounded Rosser. Night closed the action, and the adversaries entrenched to prepare for the next day's decisive struggle.[22]

At dawn on June 12, both sides faced each other, but nothing happened in the morning. Fitz Lee had attacked Custer on the other side of Trevilian Station the previous day and rejoined Hampton about noon. About 3:00 p.m., Sheridan began a series of vigorous assaults. His dismounted men, armed with repeating rifles, had a tremendous advantage over the Confederate troopers, who were armed with single-shot carbines or muskets. The fighting on June 12 was chiefly on foot, and there was good cover at places in the woods. Munford's 2nd Virginia was not actively engaged. Federal fire concentrated on Butler's brigade and on the artillery, which were able to fend off the attacks. Only 250 yards separated the opposing forces. The fighting continued until nightfall. Fitz Lee reinforced Butler's left with Wickham's brigade and took Lomax's brigade across to the Gordonsville Road to

---

20. McDonald, *Laurel Brigade*, 253–54.
21. Manly Wade Wellman, *Giant in Gray: A Biography of Wade Hampton* (New York, 1949), 151.
22. *Philadelphia Weekly Times*, April 19, 1884.

attack the Federals' right flank. Sheridan was not able to force Hampton from his position.²³

Sheridan was heavily pressed on his front and attacked on his left. He had had enough. Under the cover of darkness, Sheridan slipped away to rejoin Grant's army, abandoning his dead and wounded.²⁴

Sheridan claimed victory at Trevilian Station, but some of the Northern newspapers quickly realized that he was grossly exaggerating. For his part, Rosser was even harsher in his criticism of Sheridan's claims, stating, "Sheridan was fairly and completely beaten, and all of his apologies for his retreat, 'ammunition exhausted and presence of infantry,' are unworthy of a great soldier. Why was he there without ammunition? Didn't he expect to have some fighting? These excuses are really too ridiculous to be discussed."²⁵

Sheridan, despite a numerical superiority of five to one over Fitz Lee and three to one over Hampton, had failed to exploit his advantage and destroy Butler and Lee once they were driven apart. Then he failed to follow up when the pressure relaxed.²⁶

The Confederate victory at Trevilian Station prevented Lynchburg from falling into the hands of the Union. Captain Charles M. Blackford recalled much later:

> It is enough to say that it was one of the most brilliant and successful engagements in which our troops were involved during the war, and one which shed well-deserved renown not only on General Wade Hampton, who commanded, but on every officer and man under him. Conspicuous for their gallantry and valuable service in that battle was the Second Virginia Cavalry, under our distinguished fellow-citizen, General T. T. Munford. . . . On the day of that fight it was especially distinguished for its daring courage and for its achievements. It was in the front of the charging column which broke Custer's line and captured four out of the five caissons lost by Sheridan on that day. It captured Custer's headquarters, his sash and private wagon and papers. The wagon was used by General Munford until it was recaptured, a few days before Appomattox.²⁷

23. McDonald, *Laurel Brigade*, 255–56; *Richmond Examiner*, June 25, 1864.
24. McDonald, *Laurel Brigade*, 256.
25. Keller, *Riding with Rosser*, 39.
26. Walbrook D. Swank, ed., "The Battle of Trevilian Station: The Civil War's Greatest and Bloodiest All Cavalry Battle, with Eyewitness Memoirs," *Civil War Heritage*, vol. 4:28.
27. Captain Charles M. Blackford, "An Address delivered before the Garland–Rodes Camp of Confederate Veterans" at Lynchburg, Virginia, July 18, 1901, *SHSP*, vol. 30:286.

After the war, many of Custer's personal items taken at Trevilian were returned to Libbie Custer by Thomas T. Munford, long after Custer met his destiny at Little Big Horn in 1876. A grateful Libbie wrote to Munford:

> I feel that I can say very little with the cold medium of pen and paper to express my gratitude to you for giving back to me the precious souvenirs of my husband. Though I am not a spiritualist, I live so in the past that I can find myself unconsciously telling my husband of what I know and ignore time. The day I hung the old cap and sash in my room I could hear him say "how good of Munford," his manner of speaking is so oral to me even now and living to commemorate him as I try to do intensifies this feeling of comradeship.[28]

As the battle of Trevilian Station raged on, Union Gen. David Hunter occupied Lexington, and on June 12, his troopers torched Virginia Military Institute. Being a state arsenal and military training school, VMI was fair game for Federal attack. The cadet barracks and two faculty residences were extensively damaged, and other Institute property—most importantly the valuable library, laboratory and scientific equipment—was destroyed. The Union forces left on June 14, marching over the mountains to Lynchburg. Because of extensive damage, the Institute was closed and the cadets were furloughed until December 1864, when academic work resumed at VMI's temporary headquarters, the Alms House in Richmond. The Corps remained in Richmond until the war ended in April 1865. VMI reopened in Lexington in October that year.[29]

Meanwhile, as Federal troops retreated from Trevilian, Hampton pursued Sheridan the following day, marching parallel to his army. The 2nd Virginia camped near Frederick's Hall that night. On June 14, they crossed the North Anna and reached Chilesburg the next day on the Bowling Green Road, the whole line of march "perfumed with dead horses abandoned and shot by the enemy." The tired horsemen mounted up before dawn on June 16 and marched to Bowling Green, reaching Hanover Court House the following day. The Confederates chased Sheridan to the supply depot at White House Landing on June 18, skirmishing with Sheridan's rear guard. Hampton believed Sheridan might turn and proceed along the James River toward Richmond; he therefore moved his command via Bottom's Bridge to

---

28. Elizabeth Bacon Custer to Thomas T. Munford, August 1, 1901, Munford–Ellis Papers, DU; Thomas T. Munford to Mrs. Gen. Geo. A. Custer, July 13, 1886, Munford–Ellis Papers, DU.
29. "History of VMI," VMI Archives, Lexington, VA.

Charles City Court House. Fitz Lee wrote of the pursuit, "followed as fast as our jaded condition would allow but could not bring him to bay. His trail was strewn with dead horses, which as fast as they gave out were shot."[30]

On the evening of June 22, Fitz Lee learned Sheridan had left White House Landing and was marching via Talleyville to the Forge Bridges on the Chickahominy. At 1:00 a.m. on the 23rd, Fitz Lee led his troopers, joined there by Chambliss's brigade, down the south bank of the Chickahominy. The Confederate horsemen proceeded via White Oak Swamp, Nance's shop, and Saint Mary's Church (Samaria Church) to Salem Church in Charles City County. Sheridan had moved to the vicinity of Charles City Court House, and on June 24, he marched to the vicinity of Saint Mary's Church.[31]

Sheridan attacked Hampton's former division near Samaria Church and drove his troopers back to Nance's Shop. Fitz Lee left Lomax's brigade to protect the River Road. Reinforced with Matthew C. Butler's and Brig. Gen. Martin Witherspoon Gary's brigades from Hampton division, Fitz Lee ordered Generals Chambliss and Gary to attack and turn the Federal's right. Fitz Lee placed Butler and Wickham in line, dismounted, and attacked. The whole area was wooded. The 2nd Virginia was in front, moving up to form a battle line with its left on the country road. The 3rd and 4th Virginia formed on the left. The 2nd's skirmishers advanced with the 1st Virginia on their right. The 1st Virginia did not receive orders to advance in time, so the 2nd went forward alone, dismounted; Munford was on foot with them. Munford's rapidly moving troopers crossed an open field, attacking the Union soldiers behind two lines of breastworks, supported by artillery. Proceeding on, Munford's dismounted troops drove the Federals from their works and attacked the artillery. The Union horsemen of David M. Gregg's cavalry were driven back in some disorder, leaving their dead and wounded on the field. The Confederate pursued for five miles in the broiling hot sun before nightfall, putting an end to the chase. Lee's troopers lost 40 men killed and wounded and took 157 prisoners, including one colonel and 12 commissioned officers.[32]

---

30. Diary of J. D. Ferguson, June 15, 1864, *OR*, Supplement, vol. 7:337; Fitzhugh Lee to Dear General (Lee), December 20, 1866, Eleanor S. Brockenbrough Library, Museum of the Confederacy; Driver, *2nd Virginia Cavalry*, 126; Wittenberg, *Glory Enough for All*, 226.
31. *OR, Supplement*, vol. 7:331.
32. *OR, Supplement*, vol. 7:331; Driver, *2nd Virginia Cavalry*, 126-28; *Richmond Examiner*, July 1, 1864; J. D. Ferguson Diary, June 24, 1864, *OR, Supplement*, vol. 7:339–40.

On June 25, Sheridan crossed to the south side of the James River, supported by Federal gunboats. Fitz Lee, unable to attack because of Sheridan's gunboats, moved up the river on the north side to Chaffin's Bluff, where the Confederate pontoons were positioned. The next day, Hampton, taking Chambliss's brigade with him, crossed the James. Hampton had ordered Fitz Lee to remain near Chaffin's Bluff. Fitz finally crossed on June 28, passed through Petersburg the next day, where he received orders to proceed to Reams's Station on the Weldon Railroad. Fitz Lee kept a lookout for James H. Wilson's and August V. Kautz's cavalry divisions, since they were on raids of their own on the South Side Railroad, who were trying to get back safely to their army.[33]

The Wilson-Kautz Raid

The Wilson-Kautz Raid was a Union cavalry operation occurring early in the Richmond-Petersburg Campaign. The raid was conducted by Federal cavalry under Brigadier Generals James H. Wilson and August V. Kautz, including 5,000 horsemen and 16 artillery pieces pulled from the siege of Petersburg. The raid's purpose was to cut railroads between Lynchburg and the vital Confederate rail supply center at Petersburg. While the raid had the intended effect of disrupting Confederate rail communications for several weeks, the raiding force lost much of its artillery, all of its supply train, and almost a third of the original force, mostly to Confederate capture.[34]

Battle of Sappony Church: June 28, 1864

After more than a week of continuous operation in Confederate-held territory, Wilson's and Kautz's brigades crossed the Nottoway River, reaching the Stony Creek Depot on the Wilmington and Weldon Railroad, placing them within 10 miles of Union lines. Before they reached Stony Creek, they met an attack from Wade Hampton's cavalry division astride their path. Fitz Lee's cavalry division again caught the Union force in the rear, and the Federals were forced northward toward the crossing at Ream's Station. Federal losses amounted to 806 prisoners and all of their artillery and wagons. Lee's troopers also captured about 5,000 horses taken previously from

---

33. *OR, Supplement*, vol. 7:332.
34. Longacre, "Wilson-Kautz Raid," 34, 42.

Virginia citizens. Fitz Lee wrote, "Wilson carried nothing back with him on wheels."[35]

First Battle of Reams's Station: June 29, 1864

The exhausted Union raiders had moved toward Reams's Station on the Weldon Railroad, expecting it to be in friendly hands, but instead finding themselves almost surrounded and under attack by two small brigades of Confederate infantry under Brig. Gen. William Mahone and Fitz Lee's horsemen. Mahone's soldiers were drawn up in a line of battle across the country road intersecting the railroad at that point. Facing Wilson's and Kautz's cavalry of about 5,000 troopers, Mahone was reluctant to attack. Fitz Lee positioned his horsemen to turn the Union left flank and found a road concealed by woods. Debouching in rear of the Federal left, Lee dismounted two of Lomax's and one of Wickham's regiments, moved them along the road, and attacked. Mahone's infantry also moved ahead at the sounds of the Confederate cavalry's guns. The Federal horsemen broke and began a precipitous retreat. The remainder of Fitz Lee's command, mounted and under Wickham, charged and routed the enemy. Lee's horsemen doggedly pursued the fleeing Federals, who attempted to make a stand at Stony Creek but were chased off until about midnight. At daybreak, Lee's relentless pursuit continued. Brigade commanders Wilson and Kautz were forced to abandon their artillery, burn their remaining supply wagons, and separated, attempted breakouts eastward toward Union forces under Maj. Gen. Benjamin F. Butler. Kautz's brigade moved cross-country toward the southeast, where it met friendly lines after sundown. After suffering heavy casualties, and a loss of 500 prisoners, Wilson's brigade withdrew to the southwest, circling eastward again to re-cross the Nottoway River and finally, on July 2, northward to safety at Light House Point.[36]

Fitz Lee's command returned to Reams's Station, going into camp. He connected his pickets with W. H. F. Lee's on his left, who joined the infantry, and Hampton on his right. Meanwhile, the exhausted horsemen of the 2nd Virginia rode to Campbell's Station on June 30. The next day, the 2nd Virginia proceeded to Dinwiddie Court House and camped with the rest of Wickham's brigade, remaining there for several weeks. The season had been so arid that the area appeared as a desert, named "Camp Sahara" by the 2nd's troopers. The horses were

---

35. Whitehead, "Campaigns of Munford's 2nd Virginia Cavalry," 112–13, VHS; Driver, *2nd Virginia Cavalry*, 131.
36. *OR, Supplement*, vol. 7:332, 341-42; Diary of J. D. Ferguson, June 29, 1864.
37. Ibid.

suffering and dying off at an alarming rate. The horsemen's only duty at this time was picket duty around Reams's Station.[37]

On July 8, with things remaining quiet for several days, a group of 2nd Virginia cavalrymen led by Munford, went to Mrs. Blick's place for the evening. Accompanying Munford were J. D. Ferguson, adjutant of Fitz Lee, Garland Mitchell Ryals, Gustavus Warfield Dorsey, Isaac Wakle, and Archibald Cary Randolph. The 2nd Virginia band went along to provide entertainment.[38]

On July 12, Fitz Lee, with detachments from Wickham's and Lomax's brigades, made a reconnaissance of the Federal's lines near Lee's Mill. Here, they ran into David Gregg's cavalry on a similar mission. Captain John Owen Lashley's squadron of the 2nd Virginia cut off Gregg's advance guard of the 2nd Pennsylvania Cavalry, capturing Maj. Joseph Steele, two lieutenants, and 29 men, along with their horses and arms. Gregg broke off and returned to his line; Lee, making a narrow escape, returned to Reams's Station.[39]

On the evening of July 25, J. D. Ferguson remembered, "Generals Hampton, Butler, [Rufus] Barringer, Wickham, [James] Dearing, [John R.] Chambliss, [Lunsford] Lomax, Colonels [Tom] Munford, [Thomas H.] Owen, Captain [Joseph Van Holt] Nash, [Capt. Stith] Bowling, [and] John and Henry [Carter] Lee dined with us." On the night of July 28, Fitz Lee marched to the north side of the James River, passed through Petersburg before daylight, reaching the vicinity of Chaffin's Bluff that morning. On the night of July 31, Lee returned to Reams's Station and camped.[40]

During most of July and August 1864, Munford was assigned temporary command of Wickham's brigade. Lieutenant Colonel William F. Graves, who would have been in line to take over temporary command of the regiment, was hospitalized for dysentery through July and was again hospitalized for the first three weeks of September. Captain Cary Breckinridge took over command of the 2nd Virginia in Munford's absence until he was wounded in late August.[41]

On August 5, Fitz Lee's respite ended. In the hot August weather, amid dust clouds from thousands of horses, the 2nd Virginia left Dinwiddie Court House, marched north and across the James River. Fitz Lee's division passed through Richmond and on August 7 encamped at Ashland.[42]

---

38. Diary of J. D. Ferguson, July 8, 1864, *OR, Supplement*, vol. 7:343.
39. Ibid.
40. Ibid., 344; *OR, Supplement*, vol. 7:333; J. D. Ferguson Diary, July 12, 1864, *OR, Supplement*, vol. 7:343.
41. Thomas T. Munford, CSR; Driver, *2nd Virginia Cavalry*, 133, 199, 223.
42. Ibid., 131.

Hampton Promoted to Command the Cavalry Corps

After the death of J.E.B. Stuart on May 11, Wade Hampton had stood first in line of succession to corps commander. Robert E. Lee, however, hesitated to choose between Hampton and his nephew, Maj. Gen. Fitzhugh Lee, who also commanded a division of cavalry. Between May 12 and August 11, 1864, Gen. Robert E. Lee had both Hampton's and Fitzhugh Lee's divisions report directly to him. Over the next three months, Hampton would prove that he was ready to be a corps commander by his impressive leadership at Trevilian Station, Samaria Church, and First Reams's Station. On August 11, 1864, Hampton received his appointment as commander of the cavalry corps.[43]

Wade Hampton was a towering, bearded, 45-year-old South Carolina wealthy plantation owner and one of the South's major slaveholders. He had established himself as a man of prominence before the war, displaying leadership qualities that served him well during the conflict and, later, in politics. Although he had no formal military training or experience, he quickly established himself as a hard-fighting combat leader, an able tactician, and a trustworthy reconnaissance officer. He consistently met the growing responsibilities that befell him as a brigade commander and then as the ranking division commander in the expanding Cavalry Corps of the Army of Northern Virginia.[44]

The largest of the cavalry commands under Hampton was Maj. Gen. Rooney Lee's Third Division. Rooney Lee, second son of Robert E. Lee, had proved himself in battle. He principally relied on two of the three brigades in his division, namely, Rufus Barringer's North Carolinians and John R. Chambliss's Virginians. David Dearing's small brigade was the third of Rooney Lee's brigades. Both Barringer's and Chambliss's brigades were excellent combat units with proud traditions, led by very capable, hard-hitting commanders. When Hampton was promoted, the senior brigade commander at the time, Matthew Calbraith Butler, was in line for the command of Hampton's former division.[45]

---

43. Longacre, *Lee's Cavalrymen*, 310; Edward G. Longacre, *Gentleman and Soldier: The Extraordinary Life of General Wade Hampton* (Nashville, 2003), 183, 205; Special Order 189, *OR* 42/2:1171.
44. Boatner, *The Civil War Dictionary*, 370–71.
45. *OR* 42/2:1219.

On August 13, Grant's army began another diversion against Richmond, accompanied by a raid on the real objective: the railroads south of Petersburg. On August 14, Rooney Lee's cavalry division again was ordered north of the James, where the Federals had moved once more, this time only six miles southeast of Richmond.[46]

General Rosser took over command of Fitz Lee's division on August 30, due to Lee's bout with rheumatism. He was ordered to the Shenandoah Valley to report directly to Gen. Jubal Early and not to Brig. Gen. Lunsford Lomax, the ranking senior officer commanding Early's other cavalry division. Major General Philip H. Sheridan commanded the Federal army in the Shenandoah, with his three cavalry divisions, under Col. William H. Powell, Brig. Gen. Wesley Merritt, and Brig. Gen. George A. Custer, all under the command of Brig. Gen. Alfred T. Torbert.[47]

Colonel Munford, under the command of Rosser leading the division, headed for the Shenandoah Valley. Jubal Early, battling Philip Sheridan's army, was outmanned and in need of both infantry and cavalry reinforcements. Munford would fight well there, but the overconfident Rosser's initial successes soon turned into debacles, leading to defeat in the valley.

---

46. *NCR*, 1:434.
47. *Philadelphia Weekly Times*, March 22, 1984; Torbert was promoted to brevet major general on September 9, 1864.

Chapter Fourteen

1864 Shenandoah Valley Campaign

"The men are in good spirits—but when old Abe gets his million of new troops in the field, I think we will have to retire to west Augusta and hold the mountains and hollows. There is no chance for us now, but to fight it out and I expect we will have a rough time before we get through. I am willing to see it out, 'whichever way the wind may blow!'"

–Thomas Munford writing to his father,
November 1864.

Thomas Munford's experiences commanding a regiment, a brigade, and his knowledge gained from the 1862 Shenandoah campaign, aided him in the 1864 Valley Campaign. This able cavalry leader fought hard and well in the valley, outshining the likes of General Thomas Rosser in the ferocious fighting against a superior Federal army.

Virginia's Shenandoah Valley was a critical theater during the Civil War. A natural highway between North and South, and a richly productive agricultural region whose bounty fed the Confederate armies, the valley was fiercely contested throughout the war. More than 300 armed conflicts took place there, with Stonewall Jackson's 1862 campaign being the most famous series of actions. As the war dragged on, the Shenandoah Valley took on increasing significance as the "breadbasket" for the Army of Northern Virginia. Union forces invaded, laying waste to this region, burning its fields, farms, and towns in a devastating campaign of total warfare.[1]

Major General Jubal Early's army, of about 8,000 soldiers of all arms, achieved remarkable successes in the valley against Maj. Gen. David Hunter's army of 18,000 at Lynchburg. Early, who had replaced the ailing Richard Ewell after he had fallen from his horse at the battle of Spotsylvania Court House in May, drove Hunter into West Virginia; then marched rapidly north, defeating Maj. Gen. Lew Wallace along the Monocacy River in Maryland. Early then pushed on toward

---

1. Shenandoah Germanic Heritage Museum, Executive Summary, Shenandoah Valley Battlefields National Historic District, Management Plan, September 2000.

Washington, confronting Fort Stevens on July 11. Grant, in an effort to meet Early's threat on Washington, detached the VI Corps and part of the XIX Corps from the armies besieging Petersburg. Early retreated across the Potomac into Virginia. Defeating Maj. Gen. George Crook at Cool Spring and later at Kernstown, Early went into camp along Opequon Creek.[2]

Early's successes so alarmed the Federal high command that they dispatched Maj. Gen. Philip Sheridan to the Shenandoah Valley to deal with him. The Federal leaders, believing Early's army larger than it actually was, sent about 48,000 men, including 6,100 cavalrymen, under Sheridan, to oppose Early in the valley. Even after receiving reinforcements, Early could only muster about 12,000 soldiers of all arms.[3]

In response to Early's need of reinforcements, Robert E. Lee dispatched Maj. Wilfred E. Cutshaw's artillery battalion, Maj. Gen. Joseph B. Kershaw's infantry division of 2,700 soldiers, and Brig. Gen. Thomas Rosser's undersized, 600-man Laurel Brigade. Fitzhugh Lee's division had been dispatched to the valley earlier, arriving on August 14 at Front Royal.[4]

On August 16, with support from one of Kershaw's brigades, Fitz Lee led an aggressive cavalry assault on Wesley Merritt's troopers at Cedarville. The success of Fitz Lee's attack impressed Early enough that he named Fitz Lee as his chief of cavalry. Lee's command now included his own division, four brigades of the valley cavalry; mainly ill-disciplined and poorly armed western Virginians under Brigadier Generals John D. Imboden, William L. Jackson, John McCausland, and Bradley T. Johnson. This assignment essentially made Fitzhugh Lee a corps commander.[5]

Fitz Lee's elevation enabled him to promote Lunsford Lomax to head the reorganized Valley Cavalry Division. Brig. Gen. Williams C. Wickham commanded Fitz Lee's former division, including two brigades assigned to Colonels William H. Payne of the 4th Virginia and Reuben Boston of the 5th Virginia. Wickham's command was reduced by hard campaigning to less than 2,000 able-bodied horsemen. Lomax had slightly more riders, but they were ill-equipped with mostly single-shot, muzzle loading rifles. Colonel Munford took over command of Wickham's brigade.[6]

---

2. Bushong, *Fightin' Tom Rosser*, 111–12.
3. Ibid.
4. Bushong, *Fightin' Tom Rosser*, 112; Edward G. Longacre, *Fitz Lee: A Military Biography* (Cambridge, MA, 2005), 170–71; Driver, *2nd Virginia Cavalry*, 131.
5. Longacre, *Fitz Lee: A Military Biography*, 171–72.
6. Ibid., 172.

Needing new recruits, Munford wrote to Gen. Francis H. Smith at VMI, requesting that some of the new graduates be assigned to the 2nd Virginia. "I have lost very dearly in men and officers," he wrote, "have but fourteen officers left in my Regt out of 40—have had upwards of 260 men killed and wounded in my Regt since 1st May—but I have a noted band of men. . . . My Lt Col and Major Breckinridge are both absent, wounded. I was slightly wounded by a grape shot not long since."[7]

Sheridan's huge cavalry force, consisted of Brig. Gen. Alfred Torbert, in overall command, as well as divisions under Brigadier Generals Wesley Merritt, William W. Averell, and George A. Custer. While General Early was at Brown's Gap in the Blue Ridge Mountains preparing to resume the fight, Sheridan had been creating havoc in the upper Valley. Grant had ordered Sheridan to make the valley a "barren waste," which he largely accomplished during a 13-day burning spree from late September through early October. Sheridan's troopers concentrated on destroying barns, mills, crops, and farm equipment, while driving off livestock so that nothing could be used to aid the Confederate army. They were also retaliating for Early's burning of Chambersburg on July 30, 1864. Sheridan was so efficient that the local farmers could not provide for their own families.[8]

Battle of Third Winchester (Opequon), September 19, 1864

When Sheridan learned of the departure of Generals Anderson and Kershaw for Petersburg, he decided to attack General Early. On September 19, Sheridan advanced toward Winchester along the Berryville Pike, crossing Opequon Creek with the VI and XIX Corps. His cavalry first struck the Confederates on the Berryville Road on the morning of September 19. Fitz Lee's former division of only 1,500 troopers, now under Brigadier General Wickham, and Maj. Gen. Stephen D. Ramsuer's 1,500-man infantry division opposed Sheridan. James H. Wilson's Union cavalry struck first, moving to the left, uncovering Federal infantry under Brig. Gen. George Crook. Fitz Lee deployed Col. William H. Payne's and Wickham's brigades

---

7. Driver, *2nd Virginia Cavalry*, 133; Thomas Munford to Francis H. Smith, August 30, 1864, VMI Archives. VMI cadets had participated in the May 15, 1864 battle of New Market, suffering 10 mortally wounded or killed, and 47 wounded. General David Hunter burned most of the school down in June 1864, and it did not reopen until October 1865. Smith could not furnish Munford with any cadets.

8. *OR* 43/2:202.

(Wickham's under Munford) on Ramseur's left. Lee was soon forced to shift Munford's troopers to Ramseur's right flank in order to prevent Wilson from reaching the Valley Pike south of Winchester.[9]

Munford recalled, "I dismounted all the men I could spare from the led horses." Munford deployed them near the Berryville Pike. "They quickly collected all of the loose rocks and rails nearby," he stated, "and in an astonishing short time my men were stretched behind them, willing to take their chances." The Confederate troopers held the Federals back until Sheridan ordered up additional units. Only the timely arrival of Major Generals Robert E. Rodes and John B. Gordon's infantry divisions prevented the Confederates from being overrun. Rodes and Gordon drove the Federals back; it appeared at first that Early had won the day, but Sheridan soon ordered up George Crook's infantry division.[10]

When Munford learned General Rodes had been killed, he sadly recalled, Rodes "was a dear friend of my youth, I had known him well at the Virginia Military Institute." Munford bemoaned, "No truer knight ever flashed a blade or responded to a bugler's note." That evening, he was told that George S. Patton, his VMI classmate and roommate for two years, had also been killed.[11]

Fitz Lee moved part of Lomax's brigade to Munford's right to prevent it from being flanked, leaving Brigadier Generals John D. Imboden's and John McCausland's brigades to defend the left flank. Sheridan sent Averell's and Torbert's cavalry divisions to attack Imboden's and McCausland's brigades, driving them back. Lee then sent Payne's brigade in support, but the Confederate's mounted attack did not dissuade the advance of George Crook's VIII Corps. The Confederate cavalry fell back in disarray. Fitz Lee was wounded in the thigh and had to leave the field. Wickham's brigade, under Munford, was hastened from the Confederate right to left, occupying some works near the town and slowing the advance.[12]

Wickham, with Munford and a portion of Fitz Lee's former division, fell back on Middle Road as far as Mr. Gibbons's farm, nine miles from Winchester. There, the weary soldiers and horses rested and fed until one o'clock. According to Fitz Lee's adjutant, Maj. J.D. Ferguson, "This day's action was the first in which any portion of our army of Northern Virginia have been whipped in open field, which

---

9. Driver, *2nd Virginia Cavalry*, 135.
10. Thomas T. Munford, "Reminiscences of Cavalry Operations: Battle of Winchester, 19th September, '64," Paper No. 2, *SHSP*, vol. XII:449; Driver, *2nd Virginia Cavalry*, 135.
11. Ibid.
12. Driver, *2nd Virginia Cavalry*, 135–36.

may be attributed to injudicious disposition of our army and to the fatigues we went through the day previous, and the long and rapid march they took on the day of the fight; and also to the disgraceful behavior of a greater portion of our cavalry."[13]

Ferguson wasn't speaking of Munford's troopers, however, because they held their position at Fort Hill north of Winchester and repulsed every assault made by Averell's troopers upon the fort. Munford had only two of Breathed's guns and three regiments of dismounted cavalry. Munford held his position at least until Early's infantry had retreated from Winchester. Munford followed Early but was confronted by pursuing Federal cavalry at Red Bud Creek. He ordered a charge, and his troopers cut through the Union lines, joining the withdrawing Confederate infantry. They continued to cover Early's rear until sent to hold the fords of the Shenandoah River, near Front Royal.[14]

Confederate generals Robert E. Rodes and Archibald C. Goodwin had been killed; Fitzhugh Lee, William Terry, and Gabriel C. Wharton had been wounded. Fitz Lee, Early's cavalry commander, had just returned to duty after a bout with rheumatism before being wounded in the thigh. Union general David A. Russell was killed, and John B. McIntosh, Emory Upton, and George H. Chapman wounded. Because of its size, intensity, and result, many historians consider this the most important battle of the 1864 Shenandoah Valley Campaign.[15]

After a fatiguing night march, the retreating Confederate army reached Front Royal at 8:00 a.m. the next day. Chaplain Randolph H. McKim recalled they had had only one hour of sleep and no rations for 24 hours. The exhausted troopers rested, ate, and slept.[16]

On September 21 at 1:30 a.m., the retreating Confederates marched five miles to Middletown on the Valley Pike. Munford, with two regiments was ordered to occupy "Guard Hill" near Front Royal. Here, they all waited until the artillery came up in the rear of the army, which was falling back to Fisher's Hill. Then, they all proceeded to cross the north fork of the Shenandoah River near McCoy's Ford. There, the tired soldiers fed their jaded horses and ate breakfast. Moving on to Mr. Spangler's on the Front Royal and Muray Road, eight miles from McCoy's, they encamped. Union cavalry attempted to ford the river in Munford's front, but were checked. The Federal

13. Diary of J. D. Ferguson, September 19, 1864, Munford-Ellis Papers, DU.
14. Whitehead, "Campaigns of Munford's 2nd Virginia Cavalry," 119, VHS; Driver, *2nd Virginia Cavalry*, 136.
15. *OR* 43/1:60–61.
16. McKim, *A Soldier's Recollections*, 225–26; Driver, *2nd Virginia Cavalry*, 136.

advance on the Valley Pike reached Strasburg. In the meantime, Fitz Lee had proceeded on to Staunton, having been wounded in the thigh at Winchester. He did not return to duty for four months.[17]

At daylight on September 21, Federal cavalry of James H. Wilson's division charged Munford's troopers at Front Royal, and in the fog, succeeded in crossing the river and getting in Munford's rear. In the subsequent charges and countercharges, Capt. John O. Lasley of the 2nd Virginia was killed, and the command ran low on ammunition. The remainder of Fitz Lee's division, now under Rosser, moved down to a position four miles from Front Royal on the Luray Road in support of Munford. The Federals advanced, with most of their contingent on the Gravelly Spring Road, where Colonel Payne's troopers had been sent that morning. After some desultory artillery from the Confederates, the Union brought up three guns into position about dusk and began returning fire. Breathed's guns of Munford's brigade quickly blew up a Union gun and silenced one battery. The Confederates then retired to Mr. Spangler's and had supper. Receiving intelligence that Union supports were arriving, the Confederates withdrew during the night and concentrated at Milford on the Luray Pike, 12 miles from Spangler's.[18]

Finally, Union soldiers turned Early's left flank at Fisher's Hill just as the dismounted Southerner troopers gave way. A "disgraceful panic" seized the army, and giving way in confusion, they lost 12 to 16 artillery pieces, with many of Early's soldiers fleeing to the mountains. The remainder of Early's defeated army retreated to New Market.[19]

On September 22, the Confederates commenced fortifying their position behind Overall's Run at Milford, while remaining alert for signs of approaching Federal troops. At about 7:00 a.m., Union troopers under Alfred Torbert found Wickham's formidable position. The Confederate cavalry, deployed on a bluff above the stream, held the high ground. Their left flank was anchored on the South Fork of the Shenandoah River, while their right flank was anchored on a spur of the Blue Ridge Mountains. One brigade was positioned along the river's edge, while the other brigade was dismounted between Milford and a mountain.[20]

James H. Wilson's division made first contact with the Confederates. Torbert was reluctant to launch a full-frontal assault on such a strongly defended position. The battle ensued with artillery and

---

17. Diary of J. D. Ferguson, September 20, 1864, Munford–Ellis Papers, DU.
18. Diary of J. D. Ferguson, September 21, 1864, DU; McKim, *A Soldier's Recollections*, 227.
19. Diary of J. D. Ferguson, September 22, 1864, DU; *OR* 43/1:60–61.
20. Jay W. Simson, *Custer and the Front Royal Executions of 1864* (Jefferson, NC, 2008), 46.

carbine firing, continuing until dark. Late in the afternoon, Torbert feigned toward the Confederate brigade occupying the ground between Milford and the mountain spur. At the same time, Torbert attempted to flank the right of the Munford-commanded Confederate troopers positioned along the river.[21]

Munford was in charge of Wickham's entire division at the time, because Wickham had left the area to confer with General Early. Munford responded to Torbert's attempted flanking maneuver by dispatching a squadron to reinforce the 2nd Virginia Cavalry. It was at this time that Munford decided to employ a bit of subterfuge of his own. He sent along three buglers with the squadron, positioning them with enough space for a full regiment. At a given signal, the buglers blew a "charge." Coupled with the firing from the 2nd Virginia, Torbert lost his nerve and suspended the flanking maneuver. Torbert disengaged and withdrew down the Luray Valley.[22]

The Confederates remained in their trenches all day, with their headquarters half a mile to the rear. McKim recalled that they were so busily engaged that they had neither breakfast or lunch, but did have a "good supper." The Federal troops, held off by Wickham's troopers under Munford, had failed in an attempt to turn the Southerner's flank, allowing Early's retreating infantry to escape.[23]

Munford recalled the action:

> Off we went at a trot, and when we reached the left things looked very ugly for us. General Breckinridge and his staff were exerting themselves to rectify our infantry lines. We could see our cavalry were moving up to meet a very large force who were coming down the pike.... Averill sent a mounted regiment to take Fort Hill to the North of Winchester. General Early had no idea of allowing him to hold it, as that covered the pike below, and sent orders to me to take it and hold it up the hill we went and at them, followed by two guns of our horse artillery. We drove them from the hill, ran the two pieces into the fort, dismounted the 1st, 2nd, and 4th Virginia Cavalry, giving the 3rd Virginia the protection of the horses, and we had just gotten into the fort when Averill charged to recapture it; but we gave them a rough welcome, and sent them back faster than they came. A

---

21. Ibid.
22. Ibid., 47.
23. McKim, *A Soldier's Recollections*, 227; Whitehead, "Campaigns of Munford's 2nd Virginia Cavalry," 120, VHS.

second charge was made with the same result during which time our two guns had been doing splendid services.²⁴

Munford left Star Fort after covering the retreat, having not been driven out by a cavalry attack. When his brigade came under heavy fire from three Union batteries concentrating on Fort Jackson, Munford ordered them out. He actually had to charge and drive off some of Wilson's cavalry division which was coming up south of Winchester, as Munford withdrew. Munford's actions probably saved thousands of Early's men from capture.²⁵

Captain John William DeForest of the 12th Connecticut Infantry noted, "furious cannonade—eight or ten field pieces banging with amazing rapidity." Munford's troopers did not retreat until shells began to fall in the Fort. Munford wrote as they pulled out, "a shell . . . took off the head of one of our cannoneers. Sergeant Hawley . . . unlimbered and fired (the gun) while the dead man was being strapped on the limber chest."²⁶

The next day, September 23, the Union forces retired towards McCoy's Ford, while the Confederates remained at Milford all morning. It was there that they learned of Early's disaster at Fisher's Hill. Fitz Lee's division moved back to two miles north of Luray on the Port Royal Road and encamped. The following day, General Early ordered Colonel Payne's brigade back towards Front Royal and Munford, with the wagon train, across the Gap toward New Market to join Early's right. While Payne and his staff proceeded ahead to learn the state of affairs, Payne's brigade was attacked three miles south of Luray and forced back in disorder. Payne informed Munford of the situation, and Munford quickly came down off the mountain to assist Payne's brigade. In doing so, Munford left the wagons and artillery on top of the mountain and in danger of being cut off from the army. The

---

24. Thomas T. Munford, "Reminiscences of Cavalry Service," *SHSP*, 13:449–51. The fort to which Munford refers is Fort Jackson, which he clearly identified to Jed Hotchkiss, who made notes of his discussion with Munford and drew a sketch of the action. Fort Jackson was on the next heights south of Star Fort. Modern US 522 runs through the low ground between the two heights.
25. Shenandoah Valley Battlefield Foundation, October 9, 2013.
26. Thomas T. Munford, "Reminiscences of Cavalry Operations: Battle of Winchester, 19th September, '64," Paper No. 2, *SHSP*, Vol. XII:450; Brandon H. Beck and Charles S. Grunder, Second Edition, "The Three Battles of Winchester: A History and Guided Tour," (Berryville, Va.: The Civil War Foundation, 1988), 34. Federal reports incorrectly claimed Munford's Virginians were driven from "Star Fort" by General James M. Schoonmaker. In fact, they were never at Star Fort and repulsed Schoonmaker when he attempted to follow up his attack against the next heights, Fort Jackson, closer to Winchester.

trains could not get into Staunton Valley because the Confederate army had fallen back above New Market; they were also vulnerable from any Federal rear attack. The ordnance wagons, however, did cross the mountains and joined Early's train. The artillery and other wagons were taken up the Shenandoah River, across Bunker Hill Ford, and put on the road to Conrad's Store. Payne's brigade joined Fitz Lee's division at Bunker Hill Ford and all encamped.[27]

On September 25, Fitz Lee's division moved to Conrad's Store and was joined by General Kershaw's command. Learning that the Union cavalry was not following, the Confederates encamped in the afternoon. Receiving orders from General Early, camp was broken and Fitz Lee's division headed for Port Republic, leaving Payne's brigade and Kershaw, who were to follow the next morning. Fitz Lee's troopers reached Lomax's headquarters at Port Republic at 3:00 a.m. on the 26th, with Union forces nearby.[28]

Fitz's division, facing Union artillery which prevented them from marching through Port Republic, next moved via Mountain Road and arrived at the foot of Brown's Gap on September 26. Here, they faced artillery fire and skirmishing all day. By dusk, they proceeded to Mr. Miller's place, where they were ordered to position themselves on the road leading to Waynesboro. At daybreak the next morning, Fitz Lee's division, led by Rosser, marched to Patterson's Ford, ahead of Early's command. Here, they crossed the river, but with Wickham's "vacillating conduct," lost an opportunity to capture a Union wagon train. Fitz Lee's division then moved on to Mt. Meridian on Middle River. Confederate infantry advanced and drove Union cavalry from Port Republic. At dark, Lee's division encamped near Mr. Patterson's place.[29]

After a sunrise breakfast on September 28 at Mr. Patterson's, Fitz Lee's division headed out with Munford's brigade in the advance on the road leading up the east side of the South River toward Rockfish Gap. Meanwhile, Early's command, with Payne's brigade leading, marched by way of Mt. Meridian towards Waynesboro, with the Union in possession of the town and the roads between it and the mountains. Munford had to make a detour on the side of a mountain and arrived at the mouth of Rockfish Gap. He then led the 4th Virginia in a charge of a small Union infantry force, surprising them and driving them through Waynesboro, where the pursuit stopped because of darkness. General Wickham, having stayed behind to see General Early, nearly got cut off, but recovered by charging some

27. Diary of J. D. Ferguson, September 24, 1864, DU.
28. Ibid., September 25, 1864.
29. Ibid., September 26–27, 1864.

Union cavalry and driving them back. The Confederates finally reached Waynesboro and encamped at Captain Trice's (a conductor of the Central Railroad) place. General Early, too, arrived at Waynesboro, but did not advance against Union forces.[30]

On September 29, Fitz Lee's division broke camp and marched out of Waynesboro four miles on the road to Greenville and encamped at Mr. A. H. H. Stuart's place. They enjoyed a good supper there and received orders to move out at sunrise the next morning towards Staunton. General Early's command was still in Waynesboro.[31]

The next day, Fitz Lee's command moved at sunrise along the road from Waynesboro to Staunton at Christian's Creek, where they met Bradley Johnson's brigade, and were joined by Lomax before encamping at Mr. Hamilton's. Munford's 2nd Virginia was dispatched to Mount Sidney.[32]

Munford's troopers drove the rear guard of Federal cavalry across the river at Bridgewater and camped near Centreville. The 2nd Virginia then picketed below Mount Sidney on the Valley Pike. All could now see the skies lit up from mountain to mountain by Sheridan's troopers as they carried out their commander's scorched-earth rampage. Munford's horsemen enjoyed a brief respite in the fighting as the two opposing forces watched each other across the North River. Munford recalled with pride, "I will say here that my brigade had wonderful advantages in its recuperative abilities. I was constantly receiving accessions of boys, 'young bucks,' just eighteen. . . . I do not know how many boys had run off from home and 'jined [the cavalry]'—they would come down to bring a fresh horse for a brother, and not return."[33]

On October 1, Fitz Lee's division marched to Staunton, where the command closed up and Munford rejoined them. They proceeded down the pike six miles and encamped at Mr. Harman's place. Later that day, when they were informed that General Early was six miles out in front of them and his infantry and ordnance wagons were coming up, they broke camp and marched again down the pike to Augusta Church, turned west and moved towards Bridgewater. After proceeding about five miles, the command went into camp at Mr. Brown's.[34]

---

30. Ibid., September 28, 1864.
31. Ibid., September 29, 1864.
32. Ibid., September 30, 1864.
33. Driver, *2nd Virginia Cavalry*, 141–42.
34. Diary of J. D. Ferguson, October 1, 1864, DU.

At 8:00 a.m. the next day, Fitz Lee's division, with Munford in the advance, marched down the Harrisonburg and Warm Springs Turnpike. The 4th Virginia was sent forward to Bridgewater, where they encountered Federal cavalry, and drove them through it. The regiment, however, became so dispersed that it could not hold position, forcing it to retreat back through Bridgewater and across the river. Skirmishing between Fitz Lee's command and the Union cavalry, along with Confederate artillery fire, took place the rest of the day, but no attempt was made to cross the river. On October 3, there had still been no attempt to cross the river by either Confederate or Federal forces. General Lomax positioned his troopers on the Confederate right flank.[35]

Fitz Lee had been wounded in the thigh during the Third Battle of Winchester, and General Rosser had taken temporary command of his division, which included the brigades of Williams C. Wickham and William H. Payne. Wickham, who had been elected to the Confederate Congress a year earlier, resigned his commission on October 5, and Colonel Munford took temporary command of his brigade. Munford was a capable, efficient, and brave officer who had never been promoted to brigadier general. Munford was unhappy he had to serve under the brash and flamboyant Rosser, an officer he had once outranked, and it was indeed unfortunate that the two officers had to cooperate in the months ahead. It was reported that neither Rosser nor Munford would even enter the other's tent. The other cavalry division in the valley, commanded by Maj. Gen. Lunsford L. Lomax, comprised the brigades of John C. Imboden, John McCausland, Bradley T. Johnson, and William L. Jackson. All units were far under authorized strength due to the heavy fighting and an inability to add substantial numbers of recruits.[36]

On October 5, Rosser's brigade, under Col. Richard Dulany, and Thompson's artillery battery joined the command at dark. Munford's brigade marched on the Back Road to Brock's Gap. General Early advanced to New Market.[37]

As the Federal cavalry retired down the valley, Rosser pressed them with three days of intensive fighting. Sheridan continued his burning rampage of the valley, inciting a high-pitched level of hatred and vengeance in the Confederates, determined to get even. On October 7, Fitz Lee's division, under Rosser, with Rosser's brigade in the advance, marched through the villages of Timberville and Forestville on the Back Road. Rosser's brigade overtook the rear of the retiring Yankee

---

35. Ibid., October 2, 3, 1864.
36. Bushong, *Fightin' Tom Rosser*, 113.
37. Diary of J. D. Ferguson, October 5, 1864; Driver, *2nd Virginia Cavalry*, 142.

column near Mill Creek and charged them, capturing about 40 prisoners, nine forges, two caissons, several hundred sheep, and numerous cattle. Munford's and Payne's troopers momentarily mistook each other for the enemy, thus delaying their support of Rosser and preventing a complete rout of the Federal soldiers.[38]

On October 8, Fitz Lee's division moved out at sunrise with William Payne's brigade in the advance, followed by Munford's troopers. About three miles north of Tom's Brook, Payne ran into Union cavalry, and even though greatly outnumbered and without support (Munford was mistakenly delayed by Payne's ordnance wagons), he charged the blue horsemen and drove them across the creek. Further pursuit was delayed when the Confederates reached the Confederate works on the line of Fisher's Hill. There, they found Federal cavalry on their flank on the pike and a Union signal corps on top of Round Top Hill. Without infantry support, the gray horsemen fell back to the hill on Tom's Brook. After some artillery fire and skirmishing, Rosser retired back two miles and encamped. Colonel Payne was positioned to observe the pike, Colonel Dulany on the Middle Road, and Munford on the Back Road. Sergeant Benjamin J. Haden recalled, "I remember very well that Colonel Munford seemed very relieved when we started to retire. We fell back about a mile south of Tom's Brook, and there went regularly into camp, even taking off our saddles, which was rarely ever done in such close proximity to the enemy."[39]

Custer Gets His Revenge at Tom's Brook: "The Woodstock Races," October 9, 1864

Rosser, both brave and blunt, nevertheless became apprehensive about further pursuit of Custer because of the increased distance between his command and Early's forces. By courier, he told Early of his concerns, but "Old Jube," believing that Sheridan was leaving the valley, ordered him to continue the pursuit. Early reported that General Lomax was following the Federals on the Valley Pike, and that he had already passed New Market, where the main army was then encamped. Early felt that Sheridan would cross the Blue Ridge Mountains and rejoin Grant's army. Early urged Rosser to pursue as far north as Winchester and strike a blow if the opportunity presented itself.[40]

---

38. Diary of J. D. Ferguson, October 6–7, DU.
39. Diary of J. D. Ferguson, October 8, 1864, DU; Driver, *2nd Virginia Cavalry*, 142.
40. Jubal A. Early to Thomas L. Rosser, October 7, 1864, Thomas L. Rosser Papers, UVA; *Philadelphia Weekly Times*, March 22, 1884.

Still concerned, Rosser did continue the pursuit of Sheridan and Custer, but was mindful if he went too far north, he was in danger of being cut off from Early's army. Custer withdrew on the Back Road and joined Sheridan on the Valley Pike, while Rosser marched up the Back Road toward Winchester. Scouts then informed Rosser that Sheridan was not leaving the valley, but rather was establishing a strong position at Strasburg. At the same time, these scouts reported a large body of Federal cavalry moving from the Valley Pike to the Back Road with the obvious intention of cutting him off. Rosser quickly backtracked and struck the Federal column at Tom's Brook, six miles south of Strasburg. Making a vigorous saber charge, Rosser's horsemen drove the Federals back across Tom's Brook to Mount Olive, while Rosser established a high position on the Back Road in the vicinity of Spiker's Hill, where his 2,500 troopers encamped for the night. Lomax's division of two brigades and a battery of horse artillery, totaling about 1,000 men, bivouacked on both sides of the Valley Pike behind Jordon Run just south of the hamlet of Tom's Brook.[41]

Sheridan had had enough of Rosser's nipping at his heels. His patience was worn thin by the continuous harassment of his army by Rosser's rear guard attacks. He decided to put an end to Rosser's assaults. He knew he outnumbered the Confederate horsemen by at least two to one, in addition to having better weapons, equipment, and horses. He at once ordered Torbert to start out at daylight on October 9 and "Finish the 'Savior of the Valley." Sheridan told Torbert, "go out there in the morning and whip that Rebel cavalry or get whipped yourself." He also told Torbert that he was going to halt his army, and personally go up to the top of Round Hill to view how his orders were carried out. Torbert got the message—one did not disappoint Sheridan.[42]

General Early and his army were 25 miles in the rear, while Sheridan's army camped on the opposite bank of Tom's Brook from Rosser. This had a sobering effect on Rosser's troopers, who had gained some measure of vengeance for Sheridan's burning and plunder. On the evening of October 8, Rosser's horsemen must have wondered what tomorrow would bring, sensing they were outnumbered and far from support. Rosser did consider withdrawing southward in order to close the gap between his command and Early, but he instead convinced himself that if he faced overwhelming Federal forces in the morning, he would be able to safely withdraw—a fatal mistake. It turned out he was indeed following Sheridan's horsemen too closely.

---

41. Thomas L. Rosser Scrapbook, Thomas L. Rosser Papers. UVA; *Philadelphia Weekly Times*, March 22, 1884.
42. *OR* 43/1:327, 431; Philip Sheridan, *Personal Memoirs*, 2:56.

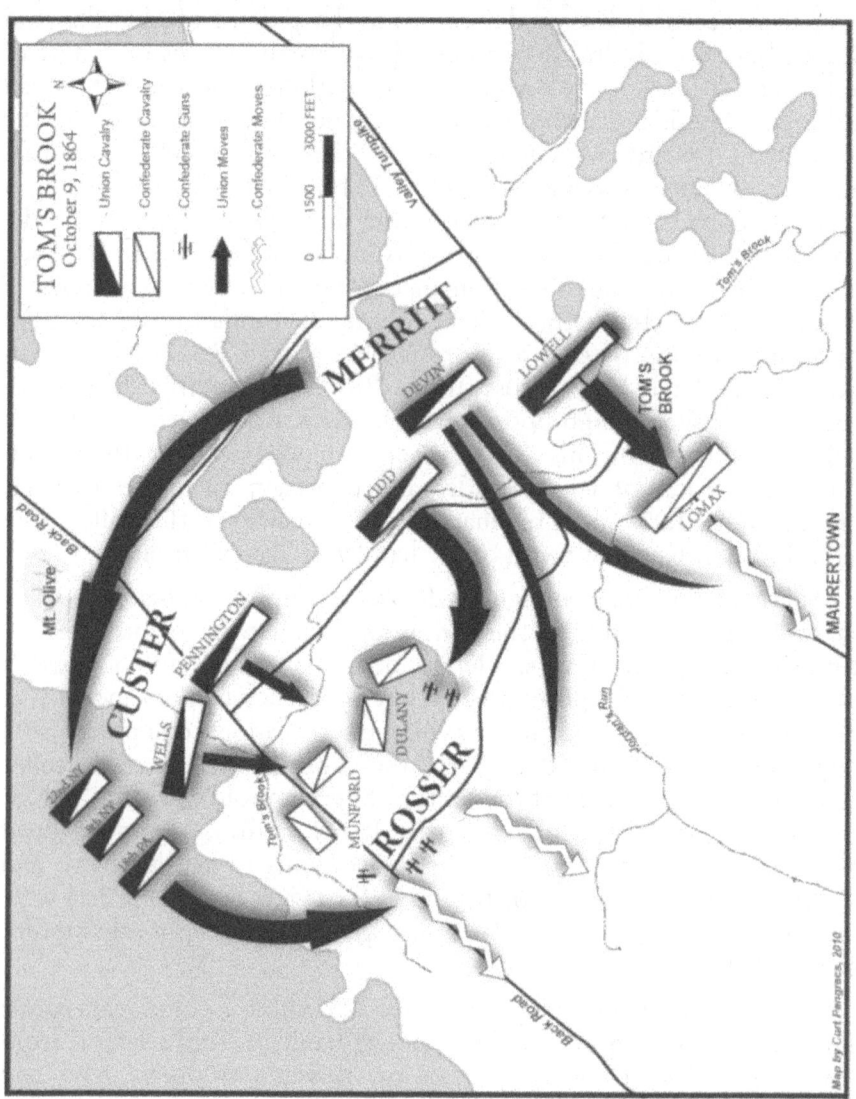

Up until this point, Rosser had pretty much had his way with the Federal cavalry in the Shenandoah Valley. Rosser's troopers bivouacked overnight on the Back Road just south of Tom's Brook, while Lomax's horsemen camped at Valley Pike near Woodstock, three miles east of Rosser. Rosser, however, had no idea of the ultimate strength of the Federal cavalry he was to face on October 9.[43]

---

43. McDonald, *Laurel Brigade*, 305–07; Whitehead, "Campaigns of Munford's 2nd Virginia Cavalry," 123, VHS; Longacre, *Lee's Cavalrymen*, 317.

The next morning, Rosser's and Lomax's troopers, numbering about 3,500, were opposed by the 6,000 Federal horsemen of Merritt's and Custer's divisions. While many of the Confederate troopers were poorly armed, the Federal troopers were well armed with Spencer repeating carbines, riding fresh mounts. Many in Lomax's command had only long rifles, which were exceedingly difficult to handle on horseback, and thus they had to fight dismounted. Merritt's cavalry division of about 3,500 men had encamped at the base of Round Top Hill at Tom's Brook. Custer's division of two brigades, totaling about 2,500 men, bivouacked behind Tumbling Run, northeast of Mount Olive on the Back Road and six miles northwest of Merritt. Torbert's plan was to bring an overwhelming force against Rosser's division on the Back Road, while holding Lomax's troopers at bay with a reinforced brigade on the Valley Pike. Lomax's main battle line was deployed behind Jordon Run on both sides of the Valley Pike and, supported by six guns. His front line was dismounted while he maintained a strong mounted reserve on the pike.[44]

As Custer approached Rosser's position on the Back Road, he recognized his friend from West Point across the way. Private George W. Hunt of the 15th New York Volunteer Cavalry recalled, "It was a magnificent place for a cavalry fight. There was room to deploy, smooth ground to ride on; all the rail fences had long ago vanished for soldiers' fires. . . . Out rode Custer from his staff, far in advance of the line, in plain view of both armies. Sweeping off his broadbrimmed hat, he threw it down to his knee in a profound salute to his foe." Rosser, viewing Custer through field glasses, returned the gesture, and his men sent up a deafening cheer. Private Hunt described what happened next:

> Custer replaced his hat, turned to his line of men and the next moment the 3d Division was sweeping on at a trot, the flaming neck tie and bright curls of Custer before all, followed by his staff, all swords out. Now the pace quickens. The rebel guns open at shorter range, bullets and shells whistling over the heads of the men. . . . The trot becomes a gallop, a wild yell from the line and they go racing across the intervening space with waving sabres, the horses wild with excitement as they race for the rebel batteries.[45]

---

44. Gary W. Gallagher, *The Shenandoah Valley Campaign of 1864* (Chapel Hill, NC., 2006), 146; U.S. Department of the Interior National Park Service, Study of Civil War Sites in the Shenandoah Valley of Virginia, "Tom's Brook," September 1992.
45. George W. Hunt Memoir, George W. Hunt Papers, William L. Clements Library, University of Michigan.

At dawn on October 9, Col. Charles Russell Lowell's brigade of Merritt's division advanced to Tom's Brook on the Pike, deployed, and pushed forward one-quarter of a mile where it found Lomax's main line, dismounted behind Jordon Run. The Confederate line was supported by six guns placed on either side of the Valley Pike and a strong mounted reserve. While Lowell was engaged, Col. James H. Kidd's brigade of Custer's division rode north along Tom's Brook to connect with Custer. Colonel Thomas Devin's brigade followed, but veered off on the Harrisville Road and advanced to the vicinity of St. Johns Church, thereby maintaining a connection with the force on the Valley Pike and extending a skirmish line to connect with Kidd's brigade on the right.[46]

Meanwhile, Rosser dismounted most of his troopers behind Tom's Brook at the base of Spiker's Hill (also known as Coffman's Hill), where they deployed behind stone fences and rudimentary fieldworks. Rosser's brigades were positioned, left to right: Munford, Payne, and the Laurel Brigade. Rosser's six guns unlimbered along the crest of Spiker's Hill, slightly behind a second line of barricades. A mounted reserve was maintained on the ridge; its right was extended toward the Middle Road by mounted skirmishers. Rosser claimed that Elijah White's battalion, which had been deployed on Rosser's front and right as skirmishers, charged one of Custer's columns while the Laurel Brigade drove Custer back across Tom's Brook.[47]

Munford observed what was happening on the left and sent for Rosser. When Rosser appeared and demanded to know what the problem was, Munford informed him that "his pickets had been driven in." Munford also told Rosser, "I could not hold my position, the country was open, and we could see two full divisions of the enemy immediately in front of us in an open field, numbering about 7,000 mounted men." Rosser arrogantly replied, "I'll drive them into Strasburg by ten o'clock." When Munford persisted, warning that they would turn Rosser's left, Rosser angrily replied, "I'll look out for that." The approaching Federals ended the conversation.[48]

Custer marched beyond Mount Olive, pushing forward three regiments of dismounted skirmishers against the main Confederate

---

46. Thomas L. Rosser Scrapbook, Thomas L. Rosser Papers, UVA; *Philadelphia Weekly Times*, March 22, 1884. Thomas Devin was promoted to brigadier general on October 19.
47. *Philadelphia Weekly Times*, March 22, 1884. For a discussion of the proper name of the Spiker's Hill, see William J. Miller, *Decision at Tom's Brook: George Custer, Thomas Rosser, and the Joy of the Fight* (El Dorado Hills, CA, 2016), Appendix C.
48. *SHSP*, vol. 13:136; Whitehead, "Campaigns of Munford's 2nd Virginia Cavalry," 123, VHS; Munford, typed history of the 2nd Virginia, p. 4, Munford–Ellis Papers, DU.

position. Three other Federal regiments and William Wells's brigade were kept mounted and behind the skirmish line. A Union battery unlimbered on the hill in front of Sand Ridge Church, engaging the Confederate artillery on Spiker's Hill. Kidd's brigade made contact with Custer's left while Custer extended his right flank along the shoulder of Little North Mountain, supporting the movement with another battery. Kidd deployed over the hill, driving Rosser's skirmishers before him. He unlimbered another battery to enfilade the Confederate position. The Confederate line was gradually forced back into a horseshoe shape around the front of Spiker's Hill. Additional Union cavalry, probably of Col. Tom Devin's brigade, marched on the Middle Road from Harrisville and positioned itself on a hill overlooking Sand Ridge Road at the intersection of Middle Road and to the right and rear of Rosser's main force. Rosser immediately ordered a withdrawal, sending his men racing to mount their horses. At this point, Wells's brigade attacked Spiker's Hill up the Back Road, and at the crest, he encountered Munford's brigade, where a mounted melee ensued. Rosser's force retreated, partly down Back Road to Pugh's Run, and partly on Sand Ridge and Middle Roads toward Woodstock. Custer's and Kidd's troopers pursued. General Sheridan watched the action from the top of Round Hill.[49]

Brevet Brigadier General George Armstrong Custer

Colonel Thomas T. Munford battled Custer many times, especially in the 1864 Valley Campaign and the Appomattox Campaign.

(Courtesy: Library of Congress)

In the meantime, fighting continued along the Valley Pike. Lowell's brigade drove Confederate pickets back to Jordon Run and

---

49. NPS, "Tom's Brook."

deployed on both sides of the pike. Kidd's 1st Michigan Brigade was supporting Lowell's right flank, while Devin's brigade moved farther to the right along the Middle Road beyond St. John's Church. As Devin maneuvered, Lomax counterattacked down the Valley Pike, driving the Reserve brigade back to Tom's Brook. Lowell, in turn, attacked until stopped by artillery.[50]

At last, Devin reached a position from which to operate against the flanks of both Lomax and Rosser. He advanced the 9th New York Cavalry and other elements against Lomax's left and rear, making Lomax's position untenable. The Confederates began to retreat up the pike toward Woodstock.[51]

Rosser retreated, losing at least two of his guns at Spiker's Hill. Munford's brigade attempted a stand behind Pugh's Run on the Back Road, but this position was quickly breached. Rosser's cavalry continued to retreat to Columbia Furnace, losing the rest of its artillery and all of its wagons. About 150 Confederate prisoners were captured during this phase of the retreat.[52]

Lomax retreated up the Valley Pike to Woodstock, where he was joined by a confused portion of Rosser's command. The forces attempted to stand behind Pugh's Run but were soon scattered. Union troopers pressed forward, driving the Confederate cavalry all the way to Mount Jackson, a distance of 25 miles. Lomax lost five pieces of artillery during this rout—two pieces at Woodstock, two at Edinburg, and the fifth beyond Stony Creek. The Union cavalry retired to the vicinity of Woodstock, where it bivouacked for the night.[53]

This disagreement between Rosser and Munford at Tom's Brook added to the existing acrimony between the two senior officers which lasted until Rosser's death. Munford, resentful of Rosser's promotion to brigadier while he remained a colonel, criticized Rosser's handling of the division at Tom's Brook. After the war, Munford referred to the fight as "the greatest disaster that ever befell our cavalry during the whole war," and accused Rosser of not reporting its extent to General Early.[54]

Munford further complained:

> To make the fight at Tom's Brook was against all the rules of discretion and judgment, and the responsibility belongs to Rosser. . . . It was a trap Sheridan set for him

---

50. *Philadelphia Weekly Times*, March 22, 1884.
51. Ibid.
52. Ibid.
53. Jack H. Lepa, *The Shenandoah Valley Campaign of 1864* (Jefferson, NC, 2003), 176–78.
54. *SHSP*, vol. 13:136.

> and was successful. . . . We had been incessantly engaged in severe skirmishing; Rosser's head seemed to be completely turned by our success, and in consequence of his rashness, and ignorance of their numbers, we suffered the greatest disaster ever befallen our command, and utterly destroyed the confidence of the officers of my brigade in his judgment--they knew that he could fight and was full of it, but he did not know when to stop, or when to retire.[55]

Munford further claimed, "if Rosser had then retired, as I suggested to him to do, he would have saved his command and his reputation; but pig-headed, in he went and ruined his command, losing everything, and then tried to put it off on old Early and two other officers, [Richard W.] Carter and [Henry] Carrington of my Brigade." In another postwar letter, Munford continued his stinging assessment of Rosser, stating "he is so very unscrupulous and not always truthful, and wants all the glory to himself, and never ought to have any rank than Col. of the 5th Va Cav."[56]

For his part, General Early never really respected or utilized his cavalry as he should have, and now his disdain for them induced him to label Rosser's Laurel Brigade "a running vine." "Buttermilk rangers" was a derisive term Early used to describe his Confederate cavalry. He characterized them, unfairly to a large degree, as "always leaving a hotter than usual conflict to sip buttermilk at a faraway farmhouse while they charmed southern belles with tales of their heroics."[57]

On the other hand, Munford believed:

> cavalry, well officered and thoroughly equipped, are able to perform any duty that any other armed troops ever did or ever will perform." He also thought "there must be sympathy between the man and the horse, each to know the other's worth. Men raised in the rural districts, who grow up with horses and ride them as boys as soon as they can hold on by themselves, are horsemen; the same class of men are accustomed to arms; such a man will give a part of an apple to his horse, and if, as a lonely picket, he sits in the chilly winds of December, without even a tree to shelter him from the cold blast or rain, when his "hard tack" rattles in his haversack and his hungry horse whinnies at the sound, he will often share

---

55. *SHSP*, vol. 13:136; Driver, *5th Virginia Cavalry*, 90; John T. Phillips to Thomas T. Munford, September 7, 1895, Munford-Ellis Papers, DU.
56. Ibid.
57. Frank E. Vandiver, *Jubal's Raid* (New York, 1960), 41.

with him his scanty ration. Do not give that man a miserable jade, but furnish him with a horse, and he will keep him a horse.⁵⁸

Referring to the battle of Tom's Brook, Lt. Robert T. Hubard of the 3rd Virginia Cavalry lamented:

> under Major General T. L. Rosser, a brave but indifferent officer, our glorious brigade that had never been defeated was subjected to the humiliation and shame of the most disastrous defeat along with the officer's whose command on the 9th of October on upper Cedar Creek. He rushed headlong upon the retreating enemy, some twenty miles ahead of the infantry, leaving his flanks exposed in the most stupid and reckless manner. Our brigade was hemmed in, its entire hospital captured a mile in its rear while it was fighting in the front and this sad news spreading among the men, they broke and fled in confusion. . . . Never was inordinate vanity and conceit more thoroughly punished than in [the] case of this peacock on that occasion.⁵⁹

Sergeant Benjamin J. Haden recalled, "the battle commenced. I said battle, but I will take that back, as there was no battle; for the enemy had nothing to do but drive our skirmish line in and it was all over; as there was nothing in reserve to support anybody or anything. The result was an ignominious rout." Trooper William C. Corson described the fight as "the most complete and disastrous cavalry stampede of the war. We lost our wagons, ambulances and 11 pieces of artillery. The blame rests with Gen. Rosser."⁶⁰

Rosser hated to lose this fight, and he claimed it was the first time the Laurel Brigade had been defeated. Merritt and Custer captured more than 300 prisoners, 47 wagons including ambulances, caissons, a battery of artillery, and the headquarters wagons of Rosser, Lomax, Wickham, and Payne.⁶¹

Custer also recovered the booty that Rosser and Munford had taken from him at Trevilian Station. One item Custer prized

---

58. *Journal of the Military Service Institution of the United States*, vol. X, No. XXXVII (March 1889), 527-28.
59. Nanzig, *Lt. Robert T. Hubart, Jr., The Civil War Memoirs of a Virginia Cavalryman* (Tuscaloosa, AL, 2007), 201.
60. Sergeant B. J. Haden, *Reminiscences of J.E.B. Stuart's Cavalry* (Palmyra, VA, 1993), 35; Driver, *1st Virginia Cavalry*, 102; William C. Corson to Jennie, October 13, 1864, William Clark Corson Papers, VHS; Corson, Blake W., Jr., ed., William Clark Corson, *My Dear Jennie: A Collection of Love Letters from a Confederate Soldier to His Fiancee During the Period 1861-1865* (Richmond, VA, 1982), 130.

Major General Jubal A. Early
Commander of Confederate forces in the 1864 Valley Campaign

He did not respect his cavalry and that cost him in the Valley Campaign.

(Courtesy: Library of Congress)

particularly was Rosser's uniform, which he later gave to his wife, Elizabeth. It is said that she, in turn, presented it to West Point, where it is on display.[62]

Sergeant-Major Richard T. Watts of the 2nd Virginia described the fight at Tom's Brook:

> In this engagement Rosser lost all of his wagons, artillery (11 pieces), camp equipment, etc., together with several hundred prisoners and horses. This was the severest blow dealt the Cavalry of the Army of Northern Va. The accumulations of four years–(spoils taken from the enemy) were lost. From this disaster they never recovered. Munford criticized Rosser for his rashness, and Rosser preferred charges against him, alleging that he did not give him cordial support, was guilty of insubordination, sedition, etc. Munford was honorably acquitted of every one of the charges and restored to his command.; the testimony of the witnesses clearly showing that no one had done more than he to save the army on that disastrous day.[63]

J. D Ferguson recalled, "The misfortunes of the day, I think, to be attributed to injudicious orders from Early, rashness on the part of Gen. Rosser and the misbehavior of 1st and 3rd Regts. Rosser's brigade was so located as to be unable to render any very efficient service in checking the advance of the enemy when first breaking our lines."[64]

Trooper John B. Philips later recalled events leading up to and including Tom's Brook:

> Now about Gen. Rosser—as you say he is so unscrupulous and not always truthful and wants all the glory for himself--and never ought to have any higher rank than Col of the 5th Va Cav. . . . You remember well. When Rosser came over in the Valley after we had been there some time with his Laurel Brgd, and they came as the Saviors of the Valley. . . . He allowed Sheridan to lead him down that back road to Tom's Brook–against your protest--nearly twenty miles from any support—and camped in sight of Sheridan Saturday night. When I understood you wanted to retire that night–which he opposed to do—but not moving had his whole command stampeded and lost every piece of artillery he had—as well as a number of his men and horses. . . . You

---

61. *OR* 43/1:521.
62. *SHSP*, vol. 13:139.
63. Driver, *2nd Virginia Cavalry*, 144.
64. J. D. Ferguson Diary, October 9, 1864, Munford–Ellis Papers, DU.

Brigadier General Thomas Lafayette Rosser – 1863

Munford's arch-nemesis. Rosser ignored Munford's warning at Tom's Brook on October 9, 1864, producing one of the worst Confederate cavalry defeats of the war. Rosser recommended Colonel William H. Payne over Munford for promotion in the fall of 1864. Rosser and Munford feuded after the war for the rest of their lives.

(Courtesy Albert and Shirley Small Special Collections Library University of Virginia)

remember that Col Carter of the first Brig and Major Carrington of the third were tried by court-martial for cowardice on the field. Carter and Carrington both ran from their commands soon in the morning. I never saw either one after that day.[65]

On a very cold and icy October 10, the Federals encamped near the scene of the Tom's Brook battle. They showed no disposition to advance. The Confederates moved back about two miles north of Cabin Point and went into camp. The next day they moved back to the vicinity of Forestville and encamped. The Federals broke camp, heading back through Winchester. On October 12, the Confederate command moved to Columbia Furnace and bivouacked while the Federals camped at Cedar Creek and Middletown.[66]

In the fight at Tom's Brook, the Union troopers routed the Confederate cavalry, impairing its morale and efficiency for the remainder of the campaign. The Confederate's flight in retreat was referred to by valley residents and victorious Union troopers as the "Woodstock Races." Custer boasted, "Never since the opening of this war had there been witnessed such a complete and decisive overthrow of the enemy's cavalry."[67]

The battle of Cedar Creek, or battle of Belle Grove, fought October 19, 1864, was the culminating battle of the Shenandoah Valley campaign of 1864. General Early launched a surprise attack against the encamped army of Union General Phil Sheridan, across Cedar Creek, northeast of Strasburg. During the morning fighting, seven Union infantry divisions were forced to fall back and lost numerous prisoners and cannons. Early failed to continue his attack north of Middletown, and Sheridan, dramatically riding to the battlefield from Winchester, was able to rally his troops to hold a new defensive line. A Union counterattack that afternoon routed Early's army.[68]

Cedar Creek dealt a crushing blow to the Confederacy in the Shenandoah Valley. Rarely have the scales of victory and defeat swung to such extremes during a battle; the morning's brilliant Confederate success was transformed by the overwhelming Federal forces and good generalship into a Union victory by day's end. Even without that fatal respite in the morning, the Confederates probably would have had little chance to carry the day. Early's hungry and ill-supplied troops lacked staying power, and so were driven from the field at day's end.

---

65. John B. Philips to General Thomas Munford, Sept. 7, 1895, Munford–Ellis Papers, DU.
66. J. D. Ferguson Diary, October 10, 12, 1864, Munford-Ellis Papers, DU.
67. *OR* 43/1:521.
68. Edward James Stackpole, *Sheridan in the Shenandoah: Jubal Early's Nemesis* (Harrisburg, PA, 1992), 397.

This battle ended large-scale fighting in the Shenandoah Valley. It also effectively ended Early's military career. Soon, both the Confederate and the Union armies were headed for the Petersburg area.[69]

Munford recalled he was on sick leave and missed the disastrous defeat at Cedar Creek on October 19. "In our fight and race at Tom's Brook, I had bruised an ugly boil, which had now turned into a severe carbuncle, giving me a fever and great pain. I got a leave of absence, and was not ready for duty, from the cause above stated, until the 14th of November, when I returned to camp and found the brigade where I had left it."[70]

Munford went at first to the hospital in Charlottesville for an undetermined stay. Even with a terrible boil on his leg, he managed to travel by train to Lynchburg. On the ride, an obnoxious, drunken officer staggered and fell on Munford's infected leg, producing terrific pain. When the train arrived at the Lynchburg depot, Munford had recovered enough to have the loathsome officer ejected from the train. It is not known if Munford proceeded to go home for a while or continued on to another hospital.[71]

Munford was still suffering from illness on November 6 and was admitted to Robertson Hospital in Richmond. On November 14, he returned to his regiment, which was still at Rude's Hill. His illness was designated "Feb. Int," probably, febrile illness, a nonspecific condition characterized by a sudden onset of fever, headaches, and body aches. "Int." probably meant "intermittent."[72]

Shortly after returning to service, Munford sent Sgt. Charles P. Preston and two others from the 2nd Virginia to locate the ambulance train. Much later, David Walker recalled he and his two companions' capture and subsequent encounters with Custer and Sheridan:

---

69. John L. Heatwole, *The Burning: Sheridan in the Shenandoah Valley* (Charlottesville, VA, 1998), 220.
70. Munford, Paper No. 3, "Reminiscences of Cavalry Operations: Operations Under Rosser," *SHSP*, vol. XIII:138.; Thomas T. Munford, CSR.
71. E. V. Anderson to Thomas T. Munford, September 4, Munford–Ellis Papers, DU.
72. Thomas T. Munford, CSR. Robertson Hospital records show Munford was admitted November 6 and released November 12, 1864; Robertson Hospital Register, Digital Collections, Virginia Commonwealth University Library, Richmond, Va. Robertson Hospital was a small, private Civil War hospital financially subsidized by the Confederate government. Located in the house of Judge John Roberts at the northwest corner of 3rd and Main Streets in Richmond, Virginia, the hospital was run by Captain Sally Louisa Tompkins, and was in operation from late July 1861 until June 1865. She was commissioned as Captain on September 9, 1861, in order to keep the hospital open after Surgeon General Samuel P. Moore closed all private hospitals in favor of large military hospitals to be run by commissioned officers.

Brigadier General William H. Payne

Promoted over Col. Thomas T. Munford in 1864, eliciting, in Payne's opinion, an offensive comment from Munford. The thin-skinned Payne challenged Munford to a duel, which Munford refused.

(Courtesy: Virginia Military Institute Archives)

We three [Davie Hunt, Asa Gills, and I] rode together to the point indicated by Munford that I would find the ambulance train at which point we rode right into a squad of Yankees—about fifteen. I had seen the squad at least four hundred yards away, but being so near in the rear of our fighting line, I naturally supposed them to be our own men—until I was halted by a Sergeant. Looking up I saw we were captured. We were carried that night first before Gen. Custer who treated me almost as a friend instead of an enemy. I sat in a room with he and his wife about three hours that night by a warm fire. It was a cold night--he and his wife treated me very affably. It was always a wonder to me that of the three of us, I was the only one to go into the General's room. Parker was initially treated the same way after he was taken to General Sheridan's Headquarters at Kernstown. At that time there were 15 prisoners instead of just three. But, Sheridan's mood changed when I was detected opening the letters of my company [Walker carried the mail for the regiment] to see if anything of value (military information) was in them then burning them. I did not answer Sheridan's questions to suit him as to our strength . . . within his lines. I told him I had seen no command but Fitzhugh Lee's brigade when in fact I knew we had three brigades fifteen miles within his lines when with an oath he ordered me out of his presence calling me a D[amn] Rebel Son of a B[itch]. He had not in him the first principle of a gentleman. I was a prisoner. What a chasm between Sheridan and Custer. No one but a coward at heart would insult a prisoner of war. Custer, generous and brave. Sheridan, (___)[73]

On November 17, Tom Munford wrote his father just after returning from the hospital in Richmond to duty:

My Regt welcomed me with three hearty cheers and the band gave me a serenade. This was very gratifying to me at this time. I addressed a very polite note to Genl Rosser, enclosing my discharge from the hospital, and the enclosed certificate and asked if any report had passed through his Head Qrts informing Genl Lee that I was absent without leave, as upon a shallow pretext—he replied, "that no such report had passed through his Head Qrts." When Genl [Fitz] Lee comes up, I intend asking him officially for the letter he received.[74]

To further exacerbate the hard feelings of Mumford for Rosser, the brassy Rosser received a recommendation for promotion to major general on November 1, while the deserving Munford was expecting a promotion to brigadier, but at that time was still a colonel. On November 4, matters were made worse for the Munford-Rosser relationship. Colonel William H. Payne received a promotion to brigadier general; it was the promotion Munford was expecting but did not get. In April 1864, Stuart had promised Munford's father that when Wickham resigned (he did so on Oct. 5), he would urge his son's promotion. But Stuart was dead, and Rosser opted for Payne, leaving Munford embittered.[75]

---

73. Letter, Nov 29, 1915, "The David Walker Family Chapter" in the book *Bedford Villages: Lost and Found* (Bedford, VA, 1998).
74. Thomas T. Munford to George W. Munford, November 17, 1864, Munford–Ellis Papers, DU.
75. General J.E.B. Stuart to George W. Munford, April 24, 1864, Private Collection of Munford's great granddaughter, Estelle Call; Munford–Ellis Papers, DU; Wert, "His Dishonored Service, CWTI, June 1985, 33. Note: Answering a letter from Fitzhugh Lee on November 2, 1864, Robert E. Lee wrote, "I have rec'd your letter of Sunday night. I have recommd [sic] Payne for Lomax's brigade, but he can be assigned where most wanted. I have had always a good opinion of Mumford [sic] & had been in view for Wickham's brigade, but at present Cannot recommend him." – Source: Robert E. Lee Papers, 1749-1975, Rubenstein Library, Duke University.

Munford was very upset at being passed over again. He must have made some very offensive remarks concerning Payne and his promotion, because Payne issued a challenge to a duel to Munford for "impeaching his veracity." Munford replied in a letter, refusing Payne's challenge and assuring Payne "that I did not intend to offer you an insult, nor to impeach your veracity." Whatever Munford exactly had stated is not known, but Munford claimed Payne's charge was untrue. Munford stated, "Patriotism and my Commission as an officer in the army (to say nothing of my professions as a Christian) would prompt me to decline to offer or accept a challenge. We had better spill our blood in defense of our cause, than to set such an example at such a time." Whatever the circumstances, the exchange ended the threat of a duel, but hard feelings continued. Payne, for his part, was rather thin-skinned; he got into numerous disputes after the war. He demanded explanations from individuals for remarks they made to others about him. After writing back and forth, these matters were settled to Payne's satisfaction before duel challenges ensued. He did issue a challenge to a duel to Col. A. W. Jones, but the difficulties were settled with an exchange of letters.[76]

William H. Payne, however, was involved in dueling activities in mid-1880. Political campaigns were the catalyst. He acted as second for Congressman George D. Wise, who dueled United States District Attorney L. L. Lewis near Warrenton in early autumn of 1880. Lewis's second was Col. John R. Paphim. Lewis had made some offensive remark about Congressman Wise which resulted in the hostilities. Payne was involved as second in another duel between Col. Thomas Smith of Fauquier and Mr. W. C. Elam, editor of the *Richmond Whig*, near Richmond in the summer of 1880. *The New York Times* reported that Payne would have probably received the Democratic nomination for Governor had it not been for his arrest and subsequent loss of political rights. In 1881, a bill was passed in the General Assembly to restore his and others' (including Rosser's) political rights that had been stripped from them earlier. Whatever the problems between Munford and Payne, they apparently were resolved to each other's satisfaction. They resumed cordial relations after the war, even corresponding with each other about remembrances of the war. Payne was supportive of Munford in dealing with erroneous accounts of others.[77]

---

76. Thomas T. Munford to General W. H. Payne, December 24, 1864, W. H. Payne Papers, Library of Virginia, Richmond, VA.
77. *The New York Times*, December 22, 1881; *Richmond Daily Dispatch*, January 11, 1882; Journal of the Senate of the Commonwealth of Virginia, (Richmond, VA, 1881), 161; William H. Payne to Thomas T. Munford, December 28, 1895, Munford–Ellis Papers, DU.

On another front dealing with Munford's feelings, Munford recalled seeing General Early and revealed his feelings about Fitz Lee:

> Since writing the above I have seen Genl Early. He seems very friendly towards me—told me that he had recommended me, but that no officer should leave his command or brig under it. That many of our best officers had ruined their prospects by absenting themselves and seemed to think a fellow had better fight & endure pain in an ambulance than to go home if he could ride. What good can an officer in this cavalry do when he cannot mount his horse? I think Genl [Fitz] Lee must have gotten his promotion from the Valley and mentioned it impudently. It is hard for a man to suffer mentally after having had as much bodily harm as I had to endure. But I hope it will all work right after a while. Hqtrs's army will date my commission from the time of Wickham's resignation. I shall be perfectly satisfied.[78]

Munford continued, "The men are in good spirits—but when old Abe gets his million of new troops in the field, I think we will have to retire to west Augusta and hold the mountains and hollows. There is no chance for us now, but to fight it out and I expect we will have a rough time before we get through. I am willing to see it out, 'whichever way the wind may blow!'"[79]

Concerned about the current state of affairs, Munford penned, "I hope our Generals will assume the defensive policy, and act strictly upon it. We haven't a man to lose—and our resources will have to be handled with economy as we will have much painful suffering."[80]

Colonel Munford concluded:

> I called upon Genl Early the night I arrived here. He received me very kindly and I heard him give a narrative of his Valley Campaign—was not impressed with his generalship by his own account. I saw many things very differently from what he did and do not think he is as well posted as he might have been more active both—physically & mentally. . . . If we only had a comprehensive head man [other than men such as Early] our army would be invincible. We want a man who can handle all of his troops. Infantry, artillery & cavalry. A man who knows when to use each and all & take the value of each and all—until we get such a man, we will

---

78. Thomas T. Munford to George W. Munford, November 17, 1864, Munford–Ellis Papers, DU.
79. Ibid.
80. Ibid.

never gain a decisive victory. We have too many heads and none of the very brilliant all imagining that they are the right one in the right place.... The Cavalry is thrown on either flank and required to perform all kind of duties. And never trusted by the infantry at a critical time if they strike the enemies cavalry to fall back when not supported and if our infantry was drawn back, we are frequently forgotten and to use a camp expression "left in the cold" to get out the best way we can.[81]

On November 22, Torbert, with two divisions of the Union cavalry, hurriedly pushed back Munford's pickets from Edinburg upon their reserve, but they were checked long enough for Munford to get his brigade ready to meet them. The Federals then entered the Broad bottoms, presenting a formidable appearance. As they moved across the river and bottoms, the Confederate horsemen kept pace with them on the north side of the Shenandoah River. General Early, being notified, moved out in line of battle with his infantry to the top of Rude's Hill. The rumbling of his artillery, the glitter of his bayonets, and an occasional shot from a battery Munford had placed in position, told the Federals that Early was still in the valley.[82]

When the Union troopers withdrew, Munford followed, hanging on their flank and rear for five or six miles, taking advantage of any opportunity of attacking their rear. As Munford's horsemen passed over the same ground returning to camp, they had a sharp encounter at Mount Jackson. They returned to camp, and soon after this, Rosser went on an expedition to New Creek. Munford's brigade remained encamped in the New Market-Mount Jackson area, picketing the Valley Pike and the Back Road, while Rosser, with some of the 2nd Virginia, conducted raids of Moorefield on November 28th and New Creek the next day. Rosser's raid netted prisoners, horses, sheep, and much needed supplies, including food stuffs for Early's half-starved soldiers.[83]

Shortly after Rosser's return from his New Creek expedition, cold weather set in, preventing operations in the field. Colonel Munford was sent to Hardy and Pendleton counties to procure forage for his horses. The 3rd division of the II Corps was sent in succession to General Lee at Petersburg. Brig. Gen. Gabriel C. Wharton's division, and most of the cavalry and most of the artillery stayed with Munford. Rosser accompanied Munford's brigade. They returned in about a

---

81. Ibid.
82. *SHSP*, vol. XIII, Paper No. 3, "Reminiscences of Cavalry Operations: Operations Under Rosser," 141.
83. Ibid.

week, bringing back a considerable drove of very fine fat cattle from Vandevender's farm, six or seven miles northwest of Petersburg; in the Moorefield Valley, as well as a large number of fat sheep said to have belonged to the United States Commissary Department.[84]

Munford recalled:

> The great North Mountain was covered deep with snow when we crossed it, but the splendid valleys below were well dotted with sweet-smelling hay, and the corn-cribs were well filled with grain. The citizens lived in a land of honey and maple-sugar, both of which were enjoyed by the soldiers. The weather was rough, but when a cavalryman could stand his horse up to his eyes in the nicest kind of hay, and had a bundle to stretch himself upon and with corn to spare for his horse, with full rations of fine, fat mutton and beef and no enemy to disturb him, it was a sad hour when he had to depart.[85]

He added: "My best efforts had to be exerted to keep whiskey out of camp in those mountains." He swore some of his men had a nose for alcohol:

> I had a few men in each regiment of the brigade whose noses were as keen as fox-hounds, or, probably, I had better say as a bee; or they had an intuitive knowledge of location. If there was a barrel, yes, a half-barrel, or a runlet of "apple jack" or "peach brandy" within a league, they would find it with absolute certainty, and when they found it they would first report to each other, and before the next morning—if you ever saw streams of ants go up and down a tree or wall and give signs—that is exactly what these fellows could do, and there would soon be a slick path to that point.[86]

Munford remembered that his expedition had been bloodless and enjoyable. They had brought back some fine cattle and sheep. "Getting back to our old lines we have had little feed. The day after our return the enemy had moved across the mountains towards Gordonsville, and we hurried in that direction over sleety roads, and I think was the roughest march we ever made. Arriving near that place we learned that Lomax had repulsed the raiding party, and we returned to Staunton and went into camp near Swope's Depot on the Virginia Central railroad."[87]

---

84. Ibid.
85. Ibid.
86. Ibid.
87. Ibid.

On December 7, Munford's brigade moved to Timberville in search of forage for their starving horses. The same day Rosser led another raid into Hardy and Hampshire counties after supplies. The Confederates raiders passed through Brock's Gap and reached Petersburg on December 9.[88]

The next day, Rosser led a raid of the Baltimore and Ohio Railroad, tearing up track and burning bridges and trestles. Fitz Lee's entire division accompanied Rosser on this trip. Rufus Peck recalled, "Twenty-five days rations of salt was given to us when we left and that was all we had. No bread, meat, or anything. Of course, we had to steal anything we ate, for we had no money to buy anything with."[89]

It was getting too cold for major movements by the infantry, and Early hoped to settle into winter quarters. The winter was to be a bitterly cold one, and the Confederates were in dire need of food, forage, and warm clothes. Beset by misery, the numbers of troops dwindled. Many of the horsemen went home, with permission, after fresh horses; and others took "French Leave." Those who remained looked forward to some rest after the exhausting campaigns. General Sheridan, however, was not quite through with his work.[90]

On December 17, Munford rejoined the 2nd Virginia. He led his troopers back to camp through Monterey and McDowell. On December 19, upon learning Custer with a force 3,000- strong was heading for Staunton, Rosser led all available horsemen, including many of Munford's 2nd Virginia, for Harrisonburg. General Early followed with infantry to Naked Creek. On December 21, in a blinding snowstorm, Rosser attacked two of Custer's brigades as they were saddling up, capturing 35 soldiers, wagons, and ambulances. Custer's 3rd brigade, however, rallied and forced the Confederates back, freeing their wagons and then withdrew down the valley. Rosser's exhausted troopers returned, the 2nd Virginia among them, going into camp at Swope's Depot.[91]

On December 23, Rosser led another mission, this time passing though Waynesboro. He crossed the Blue Ridge, and camped on the Mechum River. Here, Rosser learned that Torbert's cavalry had been turned back by Fitz Lee and Lomax; so, he headed back across the Blue Ridge. Munford was at Ivy Depot on Christmas Eve, and led his troopers back across the Blue Ridge on Christmas Day, only to re-cross the following day and encamp near Greenwood Depot. The tired

---

88. Driver, *2nd Virginia Cavalry*, 149.
89. Driver, *2nd Virginia Cavalry*, 149; Peck, *Reminiscences*, 59.
90. McDonald. *Laurel Brigade*, 331.
91. Driver, *2nd Virginia Cavalry*, 150–51.

troopers remained in camp for several days, facing sleet and snow on the 28th and bitter cold on the 29th. Finally, they headed back to Swope's Depot and encamped.[92]

Munford was recommended at least nine times for promotion to brigadier general; four times prior to the fall of 1864 and five times in the fall and winter of 1864. Among those recommending him just since the fall of 1864 were Thomas H. Ellis, Virginia Governor William Smith, Capt. Henry Lee and 67 other members of Wickham's Brigade, and 10 members of the 2nd Virginia. None of these recommendations earned him promotion.[93]

---

92. Ibid.
93. Munford, CSR. Recommendations for promotion to brigadier: September 3, 1864 by Thomas H. Ellis to Secretary of War, James A. Seddon; November 5, 1864 by Virginia Governor William Smith. R. E. Lee returned it to Secretary of War on November 9. There was activity on this recommendation at least until February 17, 1865, but no action was taken; November 29, 1864 a petition signed by Capt. Henry Lee, AAG and co-signed by 67 officers of Wickham's Brigade was forwarded to the Secretary of War; December 9, 1862 Virginia Governor John Letcher to Secretary of War James A. Seddon recommended Munford for promotion; August 17, 1863 Francis H. Smith, Superintendent of VMI, to President Jefferson Davis recommended Munford for promotion; August 5, 1863 Beverly Tucker to Secretary of War James A. Seddon recommending promotion; August 5, 1863 John Rutherford to Secretary of War James A. Seddon recommending promotion, stating he fears Munford will resign if overlooked again; January 5, 1865 Thomas H. Ellis to Secretary of War James A. Seddon recommending promotion; October 2, 1864 from 10 members of the 2nd Virginia (Messrs John P. Holcombe, James Lyons, John Goode, Jr., Charles N. Russell, ___ Johnston, A. R. Boleter, M. R. H. Garnett, Walter Preston, S. Bococh, Lt. C. D. Jarrette, and Chas. Collier), to President Jefferson Davis recommending promotion.

Chapter Fifteen

1865: Five Forks
The Waterloo of the Confederacy

"Genl George E. Picket, Genl Fitz Lee, and Genl T. L. Rosser, the three major generals (ranking) on the Confederate side, were all absent from the Battle of Five Forks—their instruction from Genl R. E. Lee was not carried out, and Genl R. E. Lee was not kept posted by them."

—Colonel Thomas Munford
on the Battle of Five Forks.

As 1864 ended with soldiers in winter quarters, the spring campaign promised a test of Petersburg's defenses. Grant was determined to breach them, forcing Robert E. Lee into an untenable position of fighting in the open or trying to flee from an overwhelming foe. Lee's troops were stretched thin, desertions were increasing, conditions were worsening, and morale was sinking. Spring would see the fall of Petersburg, the evacuation of Richmond, and the final campaign of the war: Appomattox.

After New Year's Day, 1865, many members of Rosser's division went on leave. On January 1, the men of Elijah White's battalion departed to their native counties east of the Blue Ridge Mountains. On January 3, the First Squadron of the 11th Virginia left for McDowell County. Rosser granted similar leaves to many in the 7th and 12th Virginia. By mid-January, only part of the Laurel Brigade remained in camp at Swope's Depot. Those remaining suffered greatly from lack of food. Private Beverly K. Whittle of the 2nd Virginia recalled, "Feed is very scarce, and we have to move about to get it. The horses are in wretched condition, nearly starved to death all the time; if Rosser stays in command much longer, our division will be utterly ruined by spring."[1]

---

1. Beverly Kennon Whittle Papers, Notebook, September 12, 1864-February 18, 1865, UVA, Charlottesville, VA.

Raid on Beverly, West Virginia

Rosser, still in command of Fitzhugh Lee's division, sought answers to the mounting problems. There was no help coming from others; the countryside was famine-stricken. The Confederate government could not do much. Gloom was in the air. Rosser, however, heard from his scouts that at Beverly, West Virginia, west of the Alleghenies, the Federals had stored a large quantity of army supplies. Of great interest was the fact the garrison numbered only about 1,000 soldiers of all arms. Rosser's interest piqued, and he decided to make a raid on the post. Beverly was about 75 miles from Staunton as the crow flies, but Rosser's troopers would have to travel winding roads through the Alleghenies, including war-ravaged country offering almost nothing in the way of subsistence. Most of the roads were nearly impassable, and the route was strewn with raging streams. Many gorges were blocked up with snow, some to a depth of 25 feet. The citizens living along this route were fiercely anti-Confederate.[2]

Rosser, with his raid approved by Fitzhugh Lee in General Early's absence, summoned Colonel Munford to his headquarters. Once there, Rosser ordered him to select a number of "volunteers" for the expedition, which was to leave the next morning. Munford, a capable officer, told Rosser his quartermaster was due in from Richmond with supplies and shoes for his horses. On account of the worn-down horses and dispirited men that had been on continuous duty for an extended period, Munford suggested the raid be postponed until the fresh supplies arrived, and the weather moderated. Rosser adamantly denied the request, repeating his intention to leave the next morning. Munford returned to his command and informed his officers of the orders. Captain John Lamb and Maj. Charles Old asked Munford for permission to travel to Rosser's headquarters to intercede on behalf of the dispirited men. Permission granted, Lamb and Old journeyed to Rosser's command, but Rosser was unyielding and refused their request. Lamb and Old reported they were "very indignant at his [Rosser's] reception of them, and it was evident that they had no confidence in him or his care for his men." Munford reluctantly instructed his detail to report to Col. William A. Morgan, commander of the 1st Virginia, in the morning.[3]

---

2. McDonald, *Laurel Brigade*, 334–36.
3. Thomas P. Nanzig, *3rd Virginia Cavalry*. 69; Handwritten article by Thomas T. Munford published in the *Philadelphia Weekly Times*, May 17, 1884, Munford Papers, Munford–Ellis Collection, Box 17, DU; *SHSP*, vol. 13:143–144.

At about 4:00 a.m. the next morning, Rosser sent Holmes Conrad, his adjutant and inspector general, to Munford's headquarters at Mr. Gilkerson's house to deliver Rosser's order to "mount your command." Munford strongly declined the order and reported his command unfit for duty.[4]

Rosser called for volunteers from the Laurel Brigade and Payne's brigade. He received responses from all brigades in the division, but could find only 300 horses that were suited for the trip. Some men volunteered to march on foot, but Rosser refused their offer. He divided his 300-man force about equally, half under Colonel Morgan and half under Col. Albert W. Cook, leading the 8th Virginia. The expedition started on Rosser's schedule on the morning of January 7, 1864.[5]

That same morning, Munford received a visit from Capt. R. B. Kennon, Rosser's inspector general. Kennon asked where Munford's detail was, and Munford referred him to Morgan's headquarters. Shortly, Kennon returned to Munford with a paper signed by Rosser, informing Munford that he should consider himself under arrest; he would be tried by court-martial on charges of sedition, conspiracy, and efforts to thwart Rosser's plans.[6]

Rosser conducted a risky but successful raid on Beverly, capturing the fort and gathering a large quantity of supplies before heading back. Rosser's exhausted troopers, finally back in the Shenandoah Valley, looked forward to plenty of rest before the weather improved and the spring campaign began. Fitzhugh Lee moved Payne's and Munford's brigades east of the Blue Ridge Mountains, leaving only Rosser's Laurel Brigade in the Valley.[7]

On January 23, 1865, from Wickham's brigade headquarters near Gordonsville, Munford wrote his father of his impending court-martial based on charges preferred by Rosser after the Beverley raid:

> I have just received the notice to appear in Staunton with my witnesses on Wednesday 25th. I sent you a telegram this evening but fear the sleet has broken the trains too much to get it through. Please send to Mr. Letcher immediately upon the receipt of this as I do not wish to cause a moments delay on my part. Rosser has withdrawn the charge of "Mutiny and Sedition," and modified his other charges. I do not apprehend much difficulty—but

---

4. Holmes Conrad to Thomas T. Munford, February 21, 1900, Munford–Ellis Papers, DU.
5. *Philadelphia Weekly Times*, April 5, 1884.
6. *SHSP*, vol. 13:143–44.
7. S. Roger Keller, *Riding with Rosser* (Shippensburg, PA, 1997), 61.

with Mr. T's advice shall contract the case entirely to him. The provisions are ample for the whole Brigade—Turkeys, chicks, dried figs, hams, mutton, beef, vegetables, pies, cakes, & pickles "until you can't see!" I am sick of loss and being under such people [Rosser] but hope to see it out.[8]

Upon Rosser's return from Beverly, a military court convened and held a trial, unanimously acquitting Munford. The court admonished Rosser, recommending that charges not be made against officers without sufficient foundation. A smoldering enmity between Rosser and Munford existed from then on; no one forgot the indignities.[9]

In late January, Generals Wade Hampton and Matthew C. Butler and their subordinates were ordered to South Carolina to help defend against Sherman's approaching onslaught. Robert E. Lee, with approval from Jefferson Davis, approved the reassignment, contingent upon both commanders returning to the Army of Northern Virginia by the beginning of the spring campaign. Neither officer would be able to keep that promise. Fitz Lee was assigned to command the Cavalry of the Army of Northern Virginia.[10]

The Federals continued raiding the central Virginia railroads, forcing Rosser to send Munford's brigade to help protect the valuable lines. Munford's brigade numbered only 33 officers and 394 men for duty. Another 107 were present, but their horses were in such poor condition they could not take the field. Rations for the men were scarce, and for the starving horses, even less.[11]

On February 5, Munford's regiment was ordered to march to Richmond. They reached Barboursville that evening and Trevilian Station the next day. On February 6, Munford passed through Louisa Court House, camping six miles beyond. The following day, the regiment proceeded along the Mountain Road 15 miles in a snowstorm. On February 10, within five miles of Richmond, Munford sent 60 men after deserters in Brown's Gap. Twenty deserters were captured, five were shot, and one hanged.[12]

On March 2, Sheridan defeated the remnants of General Early's army at Waynesboro and marched eastward. Munford marched his troopers northward to defend the vital railroad bridges over the North and South Anna rivers. Vastly outnumbered, Munford could only

---

8. Thomas T. Munford to George W. Munford, January 23, 1865, Munford–Ellis Papers, DU.
9. *SHSP*, vol. 13:143–44.
10. Longacre, *Lee's Cavalrymen*, 322–23.
11. Driver, *2nd Virginia Cavalry*, 153.
12. Ibid., 154.

skirmish with Sheridan's legions. On March 16, Munford led his brigade to Hanover Court House. As Sheridan moved to rejoin Grant's army, Munford shadowed him to White House Landing, harassing his rear guard. The exhausted men and their mounts rested a couple of days, beginning on March 18 at Mechanicsville. Most of the furloughed soldiers returned to duty, bringing new recruits with them.[13]

Major William F. Graves was placed in command of the 390 dismounted men of Munford's brigade and manned the trenches of the Nine Mile Road. Fitz Lee had assumed command of the cavalry of the Army of Northern Virginia after General Hampton was sent south to fight William T. Sherman. Munford took over Fitzhugh Lee's division while Col. William A. Morgan commanded the brigade. Robert E. Lee ordered Fitz Lee to move his former division, under Munford and numbering about 2,000 troopers, and with Pickett's division of infantry, to strike Phil Sheridan's command, then heading for Dinwiddie Court House. Robert E. Lee wanted to stop Sheridan before he ever got started on his mission attacking the South Side Railroad. Graves and his dismounted men were left behind.[14]

Numerous Confederate soldiers remained away from their units on sick leave, many after their supposed dates of return to service; too many for Munford's liking. On March 21, Munford penned a letter stating, "It is impossible for us to keep up the cavalry [unless] the officers at home require the men at home to report back promptly. There are a [great] many men at home upon improper paper and surgeons certificates long since out of date." The order was given to arrest the men whose names appeared on Colonel Munford's list as deserters if they could not be shown to have proper authorization.[15]

On March 29, General Grant began his spring offensive against Petersburg. He ordered Sheridan to go around the Confederate right, attempting to thereby stretch Robert E. Lee's defensive lines and force his troops out of their fortifications. Sheridan headed for Dinwiddie Court House. Per Grant's orders, General Meade ordered Maj. Gen. G. K. Warren's 15,000-man V Corps from their winter camps south of Petersburg to march north up the Quaker Road to secure the strategically important Boydton Plank Road. There, they pushed the Confederates back into their lines along the White Oak Road and took control of the Boydton Plank Road. This position afforded access for

---

13. Ibid.
14. Ibid., 155.
15. Compiled Service Records of Confederate Soldiers Who Served From Virginia 2d Cavalry (Bl–Ch), NA microfilm, M324, Roll 16, Service Record of W. H. Burnley, Private, Co. K, 2nd Regt. Virginia Cavalry.

an assault on the South Side Railroad, just three miles to the north. Meanwhile, just before nightfall in a terrible rain, Fitz Lee's former division and Rosser's division arrived at Southerland Station on the South Side Railroad.[16]

The next morning, March 30, saw the rain continuing as Fitz Lee's command headed by the most direct road to Five Forks en route to Dinwiddie Court House. Nearing Five Forks, Brig. Gen. William H. Payne's brigade, being the advance of Fitz Lee's cavalry, ran into Wesley Merritt's cavalry. General Henry E. Davies's division and his brigade had been ordered by Sheridan to occupy Five Forks. A sharp fight ensued, with General Payne being wounded and removed from the field. At once, Fitz Lee dismounted his troopers and skirmished with the Union horsemen, pushing them back to Boisseaux, about a mile and a half in the direction of Dinwiddie Court House. Lee's troopers remained there until nightfall, leaving a picket before falling back to Hatcher's Run.[17]

Also by dark, Maj. Gen. George Pickett, leading five small brigades of infantry and Lt. Col. Willie J. Pegram's battalion of artillery, joined Fitz Lee's command near White Oak Road. About the same time, Rooney Lee's and Thomas Rosser's cavalry divisions arrived, making the entire Confederate force about 8,500 men of all arms. General Pickett, the ranking major general, assumed command of the entire force. Fitz Lee headed the entire cavalry while Munford commanded Lee's former division. Colonel William B. Wooldridge led the 2nd Cavalry Brigade while Col. Reuben B. Boston commanded Payne's brigade.[18]

That same day, Warren's infantry completed fortifying their position. Across from them, Confederate Lt. Gen. Richard H. Anderson's Corps entrenched on White Oak Road. By the following day, the same day the battle of Chamberlain's Bed occurred, Rooney Lee had moved his 4,200 cavalrymen from Stony Creek to unite with Fitzhugh Lee on the White Oak Road near Five Forks, four miles northwest of Chamberlain's Bed. Five Forks was an intersection of four roads: White Oak, Scotts, Fords (or Church) and Dinwiddie Court House. Located six miles northwest of Dinwiddie Court House, it was crucial to controlling the South Side Railroad, Robert E. Lee's last supply link to Petersburg. To hold it, Lee's cavalrymen rendezvoused at Five Forks with 5,000 infantrymen commanded by Pickett.[19]

---

16. *OR* 46/1:798, 1101–02; Thomas T. Munford, "The Last Days of Fitz Lee's Division of Cavalry," VHS, Richmond, VA, 9.
17. Ibid., 9–10.
18. Ibid., 10.
19. Ed Bearss and Chris Calkins, *The Battle of Five Forks* (Lynchburg, VA,

At daylight on March 31, Confederate pickets reported to Munford on the road to Dinwiddie Court House that the sound of axes could clearly be heard, indicating the Federals were barricading and preparing to hold their ground in Munford's front. Fitz Lee ordered Munford to move to the front and position his division so as to hold the road leading to Dinwiddie Court House. Fitz Lee told him that he (Lee) would take Rooney Lee's and Rosser's divisions, supported by Pickett's infantry, and by a concealed route, reach Little Five Forks, west of Chamberlain's Bed, by crossing the Run at Fitzgerald's and Dance's Fords. Fitz Lee planned to attack the Union cavalry in the flank and rear. He ordered Munford to attack the Federals in his front on the road to Dinwiddie Court House as soon as he heard Fitz's guns, indicating a large engagement. Munford was to attack, fight through the Federals, and join Fitz Lee's command.[20]

Munford did not hear Fitz Lee's guns for many hours, not knowing that the Federals had occupied the very fords of Chamberlain's Bed that Fitz Lee was planning on crossing. Hearing the guns of Pegram's artillery at last, Munford placed the 2nd Cavalry Brigade in advance, sounded the bugle, and the whole division advanced, firing as they went. Fighting in country that was ill-suited for cavalry—swampy in places, rife with branches, ravines, briars, thickets, and stunted pines—Munford's troopers could only see a short distance ahead. Munford ordered a right oblique, but the difficulty in preserving alignment resulted in Munford's line becoming disconnected. They found themselves isolated from their support and between Union horsemen of Generals Thomas Devin and Henry Davies. Munford was forced to retreat in the general direction of Fitz Lee's division of cavalry.[21]

Passing Dinwiddie Court House, Munford established a thin line of defense. The 3rd Virginia then connected with the Confederate infantry on Munford's right rear. Munford held against Federal assaults. Fitz Lee's remaining two divisions of cavalry, preceding the infantry, moved by a concealed road, and attempted to attack and turn the Federal flank. In this action, Fitz Lee's command had to cross the fords of Chamberlain Bed in a rigorous fight with severe losses. Munford attacked at the same time, carrying the Federal works thrown up in his path, finally uniting with Fitz Lee's other divisions.[22]

1985), 8; Louis H. Manarin, *North Carolina Troops, 1861–1865, A Roster* (Raleigh, NC, 1989), vol. 2:278.
20. Thomas T. Munford, "The Last Days of Fitz Lee's Division of Cavalry," 14–15, VHS.
21. Ibid., 15–17.
22. Ibid., 17.

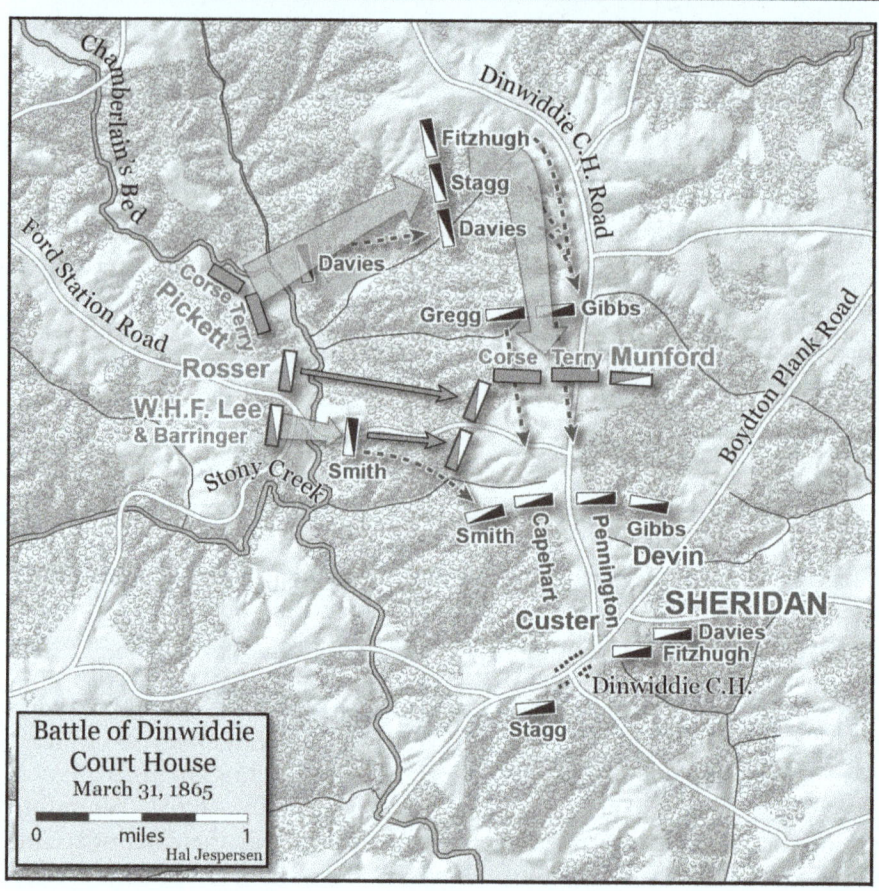

Meanwhile by about 11:00 a.m. on March 31, a detachment of Maj. Gen. Bushrod Rust Johnson's forces from Anderson's Corps attacked Warren's infantrymen. The Confederates pushed the Federals back southwest to a branch of Gravelly Run. Warren, reinforced by Brig. Gen. Nelson Miles's division of the II Corps, counterattacked. The Confederates were driven back to their works along the White Oak Road.[23]

That same day, Warren dispatched Maj. Gen. Joseph J. Bartlett's brigade to a position behind Pickett's left flank. Sensing the precariousness of his position, Pickett withdrew towards Five Forks, retreating as far as Hatcher's Run. Soon, Sheridan's cavalry and Warren's V Corps began pressing Pickett's infantry as they retreated towards Five Forks.[24]

---

23. Chris Calkins, "Hold Five Forks at All Hazards," *Blue and Gray Magazine* (April 1992), 17–18.
24. Ibid.

As the fighting ended that day, Phil Sheridan's army, instead of being able to get in the right rear of Robert E. Lee's army, found themselves in retreat back to near Dinwiddie Court House. Robert E. Lee had ordered Pickett "to drive him [Sheridan] out and break him up." Munford, in hindsight, believed Pickett should have pressed his advantage and continued to drive Sheridan, but Pickett's infantry halted. He sent his artillery back to Five Forks and bivouacked for the night. Munford complained, "It was a golden opportunity; an opportunity egregiously lost." According to Munford, Pickett's excuse was that he needed "half an hour more of daylight." This gave Sheridan time to consolidate his command and possibly be reinforced. Fitz Lee ordered Munford to send out pickets towards the Boydton Plank Road, on his left front, but to hold his position. Munford dismounted his division on the left of Gen. M. D. Corse of Pickett's infantry. By 10:00 p.m., based on information received from captured prisoners, Fitz Lee then ordered Munford to move with Pickett's army to Five Forks at dawn. He was to cover the rear of General Corse's infantry as they pulled back.[25]

Munford's command was dismounted. The horses were in the rear, about a mile away. His troopers had been in the thick of fighting all day; the mounts had been without feed or water. General Sheridan and General Merritt reported that they "pressed" Munford's horsemen all the way back to Pickett's position at Five Forks in the early morning. Munford, writing in later years, clearly disagreed with that assessment. He recalled that his troopers, knowing that the Federals had been reinforced, expected to be hurried along, but were not hard-pressed, instead undertaking a steady, controlled retreat.[26]

Five Forks—The Waterloo of the Confederacy

At the outset of the climactic battle of Five Forks on April 1, at about 9:00 a.m., Pickett placed his entrenched division of infantry north of Five Forks in a line of battle facing south along White Oak Road. Rooney Lee's and Munford's cavalry were positioned on his right and one regiment of Munford's on his left. Rosser's division was placed in reserve in the rear of the center, with Hatcher's Run between it and the others. Rosser, charged with guarding the ammunition

---

25. Thomas T. Munford, "The Last Days of Fitz Lee's Division of Cavalry," 19, 23, VHS; Thomas T. Munford to James T. Murfee, March 4, 1911, Private Collection of David Center, Highland Home, Alabama.
26. Ibid., 24–25.

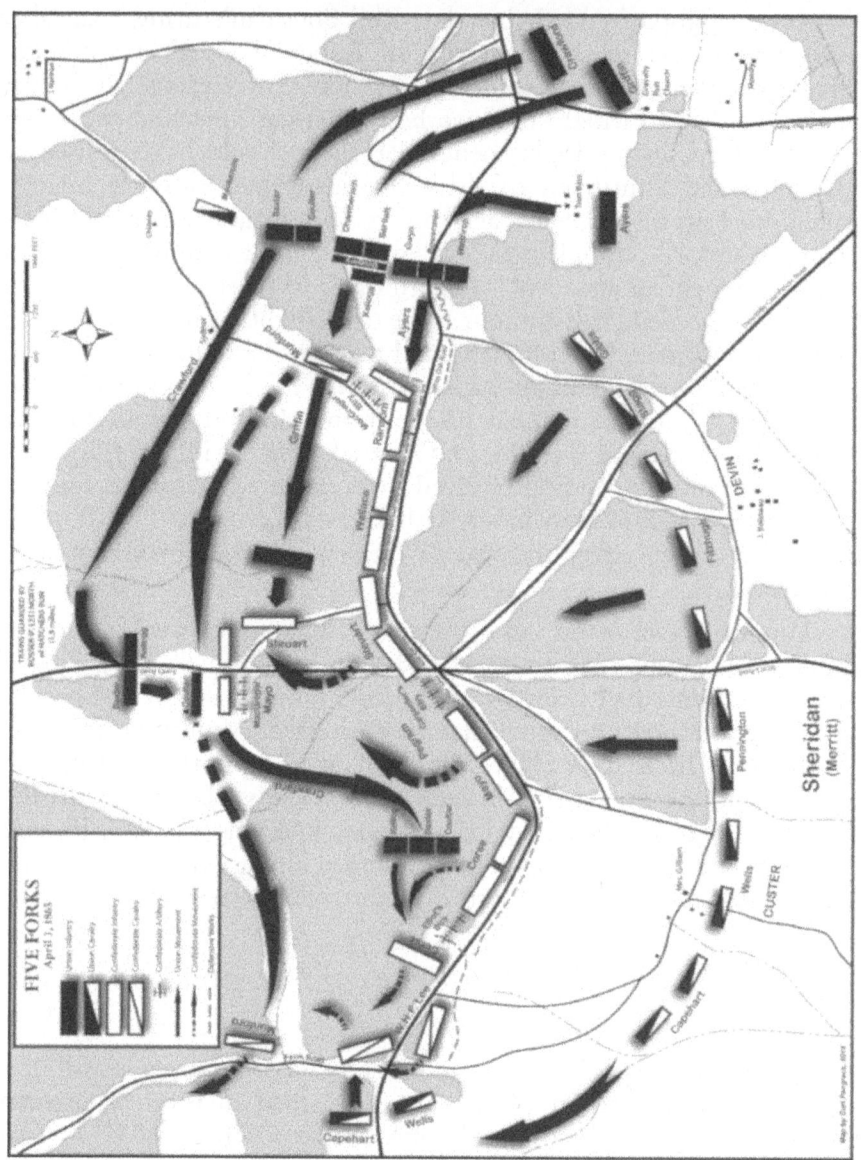

wagons, supply wagons, and ambulances, wanted to rest his jaded horses as much as possible and feed the starving animals.[27]

Pickett's men dug in and strengthened their fortifications. Their works covered a one-and-three-quarter-mile expanse, with artillery placed at strategic locations along their front. Robert E. Lee's

---

27. *OR* 46/1:1299, McDonald, *Laurel Brigade*, 366–67; Thomas T. Munford, "The Last Days of Fitz Lee's Division of Cavalry," 30, VHS.

instructions to Pickett reflected the importance of his defensive stand, "Hold Five Forks at all hazards. Protect road to Ford's Depot and prevent Union forces from striking the South Side Railroad."[28]

Between Pickett's line and the extreme right of Robert E. Lee's position at Burgess's Mill—held by Lt. Gen. Richard H. Anderson with Gen. Bushrod Johnson's division—was a gap of several miles. Brigadier General William P. Roberts's small cavalry brigade picketed the gap.[29]

Munford's division was located on the Ford Road near Fitz Lee's command, near Hatcher's Run, convenient to water the horses and close enough to send details for corn and forage from the wagon train. His headquarters was within sight of Fitz Lee's headquarters, not far from the Boisseaux house.[30]

By about 9:00 a.m., Federal cavalry opposing the Confederate forces were positioned from right to left as follows: Col. Peter Stagg's brigade, Bvt. Brig. Gen. Charles Fitzhugh's brigade, Gen. A. C. Pennington, while General Custer held the left of Rooney Lee's division.[31]

Against the backdrop of the order for Pickett to "Hold Five Forks," the infamous "shad bake" occurred. Rosser's brigade, by request, had been placed in reserve on the north side of Hatcher's Run. Rosser, who commanded a division of Virginia cavalry, had spent March 29 on the Nottoway River, 10 miles southwest of Blackstone, catching a nice supply of shad. When Rosser moved up to Five Forks on March 30-31, he brought the shad with him. As soon as he moved his division north of Hatcher's Run, he arranged for the fish to be cleaned, split, and baked over fires of dry wood. Rosser, many years later, recalled, "I had brought some excellent fresh shad from the Nottoway River with me, and I invited General Pickett to go back and lunch with me—he promised to be with me in an hour. He and Fitz Lee came back to me. . . . Some time was spent over the lunch, during which no firing was heard. We concluded that the enemy was not in much of a hurry to find us at Five Forks"[32]

---

28. Freeman, *Lee's Lieutenants*, 3:661; La Salle Corbell (Mrs. George E. Pickett), *Pickett and His Men* (Atlanta, GA, 1899), 386; Bearss and Calkins, *The Battle of Five Forks*, 76–77.
29. Munford, "The Last Days of Fitz Lee's Division of Cavalry," 30, VHS.
30. Ibid., 33–34.
31. Ibid., 31–32.
32. *Philadelphia Weekly Times*, April 5, 1895; C. Irvine Walker, *The Life of Lieutenant General Richard Heron Anderson of the Confederate States Army*, (Charleston, SC, 1917), 229–30; Thomas Rosser to Joshua Lawrence Chamberlain, August 29, 1902, Joshua Lawrence Chamberlain Papers, Curtis Library, Bowdoin College, Pejepscot Historical Society, Brunswick, Maine; Thomas Munford to Joshua Lawrence Chamberlain, January 24, 1911, Joshua Lawrence Chamberlain Papers, Curtis Library, Bowdoin College, Pejepscot

Munford spotted Fitz Lee in the saddle, ready for the two-mile ride back to Rosser's camp. Munford excitedly passed Lee a dispatch from one of his troopers on the left flank. A tide of Federal cavalry had poured over White Oak Road, scattering the brigade of William Roberts. Pickett's force appeared to be cut off from the main army. Fitz read the message too hurriedly, Munford thought, and gave no sign of concern. "Munford," he said, "go in person to see and if it is correct, order your full command to support the left and let us know about it."[33]

The message did not go to Pickett; Munford watched, surprised, as Fitz Lee rode to the rear. The troops lying in line paid no attention to the departing generals, and Rooney Lee, at the far right with his troopers, was not told of the shad bake, nor that his superiors had left the field, leaving him the senior officer.[34]

Rosser, Pickett, and Fitz Lee were feasting and probably enjoying some alcoholic beverage approximately four miles from the front, preventing any gunshot noise from reaching them. They possibly were in an "acoustic shadow." The event was a social secret. Pickett and Fitz Lee had slipped off to feast on the shad without telling anyone in their commands where they were going. Munford later complained, "they [Rosser, Pickett, and Fitz Lee] frolicked all day until just at sunset, when Pickett found his command, they were well loaded up or down with apple jack."[35]

While Rosser, Pickett and Lee feasted, the Confederates at the front skirmished with Federals in advance of Sheridan's attack. In the

---

Historical Society, Brunswick, Maine; Joshua Lawrence Chamberlain, Passing of the Armies: An Account of the Final Campaign (Lincoln, NE., 1998), 173; Fitz Lee testified at the Warren Court of Inquiry in 1880. "I personally remained in front until twelve o'clock. Everything being quiet, I left the line and rode down the road to the crossing of Hatcher's Run to see General Pickett. I found him just on the other side of Hatcher's Run. . . . I passed on further down the road . . . where our wagons were, to see General Rosser." They were in fact gathering for the shad lunch at the invitation of Rosser. See Thomas T. Munford, "The Last Days of Fitz Lee's Division of Cavalry," 32, 49, VHS.
33. Thomas T. Munford to James T. Murfee, March 4, 1911, Private Collection of David Center, Highland Home, Alabama; Munford, "Five Forks: The Waterloo of the Confederacy," 1–2, VHS, Richmond, VA.
34. Burke Davis, To Appomattox: Nine April Days, 1865 (New York, 1959), 43.
35. John B. Phillips to Thomas Taylor Munford, September 7, 1895, Munford Family Papers, DU; Akers, Thesis, 60–61, 73, 76–78, Virginia Tech; Thomas L. Rosser to A. S. Perham, August 29, 1902, Perham Collection, Library of Congress, Washington, D. C.; Thomas T. Munford, "The Last Days of Fitz Lee's Division of Cavalry," 35, 53 VHS; Thomas T. Munford to James T. Murfee, March 4, 1911, Private Collection of David Center, Highland Home, Alabama.

meantime, Sheridan was waiting impatiently for General Warren to come up and attack the left rear of the Confederate infantry. At about 2:30 p.m., Sheridan's cavalry was spotted approaching Samuel B. Gilliam's house, less than a mile southwest of the Five Forks intersection. Gilliam owned 2,800 acres of farmland that included the critical Five Forks intersection. Thus, Pickett and Fitz Lee were away from their troops when the Federals attacked in the late afternoon of April 1st. About 4:00 p.m., Sheridan drove a 9,000-man wedge of Warren's Corps between the Confederate infantry and their cavalry on the left. Munford's 2nd Virginia moved rapidly to the left of Pickett's line in a direction parallel with the line of battle as it was then raging. The rest of the brigade remained near the road in Pickett's rear. About one-quarter mile from their starting point, the 2nd Virginia ran into a column of Federal infantry moving directly across their front. Dismounted, the Confederate troopers quickly established a weak skirmish line, firing on the advancing blue-clad infantry at close range. Lieutenant Colonel Cary Breckenridge recalled, "The Federals marching in columns of fours, right shoulder shift, took little notice of us at first, but presently faced to the left [and] returned fire at a rate of about one thousand shots to one and soon swept us out of the way."[36]

The streaking Federal column turned against the left flank of the Confederate infantry, which broke and retreated. Munford dispatched trooper John B. Phillips to find Fitz Lee, finally locating Lee with Pickett under a tent fly "with a bottle of whiskey or brandy" several miles from the front. Lee told Phillips to order Munford "to do the best you could." By the time Pickett had been alerted, defeat of his troops was assured.[37]

Munford finally found Pickett as the infantry commander was returning from Rosser's long luncheon north of Hatcher's Run. Pickett galloped up to Munford and reacted to seeing Federals just 100 yards to the east by telling Munford, "Do hold them back 'till I pass to Five Forks." Pickett, "having thrown himself forward upon his horse, and leaning on the right side, ran the gauntlet, under a hot fire, for several hundred yards, and dashed forward to his broken lines ahead of him." The 2nd Virginia regained their horses and rejoined the brigade,

36. Dr. James R. Jewell, "Lieutenant Colonel Breckenridge's Account of the Second Virginia Cavalry Regiment from Five Forks to Appomattox," 2–3; Breckenridge Papers, VHS, Richmond, VA. Note: Sheridan relieved Warren of command and had him court-martialed for being late to arrive and attack. A Court of Inquiry posthumously exonerated Warren in December 1879. Munford testified at the Court of Inquiry, supporting Warren.
37. John B. Phillips to Thomas Taylor Munford, September 7, 1895, Munford–Ellis Papers, DU; Akers, Thesis, 60–61, 73, 76–78, Virginia Tech; Thomas L. Rosser to A. S. Perham, August 29, 1902, Perham Collection, LC.

and after a short respite, retired a mile or two, where the night was passed in anxious watching.[38]

It became apparent the day was lost. After the day's fight, Munford recalled "memories of his boyhood home at Richmond," his "honored parents and loving sisters, and most of what made life worth living for floated in my visions of a sacked and burned city."[39]

On April 2, Breckenridge's horsemen were not pressed, so part of the 2nd Virginia was sent forward to observe the situation. Breckenridge remembered:

> We moved in an easterly direction a mile or more, meeting no enemy, but coming [with]in hearing distance of them, deployed along the side of a bushy hill about 200 yards from their position whence we could hear them talking. Our orders were to stay there concealed, to talk only in whispers, and after the expiration of a certain to retire one by one very quietly and rejoin the brigade where it was awaiting orders. Shortly after our deployment there arose from [the] Federal position just below us, but out of sight, the greatest jubilation we ever heard. The men, seemingly many thousands of them, huzzah and cheered and the bands played the most stirring airs. This great demonstration on the part of the enemy was the announcement to us of the general breakup of the Confederate lines. We left them to their enjoyment and rejoined the brigade without further incident.[40]

The battle of Five Forks sealed the fate of the Army of Northern Virginia. Munford later called it the "Waterloo of the Confederacy." He also penned:

> It was at the battle of Five Forks, on the evening of April 1, 1865, that the sun of the Southern Confederacy went down and the star of its destiny set. No military event since the surrender of Cornwallis at Yorktown has exercised greater influence on the fate on America, or civilization itself than the disaster which destroyed the power of the South and blasted her hopes of

---

38. Munford, "The Last Days of Fitz Lee's Division of Cavalry," 45, VHS; Dr. James R. Jewell, "Lieutenant Colonel Breckenridge's Account of the Second Virginia Cavalry Regiment from Five Forks to Appomattox," 3; Breckenridge Papers, VHS.
39. Munford, "The Last Days of Fitz Lee's Division of Cavalry," 66, VHS.
40. Jewell, "Lieutenant Colonel Breckenridge's Account of the Second Virginia Cavalry Regiment from Five Forks to Appomattox," 3–4; Breckenridge Papers, VHS.

independence. . . . It extinguished the campfires of the hitherto invincible army and was the mortal wound which caused the Southern Confederacy to perish forever.[41]

Lee's last supply line to Petersburg was cut the next day, April 2, at Sutherland's Station. Lee now knew that Petersburg and Richmond were lost and ordered them evacuated. He could not move directly south to join Gen. Joseph E. Johnston's Army of Tennessee in North Carolina because Grant blocked his path. Instead, Lee decided on a rapid westward move in hopes of escaping his pursuers before moving south to join Johnston. Union losses in the climactic battle of Five Forks were about 630 killed, wounded, or missing. Confederate losses were about 545 killed and wounded and between 2,000 and 2,400 captured by the swarming Federals.[42]

Rosser blamed Pickett for the loss at Five Forks, stating "It seems to have been a surprise to General Pickett, yet one would have supposed that he would have been on alert in the presence of the enemy he had so recently been fighting, but from all I could see on the occasion, I am satisfied that all the generalship and management was on the Federal side."[43]

Fitz Lee submitted a belated report after the war upon Robert E. Lee's request for it.[44] From reading his report, Munford pointed out that one might think Fitz Lee was actually at the front at Five Forks, which he was not.

After the war, Munford wrote his friend, J. T. Murfee, "he [Pickett] was hardly worthy of such a command. No drinking man can ever be counted upon. What I mean is any man who will abandon himself, and become dependent upon whiskey, has no real character and is not himself and is not worthy to be trusted to command men."[45]

---

41. Thomas T. Munford, Draft, n.d., 73-74, Ellis–Munford Papers, Thomas Munford Division, Box 19, DU, Michael J. McCarthy, *Confederate Waterloo: The Battle of Five Forks, April 1, 1865, and the Controversy that Brought Down a General* (El Dorado Hills, CA, 2017), xi.
42. Munford, "Five Forks: The Waterloo of the Confederacy," VHS; Bearss and Calkins, The Battle of Five Forks, 113; Bryce Suderow, "Confederate Strengths & Losses." (Washington, D.C.). The National Park Service puts estimated Confederate losses at 2,950 and Union losses at 830.
43. Thomas L. Rosser Scrapbook, Thomas L. Rosser Papers, UVA, 1171a.b., Box 2, 17; *Philadelphia Weekly Times*, April 5, 1895; Walker, *The Life of Lieutenant General Richard Heron Anderson*, 229–30.
44. OR 46/1:563, 1298–1305; Morris Schaff, *The Sunset of the Confederacy* (Boston, 1912), 19–20.
45. Thomas L. Rosser to J. T. Murfree, April 10, 1911, Private Collection of David Center, Highland Home, Alabama.

Much later Munford wrote Joshua L. Chamberlain that he had written the "true story" of Five Forks and wanted to have it published. He accepted, however, recommendations from Col. Archer Anderson, Capt. William Gordon McCabe, and Maj. Robert W. Hunter that the manuscript be withheld because it would give "great grief" to families "whose husbands were active Confederates, and you will be brought into acrimonious controversy with partisans who do not agree with you." Munford penned, "There is not a word said that could not be substantiated." Munford, however, accepted the committee's recommendation and withheld the article for the time being, until such time as he and the officers in question had all died.[46]

In the same letter, Munford told Chamberlain that he had made the following statement in his manuscript:

> Genl George E. Picket, Gen' Fitz Lee, and Genl T. L. Rosser, the three major generals (ranking) on the Confederate side, were all absent from the Battle of Five Forks—and that their instruction from Genl R. E. Lee was not carried out and that Genl R. E. Lee was not kept posted by them, and that the Reserve he had had collected at his extreme right . . . under Lieu. Genl R. H. Anderson . . . were allowed to remain idle, and inactive because Picket and Fitz Lee were off at a shad lunch from 1 P.M. until 6 P.M. and had nothing to do with the fighting.[47]

In the aftermath of the debacle at Five Forks, Robert E. Lee ordered that Generals Bushrod Johnson, George Pickett, and Richard Anderson be relieved of their commands and sent to their homes. Colonel Walter H. Taylor of Lee's staff recalled that the orders were issued by Lee through him. No reasons were given by Lee, probably in the interest of sparing the families of the dismissed generals embarrassment after the war. No charges, censure, or arrests were made. General Anderson went home to South Carolina, but Pickett and Johnson could not return to their homes because they were in

---

46. Thomas T. Munford to Joshua L. Chamberlain, January 27, 1911, Joshua L. Chamberlain Papers, Catalog No. M27.1, Box 5, Folder 111, Bowdoin College Library, Brunswick, Maine; R. E. Cowart to Thomas T. Munford, September 17, 1909, Munford–Ellis Papers, DU. This letter concerns Munford's eventual publication, "Five Forks: The Waterloo of the Confederacy." Munford left instructions that the document was not to be published until 20 years after his death.
47. Thomas T. Munford to Joshua L. Chamberlain, January 27, 1911, Joshua L. Chamberlain Papers, Bowdoin College Library, Brunswick, Maine; Thomas Munford to Samuel B. Gilliam, August 30, 1908, Gilliam Family Papers, Albert and Shirley Small Special Collections Library, UVA.

Union possession. They hung on with Lee's army, without commands, until the surrender at Appomattox.[48]

---

48. Walter H. Taylor to R. E. Cowart, September 10, 1908, Munford–Ellis Papers, DU; Robert E. Cowart to Thomas T. Munford, September 17, 1909, Munford–Ellis Papers, DU. Fitz Lee escaped any admonishment.

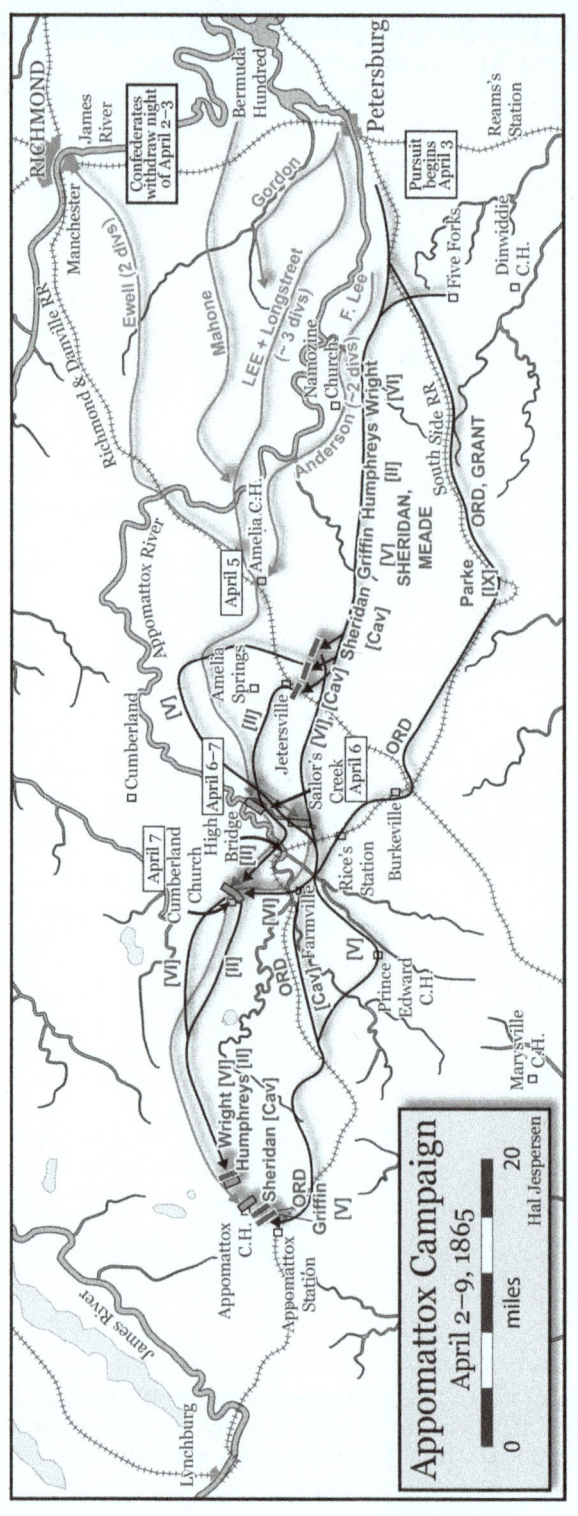

Chapter Sixteen

High Bridge, Escape to Lynchburg, and Surrender

"I feel more degraded and blue than I supposed that I would ever feel as a Virginian. . . . I feel now that we have lost all, excepting our honor."

–Thomas Munford writing to his sister, Sallie, after the surrender.

The Appomattox campaign continued with the battle of High Bridge. Soon afterward, Lee surrendered at Appomattox, but Munford escaped to Lynchburg and disbanded his command. For the Army of Northern Virginia, the war was over. Munford, still defiant, was hoping to hook up with Joseph Johnston in North Carolina, but that did not happen, as Johnston soon surrendered to William T. Sherman. Thomas Munford then returned to the life of a Virginia farmer.

On the morning of April 5, General Sheridan dispatched Brig. General Henry E. Davies's brigade of Maj. Gen. George Crook's division to scout for Confederate movements beyond Amelia Court House near Paineville, or Paine's Cross Roads, about five miles north of Amelia Springs. At Paineville, Davies discovered a headquarters wagon train guarded by Brig. Gen. Martin Gary's cavalry brigade. This was the wagon train that had left Richmond with provisions for Lee's army, including food and ammunition for Ewell's corps. Since it had followed a more circuitous route north of Genito Bridge on Paineville Road, it had only a small cavalry escort. The train crossed to the south side of the Appomattox River by the Clemmentown bridge.[1]

As Davies's brigade slowly passed Amelia Springs, the wagon train with excess artillery and equipment started up the Paineville Road from Amelia Court House toward Paineville at the same time as the wagon train from Richmond headed south on that road toward Paineville.[2]

---

1. C.C. Lews, "The Movement of Units through the War," *Civil War Times*, May 4, 2019, CivilWarTroops.Org/1865-04-06-saylers-creek.
2. Ibid.

Davies attacked the lead section of the wagon train—two companies of artillery—four miles east of Paineville and quickly rounded up 300 Confederate soldiers and as many African-American teamsters. The Union cavalrymen cut many horses and mules out of their traces, captured five new Armstrong guns, and burned more than 100 wagons of provisions. Davies's troopers destroyed Maj. Gen. Custis Lee's supplies, including all the spare ammunition. Leading wagons from the train which left Amelia Court House (including Fitzhugh Lee's headquarters baggage, Robert E. Lee's headquarters wagons with many reports, and some ambulances and medical supplies) were also taken by the Union raiders.[3]

Before Davies could return to Jetersville, his brigade was attacked near Amelia Springs by Martin Gary's cavalry brigade and a much larger force of Thomas L. Rosser's and Colonel Thomas T. Munford's divisions, under Fitzhugh Lee. Davies's force was driven back across Flat Creek. Acting as a rear guard, the 1st New Jersey Volunteer Cavalry Regiment held off the Confederate pursuers, which permitted Davies's main column with prisoners and captured horses, mules and artillery to move past Amelia Springs. At Amelia Springs, the other brigades of Crook's division under Brig. Gen. J. Irvin Gregg and Col. (Bvt. Brig. Gen.) Charles H. Smith provided reinforcements, allowing Davies's force to reach Jetersville with their prisoners, guns, and teams. Davies returned with his men to Amelia Springs to help defend against the Confederate cavalry attack.[4]

Crook's cavalry division had casualties of 13 killed, 81 wounded, and 72 missing and probably taken prisoner in three encounters during the day. Fitzhugh Lee said he counted 30 dead Union soldiers along the way. Davies captured 320 Confederate soldiers and 310 African-Americans who he described as teamsters. He also captured 400 animals and 11 flags while destroying about 200 wagons.[5]

High Bridge

Meanwhile, General Grant pressed ahead, wanting to prevent Lee from moving southward to join Joseph E. Johnston in North Carolina. Grant wanted to destroy High Bridge, which carried the South Side Railroad over the Appomattox River. Grant sent a large infantry force under Bvt. Brig. Gen. Theodore Read, chief of staff to Maj. Gen. Edward O.C. Ord, commander of the Army of the James, to

---

3. Ibid.
4. Ibid.
5. Ibid.

accomplish the task. He also dispatched a squadron of cavalry commanded by Col. Francis Washburn. The combined force numbered between 1,200 and 1,500 men.[6]

On the morning of April 6, Fitzhugh Lee ordered Rosser to take his command and report to General Longstreet at Rice's Station on the South Side Railroad. Longstreet agreed to Rosser's suggestion that he take his (Rosser's) command, along with parts of Rooney Lee's and Munford's divisions, totaling about 1,500 troopers, and attempt to save High Bridge. About 1:00 p.m., Rosser encountered Read's infantry posted behind a high fence at Watson's farm.[7]

Munford, in command of Fitz Lee's former division, dismounted his troopers and approached the Federals in front while acting Brig. Gen. James Dearing led the Laurel Brigade against Read's right flank. Colonel Francis Washburn's force charged Dearing's troopers, initiating a desperate hand-to-hand fight. Dearing, Washburn, and Read, all West Pointers, were killed or mortally wounded within a few minutes of each other. Dearing shot General Read, and shortly thereafter was mortally wounded, perhaps the victim of "friendly fire." Colonel William Miller Owen reported that Rosser personally told him on the battlefield that Dearing killed General Read in hand-to-hand fighting with sabers, and then Dearing was shot by Read's orderly.[8]

Munford deserved promotion to brigadier general, as he was Fitzhugh Lee's senior colonel and commanded Lee's former division of cavalry. Fitzhugh Lee recommended his promotion on March 20, to date from November 1, 1864, which was received and forwarded by Gen. Robert E. Lee on March 23, 1865. On March 29, Adjutant & Inspector General Samuel Cooper at the War Department received the recommendation. Before the Confederate President or Congress in Richmond could act on the recommendation, Robert E. Lee surrendered at Appomattox. Long after the war, Munford stated that trooper John E. Hull of the 2nd Virginia, was detailed as a courier with General Fitzhugh Lee on the retreat from Five Forks. Hull reached Munford at the battle at High Bridge, with "beaming countenance and announced that he had brought my promotion, and delivered the corps order sent by General Fitz Lee." Munford's "promotion" became a matter of dispute after the war, consuming

---

6. Bushong, *Fightin' Tom Rosser*, 179.
7. McDonald, *Laurel Brigade*, 375.
8. William Miller Owen, *In Camp and Battle with the Washington Artillery of New Orleans* (Baton Rouge, LA, 1999), 376; Munford's handwritten article for *Philadelphia Weekly Times*, May 17, 1884, p. 28, Munford–Ellis Papers, DU. Dearing's promotion to brigadier was never officially confirmed.

Thomas T. Munford
Circa 1866
Munford received a battlefield "promotion" from Fitz Lee during the last weeks of the war.
(Virginia Military Institute)

Munford in the task of "proving" he was a brigadier general. It also contributed to the spiteful feud with General Rosser.[9]

After High Bridge, Rosser's command retired to Rice's Station and took up a position on the right of Longstreet's infantry, which had positioned itself to confront advancing Federals. An attack was expected sometime during the night, but it never came. Little sleep was

---

9. *Richmond Dispatch*, November 6, 1904; Munford, "The Last Days of Fitz Lee's Cavalry Division of Cavalry," 77, VHS; Munford–Ellis Papers, DU; *Stanton Spectator*, October 28, 1904.

afforded the already exhausted troopers. On the evening of April 6, the Confederates abandoned Rice's Station as Fitz Lee's cavalry moved in the rear of Longstreet towards Farmville. The Federals attempted to prevent Fitz Lee from crossing the Appomattox, but Munford held off the Federal advance long enough for Fitz Lee to get over at the Cumberland Court House Road bridge. Rosser had to cross two miles upstream.[10]

Near the Cumberland Plank Road, Rosser found the Federals attacking Munford's division and assisted Munford in driving off the Union force. The Laurel Brigade struck the Federal flank, and McCausland's brigade also joined the fight. The engagement was essentially a draw. The Confederates then continued their retreat towards Appomattox. The Federals pursued, generally along the line of the railroad from Farmville to Appomattox.[11]

Fitzhugh Lee (1835-1905)
Nephew of Robert E. Lee
Commander of Division of
Cavalry in Civil War.

Commanded Detached Cavalry Corps after Wade Hampton hurried south to fight William T. Sherman's march through the Carolinas. 40th Governor of Virginia, 1886-1890.

(Courtesy: Library of Congress)

Lieutenant Colonel Gus W. Dorsey of the 1st Maryland Cavalry described Munford's actions on the retreat to Appomattox, "in a sharp fight a little west of Farmville, April 7th, 1865, a charge of [John Irvin] Gregg's division was repulsed with great loss, Gregg himself being among the captured. Such was Gen. Munford's brilliant, daring fighting all the way to Appomattox."[12]

---

10. McDonald, *Laurel Brigade*, 378.
11. Ibid.
12. Frank Dorsey, "A Sketch of Brigadier General Thomas T. Munford and Lieutenant Colonel Gus W. Dorsey," Dorsey Papers, VHS.

On the afternoon of April 9, Sgt. Robert S. Hudgins of the 3rd Virginia recalled seeing the ragged column of Lee's infantry soldiers west of Amelia:

> As I sat on my horse and watched them file past, I was almost moved to tears at the spectacle passing before me. The infantry looked like scarecrows in rags, with either no shoes or shoes so full of holes that they might as well have been barefooted. These men had not had a meal for more than a week, and were kept alive only by what they could forage as they plodded along. Regiments were now no larger than small companies. . . . Guidons and flags were now tattered and faded, though they were still borne with pride by an army only hours from exhaustion.[13]

Robert E. Lee and Ulysses S. Grant began negotiating the terms of Confederate surrender. Soon after daylight on April 9, Fitz Lee's former division of cavalry was under command of "Brigadier General" Munford, General Fitzhugh Lee being at the headquarters of the army. Munford's troopers moved through Appomattox Court House, forming a line of battle on the right of the road about one-half-mile beyond. Munford's horsemen halted briefly, then moved in column obliquely to the right and entered a heavily wooded area, where they soon met Union infantry.[14]

Throwing out skirmishers to engage them, Munford moved again to right oblique until his horsemen were struck again. He sent out more skirmishers, the first having fallen to the rear. Munford continued his rightward movement until he found a weaker place in the Federal line and made good his passage to the Lynchburg Road. At first, the Federals thought that Munford's intention was to get in the Union rear and charge while engaged in front with the infantry. Munford's intention, however, was to reach Lynchburg Road, as he at once halted and formed his men on each side. From this point, the masses of Grant's army were plainly visible, "standing as if on dress parade." The firing had by now ceased. Surrender of the Confederate army was whispered, but was heard with indignation by many, and by general consent it was determined to await events in silence.[15]

The 1st Maryland Cavalry happened to be nearest to the road and to the Federals. Its troopers dismounted, but standing to horse—the usual precaution of skirmishers in front. Everything was still. Not a

---

13. Garland C. Hudgins and Richard B. Kleese, ed., *Recollections of an Old Dominion Dragoon: The Civil War Experiences of Sgt. Robert S. Hudgins II Co. B, 3rd Virginia Cavalry* (Orange, VA, 1993), 99.
14. William Worthington Goldsborough, *The Maryland Line in the Confederate Army, 1861–1865* (Baltimore, MD, 1900), 224–27.
15. Ibid.

sound betrayed the presence of the hosts of armed men in the vicinity, and but "for the long lines of blue in sight upon the hills in front, all might have been taken for a hideous dream."[16]

Suddenly, a heavy column of Union cavalry, moving rapidly along Munford's front and parallel to his line, was seen a half-mile distant, marching toward the road. When they reached Lynchburg Road, a part of the Federal force in column advanced via the road, while the remainder rode through the fields to the right, driving back the Confederate skirmishers. As soon as the Confederate horsemen detected the scheme of the Union cavalry, Lt. Col. Gustavus W. Dorsey mounted his men and moved in column to the road, which was separated from him by a fence with manmade gaps. Through one of these gaps, the 1st Maryland passed as rapidly as they could while preserving good order. The first section of Marylanders had hardly cleared the fence when the Federals, now in full charge, began approaching, not more than 100 distant. Captain William J. Rasin of Company E, who rode with Colonel Dorsey at the head of the column, remarked, "Colonel Dorsey, we must charge those people! It is our only chance!" Scarcely had the words left his lips when Dorsey, who had already seen the necessity, gave the command, "Draw sabre! Gallop! Charge!" The little band of Marylanders hurled themselves against the heavy columns of the Federals and drove them back. Again, the Union soldiers advanced, and again the 1st Maryland charged and forced them back.[17]

While still fighting vigorously, this last charge by the Army of Northern Virginia was met by a Union officer carrying a flag of truce, who suddenly made his appearance from the right of the road. The fight instantly ceased, and the officer was asked his business. He replied that "General Lee was about to surrender; that articles of capitulation were being prepared, that hostilities had ceased, and ended by demanding that the cavalry in front should come in and lay down their arms, as being part of General Lee's army, and included in the terms."[18]

Munford's cavalry had taken a direct approach to reach the stage road to Lynchburg, rather than the circuitous back roads route that Fitz Lee and Thomas Rosser had taken. Providing guidance for Munford was his quartermaster, William H. Trent, whose home was in the area. Munford enjoyed sips from a canteen of peach brandy that Captain Trent had retrieved from his home the previous evening.[19]

---

16. Ibid.
17. Ibid.
18. Ibid.
19. William Marvel, *Lee's Last Retreat: The Flight to Appomattox* (Chapel Hill, NC, 2002), 177; Thomas T. Munford to Samuel Griffin, April 30, 1865, Munford–Ellis Papers, DU.

As Munford cleared the woods, he was spotted by Union videttes from the brigade of Gen. Henry Davies. Davies tangled with the Confederates briefly, losing a few men, but then pulled back to await reinforcements. Freed from their fight with Gen. John B. Gordon, Col. Samuel B. M. Young's and Brig. Gen. Ranald S. Mackenzie's brigades came up, and together they massed for a full-scale charge on what they believed was a flank attack. As the Federal squadrons rumbled forward, a staff officer overtook the leaders and bellowed for them to hold their fire, bringing forth the announcement of the truce. Curious at the abrupt end to the charge, Munford and some of his staff trotted forward to see what was happening. They met Union generals Davies, Young, and Mackenzie, who said Lee had asked for the cease-fire with a view to surrender. The Federal officers indicated that they would abide by that request.[20]

Colonel Munford called a council of war of his officers, and after discussing matters and taking a vote, it was determined not to surrender. The troopers rationalized in their minds that they were not subject to the treaty between Generals Lee and Grant, because their division had broken through the Union lines before a surrender had been discussed by the leaders of the two armies.[21]

Munford—again with Young, Davies, and Mackenzie—passed around the canteen of peach brandy but replied that he did not consider himself bound by the truce, since he had gotten clear of Lee's army. When the group broke up, Munford who contented himself with looking on, threw out a heavy skirmish line and retired toward Lynchburg unmolested by the enemy.[22]

Arriving at Lynchburg at night, Colonel Munford's first care was to obtain food and forage for his command, which was done without much difficulty, as large supplies had been gathered at this point with a view of meeting the necessities of General Lee's army. After feeding, Munford held another council, discussing the chances and best means of reaching Johnston's army. Without coming to any definite conclusion, they determined to move to the north side of the James River and seek supplies until some news from General Joseph E. Johnston's army could be obtained, and then unite with that army.[23]

---

20. Marvel, *Lee's Last Retreat: The Flight to Appomattox*, 178.
21. Goldsborough, *The Maryland Line in the Confederate Army, 1861-1865*, 224–27.
22. Ibid; Marvel, *Lee's Last Retreat: The Flight to Appomattox*, 178; *OR*, vol. 46, part 1, 1146, 1155–56, 1246; Thomas T. Munford to Samuel Griffin, April 30, 1906, Munford–Ellis Papers, DU. Munford reported it was General George Crook, instead of Samuel Young, who was present at the confab.
23. Goldsborough, *The Maryland Line in the Confederate Army*, 224–27.

Captain Frank S. Robertson, a close friend of the Munford family who had been on J.E.B. Stuart's staff, caught up with Munford at on the road to Lynchburg at the Munford Alpine Farm, 14 miles from Lynchburg, and stayed the night, Here, the exhausted troopers feasted and slept for almost 24 hours straight. The next day, Munford headed for Roanoke to await the unfolding events.[24]

On April 13, Munford received a note from Federal authorities directing him to report to Gen. Ranald S. McKenzie at Lynchburg. Munford replied, declining the "invitation until I can determine my status." Munford denied that he had intended on April 9 to surrender either himself or his command. He requested that the authorities submit to him the terms of Gen. R. E. Lee's capitulation, so that he could determine whether or not Lee had surrendered him (he and his command). The feisty Munford concluded by stating he would surrender to the proper authorities once evidence had been provided to him stating that Lee had included him in the terms of his surrender. He suggested that his request be sent to R. E. Lee as a simplified way to verify the situation. On April 21, Munford received a reply from Maj. Gen. John Gibbon which stated that the terms of surrender included "all the forces operating with that army on the 8th inst., except such bodies of cavalry as actually made their escape previous to the surrender." This seemed to satisfy Munford, who soon reported to Lynchburg authorities.[25]

Munford's command did not surrender at Appomattox but instead wanted to link with Joseph Johnston in North Carolina to carry on the fight. Only after Johnston surrendered to Sherman did Munford give up the fight. Earlier, Munford had reacted to the February Peace Conference in Hampton Roads, Virginia, by drafting a document which was unanimously approved by his 2nd Virginia Cavalry, urging continued resistance. Responding to the terms for peace offered by President Lincoln, Munford wrote:

> We would feel degraded and not possessed of common manhood could we accept such terms from such a source. The proud freemen of these States are told that they can have peace on no other terms than abject submission. Then we welcome war. War with all its horrors is better than life without the right to liberty and property. . . . That our slaves, after being tempted by

---

24. Robert J. Trout, ed., *In the Saddle with Stuart: The Story of Frank Smith Robertson of Jeb Stuart's Staff*, (Gettysburg, PA, 1998), 109–10; Thomas T. Munford, "The Last Days of Fitz Lee's Division of Cavalry," VHS.
25. Thomas T. Munford, "The Last Days of Fitz Lee's Division of Cavalry"; "Articles of Agreement Related to the Surrender of the Army of Northern Virginia," April 10, 1865.

every artifice to join the enemy, are not only trained and employed against us, but are now openly proclaimed to be free, without preparation for change, without providing security to the master or protection to the slave; and without home, shelter or property for the latter, other than that obtained by indiscriminate plunder and murder.[26]

Munford decried the confiscation of property, the incursion of debt owed the Federal government, and the partitioning of Virginia to form West Virginia. Under these circumstances, Munford wrote:

> we are driven, no less by 'the external law of self-preservation' than by the exalted sense of patriotic duty, to continue our resistance and to fight on, fight forever, with renewed devotion to our cause and a holy purpose under Divine favor to purchase independence; therefore, Resolved . . . we hold them, therefore, who would endeavor to reconstruct the Union, thus desecrated and perverted from its original purposes, to be traitors to our government and enemies to their country.[27]

On April 21, just 12 days after Lee's surrender at Appomattox, Munford published his Special Order No. 6 which continued his fighting tone: "We still have a country, a flag, and a government. . . . Hold yourself in instant readiness, and bring all true men with you from this command who will go." Munford passionately urged his troopers on:

> "We have sworn a thousand times by our eternal wrongs. By our sacred God-Given rights . . . that we would be free. . . . Can we kneel down by our graves of our dead, kneel in the very blood from sons yet fresh and kiss the rod which smote them down? Never! Never! Let those who were that last "organized part of the Army of Northern Virginia" strike the first blow, which, by the blessings of our gracious God, will yet come to redeem her hallowed soil."[28]

Munford's plan was to unite with Joe Johnston's army in North Carolina, but news of Johnston's surrender and the uncertainty of the whereabouts of the fleeing Confederate government prevented Munford from ever reuniting his command.[29]

---

26. R. A. Brock, ed., *SHSP*, Richmond, Virginia, 1888, vol. 16:355–56.
27. Ibid.
28. *OR* 46/3:1395
29. Dr. James R. Jewell, "In Rivulets of Gray Ink: The Bloody Battles About the War (The Munford–Rosser Feud), 2: Special Orders No. 6," Munford-Ellis Papers, DU.

Meanwhile, Lieutenant Colonel Dorsey had marched to the amicable neighborhood of Waynesboro and there awaited orders. After about 10 days he received a dispatch from Munford to move up the valley, by way of Lexington, toward Salem. From there, their cavalry was to make their way to Gen. Joseph E. Johnston's army. The 1st Maryland was immediately on the march and arrived at Cloverdale, in Botetourt County, on April 28. Lieutenant Colonel Dorsey, learning General Munford was confined to his bed by sickness, rode to the house where he was staying, and on the same day received from him the following letter, which he had prepared to be read to the 1st Maryland, and which speaks for itself. "General" Munford expressed his regret that his sickness prevented him from saying farewell to the battalion in person:

> I have just learned from Captain [George M.] Emack that your gallant band was moving up the Valley in response to my call. I am deeply pained to say that our army cannot be reached, as I have learned that it has capitulated. It is sad, indeed, to think that our country's future is all shrouded in gloom. But for you and your command there is the consolation of having faithfully done your duty.
>
> Three years ago, the chivalric Brown joined my old regiment with twenty-three Mary land volunteers with light hearts and full of fight. I soon learned to admire, respect and love them for all those qualities which endear soldiers to their officers. They recruited rapidly, and as they increased in numbers, so did their reputation and friends increase, and they were soon able to form a command and take a position of their own. Need I say when I see that position so high and almost alone among soldiers, that my heart swells with pride to think that a record so bright and glorious is in some part linked with mine? Would that I could see the mothers and sisters of every member of your battalion that I might tell them how nobly you have represented your State and maintained our cause. But you will not be forgotten. The fame you have won will be guarded by Virginia with all the pride she feels in her own true sons, and the ties which have linked us together memory will preserve. You who struck the first blow in Baltimore, and the last in Virginia, have done all that could be asked of you, and had the rest of our officers and men adhered to our cause with the same devotion, today we would have been free from Yankee thralldom.

I have ordered the brigade to return to their homes, and it behooves us now to separate. With my warmest wishes for your welfare, and a hearty God bless you, I bid you farewell. Thomas T. Munford, Brigadier–General Commanding Division.[30]

Special Order No. 6 endeared Munford to Lt. Colonel Dorsey and his Marylanders. Dorsey praised Munford as "the unselfish cavalier, the gentleman who never knew when he was whipped, the gallant officer who never deserted a command, but whose motto is 'nous vous.'" Lavish in his praise for his commander, Dorsey wrote after the war that Munford "was the best and brainiest leader of the cavalry that Virginia put in the field, except the immortal 'Jeb,' and did more hard fighting with less Richmond appreciation than any other soldier in the Confederacy." Dorsey no doubt felt obliged to heap praise on Munford, as Munford had done for him and the 1st Maryland Cavalry.[31]

Meanwhile, Thomas Munford's father, George W. Munford, knew of Robert E. Lee's surrender, having passed through Appomattox on his way to Lynchburg. He remained extremely combative nevertheless, scorning his fellow Virginians for having given up. The month after the surrender found him thinking of a way to move his family to Texas. He and his wife decided against any such move; his wife also pushed him to take the oath of allegiance.[32]

On May 9, George W. Munford wrote his wife of the dangers for their son, Thomas, yet:

> I left Lynchburg Sunday morning, that evening seeing about three hundred Yankees. They constituted a part of the Engineer Corps from Charlottesville on an expedition for the repair of the railroads. They said they intended to come up to Thom's house to catch him, for the impudence in attempting to rally his men again, and for his proclamation, and that they would burn and destroy everything he had. One of his [Thomas's] men came on immediately to inform him and the officers who were there immediately go to the mountains & I came on to Roanoke to give him warning & prevent his return, for he that day or next, was expected home. They [Yankees] returned to Charlottesville however without coming to Thom's.[33]

---

30. Goldsborough, *The Maryland Line in the Confederate Army*, 224–27.
31. Frank Dorsey, "A Sketch of Brigadier General Thomas T. Munford and Lieutenant Colonel Gus W. Dorsey," Dorsey Papers, VHS. The term "nous vous" means, "We'll go down together."
32. Marvel, *Lee's Last Retreat*, 183; George W. Munford to Lizzie Munford, May 9, 1865, Munford–Ellis Papers, DU.
33. George Munford to his wife Lizzie May 9, 1865, Munford–Ellis Papers, DU.

George Munford later recalled that he continued on to his son's home to warn him of the approaching Union cavalry. George remembered that Tom was there with several of his officers, staff, and couriers. Tom immediately dispatched pickets along the roads for about five miles. At dinner the next evening, "one of the couriers rode up at full gallop and said that a regiment of federal cavalry were on their way to capture him," having asked a local blacksmith's shop down the road as to the location of the house. With this news, the entire party dispersed, heading for parts unknown. George and Tom, riding good horses, "headed for the mountains, avoiding the main roads, and crossing by country passways with which he [Tom] was acquainted." A Union cavalry company rode up to the house, inquiring of William W. Gwalthmey, who, with his wife (Tom's older sister) had lived at Tom's house during the war, if the "General" was there. When told he was not there, they insisted on searching the premises. Not finding him, and being told the General had left about a half an hour earlier, the cavalry company moved on. Meanwhile, George and Tom proceeded to George P. Tayloe's home in the neighborhood of Big Lick. The next morning, they discovered that the Federal cavalry had continued on out of the area. George and Tom then split up, Tom returning to his home, while George proceeded to his younger sister's home in Montgomery.[34]

On May 21, 1865, Thomas Munford wrote his sister, Sallie:

> I feel more degraded and blue than I supposed that I would ever feel as a Virginian. . . . I feel now that we have lost all, excepting our honor. Had I the means to carry me, I could "speed away" to more congenial climate, once so bright and happy to me, is now almost a purgatory, changed in every way. I feel no interest in the farm, the houses or anything on it. . . . If I can make any exchanges after a while, will try my fortunes in some other country. . . .The Yankees had sent after me three times and I knew the negroes would betray me or I never would have gone down voluntarily--when I went to Lynchburg--I reported to Genl Gregg, telling him he had sent for me two or three times. I wished to know what he wanted? His reply was: to capture me. I then said to him, I am here now, what will you do with me? His reply was I will telegraph General Halleck and until I hear from him will parole you to the limits of the city. They kept me until after sundown and thereafter gave me a parole.[35]

---

34. John W. Bell, *Memoirs of Governor William Smith, of Virginia: His Political, Military, and Personal History* (New York, 1891), 220.
35. Thomas T. Munford to Sallie Munford, May 21, 1865, Munford Letters, VMI Archives, Lexington, Virginia.

Finally, and reluctantly on June 23, 1865 in Lynchburg, Thomas Munford took the Oath of Allegiance to the United States. He submitted a letter requesting a presidential pardon from President Andrew Johnson, declaring that he "made many sacrifices of property and lost dearly—am now 34 years of age—have taken the oath required by the amnesty proclamation of your Excellency . . . and on my return home, find my farm much impaired by neglect and abuse, but I am anxious to go to work with energy and to do my part to uphold the laws of the land."[36]

---

36. Confederate Applications for Presidential Pardons, 1865-1867, NARA.

Chapter Seventeen

Following the War: Farmer, Veterans Supporter, and Church Leader

"Nothing would contribute more to my happiness than to be able to help all my children, but I have arrived at that crisis both of age and pecuniary necessities as to be almost unable to help myself."

–George W. Munford to his wife, Elizabeth, after losing his wealth due to the war.

Post-Civil War

Thomas Munford returned to farming at Glen Alpine after the war. He spent much of his time after the war writing about the conflict with the goal of "setting the record straight." He also struggled to prove he was in fact a brigadier general, even though he readily admitted he never received the commission. The war ended before his recommendation to the brigadier rank could be acted upon by Richmond authorities. Munford proclaimed he had received a dispatch promoting him, which was in fact a corps order from Fitzhugh Lee, addressing him as "brigadier general." He continued his feud with Thomas L. Rosser, who readily proclaimed Munford never was promoted to brigadier general. Munford followed in his father's footsteps and cast his political lot with the Conservative Democratic Party, representing his district as a delegate twice.

After the war, 34-year-old Thomas Munford returned to his 1,000-acre Glen Alpine farm at Forest Depot in Bedford County, resuming his life as a hard-working farmer. Like many others after the war, he was financially broke. Despite being financially strapped, on April 24, 1866, Tom Munford married Elizabeth Langhorne "Emma" Tayloe of Richmond County, Virginia. Emma, 32, was Munford's late wife's first cousin, and was from a wealthy family. This, his second marriage, was solemnized by Episcopal Rev. Charles Minnegerode, in Georgetown, Washington City. Emma was the daughter of William Henry Tayloe and Henrietta (Ogle) Tayloe, who owned large farmlands in Virginia, Maryland, Mississippi, and Alabama. The couple's six surviving children were Harry Lomax Munford, Thomas Byrd Munford, Thornton Ogle Munford, Louis Sinclair Munford, Thomas Glen Munford, and Henrietta Elizabeth Munford. Their second child, Thomas Byrd Munford, was born January 9, 1868 at Glen Alpine, but died on July 9 of that same year.[1]

Soldiers returning to Lynchburg and throughout the South after the surrender, found themselves in hard times. Slaves were gone, property was in ruins, businesses wrecked, and their Confederate money useless. The Lynchburg newspaper, which had shut down, reopened in May, but was reduced to one page and passed around for folks to read. There were no banks in the city; the state banks had liquidated. The tobacco business had collapsed. The ladies took up the mantle, caring for the returning sick and weary soldiers at the Ladies Hospital and other places. The spirit of Lynchburg's people was not broken, however, and slowly things began to improve.[2]

Tom Munford had paid $10,000 for his slaves before the war, utilizing proceeds from land and slaves sold in Mississippi, which had been given to his wife by her father, William H. Tayloe. The funds from the sale were placed in the Virginia Bank in Lynchburg. Those funds, however, were worthless after the war, because the bank had failed. His father-in-law relieved Tom of this hardship, by lending him money and bequeathing the note to him in his will.[3]

In addition to farming, Munford built a cheese factory on the farm, staffed it with an Englishman and his sister, and in 1867 advertised for a "Virginia Lady" to learn the business and help with the day-to-day operations. He preferred an industrious widow of a soldier, which typified his continuing concerns for his soldiers and their families. The woman hired would be provided with a permanent home. He was able to sell cheese for as high as 28 cents per pound in Lynchburg. Cows produced three to four gallons of milk per day for six months of the year.[4]

Not long after the war, Tom Munford decided to divide up part of his Glen Alpine farm and rent it, with his tools and teams, to eight men–poor soldiers from the war who had nothing left them but their

---

1. Munford family Bible record, 1853–1913. Library of Virginia–Digital Library #21651, Bible Record Image. Bible printed 1857.
2. William Asbury Christian, *Lynchburg and Its People* (Lynchburg, VA, 1900), 239–41.
3. Thomas T. Munford's will, VHS.
4. *Richmond Whig*, January 11, 1867; M. F. Maury, LL D., *Physical Survey of Virginia; Her Resources, Climate, and Productions. Preliminary Report No. II, July 1, 1877* (Richmond, VA, 1878), 59.

willingness to work hard. Again, this was in keeping with his passion for helping soldiers in need. He recounted, "They are doing well. I have, on this place, 4 men who, by one single year's crop, have become quite independent, beginning with nothing. They have each purchased a good horse; have in store a year's supply of meat and bread, and are out of debt, with a little money in hand, besides paying me a handsome rent for my land." He also reported, "I have a neighbor who, also, works on, shares with 4 men–poor soldiers who returned penniless from the army, and divides net proceeds. His share last year was $800. There are a number of old citizens who began life as mechanics or overseers in this county, who are now in independent circumstances, owning comfortable farms and having raised large and respectable families."[5]

Munford estimated that a "good double room log house can be built for $100; a good horse can be bought for $150; a good yoke of oxen, $100; a good cow from $25 to $50; a good sow and pigs from $10 to $20; ordinary sheep from $2.50 to $4." "Such sheep," he said, "will clip from 2 to 4 pounds when allowed to run to a straw stack in winter, even though they be unsheltered all the year. Fowls are easily raised, and pay handsome returns for attention."[6]

Munford also estimated good land in Bedford County produced 15 bushels of wheat, 25 bushels of corn, and 25 to 35 bushels of oats per acre. The best lands produced from 1,000 to 1,500 pounds of tobacco. Tobacco brought from $5 to $100 per 100 pounds, depending upon the quality. The usual price of corn per bushel was from 80 cents to $1.00, wheat from $1.50 to $2.00, and oats from 50 to 75 cents. Labor costs ran from $1.50, field laborers from 30 to 50 cents per day. Land sold for $8 to $40 per acre.[7]

The 1870 Federal Census for Forest, Bedford, Virginia listed Thomas (age 37) as a farmer, with real estate valued at $25,000, Par Value of $5,000, with wife Emma (aged 35), and children George T. (age 15), Emma (age 12), George W. (age 11), William (age 9), Harry L. (age 3), and Thornton (age 1).[8]

---

5. Maury, LL D., *Physical Survey of Virginia; Her Resources, Climate, and Productions. Preliminary Report No. II, July 1, 1877* (Richmond, VA, 1878), 59.
6. Ibid.
7. Ibid.
8. Federal 1870 Census for Forest, Bedford, Virginia.

Tom's Father, George Wythe Munford, Struggles to Make a Living

Thomas's father, George Wythe Munford, like so many of the Southern elite class, lost practically all of his fortune after the war. His property had been "libeled" (Confederate officials and officers were restricted from selling their property), restricted from selling until he could obtain a pardon; he could not sell it, so he could move out of Richmond. He wrote a friend in Washington asking aid in getting himself a pardon. Time dragged on with no word on progress. His now meager funds were rapidly shrinking. He decided to go to Washington himself to seek an appointment with Secretary of State William H. Seward. Surprisingly, Mr. Seward met with him and arranged an audience with President Andrew Johnson. George Munford was successful in obtaining his pardon at a meeting with Seward and Johnson, where he was "treated respectfully and kindly by both." Released from restrictions, he sold his residence in Richmond for $20,000 and moved to Gloucester County on Virginia's middle peninsula. Here, he leased "one of the most beautiful farms and handsomest buildings in all of Virginia." It was located on the North River, near its mouth, where it emptied into Mobjack Bay. The house had 20 rooms, plenty of space for guests and family. He looked forward to the farmer's life and some fishing and sailing in a small sailboat. His wife and daughter relished the idea of country living. As George got things settled, his family stayed with Thomas at Glen Alpine in Bedford County. "All I crave now is the calm of retirement," George stated, "but I am going to hang up the fiddle and bow and take up the shovel and the hoe."[9]

During the first few years after the war, many planters became successful in utilizing a sort of slave labor, called "gang labor," paying blacks either wages or shares of crops. Most planters, including George, were forced to pay shares of the crop, because he did not possess the cash to pay wages. The sharecropping system was not always stable. Freedmen sought independence, not gang labor or shares of crops. If they could not purchase the land, then they wanted to rent it. If unable to rent it, then they wanted to sharecrop. Under the sharecropper system, cotton production began to recover. George complained that "the sharing system is a shearing system." In his mind,

---

9. George Wythe Munford to his cousin, Admiral William Radford, September 17, 1865; Sophie Radford De Meissner, *Old Navy Days: Sketches from the Life of Rear Admiral William Radford, U.S.N.* (New York, 1920), 313–15, 325.

George considered he was the one getting "sheared." Southern planters discovered sharecropping during times of falling cotton prices resulted in either economic decline or ruin for the planter.[10]

Despite his hard work, George experienced great difficulty making ends meet and therefore could not fulfill his responsibilities to provide for and protect his family from want. "Nothing would contribute more to my happiness than to be able to help all my children," George Munford wrote to his wife, "but I have arrived at that crisis both of age and pecuniary necessities as to be almost unable to help myself." George Munford diversified the crops on his Tidewater Virginia plantation and added his own hands to the labor of their production. He was not quite prepared however, for the overwhelming amount of work he had to assume in the absence of slaves. In 1867, he complained to his son, "Famers have no time to spare in these times. Oats to cut, hay to secure, corn to lay by, potatoes to work–Irish and sweet–Melons to work–turnips to sow. . . . I tell you when night comes, I drop to bed without much ceremony and I find the nights too short for my naps–I rise at four in the morning and am going at it all day long."[11]

There came a time after slavery was abolished when Southern farmers assumed new ideas about manual labor: "The best and most efficient labor performed upon the farm be done by the proprietor himself, whether it be brain work or manual labor." Expending such effort, however, did not guarantee financial success for postwar planters. After toiling on his farm for six years after the war, George Munford, remarked, "On my farm I am still getting along in a small way–working hard and realizing no profit, but having nothing else to do and no way of making money–it is root pig or die." The 1870 Federal Census reported George Munford owned real estate valued at $5,000, and his personal estate was $2,100.[12]

The amount of hard labor or time planters devoted to agriculture depended generally on their age, discipline, and proclivity for farm work. Looking forward to his 67th birthday, George Munford described the predicament he faced in his waning years, "After living in comparative ease most of the time, it is right hard to maul rails, fell

---

10. George W. Munford to Thomas T. Munford, December 4, 1870, Munford–Ellis Papers, DU.
11. George W. Munford to Elizabeth Munford, May 28, 1875, Munford–Ellis Papers, DU; Amy Feely Morsman, *The Big House after Slavery: Virginia Plantation Families and Their Postbellum Domestic Experiment* (Charlottesville, VA, 2005), 87; George Munford to William Munford, July 9, 1867, Munford–Ellis Papers, DU.
12. Morsman, *The Big House after Slavery*, 31–32; 1870 Federal Census for Ware, Gloucester County, Virginia; George W. Munford to Mrs. William P. Munford, July 25, 1871, Munford–Ellis Papers, DU.

trees, cut ditches and work from morn 'till dark." Even at his age, he did not mind the work, itself, "If I could see that I was making a living and not imposing my distresses upon my children and friends I should not mind it, but would work on cheerfully." George Munford had hopes of being able to launch his children successfully into the world once they reached adulthood. He was unable to do so, because of his own financial difficulties and because he believed he lacked the youth and vigor necessary to recover in the postwar period.[13]

George Munford needed financial help, turning in 1871 to his son, Thomas:

> I shall be greatly indebted to you for advancing the amount due Mr. Comstock. I am still hoping to obtain a loan in Richmond upon a pledge of my farm under deed of trust and although I know as you say no farmer can afford to pay twelve per cent interest. Yet to enable me to keep up my farm until I can do something else, I am forced to submit to the loss, but even with this sacrifice I have not been able to obtain the money yet. Time was when I could have raised a thousand dollars in Richmond upon my word in five minutes. Then I did not want aid—now begging won't get it with undebted security.[14]

In 1872, George still lived in Gloucester when he obtained employment by the General Assembly to codify the statutes of the state. He accomplished this work and submitted his report to the legislature. Bills were passed, enacting them into law. These codes were a significant contribution to the state of Virginia. For his efforts, Munford was paid $6,500, given a legislative committee clerkship, and provided a dozen railway passes to Richmond from Gloucester for use over a year period.[15]

Politics

Although he never ran for political office or served in public office after the war, Tom Munford followed in his father's footsteps as a lifelong conservative democrat. As a founding member and salaried Secretary of the Southern Historical Society, he furthered the spreading of the "Lost Cause" doctrine. The "Lost Cause" is the name commonly given to an intellectual movement that sought to reconcile

---

13. Morsman, *The Big House after Slavery*, 33; George W. Munford to Thomas T. Munford, December 16, 1869, Munford–Ellis Papers, DU.
14. Ibid.
15. *Daily State Journal* (Alexandria, Virginia), January 8, 1874, December 10, 1872.

the traditional white society of the South to the defeat of the Confederacy in the Civil War. Those who contributed to the movement tended to portray the Confederacy's cause as noble and most of its leaders as exemplars of old-fashioned chivalry, defeated by the Union armies through overwhelming force rather than martial skill. Proponents of the Lost Cause movement also condemned the Reconstruction period that followed the Civil War, claiming that it had been a deliberate attempt by Northern politicians to destroy the traditional Southern way of life.[16]

In the mid-1880's, Tom Munford spoke to a gathering of veterans, still advancing the Lost Cause, "To our children and our children's children, let it be our pride to teach them, as is done in every land where patriotism and self-sacrificing spirits are honored and esteemed, that the Confederates shed their blood for their mother, Virginia, defending a cause she knew to be just and right."[17]

On August 30, 1871, Tom Munford was a Bedford County delegate to the State Conservative Convention. George Wythe Munford was delegate from Gloucester, Virginia. Tom was also a delegate to the 1880 Convention in Richmond.[18]

Involved Episcopalians

Thomas and Emma Munford were active in the life of their church in Bedford County. They also became involved in St. Paul's Episcopal Church in Lynchburg after they moved to the city in 1873. Emma Munford had a strong Christian faith and lived a life of piety. Tom was a delegate representing St. Stephens Episcopal Church of Hamner Parish in Bedford County to the Episcopal Diocese of Virginia's 63rd and 66th Annual Councils in 1868 in Lynchburg and in 1871 at Petersburg. He was appointed to a lay committee at the 1871 Council to take into consideration the treasurers' reports of the different parishes with respect to the rectors' salaries.[19]

Meanwhile, in 1871, Tom's brother, Col. William Munford, was ordained a deacon in the Protestant Episcopal Church at Wilmington, North Carolina. The Right Rev. Thomas Atkinson, Bishop of North

---

16. *Richmond Dispatch*, August 24, 1901. Munford resigned as Secretary in 1874.
17. Caroline E. Janney, *Remembering the Civil War: Reunion and the Limits of Reconciliation* (Chapel Hill, 2013), 154.
18. *Staunton Spectator*, September 5, 1871; *Richmond Whig*, August 30, 1871; *Richmond Daily Dispatch*, May 6, 1880.
19. *Journals of the Sixty–Third and Sixty–Sixth Annual Councils of Episcopal Diocese of Virginia* (Richmond, VA, 1868, 1871); 1868:19, 1871:11, 25.

Carolina, officiated. Many citizens of Richmond were familiar with William Munford, and knew he was a son of Colonel George Wythe Munford. William next travelled to Memphis to became assistant to the Rev. Mr. Wheat, of St. James's Church.[20]

From Farmers to City Dwellers

By 1852, Lynchburg was a thriving city. As this region of Virginia became increasingly settled, tobacco was the money crop that fueled canals, railroads, and magnificent architecture. Lynchburg was the second wealthiest city per capita in the nation just before the Civil War, second only to New Bedford, Massachusetts with its whaling industry. During the Civil War, Lynchburg was a major Confederate hospital center, transportation hub, and supply base.[21]

Emma Munford became dissatisfied with the farming life and desired to move to the city. By 1869, Tom had concluded that "a planter could be successful by hiring negroes only when he wants them and lets them go when he has nothing for them to do." Tom, too, had had enough of farming, with a large portion of his income going to pay freedmen. He lamented, "I rejoice to be free from a farm which yielded me nothing—but I want some business to occupy my time and help to make the 'pot boil.'"[22] In 1873, Tom Munford exchanged his farm in Bedford County for the Lynchburg home, built in 1860, of John William Murrell. The Munfords received an additional $18,100 in the deal. The old Glen Alpine estate burned down in November 1904. Their Lynchburg home was located at 205 Harrison Street, at the intersection of Second and Harrison Streets in the "Garland Hill" District.[23]

As part of the property purchased, the Munfords owned what became known as "The Munford Tutor Cottage" next door at 207 Harrison Street. This Italian Villa style house was built in 1857, as the tutor's cottage and servant's quarters for William Murrell. The Tutor Cottage, originally only four rooms, was expanded to eight.[24]

---

20. *Staunton Spectator*, September 5, 1871.
21. Steven Elliot Tripp, *Yankee Town, Southern City: Race and Class Relations in Civil War Lynchburg* (New York, 1997), 7–8.
22. James L. Roark, *Masters Without Slaves* (New York: W. W. Norton & Company, 1977),179, 198-99; Thomas T. Munford to George Munford, December 20, 1874, Munford–Ellis Papers, DU.
23. 1947 Typed biography of General Munford, Jones Memorial Library, Lynchburg, Virginia; *Alexandria Daily State Journal*, Nov. 22, 1873; *Richmond Daily State Journal*, November 22, 1873.
24. Register of Virginia Historical Landmarks, Garland Hill Historic District, Lynchburg, VA.

Munford "Tutor" Home
207 Harrison Street, Lynchburg, Virginia

This house, next door to the main house purchased by General and Mrs. Munford in 1873, is of Italian Villa style and was built in 1857 as the tutor's cottage and servant's quarters for the home of William Murrell. The Tutor's Cottage, originally only four rooms, was been expanded to eight.

(Courtesy: Nancy Marion Publisher, Lynchs Ferry Magazine, Lynchburg, Virginia)

The main house, the "old Munford place," as it became known by people in Lynchburg, had wide hallways on both the first and second floors. A wide hallway also ran through the middle of the cellar and served the dining room by a dumbwaiter, which worked on a wooden pulley system in a large shaft.[25]

Tom Munford was a great believer in wholesome recreation for his sons and had a bowling alley added in the cellar. The alley was located under the porch which ran on two sides of the house. Among the rooms on the first floor was his study and library, where he was secluded from other parts on that floor. Several spacious rooms filled the attic. The house had two towers, one in the front, situated a little higher than the one in the rear. A gabled roof topped the rear tower, and the front roof gave the effect of a pagoda. Adjoining each of the bedrooms was a good-sized dressing room, where bathing in the days

---

25. Joe Young, "General's House Once a Show Place," 5, copied from *The Daily Advance*, July 19, 1949, c1–3, Jones Memorial Library, Lynchburg, Virginia; Library of Virginia, Works Projects Administration of Virginia, Historical Inventory, Virginia Conservation Commission, 1937.

*Munford Home of Thomas and Emma Munford in Lynchburg, 1873-1910
Italian Style Villa built in 1857.*

Thomas moved to his farm in Uniontown Alabama after Emma's death in 1910.

(Courtesy: Lynchburg Library)

---

preceding modern plumbing was accomplished. Water could be obtained from a cistern filled with rainwater from the roof. There was an elaborate drainage system, that permitted the roof to be washed off by the first of a rainfall, and the remainder of the water then turned into the reservoir.[26]

The flooring of the main hallway and of the wide square vestibule at the front was parquetry. In the partition between the vestibule and the hallway were windows with small panes of early red American-pressed glass. A wrought iron chandelier hung in the hall.[27]

---

26. Young, "General's House Once a Show Place," 6, copied from The Daily Advance, July 19, 1949, c1-3, Jones Memorial Library, Lynchburg, Virginia.
27. Ibid.

The 1880 Federal Census for Campbell County, Virginia, lists Thomas Munford and family residing on Harrison Street. Listed at the residence were: Thos. T. Munford (age 49), Iron Mfg; Emma (age 46), George T. (age 25), Iron Co. Agent, Emma T. (age 21), William (age 18), Clerk Iron Co., Harry L. (age 13), Thornton O. (age 11), St. Clair (age 9), Thos. G. (age 6), Ellen Feamington (age 45), and Fannie Ford (age 40), Domes Serv.[28]

George Wythe Munford's Continued Financial Woes

George Munford's experience with a government job after the war exposes even how more restrictive such work could be for elites. Munford achieved elite status, not as a member of Virginia's land gentry, but because of his long involvement in the state's legal and political circles, where he served 25 years as the Clerk of the House of Delegates and then as Secretary of the Commonwealth until the Civil War ended. It was only after the war that Munford began farming in Gloucester County. That occupation, however, did not sustain him and his family, so he supplemented his agricultural business with work as the clerk of the Committee on Courts of Justice.[29]

George moved back to Richmond in 1874, living at 117 East Franklin Street. In the late 1870s, George W. Munford succeeded in landing a job at the U. S. Census Bureau in Washington. His letters home show how far he was willing to go to keep this post. He wrote his wife that he could not take time off to come home and visit his family because he feared his boss would think badly of him. "I shall not neglect my work, not even to kiss you and shall regret exceedingly to miss Jennie," his grown daughter who was visiting. "General Walker has been very kind in promoting me," Munford explained, and he did not want to "fall out of favor with his employer." While working at the Census Bureau after the war, he discovered that the clerk working beside him had held the same high position in Maryland that he had held in Virginia before the war. Munford could not help but notice how far they both had fallen in rank. It seemed strange to him that they were now mere clerks who "had to beg for bread from the Census Bureau." He added, "Such influence as I once possessed has gone." To obtain that status again within the government bureaucracy would

---

28. Federal 1880 Census for Campbell County, Virginia; Morsman, *The Big House after Slavery*, 176.
29. Morsman, *The Big House after Slavery*, 65; James Lyons Taliaferro, "Colonel George Wythe Munford" *The Virginia Law Register* 8, No. 11 (March 1903), 784–85.

George Wythe Munford (1803-1882) Father of Thomas T. Munford

For 12 years, George Wythe Munford was Secretary of the Commonwealth of Virginia. He ran unsuccessfully for Governor of Virginia in 1863. Financially ruined after the war, he struggled to make ends meet.

(Courtesy: Rubenstein Library, Duke University)

have required a considerable amount of fawning toward his superiors. Munford did not "desire to undergo the disagreeable homage and slavishness to attempt its renewal."[30]

After moving back to Richmond, George worked for a while in the Treasurer's Office in Richmond as a clerk of accounts and was paid $1502 (less tax) per annum. He finally retired in 1880.[31]

Never recovering his fortune, on January 10, 1882, George Munford died of a heart attack at his home at the corner of 2nd and Franklin Streets in Richmond. A newspaper reported, "One of his daughters is Mrs. Charles H. Talbot. Second wife, Miss Ellis, is a sister of Colonel Charles Ellis, Sr. One of his sons is Rev. William Munford, of Columbus, Mississippi; another is General Thomas T. Munford of Lynchburg. Colonel W. P. Munford, of Richmond, is the only surviving brother of the deceased . . . His death, as is believed, was caused by "gout of the stomach, reaching towards the heart." Tom's mother, Elizabeth, died in 1900.[32]

---

30. 1882 City Directory for Richmond, Virginia; George W Munford to Elizabeth Munford, September 12, 1880, Munford–Ellis Papers, DU; George W. Munford to Elizabeth Munford, January 6, 1878, October 11, 1874, Munford–Ellis Papers, DU.
31. *Richmond Daily Dispatch*, January 3, 1880.
32. *Daily Richmond Dispatch*, January 11, 1882.

Chapter Eighteen

Thomas Munford's Business Ventures and Legal Challenges

During these trying years with his parents struggling to make ends meet, Tom Munford entered into business ventures. Some of these undertakings ended up in lawsuits. He faced several court actions involving real estate transactions and a business venture.

Tom Munford entered into various business ventures in the 1860s, 1870s, and 1880s. One partner was Wade Hampton, but there were others. In one 1872 business undertaking, Tom Munford and two other Bedford County residents bought the patent for an "Air Forcer" invention, developed by James M. Rucker. Rucker claimed the machine to be one of the most valuable inventions of the day, whereby a house could readily be supplied with water, not merely for household purposes, but so as to provide protection against fire. The investors obtained the right to make and sell the machine in 14 states, with a royalty for each machine going to Mr. Rucker.[1]

Another endeavor was the Lynchburg Iron, Steel, and Mining Company, organized about 1874, with General Bird Grubb, president, and Thomas T. Munford, vice-president and general manager. The company purchased Deane's Foundry and Rolling Mill and soon began the erection of a large blast furnace. The furnace had one heating furnace, two spike furnaces, two spike machines, one bolt machine, and one 10-inch train of rolls; steam and 108 rolling mills, water power; product, merchant iron, railroad and boat spikes, and bolts. The business became idle in 1878.[2]

That same year, the company constructed a substantial bridge, the first iron bridge ever built in Lynchburg, over Blackwater Creek, providing greater accessibility to the community of Daniels Hill. Prior to this date, a covered wooden pedestrian bridge existed at 6th Street. The new bridge could fit two wagons across and became a major thoroughfare and a vital link between Commerce and Cabell Streets.

---

1. *Richmond Daily*, August 6, 1872.
2. *Directory to the Iron and Steel Works of the United States* (Philadelphia, PA, 1878), 108.

Car traffic was removed from this bridge in 1944, but it remained as a pedestrian link until 1984 when the metal began to corrode. Munford also developed and sold the Crozier and Blue Ridge and Grubb Iron mines in Bedford and Botetourt County, Virginia.[3]

Court Cases

Tom Munford conducted his personal life with a high degree of decorum. He did, however, end up involved in several civil lawsuits, usually dealing with matters of finance. In one suit, he and Henry A. Tayloe, as executors of an estate, were sued by one of the beneficiaries of the estate. Early in 1871, an equity court ordered George Ogle to sell "Belair," a family mansion in Prince Georges County, Maryland, to satisfy a mortgage. William H. Tayloe, father of Tom Munford's second wife, Emma, proposed taking over the property prior to a public sale, but in April, before the plan could be executed, he died. George Ogle immediately sent a message to William H. Tayloe's son, Henry A. Tayloe, telling him his father and he had planned on buying the place. It could be sold at a good price to satisfy the claims, instead of sold at a public auction. Ogle pleaded that someone in the family must step up as a new financial backer. Henry A. Tayloe replied that the executors of the estate, namely he and Thomas T. Munford, would have to quickly settle the estate and attend to the sale themselves.[4]

On May 16, 1871, Belair, a magnificent, historical mansion, was offered for sale. The original Belair Mansion was built in 1745 as the plantation home of the Provincial Governor of Maryland, Samuel Ogle. Belair had been a slave-operated plantation, but the ratification of the Maryland Constitution of 1864 emancipated the slaves in the state, effectively ending its operation as a plantation. In 1867, Dr. George C. Ogle reported to the Maryland State Commissioner of Slave Statistics that he had freed 41 slaves, 24 of them 18 years of age or younger.[5]

Belair, like other plantations, consisted of huge tracts of land, but suddenly without the built-in workforce to make them productive, owners were often unable to meet mortgage debts or pay taxes. By 1870, the house had fallen into disrepair and George Ogle was in debt $7,400 to his brother-in-law, William Henry Tayloe. Ogle also had several lesser debts to others, including $2,400 to the estate of Maria

---

3. Ibid.
4. Shirley Vlasak Baltz, *A Chronicle of Belair* (Bowie, Maryland: Bowie Heritage Committee, 1984), 59, 65–67.
5. Shirley Vlasak Baltz, *Belair From the Beginning* (Bowie, Maryland: 2005), 104.

Jackson, being executed by James Mullikin. In 1871, Ogle defaulted on the latter debt, and Mullikin filed suit. The court ruled the Belair estate be sold to satisfy the debt.[6]

An advertisement described Belair as "550 acres, more or less, and one of the farms in Prince Georges County. It lies along the line of the Baltimore and Potomac Railroad, about one-quarter mile from Collington, where there will be a Depot on said Road. The improvements are a large, two-story brick dwelling house, 3 tobacco houses, corn house, granary, stables, servant's house, etc."[7]

The ad continued, "The soil is well adapted to the growth of tobacco, corn, wheat, etc. Wood and water abundant." The ad failed to mention that the house was in disrepair. Thomas Munford and Henry A. Tayloe, executors of William H. Tayloe's estate, were the highest bidders for the property with an offer of $5,100. The conditions of sale were that Rosalie Ogle retained the right to a room in the Belair house as long as she was single, and that she be paid by the purchasers the $1,500 due her from George Ogle, as specified in her father's will.[8]

Rosalie Ogle, however, took offense when the new owners' overseers moved into the mansion. In the mid-1870s, Rosalie claimed she could not live under the same roof with such people. She brought suit against Henry Tayloe and Thomas Munford, charging that she had been denied her legacy of a room in the Belair mansion. She wanted an annual allowance to provide the rental of a room equal to the one she abandoned. Tayloe and Munford countered that they had "never requested Dr. George C. Ogle or the complainant to quit the said dwelling house," and they had "offered Dr. Ogle the use of the house as long as he chose to remain there, but 'refused him the use of the farm.'" After several years' absence, Rosalie still retained the key, and the room was opened only when she sent, at various times, for her belongings. At the time of the suit, some of her furniture was still there.[9]

On June 22, 1877, the court decided against Rosalie because the defendants had met the conditions of the sale and done nothing to bar her from her room. On September 13, Thomas Munford and Henry A. Tayloe deeded Belair to Edward T. Rutter for $17,000.[10]

In another case, Tutwiler v. Munford, the Alabama Supreme Court, in its 1882 term, heard a legal ejectment case against Tom

---

6. Baltz, *A Chronicle of Belair*, 74–76; Kimberly Gatto, *Belair Stud: The Cradle of Horseracing* (Charleston, S.C., 1984), 65–68.
7. Baltz, *A Chronicle of Belair*, 1984, 73–74.
8. Baltz, *A Chronicle of Belair*, 70–73; Kimberly Gatto, *Belair Stud*, 23–24.
9. Ibid.
10. Baltz, *A Chronicle of Belair*, 70–73.

Munford. The ejectment was a legal action by which P. A. Tutwiler claimed he was wrongfully dispossessed from property and sought to recover possession, damages, and costs. A lower court had issued a verdict in favor of Munford, ruling that he was lawfully in possession of the property. Tutwiler had appealed the decision to the Supreme Court of Alabama. The land involved was sold by the Sheriff of Hale County, under writs of venditioni exponas, requiring the sale to satisfy judgments against Munford in certain attachment suits (seizure of property) brought by several of Munford's creditors. Tutwiler had bought the property at the Sheriff's sale and obtained the deed to it. Munford had obtained the property by deed of T. W. Ormand on March 5, 1874.[11]

Under the will of William H. Tayloe, his daughter Emma, wife of Thomas Munford, inherited two parcels of land, one in Prince George County, Maryland (worth about $7,000) and a lot in the town of Manchester, Virginia (worth about $1,000). On or about March 23, 1873, Tom Munford traded property with Thomas W. Ormand, receiving the Alabama property and conveying the Maryland and Virginia properties to Ormand. Instead of conveying the Alabama property to Munford's wife, Emma, Ormand inadvertently conveyed the property to Munford.[12]

Introduced into evidence was a deed dated March 28, 1876, at Lynchburg, Virginia, between Munford and his wife Emma. The deed conveyed the Alabama property to Emma for her use for life with remainder to her children, the children of them both and Munford's children born of his previous marriage.[13]

Munford testified he conveyed the property to his wife because the property conveyed to Ormond (the Virginia and Maryland properties) was Emma's inheritance from her father. He also testified he had no intention of hindering or defrauding his creditors. The Alabama property was conveyed to Munford inadvertently. He owned property valued at least $25,000 over and above his liabilities.[14]

The issue before the Supreme Court of Alabama was the legal effect of the Alabama property deed from Munford to Emma. Did it give title to Munford or did it create a trust for Emma? This issue was

---

11. John P. Tillman, *Special Reporter, Reports of Cases Argued and Determined in the Supreme Court of Alabama, during the December Terms, 1882-1888* (Montgomery, AL: Joel White, 1884), Vol. LXXIII, December Term, 1882, 308–12. Note: Thanks to the Honorable Judge Robert P. Frank, Circuit Court of Appeals for the State of Virginia, for aiding me in understanding the issues and disposition of this case.
12. Ibid.
13. Ibid.
14. Ibid.

central to whether the Alabama property was subject to attachment and sale by the Sheriff.[15]

The Supreme Court ruled that while the deed from Munford to Emma created an equitable interest in the land for Emma, legal title remained with Munford and was subject to attachment and sale by the Sheriff. Tutwiler owned the property and was entitled to have Munford's possession terminated by ejectment, despite the equitable rights of Emma and the children. The Supreme Court reversed the lower court judgment ruling which had favored Munford.[16]

In still another case, an adverse possession suit was brought by C. H. Owen involving a land dispute between himself and the trustees of Altha Grove Baptist Church. Munford owned 700 acres in Bedford County, part of which he and his wife Emma, on June 3, 1873, conveyed to Edward S. Hunter and others, as trustees for the Forest school district to build a public free school for "the colored people" of the district. The deed contained a "reverter clause," which required that if the school lot was used for any other purpose than a school or church for the "colored people," title would revert to the Munfords.[17]

Subsequently, Munford and Emma conveyed the remainder of the tract to one Murrell. Thereafter, C. H. Owen became the owner of the 224-acre tract by a deed dated August 7, 1898, from a commissioner of the Circuit Court of Bedford County. The property was described as being contiguous to and adjoining the school house lot.[18]

The school trustees built a school house on the lot. The "colored people" of Bedford obtained permission to conduct religious services therein. After the school was built, a rail fence was built on the remainder of the Munfords' tract, which cut off from that tract the school lot and a parcel containing one and one-quarter acres, lying between the school lot and the rail fence.[19]

Later, a controversy arose between Owen and the church concerning the boundary line between the school lot and Owen's property. The church filed an action enjoining Owen from interfering

---

15. Ibid.
16. Ibid.
17. Davis, et als v. Owen, 107, Va, 285; Note: "To establish to real property by adverse possession, a claimant must prove actual, hostile, exclusive, visible, and continuous possession, under a claim of right, for the statutory period of 15 years. A claimant has the burden of proving all elements of adverse possession by clear and convincing evidence." Helms v. Manspile, 277 Va. 1, 7, 671, S.E.2d 127, 130 (2009), quoting Grappo, 241 Va at 61, 400 S. 400 S.E. 2d at 170–71. Note: Thanks to the Honorable Judge Robert P. Frank, Circuit Court of Appeals for the State of Virginia, for aiding me in understanding the issues and disposition of this case.
18. Ibid.
19. Ibid.

with or trespassing upon the school property or the parcel between the rail fence and the school, a claim based on adverse possession. The church later added the school trustees as parties.[20]

Owen responded by disclaiming any right to the school house, but claimed ownership in the one and one-quarter acre parcel. The church claimed the school lot and that the one-and-one-quarter parcel by virtue of the Munfords' deed to the school trustees, claiming adverse possession for both parcels, i.e. that they have occupied those parcels for over three years, which possession has been exclusive, open, notorious, and hostile and under the cover of title.[21]

The Supreme Court of Appeals of Virginia concluded that the church's right, if any, was dependent upon and subordinate to the rights of the school trustees, who had legal title and the right of possession. Their claim was not hostile (adversarial) because they had sought permission from the school trustees to conduct religious services at the school. Further, the church never exercised possession of the one-and-one-quarter acre parcel. Some eight to nine years prior to filing this suit, the church sought and received permission to erect a building on the school property. They mistakenly erected the church and a graveyard partly on the Owen property.[22]

The Supreme Court of Appeals of Virginia rejected the church's adverse possession claim for several reasons: Their right of possession was subordinate to the school's right of possession, thus precluding a hostile possession; the church's graveyard encroaching on Owen's property occurred eight to nine years ago (not the 30 years as required under the adverse possession principles); the possession (encroachment) was by mistake and not by claim of right; the church had possession only with the consent of Owen, the owner. Thus, the Supreme Court of Appeals of Virginia affirmed the trial court's dismissal of the church's adverse possession action.[23]

---

20. Ibid.
21. Ibid.
22. Ibid.
23. Ibid.

Chapter Nineteen

Thomas Munford: President of the Board of Visitors of VMI and Life in the 1880s

The Board "had set their faces against all secret organizations [including fraternities], and will root them out, believing that the fair name of the school had been made to suffer, and that in a military school nothing is more pernicious or more antagonistic to good order and military discipline."

–Thomas Munford, writing on behalf of the VMI Board of Visitors.

Notwithstanding business ventures and court actions during the 1870s and 1880s, Thomas Munford devoted time to serve as president of the Board of Visitors of VMI from 1885 to 1888. In this position, he clashed with superintendent and long-time friend, Francis H. Smith. The difficulties arising from this struggle required legislative action to resolve. Munford and Smith, however, reconciled their differences after Munford's terms as president of the Board of Visitors.

Tom Munford's father, George Wythe Munford, was still Secretary of the Commonwealth at the close of the Civil War. As such, George was keeper of the official seal of the State of Virginia. The state's provisional governor during Reconstruction, Francis H. Pierpont, and George Munford instantly disliked each other. Pierpont, called "the Father of West Virginia," was instrumental in getting "West Virginia," a collection of western counties of Virginia which had refused to join the Confederacy, admitted to the Union as a separate state in 1863. When Arthur I. Borman was elected governor of the new state of West Virginia, Pierpont became governor of "the restored Government of Virginia," placing Northern, Norfolk, and Eastern Shore counties of Virginia under Union control. The capital of the "restored" state was Alexandria until the end of the war, with Pierpont appointed as provisional governor. The provisional government adopted a revised seal for the Commonwealth, which remained in use until 1910. Thomas Munford, along with others, such as members of the Robert E. Lee Camp of the Confederate Veterans, worked hard to see to it that the governor and legislature were petitioned to return the original seal's design which had been used since Colonial times, thus abandoning the "Pierpont seal." In 1910, Tom Munford arose from a sick bed to deliver an address at the Robert E. Lee Veterans Camp in Richmond, pleading for the cause he had for so long labored. He pleaded, "I'm am an old man. I am in my 79th year, and I should be glad and happy to see this done before I die."[1]

Governor William Smith, meanwhile, requested Tom Munford's sisters, Sallie Radford Munford Talbott and Margaret Munford, to make a new state flag to replace the existing badly worn one. The young ladies completed the project and delivered the flag to the governor. It was raised atop the historic State Capitol. At the fall of Richmond in April 1865, a Union soldier lowered the flag and took it away as a souvenir. Sixty-two years later, and after Tom Munford's death, the flag was returned to Virginia by the grandson of the Union soldier who had taken it. There was a celebration in the old halls of the House of Delegates at its return during ceremonies in the autumn of 1927, attended by Sallie Radford Munford Talbott, who was able to identify the flag as the one she and her sister had made.[2]

Thomas Munford's Tenure as President of the Board of Visitors at VMI

From 1885 to 1888, Tom Munford served as President of the VMI Board of Visitors. He inherited a bad set of circumstances enacted by the 1882 board, which had made radical changes in the general administration of the institution, resulting in a system where each administrative department was made independent of the superintendent. Purchases were made for all supplies by the commissary and military storekeeper without any contract from any quarter. The treasurer drew checks, without being countersigned by any supervising authority; confusion and conflict took the place of order and the system of administration. The result of 40 years of

---

1. *The Richmond Times Dispatch*, November 22, 1910. The seal of Virginia was restored on November 26, 1910. By 1913, Munford's efforts were rewarded with success in having the state seal restored.
2. Robert Beverley Munford, *Richmond Homes and Memories* (Richmond, VA, 1936), 8.

*Colonel Thomas Taylor Munford
in a Brigadier General Uniform
Circa 1875*

Munford served two terms as President of the VMI Board of Visitors.

(Courtesy: Anne S.K. Brown Military Collection, Brown University Library)

experience was overturned by the 1882 board, and the superintendent relegated to the position of chairman of the faculty.[3]

While serving as president of the board, Munford faced several prominent issues: hazing at the institute; the 1882 rewriting of the rules and regulations of the institute; financial troubles at the school; and relations between the board and Superintendent Francis H. Smith.

Concerning hazing at the institute, Superintendent Smith had, in earlier days of his 50-year tenure, opposed the practice, crusading to eliminate all maltreatment of new cadets. He found it impossible to weed out. By the mid-1850s, Smith changed his attitude toward hazing, reluctantly accepting it. His new assertions of hazing contributing to manliness most likely came out of frustration at being unable to curtail these abuses. Since upper-class cadets would not stop hazing new cadets, and the victims of such hazing refused to turn in their tormentors, there was little Smith could do. His vague sanctioning of hazing sent a message to all cadets that if they would not allow him to defend them, they would have to fend for themselves.[4]

By 1886, however, Smith reported hazing had in large measure been eliminated, thanks in part to the aggressive approach to the problem taken by the Munford board. Regardless of Smith's changing his attitudes towards hazing, Munford was not about to give in on the issue. Writing for the Board of Visitors, Munford pledged that the board "had set their faces against all secret organizations [including fraternities], and will root them out, believing that the fair name of the school had been made to suffer, and that in a military school nothing is more pernicious or more antagonistic to good order and military discipline."[5]

Further concerning the same hazing issue at the institute, Munford wrote long after his term as President of the Board of Visitors ended, "Things have been going on at the Institute, which make it incumbent upon [Smith's successor, Superintendent Lt. Gen. Edward Nichols] to take a firm stand. Hazing in an underhanded way has been going on, although it is correctly stated that all the plebes had pledged not to participate in the vulgar, cowardly, bullying practice." Munford recommended that a system be established tied to the "Honor System."[6]

---

3. *Annual Reports of Officers, Boards and Institutions of the Commonwealth of Virginia* (Richmond, VA, 1886), 17.
4. Superintendent Francis H. Smith to George W. Munford, 23 August 1852, Superintendent's Outgoing Correspondence, VMI Archives.
5. *Reports of Officers, Boards and Institutions of the Commonwealth of Virginia* (Richmond: Rush U. Derr, Superintendent of Public Printing, 1885), *Report of Virginia Military Institute*, 5.
6. Thomas T. Munford to James T. Murfee, March 4, 1911, Private Collection of David Center, Highland Home, Alabama.

Munford continued:

> I am of the opinion that the Board of Visitors were right in upholding the Action of the Superintendent [Nichols], wherein each cadet applying for admission under an appointment be required to take an oath affirming that they are not a member of any secret society, and if so, you renounce all connections or obligations in conflict with the "Rules and Regulations" of VMI–The question of hazing in any form is absolutely prohibited, and you affirm that you fully understand all of these conditions.[7]

The General Assembly of Virginia required an annual report "of the condition of the school." In the 1885 annual Superintendent's Report to the Board, Superintendent Maj. Gen. Francis H. Smith appealed to the board to correct an anomalous situation which the previous board had created in 1882. Smith complained that the roles and responsibilities of these departments to each other and to him were so undefined as to make it doubtful the Superintendent had the authority to require annual reports from the heads of these departments to be made to him, before they were "laid before the Board." Smith, who served as superintendent from 1839 to 1889, wrote that this was an untenable situation and needed to be corrected by the board so that he could responsibly manage the Institution.[8]

There were financial problems which the superintendent had predicted might occur under the changed system of administration. Superintendent Smith called for the board to review the 1882 regulations and make appropriate changes to "adopt such measures as shall maintain full responsibility in all accounting officers, and guard the institution against errors and mistakes and blunders which are liable to occur."[9]

Apparently, Smith's objections and recommendations were addressed by the board. Munford reported, "When this Board entered upon its duties, friction was at once detected in the ramifications of the machinery of the Institute, incident to the changes made by our predecessors (the governing power). A committee, composed of graduates of the school, after consulting with the Superintendent, Commandant of Cadets, and Finance Committee, have carefully revised the rules and regulations for the government of the Virginia

---

7. Ibid.
8. *Annual Reports of Officers, Boards and Institutions of the Commonwealth of Virginia* (Richmond: Rush U. Derr, Superintendent of Public Printing, 1885), 6.
9. Ibid., 17.

Francis H. Smith

Superintendent of Virginia Military Institute 1859-1889

During Thomas T. Munford's term as President of the Board of Visitors (1885-1888), Superintendent Smith fought with Munford and the Board over administration of the school. Smith called for a Legislative investigation, which occurred, clearing him of any misdeeds, but urging his retirement. He retired in 1889 after serving 50 years as Superintendent.

(Courtesy: V.M.I. Archives)

Military Institute, and it is believed, when this revised code is printed and promulgated, all cause for attrition will be obviated."[10]

The revised regulations gave relief from the problems of administration pointed out by Superintendent Smith and became effective March 31, 1897. Thomas Munford, however, in his portion of the report, pointed out differences between the board and the superintendent: when summer encampments were suspended at the institute, the institute's tents were sent to needy citizens in Charleston, South Carolina, without authority from the Board of Visitors. Tents would now be needed if the recommended summer encampments were to be resumed. The cost of procuring new tents had not been taken into account. Also, Munford and the board wanted to have a band as an activity at the institute. Superintendent Smith was dead-set against this, due to the costs involved, noting VMI was financially strained. Munford wrote that Smith, in his report, misrepresented the situation with respect to the band. He pointed out that the law read, "the

---

10. Ibid. 17.

Superintendent may enlist musicians." He recommended that the law be changed to read, "the Board of Visitors may direct how the post band at the Virginia Military Institute shall be organized." Smith and Munford disagreed on the difficulty of providing a band at the institute. Munford also wrote other conclusions showing, in the superintendent's view, Smith in an unfavorable light.[11]

Superintendent Smith took issue with Munford's report, sparking a dispute between the two stalwarts of the institute. Smith thought he was being persecuted by Munford and "his minions." He wrote, "Of course, I was not going to submit to such pure imputations on my official integrity." The *Alexandria Gazette* reported, "It is understood that in the last annual report of T. T. Munford, of Lynchburg, president of the Board of Visitors of the V. M. I., there are certain reflections made upon Gen. Smith, the superintendent, and the latter demands a thorough investigation."[12]

Smith hired an attorney and asked the legislature for an investigation, complaining that the report "reflected in an objectionable manner in several particulars upon the Superintendent." The legislature named a joint committee of eight members of the Senate and House to "visit the Virginia Military Institute to investigate, ascertain the facts and report upon all matters brought to their attention in reference to the management, condition and needs of that institution, and to make such recommendations as they deem proper."[13]

Smith complained that certain portions of the report of the Board of Visitors were signed only by Thomas T. Munford—as president and two other members—and reflected in an objectionable manner on the superintendent. Thus, Smith claimed the report was in fact the report of Munford alone and not the board. Smith considered the report based on hostile feelings, "disingenuous and unworthy in its character, has not been made good by the evidence, but by the contrary." The Legislative Committee found that the report was authentic as required by law, but recommended that future reports "be signed by at least a majority of the Board."[14] As to the board's complaint that finances

11. *Annual Reports of Officers, Boards and Institutions of the Commonwealth of Virginia* (Richmond: W. W. Moses, Superintendent of Public Printing, 1887), 4–5, 19.
12. Francis H. Smith to William H. Payne, March 7, 1888; Francis H. Smith Papers, Swem Library, College of William and Mary, Williamsburg, Va.; *Alexandria Gazette*, January 28, 1888; *The Richmond Dispatch*, January 28, 1888.
13. *Journal of the Senate of the Commonwealth of Virginia* (Richmond: A. R. Micou, Superintendent of Public Printing, December 7, 1887), Report of Joint Committee on Virginia Institute, Senate Document No. XXVII, VMI, 1.
14. Report of Joint Committee on Virginia Institute, Senate Document No. XXVII, VMI, December. 1987, 2.

"'were not in a shape for us to know with accuracy the condition of the indebtedness of the Institute,' the committee found that neither the superintendent nor the board at the time had had access to the most important books bearing on the finances of the Institute, because these books had been in the possession of the court of Boutetout County, which was assessing the financial condition of the Institute." The Committee believed state aid saved the institute from bankruptcy.[15]

The board had reported that "no thorough investigation has been made for years by experts as to the status of the various trust funds" of the institute. The board also pointed out that they were not compensated for their services or their time. Furthermore, they claimed the expertise required for such an undertaking was beyond their capabilities. The committee found that trust funds had been recklessly absorbed into the general expense fund, and their very existence was compromised as a result. They recommended an expert be hired to examine and straighten out this situation, which it criticized severely.[16]

Concerning the issue of the superintendent sending tents to Charleston without board authority, the committee sustained and praised the generous act of the superintendent for his action in sending the tents to those in need. On the complaints of the board as to the need for development of a better military band, the committee disagreed with Smith's estimate of the costs required and recommended adopting the board's recommendation.[17]

The committee acknowledged that since the board revised the management of the institute's finances in 1882, the superintendent had "not been in cordial and co-operative sympathy" with the new board since that time. The committee reported that it could not understand why the board and the superintendent could not now get along harmoniously. They praised the board for its conscientious service, but pointed out it had acted with at least some degree of impatience in insisting upon very prompt and immediate adoption of views altogether reasonable, albeit requiring some time to enact. The committee found that no suspicion of improper conduct in connection with the financial management of the school had been imputed to Smith. Nevertheless, the committee, while recognizing Smith's integrity and noble and faithful service, recommended that because of his age, he retire at year's end with a pension and title of "Emeritus Superintendent of the Virginia Institute." The burdens of managing the institute in the committee's opinion, required a younger man in

---
15. Ibid.
16. Ibid., 2–3.
17. Ibid., 4.

the future. The full Senate, however, rejected the committee's recommendations, and with the influence of others, such as Col. A. S. Buford, a board member, affected an adjustment in the recommendations that allowed Smith, who had set his resignation effective as of September 6, 1886, to withdraw it. He vowed to serve up to the standards of the "honorable adjustment."[18]

Munford's interest in VMI continued for the rest of his life. In 1910, dissatisfaction with the violence of football at VMI was addressed by the introduction of a bill in the legislature calling for restrictions on the game in state colleges. Munford spoke to the subject, stating he hoped the legislature would act to make football less violent. He told of three Lynchburg friends, Virginia Polytechnic Institute men who had been Confederate soldiers, but who refused to send their sons to VMI because of the violence of football. He thought "the boys in mass became riotous, and acted differently from their ordinary behavior." He begged the committee to do something to remedy the evil. He also wanted progress toward the abolition of hazing.[19]

Thomas Munford's Children

George Tayloe Munford

George Tayloe Munford attended VMI in the Class of 1875. He had trouble adapting to the military life. Tom wrote his friend, Francis H. Smith, at the institute asking for help for his son. Smith responded, "I will do for your boy what I do for my own son. Tell him to look up and when he gets out of heart—tell him to come over and see old 'Spex.' He will find he is not cross after all, but he has some tender spots left after a period of 32 years." George graduated next to the bottom of the 45 graduates of his class. He became a mining and civil engineer in West Virginia and Alabama.[20]

On June 28, 1884, George Munford, of Lynchburg, Virginia, shot and instantly killed an African-American man at "Devens's contract,"

---

18. Ibid.; Francis H. Smith to William H. Payne, March 7, 1888, Francis H. Smith Papers, Swem Library, College of William and Mary, Williamsburg, Va. Note: Smith, who wanted to retire on his own terms, did finally resign in 1889.
19. *Richmond Times Dispatch*, Feb. 9, 1910. Here again, Munford was influenced by his own experiences with hazing and by what had happened to his brother, George Wythe Munford, Jr., who had resigned from the Institute after a hazing incident. The Legislative bill was never enacted, because other state colleges did not want to restrict their football programs.
20. Francis H. Smith to Thomas T. Munford, August 15, 1871; V.M.I. Archives.

Cadet George Tayloe Munford (1854-1928)
First Son of Thomas T. Munford and
Elizabeth Henrietta "Etta" (Tayloe) Munford
George T. Munford followed in his father's footsteps to VMI.
(Courtesy: V.M.I. Archives)

one-and-one half miles east of Pocahontas, West Virginia. The man had been discharged from the work on which Munford was the "walking boss," and, becoming offended with the latter, approached him in a menacing manner, armed with an uplifted pick, whereupon Munford shot him. George went to Princeton that morning to surrender to the West Virginia authorities.[21]

The 1880 Federal census shows George Tayloe Munford as a single person living at his parent's home in Lynchburg and employed as a "General Agent of Iron" [his father's] company. George married Pauline Orchard in 1894.[22]

George's troubles continued; at times he was out of work and associated himself with the wrong crowd. He had had alcohol problems. However, he had realized he had a problem and cleaned himself of the habit. In 1916, Tom Munford wrote VMI Superintendent, Gen. E. C. Nichols, asking for aid in finding George a job. Thomas was looking for a position for his son anywhere one could be found. He vouched for George and said he would "make good," offering to pay his salary, unbeknownst to George. He was desperate to see his son get a steady job and make good on his potential. Nothing became of the request before George became disabled, spending the last years of his life as an invalid, dying in 1928.[23]

Information is scarce for Tom and Emma's other children. Thomas Glen Munford never married; he became an accountant and lived at the Munford's Lynchburg home for years. He eventually moved to London. Wythe married Lelia Oma Grogan, moved to Chickasaw, Chickasaw Nation, Indian Territory in Oklahoma, raised a family, and died there in 1913. Sinclair attended the Agricultural & Mechanical College of Alabama and married Kate Fowler of Georgia. He served as a captain in the Quartermaster Corps in the Army, serving in the Philippines during the Spanish-American War. After the war, Sinclair and Kate lived in Macon, Georgia. Thomas Ogle Munford and William Tayloe Munford remained in Uniontown, Alabama, as farmers. Thomas's daughter, Mrs. J. William Byrd, lived in Roanoke.[24]

---

21. *Richmond Dispatch*, June 29, 1884. There is no further information regarding any trial or other disposition. Perhaps, the solicitor for the district considered the matter one of self-defense and did not file any charges against Munford.
22. Federal 1880 Census for Lynchburg, Virginia.
23. Thomas T. Munford to E. C. Nichols, February 14, 1916, Thomas T. Munford Papers, VMI Archives.
24. James Longstreet to Thomas T. Munford, February 1, 1899, Munford-Ellis Papers, DU; VMI. Archives.

After Thomas's service on the board of visitors of VMI and upon the coming of the Spanish-American War, he felt the call of patriotic service. He thought of seeking a commission and serving in the war. Commenting on a letter from good friend and Congressman John Lamb suggesting Munford accompany him to Washington to see the President about such a possibility, Munford noted, "I have been thinking of going to Washington and offer my services . . . as it is, I am tired of waiting for something to do. I may ride down to Washington to see if they will take an old Confederate . . . am only sixty-six years old."[25]

Visitors to Munford's Home in Lynchburg

A frequent visitor of General Munford after the war was General P.G.T. Beauregard from Louisiana. General Beauregard was remembered as being tall and erect and always in uniform. The two men made an attractive appearance together as they would walk down the street.[26]

Another visitor was Col. Heros von Borcke, who was visiting America from his homeland in Prussia in 1884. Von Borcke wanted to visit many of his old comrades, but before beginning that trek, he desired to visit the grave of his commander, Gen. J.E.B. Stuart, at Hollywood Cemetery in Richmond. On the way out to the cemetery, accompanied by Munford, the two old soldiers stopped at a flower garden so that von Borcke could purchase flowers to put on Stuart's grave. Munford, who might have felt conflicted, claimed he had let "bygones be bygones" in his relationship with Stuart, recalling, "it was very affecting to Col. Von Borcke at the grave of his old chief. After strewing the flowers, he stood over the grave in silent prayer for several minutes."[27]

Yet another visitor was Gen. Wade Hampton of South Carolina, who prospered after the war and became a successful politician. He and Tom Munford became involved in cotton farming machinery business ventures. They had a very cordial relationship and often corresponded about the late war. Hampton once visited Munford, became very ill and ended up staying at Munford's for two weeks.[28]

---

25. Congressman John Lamb to Thomas T. Munford, June 22, 1898, Munford–Ellis Papers, DU.
26. Typed biography of Thomas T. Munford, p. 4, Jones Memorial Library, Lynchburg, Virginia.
27. *Staunton Spectator*, June 17, 1884.
28. Wade Hampton to Thomas T. Munford, December 18, 1897, June 25, 1898, Munford–Ellis Papers, DU.

Tom was gracious to his Northern counterparts in the war, whatever their rank. He encouraged good fellowship between soldiers of the North and South. He aided many Northern soldiers in their efforts to write histories of their respective units. He was invited to attend and speak at various banquets and was made an honorary member of at least one regiment, the Sixth New York Cavalry. At their reunion in 1898, Munford spoke and stated that he was not there to complain about the Civil War. "We made an attempt, and it failed. We accepted it and thank God that 'Old Glory' is ours." Munford's admiration for the abilities of the Northern commanders and their troops was appreciated and reciprocated by everyone with whom he came in contact.[29]

Tom Munford was active in the Southern SCV Camps, and served for years as Grand Commander of the Virginia SCV Grand Camp in Lynchburg.

---

29. *The Baltimore Sun*, October 8, 1898.

Chapter Twenty

Long Awaited Promotion and Bitter Feud

"It is right difficult for a gentleman to sit with folded arms and hear things which make his heart swell with indignation."

–Thomas Munford, reacting to an 1865 letter from Fitzhugh Lee to General Marcus Wright, denying Munford was promoted to brigadier.

During the ensuing years, Thomas Munford obsessively continued his struggle to be recognized as a true brigadier general. Munford let it be known that he preferred to be addressed as "General Munford." In general, the press and most people did refer to him as "General Munford." He even had a general's uniform tailored for himself, which he proudly wore to various reunion events. He had a photo taken of himself wearing it. Munford had never complained to his officers or men about the promotion, but he certainly had complained to his wife and father. The bitter Munford-Rosser feud also reached its peak, continuing until Rosser's death in 1910.

For Tom Munford, the stigma associated with never being officially promoted to the rank of brigadier general never abated. This was his Achilles heel, an easy target for his nemesis, Thomas Rosser, and others to exploit. Munford called his [lack of a] commission "a sort of pestering sore." On March 23, 1865, General Robert E. Lee recommended Munford's promotion and it was dated from November 1, 1864, after Brig. Gen. Williams Wickham's resignation. There is no record of President Davis or the Confederate Congress ever acting on the recommendation. Time simply ran out—the war ended. Munford also noted in his postwar application for pardon that he never received a commission, although he claimed he was promoted by Maj. Gen. Fitzhugh Lee in the field during the last days of the war.[1]

---

1. Munford–Ellis Papers, DU; Confederate Applications for Presidential Pardons, 1865-1867, NA; Munford, handwritten response to *Philadelphia Weekly Times* articles written by Rosser (never printed), p.1, Munford–Ellis Papers, DU.

The hatred that Rosser and Munford felt for each other was demonstrated in Munford's attempts to convince everyone that he indeed was a brigadier general in the war. Rosser dismissed Munford's pleas as untrue—Munford was still just a colonel, and Rosser wanted everyone to know it. He fought back against the case which Munford presented for acceptance of his claims.

A dinner affair in 1895 illustrates the point of the ill-will each felt towards the other. General Rosser and Thomas Munford had both been invited to attend a banquet at the Colonial Hotel in Charlottesville. General Rosser did not attend the banquet because Munford was there and contemptuously called it "Munford assemblage."[2]

A *Charlottesville Progress* reporter issued the following statement from General Rosser, touching on "General" Munford:

> Col. Munford began the War as Lieutenant Colonel of the Second Virginia Cavalry, and at the close of the war he had only risen one file and came out of the war as Colonel of the Second Virginia Cavalry. While commanding my division and Fitzhugh Lee's division of the cavalry, I was short of brigadiers and had General W. H Payne promoted, as he was the best man I had. This greatly offended Col. Munford and his friends, and I was appealed to by them to recommend Munford instead of Payne. The latter's commission was held up in Richmond until I could be heard from, but Payne being a very superior man to Munford and low on the list of colonels, I could only make use of Payne's talent by promoting him, because he was outranked by other colonels in the command.[3]

Rosser pointed out that whatever talents Munford possessed were always available, as he was a senior cavalry service colonel. Rosser continued, "Munford never forgave me for this act. His insubordination and his want of co-operation when I was preparing for the expedition to Beverly, W.Va., made it necessary for me to put him under arrest and have him court-martialed. Hence, I can readily see why he should not want me at a banquet where he was parading under a borrowed uniform." Rosser concluded his statement, "Munford was an old colonel when I was transferred to the cavalry. He had served with Jackson, Stuart and Lee, and if they had not promoted him, I

---

2. *Staunton Spectator and Vindicator*, October 28, 1904. Munford had a general's uniform tailored for himself and proudly wore it to veteran's gatherings and around town.
3. Ibid.

don't see why he should have blamed me for his not having received a commission." The trouble between Thomas Rosser and Thomas Munford found its way into public publication 20 years earlier, when a reference in an article by the latter was interpreted as a reflection upon General Rosser's brigade in a certain battle of the Civil War.[4]

General Rosser, in correspondence which followed the published article, denied that Munford had ever been commissioned a general. The *Richmond Times Dispatch* reported that Mr. John E. Hill [Hull] of Albemarle County, a courier for Munford, claimed he delivered the commission of brigadier general to Colonel Munford in April 1865. A reporter of *The Progress* called on General Rosser and asked his authority for the statement published. In reply, General Rosser produced the following copy of the record in the matter and called attention to the absence of any endorsement showing that action had been taken:

> General, I have the honor to recommend that Col. Thos. T. Munford, 2d Va. Cav, senior Col. Wickham's (old) Brigade be promoted to be Brigadier General; Wickham, resigned, and that his commission date from the acceptance of Gen'l Wickham's resignation. Very respectfully, Yr. obt. sevt, Fitz Lee, Maj (Genl. Comd'g) Hdqrs Army N. Va., March 23, 1865. Resp'y forwarded and recommended. R. E. Lee. Genl. Rec'd A. & I. G. A. March 29, 1865.[5]

The newspaper article continued, "In regard to this controversy, we have received the following letter from an old Maryland Confederate R. S. Tuck, and a member of Breathed's celebrated battalion":

> What do you think of Fitz Lee at this late day joining Tom Rosser in an attack on one of Virginia's greatest, most reliable living soldiers, Gen. Tom Munford? Fitz Lee mentioned Munford as General in his Appomattox report, April 22, 1865, and also before the Warren Court of Enquiry in 1881, when he was under oath, and now stating in a letter to Gen. Marcus J. Wright, (this is the letter Rosser is banking on) that Munford never was a Brig. General. Some months after the war Fitz Lee wrote to Gen. Munford, as I am informed, requesting him to let him have all orders, reports, etc., in his possession as he wanted to make up a report for Gen. R. E. Lee, and Gen. Munford suspecting no bad faith from a man signing

---
4. Ibid.
5. Ibid.

himself "your friend," sent everything to Fitz Lee, his order for promotion to Brig. General, among them. Fitz Lee never returned those papers, and having Munford's papers that were loaned to him writes that letter to Gen. Wright. Is this the act of a "soldier and a gentleman?" A haunting remembrance lingers still, of that most disgraceful, most disastrous banquet, April 1st, 1861, at which Pickett, Fitz Lee and Rosser were loading up with "ammunition and shad," while Tom Munford was adding his brightest laurels to his already ample wreath. That occasion is the bottom of their attack on Munford. Yours truly, Frank Dorsey.[6]

It turns out Fitzhugh Lee's letter to Maj. Gen. Marcus Wright, written in February 1865, stated, "Munford was never commissioned Brig General. . . . I was obliged to have a Brig General for a Brigade and my recollection is that I published an order being in command of the Cavalry Corps putting Munford on duty as Brig Genl and to have such commission, providing the promotion received the approval of the Confederate War Department." Fitz Lee added, "I published the order. Of course, it was perfectly illegal and I could have been held responsible for exceeding my authority."[7]

Apparently, Munford didn't know anything of Fitzhugh Lee's letter to General Wright until 1904. He saw it as a betrayal of friendship, writing to Maj. Robert W. Hunter, "It is right difficult for a gentleman to sit with folded arms and hear things which make his heart swell with indignation." He told Hunter that Lee's letter was "unworthy of an officer who pretended to be my friend." He recalled, Lee had "issued the order announcing my promotion and unsolicited by me, and it was done in the usual way." Munford took a swipe at Lee, saying, "he was willing to clip my wings, because more was accomplished without him than with him." Munford and Fitz Lee had had cordial relations up until this point, but this letter cooled their friendship. Munford had even been the grand marshal of a parade welcoming Fitz Lee to Lynchburg during Lee's successful gubernatorial campaign of 1885. Munford recalled that their friendship had never been a close one, remembering that in all the time he had served in Fitz Lee's command, he had only been invited to dine with him twice.[8]

---

6. Ibid; Fitzhugh Lee to Thomas T. Munford, February 25, 1866, Munford–Ellis Papers, DU. Fitz Lee made use of but did not include Munford's report as part of his post-dated report of the Five Forks battle.
7. Fitzhugh Lee to General Marcus J. Wright, March 4, 1865, LC.
8. Thomas T. Munford to Major Robert W. Hunter, October 22, 1904, LVA.

It is generally recognized by historians that Munford was bypassed by others less qualified than he. Lieutenant M. H. Clark of Capt. G. Gaston Otey's Company of the Virginia Light Artillery wrote Munford, "No one during the war ever realized more than I did, among your many friends, the injustice done to you in the delay of your well merited promotion, for you should have been a Major General early in 1864. You know better than I do the strings that were pulled to put less worthy officers over your head time and again, and we admired your steady performance of duty under all of this injustice." The 4th Sergeant, Company I, of the 2nd Virginia recalled, "Every man in the Brigade felt the injustice done you in the way of promotions."[9]

Postwar Feuds

The days following the Civil War witnessed a scramble by both Confederate and Union commanders to enhance their wartime reputations and shift blame for failures, producing an overabundance of feuds, which more often than not, were between comrades-in-arms. These disputes "in ink" often raged until the last of the veterans passed away. Two of the more prominent Northern feuds pitted Philip H. Sheridan against Gouverneur K. Warren and George Meade versus Daniel Sickles. The Southerners, losers in the war, and aided by the "Lost Cause" mentality, produced a broader spectrum of disputes. John S. Mosby defended J.E.B. Stuart against anyone who blamed him for the defeat at Gettysburg. Purely personal ink wars raged between Joseph E. Johnston and John Bell Hood. One of the more fascinating and bitter feuds that developed during the war and lasting for decades after was between Confederate cavalry commanders Thomas L. Rosser and Tom Munford. A primary motivation for Munford's writings after the war was to "set the record straight," acknowledging the service of men overlooked during the war, counting himself among them. He once wrote, "my object is to do justice to my men." He was also adamant in defending his own war record, particularly against the likes of Rosser.[10]

Munford took command of Fitzhugh Lee's cavalry division late in the war, leading them at Five Forks, High Bridge, and Sailor's Creek. After the war, Munford was spoken of as "General" by other

---

9. M. H. Clark to Thomas T. Munford, April 29, 1899, Munford–Ellis Papers, DU; Charles W. Chick to Thomas L. Munford, August 9, 1886, Munford–Ellis Papers, DU.
10. Dr. James R. Jewell, "In Rivulets of Gray Ink: The Bloody Battles About the War (The Munford– Rosser Feud)," np, 1–2, copy in author's possession.

Confederate soldiers. Rosser, knowing where to hit Munford to make it hurt, denied publicly that Munford made brigadier general rank, stating, "I am in a position to state positively that T. T. Munford served under me as Colonel, and was never commissioned as brigadier general."[11]

In a speech Munford gave at a 1904 reunion of the members of the old Albemarle Light Horse, Company K, Second Virginia Cavalry, he told of a then-gallant lad, John E. Hull, who was detailed as a courier with General Fitzhugh Lee on the retreat from Five Forks. Munford said that "after the battle at High Bridge, Hull came to me, with beaming countenance and announced that he had brought my promotion, and delivered the order sent by General Fitz Lee." This statement was relied on by Munford as proof that his commission as full-fledged brigadier general reached him before Lee's men reached Appomattox and before they quit fighting.[12]

Rosser may have won the argument over Munford's official rank, but it was Rosser's reputation that suffered in the postwar years. Whereas Munford was generally fair in his assessment of everyone except Rosser in his writings, his nemesis shifted blame to others, claimed successes where he should not have, and dismissed his own defeats to such an extent that he damaged his esteem in the eyes of former comrades. For example, J.E.B. Stuart's adjutant, Henry McClellan, opined, "Rosser has, I expect, killed himself in the estimation of all the old cavalrymen outside his own brigade. Stuart made him what he was."[13]

R. S. Tuck recalled the culmination of Rosser's and Munford's abhorrence of each other occurred in the winter of 1864-65:

> Gen. Rosser was camped on the Washington Swope farm, near what is yet Swope on the C. & O. Ry., with Laws' Brigade in command of Col. T. T. Munford, was also camped there, and his, Col. M.'s, headquarters were in the home of the late Samuel H. Bell, where I was boarding. Gen. Rosser conceived of making a raid into Randolph county, (now W. Va.) and capturing a post at Beverly. What the controversies were between him and Gen. [Col.] Munford, I do not know, further than told by

---

11. Thomas L. Rosser to A. S. Perham, August 29, 1902, Perham Papers, LC; *Richmond Times Dispatch*, September 19, 25, 1904.
12. *Richmond Dispatch*, November 6, 1904.
13. Dr. James R. Jewell, "In Rivulets of Gray Ink: The Bloody Battles About the War (The Munford-Rosser Feud)," np., 7; Henry B. McClellan to T. T. Munford, August 7, 1884, Munford–Ellis Papers, DU. Rosser also switched his allegiance to the Republican Party for a time, which further lowered his esteem in the eyes of many.

the official records. Gen. Rosser had his headquarters at the old Washington Swope house, now the property of Mr. L D. Myerly. I never knew why Col. Munford did not accompany that expedition, but on the morning that Gen. Rosser started for Beverley, his command passed Mr. Bell's residence where Gen. [Col.] Munford's headquarters were. Gen. [Col.] Munford and staff came out on the front porch, Gen. Rosser rode up to the gate in front of house, threw his leg over the pommel of his saddle, wrote an order which we afterwards learned was an order of arrest for Gen. [Col.] Munford and sent it in by an orderly. Col. Munford, as he then was, as well as I now recall at the time of reading the order, had on his side arms and spurs, both of which I think he then took off. Col. Munford of course did not go to Beverley, Gen. Rosser did, and captured the place with several hundred prisoners, making one of the most arduous raids of the war, his men and his prisoners suffered desperately owing to the terrible weather that set in about that time. A court martial followed in which I understand Col. Munford was honorably acquitted, but of the merits of the controversy I know nothing beyond what has long been published. But the arrest of Col. Munford on that occasion occurred as I have stated at the residence of the late Samuel H. Bell in this county, and I was an eye witness to it.[14]

In 1884, General Rosser wrote a series of articles for the *Philadelphia Weekly Times* about the Shenandoah Valley Campaign of 1864. In these he criticized Early, blaming him for failing to group cavalry in the Shenandoah Valley under Lunsford Lomax (the senior cavalry commander), instead of making two division commanders report individually to Early himself. He was also critical of Early for sending him 25 miles ahead of the infantry at Tom's Brook to engage Sheridan, when the army commander knew Sheridan had far superior numbers. Infuriating Rosser also was General Early's assertion that General Payne, and not Rosser, deserved most of the credit for the success of the New Creek and Lacey Springs engagements. Rosser concluded his remarks with a stinging attack on Early: "Incompetency is not a crime, and that you failed in the Valley is not due to your neglect or carelessness, but I know you were assiduous, but God did not make you a general, and it was Gen. R. E. Lee's mistake in trusting so important a command as you had to you before you had been more fully tried."[15]

14. *Staunton Spectator and Vindicator*, October 28, 1904.
15. Bushong, *Fightin' Tom Rosser*, 198; *Philadelphia Weekly Times*, May 17, 1884.

In response to the articles Rosser wrote for the *Philadelphia Weekly Times*, adversaries such as Early and Thomas T. Munford responded, attacking the accuracy of his accounts of the war, point by point. Munford protested, "General Rosser gallops over his campaigns as though he held a kaleidoscope in his hand, but only turns it sufficiently to exhibit his own surprising ability and tactics." The feud that began during the war burned just as hot as it had 20 years earlier. Even Rosser's death in 1910 did not assuage Munford's sense of injured personal pride. He continued his criticisms of Rosser in monologue fashion.[16]

For his part, Munford reasserted his reasons for continuing his criticisms of Rosser, noting that he had given Rosser "the most loyal support I could give them [referring to Fitzhugh Lee also] in battle," but he had been left "a drift."[17]

Munford's criticisms seemed more accurate than Early's. To widen the dispute, Col. Mottrom Dulany Ball, who had led the 11th Virginia Cavalry, criticized Early's and Munford's accounts and supported Rosser's accounts.[18]

Louis E. Fisher, of the *Minneapolis Pioneer Press*, thanked Munford for his reply to Rosser's articles, stating that "many people in this far off region who have known Rosser for a number of years, and listened to his war stories (which seem somewhat Munchausen, but which they were unable to disprove) will be delighted that one so competent as yourself has plucked some of his plumes."[19]

Rosser became so incensed over Munford's reply to the *Philadelphia Weekly Times* that he issued a challenge of satisfaction (duel) through an intermediary. Munford wrote a friend that his reply "made Rosser so indignant with me and he knew it was true; so to ease himself, he sent me a challenge to 'relieve my wrath.' It tickled me to see what a fool he was, and amused me because instead of answering it in a square, manly way in the paper, he sent a challenge to me through another medium—who neither the cause nor the facts had appeared." For this act, Rosser lost his political rights, such as the right to hold elective office. In 1890, the General Assembly of Virginia passed an act

---

16. *Philadelphia Weekly Times*, May 17, 1884; Dr. James R. Jewell, "In Rivulets of Gray Ink: The Bloody Battles About the War (The Munford–Rosser Feud)," np., 3.
17. Jewell, "In Rivulets of Gray Ink: The Bloody Battles About the War (The Munford–Rosser Feud)," np., 8; T. T. Munford to Micajah Woods, October 8, 1904, Munford–Ellis Papers, DU.
18. *Philadelphia Weekly Times*, May 17, July 12, 1884.
19. Louis E. Fisher to Thomas T. Munford, May 17, 1884, Munford–Ellis Papers, DU.

to "remove the political difficulties of Gen. T. L. Rosser and others for dueling."[20]

Concerning the battle of Five Forks, Munford wrote John S. Mosby, in part:

> That Battle was the Waterloo of the Confederacy. Gen. R. E. Lee wrote Genl Hampton, "'Had you been there with all of your cavalry, the disaster would never have occurred." That "Shad dinner" was the bottom of the Disaster. If you will read Rosser's letter, published in the Phil Weekly Times . . . you will be amazed to see he has told the truth this time—and it exhibits a picture of shame, which Virginia will never forgive.[21]

The feud stemmed, in part, from Rosser's recommending of Col. William H. Payne, junior to Munford, for promotion to brigadier general. Munford felt aggrieved, and his ill will toward Rosser continued for the remainder of his life. Rosser stated that Munford was not promoted because he was not a man of sufficient coolness and judgment to command troops in battle. In a series of articles about the 1864 Shenandoah Valley campaign, and published in the *Southern Historical Society Papers*, Munford was quite critical of Rosser's handling of the cavalry at Tom's Brook. Munford also stated that Rosser's troopers were mortified by their commander's ego, and that he did not give them proper credit for their accomplishments.[22]

Rosser wrote one final time in the press of his disdain for Munford, saying, in part:

> I do not feel that my reputation requires vindication from your feeble assaults, but I cannot repress my indignation at your deliberate falsehood, when I know that malice and a desire to injure me are your only incentives. You deliberately, willfully and basely state an untruth and make it with quotation marks as the language of Gen. Early. This is baseness which I believe no gentleman could be guilty of and, holding this opinion of you, I cannot take further notice of you through the press.[23]

---

20. Thomas Taylor Munford to Senator John W. Daniel, July 20, 1905, Munford–Ellis Family Papers, DU; Akers, Thesis, 122, Virginia Tech; *Journal of the Senate of Virginia* (Richmond, 1899), 367.
21. Thomas T. Munford to John S. Mosby, Private Collection, RR Auctions, Catalog April 2014, Item 435, Boston, MA.
22. Bushong, *Fightin' Tom Rosser*, 198–99.
23. *The St. Paul Daily Globe*, February 11, 1896.

Chapter Twenty-One

Plantation Life in Alabama and Remembering a Fallen Soldier

Colonel Munford was remembered as a "very handsome man who carried himself in such a fine manner that his slight height was hardly noticeable.... The General always dressed immaculately, wearing a large broadbrimmed hat, a black cutaway coat, and a perfectly white cravat. A gold chain crossed the front of his black waistcoat."

> –Typed biography of Thomas T. Munford, p. 4, Jones Memorial Library, Lynchburg, Virginia.

Oakland Plantation, Uniontown, Alabama

Tom Munford spent winters at his Alabama plantation, and moved there permanently after his wife's death in 1910. There, he remained for the rest of his life. He supported an impressive government crop diversification study. He also hosted festive barbeques, including one of the largest in the South. He continued his important writing about the Civil War. He became cantankerous as he aged, often at odds with his daughter-in-law, Courtney Norton Munford.

Thomas Munford's wife, Emma, had inherited a large Alabama plantation, "Oakland," from her father, William H. Tayloe. Mrs. Munford preferred living in Lynchburg to plantation life in the country, and therefore stayed in Lynchburg when Tom traveled to Oakland for extended stays, particularly over winter months. In 1900, the couple's 27-year-old son, Glen, was still living with his parents at their home in Lynchburg, a comfort to Emma when Tom was away.[1]

Thomas T. Munford arrived in Alabama to manage his inherited plantation, "in the midst of mud, worry, Negroes, and hard times." As

---

1. Thomas T. Munford to Lafayette McLaws, April 9, 1895, Munford–Ellis Papers, DU; 1900 Federal Census for Campbell County, Virginia.

time went on, "creditors threatened him with humiliating lawsuits for small sums." Merchants did not advance money, despite Munford's vast family collateral. Things got so hectic that Munford was said to have "fantasized about being a sea captain with a good crew, far away from worrying mail and telegrams."[2]

Tom, with profits from selling his mines, purchased two additional nearby cotton farms, called "Bryant" and "Ormand," in Alabama. Tom and Emma's sons, William T. Munford, Thornton Munford, and Sinclair Munford lived on, worked, and managed the Alabama farms. Mr. Cornelius Gilliam, caretaker of the Munford's home in Lynchburg, recalled that his son, Henry G. Gilliam, went south to the Munford's Alabama plantations to work for the Munfords. A skilled mechanic, Henry kept the farm machinery in good working order for William Munford on the "East Side Place." The farm had livestock, such as mules, riding horses, brood mares, a Guernsey herd, sheep, and hogs. Feed was grown for the livestock. Young Gilliam's wife became lonely and homesick after about a year, and so they moved back to Lynchburg. Gilliam and William Munford had become fast friends and remained close the rest of their lives.[3]

Tom Munford's son, Willian Tayloe Munford, remembered that 35 African-Americans worked on the plantation.[4] Tom Munford recalled that the blacks working his planation, "as a whole, they are obedient, and although not industrious, do well by being watched." Munford further observed that "the negroes in this country are wild with money and crazy for mules and horses. Planters are renting them land and resorting to every device to get them from one place to another."[5]

William Munford, a hard-working, strong-willed, positive gentleman, doted on his father, and tried to keep any problems from him. Gilliam recalled that when anything went wrong, William would plead, "don't let Dad know about it; I don't want him to worry."[6]

Tom Munford received a U. S. Patent for the invention of a metallic bale covering for cotton. Heretofore, in bailing cotton, the lint-cotton was compressed into a suitable bale and held with bands

---

2. Michael W. Fitzgerald, Reconstruction in Alabama: From Civil War to Redemption in the Cotton South (Baton Rouge, 2017), 293; T. T. Munford to H. A. Tayloe, Dec. 6, 24, 1873, Jan 6, 14, 1874, Reel 17, Tayloe Family Papers, VHS.
3. Copy of Bill in Real Estate Suit, Munford Papers, Jones Memorial Library, Lynchburg, Virginia; *The Lynchburg News*, August 2, 1953; William Tayloe Munford, *Fond Memories* (Petersburg, VA, 1992), 1.
4. William Tayloe Munford, *Fond Memories* (Petersburg, VA, 1992), 1.
5. Michael W. Fitzgerald, *Reconstruction in Alabama: From Civil War to Redemption in the Cotton South* (Baton Rouge, 2017), 234; Thomas T. Munford to H. A. Tayloe, December 8, 1869, Tayloe Papers, Reel 17, VHS.
6. *The Lynchburg News*, August 2, 1953.

Munford's Oakland Plantation, near Uniontown, Alabama before addition.

(Courtesy: Virginia Historical Society)

and ties. This, however, was not suitable as the cotton was left exposed to the elements, resulting in waste or destruction by water, fire, or theft. Munford's invention involved a covering made of metallic sheets held together by rivets, screws, nails, bolts, or other fastening devices, entirely enclosing the cotton bale, thus protecting it.[7]

Oakland, the Munford's 2300-acre plantation, was located just three miles outside of Uniontown, Alabama. Uniontown is situated in the southwestern part of Perry County and lies in the western section of the area known as the Canebrake, a portion of the Black Belt Prairie traditionally recognized as one of the richest farming areas in Alabama.[8]

Oakland was a beautiful farmstead, typical of the plain, but cozy dwellings of the new South, where Colonel Munford made a remarkable showing of what can be done by intensive farming. The home was a Victorian style frame house, with great verandas and wide-open hospitable portals, nestling amid live oaks and wide fields. Certainly, Oakwood marked the realization of the model farm of which agriculturists dream. Here, Tom, and occasionally Emma, entertained friends with that kindly, old-fashioned hospitality that has always characterized the families of the old Southern aristocracy.[9]

"Old Tom," as Tom was known, was in relatively good health at this point in his life, but he did suffer with gout. He had his own room and bath added on to the old place later, as well as his own porch, replete with rocking chair. Tom Munford had one of the largest cape jasmine bushes around, and he loved it. There were rose bushes, peacocks which screamed about, sheep, goats, and a dozen beehives. In his room were four windows, white curtains softly blowing in the air, a wood stove, a Confederate flag hanging over a roll-top desk, and a rocking chair. He had his favorite pet, an English pug. Most days, "General" Munford, as he was known by many Uniontown citizens, rode his carriage into Uniontown to visit with friends, discussing the war and other topics.[10]

William Munford married his cousin Courtenay Norton Tayloe in 1908, and William Tayloe, Jr. was born in 1910. Courtenay, who some knew as Norton, was known as a "take-charge" woman, and soon, she was supervising everything—the raising of hogs and the 300 chickens shipped to market every year. When William's wife arrived at the

---

7. United States Patent 662801A, Metallic bale–covering, August 28, 1899.
8. "The Black Belt of Alabama," *National Magazine*, May 1911, 455.
9. Ibid.
10. William Tayloe Munford, *Fond Memories* (Dietz Press, 1992), 4–5, 12. Family letters in the Munford–Ellis Papers, DU, and the Federal censuses indicate Courtenay went by her middle name, "Norton."

Thomas T. Munford sitting on the porch of his plantation, Oakland, near Uniontown, Alabama. Circa 1900

(Courtesy: Virginia Historical Society)

plantation, an indoor bathroom was installed in the house. A kitchen was also added, whereas before, cooking was done in a small room away from the house. Other out buildings included a chicken house, stables, cow barn, pigeon house, and a dairy. Norton tended to rule over everything; she and Tom Munford did not always see eye-to-eye on matters. Not helping matters was the fact that Tom had become increasingly cantankerous in his elderly years.[11]

Crop Diversification Study

In 1904, the State of Alabama, through Professor J. F. Duggar, Director of the Agricultural Experiment Station of the Alabama Polytechnic Institute, and Professor W. J. Spillman, Agriculturist in Charge of Farm Management Investigations, in conjunction with Tom and William Munford, instituted a diversification farm to study crop rotation. The test farm was established on a 65-acre hog farm, a part of

11. Ibid.

From Left to Right: William Tayloe Munford (son of Thomas Taylor Munford), William Tayloe Munford, Jr., and Thomas Taylor Munford.

Oakland Plantation, near Uniontown, Alabama
Circa 1915

(Courtesy: Virginia Historical Society)

the Munford farm. The farming method utilized included emphasis on increasing the fertility of the soil and reducing the cost of tillage by doing away with hillside ditches and adopting improved methods of cultivation.[12]

William Tayloe Munford was in "active charge" of the diversification farm. The government's policy was to furnish the planter with the seed and half the fertilizer for the first of the year and to give the Munfords the benefit of all returns from the farm. On their part, the Munfords furnished the soil and the labor, and in addition kept a close record not only of all work struck on the farm, but of matters which related to the diversification farm.[13]

---

12. M. A. Crosby, J. F. Duggar, and W. J. Spillman, Farmers' Bulletin No. 51, "A Successful Alabama Diversification Farm," (Washington, Government Printing Office, 1907), 2, 5–7, 23–24; *Roanoke Times*, August 9, 1893; William Tayloe Munford, *Fond Memories* (Dietz Press, 1992), 1.

13. The Alabama Opportunity: "Observations Upon and Descriptions of the Rapid Commercial, Industrial and Agricultural Advancement of Alabama in Recent Years, Published by the Department of Agriculture and Industries," R. R. Poole, Commissioner, October, 1906, 115.

Data was collected for three years. The results showed the farm yielded a net profit of $2,320 in the three-year period. This was an average yearly profit of about $11.90 an acre on land valued at $20 per acre, a respectable return. Included in the study was hog production, alfalfa, corn, cow peas, peanuts, sorghum, cotton, and winter barley. The three-year study proved that the methods of crop rotation used could be made profitably in southern states in regions where alfalfa can be grown successfully. The emphasis was more on increasing the fertility of the land and getting it in a good state of cultivation, rather than in a state of securing large yields.[14]

The Festive Barbeques

Barbeques were hosted by many of the plantation owners during July and August of each year. They were, for the most part, strictly gentlemen-only affairs, with large crowds gathering, dressed in their Sunday best clothes. At least a week before one of these events, pits were dug, about four feet wide, two feet deep, and at least 10 feet in length.[15]

The pig carcasses were cooked overnight over hickory fires before the festivities, while a crew of women prepared gumbo, adding chicken hens, vegetables, masses of red peppers, okra, green peppers, onions, corn, and butter beans into two huge black iron kettles suspended from tripods over the hickory fires. A neighbor—often one deemed an expert chef—supervised the entire cooking process for this and other nearby neighbor's barbeques. When Oakland hosted such an affair, Tom and son William spent most of the night going back and forth from the house to the cooking site to assure that all was going well. Even though he often spoke out about the evils of liquor, Tom Munford usually tasted the gumbo and a little bourbon.[16]

At the July 23, 1909, Munford barbeque, prior to dinner, there were several addresses by experts on the subject of diversified farming. These speakers were from the Agricultural Department of the United States, laymen from other states, as well as prominent farmers of Alabama and included Professor J. H. Spillman, of the Bureau of Plant Industry, Washington, and Professor Hunter, entomologist of the United States Agricultural Bureau. Several other authorities from the

---

14. M. A. Crosby, J. F. Duggar, and W. J. Spillman, *Farmers' Bulletin* No. 51, "A Successful Alabama Diversification Farm" (Washington, Government Printing Office, 1907), 2, 5–7, 23–24.
15. William Tayloe Munford, *Fond Memories*, 5.
16. Ibid.

Oakland Plantation Barbeque, "Largest barbeque in the South." July 23, 1909

Thomas T. Munford shown on the far right.

(Courtesy: Virginia Historical Society)

Agricultural Department spoke about the growing of alfalfa and the breeding of cattle. Tom Munford had 1,200 acres in alfalfa under cultivation on his plantation, and this crop was used as a demonstration to those wanting to grow such a crop.[17]

The 1909 Munford event was one of the largest barbeques ever held in the South. There was ice there for the drinks, but many of the men drank their bourbon "straight up." After the huge barbeque dinner attended by scores of men, some of the gentlemen lay down on the ground for a nap before returning to their homes.[18]

Just a year after the big barbeque event, Emma Munford, who had suffered heart trouble for years, finally succumbed to the disease on September 17, 1910. She died at the couple's residence in Lynchburg. In Emma's will, she bequeathed the Lynchburg home to their son, Glen. Tom knew nothing about this bequeath in advance, but honored it in respect for Emma.[19]

---

17. (Charlotte) *Evening Chronicle*, July 23, 1909.
18. Munford, *Fond Memories*, 5–6.
19. *Richmond Times Dispatch*, September 18, 1910.

After Emma's death, Tom, who continued to suffer from gout, spent the last years of his life on his plantation at Uniontown, Alabama, dying there on February 27, 1918. Eight-year-old grandson, William Tayloe Munford, Jr., recalled seeing his grandfather's body lying on a long flat table that had iron legs, "his mustache gleaming and his hair parted on the left side as always." His hands were folded over his chest, his Confederate uniform folded by his side. His body was laid in a black hearse with glass sides, pulled by two horses. Most, if not all the African-American workers on the farm stood as a group, with many of them crying in respect to "General" Munford, as the caravan rode along to the railway station, where Thomas Munford's body was loaded aboard a train and returned to Lynchburg for burial. At the funeral, young William Tayloe Munford, Jr., too small to be a pall bearer, walked up the aisle, his hands on the General's casket. He wore a VMI uniform that had been made for him. Tom Munford was buried with his saber.[20]

The funeral was held at St. Paul's Episcopal Church in Lynchburg on March 3, 1918, with full military honors. He was buried next to his wife, Emma, in the Spring Hill Cemetery. Inexplicably, an appropriate grave marker was not placed at his grave until 1953.[21]

Remembering a Fallen Soldier

"General" Munford was remembered as a "very handsome man who carried himself in such a fine manner that his slight height was hardly noticeable. . . . The General always dressed immaculately, wearing a large broadbrimmed hat, a black cutaway coat, and a perfectly white cravat. A gold chain crossed the front of his black waistcoat." He was described as "one of the handsomest men of his day. Even in old age, with snow white hair, piercing dark eyes, fine features, and an erect soldierly carriage, he bore nobly the tradition of an honored name and added luster to a high cause." Jubal Early described Munford in later life as a "small man, with dark, bright eyes, and white hair, nearly white mustache, otherwise clean shaven. Well dressed, too, and the only of the veterans that was."[22]

---

20. Munford, *Fond Memories*, 12–13; Information from Thomas T. Munford's great–granddaughter, Estelle Call.
21. Report of Commissioners of the will of Thomas T. Munford, May 6, 1918, VHS; 1947 Typed biography of General Munford, Jones Memorial Library, Lynchburg, Virginia; *The (Lynchburg) News*, March 29, 1953; William Tayloe Munford, *Fond Memories*, 12–13.
22. Typed biography of Thomas T. Munford, p. 4, Jones Memorial Library, Lynchburg, Virginia; Library of Virginia, Works Projects Administration of Virginia, Historical Inventory, Virginia Conservation Commission, 1937;

Colonel Thomas T. Munford

In his later years, had his portrait made wearing a brigadier general's uniform. He was generally recognized as having attained the rank, even though he never received a commission. The portrait is a striking life-likeness, executed by Bernard Gutman of Lynchburg, Virginia, in 1899.

(Courtesy: V.M.I. Archives)

Captain John Lamb said of Munford, "The officers and men of his command soon learned to appreciate his soldierly bearing and gave him loyal support, while his excellent qualities of head and heart endeared him to all who were thrown in social intercourse with him. In winter quarters and around camp fires the non-commissioned officers and privates conversed as freely with him as they would have in the social circle of their own homes."[23]

Lamb continued:

> During the war with Spain I made application for a commission for General Munford. Had his letter authorizing me to see the Secretary of War and the President, and offer his services to the government, been received two weeks sooner than it was, I feel sure he would have been given a commission. With his accustomed modesty, he neglected to ask for the endorsements he could so easily have obtained, and wrote me to offer his services, saying that no one knew him better than I did, and that he was satisfied to leave the matter with me.[24]

Thomas Munford left a treasure trove of information about the war as part of his legacy. His passion for "setting the record straight" and recording the events and contributions of his troopers was remarkable. Also, his obsession with making sure everyone knew and respected him as a general officer, left us with a wealth of information about the players in this drama. He was a respected, competent commander who should have been promoted to the brigadier rank by 1863.

Thomas Taylor Munford was a competent cavalry commander, at every level from regiment to division. He loved his troops as much as they loved him. He was a soldier's soldier, who often visited troops gathered around a campfire to talk with them, not as just their commander, but as a benevolent leader and friend. He knew many of the men personally. He sent sincere, heartfelt letters to the families of his men that died in service under his command. He fought and argued with his superiors for his troopers' problems or grievances. He looked after their interests. This was a man who sincerely cared about them. He was immensely proud of them and his regiment.

Leading them into battle, often at the head of a charge, he was respected by officers and troopers alike. During the conflict, he was a

---

"An Interview with Jubal A. Early," *The Journal of Southern History*, Vol. 11, No. 4 (Nov. 1945), 547–63.
23. *SHSP*, R. A. Brock, ed., (Richmond: William Ellis Jones, 1904), vol. 32:6.
24. Ibid., 10.

man of few words, direct and to the point— something he may have learned from Professor Thomas Jonathan Jackson while at VMI. Munford was passed over for promotion to brigadier general many times, sometimes by men less qualified than he. He was convinced a primary reason was he was not a member of the West Point elite, and that his commanders and the powers in Richmond were biased against him. Against that perception was the fact that other cavalry commanders, such as Wade Hampton, James Byron Gordon, and William H. Payne, none of whom attended West Point, were promoted to the brigadier rank.

Thomas Munford was not a dashing cavalryman in the mold of J.E.B. Stuart. Unlike his nemesis Thomas L. Rosser, he was not one of Stuart's protégés. From Stuart's perspective, the apex of Munford's career came in the fall of 1862 when he recommended him for promotion. However, that was before the June 9, 1863 battle of Brandy Station. It was there that Munford disappointed Stuart, even though Stuart had sent Munford ambiguous orders, calling him to Fleetwood Hill during the height of the battle. Munford misinterpreted the orders and in doing so, arrived near the end of the fight for the hill. Stuart held this tardiness against him; yet he still recommended him, however, for promotion.

For Munford's part, he thought Stuart was a great fighting commander, but he viewed him as being very vain, too much of a partier, and one who showed a disregard for the health of the cavalry's horses. Munford alleged Stuart too often took unnecessary risks with the safety of his own troopers, conducting what he thought were overly taxing, dangerous, and unnecessary raids. He also thought Stuart did Robert E. Lee a disservice during the Gettysburg campaign. Stuart must not have been completely aware of Munford's increasing contempt for him, although Munford hinted and perhaps even argued with him about the well-being of his troopers and their horses. From Brandy Station to Gettysburg, to Munford's unachieved promotion, Munford's attitude toward Stuart rose to the level of outright disdain.

Even though he never received a formal commission as a brigadier general, he deserved that promotion. In the last weeks of the war, he claimed the rank of brigadier by virtue of a battlefield promotion to brigadier, by way of a corps order from Fitz Lee. Lee's recommendation was never acted upon by either President Davis or the Confederate Senate. There simply wasn't time; the war ended. Officially, Thomas T. Munford ended the war as Robert E. Lee's most senior cavalry colonel.

Munford spent the rest of his life convincing everyone he was a general. In the postwar period, he was no longer a man of few words, but wrote and spoke volumes concerning the war. Munford urged friendly relations with Northerners, especially those soldiers he had fought in battle. He was humble in his relationships with them, showing them respect for their service. He gladly supplied them information when they requested, as they often did.

During his own life, Tom Munford played a prominent role in shaping the historical narrative about the war in Virginia. His massive effort has resulted in a true wealth of information, spread to a number of archives, for which the modern Civil War historian owes a great debt.

BIBLIOGRAPHY

Primary Sources

Manuscripts and Special Collections

Antietam National Battlefield Visitor Center Archives:
    E. A. Carmen Papers.

Boston University:
    John C. Ropes Letters.
    Brooke, Autography, VHS.

Bowdoin College, Curtis Library; Pejepscot Historical Society, Brunswick, Maine.
    Joshua Lawrence Chamberlain Papers.

Duke University, Perkins Library, Durham, North Carolina
    Diary of J. D. Ferguson, Munford-Ellis Papers.
    Diary of 1st Corporal James H. Hopkins, Munford-Ellis Papers.
    Munford-Ellis Papers.

Emory University, Atlanta, Georgia
    Stuart Papers, Robert W. Woodruff Library

Fredericksburg and Spotsylvania National Military Park
    Peter L. Huddleston Diary, typescript on file.

Jones Memorial Library, Lynchburg, Virginia
    Thomas T. Munford Papers.

Library of Congress, Washington, D. C.
    A. S. Perham Collection.
    Jedediah Hotchkiss Papers.

Library of Virginia, Richmond, Virginia.
    Williams C. Wickham Papers.
    Thomas H. Ellis Papers.

National Archives, Washington, D.C.
> Compiled Service Records of Confederate Soldiers Who Served in Organizations
> From the State of Virginia, Record Group109, 1960.
> Compiled Service Records of Confederate Generals and Staff Officers, and Nonregimental Enlisted Men, Record Group 109, 1960.
> Complied Service Record for Thomas T. Munford.
> Confederate States Army Inspection Reports.
> Confederate Applications for Presidential Pardons, 1865-1867.

New York Public Library
> E. A. Carmen Papers.
> North Carolina Division of Archives and History, Raleigh, North Carolina.
> United States Population Schedules for the 1850, 1860, 1870, 1880, and 1900 Censuses of Virginia.

Pennsylvania State Museum and Library, Harrisburg, Pennsylvania.
> Samuel M. Potter Letters.

Virginia Military Institute, Lexington, Virginia.
> Merit Roll, Virginia Military Institute, Lexington, Va., 1849-1850, 1851-1852.
> Thomas Munford Letters.
> The Cadet Newspaper.
> Diary of I. Norval Baker, 18th Virginia Cavalry.

Virginia Tech, Blacksburg, Virginia.
> Anne Trice Thompson Akers, "Colonel Thomas T. Munford and the Last Cavalry Operations of the Civil War in Virginia," Master's Thesis, 1981.

U. S. Army Military History Institute, Carlisle Barracks, Pennsylvania.
> August V. Kautz Papers.

University of North Carolina at Chapel Hill, North Carolina.
> Anne Bachman Hyde Papers.

University of Michigan, Ann Arbor, Michigan.
> George W. Hunt Memoir, George W. Hunt Papers, William L. Clements Library.

University of Virginia, Manuscripts and Special Collections, Albert and Shirley Small Special Collections Library, Charlottesville, Virginia.
> William Henry Burnley Letters.
> William Henry Burnley Letters MSS7871.

Garber Manuscript, Library of Virginia.
Irving P. Whitehead Papers, "Campaigns of (Munford's) 2nd Virginia Cavalry."
Beverly K. Whittle Papers.
Edwin R. Page Letters.
Thomas L. Rosser Papers.
Samuel B. Gilliam Papers.

Virginia Commonwealth University Library, Richmond, Virginia.
Robertson Hospital Register, Digital Collections.

Virginia Historical Society, Richmond, Virginia.
William Clark Corson Papers.
"Autobiography of St. George Tucker Brooke."
Frank Dorsey, "A Sketch of Brigadier General Thomas T. Munford and Lieutenant Colonel Gus W. Dorsey," Dorsey Papers.
Thomas T. Munford, "The Last Days of Fitz Lee's Division of Cavalry."
Thomas T. Munford, "Five Forks: The Waterloo of the Confederacy."
Colonel Cary Breckenridge Papers.

Washington and Lee University, Lexington, Virginia.
Baxter Family Papers, Washington and Lee University.
Robert E. Lee Papers.

Newspapers

Arlington (Virginia) Gazette.
Baltimore Sun.
Daily Confederate (Raleigh).
Daily Progress, Charlottesville, Virginia.
Lynchburg Daily News.
New York Times, 1865.
Philadelphia Weekly Times, 1881, 1883.
Richmond Dispatch, 1864.
Richmond Enquirer, 1861, 1864.
Richmond Whig.
Shreveport Daily News.
Staunton Spectator.

Published and Unpublished Sources

Alexander, E. P. *Military Memoirs of a Confederate: A Critical Narrative*. New York: Charles Scribner's Sons, 1907.

Allan, Elizabeth Preston. *The Life and Letters of Margaret Junkin Preston*. New York: Houghton, Mifflin, and Company, 1903.

Andrew, Rod. *Wade Hampton: Confederate Warrior to Southern Redeemer*. Chapel Hill: UNC Press, 2008.

Armstrong, Richard L. *7th Virginia Cavalry*. Lynchburg: H. E. Howard, 1992.

_____ *11th Virginia Cavalry*. Lynchburg: H. E. Howard, 1989.

Atkins, John H., ed. *1863 Civil War Diary of Corporal John Irving*. Salem, OR: Atkins Enterprises, 2014.

Baltz, Shirley Vlasak. *A Chronicle of Belair*. Bowie, Maryland: Bowie Heritage Committee, 1984.

_____ *Belair From the Beginning*. Bowie, Maryland: City of Bowie Museums, 2005.

Beale, George William, *A Lieutenant of Cavalry in Lee's Army*. Boston: The Gorham Press, 1918.

Bearss, Edward and Chris Calkins. *The Battle of Five Forks*. Lynchburg: H. E. Howard, 1985.

Beaty, John O. *John Esten Cooke, Virginian*. New York: Columbia University Press, 1922.

Beck, Brandon H. and Charles S. Grunder, Second Edition, "The Three Battles of Winchester: A History and Guided Tour." Berryville, Virginia.: The Civil War Foundation, 1988.

Besley, William B. and Gilbert Guion Wood. *History of the Sixth New York Cavalry: Second Brigade -- First Division -- Cavalry Corps*. Nabu Press, 2010.

Blackford, Captain Charles M. "An Address delivered before the Garland-Rodes Camp Of Confederate Veterans" at Lynchburg, Virginia, July 18, 1901. *Southern Historical Society Papers*, Volume 30.

Blackford, Charles Minor, III, ed., *Letters from Lee's Army*. New York: Charles Scribner & Sons, 1947.

Blackford, Susan Lee and Charles Minor Blackford. *Letters from Lee's Army*. Lincoln, Nebraska: University of Nebraska Press, 1998.

Blackford, W. W. *War Years with JEB Stuart*. Baton Rouge: LSU Press, 1993.

Bliss, George N. "A Review of Aldie." *Maine Bugle*, Vol. 1, 1894.

Borcke, Heros Von. *Memoirs of the Confederate War for Independence*. Philadelphia: J. P. Lippincott & Co., 1867.

Brock, Robert A. and Virgil A. Lewis. *Virginia and Virginians: Eminent Virginians*. Richmond: H. H. Hardesty, 1888.

Brooks, U. R. *Stories of the Confederacy*. Columbia, South Carolina: The State Company, 1912.

Brown, Philip F. *Reminiscences of the War of 1861-1865*. Richmond: Whittet and Shepperson, 1917.

Burton, Brian K. *Extraordinary Circumstances: The Seven Days Battles.* Bloomington, Indiana: Indiana University Press, 2001.

Bushong, Millard K and Dean M. Bushong. *Fightin' Tom Rosser.* Shippensburg, Pennsylvania: Beidel Printing House, Inc., 1983.

Calkins, Chris. "Hold Five Forks at All Hazards," *Blue and Gray Magazine* (April 1992).

Casdorph, Paul D. *Prince John Magruder: His Life and Campaigns.* New York: Wiley, 1996.

Carter, William R., Walbrook D. Swank, ed. *Sabres, Saddles and Spurs.* Shippensburg, Pennsylvania: Burd Street Press, 1998.

Chadwick, F. E. *Causes of the Civil War.* American Nation Series. New York, 1906, Vol. 19.

Chamberlain, Joshua Lawrence. *Passing of the Armies: An Account of the Final Campaign.* Lincoln, Nebraska: University of Nebraska Press, 1998.

Clark, Walter, ed. *Histories of the Several Regiments and Battalions in the Great War, 1861-1865.* Raleigh: North Carolina Division of Archives and History, 1901, 5 Volumes.

Cooke, John Esten. *Stonewall Jackson: A Military Biography.* New York: D. Appleton and Company, 1866.

_____ *Wearing of the Gray.* Bedford, Massachusetts: Applewood Books, 1867.

Convis, Charles L. *The Honor of Arms: A Biography of Myles W. Keogh.* Westernlore Press, 2010.

Corbell, La Salle (Mrs. George E. Pickett). *Pickett and His Men.* Atlanta: Foote and Davies, 1899.

Corson, Blake W., Jr., ed. William Clark Corson, *My Dear Jennie: A Collection of Love Letters from a Confederate Soldier to His Fiancee During the Period 1861-1865.* Richmond: 1982.

Cozzens, Peter. *General John Pope: A Life for the Nation.* Chicago: University of Illinois Press, 2000.

Cozzens, Peter and Robert I. Girardi., ed. John Pope, *The Military Memoirs of General John Pope.* Chapel Hill: UNC Press, 1998.

Crosby, M. A., J. F. Duggar, and W. J. Spillman. *Farmers' Bulletin* No. 51, "A Successful Alabama Diversification Farm." Washington, D. C.: Government Printing Office, 1907.

Cullen, Joseph P. *The Peninsula Campaign, 1862.* Harrisburg, Pennsylvania: Stackpole Books, 1973.

Current, Richard N, (Editor in Chief). *Encyclopedia of the Confederacy.* New York: Simon and Schuster, 1993. Five Volumes.

Daughtry, Mary Bandy. *Gray Cavalier: The Life and Wars of General W. H. F. "Rooney" Lee.* Cambridge, Massachusetts: Da Capo Press, 2002.

Davis, Burke. *The Last Cavalier: J.E.B. Stuart.* New York: Fairfax Press, 1988.

_____ *To Appomattox: Nine April Days, 1865.* New York: Rhinehart & Company, 1959.

Davis, Varina. *Jefferson Davis, Ex-President of the Confederate States of America: A Memoir.* New York: Belford Company, 1890.

De Meissner, Sophie Radford. *Old Navy Days: Sketches from the Life of Rear Admiral William Radford, U.S.N.* New York, Henry Holt & Company, 1920.

Downey, Fairfax. *The Clash of Cavalry: The Battle of Brandy Station.* New York: David McKay Company, Inc., 1959. Reprinted in 1987 by Olde Soldier Books, Inc., Gaithersburg, Maryland.

Driver, Robert J. *1st Virginia Cavalry.* Lynchburg, Virginia: H. E. Howard Regimental Series,1991.

_____ *2nd Virginia Cavalry.* Lynchburg, Virginia: H. E. Howard Regimental Series,1995.

_____ *5th Virginia Cavalry.* Lynchburg, Virginia: H. E. Howard Regimental Series,1997.

Dudrow, Mark. "2nd Lieutenant William A. McIlhenny: Diary of a Soldier." Emmitsville, Maryland: Maryland Historical Society. nd.

Early, Lieutenant General Jubal Anderson. *Autobiographical Sketch and Narrative of the War Between the States.* Philadelphia: J. B. Lippincott Company, 1912.

Eicher, John H., and Eicher, David J. *Civil War High Commands.* Stanford, California: Stanford University Press, 2001.

Evans, General Clement A., ed. *Confederate Military History.* 12 Vols. New York: Thomas Yoseloff.

Faust, Patricia L. *Historical Times Illustrated Encyclopedia of the Civil War.* New York: Harper Perennial, 1991.

Foner, Eric. *Reconstruction: America's Unfinished Revolution, 1863-1877.* New York: Harper & Row, 1993.

Fonerden, C. A. *A Brief History of the Military Career of Carpenter's Battery: From its Organization as a Rifle Company Under the Name of the Alleghany Roughs to the Ending of the War Between the States.* Baltimore, Maryland: Butternut Press, 1983.

Ford, Worthington C., ed. *A Cycle of Adams Letters, 1861-1865.* Two Volumes. Boston: Houghton Mifflin, 1920.

Frank, William R. "Virginia's So-Called Government: The Story of the Restored Government of Virginia, in Alexandria." n.p., n.d.

Freeman, Douglas Southall. *The South to Prosperity: An Introduction to the Writing of Confederate History.* Baton Rouge: LSU Press, 1998.

_____ *A Study in Command.* New York: Charles Scribner's Sons, 1942. Three Volumes.

_____ *Lee's Lieutenants.* 3 Volumes. New York: Charles Scribner's Sons, 1970.

_____ *R. E. Lee.* Vol. II. New York, 1934.

Frye, Dennis E. *12th Virginia Cavalry.* Lynchburg, Virginia: H. E. Howard, 1988.

Gallagher, Gary W. *The Shenandoah Valley Campaign of 1864.* Chapel Hill: UNC Press, 2006.

_____ ed., *The Spotsylvania Campaign.* Chapel Hill: UNC Press, 1998.

Garnett, Theodore Stanford. *Riding with Stuart: Reminiscences of an Aide-de-Camp*. Robert J. Trout, ed. Shippensburg, Pennslylvania: White Mane Publishing Company, 1994.

Gatto, Kimberly. *Belair Stud: The Cradle of Horseracing*. Charleston, South Carolina: The History Press, 2012.

Goldsborough, William Worthington. *The Maryland Line in the Confederate Army, 1861-1865*. Baltimore, MD: Guggenheimer, Weil & Co., 1900.

Goodhart, Briscoe, *History of the Independent Loudoun Virginia Rangers*. Washington, D.C.: McGill & Wallace, 1896.

Gracey, Rev. S. L. *Annals of the Sixth Pennsylvania Cavalry*. Philadelphia: E. H. Butler & Company, 1868.

Greeley, Horace. *American Conflict*, Vol. I. Kessinger Publishing, 2005.

Guggenheimer, W. W. *The Maryland Line in the in the Confederate Army, 1861-1865*. Baltimore: Guggenheimer, Weil & Company, 1900.

Haden, Sergeant B. J. *Reminiscences of J. E. B. Stuart's Cavalry*. Palmyra, Virginia, 1993.

Hall, Clark B. "The Battle of Brandy Station." *Civil War Times Illustrated* (May/June 1990).

Harrell, Roger H. *The 2nd North Carolina Cavalry*. Jefferson, North Carolina: McFarland and Company Publishers, 2004.

Harsh, Joseph L. Harsh. *Taken at the Flood: Robert E. Lee and the Confederate Strategy in the Maryland Campaign of 1962*. Kent, Ohio: Kent State University Press, 2000.

Hart, Albert B., Ed. *The American Nation: Slavery and Abolition, 1831-1841*. New York: Harper and Brothers, 1906.

Hartwig, David S. *To Antietam Creek: The Maryland Campaign of 1862*. Baltimore: Johns Hopkins University Press, 2012.

Hartley, Chris J. *Stuart's Tarheels: James B. Gordon and His North Carolina Cavalry*. Baltimore: Butternut and Blue, 1996.

Heatwole, John L. *The Burning: Sheridan in the Shenandoah Valley*. Charlottesville, VA: Rockbridge Publishing, 1998), 220.

Henderson, George Francis Robert. *Stonewall Jackson and the American Civil War*, Vol. I. New York: Logman's, Green and Company, 1919.

Henderson, William D. *The Road to Bristoe Station*. Lynchburg, Virginia: H. E. Howard, Inc., 1987.

Hennessy, John J. *The First Battle of Manassas*. Lynchburg, Virginia: H. E. Howard,1989.

_____ *Return to Bull Run: The Campaign and Battle of Second Manassas*. Norman, Oklahoma: University of Oklahoma Press, 1993.

Hill, Daniel Harvey. "The Land We Love." Charlotte, North Carolina: Hill and Irwin & Co., 1866-1869.

Horn, John. *The Petersburg Campaign; The Destruction of the Weldon Railroad; Deep Bottom, Globe Tavern and Reams Station; August 14-25, 1864*. Lynchburg, Virginia: H. E. Howard, Inc., 1991.

Hudgins, Garland C. and Richard B. Kleese, ed. *Recollections of an Old Dominion Dragoon: The Civil War Experiences of Sgt. Robert S. Hudgins II Co. B, 3rd Virginia Cavalry*. Orange, Virginia: Publisher's Press, Inc., 1993.

Humphreys, Andrew A. *The Virginia Campaign of 1864 and 1865: The Army of the Potomac and the Army of the James*. Reprint. New York: Da Capo Press, 1995.

Jackson, Mary Anna. *Life and Letters of General Stonewall Jackson*. 1st edition. New York: Harper, 1892.

Jewell, James R. "In Rivulets of Gray Ink: The Bloody Battles About the War (The Munford-Rosser Feud)." np. nd.

_____ "Lieutenant Colonel Breckenridge's Account of the Second Virginia Cavalry Regiment from Five Forks to Appomattox," np. nd.

Johnson, Bradley T., ed. *A Memoir of the Life and Public Service of Joseph E. Johnston*. Baltimore: R. H. Woodward and Company, 1891.

Johnston II, Angus James. *Virginia Railroads in the Civil War*. Chapel Hill: UNC Press for the Virginia Historical Society, 1961.

Jones, J. William, D. D. *Personal Reminiscences, Anecdotes, and Letters of Gen. Robert E. Lee*. New York: D. Appleton and Company, 1875.

Journal of the Senate of the Commonwealth of Virginia. Richmond: R. F. Walker, Superintendent of Public Printing, 1881.

Journal of the Military Service Institution of the United States. Volume XLIX, July-August. Governor's Island, New York, 1911.

Keller, S. Rogert. *Riding with Rosser*. Shippensburg, PA: Burd Street Press, 1997.

Kidd, James H. *Personal Recollections of a Cavalryman Riding with Custer's Michigan Cavalry Brigade*. Ionia, Michigan: Sentinel Printing Company, 1908).

Krick, Robert K. *Lee's Colonels: A Biographical Register of the Field Officers of the Army of Northern Virginia*. 4th Ed. Dayton, Ohio: Morningside, 1992.

Longacre, Edward G. *The Cavalry at Gettysburg: A Tactical Study of Mounted Operations During the Civil War's Pivotal Campaign, 9 June-14 July, 1863*. Lincoln: The University of Nebraska Press, 1993.

_____ *Lee's Cavalrymen*, Mechanicsburg, Pennsylvania: Stackpole Books, 2002.

_____ *Mounted Raids of the Civil War*. Lincoln, Nebraska and London: University of Nebraska Press, 1994.

_____ *The Cavalry at Appomattox: A Tactical Study of Mounted Operations during the Civil War's Climatic Campaign, March 27-April 9, 1865*. Mechanicsville, Pennsylvania: Stackpole Books, 2003.

_____ *Lincoln's Cavalrymen: A History of the Mounted Forces of the Army of the Potomac*. Mechanicsville, Pennyslvania: Stackpole Books, 2000.

_____ *Fitz Lee: A Military Biography*. Cambridge, Massachusetts: Da Capo Press, 2005.

_____ *Gentleman and Soldier: The Extraordinary Life of General Wade Hampton*. Nashville: Rutledge Hill Press, 2003.

_____ "The Wilson-Kautz Raid," *Civil War Times Illustrated* (May 1970).

Manarin, Louis H. *North Carolina Troops, 1861-1865, A Roster*. Raleigh: State Archives of North Carolina, 1989.

Martin, David G. *The Peninsula Campaign*. Conshohocken, PA: Combined Books, 1992.

Marvel, William. *Lee's Last Retreat: The Flight to Appomattox*. Chapel Hill: UNC Press, 2002.

M. F. Maury, M. F., LL D., *Physical Survey of Virginia; Her Resources, Climate, and Productions. Preliminary Report No. II, July 1, 1877*. Richmond, Virginia.: N. V. Randolph, 1878.

McClellan, Major Henry Brainerd. *I Rode With Jeb Stuart: The Life and Campaigns of Major General J.E.B. Stuart*. Bloomington, Indiana: Indiana University Press, 1981.

McClernand, John A. *Journal of The Military Service Institution of the United States (JMSIUS)*, Vol. 30, May, 1902.

McDonald, William N. *A History of the Laurel Brigade*. Baltimore: Johns Hopkins University Press, 2002.

McKim, Randolph Harrison. *A Soldier's Recollections*. New York: Logman's, Green and Company, 1910.

McMurry, Richard M. *Virginia Military Institute Alumni in the Civil War*. Lynchburg, Virginia: H. E. Howard, 1999.

Meade, George Gordon, ed. *Life and Letters of George Gordon Meade*, Vol. 1. New York: Charles Scribners' Sons, 1913.

Merington, Marguerite, ed. *The Custer Story: The Life and Letters of General George A. Custer and His Wife Elizabeth*. New York: The Devin-Adair Company, 1950.

Mewborn, Horace. "Herding the Yankee Cattle: The Beefstake Raid, September 14-17, 1864." *Blue and Gray Magazine*. (Summer 2005).

Miller, William J. *The Peninsula Campaign of 1862, Yorktown to Seven Days*, Vol. 2. Cambridge, Massachusetts: De Capo Publishing, 1995.

Mitchell, Adele, Ed., *Letters of James E. B. Stuart*. Stuart-Mosby Historical Association, 1990.

Moore, John S. *The History of Second Baptist Church, Richmond, Virginia, 1820-1995*. Richmond: Second Baptist Church, 1998.

Morrison, Alfred James. *The Beginnings of Public Education in Virginia, 1176-1860, Virginia State Board of Education*. Richmond: David Bottom, Superintendent of Public Printing, 1917.

Morsman, Amy Freely, *The Big House After Slavery: Virginia Plantation Families and Their Postbellum Domestic Experiment*. Charlottesville, Virginia: University of Virginia Press, 2005.

Munford, Beverley Bland. *Virginia's Attitude Toward Slavery and Secession*. New York: Longmans, Green & Company, 1909.

Munford, Robert Beverly. *Richmond Homes and Memories*. Richmond: Garrett and Massie, Inc., 1936.

Munford, Thomas T. "Reminiscences of Jackson's Valley Campaign." *Southern Historical Society Papers*, Vol. VII, No. 11. Richmond, Virginia., November, 1879.

_____ "Reminiscences of Cavalry Operations: Battle of Winchester, 19th September, '64." Paper No. 2, *Southern Historical Society Papers*, Vol. XII Nos. 10, 11, 12.

_____ "Reminiscences of Cavalry Operations: Operations Under Rosser." *Southern Historical Society Papers*, Vol. XIII, Paper No. 3.

_____ "The Maryland Campaign," Address to the Confederate Veterans Association of Savannah, Georgia, typescript, McLaws Papers, SHC.

_____ "Reminiscences," *Cavalry Journal*, Vol. 4, September, 1891.

_____ "How I Came to Know Major Thomas Jonathan Jackson," Munford-Ellis Papers, Duke University, Durham, North Carolina.

_____ "Address to the Graduates and Corps of Cadets of Marion Institute, May 23, 1916," Munford-Ellis Papers, Duke University.

_____ "The Last Days of Fitz Lee's Division of Cavalry." VHS, Richmond, VA,

_____ "Five Forks: The Waterloo of the Confederacy." VHS, Richmond, VA.

Munford, William Tayloe. *Fond Memories*. Dietz Press, Petersburg, VA., 1992.

Musick, Michael P. *The 6th Virginia Cavalry*. Lynchburg, Virginia: H. E. Howard Virginia Regimental Series, 1990.

Myers, Frank M. *The Comanches:a history of White's Battalion, Virginia Cavalry, Laurel Brig., Hampton Div., A.N.V., C.S.A.* Marietta, Georgia.: Continental Book Co., 1956.

Nanzig, Lt. Robert T. Hubart, Jr. *The Civil War Memoirs of a Virginia Cavalryman*. Tuscaloosa, Alabama: University of Alabama Press, 2007.

Neese, George M. *Three Years in the Confederate Horse Artillery*. New York: The Neale Publishing Company, 1911.

O'Neill, Robert F. "Aldie, Middleburg, and Upperville." *Gettysburg: Historical Articles Of Lasting Interest*, Issue Number 43: 20. Civil War Landscapes Association, http://www.civilwarlandscapes.org/cwla/pub/pub.htm, 1998.

_____ *Galloping Thunder*. Mechanicsburg, Pennsylvania: Stackpole Books, 2002.

Owen, William Miller. *In Camp and Battle with the Washington Artillery of New Orleans*. Baton Rouge, Louisiana: LSU Press, 1999.

Peck, Rufus H. *Reminiscences of a Confederate Soldier of Co. C of the 2nd Virginia Cavalry*. Fincastle, Virginia, 1913.

Pfanz, Donald C. *The Petersburg Campaign: Abraham Lincoln at City Point, March 20 - April 9, 1865*. Lynchburg, Virginia: H. E. Howard, Inc., 1989.

Pickett, La Salle Corbell (Mrs. George E.). *Pickett and His Men*. Atlanta: Foote and Davies, 1899.

Power, J. Tracy. *Lee's Miserables: Life in the Army of Northern Virginia from the Wilderness to Appomattox*. Chapel Hill: UNC Press, 1998.

Rafuse, Ethan S. *McClellan's War: The Failure of Moderation in the Struggle for the Union*. Bloomington and Indianapolis, Indiana: Indiana University Press, 2005.

Rarwell, Byron. *Stonewall: A Biography of General Thomas J. Jackson.* New York: W. W. Norton and Company, 1992.

Rawle, William Brook, William E. Miller, James W. McCorkell, Andrew J. Speese, and John C. Hunterson (Regimental History Committee). *History of the Third Pennsylvania Cavalry (Sixtieth Regiment Pennsylvania Volunteers) in the American Civil War, 1861-1865.* Philadelphia: Franklin Publishing Company, 1905.

Rea, D. B. "Cavalry Incidents of the Maryland Campaign." *The Maine Bugle.* Campaign II. Rockland, Maine, April, 1895.

Rhea, Gordon C. *The Battles for Spotsylvania Court House and the Road to Yellow Tavern, May 7-12, 1864.* Baton Rouge: LSU Press, 1997. Press, 2000.

_____ *To the North Anna River: Grant and Lee, May 13–25, 1864.* Baton Rouge: LSU Press, 2005.

Robertson, James I, Jr. *Stonewall Jackson: The Man, the Soldier, the Legend.* New York: MacMillan & Company, 1997.

Roman, Alfred, *The Military Operations of General Beauregard in the War Between the States, 1861-1865.* New York: Harper and Brothers, 1883.

Rosser, Thomas L. *Addresses of Gen'l T. L. Rosser, at the Seventh Annual Reunion of the Association of the Maryland Line, Academy of Music, Baltimore, Md., February 22, 1889, and on Memorial Day, Staunton, Va., June 8, 1889.* New York, 1889.

Rucker, W. A., "A Sketch of My War Experiences." From the *Rucker Family Society Newsletter,* Volume 12 Number 3, September, 2001.

Schaff, Morris. *The Sunset of the Confederacy.* Boston: J. W. Luce and Company, 1912.

Sears, Stephen W., ed. *The Civil War Papers of George B. McClellan: Selected Correspondence, 1860-1865.* New York: De Capo Press, 1992.

_____ *To the Gates of Richmond: The Peninsula Campaign.* New York: Ticknor & Fields, 1992.

_____ *George B. McClellan: The Young Napoleon.* New York: Houghton Mifflin Harcourt, 1988.

_____ *Gettysburg.* New York: Houghton Mifflin Company, 2003.

Sheridan, Philip H. *Personal Memoirs of P. H. Sheridan.* New York: Charles L. Webster, 1888.

Simon, John Y., ed. *The Papers of Ulysses S. Grant*, Vols 13, 14. Carbondale and Edwardsville: Southern Illinois University Press, 1967.

_____ and Harold Holzer, eds. *The Lincoln Forum: Rediscovering Abraham Lincoln.* New York: Fordham University Press, 2002.

Simson, Jay W. *Custer and the Front Royal Executions of 1864.* Jefferson, North Carolina: McFarland, 2008.

Smith, Francis H. *History of the Virginia Military Institute.* Evergreen, New York, 1912.

Sommers, Richard. *Richmond Redeemed: The Siege at Petersburg, The Battles of Chaffin's Bluff and Poplar Spring Church, September 29-October 2, 1864.* El Dorado Hills, CA: Savas-Beatie, 2014.

Southern Historical Society Papers. William Jones, et al, eds. Volumes 1-52. Richmond, Virginia: Southern Historical Society, 1876-1959.

Stackpole, Edward James. *Sheridan in the Shenandoah: Jubal Early's Nemesis.* Harrisburg, PA: Stackpole Books, 1992.

Starr, Stephen Z. *The Union Cavalry in the Civil War.* 3 Vols. Baton Rouge, Louisiana: State University Press, 1979-1985.

Stiles, Robert. *Four Years Under Marse Robert.* New York: The Neale Publishing Company, 1904.

Styles, Kenneth L. *4th Virginia Cavalry.* Lynchburg: H. E. Howard, 1985.

Suderow, Bryce A. "Confederate Strengths & Losses From March 25- April 9, 1865," May, 1987; revised September 29, 1991, Washington, D.C.

Swank, Walbrook D., ed. *The Battle of Trevilian Station: The Civil War's Greatest and Bloodiest All Cavalry Battle, with Eyewitness Memoirs.* Civil War Heritage, Vol. 4.

The War of the Rebellion: A Compilation of the Official Records of the Union and Confederate Armies. 70 Volumes. 128 Parts, and Atlas. Washington, D.C.: Government Printing Office, 1880-1901.

Supplement to the Official Record of the Union and Confederate Armies. Wilmington, North Carolina: Broadfoot Publishing Company, 1994-2001.

Thomas, Emory M. *Bold Dragoon: Life of J.E.B. Stuart.* New York: Vintage Books, 1988.

Tighe, Adrian. *The Bristoe Campaign: General Lee's Last Strategic Offensive with the Army of Northern Virginia October 1863.* Bloomington, IN: Xlibris Corporation, 2011.

Tillman, John P., Special Reporter. *Reports of Cases Argued and Determined in the Supreme Court of Alabama, during the December Terms,1882-1888.* Montgomery, Alabama: Joel White, 1884,

Tobie, Edward P. *History of the First Maine Cavalry,1861-1865.* Boston: Press of Emery & Hughes, 1887.

Tripp, Steven Elliot. *Yankee Town, Southern City: Race and Class Relations in Civil War Lynchburg.* New York: New York University Press, 1997.

Trout, Robert J. *Galloping Thunder: The Story of the Stuart Horse Artillery Battalion.* Mechanicsville, Pennsylvania: Stackpole Books, 2002.

_____, ed. *Memoirs of the Stuart Horse Artillery Battalion, Vol. 2: Breathed's and McGregor's Batteries.* Knoxville: University of Tennessee Press, 1910.

_____, ed. *In the Saddle with Stuart: The Story of Frank Smith Robertson of Jeb Stuart's Staff.* Gettysburg: Thomas Publications, 1998.

Trudeau, Noad Andre. *The Last Citadel: Petersburg, Virginia, June 1864-April 1865.* New York: Little, Brown & Company, 1991.

United States Federal Census, 1860-1900 & 1860 Federal Slave Schedule, Bedford County, Virginia. National Archives.

Vandiver, Frank E. *Mighty Stonewall.* College Station: Texas A&M University, 1995.

_____ *Jubal's Raid.* New York: McGraw-Hill, 1960.

Walker, C. Irvine. *The Life of Lieutenant General Richard Heron Anderson of the Confederate States Army*. Charleston, South Carolina, 1917.

Wallace, Michael M., USN. "The Use of The Virginia Military Institute Corps of Cadets as a Military Unit Before and During the War Between the States, MA Thesis presented to the Faculty of the U.S. Army Command and General Staff College in partial fulfillment of the requirements for the degree Master of Military Art and Science Military History." Tulane University, New Orleans, LA, 1999.

Warner, Ezra J. *Generals in Blue: Lives of the Union Commanders*. Baton Rouge: Louisiana State University Press, 1995.

Watkins, Raymond W. *The Hicksford Raid*. The Greensville Historical Society, April 1978.

Welsh, Jack Walsh, M. D. *Confederate Generals Medical Histories*. Kent, Ohio: Kent State University Press, 1995.

Wellman, Manly Wade. *Giant in Gray: A Biography of Wade Hampton*. New York: Charles Scribner's Sons, Inc., 1949.

Wells, Edward L. *Hampton and His Cavalry in '64*. Richmond, Virginia: B. F. Johnston Publishing Company, 1899.

Wert, Jeffrey D. *General James Longstreet: The Confederacy's Most Controversial Soldier*. New York: Simon & Schuster, 1993.

_____ *Cavalryman of the Lost Cause*. New York: Simon & Shuster, 2008.

_____ *Gettysburg, Day Three*. New York: Simon & Schuster, 2002.

Wise, Jennings C. *The Military History of the Virginia Military Institute from 1839-1865*. Lynchburg, Virginia: J. P. Bell Company, 1915.

Wise, John. *End of An Era*. New York: Houghton, Mifflin and Company, 1902.

Wittenberg, Eric J. *The Union Cavalry Comes of Age: Hartwood Church to Brandy Station, 1863*. Washington, D.C.: Potomac Books, 2003.

_____ *Glory Enough for All: Sheridan's Second Raid and The Battle of Trevilian Station*. Lincoln, Nebraska: University of Nebraska Press, 2001.

Wittenberg, Eric, J. David Petruzzi, and Michael F. Nugent. *One Continuous Fight: The Retreat from Gettysburg and the Pursuit of Lee's Army of Northern Virginia, July 4-14, 1863*. New York: Savis-Beatie, 2008.

Wright, Catherine M., ed. *Lee's Last Casualty: The Life and Letters of Sgt. Robert W. Parker, Second Virginia Cavalry*. Knoxville: University of Tennessee Press, 2008.

Yoseoff, Thomas. "North to Antietam," *Battles and Leaders in the Civil War*, Volume II. New York: Thomas Yoseoff, 1956.

Index

Military Units:

Alabama:
  4th Infantry   41
  15th Infantry   77
  47th Infantry   176

Connecticut:
  12th Infantry   252

Delaware:
  1st Cavalry   166

Georgia:
  7th Cavalry   212
  20th Battalion Cavalry   212
  Cobb Legion   152, 167, 192, 212

Illinois:
  8th Cavalry   112
  11th Cavalry   163

Indiana:
  3rd Cavalry   163

Louisiana:
  7th Infantry   35, 76

Maine:
  1st Cavalry   160

Maryland:
  1st Battalion Cavalry   193, 213
  1st Cavalry   78, 84, 109, 301,
                   302, 303, 307, 308
  1st Maryland (U.S.) Infantry
                          74, 109, 225

Massachusetts:
  1st Cavalry   132, 160, 161, 222

Michigan:
  1st Michigan Cavalry
                        106, 173, 262
  5th Michigan Cavalry
                        162, 232, 233

Mississippi:
  2nd Infantry   41
  11th Infantry   41

New Jersey:
  1st Cavalry   77
  1st Volunteer Cavalry   298

New York:
  2nd Cavalry   153, 160
  4th Cavalry   106, 132, 160, 161
  5th Infantry   74
  6th Cavalry   139, 140, 341
  8th Cavalry   152, 163
  9th Cavalry   262
  10th Cavalry   153
  15th Volunteer Cavalry   259
  124th Infantry   133
  125th Infantry   199

North Carolina:
  1st Cavalry   56, 152, 154, 173,
                  192, 195, 199, 202, 212
  2nd Cavalry   154, 167, 192, 212
  4th Cavalry   192, 198
  5th Cavalry
                  181, 192, 195, 198, 212
  N.C. Cavalry Brigade
                        186, 199, 224, 230

Ohio:
  6th Ohio Cavalry   160, 162

Pennsylvania:
  2nd Cavalry   242
  3rd Cavalry   132
  4th Cavalry   132
  8th Cavalry   143
  16th Cavalry   132, 133
  17th Cavalry   126, 143
  18th Cavalry   167, 175
  28th Infantry   59, 61, 67, 68, 74
  96th Infantry   115
  Pennsylvania Bucktails   78

Rhode Island:
  1st Cavalry   132, 160

South Carolina:
  1st Cavalry   193
  1st Infantry   176
  2nd Cavalry   152, 154, 192
  2nd Infantry   38, 44
  4th Infantry   35
  5th Cavalry   227
  6th Cavalry   234, 235
  7th Infantry   39
  8th Infantry   39, 44
  Hampton's Legion   54

Texas:
  1st Texas Infantry   176

Vermont:
  15th Cavalry   126

Virginia:
  1st Cavalry
     52, 55, 79, 123, 132, 157, 160, 161, 167, 174, 175, 177, 186, 193, 197, 203, 211, 213, 223, 224, 239, 251, 266, 280

  1st Cavalry (U.S.)   217
  1st Regiment Volunteers   39
  2nd Cavalry
     29, 31, 32, 33, 49, 53-55, 57, 60, 67, 68, 73, 75, 76, 80, 82, 89, 102-106, 108, 109, 117, 119, 120, 122, 123, 130-132, 137-140, 143, 148, 157, 160, 161, 165, 173, 176, 178, 181, 182, 186, 187, 192, 193, 196, 197, 201, 203-205, 209, 210, 212, 213, 216, 217, 222, 223, 234-236, 238, 239, 241, 242, 247, 250, 251, 254, 266, 269, 274, 276, 279, 291, 292, 299, 305, 344, 345, 348

  3rd Cavalry
     123, 132, 139, 157, 160, 161, 193, 197, 202, 213, 220, 223, 239, 251, 264, 266, 285, 302

  4th Cavalry
     36, 53, 56, 123, 126, 137, 160, 161, 193, 197, 200, 213, 223, 239, 246, 251, 253, 255

  5th Cavalry
     123, 137, 139, 160-162, 193, 246, 266

  6th Cavalry
     56, 67, 75, 76, 82, 104, 107, 112, 120, 152, 192, 213

  7th Cavalry
     80, 104, 107, 110, 112, 117, 120, 152, 192, 195, 212, 219, 236, 279

  7th Infantry   35
  8th Cavalry   281
  8th Infantry   38
  9th Virginia Cavalry
     157, 173, 180, 193, 195, 212
  10th Cavalry   156, 193, 212

11th Regiment Volunteers 39
11th Cavalry
    193, 195, 212, 213,
    219, 234, 279, 350
12th Cavalry
    80, 104, 107, 110, 112, 117,
    120, 153, 185, 192, 195,
    198, 212, 219, 279
13th Cavalry
    166, 173, 180, 193, 212
15th Cavalry 193, 220
17th Regiment Volunteers 39
17th Battn (1st Battn of
    Cavalry) 80, 112
17th Infantry 28, 46
18th Cavalry 183
24th Infantry 28, 29, 31, 34, 35
28th Infantry 31
30th Volunteer Regiment
    31, 32, 33, 34, 36, 49, 53, 54
35th Cavalry Battalion
    153, 192, 212, 219
35th Battalion 59, 68
42nd Infantry 76
58th Infantry 78
Albemarle Light Horse 348
Black Horse Troop 36, 45, 53
Chesterfield Troop 36, 45
Franklin Rangers 26
Loudoun Rangers 108
Radford Rangers 28, 33
Richmond Howitzer Battn 120
Richmond Otey Battery 29
Va Letcher Light Artillery 96
Virginia Light Artillery 347

West Virgina:
  1st Cavalry 106, 175

United States:
  1st Artillery 43, 163
  2nd Artillery 173
  4th Artillery 175
  5th Artillery 43
  5th Cavalry 222
  Union I Corps
    144
  Union II Corps
    199, 214, 215, 225, 226, 286
  Union III Corps
    144, 211
  Union IX Corps
    214-216
  Union V Corps
    199, 214-216, 220, 226, 283, 286
  Union VI Corps
    199, 211, 214, 215, 246, 247
  Union XI Corps
    140, 144, 195
  Union XII Corps
    144, 195
  Union XIX Corps
    246, 247

Abercrombie, John J. 67
Accotink, Virginia 126
Adams, Charles 161
Adams, William 160
Agriculture Exper. Station 357
Air Enforcer 323
Alabama, Agriculture and
    Mechanical College of 339
Alabama Polytechnic Institute 357
Alabama Supreme Court 325, 327
Albemarle County, Virginia
    32, 205, 211, 345
Aldie, Battle of 159

Aldie, Virginia
    34, 67, 147, 160, 161, 162, 163
Alexander, Edward Porter   43
Alexander, John D.   32
Alexandria Gazette   335
Alexandria Line   49, 52
Alexandria, Va   36, 39, 52, 164
Allan, John   6
Alleghney Mountains   280
Almond, Charles H.   235
Alms House, Virginia   238
Altha Grove Baptist Church   327
Ambrose P. Hill's III Corps   158
Amelia Court House, Va   297, 298
Amelia Springs, Virginia 297, 298
Amherst County, Virginia   32
Amissville, Virginia 103, 138, 186
Anderson, Archer   294
Anderson, George   176
Anderson, Richard H.
    127, 221, 247, 284, 286, 289, 294
Andrews, Clinton   225
Annandale, Virginia   52, 165
Antietam, Battle of   117
Antietam Creek   117
Antietam, Maryland   34, 59, 147
Appomattox Campaign
                       34, 261, 297
Appomattox County, Virginia
                            32, 33
Appomattox Court House   302
Appomattox River   297, 298, 301
Appomattox, Virginia
    125, 235, 236, 295, 297, 299,
    301, 305, 308
Aquia, Virginia   126
Arlington, Virginia   46
Armistead, Lewis A.   118

Army of Northern Virginia
    49, 54, 64, 84, 102, 109, 117,
    123, 124, 139, 147, 158, 159,
    174, 183, 197, 203, 206, 214,
    229, 230, 245, 248, 266, 282,
    283, 303, 306
Army of Tennessee   195, 214, 293
Army of the Potomac
    35, 36, 50, 53, 91, 93, 103, 121,
    123, 129, 136, 139, 147, 158,
    204, 214
Army of the Shenandoah
    Valley   40, 41
Army of Virginia   100
Ashby, Turner
            66, 69, 72, 76-80, 89
Ashby's Gap Turnpike, Va
                      159, 161, 163
Ashland, Virginia   89, 222, 242
Atkinson, Rev. Thomas   317
Atlanta, Georgia   230
Atlantic and North Carolina
    Railroad   64
Atlee's Station, Virginia   226
Auburn Mills, Virginia   199
Auburn, Virginia
              197, 198, 200, 201, 203
Augusta Church, Virginia   254
Averell, William W.
    132, 134, 136, 137, 139, 205,
    206, 247-249, 251
Ayers, R. B.   40
Back Road, Virginia
            255-259, 261, 262, 274
Bacon, Thomas G.   39
Baker, I. Norval   183
Baker, Laurence
            173, 176, 185, 186, 192
Ball, Mottrom Dulany   350

Ball, William B. 36, 53
Ball's Bluff, Virginia 53, 56
Ball's Ford 45
Baltimore and Ohio Railroad
    118, 120, 122, 166, 186, 276
Baltimore and Potomac Railroad
    325
Baltimore Pike, Pennsylvania
    170, 172
Baltimore, Maryland 108
Bank's Dept of the Shenandoah
    66
Bank's Ford, Virginia 145
Banks, Nathaniel
    65, 67, 70, 72-75, 101, 102
Banks's Ford, Virginia 127
Banyard, George D. 104
Barboursville, Virginia 196, 282
Bark Milford, Virginia 127
Barringer, Rufus
    202, 230, 242, 243
Bartlett, Joseph J. 286
Bartow, Francis S. 41, 43
Bath, Virginia 65
Baxter, Thorton R. 107
Bayard, George D. 124
Beauregard, Pierre G.T.
    34-38, 40, 41, 43, 44, 47, 53, 54,
    60, 61, 63, 191, 340
Beaver Creek, Maryland 181
Beaver Dam Road, Virginia 222
Beaver Dam Station, Virginia 223
Beaver Dam, Virginia 218
Beckham, Robert F.
    148, 150, 152, 199
Bedford County, Virginia
    22, 27, 28, 32, 33, 68, 209, 311,
    313, 314, 317, 318, 323, 324, 327
Bee, Bernard Elliot 41, 43

Belair Mansion, Md. 324, 325
Bell, Samuel H. 348, 349
Belle Grove, Virginia 268
Belmont Farm, Virginia 216
Benjamin F. Davis 115
Berea Church, Virginia 133
Berlin, Maryland 183
Berlin, Virgnia 121
Berry, William W. 33
Berry's Ferry, Virginia 120
Berryville Pike, Virginia 247, 248
Berryville Road, Virginia 247
Berryville, Virginia 120
Beverly Ford Road, Virginia 152
Beverly Ford, Virginia
    150, 152, 154, 156, 203
Beverly, West Virginia
    280, 282, 344, 348, 349
Big Lick, Virginia 309
Big Round Top Mountain
    (Gettysburg) 174
Big Round Top-Emmitsburg Road
    (Gettysburg) 172
Birney, David B. 225
Black Belt Prairie, Alabama 356
Black, John L. 153
Blackburn's Ford 39, 41, 46
Blackford, Charles Minor
    55, 124, 179, 182, 237
Blackford, William W. 165
Blackstone, Virginia 289
Blackwater Creek, Lynchburg, Va
    323
Blenker, Louis 66
Blick, Mrs. 242
Blue Ridge Iron mine, Va 324
Blue Ridge Mountains
    23, 25, 62, 69, 70, 71, 87, 121,
    121, 137, 159, 163, 164, 186,

204, 205, 247, 250, 256, 276, 279, 281
Boisseaux House 289
Boisseaux, Virginia 284
Bolivar Heights, Virginia 75
Bonham, Milledge Luke
   35, 36, 38, 40, 41, 44, 46, 52, 54
Boonsboro Road, Pa. 178
Boonsboro, Md. 115, 178-181
Borcke, Heros von 140, 340
Borman, Arthur I. 329
Boston, Reuben
   160, 162, 246, 284
Boteler's Ford, Md. 117, 118
Botetourt County, Virginia
   21, 22, 25, 27, 32
Bottom's Bridge, Virginia 238
Botts, John Minor 148
Boutetort County, Virginia
   307, 324, 336
Bowling Green Road 238
Bowling Green, Virginia 238
Bowling, Stith 242
Boydton Plank Road 283, 287
Braddock Road 37
Brandy Station, Virginia
   34, 104, 110, 123, 136, 139, 147, 148, 150, 152, 154, 155, 158, 159, 190, 197-199, 203, 364
Breathed, James
   137, 156, 157, 161, 172, 197, 201, 211, 212, 223, 234, 249, 250, 345
Breckinridge, Cary
   33, 95, 107, 140, 209, 212, 242, 247, 291, 292
Breckinridge, James 157
Brent, George W. 46
Brentsville, Virginia 164

Bridgewater, Virginia 254
Bristoe Station Campaign
   34, 196, 197, 201, 203
Bristoe Station, Virginia
   105, 164, 183, 196, 199
Bristol, Virginia 31
Broad Run, Virginia 200, 201
Brock Road 143, 219, 225, 220
Brock's Gap, Virginia 255, 276
Brooke, Henry St. George Tucker
   205, 210, 222, 227
Brooks, William T. H. 115
Brown, John 15
Brown, Ridgley 84
Brown's Gap, Virginia
   82, 247, 253, 282
Brownsville Gap, Maryland 114
Brownsville, Virginia 206
Brunswick County, Virginia 2
Bryant Farm, Alabama 354
Buchanan, Virginia 206
Buckeystown Road 112
Buckittsville, Md. 113, 115, 116
Buckland Mills, Virginia 197
Buckland Races, Virginia 203
Buckland, Virginia 200-203
Buckton Depot, Virginia 72
Buena Vista Land Company 22
Buena Vista, Virginia 22, 23, 209
Buford, A. S. 337
Buford, John
   104, 106, 150, 152-154, 167, 174, 178, 181-183, 195, 197-199
Bull Run, Battle of First and Second   *see Manassas*
Bull Run (Manassas), Virginia
   35, 36, 38-40, 43, 45
Bull Run Mountains, Virginia
   105, 121, 160, 200

Bunker Hill Ford, Virginia 253
Bunker Hill, Virginia 185
Bureau of Plant Industry 359
Burgess's Mill, Virginia 289
Burke, William 5, 6, 7
Burke's Station, Virginia 164
Burkesville, Virginia 231
Burks, Richard H. 32
Burnley, William H. 69, 77
Burnside, Ambrose
    64, 101, 122-124, 129, 214-216
Burnside's Mud March 129
Burwell, Thomas N. 25
Bushman, George 175
Bushman's Hill, Pennsylvania 172
Butler, Benjamin F. 224, 241
Butler, Matthew C.
    152, 154, 192, 227, 232-237, 239,
    242, 243, 282
Butterfield, Daniel 133
Byrd, Mrs. J. William 339
Cabin Point, Virgina 268
Cake, H. L. 115
Camp Pickens, Virginia 34
Campbell County, Va 32, 321
Campbell's Station, Virginia 241
Caperton, George H. 60
Carlisle, Pennsylvania 168
Carpenter's Ford, Virginia 232
Carrington, Henry 263, 268
Carroll, Samuel 83
Carson, Joseph W. 222
Carter, Franklin 159, 160
Carter, Richard W. 263, 268
Carter, William R. 132, 203
Cash, E.B. 39
Cash, E.C.B. 44
Cashtown Pass 176
Cashtown Road 177

Cashtown, Pennsylvania 174, 178
Cassell County, Mississippi 22
Catharpin Road, Virginia 216
Catherine Furnace Road 219
Catlett's Station, Virginia 137, 198
Catoctin Mountain, Md. 113, 177
Cavalry Reorganization 192
Cedar Creek, Va 102, 268, 269
Cedar Mountain, Va 102, 196
Cedar Point, Virginia 72
Cemetery Ridge, Gettysburg 175
Centreville, Virginia
    34-36, 38, 39, 46, 50, 52-54, 57,
    61, 65, 106, 112, 199, 200, 254
Chadwick, F. E. 25
Chaffin's Bluff, Virginia 240
Chamberlain, Joshua L. 294
Chamberlian's Bed, Va 284, 285
Chambersburg Pike 176
Chambersburg, Pa 119, 247
Chambliss, John R.
    159, 166, 167, 172, 173, 177, 178,
    180, 186, 212, 239, 240, 242, 243
Chancellorsville, Battle of 139
Chancellorsville, Virginia
    17, 34, 129, 139, 140, 145, 147,
    148, 158, 159, 216
Chapman, George H. 249
Charles City County, Va 239
Charles City Court House, Va
    226, 239
Charles Town, Pennsylvania 173
Charleston, SC 334, 336
Charlestown, Va 75, 118, 120
Charlestown, West Virginia 185
Charlottesville, Virginia
    77, 87, 127, 210-212, 231, 236,
    269, 308, 344
Chattanooga, Tennessee 194

Chesapeake & Ohio Railroad	165	Columbia Bridge	70
Chesapeake Bay, Va	2, 63, 137	Columbia Furnace, Va	262, 268
Chesnut Hill, Virginia	201	Columbia Turnpike	52
Chesnut, James	37	Committee on Courts of	
Chester Gap	69, 70, 186	Justice	321
Chesterfield Bridge, Virginia	226	Commonwealth of Virginia	9, 27
Chesterfield Station, Virginia	224	Confederate Congress	192
Chew, Roger Preston		Confederate Senate	364
78, 80, 84, 104, 109, 110, 112,		Confederate War Dept	346
114, 120, 199, 211, 212, 233-236		Conrad, Holmes	281
Chewsville, Maryland	178, 180	Conrad's Store, Virginia	
Chickahominy River, Virginia		69, 71, 83, 86, 253	
91, 93, 211, 223, 224, 230, 239		Conservative Democratic Party,	
Chickamauga, Georgia	195	Virginia	311
Chickasaw Nation	339	Cook, Albert W.	281
Chickasaw, Oklahoma	339	Cooke, Flora	5
Chilesburg, Virginia	238	Cooke, John Esten	
Chinn Ridge, Manassas	44	5, 6, 7, 98, 119, 165	
Chipley, T.L.M.	80	Cooke, John Rogers	5
Christian's Creek, Virginia	254	Cooke, Philip St. George	
Churchman, Caleb	166	5, 35, 40, 44	
Clark, M. H.	347	Cookesville, Maryland	166
Clayton's Store, Virginia	232	Cook's Ford, Virginia	212
Clemmingtown Bridge, Va	297	Cool Spring, Virginia	246
Clifton Forge, Virginia	206	Cooper, Samuel	37, 38, 40, 299
Cobb, Howell	113, 114	Cooperstown, Maryland	177
Cobb, Thomas R.R.	125	Corbin Bridge, Virginia	218
Cobbler's Mountain, Virginia	138	Corbit, Charles	166
Coffee, Virginia	23	Corse, Montgomery D.	
Coffman's Hill, Virginia	260	28, 46, 287	
Cold Harbor, Virginia		Corson, William C.	264
34, 225, 226, 229		Covington, Virginia	206
Cole, Henry A.	109	Cowles, W.H.H.	154, 202
William and Mary, College of	3	Craig's Creek, Virginia	206
Collierstown, Virginia	206	Craig's Meeting House, Va	
Collington, Maryland	325	216, 218	
Collins, Charles R.	220	Crampton's Gap, Md.	
Colston, Edward	173	113, 114, 116	
Colston, Raleigh E.	14, 143, 144	Crenshaw's, Virginia	230

Cress Ridge, Pennsylvania 172
Criglersville, Virginia 213
Crook, George 246-248, 297, 298
Cross Keys, Virginia 76, 82, 83
Crozet, Claudius 5
Crozier, Virginia 324
Crutchfield, Stapleton
   14, 94, 140, 143
Cub Run, Mannassas 45, 46
Culpeper County, Virginia
   136, 148, 203
Culpeper Court House, Va
   67, 69, 70, 103, 104, 121, 127,
   131, 137, 138, 148, 150, 188,
   195, 197, 198, 199, 215
Culpeper, Virginia
   132, 136, 148, 150, 156, 158,
   195, 196, 199
Cumberland C. H. Road Bridge,
   Virginia 301
Cumberland Plank Road 301
Cummiins, F. M. 133
Cunningham, J. N. 211
Custer, Elizabeth 'Libbie'
   229, 235, 238, 266
Custer, George A.
   202, 211, 232, 257, 259, 260,
   167, 172, 173, 174, 178, 201,
   203, 212, 219, 219, 227, 229,
   233, 234, 235, 236, 237, 238,
   244, 147, 256, 260, 264, 268,
   269, 270, 271, 276, 289
Cutshaw, Wilfred E. 246
Dahlgren, Ulric 211
Dance's Ford, Virginia 285
Dandridge, Stephen 118, 185
Daniels Hill, Lynchburg 323
Danville, Virginia 231
Darkesville, Virginia 119

Davies, Henry E., Jr.
   195, 201, 284, 285, 297, 298, 304
Davis Ford, Virginia 126
Davis, Benjamin F. 152
Davis, Eugene 32, 45
Davis, Jefferson
   37, 38, 40, 41, 47, 60, 61, 89, 92,
   147, 189, 211, 282, 343, 364
Davis, Lucius 156
Deane's Foundry, Lynchburg 323
Dearing, David 243
Dearing, James 242, 299
DeForest, John William 252
Department of N. Carolina 110
Devil's Den, Gettysburg 176
Devin, Thomas
   219, 235, 260, 262, 285
Dinwiddie C. H. Road 284
Dinwiddie Court House, Va
   241, 242, 283-285, 287
Dorsey, Frank 346
Dorsey, Gustavus W.
   242, 301, 303, 307, 308
Dover Mills, Virginia 160
Dover, Pennsylvania 168
Downsville, Maryland 178, 180
Drake, James H. 132, 186
Dranesville, Virginia 55, 59, 165
Drewry's Bluff, Virginia 224
Duggar, J. F. 357
Dulany, R. H. 236
Dulany, Richard 255
Dumfries, Virginia 126, 127, 165
Early, Jubal A.
   31, 32, 34, 44, 123, 147, 183,
   204, 206, 230, 244, 245, 246,
   249, 250, 251, 252, 253, 254,
   255, 256, 257, 263, 265, 266,
   268, 273, 274, 276, 280, 282,
   349, 350, 362

East Cavalry Field, Gettysburg 173, 174
Edinburg, Virginia 262, 274
Elam, W.C. 272
Elk Run Church, Shenandoah Valley 62
Ellis, Charles 6, 27, 24
Ellis, Charles, Sr. 322
Ellis, Elizabeth Thorowgood 6
Ellis, Lucy Thorowgood 1
Ellis, Powhatan, Jr. 22
Ellis, Thomas H. 277
Ellis's Ford, Virginia 104
Elon J. Farnsworth 112
Ely's Ford Road 129, 143, 144
Ely's Ford, Virginia 139, 204, 205, 211, 215
Elzey, Arnold 44
Emack, George M. 307
Emmitsburg Road, Gettysburg 176
Emmitsburg, Maryland 177, 178
Emory and Henry College 32
Enon Church, Virginia 227
Evans, Nathan G. 35, 43, 53, 54
Evansport, Virginia 52
Evelington Heights, Peninsula Campaign 99
Ewell, Richard S. 35, 37, 62, 67, 69, 70, 76, 77, 78, 85, 87, 105, 147, 150, 164, 166, 168, 172, 177, 193, 205, 214, 217, 225, 245, 297
Ewell's II Corps 158
Fair Oaks, Virginia 91
Fairfax Court House, Virginia 35-40, 46, 50, 52-55, 108, 126, 127
Fairfax Station, Va 35, 52, 164
Fairfield, Pa 174, 176, 178
Fairview, Pennsylvania 119
Falling Waters, Maryland 179, 182, 183, 185
Falls Church, Virginia 52
Falmouth, Virginia 132, 133, 148
Farmville, Virginia 301
Farnsworth, Elon J. 110, 166, 167, 172, 174, 175, 176
Fauquier Springs, Virginia 67
Fauquier, Virginia 272
Feamington, Ellen 321
Ferguson, J. D. 242, 248, 249, 266
Ferguson, Milton J. 157, 172, 177
Field, Charles W. 56, 60
Fincastle, Virginia 206
Fisher, Charles F. 38
Fisher, Louis E. 350
Fisher's Gap 122
Fisher's Hill, Virginia 249, 250, 252, 256
Fitzgerald's Ford, Virginia 285
Fitzhugh Lee 168
Fitzhugh, Charles 289
Five Forks 279, 284, 286, 287, 289, 291, 292, 293, 294, 298, 347, 348, 351
Five Forks, Battle of 279
Fleetwood Hill, Brandy Station 147, 153, 154, 156, 198
Flint Hill, Shenandoah Valley 52, 69, 71
Flood, Joel 32, 38
Flournoy, Thomas S. 67, 72, 76, 107
Ford Road, Virginia 289
Ford, Fannie 321
Ford's Depot, Virginia 289
Ford's Road, Virginia 284
Forest Depot, Virginia 311

Forest School District, Bedford
   County, Virginia 327
Forest, Virginia 313
Forestville, Virginia 255, 268
Forge Bridges, Virginia 239
Fort Hill, Virginia 249, 251
Fort Powhatan, Virginia 226
Fort Stevens, Maryland 246
Fort Sumter, South Carolina 28
Fortress Monroe, Virginia 64
Fowler, Kathe 339
Fox, Edward 203
Fox's Ford, Virginia 198
France 108
Franklin County, Virginia 32
Franklin Debating Society 7, 10
Franklin, Virginia 72
Franklin, William B.
   41, 93, 113, 115, 116, 114, 124
Frayser's Farm, Virginia 93
Frederick City, Maryland 112
Frederick County, Virginia 66
Frederick, Maryland 177
Frederick's Hall, Virginia 238
Fredericksburg, Virginia
   34, 38, 59, 63, 64, 67, 70, 88,
   123, 124, 125, 127, 129, 132,
   134, 136, 139, 145, 148, 158,
   187, 189, 225
Fredericksburg, Battle of 101, 123
Fredericksburg and Potomac
   Railroad 63
Fremont, John C.
   72, 75, 76, 82, 83, 87
Fremont's Mountain Dept 66
French and Indian War 2
Front Royal, Virginia
   70, 72, 74, 186, 246, 249, 250
Frying Pan Church, Virginia 34

Frying Pan, Virginia 127
Fulkerson, Samuel V. 66
Funkstown, Maryland 179, 181
Funkstown, Pennsylvania 178
Funsten, Oliver 80, 84, 219
Gaines' Cross Roads, Virginia
   69, 70, 186
Gaines's Mill, Virginia 93
Gainesville, Va 65, 103, 164, 200
Gamble, William 163
Garber, Thomas M. 117(n)
Garland Hill District 318
Garnett, Richard B. 37, 66
Gary, Martin W. 239, 297, 298
Geary, John W. 59, 61, 67-69
General Assembly of Virginia
   333, 350
Genito Bridge, Virginia 297
Georgetown, Virginia 311
Germanna Ford, Va 139, 204, 215
Germanna Plank Road 216
Germantown, Maryland 52
Gettysburg Campaign
   136, 147, 190, 364
Gettysburg, Pennsylvania
   34, 147, 158, 164, 167, 168, 177,
   181, 185, 193, 206, 347
Gibbon, John 305
Gibbon's farm, Virginia 248
Gilham, William 14, 15, 18
Gilkerson's house, Virginia 81
Gilliam, Cornelius 354
Gilliam, Henry G. 354
Gilliam, Samuel B. 291
Gills, Asa 270
Gilmer, William 87
Glascock's Gap, Va 103, 164
Glen Alpine, Virginia 23,
   134, 209, 305, 311, 312, 314, 318

Glendale, Virginia 93
Gloucester County, Virginia
    314, 316, 321
Gloucester, Virginia 317
Goldsboro, North Carolina 64
Goldsborough, R. H. 156
Goode, Robert W. 177
Goods Farm, near Harrisonburg,
    Virginia 77
Goods Mill, near Port Republic,
    Virginia 77
Goodwin, Archibald C. 249
Goose Creek, Virginia 163
Gordon, James Byron
    181, 192, 199, 201,
    212, 216, 224, 364
Gordon, John B. 225, 248, 304
Gordon, William M. 18, 19
Gordonsville Road 232-234, 236
Gordonsville, Virginia
    36, 67, 68, 70, 102, 122, 231,
    232, 275, 281
Graham's Shop, Virginia 210
Grant, Ulysses S.
    147, 214-216, 219, 221, 225, 226,
    229, 230, 246, 283, 293, 298,
    302, 304
Gravelly Spring Road, Va 250
Graves, William F. 242, 283
Great Britain 108
Green Spring Valley, Va 231
Green, Charles A. 172
Green, Dr. Daniel
    153, 156, 157, 203
Greencastle Road, Maryland 181
Greencastle, Pennsylvania 176
Greenville, Virginia 205, 254
Greenwich, Virginia 201
Greenwood Church, Va 26
Greenwood Depot, Va 276
Greenwood, Pa 176, 178
Gregg, David M.
    152-154, 159, 162, 163, 167, 172,
    173, 214-216, 218, 220, 224, 227,
    231, 239, 242, 309
Gregg, John Irvin
    172, 178, 298, 301
Gregg, Maxcy 125
Griffin, Charles 43, 44, 217
Griffin, Wiley H. 199
Griffinsburg, Virginia 131
Grogan, Oma 339
Grubb Iron mine, Virginia 324
Grubb, Bird 323
Guard Hill, Virginia 249
Gwalthmey, W. M. 28
Gwalthmey, William W. 309
Haden, Benjamin J. 256, 264
Hagerstown Pike, Md 117
Hagerstown, Maryland 178, 180
Hale, Giles W. B. 32, 36, 53
Halifax County, Virginia 2
Halleck, Henry W.
    102, 122, 200, 309
Hamilton's Crossing, Va 213, 216
Hammond, George N. 203
Hamner Parish, Virginia 209, 317
Hampden-Sydney College 11
Hampshire County, Va 210, 276
Hampton, Frank 154
Hampton, Virginia 64
Hampton, Wade 38, 43, 95,
    109, 118, 127, 148-150, 152-154,
    164, 165, 167, 172-174, 176, 177,
    188, 191, 192, 200, 204, 212,
    216, 220, 226, 228, 229, 231,
    233-238, 240, 241, 242, 243, 282,
    283, 323, 340, 351, 364

Hancock, Winfield Scott
    120, 164, 214-219, 225, 226
Hanover County, Va   159, 227
Hanover Court House, Va
    130, 131, 238, 283
Hanover Junction, Va   222
Hanover Road, Pennsylvania   172
Hanover, Pa   166, 167, 172
Hanovertown, Virginia   228
Harbaugh's Valley, Maryland   177
Hardy County, Va   210, 274, 276
Harman, Asher W.
    104, 107, 112, 113, 153, 154, 185
Harness, William H.   80
Harpers Ferry, Virginia
    15, 50, 65, 74, 75, 113, 114, 115,
    116, 118, 120, 122, 185, 186
Harris Farm, Virginia   225
Harrisburg, Pennsylvania   148
Harrisonburg, Virginia
    69, 74, 77, 82-84, 86, 87, 89,
    255, 276
Harrison's Landing, Virginia
    93, 98, 99, 230
Harrisville Road, Virginia   260
Harrisville, Virginia   261
Hart, James F.   109, 150, 152, 234
Hartwood Church, Va   132, 133
Hatcher's Run, Virginia
    230, 284, 286, 287, 289, 291
Hawley, Sergeant   252
Haw's Shop, Virginia   34, 227
Haxall's Landing, Virginia   224
Hazel River, Virginia   157
Hedgeman River, Virginia   198
Hedgesville, Maryland   118
Hedgesville, Virginia   185, 186
Heintzelman, Samuel P.
    36, 39-41, 43, 44
Henagen's Redoubt, Va   226
Henry Hill, Manassas, Va   43, 44
Henry, Patrick   2
Herring Creek, Virginia   99, 230
Hess, Joseph T.   80
Heth, Henry   199
Hickman's Farm, Virginia   143
Higginson, Henry Lee   161
High Bridge, Virginia
    297, 298, 299, 300, 347, 348
Highland County, Virginia   72
Hill, Ambrose P.
    102, 144, 147, 150, 158, 177, 196,
    199, 204, 214, 217-219, 226
Hill, Daniel Harvey   56, 59-61
Hinson's Hill, Virginia   103
Holland, T. B.   113
Holland, Thomas B.   138
Hollins University   22
Hollywood Cemetery, Richmond
    5, 340
Holmes, Theophilus   38
Hood, John Bell   176, 347
Hood's Mill, Maryland   166
Hooker, Joseph
    124, 129, 133, 136, 139, 140,
    145, 148, 150, 158, 160, 163
Hopkins, E. P.   222
Hopkins, James H.   54(n), 57(n)
Hotchkiss, Jedediah   86, 145
House of Delegates, Virginia   330
Howard, Oliver Otis
    44, 140, 143, 144
Hubard, Robert T.   264
Huddleston, Peter   131, 212, 213
Hudgins, Robert S.   302
Huey, Pennock   181
Hull, John E.   299, 345, 348
Humphreys, Andrew A.   120

Hunt, Davie 270
Hunt, George W. 259
Hunt, Henry J. 214
Hunter, David
    41, 43, 231, 238, 245
Hunter, Edward S. 327
Hunter, Robert W. 294, 346
Hutton, Eppa 38
Imboden, John D.
    182, 176, 178, 206, 246, 248, 255
Inlet Station, Virginia 149
Iverson, Alfred 144, 180
Ivy Depot, Virginia 276
Ivy Station, Virginia 205
J.E.B. Stuart 154
J.E.B. Stuart's Christmas Raid 125
Jack Mountain Pass, Pa 176
Jack Mountain, Pa 174, 176
Jackson, Conrad F. 124
Jackson, Maria 325
Jackson, Thomas E. 172
Jackson, Thomas Jonathan
    7, 14-18, 33, 41, 43, 44, 65-67,
    69-77, 80, 83, 84, 86, 87, 89, 91,
    93-96, 98, 99, 102, 103, 105-107,
    112, 115, 116, 118, 121-124, 129,
    139, 140, 143, 144, 161, 191, 364
Jackson, William L. 246, 255
James City, Virginia 197
James River
    6, 62-64, 93, 98, 127, 224-226,
    230, 238, 240, 242, 244, 304
Janney, John 108
Jeff Davis Legion
    56, 152, 154, 173, 192, 212
Jefferson, Maryland 113
Jefferson, Pennsylvania 168
Jeffersonton, Virginia 103, 198
Jenkins, Albert G.
    172, 177, 178, 180, 186

Jericho Mills, Virginia 226
Jetersville, Virginia 298
John Lamb 340
Johnson, Andrew 310, 314
Johnson, Bradley T.
    213, 246, 254, 255
Johnson, Bushrod Rust
    286, 289, 294
Johnston, Albert Sidney 54, 60
Jones, A. W. 272
Johnston, Joseph E.
    35-37, 40, 41, 44-47, 49, 52, 53,
    62, 63, 91, 92, 214, 230, 293,
    297, 298, 304-307
Jones, David R. 35
Jones, Hilary P. 172
Jones, William E.
    33, 49, 55, 109, 118, 120-122,
    136, 148-150, 152, 153, 164, 176,
    178, 180, 188, 192, 193, 209
Jordan Run, Va 257, 259, 260, 261
Jordan, T. J. 47
Joseph E. Johnston 60
Joseph J. Bartlett 115
Kasey, John S. 33
Kautz, August V. 240, 241
Kearney, Philip 98
Keedysville, Maryland 115
Kelly's Ford Road 153
Kelly's Ford, Virginia
    34, 104, 126, 132, 133, 136, 137,
    139, 150, 152, 153, 158, 204
Kemper, Del 44, 45
Kenly, John R. 72, 74
Kennon Landing, Virginia 226
Kennon, R. B. 281
Kernstown, Virginia
    65, 66, 71, 75, 76, 246, 270

Kershaw, Joseph B.
    38, 44, 45, 246, 253
Key Ferry, Virginia   75
Keystone State   148
Kidd, James H.   260-262
Kilpatrick, H. Judson
    160, 161, 167, 172, 176, 178, 180-183, 193, 201, 211
Kilpatrick-Dahlgren Raid   211
Kimball, Nathan   66
Knight, Napolian B.   166
Lacey Springs, Virginia   349
Lakes, John W.   183, 204, 212, 213
Lamb, John   122, 203, 280, 363
Lamont Point, Virginia   67
Lane, John   123
Langhorne, Daniel A.   31
Langhorne, John   45, 46
Langhorne, John S.   32, 36
Langley, Virginia   50
Langyher's Mill, Virginia   200
Lasley, John Owen   242, 250
Laurel Brigade
    117, 212, 219, 246, 260, 263, 264, 266, 281, 299, 301
Law, Evander M.   176, 349
Lawton, Alexander   118
Ledlie, James H.   226
Lee, Curtis   298
Lee, Fitzhugh
    33, 79, 103, 104, 107, 109, 118, 120, 122, 123, 125-127, 130-133, 136, 137, 139, 143, 145, 148, 159, 160, 162-167, 172-174, 176-178, 180-182, 185, 186, 188, 192, 194, 197, 199-202, 205, 206, 211-213, 216, 218-227, 231, 232, 234, 236, 237, 239, 240, 242-244, 246-250, 252-255, 264, 271, 273, 276, 279-283, 285, 287, 289-291, 293, 294, 298-303, 311, 343-348, 350, 364
Lee, Henry   277
Lee, Henry Carter   156, 242
Lee, John   242
Lee, Robert E.
    29, 31, 32, 34, 37, 49, 77, 79, 92, 93, 96, 99, 101, 102, 108, 109, 115, 116, 118, 122-124, 127, 129-132, 136, 138-140, 144, 145, 147-149, 158, 159, 163, 164, 166, 169, 170, 174, 176, 177, 182, 186, 190, 192-197, 199, 200, 203-205, 214-217, 219, 221, 223, 224, 225, 227, 229, 230, 243, 246, 279, 282, 283, 287, 288, 293, 294, 298, 299, 302-305, 308, 343, 345, 350, 351, 364
Lee, W. H. F. 'Rooney'
    118, 125, 127, 137, 148, 150, 152-154, 156, 159, 160, 164, 166, 186, 193, 212, 216, 226, 230, 241, 243, 244, 284, 285, 287, 289, 290, 299
Leesburg, Virginia
    34, 35, 52-54, 56, 59, 108, 121, 159
Leestown Road   186
Leestown, Virginia   118, 185, 186
Leitersburg, Maryland   177, 178
Letcher Light Artillery   29, 98
Letcher, John
    5, 26, 31, 121, 134, 203, 281
Lewis Farm   107
Lewis Ford, Virginia   101
Lewis, L. L.   272
Lexington, Virginia
    9, 10, 19, 205, 231, 307
Liberty Mills, Va   68, 195, 196

Light House Point, Virginia 241
Lillestown, Maryland 166
Lincoln, Abraham
  26, 28, 31, 53, 63, 64, 158, 214, 305
Linden Station, Virginia 62
Litchfield, C. T. 157
Little Big Horn 229, 238
Little Five Forks, Virginia 285
Little North Mountain, Va 261
Little River Pike 159
Little River Turnpike 37, 159
Little River, Virginia 160
Littlestown, Maryland 166
Lomax, Lunsford
  181, 188, 192-194, 210, 213, 216,
  217, 220, 223, 234, 236, 241,
  242, 244, 246, 248, 254-259,
  262, 264, 275, 349
Long's Depot, Virginia 205
Longstreet, James
  35, 39, 41, 46, 53, 54, 84, 102,
  105, 107, 122, 124, 130, 147,
  150, 159, 163, 177, 186, 190,
  195, 214, 219, 299, 300
Longstreet's I Corps 158
Loring, William W. 65
Lost Cause Doctrine 316, 317, 347
Loudoun County, Virginia
  35, 54, 59, 67, 159, 183
Loudoun Valley, Virginia 163
Louisa C. H. Road, Va 232
Louisa Court House, Va
  231, 232, 282
Louisiana Guard Artillery 172
Low Dutch Road, Pa 170, 172
Lowell, Charles Russell 260-262
Lunenburg County, Virginia 2
Luray Pike 250
Luray Road 250
Luray, Virginia 70, 72, 252
Lynchburg Depot, Virginia 269
Lynchburg Iron, Steel, and Mining
  Company 323
Lynchburg Road 302, 303
Lynchburg, Virginia
  28, 31, 32, 34, 206, 209, 231,
  236, 238, 245, 269, 303-305,
  308, 310, 312, 317-319, 326, 335,
  337, 339-341, 346, 353, 354, 360,
  361
Mackenzie, Ranald S. 304, 305
Macon, Georgia 339
Madison County, Virginia 211
Madison Court House, Va
  69, 71, 76, 122, 195, 211, 212
Madison Hall 77
Madison, James 210
Magruder, James W. 203
Magruder, John B. 91
Mahone, William 114, 127, 241
Malvern Hill, Battle of
  29, 94, 96, 98
Manassas, Battle of First
  28, 31, 33, 49, 50, 55, 63
Manassas, Battle of Second
  34, 59, 69, 101, 108, 133, 143
Manassas Gap Railroad
  65, 68, 69, 71, 164
Manassas Gap, Virginia 73, 186
Manassas Junction
  34, 35, 36, 39, 40, 53, 63, 105,
  118, 159, 200
Manassas, Virginia
  32, 34, 36, 37, 38, 39, 40, 52, 53,
  61, 63, 65, 106, 196, 200
Marcy, Randolph B. 64
Margaret Nimmo Munford 1
Marion, Pennsylvania 176

Marquiz Road 232
Marshall, Charles 169
Martin, William T. 56
Martinsburg, Va 75, 185, 186
Maryland 164
Maryland Campaign
    101, 109, 111, 116
Maryland Heights 113-115
Mason, Judge John Y. 19
Massanutten Mountain 72, 76
Massaponax Church, Va 216
Matthew C. Butler 192
Matthew's Hill 43
Matthews, Henry H. 112, 161
Mayre's Heights 123, 124, 145
McCabe, James P. 197
McCabe, William Gordon 294
McCausland, John
    246, 248, 255, 301
McClellan, George B.
    47, 52, 53, 56, 61, 63, 64, 66, 91-93, 98, 99, 102, 118, 121, 122
McClellan, Henry B.
    169, 170, 172, 195, 348
McCoy's Ford, Virginia
    72, 119, 249, 252
McDaniel, Albert 23, 33
McDaniel, Catherine S. 23
McDonald, Edward H. 80
McDowell County, Virginia 279
McDowell, Irvin
    36, 39, 40, 41, 43, 44, 46, 60, 63, 64, 67, 70, 88, 101
McDowell, Virginia 72, 276
McDowell's Dept of the
    Rappahannock 66
McGregor, William M.
    167, 172, 199, 211
McGuire, Hunter 96

McIlhenny, William A. 109
McIntosh, John B. 172-174, 249
McKim, Randolph H. 249, 251
McLaws, Lafayette 113-116, 123
McMurry, Robert M. 13(n)
McVicar, Duncan 140
Meade, George Gordon
    158, 195-197, 199, 200, 204, 205, 211, 215-219, 221, 228, 283, 347
Meadow Bridge 224
Means, Samuel C. 61, 108, 109
Mechanicsville, Virginia
    93, 211, 225, 283
Mechum River, Virginia 276
Mechum's River Station, Va 72
Mecklenburg County, Va 2, 3
Memphis, Tennessee 318
Mercersburg, Pennsylvania 119
Meredith, Samuel H. 32
Meriweather, Francis 33
Merritt, Wesley
    174, 176, 220, 224, 244, 235, 246, 247, 259, 260, 264, 284, 287
Merritt's bridge, Pennsylvania 176
Mexican-American War 15
Middle River, Virginia 253
Middle Road 248, 256, 260-262
Middleburg Road 161
Middleburg, Va 67, 121, 123, 127, 159, 160, 162, 163
Middletown, Virginia
    74, 113, 115, 249, 268
Mile Hill, Virginia 109
Miles, Dixon S. 116
Miles, Nelson 286
Milford Mills, Virginia 34
Milford, Virginia 250-252
Miliam's Gap, Virginia 204
Mill Creek, (Port Republic) 77

Mill Creek, Virginia	256	Munford, Anne Bland	1
Miller's Furnace, Virginia	205	Munford, Beverly Carlton	134
Millwood, Virginia	186	Munford, Carlton Beverly	22
Mine Run Canpaign, Virginia	34	Munford, Caroline Homasselle	1
Mine Run, Virginia	183, 204	Munford, Charles Ellis	
Minneapolis Pioneer Press	350		1, 2, 27, 29, 97
Minnegerode, Charles	311	Munford, Courtney Norton	
Mitchell's Ford	38, 40, 41		353, 357
Mobjack Bay, Virginia	314	Munford, Elizabeth Henrietta	
Monocacy Church, Maryland	112	'Etta' (Tayloe)	
Monocacy River, Virginia	245	22, 23, 28, 134, 209, 338, 339	
Monterey Pass, Pennsylvania	177	Munford, Elizabeth Thorowgood	
Monterey, Virginia	276	Ellis	22, 98
Montgomery, Alabama	28	Munford, Emma Tayloe	
Montgomery, Virginia	309	313, 317, 318, 319, 320, 321, 326,	
Moorefield Valley, Virginia	275	327, 328, 353, 356, 360, 361	
Moorefield, Virginia	274	Munford, Etta Wythe	1
Mooresville, Virginia	125	Munford, Frances Ellis	1
Moorman, M. M.	211, 212	George Tayloe Munford	338
Morgan, William A.	280, 281, 283	George Wythe Munford	22
Morrisville, Virginia	132, 133	Munford, George Tayloe	
Morton's Ford, Virginia	197, 199		5, 22, 313, 337, 339
Mosby, John S.	347, 351	Munford, George Wythe	
Moss Neck, Virginia	126	1, 3, 4, 6, 9, 21, 24, 27, 121, 194,	
Mount Crawford, Virginia	84	308, 309, 311, 313-318, 322, 329	
Mount Jackson, Virginia		Munford, George Wythe, Jr.	1
	82, 262, 274	Munford, Glen	353, 360
Mount Olive, Virginia		Munford, Harry Lomax	
	257, 259, 260		312, 313, 321
Mount Olivet Cemetery, Pa	167	Munford, Henrietta Elizabeth	312
Mount Sidney, Va	86, 87, 254	Munford, Jane Beverly	1
Mount Zion Church, Va	204	Munford, Jennie	97
Mountain Road, Va	223, 253, 282	Munford, Louis Sinclair	312
Mountville, Virginia	67	Munford, Lucy Harrison	1
Mt. Meridan, Virginia	253	Munford, Lucy Taylor	1
Mullikin, James	325	Munford, Margaret	330
Mumford Tutor Cottage	318, 319	Munford, Rev. William	322
Mumford, William Tayloe	357	Munford, Robert	1, 2
Munford Lynchburg home	320	Munford, Rosalie	1

Munford, Sally   209, 210, 297, 309
Munford, Sallie Radford   1
Munford, Sinclair   321, 339, 354
Munford, Thomas (ancestor)   2
Munford, Thomas Byrd   312
Munford, Thomas Glen
   312, 321, 339
Munford, Thomas Ogle   339
Munford, Thorton Ogle
   312, 313, 321, 354
Munford, W. P.   322
Munford, William
   1, 22, 29, 46, 313, 317, 318, 321
Munford, William (grandfather) 3
Munford, William Tayloe
   339, 354, 358, 359
Munford, William Tayloe, Jr.
   356, 358, 361
Munford, Wythe   19, 21, 22, 339
Muray Road   249
Murfee, J. T.   293
Murfee, James T.   13(n)
Murfee, James T.   14
Murrell, John William   318
Murrell, William   318, 319
Myerly, L. D.   349
Myers, Frank   110
Myers, Frank M.   68
Myers, George W.   80
Myers, S. B.   106
Naked Creek   276
Nance's Shop, Virginia   230, 239
Nash, Joseph Van Holt   242
Nathaniel P. Richmond   180
National Road   116
Neese, George M.   235
Netherland Tavern   234
New Baltimore, Virginia   123, 200
New Bedford, Mass.   318

New Berne, N.C.   64
New Creek, Virginia   274, 349
New Market Gap, Va   72, 74
New Market, Virginia
   69, 70, 76, 82, 84, 86, 206, 250,
   252, 253, 255, 256, 274
New Orleans, Louisiana   60
New York Times   272
Newport News, Virginia   64
Newton, John   115
Newton, William B.   197
Newtown, Virginia   73
Nichols, E. C.   339
Nichols, Edward   332, 333
Nine Mile Road   283
Nolan, B. P.   61
Norfolk and Petersburg Railroad
   230
Norfolk, Virginia   11
North Anna River
   183, 225, 226, 229, 232, 238, 282
North Anna, Battle of   225, 226
North Mountain, Maryland   118
North Mountain, Virginia   275
North River bridge   83
North River   254, 314
Northrop, Lucius B.   60
Nottoway River, Va   240, 241, 289
Oak Grove, Virginia   92
Oak Shade, Virginia   67, 68, 156
Oakland Plantation, Uniontown,
   Alabama   353, 354, 356-360
Occoquan River
   35, 36, 39, 126, 164
Occoquan, Virginia   125
Ogle, Dr. George C.   324, 325
Ogle, George   324, 325
Ogle, Rosalie   325
Ogle, Samuel   324

Old Wilderness Tavern	216	Partridge, Alden	9
Old, Charles	280	Pate, Henry C.	137
Opequan River, Virginia	246	Patrick, William	80

Opequon Creek, Virginia 247
Orange and Alexandria Railroad
   39, 52, 68, 103, 105, 164, 196,
   198-200, 203
Orange County, Virginia 148
Orange Court House, Virginia
   62, 196, 204, 215, 216
Orange Plank Road 140
Orange Road 219
Orange Springs, Virginia 196
Orange Turnpike, Virginia 216
Orchard, Pauline 339
Ord, Edward O. C. 298
Orleans 103
Orleans, Virginia 65
Ormand farm, Alabama 354
Ormand, T. W. 326
Otey, G. Gaston 347
Overall's Run, Virginia 250
Overland Campaign, Virginia
   214, 221, 225
Owen, C. H. 327, 328
Owen, Thomas H.
   197, 198, 200, 201, 203, 220, 242
Owen, William Miller 299
Ox Ford, Virginia 226
Page, Edwin R. 54, 56
Paine's Cross Roads, Va 297
Painesville Road, Virginia 297
Painesville, Virginia 297, 298
Pamunkey River, Va 93, 131, 227
Paphim, John R. 272
Parham, William A. 114
Parker, Robert W.
   53, 67, 145, 180, 198, 200
Parker's Store, Virginia 216, 218

Patterson, Robert
   37, 40, 41, 43, 64
Patterson's Ford, Virginia 253
Patton, George Smith 9, 82, 246
Payne, William H.
   36, 45, 46, 167, 246-248, 250,
   252, 253, 255, 260, 264, 267,
   270, 271, 272, 281, 284, 344,
   349, 351, 364
Peace Conference of Hampton
   Roads 305
Peaks of Otter, Virginia 23
Pealy Mills, Virginia 213
Peck, Rufus
   40, 54, 55, 62, 165, 196-198,
   210, 217, 276
Pegram, William 96, 97
Pegram, William J. 284, 285
Pelham, John 109, 114, 137
Pendleton County, Virginia 274
Pendleton, A. S. 'Sandie' 75
Pendleton, William N. 117, 214
Peninsula Campaign
   34, 59, 64, 66, 77, 91, 94, 99
Peninsula, Virginia 65, 103
Pennington, A. C. 289
Pennington, Alexander 173, 234
Pennsylvania 108, 148
Pennsylvania Raid 118
Perry County, Alabama 356
Petersburg and Weldon Railroad
   231
Petersburg, Virginia
   225, 230, 240, 242, 246, 247,
   269, 274, 275, 276, 279, 283,
   284, 293, 317

Pettigrew, James J. 182
Philadelphia Weekly Times
    349, 350, 351
Philadelphia, Pennsylvania 148
Philips, John B. 266
Phillipines 339
Phillips Legion 192, 234, 235
Phillips, Jefferson C. 166
Phillips, John B. 291
Philomont, Virginia 163
Pickett, George E.
    279, 283-291, 293, 294, 346
Pierpont, Frank H. 329
Pitzer, Andrew L. 32
Plank Road 143, 216, 217
Pleasant Valley, Maryland 114
Pleasonton, Alfred
    113, 121, 133, 144, 148, 150,
    159, 172, 174, 198
Plum Creek, Pennsylvania 167
Po River, Virginia 218
Pocahontas, West Virginia 339
Poe, Edgar Allan 6
Point of Rocks, Maryland
    59, 109, 113
Poolesville, Md 110, 112, 113
Pope, John
    84, 99, 100, 101, 103-106
Poplar Ford, Manassas 41
Port Republic, Virginia
    72, 76, 77, 80, 82, 83, 86, 87, 253
Port Royal Road, Virginia 252
Port Royal, Virginia 125, 127
Porter, Fitz John 93, 98, 106, 118
Posey, Carnot 127
Potomac River
    34, 35, 47, 50, 52, 56, 59, 75,
    109, 117-119, 121, 122, 127, 147,
    164, 165, 176, 177, 180, 182,
    183, 185, 186, 246

Powell, E. B. 54
Powell, William H. 244
Powhatan County, Virginia 21
President of VMI Board of
    Visitors 330, 334
Preston, Charles P. 269
Preston, John S. 37
Preston, John T. L. 10, 11
Preston, Margaret Junkin 205
Preston, R. T. 31
Prince George's County,
    Maryland 324-326
Princeton, West Virginia 339
Pritchard Hill 66
Prussia, Europe 340
Pugh's Run, Virginia 261, 262
Purcellville, Virginia 121
Quaker Road, Virginia 283
Raccoon Ford, Virginia
    104, 139, 197, 205
Radford, Edmund Winston 32, 45
Radford, Richard C. W.
    31, 32, 34-36, 38-41, 44-46, 49,
    52, 55, 60, 61, 68, 79
Ramsuer, Stephen D. 247, 248
Randolph County 348
Randolph, Archibald Clay 242
Randolph, John 79
Randolph, Robert 200
Randolph-Macon College 32
Ransom, Robert 56, 79, 123
Rapidan River, Virginia
    103, 104, 127, 139, 187, 195-197,
    199, 204, 205, 210, 211, 215, 219
Rapidan Station, Virginia 196
Rappahannock Bridge, Va 203
Rappahannock Ford, Va 137

Rappahannock River
  36, 52, 61, 64, 67, 68, 103, 104,
  123, 125-127, 129-132, 133, 136,
  139, 145, 148, 150, 156, 158,
  183, 187, 195, 197-200, 203, 204
Rappahannock Station, Va
  67, 196, 197
Rasin, William J.   303
Read, Theodore   298, 299
Reams' Station, First Battle of 241
Reams's Station, Virginia   240-243
Rectortown, Virginia   123, 160
Red Bud Creek, Virginia   249
Reno, Jesse L.   101
Reynolds, John F.   144
Rice's Station, Virginia   299, 301
Richard C. W. Radford   33
Richard's Ford, Virginia   131
Richardson, Israel B.   39, 41, 46
Richmond Academy   6, 7
Richmond County   311
Richmond Dispatch   38
Richmond Times Dispatch   345
Richmond Whig   272
Richmond, Virginia
  1, 3, 5, 7, 19, 28, 38, 62, 64, 66,
  74, 77, 83, 87, 88, 91-93, 98, 99,
  102, 119, 122, 123, 131, 136,
  145, 186, 211, 215, 217, 218, 223-
  225, 229, 230, 238, 242, 244,
  269, 271, 272, 279, 280, 282,
  292, 293, 297, 299, 308, 314,
  316, 318, 321, 322, 330
Richmond-Petersburg Campaign
  240
Ricketts, James B.   43, 44, 102
Riddle's Shop, Virginia   230
Ridge Road, Virginia   132, 133
Rio Ridge, Virginia   211, 212

Rivanna River, Virginia   211
Rixey's Ford, Virginia   157
Roanoke College   22
Roanoke Valley Union Seminary
  22
Roanoke, Virginia
  21, 22, 27, 209, 305, 339
Robert E. Lee Camp of
  Confederate Veterans   330
Roberts, William P.   289, 290
Robertson Hospital   269
Robertson, Beverly H.
  33, 56, 80, 82, 87, 89, 96, 103,
  104, 106-110, 158, 148, 150, 153,
  160, 164, 174, 176, 178, 180,
  185, 186, 209
Robertson, Frank S.   305
Robertson, Wyndam   3
Robinson River
  196, 204, 210, 211, 212
Rock Spring Farm   21, 23
Rockfish Gap, Virginia   253
Rockford Road   186
Rockingham County, Va   82
Rockville, Maryland   165
Rodes, Robert E.
  14, 143, 144, 225, 248
Rogers, Asa   162
Rolling Mill, Lynchburg, Va   323
Romney, Virginia   65
Rosecrans, William S.   65
Rosser, Thomas L.
  145, 157, 160-162, 168, 188, 193,
  194, 195, 201, 209, 212, 213,
  218, 219, 227, 231, 232, 234-237,
  244, 246, 250, 253, 255-264,
  266, 267, 271, 272, 274, 276,
  279-282, 284, 285, 287, 290,
  291, 293, 294, 298-301, 303, 311,
  343-351, 364

Index

Round Hill, Virginia 257, 261
Round Top Hill, Va 256, 259
Round Top, Gettysburg 176
Rowzer's Mill Ford 165
Rucker, James M. 323
Rude's Hill, Virginia 269, 274
Rummel, John 172, 173
Russell, David A. 249
Rutter, Edward T. 325
Ryals, Garland Mitchell 242
Sailor's Creek, Virginia 347
Saint Mary's Church, Va 239
Salem Church, Va 139, 145, 239
Salem Depot, Virginia 164
Salem, Virginia 68, 307
Samaria Church, Va 230, 239, 243
Sand Ridge Church 261
Sand Ridge Road 261
Sandy Hook, Maryland 50
Sandy Ridge, Virginia 66
Sangster's Cross Roads, Va 52
Sangster's Station, Virginia 37
Sappony Church, Virginia 240
Savage's Station, Virginia 93
Scott, John 45
Scott, Winfield 63
Scott's Road, Virginia 284
Second Virginia Company of London 2
Secretary of the Commonwealth of Virginia 3, 5, 321, 322, 329
Seddon, James A. 136, 138
Sedgwick, John 65, 140, 145, 214-217
Seven Days Battles 92, 93, 96, 99, 101, 143
Seven Pines, Virginia 91, 92
Seward, William H. 314
Shad Bake 289, 351
Shady Grove Church, Va 216
Sharpsburg Pike 181
Sharpsburg, Md 117, 122, 178
Shenandoah Mountain, Va 87
Shenandoah River, Virginia 72, 77, 83, 185, 186, 249, 250, 253, 274
Shenandoah Valley Campaign (1862) 7, 16, 34, 59, 71, 79, 85, 88, 143
Shenandoah Valley Campaign (1864) 245, 249, 261, 273, 349, 351
Shenandoah Valley 18, 34, 36, 37, 40, 41, 43, 60, 65, 66, 69, 72, 76, 82, 93, 102, 108, 148, 150, 159, 204, 205, 212, 231, 244, 246, 258, 269, 281
Shepherdstown, Maryland 117, 118, 120
Shepherdstown, WV 34, 185, 186
Sheridan, Philip H. 214-216, 218-221, 223, 224, 228, 231, 236-240, 244, 246-248, 254, 256, 257, 266, 268-271, 276, 282, 287, 290, 291, 297, 347, 349
Sheridan's Richmond Raid 34
Sheriff of Hale County, Al 326
Sherman, William T. 214, 230, 282, 283, 297, 305
Shields, James 65, 69, 70, 75
Shippensburg, Pa 168
Shoemaker, John J. 219
Sickles, Daniel 133, 144, 347
Siege of Petersburg 34, 229
Sigel, Franz 101, 123, 231
Sindler, E. L. 217
Slocum, Henry W. 112, 115, 139
Smith, Charles H. 298

Smith, Frances H.
    11, 12, 14, 247, 329, 332-337
Smith, Kirby   44
Smith, Thomas   272
Smith, William   277, 330
Smithfield, Virginia   120
Smithtown, Maryland   177
Snicker's Gap Pike, Virginia
                62, 159, 160, 163
Snicker's Gap Turnpike, Va   161
Snickersville Road   160, 161
Snickersville, Virginia   121
Somerville Ford, Virginia   196
South Anna River   282
South Mountain, Maryland
                      113, 116, 193
South Mountain, Pa.   177
South River   253
South Side Railroad
    231, 240, 283, 284, 289, 298, 299
Southern Historical Society   316
Southern Historical Society
    Papers   351
Spangler, Mr.   250
Spanish-American War   340
Sperryville Bridge, Virginia   70
Sperryville Turnpike, Virginia 70
Sperryville, Virginia   70, 138, 213
Spiker's Hill, Va   257, 260-262
Spillman, J. H.   360
Spillman, W. J.   357
Spotsylvania, Battle of   221
Spotsylvania Campaign   214
Spotsylvania County, Va   139
Spotsylvania Court House, Va
          123, 139, 140, 214, 216,
          219-221, 226, 245
Spotsylvania, Virginia
                    34, 221, 229

Spring Hill Cemetery, Lynchburg,
    Virginia   361
Springfield Station, Virginia   52
St. James Church of Memphis,
    Tennessee   318
St. James Church, Brandy Station
                          152, 153
St. John's Church, Va   260, 262
St. Paul's Episcopal Church,
    Lynchburg, Virginia   317, 361
Staggs, Peter   289
Stahel, Julius   82
Stannardsville, Virginia   212
Stanton, Edwin M.   63, 122
Star Fort, Virginia   252
State Conservative Convention,
    Virginia   317
Staunton Valley, Virginia   253
Staunton, Virginia
          72, 205, 250, 254, 275, 276
Stedman, William   162
Steele, Joseph   242
Steptoe, William   33
Steuart, George S.   72-76
Stevensburg, Virginia
                104, 139, 197, 198, 211
Stone Bridge, Manassas
            41, 43, 45, 55, 60, 61, 107
Stone Church, Virginia   75
Stone, Charles P.   53, 56
Stoneman, George
                    130, 139, 145, 148
Stonewall Brigade   66
Stony Creek Depot, Virginia   240
Stony Creek, Virginia
                    240, 241, 262, 284
Stony Ridge   105
Stoughton, Edwin H.   126

Strasburg, Virginia
    65, 72-76, 87, 118,
    250, 257, 260, 268
Stratton, William H. 222
Stuart J.E.B. 5
Stuart's Pennsylvania Raid 120
Stuart, A. H. H. 254
Stuart, Flora 110
Stuart, James Ewell Brown
    35, 43, 49, 52, 55-57, 60, 67, 79,
    93, 96, 99, 102, 104, 107, 109,
    110, 114, 115, 118-123, 125, 126,
    130, 131, 134, 139, 144, 145,
    147-149, 152, 153, 155, 156, 158,
    159, 162, 164-170, 172-174, 176-
    178, 180, 182, 183, 185, 187-190,
    192-195, 198-201, 203-205, 209,
    212-214, 216, 218, 219, 221-224,
    232, 243, 340, 344, 347, 348,
    364
Stuart's Horse Artillery 112, 180
Stuat's Chambersburg Raid 120
Sudley Ford 41, 43
Sudley Springs 43
Sudley, Virginia 41
Sugar Loaf Mountain, Md 112
Sumner, Edwin V. 124
Supreme Court of Alabama 326
Supreme Court of Appeals of
    Virginia 328
Susquehanna River 167
Sweeney, Sam 55, 119, 120, 126
Swift Run Gap 69, 80
Swope, Washington 348, 349
Swope's Depot, Va 275-277, 279
Sykes, George 44
Sykesville, Maryland 166
Talbot, Mrs. Charles H. 322

Talbot, Sallie Radford Munford
    330
Taliaferro, John 46
Talleyville, Virginia 239
Tayloe, Courtney Norton 356
Tayloe, Elizabeth Henrietta 22
Tayloe, Elizabeth Langhorne
    'Emma' 311
Tayloe, George Plater 22, 309
Tayloe, Henrietta Ogle 312
Tayloe, Henry A. 324, 325
Tayloe, Lomax
    33, 131, 134, 182, 186
Tayloe, Mary Elizabeth
    Langhorne 22
Tayloe, William Henry
    311, 312, 324-326, 353
Taylor, Lucy Singleton 1
Taylor, Walter H. 294
Telegraph Road, Virginia
    132, 223, 226
Tennessee 195
Tennessee and Virginia Railroad
    205
Terrett, George H. 35
Terry, William R. 32, 249
The Bower (Dandridge Estate)
    118, 119, 121, 185
The Commanches 68
The Maryland Campaign 108
The Progress, Albermarle County,
    Virginia 345
The Wilderness 204
The Woodstock Races 256
Third Winchester, Battle of
    247, 255
Thomson, James W. 219, 233, 255
Thoroughfare Gap
    62, 65, 103, 105, 106, 160

Thorton, Thomas R. 15
Thorton's Gap 69
Tidewater, Virginia 315
Timberville, Virginia 255, 276
Tobacco Stick Ford 103
Todd's Tavern, Virginia
    34, 139, 216-220
Tom's Brook, Virginia
    256-260, 262, 264, 266,
    268, 269, 349, 351
Torbert, Alfred
    115, 214, 215, 216, 219, 220, 227,
    232, 244, 247, 248, 250, 251, 256,
    257, 274, 276
Totopotomoy Creek 227
Trent, William H. 33, 303
Trevilian Station, Virginia
    243, 264, 282
Trevilian Station Road 232
Trevilian Station, Virginia
    34, 229, 231, 232, 234, 236, 238
Trimble, Isaac R. 82
Tuck, R. S. 345, 348
Tucker, Beverly 195(n)
Tucker, Nathaniel Beverly 188(n)
Tumbling Run, Virginia 259
Turkey Ridge 69, 229
Tutwiler v. Munford 325
Tutwiler, P. A. 326, 327
Twyman's Farm, Virginia 205
Twyman's Mill, Virginia 204
Tyler, Daniel 39, 40, 43
Tyler, Erastus B. 66, 82, 83
Union Church, Port Republic,
    Virginia 77
Union Mills, Maryland 166
Union, Virginia 163
Uniontown, Alabama
    320, 339, 355-358, 361

U.S. Agriculture Bureau 359
University of Virginia 7, 32, 33
Upperville, Virginia 34, 121, 163
Upton, Emory 249
Urbanna Plan 63, 64
Valley Pike, Virginia
    248, 249, 250, 254, 256-262, 274
Vandevender's Farm 275
Venable, Charles 169
Verdiersville, Virginia 196
Vicksburg, Mississippi 147
Vienna, Virginia 50
Virginia 28
Virginia and Tennessee Railroad
    231
Virginia Bank 312
Virginia Central Railroad
    102, 205, 223, 231, 275
Virginia Military Institute
    6, 7, 11, 13, 14, 15, 17, 18, 19,
    32, 33, 143, 238, 247, 248, 329,
    335, 337, 364
Virginia Polytechnic Institute 337
Virginia Secession Convention 28
VMI Board of Visitors
    329, 332, 333, 335, 340
Wakle, Isaac 242
Walker, David 269
Walker, James A. 9, 70
Wallace, Lew 245
Walper's Cross Roads, Va 120
Walton, William 160, 161
Warm Springs Turnpike, Va 255
Warren County, Virginia 74
Warren Court of Inquiry (1881)
    345
Warren, Gouverneur K.
    199, 214-217, 220, 221, 226,
    237, 283, 284, 286, 291

Index

Warrenton Junction, Virginia 62
Warrenton Pike, Virginia 201
Warrenton Post Road 132, 133
Warrenton Springs, Va 157, 198
Warrenton Turnpike 41, 105
Warrenton, Virginia
    39, 62, 70, 122, 196-198, 200, 201, 271
Washburn, Francis 299
Washington City
    26, 36-38, 46, 47, 50, 52, 60, 62, 63, 65-67, 71, 74, 102, 107, 108, 119, 121, 148, 158, 164, 165, 183, 196, 206, 246, 311, 314, 321, 340
Washington College, Lexington, Virginia 10, 32
Washington County, Md 180
Washington Road 166
Waterford, Virginia
    52, 54, 59, 60, 61, 109, 121
Waterloo of the Confederacy 292, 351
Watson's Farm 299
Watts, Charles E. 165
Watts, James W.
    106, 107, 126, 140, 143, 157, 162
Watts, Richart T. 266
Waynesboro, Virginia
    253, 254, 276, 282, 307
Weldon Railroad 64, 240, 241
Welford's Farm, Virginia 203
Welford's Ford, Virginia 152, 156, 157
Wells, William 261
West Point (U.S. Military Academy) 9, 33
West Point, NY
    10, 12, 31, 191, 266
Westminster, Md 166

Wharton, Gabriel C. 249, 274
Wheat, Chatham R. 35
White House Landing, Virginia 93, 238, 239, 283
White Oak Bridge 93
White Oak Road 283, 284, 286, 287, 290
White Oak Swamp 91, 93-96, 230, 239
White Plains, Virginia 65
White, Elijah V. 59, 68, 153, 219, 234, 236, 260, 279
White, G. D. 157
Whitehead, Edgar 32, 53, 138, 143, 204, 222
Whittle, Beverly K. 210, 213, 279
Wickham, Williams C.
    33, 38, 54, 56, 136, 145, 156, 159, 160, 192, 193, 196-198, 200, 201, 203-205, 209, 212, 213, 220, 222, 223, 226, 227, 236, 239, 241, 242, 246-248, 250, 251, 253-255, 264, 272, 273, 277, 343, 345
Wilcox, Cadmus 127, 196
Wilcox's Landing, Virginia 230
Wilderness Campaign 214
Wilderness, Va 215, 217, 219, 221
Willcox, Orlando 44
William and Mary, College of 7
William Henley Burnley 76(n)
William Munford 28
Williams, Alfred S. 65
Williams, Alpheus S. 133
Williams, Solomon 154
Williamsport, Md 178, 180, 181
Williamsport, Pennsylvania 176
Williamsport, Virginia 75

Wilmington and Weldon Railroad
                                240
Wilmington, NC   317
Wilson, James H.
        32, 214-216, 218, 240,
        247, 250, 252
Wilson, Robert C.   227
Wilson-Kautz Raid   240
Winchester, Virginia
    35, 50, 65, 66, 72, 74, 75, 87, 118,
    121, 182, 247-252, 256, 257, 268
Winder, Charles S.   77, 120
Wise, George D.   272
Wise, Henry A.   15
Wofford, William T.   178
Wolf Run Shoals, Va   36, 39, 164
Wolftown, Virginia   69
Woodstock Races   268
Woodstock, Va   76, 258, 261, 262
Wooldridge, William B.   284
Wright, Gilbert J.   232, 235
Wright, Marcus J.   343, 346
Wyndham, Sir Percy   77
Wythe, George   3
Yellow Tavern, Battle of   223
Yellow Tavern, Va   34, 223, 224
Yew Hills, Brandy Station   153
Yew Ridge, Brandy Station   153
York Pike   170, 172, 174
York River,   63, 64
York, Pennsylvania   168
Young, Pierce M.B.
        153, 167, 192, 201, 211,
        212, 216, 232, 234
Young, Samuel B. M.   304
Zion Church, Maryland   177

About the Author

Sheridan R. Barringer retired from NASA where he worked as a mechanical engineer and project manager at Langley Research Center for 37 years. He graduated from Virginia Tech in mechanical engineering in 1965. He is the author of *Fighting for General Lee: General Rufus Barringer and The North Carolina Cavalry Brigade* about his ancestor for which he won the Douglas Southall Freeman Best Southern History Book Award and the North Carolina Society of Historians History Book Award in 2016. He is also the author of *Custer's Gray Rival* about the life of Confederate Major General Thomas L. Rosser. He continues work on other cavalry figures from the Army of Northern Virginia. He and his wife Pam have two grown children and reside in Virginia.